Achieving Real-Time in Distributed Computing:

From Grids to Clouds

Dimosthenis Kyriazis
National Technical University of Athens, Greece

Theodora Varvarigou
National Technical University of Athens, Greece

Kleopatra G. Konstanteli
National Technical University of Athens, Greece

A volume in the Advances in Systems
Analysis, Software Engineering, and High
Performance Computing (ASASEHPC)
Book Series

Senior Editorial Director:	Kristin Klinger
Director of Book Publications:	Julia Mosemann
Editorial Director:	Lindsay Johnston
Acquisitions Editor:	Erika Carter
Development Editor:	Joel Gamon
Production Editor:	Sean Woznicki
Typesetters:	Natalie Pronio, Jennifer Romanchak, Milan Vracarich, Jr.
Print Coordinator:	Jamie Snavely
Cover Design:	Nick Newcomer

Published in the United States of America by
Information Science Reference (an imprint of IGI Global)
701 E. Chocolate Avenue
Hershey PA 17033
Tel: 717-533-8845
Fax: 717-533-8661
E-mail: cust@igi-global.com
Web site: http://www.igi-global.com

Library of Congress Cataloging-in-Publication Data

Achieving real-time in distributed computing: from grids to clouds / Dimosthenis P. Kyriazis, Theordora A. Varvarigou, and Kleopatra Konstanteli, editors.
    p. cm.
 Includes bibliographical references and index.
 Summary: "This book offers over 400 accounts from a wide range of specific research efforts on methodologies, tools, and architectures for complex distributed systems that address the practical issues of performance guarantees, timed execution, real-time management of resources, synchronized communication under various load conditions, satisfaction of QoS constraints, as well as dealing with the trade-offs between these aspects"-- Provided by publisher.
 ISBN 978-1-60960-827-9 (hardcover) -- ISBN 978-1-60960-828-6 (ebook) -- ISBN 978-1-60960-829-3 (print & perpetual access) 1. Real-time data processing. 2. Electronic data processing--Distributed computing. I. Kyriazis, Dimosthenis P., 1973- II. Varvarigou, Theordora A., 1966- III. Konstanteli, Kleopatra, 1981-
 QA76.54.A328 2011
 004'.33--dc23
                            2011016061

This book is published in the IGI Global book series Advances in Systems Analysis, Software Engineering, and High Performance Computing (ASASEHPC) Book Series (ISSN: 2327-3453; eISSN: 2327-3461)

British Cataloguing in Publication Data
A Cataloguing in Publication record for this book is available from the British Library.

Advances in Systems Analysis, Software Engineering, and High Performance Computing (ASASEHPC) Book Series

Vijayan Sugumaran
Oakland University, USA

ISSN: 2327-3453
EISSN: 2327-3461

MISSION

The theory and practice of computing applications and distributed systems has emerged as one of the key areas of research driving innovations in business, engineering, and science. The fields of software engineering, systems analysis, and high performance computing offer a wide range of applications and solutions in solving computational problems for any modern organization.

The **Advances in Systems Analysis, Software Engineering, and High Performance Computing (ASASEHPC) Book Series** brings together research in the areas of distributed computing, systems and software engineering, high performance computing, and service science. This collection of publications is useful for academics, researchers, and practitioners seeking the latest practices and knowledge in this field.

COVERAGE

- Computer Graphics
- Computer Networking
- Computer System Analysis
- Distributed Cloud Computing
- Enterprise Information Systems
- Metadata and Semantic Web
- Parallel Architectures
- Performance Modeling
- Software Engineering
- Virtual Data Systems

IGI Global is currently accepting manuscripts for publication within this series. To submit a proposal for a volume in this series, please contact our Acquisition Editors at Acquisitions@igi-global.com or visit: http://www.igi-global.com/publish/.

Titles in this Series

For a list of additional titles in this series, please visit: www.igi-global.com

Service-Driven Approaches to Architecture and Enterprise Integration
Raja Ramanathan (Independent Researcher, USA) and Kirtana Raja (Independent Researcher, USA)
Information Science Reference • copyright 2013 • 367pp • H/C (ISBN: 9781466641938) • US $195.00 (our price)

Progressions and Innovations in Model-Driven Software Engineering
Vicente García Díaz (Universidad de Oviedo, Spain) Juan Manuel Cueva Lovelle (University of Oviedo, Spain) B. Cristina Pelayo García-Bustelo (University of Oviedo, Spain) and Oscar Sanjuan Martinez (University of Oviedo, Spain)
Engineering Science Reference • copyright 2013 • 352pp • H/C (ISBN: 9781466642171) • US $195.00 (our price)

Knowledge-Based Processes in Software Development
Saqib Saeed (Bahria University Islamabad, Pakistan) and Izzat Alsmadi (Yarmouk University, Jordan)
Information Science Reference • copyright 2013 • 318pp • H/C (ISBN: 9781466642294) • US $195.00 (our price)

Distributed Computing Innovations for Business, Engineering, and Science
Alfred Waising Loo (Lingnan University, Hong Kong)
Information Science Reference • copyright 2013 • 369pp • H/C (ISBN: 9781466625334) • US $195.00 (our price)

Data Intensive Distributed Computing Challenges and Solutions for Large-scale Information Management
Tevfik Kosar (University at Buffalo, USA)
Information Science Reference • copyright 2012 • 352pp • H/C (ISBN: 9781615209712) • US $180.00 (our price)

Achieving Real-Time in Distributed Computing From Grids to Clouds
Dimosthenis Kyriazis (National Technical University of Athens, Greece) Theodora Varvarigou (National Technical University of Athens, Greece) and Kleopatra G. Konstanteli (National Technical University of Athens, Greece)
Information Science Reference • copyright 2012 • 330pp • H/C (ISBN: 9781609608279) • US $195.00 (our price)

Principles and Applications of Distributed Event-Based Systems
Annika M. Hinze (University of Waikato, New Zealand) and Alejandro Buchmann (University of Waikato, New Zealand)
Information Science Reference • copyright 2010 • 538pp • H/C (ISBN: 9781605666976) • US $180.00 (our price)

DISSEMINATOR OF KNOWLEDGE

www.igi-global.com

701 E. Chocolate Ave., Hershey, PA 17033
Order online at www.igi-global.com or call 717-533-8845 x100
To place a standing order for titles released in this series, contact: cust@igi-global.com
Mon-Fri 8:00 am - 5:00 pm (est) or fax 24 hours a day 717-533-8661

Manuel Stein, *Alcatel Lucent Bell Labs, Germany*

Theodora A. Varvarigou, *National Technical University of Athens, Greece*

Wolfgang Ziegler, *Fraunhofer-Institut für Algorithmen und Wissenschaftliches Rechnen SCAI, Germany*

Table of Contents

Section 1
Software as a Service

Chapter 1

Matthew Addis, University of Southampton IT Innovation Centre, UK
Michael Boniface, University of Southampton IT Innovation Centre, UK
Juri Papay, University of Southampton IT Innovation Centre, UK
Arturo Servin, University of Southampton IT Innovation Centre, UK
Zlatko Zlatev, University of Southampton IT Innovation Centre, UK
George Kousiouris, National Technical University Athens, Greece

Chapter 2

Luis Costa, SINTEF ICT, Norway
Neil Loughran, SINTEF ICT, Norway
Roy Grønmo, SINTEF ICT, Norway

Chapter 3

Gregory Katsaros, National Technical University of Athens, Greece
Tommaso Cucinotta, Scuola Superiore Sant'Anna, Italy

Section 2
Platform as a Service

Section 3
Infrastructure as a Service

Detailed Table of Contents

Section 1
Software as a Service

Chapter 1

> *Matthew Addis, University of Southampton IT Innovation Centre, UK*
> *Michael Boniface, University of Southampton IT Innovation Centre, UK*
> *Juri Papay, University of Southampton IT Innovation Centre, UK*
> *Arturo Servin, University of Southampton IT Innovation Centre, UK*
> *Zlatko Zlatev, University of Southampton IT Innovation Centre, UK*
> *George Kousiouris, National Technical University Athens, Greece*

The complexity of determining resource provisioning policies for applications in such complex environments introduces significant inefficiencies in the cloud. Novel approaches are needed to efficiently model and analyse QoS for such applications, especially those with real-time constraints. This chapter investigates some of the techniques that can be used to explore these trade-offs and to find business models where value can be provided at all stages in the value-chain. For example, how can an application user identify a set of service providers that in combination provide the best solution to their workflow? How much risk is involved, e.g. what is the probability and impact of a failure of a service provider to deliver the QoS they promise? How can Service Level Agreements be specified that provide the flexibility to accommodate variability in service use, yet don't result in unnecessarily high cost to the consumer due to the service provider having to use massive over-provisioning of resources to ensure they can meet times of peak-load?

Chapter 2

> *Luis Costa, SINTEF ICT, Norway*
> *Neil Loughran, SINTEF ICT, Norway*
> *Roy Grønmo, SINTEF ICT, Norway*

Model-driven software engineering (MDE) has the basic assumption that the development of software systems from high-level abstractions along with the generation of low-level implementation code can improve the quality of the systems and at the same time reduce costs and improve time to market. This chapter provides an overview of MDE, state of the art approaches, standards, resources, and tools that support different aspects of model-driven software engineering: language development, modeling services, and real-time applications. The chapter concludes with a reflection over the main challenges faced by projects using the current MDE technologies, pointing out some promising directions for future developments.

Chapter 3

Gregory Katsaros, National Technical University of Athens, Greece
Tommaso Cucinotta, Scuola Superiore Sant'Anna, Italy

Research in the fields of Grid Computing, Service Oriented Architectures (SOA), as well as virtualization technologies has driven the emergence of Cloud service models such as Software-as-a-Service (SaaS), Platform-as-a-Service (PaaS), and Infrastructure-as-a-Service (IaaS). The appearance of different business roles according to this classification, potentially with differing interests, introduces new challenges with regard to the tools and mechanisms put in place in order to enable the efficient provisioning of services. Security, QoS assurance, and real-time capabilities are just a few issues that the providers are trying to tackle and integrate within the new products and services that they offer. In this chapter, we make an overview of the approaches that aim to APIs for real-time computing. In the first part of this chapter, several real-time application interfaces will be presented and compared. After that, we will document the state-of-the-art regarding the Cloud APIs available and analyze the architecture and the technologies that they support.

Chapter 4

Fotis Aisopos, National Technical University of Athens, Greece
Magdalini Kardara, National Technical University of Athens, Greece
Vrettos Moulos, National Technical University of Athens, Greece
Athanasios Papaoikonomou, National Technical University of Athens, Greece
Konstantinos Tserpes, National Technical University of Athens, Greece
Theodora A. Varvarigou, National Technical University of Athens, Greece

In this chapter, we present the current state-of-the-art technology and methodologies, regarding the evaluation of the provided QoS in service oriented environment. With the emergence of service provisioning infrastructures and the adoption of Service Level Agreements acting as electronic contracts between service providers and customers, the need to control and validate the offered quality has appeared throughout the service lifecycle. This monitoring is performed either in the client side, using the customer's quality of experience and employing trust and reputation mechanisms for the service selection and evaluation phase, or in the provider side, dynamically reconfiguring the service and allocating resources accordingly, in order to optimize the quality metrics guaranteed. The latter, of course, initially requires mapping of the high-level quality parameters, which are closer to the customer perception, to low-level computing terms related to the resource management process. Dynamic resource allocation based on monitoring and evaluation can lead to optimizing resource utilization and provider's profits.

Section 2
Platform as a Service

Chapter 5

George Kousiouris, National Technical University of Athens, Greece
Dimosthenis P. Kyriazis, National Technical University of Athens, Greece
Theodora A. Varvarigou, National Technical University of Athens, Greece
Eduardo Oliveros, Telefónica Investigación y Desarrollo, Spain
Patrick Mandic, Rechenzentrum Universität Stuttgart, Germany

Service discovery mechanisms are gaining interest in the last years due to the growing bulk of information available, especially to distributed computing infrastructures like Grids and Clouds. However, a vast number of characteristics of these implementations exist, each one suitable for a number of purposes. The aim of this chapter is to extract a taxonomy of these characteristics found in modern Service Discovery systems and produce a categorization of existing implementations in a grouped and comparative way, based on these features. Furthermore, the mapping of these characteristics to the Cloud business model is produced, in order to assist in selecting the suitable solutions for each provider based on his/her location in the value chain or identify gaps in the existing implementations.

Chapter 6

Eduardo Oliveros, Telefónica Investigación y Desarrollo, Spain
Tommaso Cucinotta, Scuola Superiore Sant'Anna, Italy
Stephen C. Phillips, University of Southampton IT Innovation Centre, UK
Xiaoyu Yang, University of Southampton IT Innovation Centre, UK
Stuart Middleton, University of Southampton IT Innovation Centre, UK
Thomas Voith, Alcatel-Lucent, Germany

Monitoring and Metering are essential activities for Service Oriented Infrastructures (SOI) and Cloud services. The information collected through monitoring is necessary to ensure the correct execution of the applications in the Cloud and the monitoring of the SLA compliance. This chapter will present the reasons and difficulties for monitoring and metering on Cloud infrastructures. The approaches for monitoring of the execution environment and the network on virtualised infrastructures will be described together with the existing monitoring tools present on different commercial and research platforms.

Chapter 7

Spyridon V. Gogouvitis, National Technical University of Athens, Greece
Kleopatra G. Konstanteli, National Technical University of Athens, Greece
Dimosthenis P. Kyriazis, National Technical University of Athens, Greece
Gregory Katsaros, National Technical University of Athens, Greece
Tommaso Cucinotta, Scuola Superiore Sant'Anna, Italy
Michael Boniface, University of Southampton IT Innovation Centre, UK

With the advent of Service Oriented Architectures, more applications are build in a distributed manner based on loose coupled services. In this context, workflow management systems play an important role, as they are the means to both define the processes that realize the application goals and implement the orchestration of the different services. The purpose of this chapter is to give an overview of various solutions regarding workflow semantics and languages as well as their enactment within the scope of distributed systems. To this end, major focus is given to solutions that are aimed at Grid environments. Scheduling algorithms and advance reservation techniques are also discussed as these are one of the hottest research topics in workflow management systems.

Chapter 8

Service Level Agreements (SLAs) are nowadays used as a cornerstone for building service-oriented architectures. SLAs have been closely investigated in the scope of distributed and Grid computing and are now gaining uptake in cloud computing as well. However, most solutions have been developed for specific purposes and are not applicable generally, even though the most approaches propose a general usability. Only rarely have SLAs been applied to real-time systems. The purpose of this chapter is to analyze different fields where SLAs are used, examine the proposed solutions, and investigate how these can be improved in order to better support the creation of real-time service-oriented architectures.

Chapter 9

Enterprise adoption of cloud computing for real-time interactive applications processes is limited by their ability to meet inter-enterprise security requirements. Although some clouds offerings comply with security standards, no solution today allows businesses to assess security compliance of applications at the business level and dynamically link to security countermeasures on-demand. In this chapter we examine cloud security, privacy, and trust issues from three levels; business, jurisdiction, and technical. Firstly, we look at the business level to identify issues arising from the motivations and concerns of business stakeholders. Secondly, we explore jurisdictional level to identify risks that arise from legislation, gaps in legislation, or conflicts between legislation in different jurisdictions related to a cloud deployment, given the concerns of stakeholders. Finally, we examine the technical level to identify issues that arise from technical causes such as ICT vulnerabilities, and/or require technical solutions, such as data confidentiality and integrity protection.

    Eduardo Oliveros, Telefónica Investigación y Desarrollo, Spain
    Jesús Movilla, Telefónica Investigación y Desarrollo, Spain
    Andreas Menychtas, National Technical University of Athens, Greece
    Roland Kuebert, University of Stuttgart, Germany
    Michael Braitmaier, University of Stuttgart, Germany
    Stuart Middleton, University of Southampton IT Innovation Centre, UK
    Stephen C. Phillips, University of Southampton IT Innovation Centre, UK
    Michael Boniface, University of Southampton IT Innovation Centre, UK
    Bassem Nasser, University of Southampton IT Innovation Centre, UK

Service Oriented Infrastructures (SOIs) have recently seen increased use, mainly thanks to technologies for data centre virtualization and the emergence and increasing commercial offering of Cloud solutions. Web Services have been seen as a tool to implement SOI solutions thanks to their versatility and interoperability, but at the same time, Web services have been considered not suitable for providing interactive real-time solutions. In this chapter the state of the art of Web service technology will be analysed, and their different communication mechanisms and the existing implementations will be compared. Firstly, the different standardisation bodies working on Web service specifications relevant to SOI will be introduced. The various approaches to implement Web services will be described followed by the Web service specifications and the middleware that make use of those specifications, including the description of the commercial interfaces and development tools to create services for the cloud. In the last part of the chapter, the interoperability problems present on the different frameworks and the existing solutions to minimize those interoperability problems will be explained.

Section 3
Infrastructure as a Service

    Dominik Lamp, University of Stuttgart, Germany
    Sören Berger, University of Stuttgart, Germany
    Manuel Stein, Alcatel-Lucent Bell Labs, Germany
    Thomas Voith, Alcatel-Lucent Bell Labs, Germany
    Tommaso Cucinotta, Scuola Superiore Sant'Anna, Italy
    Marko Bertogna, Scuola Superiore Sant'Anna, Italy

Both real-time systems and virtualization have been important research topics for quite some time now. Having competing goals, research the correlation of these topics has started only recently. This chapter overviews recent results in the research literature on virtualized large-scale systems and soft real-time systems. These concepts constitute the fundamental background over which the execution environment of any large-scale service-oriented real-time architecture for highly interactive, distributed, and virtualized applications will be built in the future. While many aspects covered in this chapter have already been adopted in commercial products, others are still under intensive investigation in research labs all over the world.

Chapter 12

Manuel Stein, Alcatel-Lucent Bell Labs, Germany
Karsten Oberle, Alcatel-Lucent Bell Labs, Germany
Thomas Voith, Alcatel-Lucent Bell Labs, Germany
Dominik Lamp, University of Stuttgart, Germany
Sören Berger, University of Stuttgart, Germany

Service Oriented Infrastructures (SOI) build upon previous advancements in distributed systems, Grid computing, Cloud computing, virtualization, SOA, and technologies alike. Capabilities merged under the banner of SOI offer a solution serving long-standing business needs, but also meet increasing demand for infrastructures enabling the fast and flexible deployment of new services. However, typical current SOI realizations, e.g., Grid or Cloud solutions, do not take the network infrastructure, necessary for flawless service interaction, sufficiently into consideration. In most cases, those frameworks focus on providing huge and extremely divisible applications with hardware resources possibly distributed over several provider domains. They manage just computing related resources like CPU and RAM or Storage, but network connectivity is typically taken for granted, while network QoS aspects (e.g., jitter, delay) of the data exchange is usually not considered. Consequently, the data exchange between changeably deployed components cannot be comprehensively treated. This chapter provides an overview on related state of the art technologies regarding topics such as QoS provisioning, virtualization, and network resource management. This background is enriched with latest research results on future trends and advances in state of the art in Network Management.

Chapter 13

Sai Narasimhamurthy, Xyratex, UK
Malcolm Muggeridge, Xyratex, UK
Stefan Waldschmidt, Digital Film Technology, Germany
Fabio Checconi, Scuola Superiore Sant'Anna, Italy
Tommaso Cucinotta, Scuola Superiore Sant'Anna, Italy

The service oriented infrastructures for real-time applications ("real-time clouds") pose certain unique challenges for the data storage subsystem, which indeed is the "last mile" for all data accesses. Data storage subsystems typically used in regular enterprise environments have many limitations which impede direct applicability for such clouds, particularly in the ability to provide QoS for applications. Provision of QoS within storage is possible through a deeper understanding of the behaviour of the storage system under a variety of conditions dictated by the application and the network infrastructure. We intend to arrive at a QoS mechanism for data storage keeping in view the important parameters that come into play for the storage subsystem in a soft real-time cloud environment.

The need for guaranteed QoS and efficient management in Service Oriented Infrastructures is an essential requirement for the deployment, execution, and management of modern business applications. In that frame, the capabilities for fault detection and recovery in all layers of a Service Oriented Infrastructure are essential for the smooth operation of the business applications and the wide adoption of these solutions in the global market. In this chapter, we present the concepts of fault detection and recovery, including terminology, classification of faults, and analysis of the key processes taking place in a system in order to diagnose and recover from failures. The state of the art mechanisms and techniques for fault detection and recovery are also analyzed while recommendations for applying them in Service Oriented Infrastructure are presented.

Chapter 15

General-Purpose Operating Systems (GPOSes) are being used more and more extensively to support interactive, real-time, and distributed applications, such as found in the multimedia domain. In fact, the wide availability of supported multimedia devices and protocols, together with the wide availability of libraries and tools for handling multimedia contents, make them an almost ideal platform for the development of this kind of complex applications. However, contrarily to Real-Time Operating Systems, General-Purpose ones used to lack some important functionality that are needed for providing proper scheduling guarantees to application processes. Recently, the increasing use of GPOSes for multimedia applications is gradually pushing OS developers towards enriching the kernel of a GPOS so as to provide more and more real-time functionality, thus enhancing the performance and responsiveness of hosted time-sensitive applications. In this chapter, an overview is performed on the efforts done in the direction of enriching GPOSes with real-time capabilities, with a particular focus on the Linux OS. Due to its open-source nature and wide diffusion and availability, Linux is one of the most widely used OSes for such experimentations.

Foreword

Whenever I think of the pace at which technology evolves I think of tennis; tennis racquets, to be more specific. Wooden racquets existed in more or less the same form for one hundred years. In less than ten years after the first steel racquet became commercially available, aluminum racquets hit the market, and then within five years, racquets made of composites were being sold.

The world of Information and Communication Technology, of course, changes a lot faster than the design of tennis racquets. Development in sports equipment tends to be constrained by rules of the game, whereas advances in ICT open more opportunities for further innovations.

In the space of just a few years, Cloud Computing has become an extremely hot trend. Indeed, the cloud may be the solution for the "perfect storm" of issues that the ICT world has to contend with today – exponentially spiraling demands on storage and computing power, rising costs for energy to run and cool data centers, the push for lower power consumption, the shift to a "release early, release often" philosophy for software development, et cetera. However, there is still a lot of research to be done. Service providers on host clouds still have concerns about issues such as security and vendor lock-in. Besides needing to solve the concerns of service providers, cloud infrastructure providers are motivated to continue to find ways to take advantage of virtualization technologies to increase utilization of their hardware infrastructure to reduce CAPEX and OPEX costs.

Even while the cloud infrastructure continues to develop, we are seeing different models for the use of cloud computing emerge. Software-as-a-Service (SaaS) is perhaps the most recognizable to the average user today who gets free email service and video streaming from the Web. Platform-as-a-Service (PaaS) is rapidly growing, offering easily deployable Web platforms for application development. At a lower level, Infrastructure-as-a-Service (IaaS) is proving highly desirable for small to mid size businesses with its "pay for use" model for computing and storage resources.

The organizational use of clouds, too, is being defined. Public clouds, typically hosted by large, external companies, can offer economies of scale to keep costs low, but a risk level to which enterprises are typically unwilling to trust business critical data. Private clouds, owned by the business, are a much more secure environment, but come at a higher price in terms of capital costs and maintenance. And, of course, between these two models lay various other flavors typically enabled by "cloud bursting," or dynamic federation of clouds. Interesting times ahead.

Real-time systems are of importance to a large number of university laboratories and research institutes worldwide. This book represents the integration and discussion of many research efforts which can be exploited differently by the readers. For example, researchers may consider the future trends section as a "research agenda" for future projects, which students may identify potential PhD areas. Additionally it classifies more than four hundred research efforts under main areas, compares them, and highlights future trends.

Eliot Salant
IBM Haifa Research Labs, Israel

Eliot Salant *is the manager of the Virtualisation and Systems Management group at the IBM Haifa Labs and has been the Project Coordinator for a number of large European Union sponsored FP7 projects. He has a B.Eng. degree in Mechanical Engineering from McGill University, an M.S. degree in Biomedical Engineering from The Technion – Israel Institute of Technology, and an M.S. degree in Computer Science from Union College. He has been at IBM for over 15 years where he has held a variety of management and development positions. Before joining IBM, Mr. Salant worked at the General Electric Corporate Research and Development Center in Schenectady, New York.*

Preface

INTRODUCTION

Various attempts are conducted nowadays in order to bridge the gap between two worlds: *real-time and distributed computing*, where processing, storage, and networking need to be combined and delivered with guaranteed levels of service. The publication aims at becoming a reference point for the research community by providing a detailed analysis on the outcomes of the work performed on real-time technologies and concepts for Service Oriented Infrastructures (SOIs) - including more than 400 references to innovative works - since real-time is considered to be a multidisciplinary approach. Furthermore, each section that describes a specific area (e.g. workflow management) also presents comparisons of the research outcomes and Future Trends in order to highlight the potentials for future work in the field.

REAL-TIME & DISTRIBUTED COMPUTING

Traditionally, "real-time" refers to hard real-time systems, where even a single violation of the desired timing behavior is not acceptable, for example because it leads to total failure, possibly causing loss of human lives. However, there is also a wide range of applications that also have stringent timing and performance needs, but for which some deviations in Quality of Service (QoS) are acceptable, provided these are well understood and carefully managed. These are soft real-time applications and include a broad class of interactive and collaborative tools and environments, including concurrent design and visualization in the engineering sector, media production in the creative industries, and multi-user virtual environments in education and gaming. Soft real-time applications are traditionally developed without any real-time methodology or run-time support from the infrastructure on which they run. The result is that either expensive and dedicated hardware has to be purchased to ensure good interactivity levels and performance, or that general-purpose resources are used as a compromise (e.g. commodity operating systems and Internet networking) with no way to guarantee or control the behavior of the application as a result.

Real-time attributes in SOIs require time-constrained operation of services, both to satisfy deadlines of executing tasks that have been set by users and to sustain appropriate throughput levels. In particular, this time critical operation involves synchronous communication between services, something which has a direct impact in the design, implementation, and integration of services oriented infrastructures.

The most challenging aspect is the integration of real-time attributes into all levels of service oriented systems. Major focus is given to the need for methodologies, tools, and architectures for complex distributed systems that address the practical issues of performance guarantees, timed execution, real-time management of resources, synchronized communication under various load conditions, satisfaction of QoS constraints, as well as dealing with the trade-offs between these aspects.

The *main objective* of this publication is to provide an integrated view of the outcomes in the multidisciplinary area of real-time in distributed computing. In the core of the chapters, the readers can find answers to questions such as: what is the state of the art in the field with regard to real-time, how are the presented approaches compared, and what are the potentials in each area. Therefore, the chapters also include reflections on what are the merits and limits of the relevant approaches. The publication describes and compares more than 400 research efforts.

ORGANIZATION OF THE BOOK

Service Oriented Architectures refer to a specific architectural paradigm that emphasizes implementation of components as modular services that can be discovered and used by clients. Through the agility, scalability, elasticity, rapid self-service provisioning, and virtualization of hardware, Service Oriented Architecture principles are reflected into Grids and Clouds, which provide the ability to efficiently adapt resource provisioning to the dynamic demands of Internet users. Many architectural paradigms from distributed computing such as service-oriented infrastructures, Grids, and virtualization are incorporated into Clouds. According to these, there are three main classes in the cloud services stack which are generally agreed upon:

- Software as a Service (SaaS), which refers to the provision of an application as a service over the Internet or distributed environment.
- Platform as a Service (PaaS), which refers to the provision of a development platform and environment providing services and storage, hosted in the distributed system.
- Infrastructure as a Service (IaaS), which refers to the provision of "raw" machines (computing, storage, networking and other devices) on which the service consumers deploy their own software.

Based on the above, in this book the research efforts in different areas of real-time distributed systems are presented, classified under the aforementioned cloud services stack (i.e. SaaS, PaaS, IaaS). The book includes fifteen (15) chapters contributed by forty-three (43) scholars. In the first section (named "Software as a Service"), Chapter 1 introduces specific techniques used to model and analyze the required QoS level for real-time applications as well as mechanisms to find business models where value can be provided at all stages in the value-chain. For example, how can an application user identify a set of service providers that in combination provide the best solution to a workflow, how much risk is involved, et cetera. Authors of Chapter 2 provide an overview of model-driven engineering approaches, standards, resources, and tools that support different aspects of model-driven software engineering: language development, modeling services, and real-time applications. Chapter 3 discusses on the research efforts that aim to APIs for real-time computing, including real-time application interfaces, as well as available cloud APIs, along with the architecture and the technologies that they support. The last chapter of the first section, Chapter 4 presents the current state-of-the-art technology and methodologies regarding the evaluation of the provided QoS in service oriented environments.

Section 2 (named "Platform as a Service"), starts with Chapter 5, in which authors extract a taxonomy of characteristics found in modern service discovery systems and produce a categorization of existing implementations in a grouped and comparative way, based on these features. Furthermore, the authors introduce a mapping of these characteristics to the cloud business model, in order to assist in selecting the suitable solutions for each provider based on his location in the value chain or identify gaps in the existing implementations. Chapter 6 introduces the reasons and difficulties for monitoring and metering on Cloud infrastructures. The approaches for monitoring of the execution environment and the network on virtualized infrastructures are described along with the existing monitoring tools present on different commercial and research platforms. Still in the PaaS section of the book, Chapter 7 gives an overview of various research efforts regarding workflow semantics and languages as well as their enactment within the scope of distributed systems. Scheduling algorithms and advance reservation techniques are also discussed as these are one of the hottest research topics in workflow management systems. Authors of Chapter 8 analyze different fields where Service Level Agreements are used, examine the proposed solutions, and investigate how these can be improved in order to better support the creation of real-time service-oriented architectures. Addressing security concerns is the topic of Chapter 9, in which authors examine cloud security, privacy, and trust issues from three levels: business (to identify issues arising from the motivations and concerns of business stakeholders), jurisdiction (to identify risks that arise from legislation, gaps in legislation, or conflicts between legislation in different jurisdictions related to a cloud deployment), and technical (to identify issues that arise from technical causes such as ICT vulnerabilities, and/or require technical solutions, such as data confidentiality and integrity protection). The last chapter of the second section of the book, Chapter 10, introduces different Web service specifications, analyses their different communication mechanisms, and compares the existing implementations. Moreover, various approaches to implement Web services are described by the authors followed by the middleware that makes use of specific web service specifications, including the description of the commercial interfaces and development tools to create services for distributed systems. Interoperability problems are also mentioned in Chapter 10.

The last section of the book, named "Infrastructure as a Service," discusses how different research efforts address issues related to virtualization of computing, storage, and network resources on the infrastructure level. In this context, Chapter 11 provides recent results in the research literature on virtualized large-scale systems and soft real-time systems. These concepts constitute the fundamental background over which the execution environment of any large-scale service-oriented real-time architecture for highly interactive, distributed, and virtualized applications will be built in the future. Authors of Chapter 12 introduce related state of the art technologies regarding topics such as QoS provisioning, virtualization, and network resource management. This background is enriched with latest research results on future trends and advances in network management. Storage approaches are tackled in Chapter 13. Authors discuss how QoS provision within storage in distributed systems is possible given the behavior of the storage system under a variety of conditions dictated by the application and the network infrastructure. Besides, the authors present a QoS mechanism for data storage keeping in view the important parameters that come into play for the storage subsystem in a soft real-time cloud environment. Chapter 14 presents the concepts of fault detection and recovery, including terminology, classification of faults, and analysis of the key processes taking place in a system in order to diagnose and recover from failures. The state of the art mechanisms and techniques for fault detection and recovery are also analyzed, while recommendations for applying them in Service Oriented Infrastructure are presented. The last book chapter, Chapter 15 provides an overview of different research efforts in the direction of enriching general purpose operating systems with real-time capabilities, with a particular focus on the Linux OS, since due to its open-source nature and wide diffusion and availability, Linux is one of the most widely used operating systems for such experimentations.

TARGET AUDIENCE

The target audience for the specific book ranges from PhD or Master's students to researchers and teachers. The publication is a point of reference for real-time distributed systems, classifying more than 400 research efforts, to which the aforementioned audience can refer. From the domain or community point of view, researchers in real-time and distributed systems are naturally meant since they could discover through this book the particularities, strengths, weaknesses, and future trends of different research areas and potentially draft a "research agenda" for future projects according to these. Given the number of laboratories in universities and research institutes worldwide that deal with real-time systems, we expect this book to become a point of reference for the students and researchers in the multidisciplinary area of real-time in distributed computing.

CONCLUSION

Today, the Internet is the backbone of modern society and the global economy supporting almost every aspect of social and business interaction. The success of the global connectivity principle within the original Internet architecture has created and promoted new continuously evolving interaction models offering faster, more efficient, and richer collaborative and community experiences. In this context and given that sensors networks are emerging, focus is being put upon infrastructures that will be able to process and deliver in real-time interactive applications. To this direction, the publication provides a point of reference for the research community in the field of distributed environments that allows for the adoption of interactive real-time applications.

Dimosthenis P. Kyriazis
National Technical University of Athens, Greece

Theodora A. Varvarigou
National Technical University of Athens, Greece

Kleopatra G. Konstanteli
National Technical University of Athens, Greece

Acknowledgment

Several collaborators and colleagues, mainly from the European funded IRMOS Project, have contributed greatly to this comprehensive book. Without their help, the preparation of this book would be impossible. The editors would take this chance to thank all book chapter authors, who have contributed their research results to this book. We also owe a debt of gratitude to the reviewers who have provided valuable comments on the book chapters. We also wish to record our sincere thanks to the Editorial Advisory Board members. Last but not least, special thanks are given to Mr. Joel Gamon of IGI Global for his assistance in the book preparation.

Dimosthenis P. Kyriazis
National Technical University of Athens, Greece

Theodora A. Varvarigou
National Technical University of Athens, Greece

Kleopatra G. Konstanteli
National Technical University of Athens, Greece

Section 1
Software as a Service

Chapter 1
Modelling and Analysing QoS for Real–Time Interactive Applications on the Cloud

Matthew Addis
University of Southampton IT Innovation Centre, UK

Arturo Servin
University of Southampton IT Innovation Centre, UK

Michael Boniface
University of Southampton IT Innovation Centre, UK

Zlatko Zlatev
University of Southampton IT Innovation Centre, UK

Juri Papay
University of Southampton IT Innovation Centre, UK

George Kousiouris
National Technical University Athens, Greece

ABSTRACT

The complexity of determining resource provisioning policies for applications in such complex environments introduces significant inefficiencies in the cloud. Novel approaches are needed to efficiently model and analyse Quality of Service for such applications, especially those with real-time constraints. This chapter investigates some of the techniques that can be used to explore these trade-offs and to find business models where value can be provided at all stages in the value-chain. For example, how can an application user identify a set of service providers that provide the best solution to their workflow in combination? How much risk is involved, e.g. what is the probability and impact of a failure of a service provider to deliver the QoS they promise? How can Service Level Agreements be specified that provide the flexibility to accommodate variability in service use, yet don't result in unnecessarily high cost to the consumer due to the service provider having to use massive over-provisioning of resources to ensure they can meet times of peak-load?

DOI: 10.4018/978-1-60960-827-9.ch001

OVERVIEW

Cloud computing must support complex service-oriented workflows where multiple actors at different geographical locations interact 'in real-time' using a range of software applications that are accessible as services and are executed at one or more service provider facilities. Determining the resource provisioning policies for applications in such complex environments has created the need for novel approaches to efficiently model and analyse Quality of Service for Real-time Interactive Applications on the Cloud. These tools and techniques form part of a new class of infrastructure called Platform-as-a-Service (PaaS). PaaS must provide a choice of models for provision and use of resources, e.g. 'in house', 'outsource', 'share', which includes the location of the people using these resources. This choice is not a simple one and typically involves trade-offs between cost, QoS, flexibility, security and other factors. Therefore, once the resource requirements of an application are known, there needs to be a straightforward interface to the Infrastructure-as-a-Service (IaaS) to reserve and monitor resources. The challenge of course is to know what resources are needed. This is where significant uncertainty comes into play. Mapping from application needs (e.g. rendering at a certain frame rate) to resource requirements (processing power, memory, bandwidth) is typically non-deterministic. Stochastic variations occur, especially in interactive applications where application users are able to adjust application settings during application execution (e.g. making tweaks to the parameters of a render code, or changing the number of frames to be rendered). In some cases, the workflow itself may evolve at 'execution time' and it is not possible to define the steps or paths through the workflow until at least some of the steps have been executed. In summary, Clouds needs to support provisioning of multiple services to support applications where there is uncertainty in data volumes, data rates, computational needs, number of users, workflow steps and paths etc. If resources are underestimated then it is likely that the application workflow will fail or degrade unacceptably. If resources are overestimated then consequent charging by service providers of what resources were reserved rather than what were used may cause costs to rise and applications to be uneconomic.

The challenge is to identify the range of resource requirements that bound application execution and the likelihood that execution will be within this range. The decision is then one of cost of provisioning for this range (and the cost incurred for deviations from the range) against the risk (probability and impact) that execution deviates from the range. This is a risk management problem and one that can only be tackled in terms of probabilities.

The same type of problem exists for various actors in the value chain, be it a post-house who have a deadline to meet and want to identify the set of service providers that give them the best chance of meeting this deadline at the lowest cost, or a service provider who wants to optimise the return on their investment in resources by achieving the best balance between honouring SLA commitments and penalties incurred if they breach these SLAs.

This chapter investigates some of the techniques that can be used to explore these trade-offs and to find business models where value can be provided at all stages in the value-chain. For example, how can an application user identify a set of service providers that in combination provide the best solution to their workflow? How much risk is involved, e.g. what is the probability and impact of a failure of a service provider to deliver the QoS they promise? How can Service Level Agreements be specified that provide the flexibility to accommodate variability in service use, yet don't result in unnecessarily high cost to the consumer due to the service provider having to use massive over-provisioning of resources to ensure they can meet times of peak-load?

Figure 1. Development of platform-independent load models

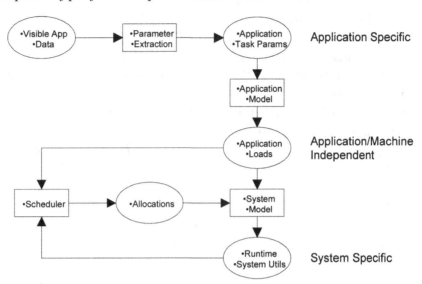

APPROACHES, IMPLEMENTATIONS AND COMPARISONS

In the following sections we consider some of the most significant areas of research that have been considered in qualitative and quantitative analysis and modelling with respect to service-oriented infrastructures.

Analytical Characterisation Models

Analytical characterisation models use simple algebraic expressions that enable to characterise Service Oriented Infrastructures (SOI). This approach assumes numerous approximations that make the system analytically tractable. The predictions obtained by characterisation are less accurate, however they provide a quick estimation of the impact of various parameters. Examples of this approach include IT Innovation's work on analytical models that cover a range of applications including large scale engineering simulations, multi-user environments and transaction processing (Floros, Meacham, Papay, & Surridge, 1999; Meacham, Floros, & Surridge, 1998; Risse, Wombacher, Surridge, Taylor, & Aberer, 2001).

The key aspects of the characterisation methodology used in analytical modelling are described below.

The first step is to develop machine-independent application models, in which the load associated with an application, could be represented in terms of basic resource requirements (CPU, memory size, I/O traffic and disk volume). The run-time could then be found using an application-independent machine model, describing the performance of the machine in terms of these basic resources. After the factorisation of analytical performance models the intermediate application- and machine-independent load models can be derived. These models then can be used to compare tasks prior to making scheduling decisions about which machine each would run on. The overall scheduling process is illustrated in Figure 1.

The accuracy of performance predictions obtained by this technique was illustrated by several case studies drawn from the domain of mechanical simulations (Risse et al, 2001). It is important to stress that, as is commonly the case for commercial software codes, the source code for the application is not available for instrumentation and all analytical models have therefore to be derived from benchmarking the application on different computer architectures. During benchmarking, the run-time, memory, disk traffic, disk space parameters are measured. These measurements are then used for the development of the analytical performance models.

The advantage of an analytical approach is that it provides simple mathematical expressions that include the key parameters governing the performance of the application. The models are easy to understand and they are suitable for "back of the envelope" calculations. The main drawback is that the development of these models requires substantial benchmarking effort and also some knowledge of the application. Often numerous approximations are required in order to make the problem analytically tractable. Furthermore, it is almost impossible to obtain high accuracy for arbitrary inputs from a single model of a complex industrial application. Nevertheless, these experiments demonstrate that good accuracy can be obtained for reasonably large classes of inputs (e.g. pure shell or pure solid models for engineering simulations) even for industrial codes for which the source code is not available.

The use of neuro-fuzzy models represents a step towards the automatic generation of performance models, and was investigated in the COPE project (Floros, 1999). The experience with hand-tuned performance modelling has shown that this approach requires a substantial knowledge of the governing parameters and the relationship between them if we wish to derive accurate mathematical models. The neuro-fuzzy technique offers a more promising approach since it provides learning capability and also higher accuracy. It is also important to mention that no detailed knowledge of the application is required in order to generate prediction models. Aside from the high accuracy achieved (as good if not better than our previous analytical models), this approach has the advantage that operational measurements are used to enhance the performance models. This means that the model that emerges from the neuro-fuzzy

estimator will be well matched to the users of the system. However, we should underline that it is not a silver bullet; the accuracy of this method depends on the quality and amount of input data and on the initial assumptions that serve as a seed for the modeling process, and the models may be difficult to interpret.

Queuing Network Models

The Queuing Network approach has been used for many years for modelling distributed systems. These models for the simplest cases can be evaluated analytically and by using simulations. Although the analytical models provide quick results, however they are applicable only for the analysis of simplest cases. An example of this approach is described by Kraiss et al. (Hey, Papay, & Surridge, 2005)where an M/G/1 model was used for the performance evaluation of a message passing system. Extending Queuing Networks with parameters representing QoS is an intensive research area (Kraiss, Schoen, Weikum & Deppisch, 2001; Woodside & Menascé, 2006). The TAPAS (http://tapas.sourceforge.net) project represents a promising approach that enables to generate queuing models directly from the UML specification. This allows the user to assess the performance cost of various design options at an early stage of development.

Soft Real-Time Behaviour Modelling and Verification

End users will have a variety of workflows that accompany requirements use cases. These workflows define threads of concurrent behaviour that must be sufficiently monitored and controlled with respect to QoS criteria. These behaviours have QoS properties that need modelling and verifying prior to runtime and potentially prior to SLA negotiation.

Modelling will consist of two types of simulation/verification activities. In the first case global constraints will be checked for parameters that capture user defined values. For example, perhaps that certain frame rates are achieved at a particular resolution within a specific time frame. The second type of simulation/verification will be used to prove that workflows cause system events to be scheduled within the appropriate temporal order of a system execution, no matter what asynchronous interleaving occurs between the different threads of activity permitted by the workflow. For example, if a large scale battle scene for a blockbuster film requires multiple additional FX elements then these need to be rendered to a suitable resolution, which may occur concurrently across appropriate resources that synchronise within a given time frame after which appropriate lighting, shading and textures will be added to complete the scene. Different users in a distributed network may be responsible for attributes of various subsets of these FX elements. In addition during FX content creation circumstances may dynamically change again requiring additional post house involvement from perhaps multiple such post houses.

Any real-time behaviour models need to take into account that practitioners usually define systems that are at best partially defined and ambiguous. Thus simulation and verification techniques need to avoid false positives that can cause exceptions to be raised in SLAs whilst capturing genuine issues that affect overall performance and quality. Approaches include but are not limited to:

Soft real-time behaviour abstractions: user events and interactions through service interfaces will most likely be modelled within an MDE framework. That will require a UML soft real-time SOI profile to define suitable abstractions. The IST project SENSORIA (http://www.sensoria-ist.eu) has adopted UML as part of a software engineering methodology for designing and verifying SOI systems. Many of the foundational themes they have been investigating are related to those which will need to be adapted to suit the cloud, and are referenced in the following sections. SENSORIA are investigating SOA software engineering in the broader context rather than focusing on real-time issues for distributed multimedia content creation over an SOI.

Model driven engineering for soft real-time systems: OMG have published two profiles concerning real-time embedded systems and QoS of UML models (OMG, 2002), but as yet have not produced any proposals for adapting these for SOI. UML seems an ideal vehicle for describing partially defined service behaviours in a form that will be relevant to the many stakeholders in the cloud. SENSORIA (http://www.sensoria-ist.eu) are developing a UML profile UML4SOA that considers service orchestration and workflow modelling, but for the most part at the analytical level. Figure 2 shows one of the class diagrams from UML4SOA describing the compensation architecture.

SENSORIA have been investigating qualitative analysis of service behaviour with respect to QoS concerns, but so far their work is complementary to the issues that need to be addressed for cloud computing. UML4SOA integrates several of the QoS catalogue elements from the OMG standard (OMG, 2004) in order to define a coherent extension of the existing standards. Where SENSORIA considers QoS performance issues it has so far been with respect to management of resources within a single domain with central control, as opposed to the cross-domain cloud scenarios where no such central control will exist and resource control may be spread across many domains with individual SLAs defining the performance characteristics of the SOI.

Sequence and activity diagrams: Partial behaviours for distributed systems are commonly described with UML sequence and activity diagrams. Sequence diagrams have a simple mechanism for describing timing constraints that makes it relatively straightforward to directly represent QoS properties visually. Sequence diagrams are very common in standards based activities for telecommunications protocols (Koch, Mayer, Heckel, Gönczy, & Montangero, 2007). Sequence

Figure 2. UML4SOA Compensation Class Diagram

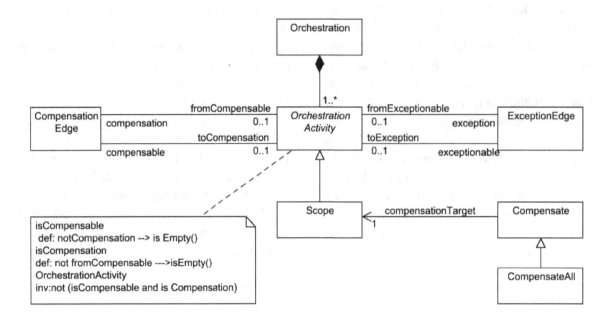

diagrams are appealing since they naturally capture workflow behaviours and relate them to user based events from requirements specifications. Although general property checking does not allow decisions for sequence diagrams (ETSI, 2001) certain types of behaviours can be checked effectively for them such as deadlocks and race conditions (Alur & Yannakakis, 1999; Mitchell, 2008). Sequence diagrams may represent a usable mechanism for describing QoS constraints as they relate to workflows that are amenable to automated analysis and reasoning with respect to SLAs. Some work towards formalising a translation between sequence diagram descriptions of service behaviours and process algebras has already been done in (Mitchell, 2005). Activity diagrams are another form of interaction type diagram that is useful for describing partially defined system interactions. The underlying semantics for an activity diagram can be captured in much the same manner as for sequence diagrams. Hence, from the point of view of simulation and verification they serve much the same purpose. As mentioned sequence diagrams

provide a more direct mechanism for defining timing constraints.

Figure 3 represents a hypothetical high level sequence diagram that represents an example of the type of QoS concern that may be relevant to end users of the cloud. It attempts to capture the scenario of physically dislocated employees logging into a video streaming server in order to collaboratively review content for a project they are jointly working on. To simplify the diagram we have not included formal UML notations for timing constraints and have assumed there will be exactly two employees. Instead we have simply annotated the diagram with intuitive user level requirements. The diagram is interesting from cloud perspective since it mixes real-time user constraints with asynchronous workflow control requirements. It also highlights the partial and incomplete nature of user requirements.

Despite the ambiguities inherent in this example it is does impose several formal constraints on message flows between actors and other stakeholders, which will require analysis and validation with any model. For example:

Figure 3. High Level Example of UML User QoS Constraint

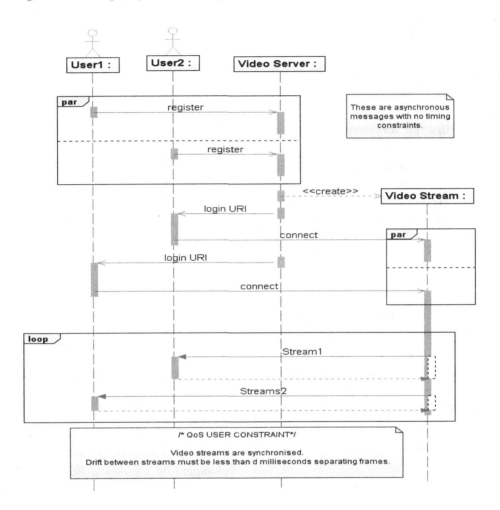

- are the asynchronous exchanges logically consistent
- will there be any potential deadlocks caused by incorporating this scenario within a partially constructed model
- are there any race conditions resulting from these requirements
- how do we extend this scenario to many users joining the system
- how do we decompose the requirements of the video stream into meaningful requirements for the video server and underlying network

Notice that none of these constraints are specific to real-time issues. They do not even begin to address the timing constraint requirements. Hence, there will be many analytical verification issues that need to be addressed in conjunction with quantitative analysis of performance issues. However, real-time constraints may well impact on the analytical verification process, since timing constraints will significantly affect causal relationships between services that are critical in defining any state based behavioural model.

There has also been some work considering how to describe service behaviour in the form of Message Sequence Charts (MSCs) (which are equivalent to UML sequence diagrams) and then translate them to a process algebra (Mitchell, 2005; Broy, Krugger, & Meisinger, 2007). That work also considers how to represent the resulting behaviour within AspectJ. Those works attempt to address the issue of partially specified service behaviour.

Process algebras for services: Process algebras, such as CCS and CSP, arose from the need to have an algebraic means of describing interleaving behaviour of communicating distributed systems at an abstract level that provided a mechanism for formal verification. They are ideal in situations where there is a need to model systems in order to cope with:

- compositionality, where systems have to be considered as interacting subsystems
- formality, ensuring there are exact descriptions with no ambiguity, which can be shared between all stakeholder toolsets
- abstraction, the ability to seamlessly move between different layers of system descriptions that are relevant to particular layers within an architecture

For SOI however there are some shortcomings of these original algebras. For example, traditional process algebras are not well suited to describing compensation or long running transactions and it is difficult to adequately handle composition of services in an elegant way. (Krugger & Matthew, 2004; Bruni, Melgratti, & Montanari, 2005) have developed calculi in an attempt to address these issues. (Bocchi, Laneve, & Zavattaro, 2003; Guidi, Lucchi, Gorrieri, Busi, & Zavattaro, 2006) have developed further calculi in order to address some of the wider issues of service behaviour. Verifying properties of choreography of web services is also an area where bespoke process algebras have been developed, (Mitchell, 2005; Guidi, 2007). Another current effort along these lines is Stochastic COWS (Li, He, Zhu, & Pu, 2007; Lapadula, Pugliese, & Tiezzi, 2007) process algebra. This

Figure 5. Example of inverse exponential probability density function

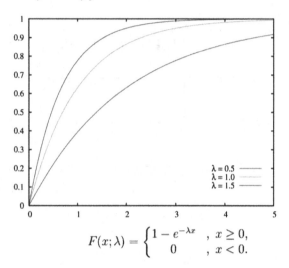

$$F(x; \lambda) = \begin{cases} 1 - e^{-\lambda x} & , \ x \geq 0, \\ 0 & , \ x < 0. \end{cases}$$

is one of several process algebras that adopt the approach of generating a continuous time Markov chain (CTMC) from a process algebra term. In this case the resulting CTMC is used as input to the PRISM stochastic model checker (Prandi & Quaglia, 2007).

PEPA: The PEPA tool set (http://www.dcs.ed.ac.uk/pepa) has been continuously under development by a group at Edinburgh University UK since 1991. The PEPA Eclipse plug-in has been adopted within the SENSORIA consortium as one of the formal tools they are integrating into their work. It represents a good example of what is achievable with such tools.

The PEPA process algebra uses normal process algebra operators such as sequential composition, choice, and cooperative concurrent composition. Actions within a process term are also annotated with stochastic values that represent the probable duration of the event. The probability is defined as an inverse exponential distribution (see Figure 5) in order to be able to derive a CTMC from the model. Such inverse probability density functions are known as rates, and characterise the probability distribution for the duration of the event.

Table 1. PEPA Example of Elementary Web Server

```
// A PEPA model of a web server
// http://www.dcs.ed.ac.uk/pepa/webserver/ws-3-3-2-2.pepa

// Rate definitions
rsf = 1.0;
rsw = 1.0;
rwbw = 1.0;
rrsrr = 1.12;
rsrl = 0.94;
rsfr = 3.0;
rsfsw = 0.9;
rwra = 1.0;
rsgsfra = 2.0;

// Server definitions
Server = (s_read_request, infty).Server_read
         + (s_fail, rsf).Server_fail + (s_write, rsw).Server;
Server_read = (s_read_lookup, rsrl).Server;
Server_fail = (s_fail_recover, rsfr).Server
              + (s_fail_recover_all, infty).Server +
                (s_write, rsfsw).Server_fail;

// Server groups
Server_group_0 = (s_fail, infty).Server_group_1;
Server_group_1 = (s_fail, infty).Server_group_2 +
                 (s_fail_recover, infty).Server_group_0;
Server_group_2 = (s_fail, infty).Server_group_3 +
(s_fail_recover, infty).Server_group_1;
Server_group_3 = (s_fail_recover_all, rsgsfra).Server_group_0;

// Write buffer
Write_buffer_0 = (b_write, infty).Write_buffer_1;
Write_buffer_1 = (b_write, infty).Write_buffer_2 +
                 (s_write, infty).Write_buffer_0;
Write_buffer_2 = (b_write, infty).Write_buffer_3 +
                 (s_write, infty).Write_buffer_0;
Write_buffer_3 = (s_write, infty).Write_buffer_0;

// Writer definition
Writer = (b_write,rwbw).Writer_writ;
Writer_writ = (rw_reset_all,infty).Writer;

// Reader component
Reader = (s_read_request,rrsrr).Reader_next;
Reader_next = (s_read_lookup, infty).Reader_read;
Reader_read = (rw_reset_all, infty).Reader;

// Reader/Writer reset
RW_reset = (rw_reset_all, rwra).RW_reset;

// System equation
((Writer <rw_reset_all> Writer <rw_reset_all> (
  Reader <rw_reset_all> Reader) <rw_reset_all> RW_reset)
<b_write,s_read_request,s_read_lookup> (
((Server <s_write,s_fail_recover_all> Server
        <s_write,s_fail_recover_all> Server)
<s_fail,s_fail_recover,s_fail_recover_all> Server_group_0
) <s_write> Write_buffer_0))
```

Figure 4. Some PRISM operators for constructing Stochastic Buchi Automaton

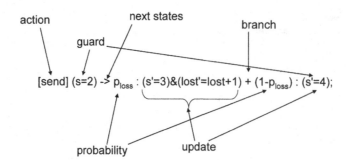

Table 1 shows a PEPA example for an elementary Web Server taken from the DCS web site at Edinburgh. It captures the idea of a server that allows clients to read or write content to the server, with possible contention through queuing to the read write buffers on the server. Such a process algebra provides a compact elegant formal representation of system behaviour. It is ideal as a target language for a high level workflow analysis tool that translates a formal graphical representation of requirements into an analytical/ quantitative description for V&V purposes.

The PEPA tool can perform a number of stochastic analyses on the CTMC derived from a process algebra model. The tool can also present these in graphical form. PEPA can perform throughput, utilization, and population analysis. Some preliminary work has investigated how PEPA could be used in describing QoS values within a process algebra in order to reason formally about SLA constraints (Clark & Gilmore, 2006). In that example the SLA constraints are reasoned about directly in order to discover if the high level model can deliver a service within the QoS requirements. For that work the authors are not concerned with mapping high level QoS parameters to lower level networking parameters. It is also not concerned with multiple SLAs and instead considers a central controlling service which has sole responsibility for ensuring compliance.

One of the strengths of stochastic process algebras is the ability to generate a CTMC from a process term. It is then possible to perform general stochastic model checking on such a CTMC using a tool such as Matlab or PRISM (http://www.prismmodelchecker.org).

PRISM was originally developed by the University of Birmingham. This group has now moved to Oxford University. PRISM can use a probabilistic temporal logic (PCTL) to describe arbitrary causal interrelationships that can then be verified automatically. PRISM can also output Matlab and Mathematica model descriptions for other forms of quantitative analysis. The following expression in Figure 4 illustrates some typical language constructs in PRISM.

Petri nets: Petri nets are able to more closely represent true concurrency than process algebras, which model concurrent behaviours with interleaving semantics. The cost of this is an increase in computational complexity and a greater complexity in constructing compositions of services. Although there is an apparent increase in expressive power it is not yet clear that this gives real advantages over the more streamlined process algebra approaches, which have generally shown a greater flexibility in modelling just those aspects of a system that need to be reasoned about. Petri nets are a mature formalism with a plethora of verification and modelling tools, a list of some of these can be found here (Clark & Gilmore, 2006).

(Schmidt & Stahl, 2004; Kang, Yang, & Yuan, 2007) have considered how to represent services described in WS-BPEL in terms of colored petri nets. In particular they considered how to verify that WS-BPEL services when composed in certain configurations are valid. (Wang, H. & Wang, 2007) considered how to incorporate object oriented concepts within a colored petri net formalism to facilitate modelling service composition and facilitate mapping to OO modelling tools. (Li, Liang, Song & Zhou, 2007) considered how to incorporate some aspects of QoS within a colored petri net model. They considered compositional aspects of services with respect to QoS properties and how to establish whether QoS would be preserved through composition.

Discrete event models: Discrete Event Simulation (DES) provides a powerful technique with which to model complex systems. In the simplest case we can represent use of a service by a time delay. This time delay is a result of contribution of many factors such as the amount of computation, the resources used by individual tasks, the load on the computer, etc. In the cloud, DES provides a candidate technology since:

- It is necessary to model a complex non-determistic system with numerous stochastic variables
- DES is a mature technology proven in many industrial applications
- There is a strong tool support
- DES enables us to model systems with humans in the loop and from the perspective of different categories of users that have been identified in the value chain
- The terminology used by DES is well understood and can serve for communicating ideas between project partners

DES also allows an incremental approach, for example by allowing to start with an initial simple set of assumptions and then move on to more sophisticated models. For example, to start with one can represent service duration by a time delay of initially fixed duration and then later add a stochastic boundary. Multiuser models can be

introduced through service queues. Workflows can be represented through chains of services. We can refine distribution functions based on empirical data collected in test beds.

There are some initial studies investigating the feasibility of discrete event simulation approach to modelling of SOA that need to be carefully assessed whether they meet the requirements of the project (Sloane et al, 2007; Schruben, 2000).

Related Integrated Projects

There are three other IPs that have been investigating complementary work relevant to this section. SENSORIA referred to in section 0, EUQoS (http://www.euqos.eu) and TAPAS (http://tapas.sourceforge.net). This section briefly mentions the relevant parts of these projects that were not discussed earlier.

TAPAS (Trusted and QoS-Aware Provision of Application Services): TAPAS is an exploratory project with an emphasis on the development of novel techniques for provisioning and construction of Internet Application Services (IAS) (Cook, Shrivastava, & Wheater, 2003; Denaro, Polini, & Emmerich, 2004; Kaveh, & Emmerich, 2003). The main focus areas of the project are:

- Service Level Agreements (SLAs) between application services
- QoS of middleware services
- Trust and security between IAS service providers
- Model Driven Service Architectures
- SLA composition and validation

One of the key objectives is the extension of SLAs with QoS aspects and their application in a real service oriented architecture. The project also aims to develop a model checking tool that enables to reason about QoS characteristics of components. The project uses the UML standard for modelling and analysis of mechanisms and interactions between IASs. Using UML allows the user to assess the performance cost of various design options at an early stage of development. The main features of the QoS aware architecture are:

- Support for real-world auction scenarios with strong trust and QoS aspects
- Monitoring SLA violations
- Dynamic service composition and deployment
- Contract Monitoring and enforcement
- Middleware for trusted coordination
- QoS metric collection
- QoS monitoring and violation detection

The initial study of the TAPAS project indicates that there are several aspects of this project that might be relevant for cloud computing as well. These concern the QoS and SLA related work.

EUQoS: To quote from the EUQoS web site: ` The key objective of EuQoS is to research, integrate, test, validate and demonstrate end-to-end QoS technologies to support the infrastructure up-grade for advanced QoS-aware applications - voice, video-conferencing, video-streaming, educational, tele-engineering and medical applications - over multiple, heterogeneous research, scientific and industrial network domains.'

EUQoS have considered a number of scenarios for QoS provision over existing network standards, such as WiFi, LAN, UMTS and xDSL. For these networks the project considers a suite of multimedia content to be delivered over the networks, such as voice over IP (VoIP), video tele-conferencing and video on demand. The EUQoS project has investigated a variety of techniques for prioritising traffic and allocation of resource. An overview of their work can be found in deliverable D2.1.2 Validation of the EuQoS system by simulation. EUQoS have followed ITU and IEEE standards for their simulation work, so their results may be relevant to the cloud.

FUTURE TRENDS: HOW DO WE PROCEED BEYOND THE STATE OF THE ART?

Much of the current work in modelling a SOI is focussed on UML profiles and applying formal analysis techniques to those models. For example formal reasoning about concurrent protocols for service implementation; or stochastic modelling of utilisation, latency and jitter in networks of activates within a virtualized network topology. For the cloud it is important to continue with this trend and apply UML to describe the integration of the real-time aspects of service execution with the non-real-time workflow creation, management and enactment aspects.

Research themes modelling and analysing QoS for Real-time Interactive Applications on the Cloud include

- Development of a UML profile for real-time concepts that is compatible with the existing UML4SOA and other OMG profiles for QoS and real-time behaviour
- Development of behavioural models within the UML profile for SLA negotiation that includes the comparison of different QoS user parameters within the selection and negotiation process
- Determine formal reasoning languages that can correctly model the profile behaviours
- Formally describe the SLA concepts that determine how a service needs to be monitored and evaluated against its QoS characteristics during execution
- Development of a methodology for applying stochastic and formal analysis techniques that can be integrated into the behavioural components of a the UML profile for service-oriented workflows

REFERENCES

Alur, R., & Yannakakis, M. (1999). Model checking of message sequence charts. In *Proceedings of the Tenth International Conference on Concurrency Theory, LNCS 1661*, (pp 114–129). Springer.

Bocchi, L., Laneve, C., & Zavattaro, G. (2003). A calculus for long-running transactions. In *Proceeding Conference on Formal Methods Open Object-based Distributed Systems* (FMOOD), *LNCS 2884*, (pp. 124–138).

Broy, M., Krugger, I., & Meisinger, M. (2007). A formal model of services. *ACM Transactions on Software Engineering and Methodology, 16*(1). doi:10.1145/1189748.1189753

Bruni, R., Melgratti, H. C., & Montanari, U. (2005). *Theoretical foundations for compensations in flow composition languages.* In Symposium on Principles of Programming Languages (PoPL), (pp. 209–220).

Clark, A., & Gilmore, S. (2006). Evaluating quality of service for service level agreements. In L. Brim & M. Leucker (Eds.), *Proceedings of the 11th International Workshop on Formal Methods for Industrial Critical Systems, LNCS vol. 4346* (pp. 181-194). Springer-Verlag.

Cook, N., Shrivastava, S., & Wheater, S. (2003, November). Middleware support for non-repudiable transactional information sharing between enterprises. In *Proceedings of 4th IFIP International Conf. on Distributed Applications and Interoperable Systems.*

Denaro, G., Polini, A., & Emmerich, W. (2004, January). Early performance testing of distributed software applications. In *Proceedings of the 4th Int. Workshop on Software and Performance*, San Francisco, ACM Press.

ETSI. (2001). *Methodological approach to the use of object-orientation in the standards making process. ETSI EG, 201*, 872.

Floros, N., Meacham, K., Papay, J., & Surridge, M. (1999). Predictive resource management for unitary meta-applications. *Future Generation Computer Systems, 15*, 723–734. doi:10.1016/S0167-739X(99)00022-9

Guidi, C. (2007, March). *Formalizing languages for service oriented computing.* (Technical Report, UBLCS-2007-07), Department of Computer Science, University of Bologna.

Guidi, C., Lucchi, R., Gorrieri, R., Busi, N., & Zavattaro, G. (2006). SOCK: A calculus for service oriented computing. In *International Conference on Service Oriented Computing (ICSOC), LNCS 4294*, (pp. 327–338).

Hey, T., Papay, J., & Surridge, M. (2005). The role of performance engineering techniques in the context of the Grid. *Concurrency and Computation: Practice and Experience, 17*(2-4), 297-316. ISSN 1532-0626

Kang, H., Yang, X., & Yuan, S. (2007, September). Modeling and verification of Web services composition based on CPN. In *Proceedings of IFIP international Conference on Network and Parallel Computing Workshops*, (pp. 613-617). NPC. Washington, DC: IEEE Computer Society.

Kaveh, N., & Emmerich, W. (2003). Validating distributed object and component designs in formal methods for software architecture. [Springer Verlag.]. *Lecture Notes in Computer Science, 2804*, 63–91. doi:10.1007/978-3-540-39800-4_5

Koch, N., Mayer, P., Heckel, R., Gönczy, L., & Montangero, C. (2007). *D1.4a: UML for service-oriented systems, Sensoria software engineering for service-oriented overlay computers.* Retrieved from http://www.pst.ifi.lmu.de/ projekte/Sensoria/del_24/D1.4.a.pdf

Kraiss, A., Schoen, F., Weikum, G., & Deppisch, U. (2001). Towards response time guarantees for e-service middleware. *A Quarterly Bulletin of the Computer Society of the IEEE Technical Committee on Data Engineering, 24*(1), 58–63.

Krugger, I., & Matthew, R. (2004). Systematic development and exploration of service-oriented software architectures. In *Proceedings of the 4th Working IEEE/IFIP Conference on Software Architecture* (WICSA) (Oslo), (pp. 177–187).

Lapadula, A., Pugliese, R., & Tiezzi, F. (2007). *Calculus for orchestration of Web services*. In *Proc. European Symposium on Programming* (ESOP). *LNCS, vol. 4421*, (pp. 33–47). Heidelberg, Germany: Springer. Retrieved from http://rap.dsi.unifi.it/cows

Li, J., He, J., Zhu, H., & Pu, G. (2007). Modeling and verifying Web services choreography using process algebra. In *Proceedings of the 31st IEEE Software Engineering Workshop*, (pp. 256-268). Washington, DC: IEEE Computer Society. (March 06-08, 2007).

Li, W., Liang, X., Song, H., & Zhou, X. (2007, June). QoS-driven service composition modeling with extended hierarchical CPN. In *Proceedings of the First Joint IEEE/IFIP Symposium on Theoretical Aspects of Software Engineering*, (pp. 483-492). Washington, DC: IEEE Computer Society. Retrieved from http://dx.doi.org/10.1109/TASE.2007.39

Meacham, K. E., Floros, N., & Surridge, M. (1998). *Industrial stochastic simulations on a European meta-computer.* Euro-Par'98 Parallel Processing, Springer . *Lecture Notes in Computer Science, 1470*, 1131–1139. doi:10.1007/BFb0057975

Mitchell, B. (2005). Resolving race conditions in asynchronous partial order scenarios. *IEEE Transactions on Software Engineering, 31*(9), 767–784. doi:10.1109/TSE.2005.104

Mitchell, B. (2008). Characterising communication channel deadlocks in sequence diagrams. *IEEE Transactions on Software Engineering, 34*(3), 305–320. doi:10.1109/TSE.2008.28

OMG. (2002). UMLTM profile for modeling quality of service and fault tolerance characteristics and mechanisms, *2002*.

OMG. (2008). *A UML profile for MARTE: Modeling and analysis of real-time embedded systems*, 2008.

Prandi, D., & Quaglia, P. (2007). Stochastic COWS. In *Proc. 5th International Conference on Service Oriented Computing, ICSOC~'07. LNCS vol. 4749*.

Risse, T., Wombacher, A., Surridge, M., Taylor, S., & Aberer, K. (2001, August). Online scheduling in distributed message converter systems. *Proceedings of 13th Parallel and Distributed Computing and Systems* (PDCS 2001), Anaheim, CA.

Schmidt, K., & Stahl, C. (2004). A Petri net semantic for BPEL4WS validation and application. In *Proceedings of the 11th Workshop on Algorithms and Tools for Petri Nets*, (pp. 1-6).

Schruben, L. (2000). *Mathematical programming models of discrete event system dynamics*. In: Winter Simulation Conference 2000, (pp. 381-385). Retrieved from http://ieeexplore.ieee.org/iel5/7220/19454/00899742.pdf

Sloane, E. (2007, April). A hybrid approach to modeling SAO systems of systems using CPN and MESA/EXTEND. In *Proceedings of 1ˢᵗ IEEE Systems Conference Waikiki Beach*, Honolulu, Hawaii, USA. Retrieved from http://ieeexplore.ieee.org/ iel5/4258845/4258846/ 04258897.pdf

Wang, C. H., & Wang, F. J. (2007). An object-oriented modular Petri nets for modeling service oriented applications. In *Proceedings of the 31st Annual international Computer Software and Applications Conference* (pp. 479-486). COMPSAC. Washington, DC: IEEE Computer Society. Retrieved from http://dx.doi.org/10.1109/COMPSAC.2007.68

KEY TERMS AND DEFINITIONS

Analytical Models: A tool for the characterization of Service Oriented Infrastructures based on algebraic expressions.

Quality of Service: A guarantee on performance as measured by a service provider.

Real-Time System: A system where the absolute correctness depends not only on the correctness of the output, but also on the time that this is produced.

Risk: The combination of the probability of an event and its consequences, positive and negative.

Service Level Agreement: A negotiated agreement between a customer and service provider that defines services, obligations, QoS guarantees, and penalties.

Stochastic Process Models: A tool for estimating probability distributions of potential outcomes by allowing for random variation in one or more inputs over time.

System Performance: A measure of the ability for a system to get work done considering time and results (e.g response time, capacity, latency, throughput, scalability, etc).

Chapter 2

Model–Driven Engineering, Services and Interactive Real–Time Applications

Luis Costa
SINTEF ICT, Norway

Neil Loughran
SINTEF ICT, Norway

Roy Grønmo
SINTEF ICT, Norway

ABSTRACT

Model-driven software engineering (MDE) has the basic assumption that the development of software systems from high-level abstractions along with the generation of low-level implementation code can improve the quality of the systems and at the same time reduce costs and improve time to market. This chapter provides an overview of MDE, state of the art approaches, standards, resources, and tools that support different aspects of model-driven software engineering: language development, modeling services, and real-time applications. The chapter concludes with a reflection over the main challenges faced by projects using the current MDE technologies, pointing out some promising directions for future developments.

1 MODEL DRIVEN ENGINEERING

1.1 Overview

Model-driven software engineering (MDE) (Kent, 2002) refers to the generation of software systems from high-level abstractions using *meta-models* and *models*. A meta-model provides the language

abstraction of a system, while models, i.e. instances of the meta-models, allow the specification of an intended application based upon the constraints imposed by the meta-model. Typically, MDE is used in the building of a *domain specific language* (DSL) (Fowler & Pearson, 2010). A DSL, as opposed to a general purpose low-level language like Java or C++, is a high-level language containing abstractions that are specific to a certain appli-

DOI: 10.4018/978-1-60960-827-9.ch002

cation area or task. For example, the language constructs for a DSL in the automotive domain may refer to concepts relating directly to automotive concepts (e.g. vehicle type, engine capacity, transmission, etc.).

The architecture of such languages typically consists of two key elements: the *abstract* and the *concrete* syntax. The abstract syntax is usually defined using a model. As this model is actually a model of other models it is called a meta-model. The meta-model describes the different concepts of the language and the relationships between them. The concrete syntax describes what syntactic elements constitute the language, or how the elements of the abstract syntax are to be presented or specified. One example is that in the Unified Modeling Language (UML) (OMG, 2010c) a Class is represented by a box. A language may have several concrete syntaxes for the same abstract syntax. For example it can have both a graphical notation (diagrams) and a textual notation. The field of language engineering is not new, but in recent years tool support has improved considerably. This eases the creation of both abstract and concrete syntaxes and the connections between them. Examples of such tools are the Eclipse Graphical Modeling Framework (GMF) (Eclipse, 2010b) and MetaEdit from MetaCase (Metacase, 2010). The Object Management Group (OMG) (OMG, 2010a), the standardisation organisation behind the UML, typically when standardising such specific languages requires a meta-model and a UML profile representing the concrete syntax.

In this chapter we describe a number of the state of the art approaches in modeling with respect to language development, services and real-time modeling.

2 MODELING TECHNOLOGIES

In this section we investigate a range of the state of the art in model-driven engineering techniques within the UML and Eclipse worlds.

2.1 MOF

The Meta Object Facilities (MOF) (OMG, 2010b) proposed by the OMG provides a *meta-metamodel* at its top layer. If we consider a meta-model as concepts for describing models, then a meta-metamodel can be considered as the concepts used for describing a given meta-model. MOF is based on the object-oriented paradigm and there are different flavours in existence: Complete MOF (CMOF), Essential MOF (EMOF) and Semantic MOF (SMOF). CMOF is the whole of the MOF specification, whereas the EMOF contains only a subset of the main elements of MOF. SMOF is currently a proposal for adding additional semantics to MOF. MOF is currently utilised by UML and Ecore, i.e. the meta-model of the Eclipse Modeling Framework (Eclipse, 2010a).

2.2 UML

The Unified Modeling Language (UML) (OMG, 2010c) is a standardized general-purpose modeling language used in software engineering to model systems. UML provides a standard notation to deal at a high level with several facets of complexity of a system. In section 2.2.1 we give an overview of the UML language and in section 2.2.2 we list some of the commonly used UML tools.

2.2.1 The Language

A UML model consists of elements such as packages, classes, and instances. UML diagrams are graphical representations of parts of the UML model. UML diagrams are formed by graphical elements (nodes connected by paths) that represent elements in the UML model. In this sense, the different diagram types of UML (see Figure 1) try to define and express the functionality of a system from different points of view.

UML is defined using MOF and is a central aspect of MDE today as it is the most wide-spread modeling language in general, and it is com-

Figure 1. Diagram types of UML (from (Wikipedia, 2010))

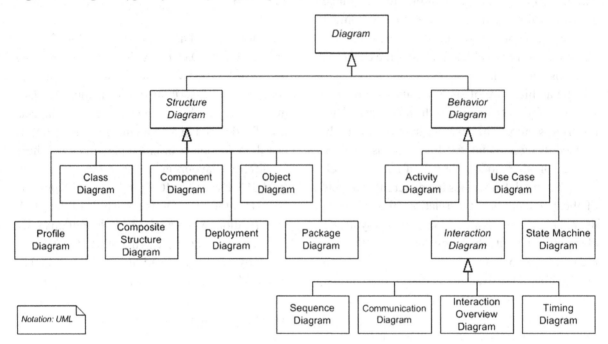

monly used to define models used for further processing through transformations and refinements.

It is out of the scope of this chapter to give a full overview of all the diagram types available in UML, but we will give a basic description of the ones we believe can be more relevant for the domain of this book.

Class diagrams describe the structure of a system by showing the classes, their properties, the relationships between the classes of a system and the operations that they can perform. Figure 2 depicts a simple example of a class diagram. The class diagram models two types of bank accounts named Standard Bank Account and VIP Bank Account. They share some characteristics (properties and operations) given in the common supertype Bank Account, but they also have specific properties and operations.

Composite structure diagrams show the internal structure of a class and the existing collaborations within this structure. This diagram can include internal parts, ports (which enable the parts

to interact with each other or the instances of the class to interact with other classes), and connectors between parts or ports. Figure 3 illustrates how a class (in this case System X) can be specified by its parts (Component 1 and Component 2) and ports which enable the components to interact with each other and an additional port which enables the class to communicate with other classes (the port on the boundary of the class).

Activity diagrams can be used to describe the control flow between the components in a system. They contain elements supporting choice, iteration and concurrency. Figure 4 exemplifies how part of the behavior of a system can be modeled: here the first action is to start a server; after that the system checks periodically whether the server is ready and when that happens the client component is started too.

State machine diagrams use directed graphs where the nodes represent states and the connectors represent state transitions. The transitions are labeled with the triggering events and can also

Figure 2. Class diagram

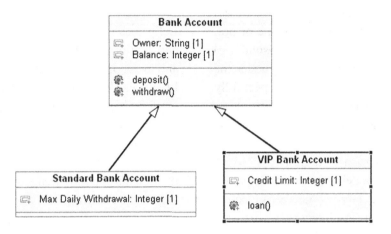

have an associated list of actions to be executed. See Figure 5, for a simple example of a diagram representing the behavior of a system: after startup, this system can receive requests which in turn can be successfully processed or force the system into a recovery mode. The system stays in the recovery mode until it manages to return to normal operation.

UML has three generic extension mechanisms that enable the customization of models for particular domains and platforms: stereotypes, tag definitions, and constraints. These extension mechanisms can be applied to specific model elements, like Classes, Properties and Ports in order to further refine and specify those elements. A so called Profile is then a collection of such extensions that customize a UML model for a

particular domain (e.g., railway, education or banking) or platform (e.g., NET, Java).

2.2.2 UML Tools

UML modeling tools are software applications supporting the creation, maintenance and processing of UML models and diagrams. There

Figure 4. Activity diagram

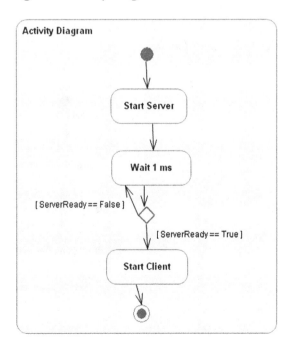

Figure 3. Composite Structure diagram

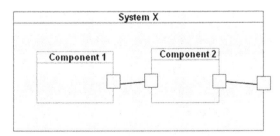

are a considerable number of tools, varying in the supported functionalities, licensing model and whether their source code is public or not. One example is Papyrus (www.papyrusuml.org) which is open source and distributed under the Eclipse Public License. It claims to respect fully the UML2 standard, but has some usability issues. Additionally there are a number of commercial products like Enterprise Architect (www.sparx-systems.com/products/ea), Magic Draw (www.magicdraw.com), Modelio (www.modeliosoft.com), Objecteering (www.objecteering.com/) and Rational Software Architect (www-01.ibm.com/software/awdtools/swarchitect/websphere/) which have more professional interfaces and are probably more adequate to use in industrial settings.

For a more comprehensive list of tools that support the UML standard please check the directory of vendors of UML-based modeling tools maintained by the OMG at http://uml-directory.omg.org/

2.3 Eclipse-Based Technologies

Eclipse can be described as both a community and platform with a special focus on building and managing software at different phases of the lifecycle. The open source nature of the Eclipse platform has meant that there are a wide variety of frameworks, languages, tools and utilities which all, at least potentially, should work with one another in a unified way. The Eclipse platform itself features a fully fledged integrated development environment (IDE) which can be used with a wide variety of programming languages. A key part of the Eclipse platform is in the provision of multiple MDE technologies covering many different aspects of language design, transformation technologies, processes and software development. In the following sections we detail some of the key state of the art MDE-related technologies currently being employed within Eclipse.

2.3.1 Eclipse Modeling Framework (EMF)

The Eclipse Modeling Framework (Eclipse, 2010a) origins come from an implementation

Figure 5. State Machine Diagram

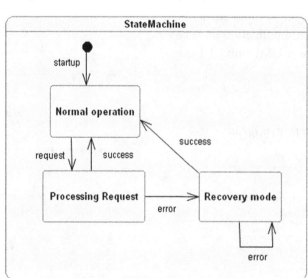

of MOF (mostly aligned with OMG's EMOF). However it developed from there based on the experience obtained from implementing a large set of tools using the framework. EMF can be looked at as a very efficient Java implementation of a core subset of the MOF API. EMF has three main components: *core*, *edit* and *codegen*. Whereas the *core* component contains the Ecore meta-metamodel, persistence, serialization, a model tracer (change notification and recording) and a validation framework, *edit* includes a default model viewer and supports building rich user interfaces (viewer, editor) for models. Finally the *codegen* component provides a code generator for Ecore based models and several importers.

2.3.2 Graphical Editing Framework (GEF) and Graphical Modeling Framework (GMF)

GEF (http://www.eclipse.org/gef/) enables developers to create rich graphical editors from existing application models.

GMF (http://www.eclipse.org/modeling/gmp/) provides a generative component and runtime infrastructure supporting the development of graphical editors based on EMF and GEF.

GEF includes two plug-ins. While the *org. eclipse.draw2d* plug-in provides a layout and rendering toolkit for displaying graphics, the org. eclipse.gef plug-in provide tools like Selection, Creation, Connection and Marquee tools and a Palette for displaying those tools. Additionally the latter plug-in provides handles for resizing objects and bending connections, two types of GEF Viewers (Graphical and Tree) and Undo/Redo support.

The developer can use many common operations provided in GEF and/or extend them for the specific domain that he is dealing with. GEF has an MVC (model-view-controller) architecture that enables simple changes to be applied to the model from the view.

GEF is completely application independent and provides the basis to build almost any application like for example activity diagrams, GUI builders, class diagram editors, state machines, and even WYSIWYG text editors.

GMF is not in any sense a replacement for EMF: GMF uses and therefore is dependent on EMF. EMF provides core facilities for defining models and generating java code and manipulating instances of those models. As it is very common that GEF editors manipulate an object model, it turns out that GEF pairs very well with EMF and these two frameworks have become a popular combination. The main goal of the GMF project is to simplify the combination of these two technologies by allowing GEF editors to be specified and generated using models i.e. GMF allows developers to generate GEF editors that can be used to manipulate EMF models.

The Logic Example, one of the examples provided in the GEF documentation, is pictured in Figure 6. This GEF-based editor allows a user to specify logic circuit diagrams by selecting and dragging graphical elements from the palette onto the model view.

2.3.3 Modeling Workflow Engine (MWE)

An important task when developing Eclipse-based languages incorporating many different technologies concerns itself with the orchestration and the ordering of different calls involved in execution of different Eclipse components. The MWE project is a project which uses a framework based upon dependency injection for developing workflows using declarative XML. Currently, there is only one language being actively developed within the MWE project and that is the workflow engine from the OpenArchitectureWare project (see Section 2.3.5.2).

2.3.4 Model Transformation Technologies

There are a number of transformation languages available with respect to the Eclipse platform.

Figure 6. Example of GEF application

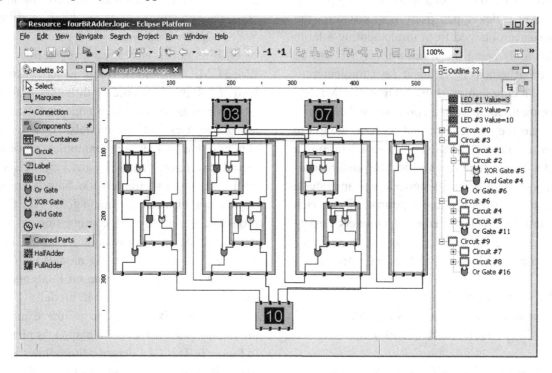

It should be noted that these approaches can be utilised with UML models as well as other models. In the next subsections we describe some of the more prominent approaches.

2.3.4.1 Model to Text Transformation (M2T)

M2T concerns itself with the generation of textual artefacts from models. Examples of such textual artefacts are program code, configuration scripts and even documentation. At least originally, XSLT was the prominent technology for developing textual transformations from models. However, XSLT seems to have fallen out of favour mainly due to its obscure syntax and its missing relation to the metamodel.

Today, there are a wide variety of M2T approaches offering advanced IDE support, constraints, syntax highlighting, code completion, error checking, etc. The leading M2T approaches provide the user with source model elements as first class citizens based on a given source metamodel.

JET (Java Emitter Templates) (Eclipse, 2010c) is the original Eclipse M2T transformation language. It uses a Java Server Pages (JSP) style syntax and, although the name would express otherwise, can be used to generate SQL, XML and other textual artefacts. There are many M2T approaches which provide a similar functionality to JET. Acceleo (Obeo, 2010) is an M2T tool which can be used from Eclipse- and XMI-based tools such as Papyrus. Acceleo code is written as a set of template rules where a simplified version of OCL (Object Constraint Language) plays a key role. Xpand (OpenArchitectureWare, 2010b) is the M2T approach developed in the OpenArchitectureWare project (see Section 2.3.5.2). Xpand uses an XML-style approach (albeit with the guillemot bracketing style). MOFScript (Oldevik et al., 2005) is an approach using an imperative programming style. Overall, the selection of a particular M2T approach over another is largely motivated by personal preference than by the features offered.

2.3.4.2 Model to Model Transformation (M2M)

M2M concerns itself with the transformation of models into other models. In contrast to the M2T approach M2M does not necessarily concern itself directly with the textual output (although of course, the actual output of models can be text based). There are a number of M2M approaches being utilised in the modeling world, with some of the most prevalent being ATL (Jouault & Kurtev, 2006), Xtend (OpenArchitectureWare, 2010a) and Kermeta (Muller et al., 2005). These model transformation languages largely follow a textually based imperative programming style. Like the aforementioned M2T approaches, the choice of one M2M approach over another is largely down to personal preference.

2.3.4.3 Textual Modeling Framework (TMF)

The TMF project focuses on the development of meta-models from textual descriptions. At present XText, from the OpenArchitectureWare project, is the only project on the Eclipse project site dealing with textual model descriptions. However, there are other initiatives such as TextUML (Abstratt Technologies, 2010) also dealing with the development of meta-models from textual descriptions.

The TMF project is interesting as it concerns itself with the development of textual languages using grammar rules. The XText project is used to develop domain specific languages. Using XText the developer creates a grammar and then invokes a workflow which in turn creates the necessary Java code for a language IDE. The developer also needs to express the necessary constraints for instances of the language (models) using an OCL-like language known as *Check*. The workflow may also invoke numerous model transformation files (M2T/M2M) and Java components.

2.3.5 Eclipse Tool Suites

In the last few years a number of Eclipse-based MDE tool suites have appeared which offer families of technologies covering the different aspects of language modeling. The primary advantage of such frameworks is that the individual technologies incorporated within them (e.g. modeling languages, transformation languages, workflow languages, etc.) are designed from the outset to be utilised together in an integrated fashion. This interoperability means that less time is spent on problems regarding configuration issues and dependency conflicts with respect to Eclipse which can be encountered when using individual technologies. Two of the prominent Eclipse tool suits to emerge in recent years are Epsilon (Epsilon, 2010) and OpenArchitectureWare (OpenArchitectureWare, 2010a).

2.3.5.1 Epsilon

The Epsilon tool suite contains an array of task-specific languages for performing duties relating to model transformation, model-composition, code generation and so forth. EOL (Epsilon Object Language) is used for model management and definition of operations which other languages can use. EVL (Epsilon Validation Language) is used to specify constraints on model instances using an OCL like syntax. ETL (Epsilon Transformation Language) is essentially the M2M language of Epsilon. Likewise, EGL (Epsilon Generation Language) is used for M2T transformations. There are also other languages in Epsilon covering other aspects (e.g. model merging, model comparison, etc.).

2.3.5.2 OpenArchitectureWare

OpenArchitectureWare (oAW) is a tool suite which includes a number of different languages for dealing with different aspects of model driven software development. The *Xtext* language provides the means for developers to create textual-based domain specific languages using an Extended Backus-Naur Form (EBNF) notation to define a grammar. From this grammar oAW creates a parser, meta-model and the basis of an Eclipse editor with code completion, outline view and syntax highlighting. The grammar may support references to model elements and linkage to other model files by way of imports. The *Xpand* language is used to turn models into code. The *Check* language is used to define constraints on models and also provide explicit support for error messages and warnings. The *Xtend* language is used for defining operations, meta-model extensions and model transformations. These operations can be called from other languages within the oAW framework. *Workflows,* with respect to oAW, are XML based scripts that specify an order in which certain operations and components within the oAW environment or generated DSL are called and executed. Workflows can call different languages within the oAW framework and other workflows as well as Java based extensions and executables (e.g. Ant script). Since the latter part of 2009, the individual technologies within the oAW environment have become available as separate Eclipse projects.

2.4 UML Based Technologies Specific to Real-Time and/ or Service Modeling

The Object Management Group (OMG) has three language specifications that are relevant to interactive real-time applications and service modeling: the *UML Profile for Modeling and Analysis of Real-time and Embedded Systems (MARTE)*, the *UML profile for Modeling Quality Of Service and Fault Tolerance Characteristics and Mechanisms (QoSFTC)* and the *Service-Oriented Architecture Modeling Language* (SoaML).

These standards mean that now UML allows real-time aspects of streaming multimedia applications to be incorporated within a MDE design methodology. This style of UML is particularly relevant during the application service design phase. UML models can then be used to define application service capabilities and interfaces between architecture components.

2.4.1 MARTE

The MARTE profile (OMG, 2009b), aims at using UML in the specific domain of real-time and embedded systems. This is a significant area to cover, and the resulting standard is therefore considerable large.

The MARTE specification is organized in four packages: *Foundations, Design Model, Analysis Model* and *Annexes* (see Figure 7).

MARTE provides a good support for the definition of Non Functional Properties (NFP). While Functional Properties define the purpose of a system or application, NFPs are concerned with the systems fitness to its purpose. NFPs can include information about for example memory and CPU usage, throughputs, delays and deadlines. MARTE supports the definition of NFPs and their usage to annotate UML models.

NFPs are classified into two main categories: qualitative or quantitative. The quantitative ones are measurable properties that may be specified using units with a meaningful semantic. On the other hand the qualitative NFPs denote characteristics that may not be measured directly. These can only be dealt with properly by analysts and analysis tools. The NFP package also provides a set of probability distribution operations which can support more mathematically founded modeling.

Some basic types are defined in MARTE (see Figure 8). MARTE extends UML adding specific semantics to deal with NFPs that are relevant to real-time systems like memory allocation, power consumption, reliability and safety. In addition specific non functional properties can be defined by the user following the specification. The concrete coupling among the units and measurements provides a specific and accurate semantic for the meaning of these properties, leading towards a unified semantic in the embedded system domain.

NFPs are typically specified using the Value Specification Language (VSL). VSL expressions can be used to specify non-functional values, parameters, operations, and dependencies between

Figure 7. Architecture of the MARTE profile (from the Papyrus implementation of the MARTE profile (Papyrus, 2010))

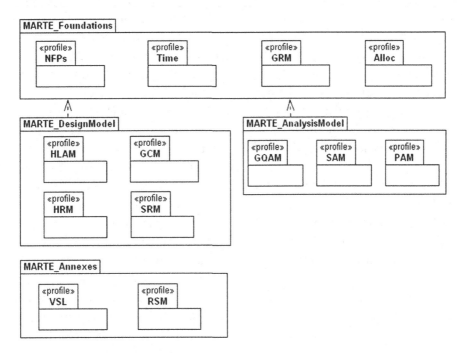

Figure 8. Extract of the library of pre-declared NFP types (from the Papyrus implementation of the MARTE profile (Papyrus, 2010))

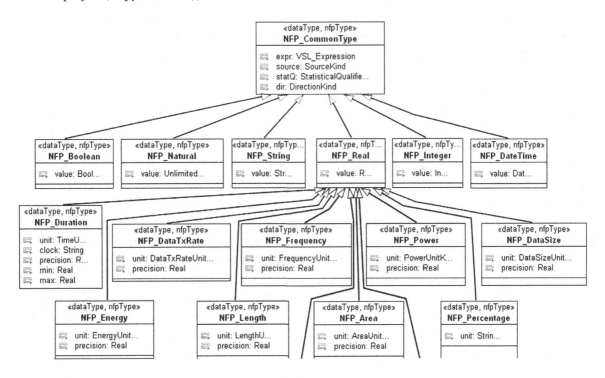

different values in a UML model. UML modelers can use VSL to specify non-functional constraints in their models.

VSL provides syntax for structural values, time and algebraic expressions, that cannot be expressed in a formal way in UML 2.

Relationships among properties can be defined with support on arithmetic, logical, relational and conditional expressions. Furthermore, VSL provides a way of supporting time values and assertions.

The VSL language provides full support for the definition of expressions, time values, etc., needed in MARTE. Although variables can be created using VSL expressions, they can be also alternatively declared by means of extended UML properties.

In real-time systems time and behavior are closely coupled which stresses the importance of timing constraints in the modeling of these systems.

Even though time is considered in other standards like SysML (OMG, 2008b) and UML, the timing model available in MARTE has some advantages concerning time constraints.

The time model in MARTE extends the Simple Time package proposed by UML 2 and provides a broad range of capabilities to deal with real-time requirements. This extension is based on the concept of temporal ordering of instants. MARTE's approach is to relate events, behaviors and objects with a time structure. Events, behaviors and objects may also be explicitly related to a clock.

Time in MARTE can be modeled using three main classes of time abstraction: physical/real-time, causal/temporal and clocked/synchronous.

Physical/real-time models require the precise modeling of real-time duration values, to address scheduling issues.

In causal/temporal models, the main concern is about precedence and dependency between the different entities.

Finally clocked/synchronous models add the concept of simultaneity and divide the time scale in a discrete succession of instants. These models can relate to several user-defined clocks. This allows the definition of time restrictions based on an ideal clock, or using different clock definitions, covering a wider map of situations and system requirements that can be very useful for modeling systems in the real-time domain. The *Clock* stereotype (Figure 9) provides access to the time structure. In order to specify time constraints, MARTE provides a new clock constraint specification language (CCSL) within the UML.

This timing definition provides an explicit way of expressing relationships among events, actions and messages specifying the behavior of a system. MARTE time definition is based on the assumption that every event, message or time element can be associated to a *clock*. Time structures allow the relationship among several interdependent clocks. This allows an explicit definition of the schedulability among the different elements involved in the design of a system.

Regarding the area of Design, MARTE includes the concept of a General component. This builds on the UML Structured Classifier (the typical component representation in UML) adding concepts that are relevant to real-time systems such as Flow Ports. These elements allow the specification of flow-oriented communication between components.

MARTE offers support to model platforms for executing real-time applications. Different types of resources are provided which can be also extended through the Generic Resource Modeling (GRM) sub-profile, which allows modeling of embedded platforms at the high level including both software and hardware in a generic way (Figure 10).

The third part of MARTE focuses on analysis. The goal of MARTE's analysis package is to support accurate and trustworthy evaluations using formal quantitative analyses based on sound mathematical models. This package provides a Generic Quantitative Analysis model and includes two sub-profiles: performance analysis and schedulability analysis.

Figure 9. UML extensions for time modeling: Clock element (from the Papyrus implementation of the MARTE profile (Papyrus, 2010))

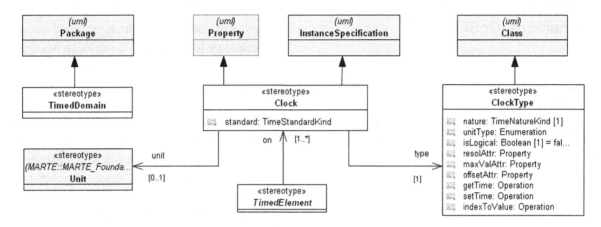

Quantitative analysis techniques can be used to estimate values for the output NFPs based on data provided by the input NFPs. Key terms in this context are *Workload Behaviour* which contains a set of end-to-end system level operations with defined behavior and *Resources Platform* which is a container for the resources used by the mentioned behavior. A *Workload behaviour* contains scenarios each constituted by a set of steps.

Performance Analysis Modeling describes the analysis of temporal properties of best effort and soft-real-time systems including multimedia and networked services.

Schedulability analysis is crucial to calculate guaranteed bounds on response times and resource processing loads. The schedulability analysis provided by MARTE allows the attachment of quantitative annotations at the level of detail desired by the designer.

Figure 10. Types of resources considered in GRM (from the Papyrus implementation of the MARTE profile (Papyrus, 2010))

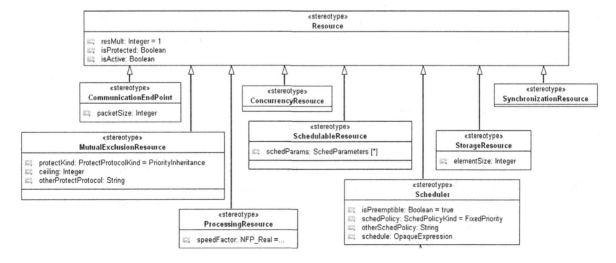

2.4.2 UML Profile for Modeling Quality of Service and Fault Tolerance Characteristics and Mechanisms (QoSFTC)

QoSFTC (OMG, 2008a) is more limited in scope than MARTE, and relates to the NFP part of MARTE.

The key concepts of QoSFTC are Quality Characteristics, Quality Constraints and Quality Levels.

A quality characteristic is a set of quality attributes that are the dimensions along which to describe quality satisfaction.

The stereotype *QoSCharacteristic* represents the quantifiable quality characteristics of services. This is specified independently of the elements being qualified. *QoSCharacteristic* is the constructor used for the description of non-functional aspects like for example latency, throughput, capacity, availability, etc. These are examples of general characteristics, but specific domains may require modeling of specific characteristics.

The *QoSCharacteristic* definition may require some parameters like for instance, the parameterization of the units and types to describe value definitions, or specific methods for the quantification of the values. The *QoSParameter* stereotype supports the definition of such parameters.

QoSDimensions are the dimensions used for the quantification of *QoSCharacteristics*. It is possible to define *QoSCharacteristics* using different methods (e.g., absolute values, maximum and minimum values, statistical values). As an illustration, it is possible to quantify the latency of a particular function of a system as the end-to-end delay of that function, the mean time of all executions, or the variance of time delay. A *QoSCharacteristic* may require more than one type of value for its quantification. For example for the characteristic *Reliability*, one may want to use dimensions like time to repair, time to failure and number of failures supported.

To make a relational comparison between two values of *QoSDimensions*, it is essential to know the relational precedence of the domain values. The property *direction* (which is typed as an enumeration with the possible values *increasing, decreasing,* and *undefined* values) defines the type of order relation. For instance, in most of the systems, a low *response time* is better than a high *response time*; in this case, the value of this property is set to *decreasing*. *Rate transmission* on the other hand is an example where this property would be set to *increasing*, since, in general, a high transmission rate is preferred.

The property *unit* enables the specification of units for the values of a dimension and the property *statisticalQualifier* indicates the type of statistical qualifier when the value of a dimension is represented as a statistical value. The types of statistical qualifiers supported are *maximum value, minimum value, range, mean, variance, standard deviation, percentile, frequency, moment* and *distribution*.

When the number of *QoSCharacteristics* is large, or they are particularly complex, a mechanism for grouping them can be extremely useful. The stereotype *QoSCategory* enables the creation of groups of closely related *QoSCharacteristics*.

The *QoSConstraint* stereotype is an abstract metaclass that restricts the allowed values of one or more *QoSCharacteristics*. Application requirements or architectural decisions may limit the allowed values of quality and the *QoSConstraints* describe these limitations.

The *QoSContext* stereotype enables the definition of which *QoSCharacteristics* and functional elements are involved in a *QoSConstraint*. The stereotype *QoSContext* establishes the vocabulary of the constraint, and the *QoSConstraint* allowed values. One can use two different approaches for the description of these values: 1. The enumeration of the values allowed for each of the *QoSCharacteristics* involved in the *QoSContext* independently; 2. The expressions that must be fulfilled by the *QoSCharacteristics*. These expressions can define maximum and minimum values, and the dependencies between *QoSCharacteristics*. The latter approach is more flexible than the previous one, because it is possible to identify not only the limits but also the dependencies between the supported *QoSCharacteristics*.

Quality constraints can be seen from two perspectives: from the client's point of view and from the provider's point of view. Additionally there are two different types of constraints: the required constraints and the offered constraints by each of the actors.

When a client defines a *QoSRequired* constraint, he is expecting the service provider to offer services with quality levels that achieve these requirements. Basically he is limiting the space of valid values for the *QoSCharacteristics* describing the service. The *QoSCharacteristics* are the dimensions of the quality space, and the *QoSRequired* constraints define the valid values for this space.

When the provider defines its *QoSRequired* constraints, he is asking the client to achieve some quality requirements in order to get the offered quality. An example of *QoSRequired* constraint defined by a provider can be the maximum frequency of invocation from its client.

A *QoSOffered* constraint has associated the set of *QoSCharacteristics* that a service takes into consideration (*QoS Characteristics* are an integral part of the specification of *QoSContext*). A *QoSOffered* constraint defines the space of quality (ranges of quality values) supported by the service.

When a quality does not appear in the context of the *QoSOffered* constraint, the service does not take it into account, and therefore the service does not guarantee this quality. When the provider defines a *QoSOffered* constraint, he is responsible to achieve this constraint. When it is the client who defines a *QoSOffered* constraint, he must achieve the constraint when using the service.

A *QoSContract* is basically an agreement between all the constraints at stake: the quality

values supported by the provider, its requirements to the clients, the quality values required by the client and the quality assured by the client.

In general, the required quality values by the client must be a subset of values supported by the provider, and the required values by the provider must be a subset of the values supported by the client. If the provider does not support the QoS required by the client, the contract needs to be negotiated in order to agree (or not) on new QoS values.

In some cases, a model element does not have a single mode of execution or can adapt its execution to provide different quality levels. This means that the quality offered or required can be a combination of a set of quality constraints, and each constraint is associated to a specific level or execution mode. The stereotype *QoSCompound-Constraint* is the combination of a set of constraints that in conjunction represent a QoSConstraint for the model element.

A *QoSLevel* represents the different modes of QoS supported by a service. Depending on its configuration, a service can support different working modes, and these working modes provide different qualities. A *QoSLevel* should be specified for each working mode.

QoSLevels represent states in the system from a quality point of view. The *QoSLevel* at each time depends on the current resources available and the quality required.

For each *QoSLevel* the resources required are different. In general, the resources offer different quality depending on the load that they are submitted to. A *QoSLevel* is associated with one or more *QoSConstraints* that state the conditions that the service must accomplish to be able to stay in that specific *QoSLevel* (relation *allowedSpace*).

The *QoSTransition* stereotype models the allowed transitions between *QoS Levels*.

A *QoSLevel* changes when the *allowedSpace* of the current *QoSLevel* becomes false, and a transition fires. This change requires the existence of one enabled transition from the current *QoSLevel* to a new *QoSLevel*. If there is not an enabled transition, the system is in a state where it cannot achieve its QoS requirements. It will continue in the current state, but it cannot guarantee the compliance with its QoS contracts.

A *QoSCompoundLevel* includes all the *QoS-Levels* that define the quality behavior of a model element. These *QoSLevels* have associated a set of *QoSConstraints* which in conjunction define the *QoSCompoundConstraint* associated to the *QoSCompoundLevel*.

General QoS characteristics and categories can be reused in different domains. These include characteristics whose quantification dimensions are not problem specific. The QoSFTC specification document (OMG, 2008a) also proposes a general QoS catalog including a set of general characteristics and categories that are not specific of projects or domains. The focus behind the creation of this catalog was the selection of characteristics which are important to real-time and high confidence systems and create a common framework relating them all.

This general catalog is extendable with domain specific characteristics in order to define a domain QoS catalog, and each domain QoS catalog can be specialized for specific projects.

Latency, Efficiency, Reliability, Availability and Integrity are just some examples of the QoS categories included in the general QoS catalogue.

2.4.3 Service-Oriented Architecture Modeling Language (SoaML)

SoaML is a modeling language standardized in OMG (OMG 2009c). It describes a UML profile and a metamodel for designing services. The main goals of SoaML are supporting the activities of service modeling and design and to contribute into an overall model-driven development approach.

The basic concepts of SoaML are:

1. Participants which are the service providers and consumers in a system. A *Participant*

can play the role of service provider, consumer or both. When a participant acts as a provider it contains a *Service*, and when a participant acts as a consumer it contains a *Request*.

2. Service interfaces which describe the operations provided and required to complete the functionality of a *Service*. A *ServiceInterface* is used as the protocol for a *Service* or a *Request*.

3. Service contracts which describe the interaction patterns between service entities. A *ServiceContract* is used to model agreements between two or more parties. A *ServiceContract* is associated with several service roles which in turn have each a *ServiceInterface* type usually representing a provider or consumer.

4. Service data which describes the service's messages and message attachments. *MessageType* is used to specify the messages exchanged between services. The information itself is not contained in the messages, is instead attached to them.

5. Services architectures that define how a number of participants work together for some purpose by providing and using services specified as *ServiceContracts*.

The main advantage of the SoaML profile is an easier integration with state of the practice UML modeling tools, whereas the SoaML Metamodel has as advantage its easier use for transformation and model automation.

As both the SoaML Metamodel and the SoaML profile focus on the representation of the same set of concepts and extend UML2 in the same main areas, this section will focus only on one of these formalisms, namely the SoaML profile.

The SoaML profile supports the range of requirements posed on modeling service-oriented architectures. These include the specification of systems of services, individual service interfaces and service implementations. The SoaML profile

Figure 11. Service participants and interfaces (from (Hahn et al., 2009))

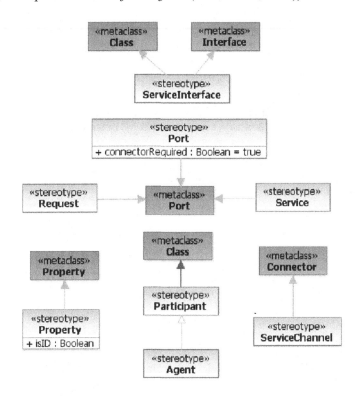

extends the UML2 metamodel in order to support explicit service modeling in distributed environments. This extension aims to support different service modeling scenarios like for example single service descriptions, service-oriented architecture modeling and service contract definitions.

The SoaML Profile includes stereotypes that refine UML. The provided stereotypes differentiate service related elements from regular UML modeling elements. For example, using the profile it is possible to distinguish a normal interface from a service interface and manage them in the appropriate way.

As mentioned earlier, the specification of participants defines who are the service providers and consumers in a system. Service interfaces explicitly model the operations provided and required to complete the functionality of a service. Figure 11 shows the stereotypes that support the specification of *Participants*, *ServiceInterfaces* and other related concepts.

ServiceContracts describe the interaction patterns between service entities. *ServicesArchitectures* describe the participant's architectures, not necessarily going deeply into the interaction between them. Figure 12 presents the stereotypes supporting the representation of *ServiceContracts*, *ServicesArchitectures* and related concepts.

The SoaML profile also provides elements such as attachments and message types which are relevant concepts for modeling services' data. Figure 13 describes the stereotypes that support the representation of *Attachment* and *MessageType* and their related concepts.

2.5 Eclipse Based Technologies Specific to Real-Time and/or Service Modeling

In the following subsections we describe some of the prominent Eclipse based projects concerning

Figure 12. Service contracts and architectures (from (Hahn et al., 2009))

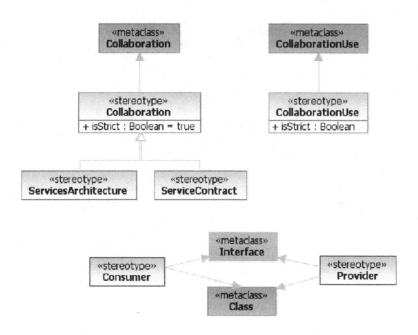

themselves with real-time and/or service modeling.

2.5.1 RT-Druid

RT-Druid (RT-Druid, 2004) is an integrated set of tools enabling the modeling, analysis and simulation of timing behaviour in real-time systems. The tool set was developed with aims of achieving modularity, interoperability, portability and extensibility. Figure 14 illustrates the RT-Druid architecture. Repositories capture information relating to functional and architectural models. A kernel provides the management of the data and GUI to different functions with respect to mapping, scheduling and tracing, etc.

2.5.2 Real-Time Software Components (RTSC)

RTSC (RTSC, 2010) is an Eclipse project with a special focus on tool development for the creation and configuration of highly constrained devices. The project is primarily concerned with embedded

Figure 13. Message types and attachments (from (Hahn et al., 2009))

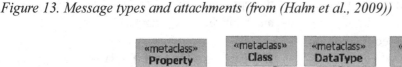

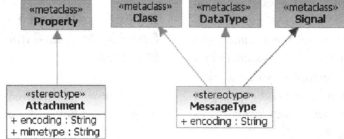

Figure 14. RT-Druid architecture (from whitepaper (RT-Druid, 2004))

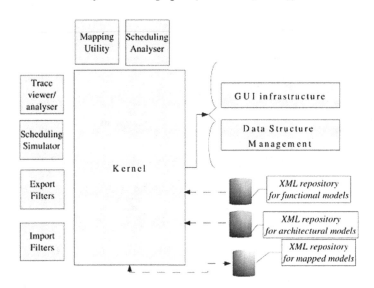

software development in C/C++ with respect to digital signal processing and micro-controllers. The component model itself is based upon the notions of modules, interfaces and packages for the 'content structure' (Figure 15). Modules encapsulate sets of operations and types and are somewhat akin to class definitions, whereas interfaces and packages are equivalent to their notions in languages such as Java. Modules and interfaces co-exist in both the meta (configuration) and target (execution) domains. Packages are the primary artefact and the content management covers the necessary life-cycle operations (build, deploy, etc.).

A core set of tools for defining interfaces, configuring components and generating artefacts is provided. Additionally there are tools for displaying the runtime characteristics of components. The project intends to utilise EMF and UML to facilitate the specification of components.

2.5.3 Service Oriented Architecture Approaches in Eclipse

SOA in Eclipse is covered under the umbrella of the Eclipse SOA initiative. The initiative is split up into technologies covering the *design* and *runtime* considerations of SOA.

Figure 15. RTSC concepts (from (RTSC, 2010))

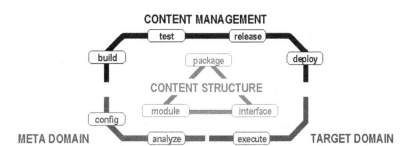

Figure 16. Composite structure designer in STP (from (SCA, 2010))

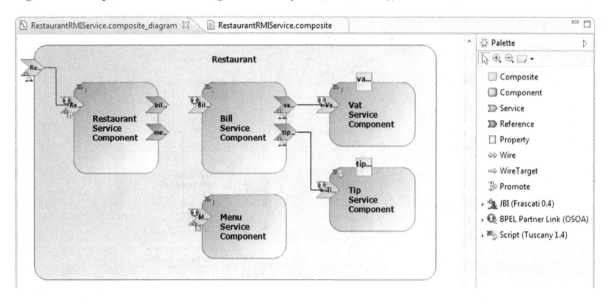

Service-Oriented Architecture Tools Platform Project (STP) is an Eclipse-based project concerning itself with the activities of design, configuration, assembly, monitoring and management of applications based around SOA. It contains four active subprojects focusing on specific tasks within SOA. The STP BPMN project is focused on providing tools for modeling business processes. It uses EMF for its meta-model and GMF for the graphical notation. The STP Intermediate Metamodel project focuses on content sharing of information between STP editors by acting as a bridge between workflows and processes. The STP Policy Editor project provides graphical tooling for editing XML based policy files. The STP Service Component Architecture project (SCA, 2010) consists of a number of tools, e.g. composite structure designer (as illustrated in Figure 16), form editor, XML editor, Java code skeleton generator etc., for developing service oriented related artefacts.

The runtime of the EclipseSOA initiative is the main focus of the Swordfish technology (Swordfish, 2010). Swordfish provides the ability to develop OSGi bundles for enterprise-wide SOA. It is based upon open source technologies

from Apache, i.e. ServiceMix (Apache, 2010) and CXF (CXF, 2010), and Eclipse Equinox (Equinox, 2010). Swordfish provides facilities dealing with runtime service discovery, security, monitoring and remote configuration.

STP represents a considerable effort in creating an integrated set of tools for dealing with the demands of service oriented application modeling. However, the approach is still somewhat in its early stages with rather rudimentary documentation, thus it is unclear how flexible the approach is in dealing with the demands of application developers.

2.6 Other Technologies

There are of course many modeling-based technologies, tools and approaches which are neither Eclipse or UML-based. Here we briefly mention a few of these approaches.

2.6.1 MATLAB and Scilab

MATLAB (Mathworks, 2010) is an environment containing a programming language and a wide variety of data modeling, processing and manipulation, visualisation and analysis functions. It is used to perform computationally intensive tasks. MATLAB supports a restricted object-oriented programming language and can interface with existing general purpose languages like Java and C++. One of the primary motivators for using MATLAB is its ability to generate C code automatically using a subset of the language known as Embedded MATLAB and also to assist in the development of simulations. MATLAB has achieved a wide acceptance in industry due to its inherent user-friendliness, high quality numerical analysis functions, high quality graphics and its ability to interface with other languages.

Scilab (Scilab, 2010) is an open source project that is somewhat derivative of MATLAB. It has been in development since the 1990s and offers the same kind of functionality. Indeed, MATLAB code can be transformed into Scilab code via a source code translator.

2.6.2 MetaEdit+

MetaEdit+ (Metacase, 2010) can be described as a development environment for the creation of domain specific languages and generators. Meta-edit provides a concept editor for defining the concepts which will be part of the language. A rule language then states the constraints upon the language. Then a symbol editor is used for connecting the concepts and rules to a notation. Finally, a code generation language facility translates the models into code or documentation. The Meta-Edit approach can be seen as a direct competitor to the Eclipse frameworks.

2.6.3 Business Process Modeling Notation (BPMN)

BPMN (OMG, 2009a) is an OMG specification for modeling service compositions with a graphical notation. BPMN aims to be intuitive and easy to use for domain experts and system designers as an alternative to the XML-based composition

languages that can be hard to understand for the users.

BPMN provides three basic sub-model types: process, choreography and collaboration. A process consists of an ordered flow of activities and is executed by a single controller. A choreography also consists of an ordered flow of activities, but with different controllers for each involved process. A collaboration depicts interactions between several processes. Collaborations include the concept of conversation which can model a dialogue of communication between two entities. This is in contrast to executing each entity only once in a process specification. A process can be mapped to a BPEL document. A choreography will be mapped to several BPEL documents, one for each process.

BPMN combines a procedural way of specifying the order of activities and an event-based model. This allows for rich support of the control flow patterns identified by (van der Aalst et al., 2003). BPMN provides the basic control flow constructs, such as start, end, event and its gateways. Gateways are used to model advanced control flow patterns in addition to branching of standard types e.g., *or*, *xor*, *and*. There is rich support for exception handling, transactions, recovery and compensation mechanisms.

Activities are depicted with a small icon in the top left part to indicate its task type. Possible task types include service, human and manual. A service task is fully automatic, a human task is performed by a human and a manual task is performed by a human in interaction with tool support.

2.6.4 Petri Nets

A Petri net (Petri, 1962) is a modeling language for the specification and analysis of information systems of a parallel, distributed, concurrent or non deterministic nature. The language using a graphical notation consisting of place nodes, transition nodes and directed arcs which connect places to transitions. In the graphical notation places are drawn as circles, transitions as boxes and arcs are stated with their weights. Since Petri nets are mathematical models, the generation of application code from these models is possible.

3 FUTURE RESEARCH DIRECTIONS

MDE is a constantly evolving area and thus there are new tools, techniques and approaches being developed all the time. Therefore, there is a great deal of promise for future research in the area. There are however a number of issues involved here. They concern themselves principally with:

- Modeling of real-time applications in general
- Tool usability
- Complexity of transformations and iterative development
- Methodologies and consolidation of technologies

3.1.1 Tool Usability

There are many MDE tools available for developing applications relating to real-time and service modeling. However, the usability of such tools often leaves a lot to be desired. Open source projects often do not provide robust environments needed to develop complex applications, and even the commercial tools come up short. For example, even specifying a value to a given parameter often involves the developer clicking on multiple context menus and property boxes. This seems at odds with one of the main objectives of MDE which is saving time via the usage of model specifications. This particular observation has been the motivation for the TextUML Toolkit (Abstratt Technologies, 2010) where UML models are created in a textual format rather than the usual graphical one. At present TextUML only concerns itself with the class models although there are plans to extend the approach to cover UML features relating to activity, state, components and deployment.

3.1.2 Complexity of Transformations and Iterative Development

One of the major challenges in MDE involves the writing of transformations. As meta-models become more complex so does the nature of the transformations. The UML meta-model itself consists of 246 classes and 583 properties; add the notions of profiles and extensions and even the development of the simplest of transformations is non-trivial. In this respect, there is a need for better tooling for developing transformations. At present the prominent M2T and M2M transformation approaches are text-based, offering no graphical support for mapping constructs from the source model to the target model. A graphical transformation language would therefore seem a logical next step in this regard. The MOLA (Model transformation Language) project (MOLA, 2010) aims to provide a way to develop a transformation language along these lines allowing model transformation constructs associated with mapping source and target along with branching, conditions and so on to be captured in a graphical way.

Other important issues are the activities of iterative development and evolution. At least in principle, MDE would seem the ideal technology for dealing with rapid iterative development and evolutions brought on by changes in system specifications, in that changes specified via the model will automatically make the required changes to the code. However, in practice this is only true if the meta-models and transformations are sufficiently rich to accommodate such changes in the first place. Typically, in many cases MDE is not utilised to generate 100% of the code solution and thus handcrafted code in addition to the generated code is obligatory. While there are many code protection and modularisation techniques (e.g. inheritance, Aspect-oriented programming (Filman et al., 2004), mixins, partial classes

(Microsoft, 2010b), generics (Microsoft, 2010a) in use by programmers there are generally no commonly accepted guidelines in place stating the best practices with regard to iterative MDE development or MDE evolution.

The main problem is that evolutions to system specifications generally entail evolution to not only code but also multiple artefacts in the MDE process i.e. workflow files, transformations, validation functions, etc. In particular the editing of transformation files can be an arduous process especially if the editors do not give the programmer sufficient feedback and validation. The problems described above are particularly felt when developing DSLs using the Eclipse platform where multiple frameworks (e.g. TMF, GMF, GEF, MWE, etc.) are used. The EuGENia project (EuGENia, 2010) concerns itself with a tool that generates a large part of the Java code associated with a GMF editor. It allows rapid prototyping of graphical based editors from an annotated EMF model. While the approach does not entirely obviate the manual writing of Java code it shows an approach where changes to the meta-model can be automatically accommodated and transformed into a graphical editor's code.

From our own experiences with UML we have observed that some of the problems associated with graphical interfaces in Eclipse using GMF/GEF, i.e. the need for the development of handcrafted Java code, are obviated although the evolutions to profiles do require that the associated model transformation files are also updated.

There are, however, some interesting approaches dealing with meta-model evolution and the associated model instances. COPE (COPE, 2010) (Coupled Evolution of Meta-models and Models) is an approach to easing the migration of models as a meta-model evolves. The approach works by recording changes to the meta-model. However, the approach requires some overhead from the user in terms of following a prescribed procedure. Similarly, the Eclipse Edapt project (Edapt, 2010) is a proposal for capturing the

changes from different meta-model instances using the EMF Compare project (EMF Compare, 2010).

3.1.3 Methodologies and Consolidation of Technologies

As can be ascertained by the material in this chapter, there are a wide variety of tools and approaches dealing with general application modeling, model transformations, real-time application modeling and service modeling. Many of the approaches work with a common meta-model developed in either EMF or UML, thus the tools, at least in principle, ensure some level of interoperability. However, the reality is somewhat different. Many of the approaches are immature and lack the integration required. One of the problems with having such diversity is one of tool consolidation and lack of an associated defined methodology guiding the developer through each stage. In other words, where do the developers start and what are the steps they need to take in order to develop their intended application? The SHAPE Project (Bastida et al., 2009) is an example of a project which aims to define a methodology where the best practices in existing MDE and SOA development are combined. While there are a number of methodologies associated with MDE, as illustrated by (Bastida et al., 2009), they tend to be heavyweight and somewhat vague.

Another project with a strong focus on supporting the specification of methodologies is the EPF project (http://www.eclipse.org/epf/). This project has two main goals: 1. Providing an extensible framework and exemplary tools for software process engineering which address method and process authoring, library management and configuring and publishing of processes. 2. Providing exemplary and extensible process content for a range of software development and management processes supporting iterative, agile, and incremental development that can be applied to a broad set of development platforms and applications.

Similarly, no common SOA platform has been adopted by the industry which has meant that there is a lack of interoperability. The Eclipse SOA project and SoaML approach are intended to standardise the development of SOA applications. However, they are still somewhat new technologies and under development.

REFERENCES

Abstratt Technologies. (2010). *TextUML toolkit*. Retrieved from http://abstratt.com/

Apache. (2010). Apache ServiceMix. Retrieved from http://servicemix.apache.org /home.html

Bastida, L., Berre, A. J., Elvesæter, B., Hahn, C., Johnsen, S. G., Kämper, S... Stollberg, M. (2009). *Model-driven methodology and architecture specification*. (SHAPE project deliverable D2.1).

Compare, E. M. F. (2010). *EMF Compare*. Retrieved from http://wiki.eclipse.org/ index.php / EMF_Compare

COPE. (2010). *COPE – Coupled evolution of metamodels and models*. Retrieved from http:// cope.in.tum.de/ pmwiki.php

CXF. (2010). *Apache CXF: An open source service framework*. Retrieved from http://cxf.apache.org/

Eclipse. (2010a). *Eclipse modeling framework* (EMF). Retrieved from http://www.eclipse.org/ modeling/emf/

Eclipse. (2010b). *Graphical modeling project* (GMP). Retrieved from http://www.eclipse.org/ modeling/gmp/

Eclipse. (2010c). *Java emitter templates* (JET) Retrieved from http://www.eclipse.org/ modeling/ m2t/?project=jet

Edapt. (2010). *Edapt - Framework for Ecore model adaptation and instance migration*. Retrieved from http://www.eclipse.org / proposals/ edapt/

Epsilon. (2010). *Epsilon*. Retrieved from http:// www.eclipse.org/ gmt/epsilon/

Equinox. (2010). *Equinox*. Retrieved from http:// www.eclipse.org/ equinox/

EuGENia. (2010). *EuGENia*. Retrieved from http://www.eclipse.org/ gmt/ epsilon/ doc/ eugenia/

Evidence. (2010). *ERIKA Enterprise and RT-Druid website*. Retrieved from http://www.evidence. eu.com / content/ view/ 28/51/

Filman, R., Elrad, T., Clarke, S., & Aksit, M. (2004). *Aspect-oriented software development*. Addison Wesley.

Fowler, M., & Pearson, R. (2010). *Domain specific languages*. Addison Wesley.

Hahn C., Cerri, D., Panfilenko, D., Benguria, G., & Sadovyhk, A. (2009). *Model transformations and deployment – From UPMSHA to WSA, agents, P2P, grid and SWS platforms*. (SHAPE project deliverable D5.3).

Jouault, F., & Kurtev, I. (2006). *Transforming models with ATL*. In Satellite Events at the MoDELS 2005 Conference, Revised Selected Papers, volume 3844 of Lecture Notes in Computer Science. Springer. Kent, S. (2002). Model driven engineering. *Proceedings of IFM2002, LNCS 2335* (pp. 286-298). Springer.

Mathworks. (2010). *MATLAB - The language of technical computing*. Retrieved from http://www. mathworks.com/ products/ matlab/

MetaCase. (2010). *Domain-specific modeling with MetaEdit+*. Retrieved from http://www. metacase.com/

Microsoft. (2010a). *C# programming guide on generics*. Retrieved from http://msdn.microsoft. com/ en-us/ library/ ms379564(VS.80).aspx

Microsoft. (2010b). *C# programming guide on partial classes.* Retrieved from http://msdn.microsoft.com/ en-us/ library/ wa80x488(VS.80).aspx

MOLA. (2010). *MOLA - Model transformation language.* Retrieved from http://mola.mii.lu.lv/

Muller, P. A., Fleurey, F., & Jézéquel, J.-M. (2005). Weaving executability into object-oriented meta-languages. In *Model Driven Engineering Languages and Systems, 8th International Conference, MoDELS, volume 3713 of Lecture Notes in Computer Science*, (pp. 264–278). Springer.

Obeo. (2010). *Acceleo: MDA generator.* Retrieved from http://www.acceleo.org / pages/ home/en

Oldevik, J., Neple, T., Grønmo, R., Aagedal, J. Ø., & Berre, A.-J. (2005). Toward standardised model to text transformations. In Hartman, A., & Kreische, D. (Eds.), *ECMDAFA 2005. LNCS* (*Vol. 3748*, pp. 239–253). Heidelberg, Germany: Springer.

OMG. (2008a). *UML profile for modeling quality of service and fault tolerance characteristics and mechanisms*, v1.1. Retrieved May 31, 2010, from http://www.omg.org / spec/ QFTP/

OMG. (2008b). *OMG systems modeling language* (OMG SysML) version 1.1. Retrieved June 7, 2010, from http://www.omg.org/ spec/ SysML/

OMG. (2009a). *Business process model and notation* (BPMN) *FTF beta 1 for version 2.0.* OMG. Retrieved June 12, 2010, from http://www.bpmn.org/

OMG. (2009b). *UML profile for MARTE: Modeling and analysis of real-time embedded systems*, version 1.0. Retrieved June 3, 2010, from http://www.omg.org /spec/ MARTE/

OMG. (2009c). *Service oriented architecture modeling kanguage (SoaML) - Specification for the UML profile and metamodel for services* (UPMS). Retrieved June 12, 2010, from http://www.omg.org/ spec/ SoaML/

OMG. (2010a). *Object management group.* Retrieved from http://www.omg.org

OMG. (2010b). *OMG's meta-object facility.* Retrieved from http://www.omg.org/ mof/

OMG. (2010c). *Unified modeling language, infrastructure version* 2.3. Retrieved June 3, 2010, from http://www.omg.org/ spec/ UML/

OMG. (2010d). *MOF support for semantic structures RFP.* (Document ad/06-06-08). Retrieved from http://www.omg.org/ cgi-bin/ doc?ad/ 2006-6-8

OpenArchitectureWare. (2010a). *OpenArchitectureWare.* Retrieved from http://www.openarchitectureware.org/

OpenArchitectureWare. (2010b). *Xpand language.* Retrieved from http://wiki.eclipse.org/ Xpand

Papyrus. (2010). *Papyrus.* Retrieved from http://www.papyrusuml.org

Petri, C. A. (1962). *Kommunikation mit Automaten.* Schriften des Rheinisch- 6 Westfälischen Institutes für Instrumentelle Mathematik an der Universität Bonn Nr. 2, 1962.

RT-Druid. (2004). *RT-Druid: A tool for architecture level design of embedded systems.* White paper, Evidence S.r.l. 2004.

RTSC. (2010). *Real-time software components.* Retrieved from http://www.eclipse.org/ proposals/ rtsc

SCA. (2010). *STP service component architecture project.* Retrieved from http://www.eclipse.org/ stp/ sca/

Scilab. (2010). *The free platform for numerical computation.* Retrieved from http://www.scilab.org/

SHAPE. (2010). *SHAPE project.* (EU STREP – fp7 ICT-2007-216408). Retrieved from http://www.shape-project.eu

Swordfish. (2010). *Swordfish SOA runtime framework project.* Retrieved from http://www.eclipse.org/ swordfish/

van der Aalst, W. M. P., ter Hofstede, A. H. M., Kiepuszewski, B., & Barros, A. P. (2003). Workflow patterns. *Distributed and Parallel Databases, 14*(1), 5–51. doi:10.1023/A:1022883727209

Wikipedia. (2010). *Unified modeling language.* Retrieved from http://en.wikipedia.org/ wiki/ Unified_Modeling_ Language

Chapter 3
Programming Interfaces for Realtime and Cloud-Based Computing

Gregory Katsaros
National Technical University of Athens, Greece

Tommaso Cucinotta
Scuola Superiore Sant'Anna, Italy

ABSTRACT

Research in the fields of Grid Computing, Service Oriented Architectures (SOA) as well as virtualization technologies has driven the emergence of Cloud service models such as Software-as-a-Service (SaaS), Platform-as-a-Service (PaaS), and Infrastructure-as-a-Service (IaaS).

The appearance of different business roles according to this classification, potentially with differing interests, introduces new challenges with regard to the tools and mechanisms put in place in order to enable the efficient provisioning of services. Security, Quality of Service (QoS) assurance, and real-time capabilities are just a few issues that the providers are trying to tackle and integrate within the new products and services that they offer. In this chapter, we make an overview of the approaches that aim to APIs for real-time computing. In the first part of this chapter, several Real-Time Application Interfaces will be presented and compared. After that, we will document the state-of-the-art regarding the Cloud APIs available and analyze the architecture and the technologies that they support.

DOI: 10.4018/978-1-60960-827-9.ch003

INTRODUCTION

New generation interactive distributed applications, such as various multimedia, virtual collaboration and e-learning applications, have significant demands on processing, storage and networking capabilities, as well as stringent timing requirements. For these applications, the time at which individual computations and data transfers are terminated is as important as their functional correctness. Contrarily to the traditional domain of hard real-time systems, where a single violation of the timing constraints is not acceptable because it would lead to potential overall system failures and/or life losses, the mentioned applications posses instead soft timing constraints, whose violation leads to degradation of the offered Quality of Service and interactivity level.

Soft real-time applications, and especially multimedia ones, would greatly benefit from a real-time run-time support like commonly available on Real-Time Operating Systems. In fact, this type of OS usually provides those features that allow for a well-known, predictable and analyzable timing behavior of hosted applications: all kernel segments are characterized with well-known worst-case durations, scheduling latencies and interrupt latencies which may be controlled through the appropriate tuning of the interrupt and process schedulers. A set of real-time scheduling policies is available for the system designer and programmers. Time may be measured (and timers may fire) with a high precision (typically sub-millisecond) while there are tools available for WCET estimation and (off-line) analysis, as well as for schedulability analysis. Unfortunately, such OSes are designed for embedded control applications, thus they imply serious constraints on the supported hardware and available high-level software infrastructures.

Nowadays multimedia applications are increasingly complex and they tend to be distributed, thus their development on a hard real-time OS may be overly prohibitive, due to the lack of such OS functionality as: compression libraries, the support for a wide range of multimedia devices and protocols, including the possibility to handle various types of media, and the availability of a complete networking stack.

On the other hand, General-Purpose Operating Systems (GPOS) constitute the ideal development platform for multimedia applications. Unfortunately, GPOSes are not designed to provide the run-time support that is necessary for meeting timing requirements of individual applications. Therefore, in recent years, various efforts have been done towards the integration of real-time technologies within GPOSes, particularly within Linux, for the availability of its kernel as open-source and its worldwide diffusion. Various drawbacks make the Linux kernel, as well as most of the GPOSes, particularly unsuitable for running real-time applications: the monolithic structure of the kernel and the wide variety of drivers that may be loaded within, the impossibility to keep under control all the non-preemptable sections possibly added by such drivers, the general structure of the interrupt management core framework that privileges portability with respect to latencies, and others. As a result, the latency experienced by time-sensitive activities can be as large as tens or hundreds of milliseconds. This makes Linux non-suitable for hard real-time applications with tight timing constraints. Though, soft real-time applications may run quite well within such an environment, especially when the original kernel is modified so to integrate the necessary real-time capabilities.

Furthermore, research in the fields of Grid Computing, Service Oriented Architectures (SOA) as well as Virtualization technologies has driven the emergence of Cloud service models such as Software-as-a-Service (SaaS), Platform-as-a-Service (PaaS), and Infrastructure-as-a-Service

Table 1. Taxonomy of the major Cloud solutions and APIs

Providers/APIs	SaaS	PaaS	IaaS	Open Source	Commercial
Amazon EC2			x		x
Vmware vCloud			x		x
Sun Cloud			x	x	
OCCI			x	x	
Google AppEngine		x		x	x
Microsoft Azure		x			x
jCloud	x			x	
libCloud	x			x	
deltacloud	x			x	

(IaaS). Moreover, the emergence of different business roles according to this classification, potentially with differing interests, introduces new challenges with regard to the tools and mechanisms put in place in order to enable the efficient provisioning of services. Security, Quality of Service (QoS) and efficiency are just a few issues that the providers are trying to tackle and integrate within the new products and services that they offer. In general, the SaaS provider offers an application as a service over a distributed environment to the end users. The PaaS provider offers a development platform and environment consisting of services and storage units hosted on the cloud, while the IaaS provider offers resources on demand depending on each deployed instance. The PaaS offerings include services for binding all the involved parties, in addition to the end user of the infrastructure. This includes adapting the application in order to be executed on a service oriented and distributed infrastructure, describing it in a machine understandable way and enabling it in order to be executed on virtualized environments. To this end, several Application Programming Interfaces have been published serving different layer of the Cloud architecture. In the following table (Table 1) we try to map the important ones regarding their characteristics.

Amazon and Vmware provide commercial solutions for IaaS layer (EC2 and vCloud). The first one offers packages for accessing and utilizing Amazon's servers while with the vCloud you can build your own Cloud infrastructure. OCCI is a specification that is being developed for IaaS providing supported by the Open Grid Forum (OGF) community while Sun Cloud is the solution that Sun Microsystems published in the same context. From the other hand, there are APIs that are trying to cover the intermediate layer of the platform (PaaS) such as Microsoft Azure and Google App Engine. The first offers components and tools for developing and deploying applications within Microsoft's data centers. It is commercial product that allows you to deploy Windows applications on Microsoft's data centers. Google's App Engine on the contrary, provides an API for developing and executing Cloud-based applications for free, with specific utilization boundaries and limits. Extension of those quotas can be achieved by joining the billing mode of that service. Finally, there are several cross platform Cloud APIs like jClouds, libCloud, deltacloud and others, that allow you to develop applications using various programming languages (e.g. Java, Python) and deploy them onto proprietary as well as open Cloud infrastructures.

In what follows we make an overview of the approaches that aim to APIs for real-time computing. In the first part of this chapter, several Real-Time Application Interfaces will be presented and compared. After that, we will document the state-of-the-art regarding the Cloud APIs available and analyze the architecture and the technologies that they support.

PROGRAMMING INTERFACES FOR REAL-TIME COMPUTING

Approaches, Implementations and Comparisons

POSIX

POSIX stands for Portable Operating System Interface and is the collective name of a family of standards, also referred as IEEE 1003 or ISO/IEC 9945, jointly developed by the IEEE Portable Application Standards Committee (PASC) and the Austin Common Standards Revision Group (CSRG) of The Open Group.

In 1998, the first real-time profile, IEEE Std 1003.13-1998, was published enabling POSIX to address real-time applications, even for embedded systems and small footprint devices. It must be said that support for most of these functionalities is not mandatory in a POSIX-conforming implementation and the 1003.1-2001 standard defines the X/Open System Interface (XSI) extensions that groups together several of these optional features in the so-called XSI Option Groups. A compliant XSI implementation has to support at least the following options: file synchronization, memory mapped files, memory protection, threads, thread synchronization, thread stack address attribute and size, and may also support a bunch of other option groups among whom: Realtime (grouping together asynchronous, synchronized and prioritized I/O, shared memory objects, process and range based memory locking, semaphores, timers, realtime

signals, message passing and process scheduling), Advanced Realtime (grouping together clock selection, process CPU-time clocks, monotonic clock, timeouts and typed memory objects), Realtime Threads (grouping together thread priority inheritance and protection, and thread scheduling), Advanced Realtime Threads (grouping together thread CPU-time clocks, thread sporadic server, spin locks and barriers).

By means of the just listed features, the standard allows for a precise timing of real-time processes and threads on a system, and for a certain control over the scheduler configuration for individual processes and threads. This last aspect is critical: a real-time application should not compete for the access to the shared physical resources, first of all the CPU, with all the other non real-time processes on the system. In fact, POSIX defines a multi-queue priority-based regulated access to the CPU, where a set of system calls can be used in order to set the scheduling policy of each process to SCHED_FIFO, SCHED_RR or SCHED_OTHER:

- int sched_setscheduler(pid_t pid, int policy, const struct sched_param *param)
- int sched_getscheduler(pid_t pid)
- int sched_rr_get_interval(pid_t pid, struct timespec * tp)
- int sched_get_priority_max(int policy)
- int sched_get_priority_min(int policy)

The SCHED_FIFO and SCHED_RR policies allow the programmer to specify the real-time priority at which a process will be scheduled (by setting the priority field of the sched_param structure). The available priorities range for a given policy may be retrieved by using the sched_get_priority_min() and sched_get_priority_max() system calls. In case multiple processes are assigned the same priority, SCHED_FIFO simply schedules them in FIFO order, whilst SCHED_RR applies a Round-Robin policy with a fixed time-slice (whose duration may be retrieved using the sched_rr_get_interval() system call).

All other non real-time processes in the system have the default SCHED_OTHER policy, meaning that they are scheduled in the background of the real-time processes, allowing real-time processes to exhibit a far better responsiveness than non real-time ones.

In the context of cloud-computing and virtualized infrastructures, the POSIX API for real-time computing is relevant in those contexts in which a host Operating System (OS) is exploited as hypervisor for hosting multiple Virtual Machines (VM), along with the guest OSes running inside. In fact, in this scenario, each VM is seen by the host OS as a process, thus its scheduling policy and real-time scheduling priority may be manipulated by leveraging the POSIX API. For example, this kind of scenario is realized by the Kernel Virtual Machine (KVM) hypervisor on the Linux OS.

With the mentioned POSIX priority-based scheduling policies, the actual guarantees a real-time process receives depend basically on what other real-time processes run into the system at a higher real-time priority. The SCHED_FIFO and SCHED_RR POSIX scheduling classes have the heavy drawback that a higher priority process can indefinitely delay the execution of all other lower priority ones, and there is no run-time mechanism that ensures temporal encapsulation among real-time processes.

Such problem is mitigated by the SCHED_SPORADIC optional POSIX real-time scheduling class. In this model, the developer may reserve the CPU for a real-time task by specifying a *budget*, a *period*, a *real-time priority* and a *low priority*. The kernel runs the process at the specified real-time priority for an overall time duration not exceeding the budget in each time window as wide as the period. When the budget is exhausted, the process is downgraded to the low priority. The advantage of such a scheme is that, with proper refinements (Mark Stanovich et al., 2009), (Dario Faggioli et al., 2010) it is possible to rely on classical Fixed-

Priority analysis for checking schedulability of the real-time processes on the system. Also, if an application tries to consume more CPU than the maximum value theoretically foreseen in the analysis, i.e., the reservation budget, it is downgraded to the low real-time priority. Therefore, it is possible to keep under control the maximum interference that a higher priority real-time process may have on lower priority ones.

Unfortunately, being optional, the SCHED_SPORADIC scheduling class is not widely implemented on POSIX compliant OSes. On Linux, an implementation of SCHED_SPORADIC has been developed in the context of the IRMOS European Project by Faggioli et al. and made available as a kernel patch (Faggioli).

When using Fixed-priority scheduling, the optimum assignment of priorities is the well-known Rate-Monotonic, which needs knowledge of the entire set of real-time tasks running on the system, in order to set each one priority. Interfaces that are more suitable to open, dynamic real-time systems are based on EDF scheduling and they allow each application to request to the OS scheduling guarantees in terms of a minimum budget to be granted every application period. This model is also capable of theoretically saturating a single-processor system with real-time tasks, conversely to what happens with Fixed-priority scheduling. For example, such an API has been developed for Linux in the context of various academic projects, such as the ones summarized in what follows. (Mark Stanovich et al., 2009) (Dario Faggioli et al., 2010) (Faggioli).

The AQuoSA API

The AQuoSA framework (Luigi Palopoli et al., 2008), (OCERA – Open Components for Embedded Real-time Applications), (OCERA Project Deliverable D1.1 - RTOS), (S.Oikawa et al., 1999), enhances a standard GNU/Linux system with scheduling strategies based on the Resource Reservation techniques (Tommaso Cucinotta,

2008). AQuoSA features a well-designed C API allowing for an easy use of the EDF-based real-time scheduling capabilities available on the platform. This is exposed to applications in form of a set of header files and a dynamically loadable library that needs to be linked to the executables.

The most important API calls, available after inclusion of the <aquosa/qreslib.h> header file, are the following:

- **creation** and **destruction** of resource-reservation "servers":
  - qos_rv qres_create_server (qres_ params_t * p_params, qres_sid_t *p_sid)
  - qos_rv qres_destroy_server (qres_ sid_t sid)

where parameters to be provided via the qres_ params_t structure are a minimum guaranteed budget (Q_min) that is always granted once the reservation is accepted, a desired budget (Q) that is granted only if available, and the reservation period (P); once created, a server is identified via a qres_sid_t identifier;

- **attach** and **detach** of threads to the created server:
  - qos_rv qres_attach_thread (qres_ sid_t server_id, pid_t pid, tid_t tid)
  - qos_rv qres_detach_thread (qres_ sid_t sid, pid_t pid, tid_t tid)

where the thread to be attached is identified by its POSIX process identifier (pid) and the Linux-specific thread identifier (tid), which can be obtained via the Linux gettid() system call;

- dynamic **setting** and **retrieval of scheduling parameters** for a server:
  - qos_rv qres_get_params (qres_sid_t sid, qres_params_t *p_params)
  - qos_rv qres_set_params (qres_sid_t sid, qres_params_t * p_params)

The FRSH API

The FRSH API has been developed in the context of the FRESCOR project for the purpose of allowing writing complex embedded real-time applications which may be portable across multiple hard and soft real-time platforms and OSes. In fact, the FRSH API is available on the MarteOS, Partikle and Enea OSE OS Hard Real-Time OSes, and on the Linux General-Purpose OS. From an API and programmability perspective, the portability has been achieved mainly by realizing a POSIX-like common API layer, the FRESCOR Operating System Abstraction Layer (FOSA), which subsumes a minimum set of POSIX capabilities that are needed in order to realize complex, distributed real-time embedded applications.

When considering complex distributed Cloud Computing applications with real-time requirements, the FRSH API may be used in order to provide scheduling guarantees to Virtual Machines hosted on a Linux-based machine by means of the KVM hypervisor.

The FRSH API is divided into multiple modules. The most important ones are the following:

- the **Core Module** provides applications with fundamental real-time scheduling services;
- the **Shared Objects Module** allows for realizing atomic operations where the access to the shared resources is governed according to well-designed real-time protocols;
- the **Hierarchical Scheduling Module** provides applications with hierarchical scheduling capabilities, allowing for example to nest Fixed-Priority scheduling inside Resource-Reservation scheduling, etc.
- the **Distribution Module** provides services for distributed real-time applications, such as the capability to negotiate the allocation of resources atomically on a set of distributed physical nodes;

- the **Feedback Control Module** provides applications with adaptive reservation strategies, where the resource allocation can be varied dynamically following the actual instantaneous application workload;
- the **Energy Management Module** allows applications to specify their resource requirements in presence of dynamic voltage scaling capabilities of the CPU.

In what follows, we focus on FRSH Core Module. The reader may refer to for a complete description of the FRSH API.

The most important functions of the FRSH Core Module are the following:

- **preparation** of the **scheduling parameters**, referred to as *contracts*, to be negotiated with the OS:
  - int frsh_contract_init (frsh_contract_t *contract)
  - int frsh_contract_set_basic_params (frsh_contract_t*contract, const frsh_rel_time_t *budget_min, const frsh_rel_time_t*period_max, ...)
  - int frsh_contract_set_timing_reqs (frsh_contract_t*contract, const boold_equals_t, const frsh_rel_time_t*deadline, ...)
- **negotiation** of the **contract** with the OS:
  - int frsh_contract_negotiate (const frsh_contract_t*contract, frsh_vres_id_t*vres)
  - int frsh_contract_cancel (const frsh_vres_id_t vres)
  - int frsh_contract_renegotiate_sync (const frsh_contract_t*new_contract, const frsh_vres_id_t vres)

where, after negotiation, the granted reservation is referred to by means of a frsh_vres_t identifier, and its parameters may be also changed via the renegotiation function, if needed;

- **binding** and **unbinding of threads** to a negotiated contract:
  - int frsh_thread_bind (const frsh_vres_id_t vres, const frsh_thread_id_t thread)
  - int frsh_thread_unbind (const frsh_thread_id_t thread)
- **querying the run-time status** of the scheduler:
  - int frsh_vres_get_remaining_budget (const frsh_vres_id_t vres, frsh_rel_time_t*budget)

this function is useful for realizing anytime computing real-time algorithms, where some optional computations in the algorithm may be performed or suppressed depending on the availability of residual budget granted by the OS till the deadline.

The IRMOS Real-Time Schedulers

In the context of the IRMOS European Project, a new multi-processor real-time scheduler for Linux has been developed, with hierarchical scheduling capabilities.

In this case, the real-time computing capabilities of the kernel are not exposed to applications through an API, but rather the Linux cgroup virtual file-system is exploited.

Therefore, the main operations related to real-time scheduling may be achieved as follows:

- first of all, the cgroup special file-system (and specifically the CPU controller) needs to be mounted somewhere on the system, e.g., for mounting it in /cg/ the following shell command can be used:
  - mount -t cgroup -o cpu cgroup /cg
- for **creating a new reservation**, a group must be created by creating a folder in /cg/, e.g.:
  - mkdir /cg/myresv1

- for **setting the scheduling parameters**, i.e., a given budget (a.k.a., runtime) and period, the corresponding quantities (in microseconds) need to be written into special entries available in the group folder, e.g., for creating a reservation of 10ms every 100ms:
  - echo 100000 > /cg/myresv1/cpu. rt_period_us
  - echo 10000 > /cg/myresv1/cpu. rt_runtime_us
  - echo 100000 > /cg/myresv1/cpu. rt_task_period_us
  - echo 10000 > /cg/myresv1/cpu. rt_task_runtime_us

where the cpu.rt_*_us entries decide the parameters for the entire group, comprising possible subgroups that one might want to create, whilst the cpu.rt_task_*_us entries decide the parameters dedicated to the tasks attached at this very level of the hierarchy

- for **attaching a task** to a group, its Linux TID (similar to the POSIX PID) needs to be written into the tasks special entry available in the group, e.g., if the TID of the task we're interested into is 1421:
  - echo 1421 > /cg/myresv1/tasks
- for **detaching a task** from a group, its Linux TID needs to be written into the tasks special entry at the root cgroup level, e.g.:
  - echo 1421 > /cg/tasks
- finally, in order to **allow tasks to actually exploit real-time scheduling**, they need to be scheduled according to the needed POSIX real-time scheduling class (SCHED_RR or SCHED_FIFO), and a real-time priority needs to be assigned, e.g.:
  - chrt -r -p 20 1421

For the convenience of the programmer, the above operations are made available to C programs through an adaptation layer written in C implementing the AQuoSA API already detailed above, and to Python scripts via an adaptation layer written in Python realising a similar API.

RTLinuxFree and RTAI

- RTLinux and RTAI (Setz) are projects mainly aimed to support real-time in the context of industrial control, and they do not generally target complex, distributed multimedia applications on Linux, nor general cloud-computing applications running in virtualized infrastructures. In fact, in these projects a real-time task is generally written as a kernel module for the Linux kernel, which may use a proper API in order to set its own real-time scheduling class and related parameters. Such an approach is perfectly viable for relatively simple control applications that need to periodically read information from a sensor, apply some control logic then drive an actuator, but it is not easy at all to realize complex real-time distributed applications in form of kernel modules.

RTSJ

To address the problems that Java has when used in real-time systems, the Real-Time Specification for Java has been developed. Among other features, RTSJ basically exposes at the Java programming level the POSIX real-time scheduling capabilities of the underlying OS. Also, in order to face with the well-known problem of the Garbage Collector that can interfere with Java applications in unpredictable ways, RTSJ defines immortal and scoped memory areas to supplement the standard Java heap. These areas allow applications to use memory without being required to block if the garbage collector needs to free memory in the heap. Objects allocated in the immortal memory area are accessible to all threads and are never collected. Because it is never collected, immortal memory is a limited resource that must be used carefully. Scoped memory areas can be created and destroyed under programmer control, through specific API available to the programmer.

PROGRAMMING INTERFACES IN CLOUD COMPUTING

Amazon EC2 API

Amazon is considered to be the leader Cloud Provider in the current market. The Cloud solution offered by Amazon is called Amazon Web Services (AWS) and was initially launched in 2002. In principle AWS is a collection of Web services that together are forming the Amazon's Cloud platform. The company offers a variety of Cloud related products such as Elastic Compute Cloud (Amazon EC2), Simple Storage Service (S3), Simple Queue Service (SQS), CloudFront, Simple DB and more. It is not in the context of this chapter to elaborate on the services and products offered by Amazon so we will only mention the basic characteristics of the two basic services: EC2 and S3, before elaborating on the Amazon EC2 API (Amazon EC2 API).

EC2 is a Web service that allows you to deploy and manage server instances with a variety of operating systems in Amazon's Data Centers. It offers specific API and utilities to control the computing resources and manage the network's access permission and therefore launch a custom application environment. Apart from the complete control that you have on the instances, scalability is another key feature of EC2 service. As the name of the service implies (*Elastic*), the computing capacity of each resource can be adjusted manually or automatically by the application through the provided API.

Amazon S3 service offers an on-line storage space that can be accessible by any individual or application on the Web. It appears as an alternative of local storage systems and is one of the major services of the whole AWS collection. Similar with EC2, Amazon provides an S3 API for storing and retrieving data from their Data Centers. In addition, Amazon is committed to provide 99.99% durability and availability of the stored data as described in the Amazon S3 Service Level Agreement.

For better understanding of EC2 service we will explain the terminology that Amazon uses for the specification of the related API. An *instance* is a virtual server that runs over the physical host within Amazon's Data Centers. The templates from which the instances are been created are called *Amazon Machine Images* (AMIs) and include options of operating system or other properties than you can select in order to define the individual instance that you want to utilize. To access your instances you can use Amazon's Elastic IP Addresses that are actually static IP addresses designed for dynamic Cloud computing. That IP address is associated with your account in Amazon and you can reconfigure to point to a different instance. *Elastic Block Storage* (EBS) is the persistent storage of each EC2 instance that keeps the state of the instance. In addition, you can create a *snapshot* of the state that will be stored within the S3 service for long term durability. Like presented in Figure 1, the basic flow when using the EC2 starts by finding an existing public AMI and customizing to our needs or building one from scratch. The next step is to create the instance for the AMI using the provided EC2 API. The result of this bundling process is an AMI ID that you can use in order to launch as many instances of the AMI as you want. Finally, through the available tools of the API you can administer and use the instances as you want with any servers.

Amazon EC2 API provides access to EC2 Web service either using the SOAP API or the Query API. When using the SOAP Web Services messaging protocol, the interfaces are defined by a Web Service Description Language (WSDL) xml document. While the SOAP requests and re-

Figure 1. Amazon EC2 AMI deployment flow

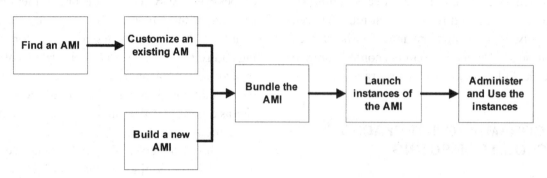

sponses in Amazon EC2 follow current standards, any programming language supporting those standards (e.g. Java, C++, C#, Python, Perl and Ruby) could be used within Amazon's Cloud. The Query API interface is a REST-based interface that supports GET and POST method to perform any request. The Query interface is seems to be preferred by the Amazon's developers and is provided for almost all AWS. Moreover, many browsers do not support the full range of HTTP methods, while all Web browsers can handle GET and POST requests.

VMware vCloud Computing Interface

VMware as a leading company in the field of virtualization released in 2009 the vCloud API (VMware vCloud), an OVF 1.0 standards-based Programming Interface for providing and consuming virtual resources from the cloud. The vCloud API was a result of a combined effort from VMware and its partners in order to deliver an easy to use Cloud Interface, extensible and based on various established open standards such as XML, HTTP, OVF etc. In more details, the vCloud API can be distinguished in two parts: the Administrative API which is used for creating, managing and monitoring resources, users and roles within a vCloud and the Users API which provides browsing and discovering resources operations as well as creating, modifying and deploying operating virtual appliances. The VMware vCloud API

enables application developers to create clients of vCloud services using a RESTful application development style. vCloud API clients and servers communicate over HTTP, exchanging XML representations of vCloud entities.

The vCloud defines several resources and entities illustrated in Figure 2. All kind of objects (resources and other entities) are being described through XML. In addition, the vCloud API elaborates and defines in detail with links the context of a resource, list other relevant resources, and define how they relate to the current resource. These links are the primary way that a server delivers information to a client about how to access and operate a resource.

Organization: A vCloud can include more than one organization each one of them is a administrative superset of users, groups and resources.

vDC: A vCloud virtual datacenter (vDC) is a mechanism for allocating computing resources such as networks, storage, CPU, and memory. Within a vDC the resources are fully virtualized and either are reserved on demand or pre-defined through the SLA. There are Provider vDCs, containing the available resources of a vCloud Service Provider and Organization vDCs (Org. vDCs) that provide an environment where the virtual systems can be stored, deployed and operated.

Catalogs: Catalogs contain references to the organization's virtual datacenters and media images. A catalog can be visible only to its creators

Figure 2. Resources entities in vCloud

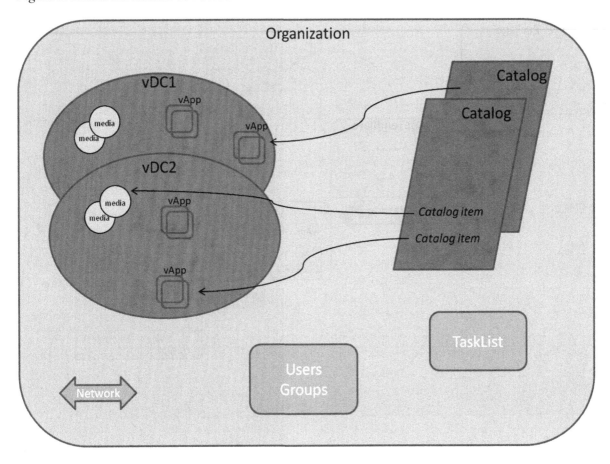

or could be published and become visible to other members of the organization as well.

Network: Network represents the allocated network capacity of a vDC provider within the organization.

User & Groups: An organization can contain several Users or Groups that are being created from the Organization Administrator or imported from the Directory Service (LDAP). Roles and specific rights are being assigned from the Administrator for setting the users permissions.

TasksList: The tasks that are being created by the execution of long-running operations are kept within the TaskList of the Organization.

Virtual Systems and Media Images: A vDC can include several Virtual Systems and Media Images. References of those can be listed within

the catalog, while the Media Images are stored in their native representation (ISO, floppy) and the Virtual Systems are stored as template based on the OVF 1.0 standard format. Those templates can then be retrieved from the catalog and be instantiated to become vApps. A vApp resource can contain even more than one Virtual Machine (VM) including the operational parameters such as: connection links between the VMs, the hierarchy of powering on and off the VMs, the End-user license agreements for each VM, the deployment terms and conditions that constrain the vDC resources consumption, access control and user permissions etc.

The vCloud API supports multiple operations for enabling the two-way transfer of Media Images and OVF packages between the client and

Figure 3. vApp lifecycle

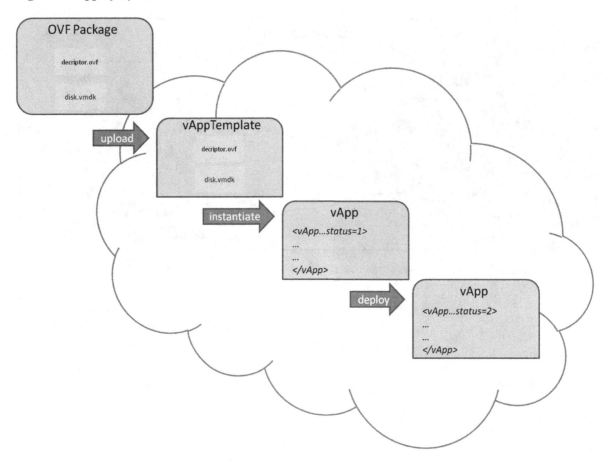

the cloud. Those upload and download operations are implemented by POST and GET requests respectively. In this context, the vApp Lifecycle includes three major steps:

- Uploading the OVF package
- Instantiating the vApp template
- Deploying the vApp

In order to create a vApp template an OVF package must be uploaded to the cloud through a vCloud API client. The steps that must be fulfilled are:

1. The client POSTs an initial request that specifies a name for the template, a transfer format for the data, and an optional description.

2. The server returns an unresolved (status="0") vAppTemplate document that includes an upload URL for the OVF package.

3. The client uses an HTTP PUT request to upload the OVF package descriptor (the .ovf file) to the upload URL.

4. The server reads the descriptor and constructs a complete vAppTemplate document (one that includes an upload URL for each file listed in the References section of the descriptor). While the server is constructing this document, the client makes periodic requests for it and examines the response for additional upload URLs. When the response contains any upload URIs beyond the one returned in Step 2, template is complete

5. The client uses HTTP PUT requests to upload each of the files.
6. If the OVF package includes a manifest file, the entire upload is validated against the contents of the manifest file.

The Instantiation process is a prerequisite to deployment and is based on the uploaded vApp Template. The template includes specific details of the vApp such as virtual disks that the cApp requires, CPU, memory and network connections that must be allocated by the vDC etc. A client can trigger the instantiation either using the default parameters of a vDC or he can override the vDC parameters with his own set. Instantiation parameters allow you to specify certain properties of a vApp, including: details of its vApp network, lease settings for the vApp, startup and shutdown parameters for the vApp. Instantiation parameters also include a way to indicate that any terms and conditions (such as license agreements) contained in the vApp have been accepted.

For the deployment and powering on a vApp a POST request is again being used. The client makes the request to the respective action/deploys URL and all VMs that are included within the vApp are being deployed. Similar requests for the operation of undeploy, power-off, reset, suspend and other are supported by the API.

Google App Engine

The introduction of Google into the Cloud computing technologies and the related marketplace was realized through Google's App Engine. In contrast with other providers and solutions that implement IaaS (e.g. Amazon AWS), the App Engine is a PaaS system. In principle, Google App Engine is a platform through which a developer can deploy and execute web application to Google's Data Centers. Currently the platform supports application written in Java and Python but can also serve other JVM related languages like Groovy, JRuby and Scala. Apart from the

SDK that is available for both languages (Java and Python) there is also an Eclipse plugin provided for development. Moreover, the data handling at Google's Cloud-enabled platform is provided with the Datastore API. In the case of Java development, the Datastore API stores and performs queries over data objects, known as entities. Each entity has a unique identifier (key) and one or more properties, as values of specific data types. The Datastore supports Java Data Objects (JDO) 2.3 and Java Persistent API (JPA) 1.0 standard interfaces. When building Python applications the Datastore in implemented through an SQL-like language called QGL. It does not support Join statements while it is inefficient when queries span over multiple machines. In this context, GQL is not a relational database in the common SQL sense but such a modeling can be accomplished through specific mechanism provided by the API (e.g. ReferenceProperty()).

When it comes to build an application, Google App Engine API provides a development environment either for Java (Eclipse plugin) or for Python. This environment simulates Google App Engine (including local Datastore, Google accounts etc.) and gives you the ability to deploy (*upload*) the application directly to Google App Engine. As a result, the whole process includes the following steps:

- Develop the application through the provided tools and APIs
- Register an Application ID on Google App Engine through the Administration Console
- Uploading the actual application files
- Accesses the Web application using a specific URL based on the Application ID

Google offers usage quotas for deploying application for free with certain limits. Developers can always enable billing in order to extend their usage on CPU, bandwidth, storage and e-mails. An

Table 2. Google App Engine free quota

Quota	Limit
Apps per developer	10
Time per request	30 sec
Blobstore size (total file size per app)	1 GB
HTTP response size	10 MB
Datastore item size	1 MB
Application code size	150 MB

indication of the free provided usage is presented on Table 2.

Open Cloud Computing Interface (OCCI)

During the OGF25 in March 2009 Ignacio M. Llorente (UCM – OpenNebula) and Thijs Metsch(Sun Microsystems - RESERVOIR project) founded the Open Cloud Computing Interface Working Group (OCCI) with the initial name of Cloud API (CAPI). At the following OGF26 and OGF27 the group was renamed to the current OCCI and the first results were presented. The goal of the OCCI-wg is to develop a clean, open API for 'Infrastructure as a Service' (IaaS) based Clouds. It has active membership of over 200 individuals and is led by four chairs from industry, academia, service providers and end-users. Several members are from commercial service providers that are committed to implementing the OGF-OCCI specification. OCCI will provide a slim and extensible RESTful based API. Every resource defined through OCCI will hold a unique address using a Uniform Resource Identifier (URI). The API implements CRUD operations: Create, Retrieve, Update and Delete, each one mapped to HTTP

verbs POST, GET, PUT and DELETE respectively. The types of resources that are currently supported are storage, network and compute resources and can be linked together to form a virtual machine with assigned attributes.

The Specification of OCCI is designed to be modular and is described to individual document deliverables:

- The OCCI Core & Models
- The OCCI Infrastructure Models

Figure 4. Alignment of OCCI URI to IaaS Resources

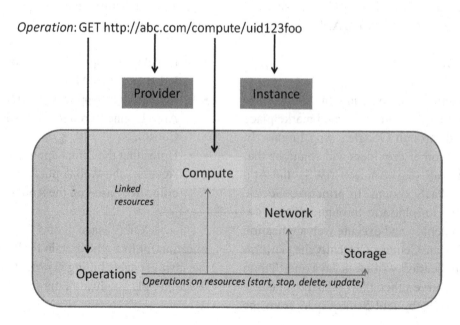

- OCCI XHTML5 rendering
- OCCI HTTP Header rendering

Currently the group is working on finalizing the specification while draft documents for all previous modules are available on SourceForge.

Azure (.NET)

The rapid evolution of Cloud Computing and the related technologies could not leave Microsoft out of this field. As a result, Microsoft published the Windows Azure solution as a Cloud service operating system. In principle, Azure is a service platform that allows the developer to deploy and run Windows applications and store data on Microsoft's data centers. The developers could write applications with the common Windows languages (C#, C++, VB etc) through the Microsoft Visual Studio suite but it also supports Java, Ruby, PHP and Python. The Azure platform is consisted by three major parts: Compute Service, Storage Service and Application Fabric. The first, provides the appropriate interfaces and support for the applications developed with the pre-mentioned technologies and can have multiple instances deployed. All kind of applications can utilize the storage service and have access to data resources throughout a RESTful approach. The storage service provides BLOBs for storing binary large objects, tables and queues for managing data. For applications that are more demanding on data management, Windows offers the SQL Azure Database, a cloud-based data management system (DBMS). The system is based on the Microsoft SQL Server and offers a similar management environment within the cloud. The data can be then accessed using ADO.NET or other Windows access interfaces. The cloud-based infrastructure service of the Azure solution is implemented by the Application Fabric mechanism. To this end, each application can expose endpoints using the Service Bus component of the Application Fabric in order to be accessed by other application of the

cloud or on-premise applications. The connection of a RESTful client towards an application is managed by the Access Control component of the Application Fabric mechanism. The developers can create applications with either *Web role* or *Worker role*, and define how many instances he wants to execute within the Windows Virtual Machines (VMs). Those VMs are not created by the developer but provided by the hypervisor that is specifically designed for use in the cloud. Applications with Web role are usually implemented with ASP.NET and are intended to accept and process HTTP requests using IIS. Apart from the Web applications, the Worker instances are batch jobs that interact with the Web role instances through the Storage Service.

Sun Cloud API

Sun Microsystems got involved into the Cloud technologies in 2009 by presenting their cloud computing infrastructure and API with the name Sun Open Cloud. Like the words imply, Sun's Cloud system is an open source solution with the API published under the Creative Common license which in principle allows anyone to use it in any way. SUN's Open Cloud is consisted by two core components: Sun Cloud Storage Service and Sun Cloud Compute Service. The first is a set of web services and WebDAV protocols that provide the functionality for accessing and storing data in various formats. It is also compatible with Amazon's S3 API. The Sun Cloud Compute Service provides to the developer all the tools and interfaces to build and operate a data center in the cloud or as Sun names, a Virtual Data Center (VDC). The VDC offers an easy to use integrated graphical interface, accessible via any browser through which you can design an application running on various operating systems within the cloud (Windows, Solaris, Linux etc). This user friendly interface supports drag-and-drop features as well as specific APIs and command-line-client for provisioning compute, storage and network resources.

SUN's Cloud API is a RESTful programming interface, with every entity be represented as cloud resources (compute, storage, networking components etc). The usage of the API is realized via HTTP protocol through the common GET, POST, PUT and DELETE requests. The API operates in the context of various resource types:

- Cloud: A top-level construct which groups all the Virtual Data Centers to which an API user has access.
- Virtual Data Center (VDC): An isolated container which is populated with Clusters, Private Virtual Networks, Public Addresses, Storage Volumes, Volume Snapshots.
- Cluster: An administrative grouping of Virtual Machines, useful for access control, copying or cloning, geographic isolation, and scripting automation.
- Virtual Machine (VM): A server.
- Private Virtual Network (VNet): A subnet, not connected to the Internet, which may be used to connect Virtual Machines within a VDC.
- Public Address: A connection to the Internet.
- Storage Volume: A storage resource which may be accessed via WebDAV and other storage protocols.
- Volume Snapshot: A snapshot of the state of a Storage Volume.

More information about the API specification can be found at the Kenai project wiki, where documentation as well as the actual source code and binaries are provided.

Cross Platform Cloud APIs

Apart from the Cloud Provider specific APIs there are several platform independent programming

interfaces for Cloud Computing. Jclouds is a Java-enabled open source framework for developing applications, supporting many cloud-aware features. Using the framework you can develop applications for various Cloud Providers such as Amazon, VMWare, Azure and others. Deltacloud is an open source RESTful API, provided by Red Hat and is compatible with EC2, Rackspace, GoGRID and other Cloud Providers. Deltacloud offers drivers for every supporting Cloud as a translation layer between the client and the provider's native API. In the same context, libcloud is Python client library that allows your application to interact with various providers. It is distributed under the Apache Software License and serves through specific drivers provided by the API the most common Clouds in the market.

CONCLUSION

Through this chapter we documented the basic Application Programming Interfaces for integrating Real-Time capabilities to Linux kernels. Several approaches were presented and compared in the context of executing soft as well as hard real-time applications. From the other hand, the emergence of Cloud computing brought a revolution and a new perception on application development and execution. All major Service Providers of the global marketplace, sooner or later got involved into Cloud-enabled technologies and related products. In the previous section, we presented various solutions and APIs covering all three layers of Cloud service model (SaaS, PaaS and IaaS). After investigating all most of the APIs available, either commercial and open source, we concluded that while the last three years there is a vast explosion of Cloud solutions published, still many aspects should be further explored. One important drawback detected was that the Cloud technology available lacks in standardization. The field of Cloud Computing is quite immature and still under development. Every Service Provider publishes its own API to serve their Data Centers and there only a few open source Cloud APIs. As a result, this affects interoperability in a very important way and the SaaS APIs (jCloud, libcloud etc) have to implement specific libraries and plugins for every individual Cloud (IaaS). When it comes to real-time capabilities in Cloud not much can be found in literature. The technology is relatively young and the Cloud-enabled APIs are focusing into the virtualization of resources, the deployment of applications and the control of the virtual environment. From the other hand, the integration of real-time capabilities into the Linux kernel is an active topic for more than a decade with several really promising results. In total, Cloud Computing, regardless the current deficiencies will remain the buzzword the following years and its capabilities will evolve to meet the requirements of the contemporary interactive and distributed applications.

REFERENCES

Amazon EC2 API. (n.d.). Retrieved from http://docs.amazonwebservices.com /AWSEC2/2009-11-30/ APIReference/

Amazon EC2. (n.d.). Retrieved from http://aws.amazon.com/ec2/

Cucinotta, T. (2008). *Access control for adaptive reservations on multi-user systems*. 14th IEEE Real-Time and Embedded Technology and Applications Symposium. St. Louis, MO, United States.

Deltacloud. (n.d.). Retrieved from http://www.deltacloud.org/

DMTF. (n.d.). *DSP0243 open virtualization format specification 1.1.0.*

Enea, O. S. E. O. S. (n.d.). Retrieved from http://www.enea.com/Templates/ Product____27035.aspx

Faggioli, D. (n.d.). *POSIX SCHED_SPORADIC implementation for tasks and groups*. Retrieved from http://lwn.net/Articles/293547/

Faggioli, D., et al. (2010). Sporadic server revisited. *Proceedings of 25th ACM Symposium On Applied Computing*. Sierre, Switzerland.

FRESCOR – Framework for Real-time Embedded Systems. (n.d.). *European project no. FP6/2005/ IST/5-034026*. Retrieved from http://www.frescor.org

González Harbour, M., et al. (2008). *FRESCOR deliverable D-AC2v2 – Architecture and contract model for integrated resources II.*

Google App Engine. (n.d.). Retrieved from http://code.google.com/appengine/

IBM jrtj. (n.d.). Retrieved from http://www.ibm.com/ developerworks/java/library/ j-rtj1/index.html?S_ TACT=105AGX02& S_CMP=EDU

Java, A. P. I. (n.d.). Retrieved from http://code.google.com/ appengine/docs/java/ overview.html

Javolution. (n.d.). Retrieved from http://javolution.org

jClouds. (n.d.). Retrieved from http://code.google.com/p/jclouds/

KENAI Project. (n.d.). Retrieved from http://kenai.com

KVM. (n.d.). Retrieved from http://www.linux-kvm.org

libCloud. (n.d.). Retrieved from http://ci.apache.org/ projects/libcloud

Litchfield, J. (2007). *The foundations of Solaris realtime*. Retrieved from http://blogs.sun.com/thejel/ entry/the_foundations_of_solaris_realtime

Marte, O. S. (n.d.). Retrieved from http://marte.unican.es

Menage, P. (n.d.). *CGROUPS.* Retrieved from http://www.mjmwired.net/ kernel/Documentation/ cgroups.txt

OCCI. (n.d.). Retrieved from http://www.occi-wg.org

OCCI specification. (n.d.). Retrieved from http:// forge.ogf.org/sf/docman /do/listDocuments/ projects.occiwg /docman.root.drafts. occi_specification

OCERA – Open Components for Embedded Real-time Applications. (2001). (European Project No. IST-2001-35102). Retrieved from http://www. ocera.org

OCERA Project deliverable D1.1 - RTOS. (n.d.). Retrieved from http://www.ocera.org/download /documents/ documentation/wp1.html

OGF. (n.d.). *Cloud storage for cloud computing.* Retrieved from http://ogf.org/Resources/ documents/CloudStorage ForCloudComputing.pdf

Oikawa, S., et al. (1999). *Portable RK: A portable resource kernel for guaranteed and enforced timing behavior.* Fifth IEEE Real-Time Technology and Applications Symposium. Vancouver.

Opennebula. (n.d.). Retrieved from http://www. opennebula.org/

Palopoli, L. (2008). AQuoSA - Adaptive quality of service architecture. *Software, Practice & Experience, 39*(1).

Partikle. (n.d.). Retrieved from http://www.e-rtl. org/partikle

Python, A. P. I. (n.d.). Retrieved from http://code. google.com/ appengine/docs/python/ overview. html

Rajkumar, R., et al. (1998). *Resource kernels: A resource-centric approach to real-time and multimedia systems.* SPIE/ACM Conference on Multimedia Computing and Networking.

Reservoir Project. (n.d.). Retrieved from http:// www.reservoir-fp7.eu

Rtsj. (n.d.). Retrieved from http://www.rtsj.org/ specjavadoc /book_index.html

Setz, J. (2007). *Inter-process communication in RTAI and RTLinux.* Saarland University.

Stanovich, M., et al. (2009). *Defects of the POSIX sporadic server and how to correct them.*

Sun Microsystems. (n.d.). *SUN Cloud.* Retrieved from http://developers.sun.com/cloud/

Timesys. (n.d.). Retrieved from http://www.time-sys.com/java

vCloud API Programming Guide. (n.d.). Retrieved from http://communities.vmware.com /servlet/ JiveServlet/previewBody/ 12463-102-1-13007/ vCloud_API_Guide.pdf

VMware vCloud. (n.d.). Retrieved from http:// www.vmware.com/ products/vcloud/

Windows Azure. (n.d.). Retrieved from http://www. microsoft.com/ windowsazure/windowsazure/

Chapter 4
Service Quality Model Evaluation

Fotis Aisopos
*National Technical University of Athens,
Greece*

Athanasios Papaoikonomou
*National Technical University of Athens,
Greece*

Magdalini Kardara
*National Technical University of Athens,
Greece*

Konstantinos Tserpes
*National Technical University of Athens,
Greece*

Vrettos Moulos
*National Technical University of Athens,
Greece*

Theodora A. Varvarigou
*National Technical University of Athens,
Greece*

ABSTRACT

In this chapter, we present the current state-of-the-art technology and methodologies regarding the evaluation of the provided quality of service in service oriented environments. With the emergence of service provisioning infrastructures and the adoption of Service Level Agreements acting as electronic contracts between service providers and customers, the need to control and validate the offered quality has appeared throughout the service lifecycle. This monitoring is performed either in the client side, using the customer's Quality of Experience and employing trust and reputation mechanisms for the service selection and evaluation phase, or in the provider side, dynamically reconfiguring the service and allocating resources accordingly, in order to optimize the quality metrics guaranteed. The latter, of course, initially requires mapping of the high-level quality parameters, which are closer to the customer perception, to low-level computing terms related to the resource management process. Dynamic resource allocation based on quality monitoring and evaluation can lead to optimizing resource utilization and provider's profits.

INTRODUCTION

For a long time now, the evaluation of service quality has been a central theme in research from various disciplines. Even though the notion still remains fuzzy, the paramount importance of quality is undeniable to firms and customers. Thus, researchers along with marketers have always tried to model quality in order to provide the means to evaluate it. In certain domains and applications,

DOI: 10.4018/978-1-60960-827-9.ch004

quality quantification has been achieved but still its requirements are not easily defined by customers (Parasuraman, Zeithaml, & Leonard, 1985), (Takeuchi & Quelch, 1983) and as a result the service model complies only with the understanding of the service provider.

This is particularly true when it comes to electronic services, and especially service provisioning environments such as those implemented using Service Oriented Architectures (SOA). The ever-changing nature of service provisioning technologies, the possible "lack of computer literacy" by consumers and the complex hierarchy of the modern businesses that make it difficult to identify who the actual end-user is, all add up to making the problem of modeling quality extremely difficult.

This work provides a high-level view of this problem, studying solutions that have been proposed in various situations on the aspect of service quality evaluation. The document is structured as such: The following section elaborates on the service quality modeling techniques and the various options that exist. It explains the notion of Quality of Experience and how it is nowadays used for evaluation purposes, and describes the techniques that have been proposed for evaluation of service quality from the customer side, as well as for the corresponding side of the provider. After this, the future research directions are briefly presented, while the final section provides the generic conclusions that yield from this research.

SERVICE QUALITY MODELING

In the beginning of 2000 a term has been coined perhaps more than any other in relation to Quality of Service (QoS) and Service-Oriented Computing (SOC), that is, of the Service Level Agreement (SLA) (Tian, Gramm, Naumowicz, Ritter, & Schiller, 2003), (Sahai, Machiraju, Sayal, Jin, & Casati, 2002), (Keller & Ludwig, 2002). Of course, the term itself had been defined a long time ago as "… an agreement between the provider

of a service and its customers which quantifies the minimum quality of service which meets the business need" (Hiles, 1994). In short, SLAs are the formalization of a provable, quantitative assessment of QoS upon which both the provider and the consumer negotiate and agree. Upon agreement the provider must commit the necessary resources so as to satisfy the consumer requirements. The consumer is then able to evaluate the outcome of the service against the set of SLA terms. There are various negotiation models that differentiate this procedure. The main differentiation axes (Figure 1) are the lifetime of the SLAs and the granularity of the SLA terms. The differentiation mainly affects the side (provider or customer) that has to do the evaluation and in turn the side which is more susceptible to SLA violations (normally these sides are opposites).

Generally, using longer SLA lifetimes will require the adoption of advance reservation schemes by the provider in order to estimate future resource requirements and ensure optimal resource allocation and the minimization of violations. In addition, it only makes sense for the customer to hold long-term SLAs (initially referred to and used in (Aisopos, Tserpes, Kardara, Panousopoulos, Phillips, & Salamouras, 2010)) in cases where the application permits it (e.g. provision of Cloud computing services as part of the business process workflow (Patel, Ranabahu, & Sheth, 2009)). If that is the case, then it is most likely that the SLA terms will be resource-oriented, either directly describing the amount and type of resources that will be assigned to the customer each time he invokes the service or over a specific time period (e.g. 4 CPUs), or generically referring to the provision of resources from the provider (e.g. availability and reliability). In addition to defining the promised QoS to be delivered by the provider, SLAs may also impose limitations to the amount of resources that the consumer is able to use. If the customer exceeds usage defined in the SLA then he is bound to the violation terms. Such models are supported by environments such as

Figure 1. Variety in SLA models. The further right we move on the "SLA lifetime" axis, the more a provider has to reserve its resources for the customer. The further up we move on the "granularity" axis, the closer we get to the use of terms that match the customer's understanding

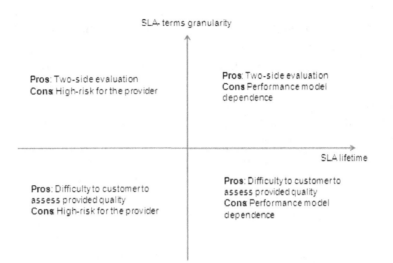

the GRIA middleware (Boniface, Phillips, Sanchez-Macian Perez, & Surridge, 2007) that focuses on capacity management and Infrastructure as a Service (IaaS) solutions (Waheed Iqbal, 2009), (Amazon: Service level agreement for ec2, 2008).

Short-term SLAs, require (soft-) real time monitoring and evaluation mechanisms as well as (near-) optimal resource allocation schemes. A major challenge for the provider is to have a real-time monitoring of its resources capacity for dynamically deciding if new SLAs can be accepted based on the current workload. Suggestions for such mechanisms and schemes have been proposed by IRMOS project (e.g. (Cucinotta, Checconi, Abeni, & Palopoli, 2010) and (Addis, Zlatev, Mitchell, & Boniface, 2009)) however, the probably most complete proposal comes from (Raimondi, Skene, & Emmerich, 2008). In contrast to long-term, short-term SLAs infuse an inherent difficulty for the provider to manage and monitor its resources adequately because of tight time constraints.

The other axis of differentiation that was mentioned above is the SLA term granularity.

The service quality model can be either closer to low-level, resource-oriented terms or closer to high-level, application-oriented terms. For each option, a number of languages and mechanisms have been developed and some of them are widely used. The most broadly accepted framework for resource description is the Resource Description Framework (RDF) (Lassila & Swick) the purpose of which is to define a mechanism for describing resources that makes no assumptions about a particular application domain, nor defines (a priori) the semantics of any application domain. On the other side, we have domain-specific languages (DSML) for SLAs such as the Platform-Independent Component Modeling Language (PICML) proposed in (Balasubramanian, Balasubramanian, Parsons, Gokhale, & Schmidt, 2007) and the framework proposed by Skene et al. in (Skene, Raimondi, & Emmerich, 2009). The quality modeling achieved using DSML is usually referred to as Quality of Business (QoBiz) and the quantified terms to express quality in that context are also called QoBiz metrics (Moorsel, 2001).

The weaknesses of each model are related to the difficulty of each side in monitoring and evaluating QoS against the SLA when the terms are closer to the understanding of the other side. Languages such as RDF are commonly accepted by service providers as descriptors of the service quality model, but the fact that they do not allow external access to their resources means that the customer cannot assess the provided quality using the SLA terms. On the other hand, adopting a DSML for SLA representation implies that the provider must have a very accurate performance model in place, which is something that experience shows that we cannot rely upon unless we focus on specific applications, implementations and infrastructures.

Unfortunately, in SOC, where the provider is usually application-agnostic, there is only a very small chance that the provider will be willing to accept a high-level service quality model. Therefore, in most of the cases the SLA terms are resource-level which creates an important leak in the evaluation process: The typical lifecycle of the SLA management in SOC involves the provision, negotiation, agreement, monitoring and evaluation. Throughout this lifecycle both parties are in control of the SLA and its terms but in one, that is, monitoring. Only the provider has access to its resources and directly evaluates their usage against what has been promised in the SLA. This creates a trust issue, as only the provider can actually evaluate the quality, leaving the consumer out of the picture. (Tserpes, Kyriazis, Menychtas, & Varvarigou, 2008)

A proposal for a trusted third party has been made by some such as (Molina-Jimenez, Shrivastava, Crowcroft, & Gevros, 2004), (Overton, 2002) and (Keller & Ludwig, 2002) where the monitoring and evaluation service can be provided by a third party that is a domain expert. The issue in this case is whether there is such party that the customer would trust for monitoring and evaluation and at the same time the provider would give access to its resources. This is exactly the weakness of an otherwise ideal solution. Ideal because the mapping between QoS and QoBiz will be done by another party that guarantees that it is doing it correctly and fairly but not viable because it is almost impossible to get such a trusted third party.

Given all the above, the common practice regarding the quality model evaluation is by using low-level SLA terms leaving the customer to rely upon his own experience to evaluate whether the provider was honest or not. The following Section further elaborates on that topic.

Quality of Experience

Common service-based systems dictate the use of resource-level models to monitor quality, however, there are quite a few researchers claiming otherwise. Work in (Tserpes, Kyriazis, Menychtas, Litke, Christogiannis, & Varvarigou, Evaluating Quality Provisioning Levels in Service Oriented Business Environments, 2008), (Goiri, Julià, Fitó, Macías, & Guitart, 2010), (Gu, Nahrstedt, Yuan, Wichadakul, & Xu, 2002) and (Lamanna, Skene, & Emmerich, 2003), states that the adoption of a common "language" for defining quality between the customer and provider are necessary. The only way for this to happen is to use application-level terms (QoBiz or as sometimes is also called: "service-level metrics") putting the weight to the provider to translate them into more tangible, resource related parameters. There are various ways for this "translation" to take place and most of them involve the production of an intermediate performance model that can be created using fuzzy logic techniques (e.g. (Varvarigou, Tserpes, Kyriazis, Silvestri, & Psimogiannos, 2010)) or semi-static QoS-QoBiz correlation as presented in (Kim, Lee, Lee, Lee, Lyu, & Choi, 2008).

Still, in most of the cases, the customer has to usually rely on his own experience as a domain expert in order to measure the delivered quality. This is related to the customer's subjective perception of quality. This is usually referred to as Quality of user Experience (QoE) and even though it may have no impact on the actual SLA, it has a direct impact on the assessment of the provider reputation from the customer. But the assessment of the provider is unique to the customer who conducts it since requirements as well as the experience to the domain, varies from expert to expert (Li-yuan, Wen-an, & Jun-de, 2006). Furthermore, there is no way to incorporate QoE terms in the SLAs, as there is no direct match to translate them to resource-level terms.

As such there are quite a few proposals for creating history-based evaluation mechanisms that record the reputation of the providers and providing decision support to future service selection. Similarly, there are a number of proposals and implementations related to the objective use of the QoE evaluation by more than one service customers. The most prominent are presented in the following Section.

Customer-Side Evaluation

Exploiting the concept of QoE, service customers can evaluate the QoS offered by antagonistic providers themselves, or via third party universal supporting systems that provide recommendations based on previous invocations (potentially by various customers) of each service, as well as on client preferences. Thus, in general client side QoS monitoring is performed through:

- A broker that intercepts the communication between service provider and service consumer and collects data concerning the service performance. The information analyzed here tends to be more objective, however this solution may be expensive if it is done in large scale, and also there can be latency problems.
- Third-party trust and reputation systems, in which all users participate and provide their feedback. Users of such systems should be able to somehow assess the QoS they receive, with the credibility of

users being the most essential issue to be resolved.

Of course, as long as a third party service is involved in the service evaluation/selection process, issues of trust and security also arise and need to be dealt with, as will be discussed below.

Maximilien and Singh (Maximilien & Singh, 2002) first presented a Conceptual Model of Web Service Reputation, using a Web Service Agent Proxy (WSAP) acting as a proxy for clients of Web services. In this model, all communications with UDDI registries and bindings occur via the WSAP for a service. This way, WSAP, which consults outside registries as well as reputation and endorsement agencies, records any client feedback and helps finding appropriate providers, by learning and sharing its knowledge with external agencies and other WSAPs. Thus, this proxy overall implements a reputation system, facilitating customers during the service selection process. A similar proxy-oriented approach was also followed by Lo and Wang (Lo & Wang, 2007), to create an evaluation and selection framework (CosmosQoS) for QoS-required Web services. The intention was again to better support service requesters such that they can select suitable Web services based on their QoS requirements, using a more centralized service reputation appraisal mechanism, with a universal proxy. Cao et al. (Cao, Huang, Wang, & Gu, 2009) proposed a QoS and user preference based evaluation model called Q-WSEM (QoS based Web Service Evaluation Model), introducing an external Service Center to support web service QoS evaluation. This component collects the QoS information about candidate web services that may provide qualified services to users, stores and updates the QoS information in UDDI Registry, provides interface for user constraints and preference configuration and executes web service filtering and evaluating process via a sophisticated algorithm taking into account qualitative and quantitative criteria.

An important innovation of the WSAP model was the use of semantics to describe web service attributes concretely. Semantics were also used by Wang et al. (Wang, Vitvar, Kerrigan, & Toma, 2006) to create a QoS-Aware Service Selection Model based on a QoS Ontology defined using the Web Services Modeling Ontology (WSMO), that filters available services using quality metrics with a combinational selection algorithm. Frutos et al. (Muñoz Frutos, Kotsiopoulos, Vaquero Gonzalez, & Rodero Merino, 2009) extended this work to a QoS conceptual model formed as a QoS ontology and selection algorithm, while Chaari et al. (Chaari, Badr, & Biennier, 2008) applied ontological concepts and extended the WS-Policy Specification (Bajaj, Box, & Chappell, 2006) to represent QoS policies, so as to provide QoS Policy Matching in service selection. In (Maximilien & Singh, 2004) Maximilien and Singh worked on Autonomic Web Services Trust and Selection, proposing a QoS motivated multi-agent approach, with a QoS ontology allowing to match services semantically and dynamically. A simple matching algorithm was provided, so as to match consumer policies to advertised provider service policies, based on nonfunctional attributes such as Service quality reputation and trust. Wang and Vassileva (Wang & Vassileva, 2007) further investigated Trust and Reputation for Web Service Selection based on service characteristics such as QoS, cost, etc., having a Central QoS Registry collecting and storing QoS information of the system and an third party supervising the whole process. Finally, Serhani et al. (Serhani, Dssouli, Hafid, & Sahraoui, 2005) presented a broker based architecture, having a QoS broker performing a semantic verification of each service's QoS parameters description, comparing metrics' values with the claimed one to verify web service conformity and evaluating and selecting the appropriate service for the customer.

In (Ma, Wang, Li, Xie, & Liu, 2008) Ma et al. combined semantic technologies and Constraint Programming to provide QoS-aware services

discovery. Their discovery framework consists of three layers: The first layer is the *Semantic Matchmaking Layer*, which uses Description Logic (DL) reasoners to guarantee that QoS data of a web service advertisement are semantically compatible with the user query. On top of that, there is the constraint programming layer, where QoS constraints are treated as a Constraint Satisfaction Problem. Finally, there is the QoS Selection Layer that processes the candidate web services list provided by the CP layer, to return best offer for a QoS requirement. Garcia et al. (García, Ruiz, Ruiz-Cortés, Martín-Díaz, & Resinas, 2007) proposed a hybrid discovery mechanism, which consists of an n-stages discovery process. Each stage is served by the best suited engine. In particular, the QoS-based discovery is based on Constraint Programming, while the functional discovery is performed by DLs reasoners.

An essential problem when using QoS for web services discovery is the place that the QoS information is stored and evaluated against the user requirements. Many researchers, like Blum (Blum, 2004) and Ziqiang et al. (Xu, Martin, Powley, & Zulkernine, 2007), enhance UDDI's *tModels* to include QoS information in the UDDI. In (Ran, 2003), Ran recommended a new discovery model for Web services with the addition of a new component called *QoS Certifier*. The Certifier component verifies the advertised QoS claims of the web service. If the procedure is successful, the web service providers receive a Certification ID, which enables them to register with the UDDI so that the QoS information for services can be retrieved from there. Zhang et al. (Zhang, Zheng, & Lyu, 2010) proposed a different approach by presenting a web service searching engine, called WSExpress, which covers both the QoS evaluation and service selection functionality. The search engine consists of three components: Non-functional evaluation, Functional evaluation and QoS-aware Web Service ranking. For the functional part, WSExpress performs a WSDL preprocessing of all available services, to identify useful terms (e.g.

input/output parameters) and then it performs a similarity computation with the user query. For the non-functional part (QoS), normalization and utility computation techniques provide a list of candidate web services that satisfy the QoS requirements. Finally, the outcomes of these stages are combined and a web service list that fulfills both the functional and non-functional requirements is returned to the user. Schlosser et al. (Schlosser, Sintek, Decker, & Nejdl, 2002) proposed a P2P infrastructure instead of the centralized UDDI model. Peers in the P2P network are organized into a graph structure based on hybercubes. Peers with similar services are grouped into concept clusters. Ideally, the P2P network should be able to route a user query to those peers that can answer the query. A similar P2P approach is followed by Vu et al. (Vu, Hauswirth, & Aberer, 2005), where all ontological concepts representing inputs/outputs of a web service advertisement/service request are categorized in Concept Groups based on their semantic similarity. Each semantic service description (advertisement or query) is associated with a multi-key vector, called *"characteristic vector"*, which is used to assign service advertisements to peer registries. The characteristic vector is actually the list of the Bloom keys of the corresponding concept groups to which the service's inputs and outputs belong. The semantic service discovery is based on Bloom filters.

Ontology solutions mentioned above designed their models dependent only on the service providers' SLA Templates and QoS attributes definitions in the WSDL and not taking into account other consumers' opinions. Most reputation systems based on the client-side QoS Evaluation, however, collect and combine evaluations by many users and work totally independent from the web service providers, without the latter even being aware of their existence. Wang et al. (Wang, Lee, & Ho, 2007) presented a method that considers not only the objective factors described by service providers, but also the subjective trust evaluations from clients that use the services. In this work, a

QoS-supported recommender agent captures QoS information from a UDDI Registry and also collects users' appraisals in order to reach a specific recommendation for service selection through a Genetic algorithm (GA). Subjective information was also studied by Ding et al. (Ding, Li, & Zhou, 2008), that worked on Reputation-based Service Selection in a Grid environment, using an evaluator component collecting and interpreting client observations to assist grid customers to select the 'best' service provider from a services list. As the trustworthiness of the subjective client's QoS evaluations now comes into play, decision support systems are considered more appropriate to be engaged to provide recommendations in the service selection process. Wu et al. (Wu, Chang, & Thomson, 2005) presented a Decision Support System for QoS-enabled Distributed Web Services Architectures, using the Decision Support Systems Module (DSS Module) to select the most appropriate service providers. The DSS module integrated into this solution includes a QoS Analyzer component and a Trust Model, that use the History QoS data from a QoS Database, generating the output of trustworthiness values for involved web services to provide a final ranking list of the services. Tong and Zhang (Tong & Zhang, 2006) proposed a Fuzzy Multi-Attribute Decision Making Algorithm for Web Services Selection Based on QoS, using quality of Web services metrics advertised by the service providers and computed by the registries, while Tserpes et al. (Tserpes, Aisopos, Kyriazis, & Varvarigou, 2010) presented a third-party Decision Support system performing collaborative filtering techniques over QoS customer ratings for a web service to provide a recommender mechanism. Vu et al. (Vu, Hauswirth, & Aberer) presented a QoS-based selection and ranking approach, which uses trust and reputation evaluation techniques to predict the future quality of a service. Quality properties of web services are described by concepts from a QoS ontology defined in WSMO and a forecasting technique to predict their future quality conformance from past data, while in the same time performing trust and reputation management. Credibility of user feedback is also a major problem in electronic business, in case subjective information comes into play, as mentioned above. Reputation systems should be able to filter out malicious reports. In (Vu, Hauswirth, & Aberer, 2005) Vu et al. propose a model based on trusted agents. These agents always produce credible QoS reports that can be used to evaluate the behavior of other users.

A special case of service selection is Service Composition, the combination of a set of elementary services, often from different providers, that will interconnect with each other and provide a new customized service. In this case, the selection of elementary services is usually related with end-to-end QoS requirements; hence QoS-aware service composition is needed in order to find the best combination of services such that their aggregated QoS values meet these end-to-end requirements. Alrifai and Risse (Alrifai & Risse, 2010) proposed an efficient QoS-aware Service Composition solution using mixed integer linear programming (MILP) to find the optimal decomposition of global QoS constraints into local constraints and searching locally to find the best web services that satisfy these local constraints. Kyriazis et al. (Kyriazis, Tserpes, Menychtas, Sarantidis, & Varvarigou, 2009) presented an approach for service selection using QoS criteria, allowing for different mappings of application workflow processes to Grid services, so as to maximize the user benefit in terms of the offered QoS level. This is achieved through Supervision, Workflow mapping and Decision Support components, controlling concrete workflows' definition processes, mapping workflow processes to service instances and evaluating historical information regarding the service providers' behavior.

Provider-Side Evaluation

The previous chapters have addressed the issue of service evaluation from the service consumer's perspective, focusing on ranking services based on the delivered QoS and using this knowledge to build decision support systems that help consumers with their service selection decisions. In terms of service evaluation, the customer need not know the internal service level management SLM (Sturm, Morris, & Jander, 2000) processes that take place on the provider's side as long as the promised level of service is delivered.

The current section aims to examine service evaluation from a provider's side by investigating in what ways service providers can evaluate their own services and use the evaluation results for gaining business benefits. For a provider, being able to promise and deliver a high level of QoS would translate to a competitive advantage over other providers offering a similar service.

Early on in the decade, component based architectures built on top of Web Services such as the Open Grid Services Architecture (OGSA) (Foster, Kesselman, Nick, & Tuecke, 2002) introduced a new generation of systems built as a pool of services, possibly from different providers, interconnecting with each other in order to offer an end-to end service to the customers. Despite the fact that the hype around the Grid failed to deliver a new generation of viable commercial Grid Computing providers, the concept of centralized facilities operated by third-party computing and storage utilities was incorporated in a new computing paradigm, Cloud Computing (Foster, Yong Zhao Raicu, & Lu, Cloud Computing and Grid Computing 360-Degree Compared, 2008). Cloud computing involves over-the-Internet provision of not only dynamically scalable but also highly abstracted and virtualized resources.

In distributed service oriented environments such as grids and clouds, Service Level Agreements, as previously discussed in the Introduction, have established themselves as the standard tool for specifying the QoS guarantees promised by the provider to the consumer with service management in such systems becoming increasingly SLA-driven. An important step towards that direction was the publication of the Web Service Level Agreement (WSLA) framework (Keller & Ludwig, 2002), introducing specifications for the definition and monitoring SLAs of Web Services which set the basis for the design of numerous service oriented architectures as well as was integrated with existing management models. In (Debusmann & Keller, 2003) authors investigated how WSLA can be adapted for a service provider who uses a traditional management system such as the Common Information Model (Force, 1999).

In order to attract more customers and improve their reputation, service providers need to not only offer more attractive SLAs but more importantly to be able to deliver the promised QoS. For SLA driven systems, this translates to a set of challenges: dynamically deciding whether new SLAs can be accommodated based on the current capacity; the dynamic negotiation of SLA parameters in order to create new SLAS; the continuous monitoring of resources and applications; the evaluation of monitoring results with SLA parameters in order to decide whether the SLA terms have been fulfilled; and in case the SLA terms have not been fulfilled deciding what action should be taken for handling the violation.

A key requirement for all the aforementioned challenges is the appropriate mapping of high-level to low-level parameters. The low level parameters, or Resource Metrics as defined in (Tian, Gramm, Naumowicz, Ritter, & Schiller, 2003), are retrieved directly from the managed resources such as counters and gauges. The combination of several resource metrics according to a specific algorithm defines a Composite Metric or high level parameters. Examples of composite metrics are maximum response time of a service, average availability of service, or minimum throughput of a service. Examples of resource metrics are system uptime, service outage period, number of service

invocations. SLA parameters associate composite metrics to a range of values for the metric that are specific to a particular customer. So, essentially, an SLA parameter defines the promised performance of the service with regards to this specific metric.

An incorrect mapping between resource and composite metrics means that the provider will either allocate more resources than necessary for a specific job in order to ensure that the SLA is fulfilled or accept more SLAs that he can accommodate leading to SLA violations. Authors in (Rosenberg, Platzer, & Dustdar, 2006) identified important QoS attributes and presented mapping techniques for combining resource metrics into composite metric in order to form SLA parameters for a specific domain, without however taking into account the monitoring results of resource usage. The monitoring and evaluation of services can help the provider gather statistics of the services' performance which can be used for a long term analysis. The gained knowledge from this analysis will help the provider do a better mapping between high level and low level parameters and thus improve the utilization of his resources and minimize SLA violations. In (Emeakaroha, C., Brandic, Maurer, & Dustdar, 2010) Emeakaroha et.al propose a framework for managing the mappings of the low-level resource metrics to high-level SLAs by analyzing the monitored usage of the resourced metrics. Also, Tserpes et al. in (Tserpes, Kyriazis, Menychtas, & Varvarigou, 2008) have developed a novel mechanism that monitors the service provider's performance throughout its lifetime and uses the historical data in order to better define high-level parameters in relation to resource metrics.

In addition to the long term analysis, efficient monitoring and violation detection can help the provider do optimization during runtime by using a dynamic resource management mechanism that enables the reallocation and migration of running applications. Authors in (Ferretti, Ghini, Panzieri, Pellegrini, & Turrini, 2010) introduce a middleware architecture that enables SLA-driven dynamic configuration, management and optimization of cloud resources and services. The proposed architecture includes a load balancer that distributes the computational load across the platform resources, and monitors the QoS in order to ensure optimal resource usage. If a deviation to the promised QoS is detected that could lead to an SLA violation, the platform is reconfigured dynamically in order to use additional resources. Similarly, if it is detected during runtime that the SLA can be fulfilled with fewer resources than those initially allocated, platform reconfiguration occurs to release those unused resources.

In (Lodi, Panzieri, Ross, & Turrini, 2007) Lodi et al have defined a middleware architecture for enabling SLA-driven clustering of QoS-aware application servers. Application server technology without QoS support offers clustering and load balancing mechanisms for handling scalability and availability requirements. In order to enhance the abovementioned mechanism with SLA Enforcement functionality, the featured architecture supports dynamic resource management as application servers can dynamically change the amount of clustered resources assigned to hosted applications on-demand so as to meet application-level QoS requirements.

In addition to the dynamic reallocation of resources, gathering monitoring data at runtime can be used by the providers for dynamically adjusting the SLA templates they propose to the customers based on the resources' performance. In (Spillner & Schill., 2009) authors propose an innovative mechanism that gathers monitoring results and feeds it back into the service registry to adjust the values of non-functional properties in service descriptions depending on the service's runtime behavior. Using these updated properties, the respective constraints in the SLA templates are adjusted semi-automatically aligned with business goals.

For a service provider it is important not only to satisfy their consumers' demand for high level QoS, but also to satisfy their own business objec-tives by cost-effectively minimizing the business impact of SLA violations). In (Buco, Chang, Luan, Ward, Wolf, & Yu, 2004) Buco et al. present the design specifications for a business-objectives-based utility computing SLA management system, SAM. SAM is a distributed SLA management system that enables a utility computing provider to reduce the financial risk of service level violations by fulfilling SLA demands in accordance with the provider's business requirements.

A special case for the problem of resource metering is when the role of the provider is twofold: he can act either as the owner of the resources or as a sub-contractor. In order to satisfy their customers' needs, more and more companies use outsourcing in combination with their own resources, becoming a provider and client at the same time. This poses an additional requirement for the monitoring and evaluation mechanism: the provider will now need to monitor the QoS provided by external resources in addition to his own as well as take into account the extra cost for renting those resources. A dynamic resource allocation scheme based on monitoring will help the provider achieve resource optimization and maximize his profits. For example, if during runtime the provider's own resource utilization is low he might consider the option to free some rent-resources to lower the costs without in the meantime breaching any of the SLAs.

FUTURE RESEARCH DIRECTIONS

It is quite clear that the research direction towards which the service quality evaluation is leaning to, is the use of collaborative intelligence to evaluate service provisioning as the only seemingly objective and viable evaluation method. Furthermore, the automatic definition of high-level parameters that will accurately define the quality but in service consumer terms will greatly improve this particular evaluation technique. It will allow for the formation of expert domains limiting the amount of services that each consumer needs to evaluate as well as creating networks of trust between people who understand (and actually consume) certain types of the provided services. This, of course, presupposes the development of more efficient mechanisms and semantics that help translating these high-level parameters to low-level computing terms, more useful for the resource management process within the service provider.

CONCLUSION

The quality evaluation in service-oriented environments is undeniably a very crucial aspect, especially when it comes to business. Customers and providers have to agree to tangible and measurable metrics that will allow the undisputable evaluation of quality by both sides when the outcome is delivered. However, this is not always feasible especially because modern service provisioning environments are application-agnostic (e.g. Cloud infrastructures) and based on distributed infrastructures. It is therefore difficult to map the performance model of the infrastructure to application-specific quality terms.

In most of the market systems that fall into the category of service-provisioning platforms described in the previous paragraph, the practice is to use resource-level terms to model the agreed levels of quality between the two sides. These can be easily monitored by the provider and they are application-independent. The problem in this case is the difficulty of the customer to monitor and evaluate quality, especially when the customer is a home-user. Various works advocate that the solution for that is to have customers assess the provider's reputation based on their own invocation history or on collaboration with other customers. The implementation of concepts such as the Internet of Services will greatly contribute towards that direction.

REFERENCES

Addis, M., Zlatev, Z., Mitchell, W., & Boniface, M. (2009). *Modelling interactive real-time applications on service oriented infrastructures. 2009 NEM Summit – Towards Future Media Internet.* St Malo.

Aisopos, F., Tserpes, K., Kardara, M., Panousopoulos, G., Phillips, S., & Salamouras, S. (2010). Information exchange in business collaboration using Grid technologies. *Identity in the Information Society, 2,* 189–204. doi:10.1007/s12394-009-0028-0

Alrifai, M., & Risse, T. (2010). Efficient QoS-aware service composition. In Alrifai, M., Risse, T., Calisti, M., Walliser, M., Brantschen, S., & Herbstritt, M. a. (Eds.), *Emerging Web services technology (Vol. III,* pp. 75–87). Whitestein Series in Software Agent Technologies and Autonomic Computing, Birkhäuser Basel. doi:10.1007/978-3-0346-0104-7_5

Amazon. (2008). *Service level agreement for ec2.* Retrieved from http://aws.amazon.com/ ec2-sla

Bajaj, S., Box, D., & Chappell, D. (2006). *Web services policy framework* (WS-Policy). Retrieved from http://www-128.ibm.com/ developerworks/ library/ specification/wspolfram/

Balasubramanian, K., Balasubramanian, J., Parsons, J., Gokhale, A., & Schmidt, D. C. (2007). A platform-independent component modeling language for distributed real-time and embedded systems. *Journal of Computer and System Sciences, 73*(2), 171–185. doi:10.1016/j.jcss.2006.04.008

Blum, A. (2004, June 4). *UDDI as an extended Web services registry: Versioning, quality of service, and more.* SOA & WOA: Article.

Boniface, M. J., Phillips, S., Sanchez-Macian Perez, A., & Surridge, M. (2007). *Dynamic service provisioning using GRIA SLAs.* NFPSLA-SOC'07. Vienna.

Buco, M. J., Chang, R. N., Luan, L. Z., Ward, C., Wolf, J. L., & Yu, P. S. (2004). *Utility computing SLA management based upon business objectives.*

Cao, J., Huang, J., Wang, G., & Gu, J. (2009). *QoS and preference based Web service evaluation approach.* Eighth International Conference on Grid and Cooperative Computing, (pp. 420-426).

Chaari, S., Badr, Y., & Biennier, F. (2008). *Enhancing Web service selection by QoS-based ontology and WS-policy.* ACM Symposium on Applied Computing, SAC '08 (pp. 2426-2431). Fortaleza, Ceara, Brazil: ACM.

Cucinotta, T., Checconi, F., Abeni, L., & Palopoli, L. (2010). *Self-tuning schedulers for legacy real-time applications.* EuroSys '10, 5th European Conference on Computer Systems (pp. 55-68). Paris, France: ACM.

Debusmann, M., & Keller, A. (2003). *SLA-driven management of distributed systems using the common information model.* IFIP/IEEE International Symposium on Integrated Management. Kluwer Academic Publishers.

Ding, Q., Li, X., & Zhou, X. H. (2008). *Reputation based service selection in Grid environment.* International Conference on Computer Science and Software Engineering, 3, (pp. 58-61).

Emeakaroha, C. V., Brandic, I., Maurer, M., & Dustdar, S. (2010). *Low level metrics to high level SLAs - LoM2HiS framework: Bridging the gap between monitored metrics and SLA parameters in cloud environments.* IEEE 3rd International Conference on Cloud Computing.

Ferretti, S., Ghini, V., Panzieri, F., Pellegrini, M., & Turrini, E. (2010). QoS–aware clouds. IEEE 3rd International Conference on Cloud Computing.

Force, D. M. (1999, June). *Common information model* (CIM) version 2.2. Specification.

Foster, I., Kesselman, C., Nick, J., & Tuecke, S. (2002, July). Retrieved from Globus Project.

Foster, I., Yong Zhao Raicu, I., & Lu, S. (2008). *Cloud computing and Grid computing 360-degree compared.* Grid Computing Environments Workshop, GCE.

García, J. M., Ruiz, D., Ruiz-Cortés, A., Martín-Díaz, O., & Resinas, M. (2007). *An hybrid, QoS-aware discovery of Semantic Web services using constraint programming.* 5th International Conference on Service-Oriented Computing, (pp. 69-80). Vienna.

Goiri, Í., Julià, F., Fitó, J. O., Macías, M., & Guitart, J. (2010). Resource-level QoS metric for CPU-based guarantees in cloud providers. In *Economics of Grids, clouds, systems, and services, LNCS 6296* (pp. 34-47).

Gu, X., Nahrstedt, K., Yuan, W., Wichadakul, D., & Xu, D. (2002). An XML-based quality of service enabling language for the Web. *Journal of Visual Languages and Computing, 13*(1), 61–95. doi:10.1006/jvlc.2001.0227

Hiles, A. N. (1994). Service level agreements: Panacea or pain? *The TQM Magazine, 6*(2), 14–16. doi:10.1108/09544789410053966

Keller, A., & Ludwig, H. (2002). *The WSLA framework: Specifying and monitoring of service level agreements for Web services. Research report.* IBM.

Kim, H. J., Lee, D. H., Lee, J. M., Lee, K. H., Lyu, W., & Choi, S. G. (2008). *The QoE evaluation method through the QoS-QoE correlation model.* Fourth International Conference on Networked Computing and Advanced Information Management, NCM '08, (pp. 719-725).

Kyriazis, D., Tserpes, K., Menychtas, A., Sarantidis, I., & Varvarigou, T. (2009, April). Service selection and workflow mapping for Grids: An approach exploiting quality-of-service information. *Concurrency and Computation, 21*(6), 739–766. doi:10.1002/cpe.1343

Lamanna, D., Skene, J., & Emmerich, W. (2003). *SLAng: A language for defining service level agreements.* The Ninth IEEE Workshop on Future Trends of Distributed Computing Systems (FTDCS'03), (pp. 100- 106).

Lassila, O., & Swick, R. R. (n.d.). *Resource description framework (RDF) model and syntax.* Retrieved from http://citeseerx.ist.psu.edu/ viewdoc/download?doi=10.1.1.44.6030&rep=rep1&type=pdf

Li-Yuan, L., Wen-An, Z., & Jun-De, S. (2006). *The research of quality of experience evaluation method in pervasive computing environment.* 1st International Symposium on Pervasive Computing and Applications, (pp. 178-182).

Lo, N., & Wang, C.-H. (2007). *Web services QoS evaluation and service selection framework - A proxy-oriented approach.* IEEE Region 10 Conference TENCON 2007, (pp. 1-5).

Lodi, G., Panzieri, F., Ross, D., & Turrini, E. (2007, March). SLA-driven clustering of QoS-aware application servers. *IEEE Transactions on Software Engineering, 33*(3). doi:10.1109/TSE.2007.28

Ma, Q., Wang, H., Li, Y., Xie, G., & Liu, F. (2008). *A semantic QoS-aware discovery framework for Web services.* IEEE International Conference on Web Service, ICWS '08, (pp. 129-136).

Maximilien, E. M., & Singh, M. P. (2002). Conceptual model of web service reputation. *SIGMOD Record, 31*(4), 36–41. doi:10.1145/637411.637417

Maximilien, E. M., & Singh, M. P. (2004). *Toward autonomic Web services trust and selection.* 2nd International Conference on Service Oriented Computing, ICSOC '04 (pp. 212-221). New York, NY: ACM.

Molina-Jimenez, C., Shrivastava, S., Crowcroft, J., & Gevros, P. (2004). *On the monitoring of contractual service level agreements.* First IEEE International Workshop on Electronic Contracting, (pp. 1- 8).

Moorsel, A. V. (2001). *Metrics for the Internet age: Quality of experience and quality of business.* 5th Performability Workshop.

Muñoz Frutos, H., Kotsiopoulos, I., Vaquero Gonzalez, L. M., & Rodero Merino, L. (2009). *Enhancing service selection by semantic QoS.* 6th European Semantic Web Conference on the Semantic Web: Research and Applications (pp. 565 - 577). Heraklion: LNCS.

Overton, C. (2002). On the theory and practice of Internet SLAs. *Journal of Computer Resource Measurement,* 32–45.

Parasuraman, A., Zeithaml, V. A., & Leonard, L. (1985). A conceptual model of service quality and its implications for future research. *Journal of Marketing, 49*(4), 41–50. doi:10.2307/1251430

Patel, P., Ranabahu, A., & Sheth, A. (2009). *Service level agreement in cloud computing. OOPSLA 2009, 24th ACM SIGPLAN.* ACM.

Raimondi, F., Skene, J., & Emmerich, W. (2008). *Efficient online monitoring of Web-service SLAs.* 16th ACM SIGSOFT International Symposium on Foundations of Software Engineering. Atlanta, GA: ACM.

Ran, S. (2003). *A model for Web services discovery with QoS. SIGecom Exch* (pp. 1–10). ACM.

Rosenberg, F., Platzer, C., & Dustdar, S. (2006). *Bootstrapping performance and dependability attributes of Web service.* ICWS.

Sahai, A., Machiraju, V., Sayal, M., Jin, L. J., & Casati, F. (2002). *Automated SLA monitoring for Web services.* HP.

Schlosser, M., Sintek, M., Decker, S., & Nejdl, W. (2002). *A scalable and ontology-based P2P infrastructure for Semantic Web services*. Second International Conference on Peer-to-Peer Computing (P2P'02), (p. 104).

Serhani, M., Dssouli, R., Hafid, A., & Sahraoui, H. (2005). *A QoS broker based architecture for efficient Web services selection*. IEEE International Conference on Web Services, ICWS 2005, (pp. 113- 120).

Skene, J., Raimondi, F., & Emmerich, W. (2009). Service-level agreements for electronic services. *IEEE Transactions on Software Engineering, 99*, 288–304.

Spillner, J., & Schill, A. (2009). *Dynamic SLA template adjustments based on service property monitoring*. IEEE Conference on Cloud Computing.

Sturm, R., Morris, W., & Jander, M. (2000). *Foundations of service level management*. SAMS Publishing.

Takeuchi, H., & Quelch, J. (1983). Quality is more than making a good product. *Harvard Business Review*.

Tian, M., Gramm, A., Naumowicz, T., Ritter, H., & Schiller, J. (2003). *A concept for QoS integration in Web service*. Fourth International Conference on Web Information Systems Engineering Workshops (WISEW'03), (pp. 149-155). Rome.

Tong, H., & Zhang, S. (2006). *A fuzzy multi-attribute decision making algorithm for Web services selection based on QoS*. IEEE Asia-Pacific Conference on Services Computing, APSCC '06., (pp. 51-57).

Tserpes, K., Aisopos, F., Kyriazis, D., & Varvarigou, T. (2010). Service selection decision support in the Internet of services. In J. Altmann, & O. Rana (Ed.), *GECON 2010. LNCS 6296*, (pp. 16-33). Springer.

Tserpes, K., Kyriazis, D., Menychtas, A., Litke, A., Christogiannis, C., & Varvarigou, T. (2008). *Evaluating quality provisioning levels in service oriented business* environments. 12th International IEEE Enterprise Distributed Object Computing Conference, (pp. 309-315).

Tserpes, K., Kyriazis, D., Menychtas, A., & Varvarigou, T. (2008). A novel mechanism for provisioning of high-level quality of service information in Grid environments. *European Journal of Operational Research, 191*(3), 1113–1131. doi:10.1016/j.ejor.2007.07.012

Varvarigou, T., Tserpes, K., Kyriazis, D., Silvestri, F., & Psimogiannos, N. (2010). A study on the effect of application and resource characteristics on the QoS in service provisioning environments. *International Journal of Distributed Systems and Technologies, 1*(1), 55–75. doi:10.4018/jdst.2010090804

Vu, L. H., Hauswirth, M., & Aberer, K. (2005). *Towards P2P-based Semantic Web service discovery with QoS support*. Workshop on Business Processes and Services (BPS). Nancy.

Vu, L.-H., Hauswirth, M., & Aberer, K. (2005). *QoS-based service selection and ranking with trust and reputation management. CoopIS; DOA; ODBASE. On the move to meaningful Internet systems*. Springer.

Waheed Iqbal, M. D. (2009). *SLA-driven adaptive resource management for Web applications on a heterogeneous compute cloud. Lecture Notes in Computer Science*. LNCS.

Wang, H.-C., Lee, C.-S., & Ho, T.-H. (2007). Combining subjective and objective QoS factors for personalized Web service selection. *Expert Systems with Applications, 32*(2), 571–584. doi:10.1016/j.eswa.2006.01.034

Wang, X., Vitvar, T., Kerrigan, M., & Toma, I. (2006). A QoS-aware selection model for semantic Web Services. In A. Dan, & W. Lamersdorf (Ed.), *ICSOC 2006. LNCS 4294*, (pp. 390–401). Springer.

Wang, Y., & Vassileva, J. (2007). *A review on trust and reputation for Web service selection*. 27th International Conference on Distributed Computing Systems Workshops, ICDCSW '07, (p. 25).

Wu, C., Chang, E., & Thomson, P. (2005). A decision support system for QoS-enabled distributed Web services architecture. In H. Hess, L. Franquelo, A. Malinowski, & M. Chow (Ed.), *Industrial Electronics Society Conference*, IECON 2005.

Xu, Z., Martin, P., Powley, W., & Zulkernine, F. (2007). *Reputation-enhanced QoS-based Web services discovery*. IEEE International Conference on Web Services, ICWS 2007, (pp. 249-256).

Zhang, Y., Zheng, Z., & Lyu, M. R. (2010). *WS-Express: A QoS-aware search engine for Web services*. IEEE International Conference on Web Services, ICWS 2010, (pp. 91-98).

KEY TERMS AND DEFINITIONS

Ontology: A formal representation of knowledge as a set of concepts and relationships between them within a domain.

Quality of Experience (QoE): A subjective measure of a customer's experiences with a service provider.

Quality of Service (QoS): Quality measure of the provided service with regards to predefined performance evaluation parameters.

Resource Allocation: Assignment of available resources in an economic way by the provider taking into consideration both the resource availability and the activities' deadlines.

Semantics: Machine-readable metadata that are used to provide a formal description of concepts, terms, and relationships within a given knowledge domain.

Service Evaluation: Evaluation of the performance of a service.

Service Level Agreement (SLA): Contract between the service provider and the customer where the level of service is formally defined.

Service Oriented Computing (SOC): Design paradigm in which functionality is provided as a set of loosely coupled interoperable services that can be used within multiple separate systems from several business domain.

Section 2
Platform as a Service

Chapter 5

Taxonomy and State of the Art of Service Discovery Mechanisms and Their Relation to the Cloud Computing Stack

George Kousiouris
National Technical University of Athens, Greece

Dimosthenis P. Kyriazis
National Technical University of Athens, Greece

Theodora A. Varvarigou
National Technical University of Athens, Greece

Eduardo Oliveros
Telefónica Investigación y Desarrollo, Spain

Patrick Mandic
Rechenzentrum Universität Stuttgart, Germany

ABSTRACT

Service Discovery mechanisms are gaining interest in the last years due to the growing bulk of information available, especially to distributed computing infrastructures like Grids and Clouds. However a vast number of characteristics of these implementations exist, each one suitable for a number of purposes. The aim of this chapter is to extract a taxonomy of these characteristics found in modern Service Discovery systems and produce a categorization of existing implementations in a grouped and comparative way, based on these features. Furthermore, the mapping of these characteristics to the Cloud business model is produced, in order to assist in selecting the suitable solutions for each provider based on his/her location in the value chain or identify gaps in the existing implementations.

DOI: 10.4018/978-1-60960-827-9.ch005

Figure 1. Service Discovery Generic Architecture

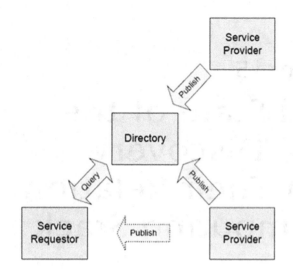

INTRODUCTION

Locating resources in a large scale, heterogeneous network is a non-trivial task. There may be several providers, each one with different characteristics, thus offering a variety of different levels of user-requirement fitness. In order to allow awareness about the status and the availability of these resources, a Service Discovery (SD) mechanism must be installed. All Service Providers will require registering in such a mechanism, along with all the necessary information such as URL, rates, compatibility and interface, so that their services are advertised to the end user. The information service then makes all of these available to potential clients, by matchmaking the request with the available resources and returns back the results. A high-level overview of SD's generic architecture is illustrated in the following figure (Figure 1).

In the current model of distributed infrastructures, a number of different artifacts may be addressed. What needs to be discovered is services, their interfaces, resources and their interfaces and their matchmaking in order to produce added value.

During recent years, specific focus has been given to adding value to such mechanisms, through adding functionality on top of this registry. This may refer to the way the registry mechanism is built, deployed or enriched, to more advanced protocol usage that enhances interoperability and management or the use of semantics and processing for increased functionality.

The basic aim of this chapter is to provide an in-depth presentation of the State of the Art with regard to Service Discovery systems and methodologies in distributed computing. This is combined with an identification of the most important characteristics of such systems, taxonomy of them based on the latter and comparison. Finally an identification of future trends will be pursued, in order to suggest which of the presented solutions show the higher perspective. The structure of this work is heavily based on the structure of Yu and Buyya (2005), which to the view of the authors is a model example of how to write taxonomies and surveys. In comparison to this, what is pursued is a specific focus on Service Discovery systems and not in general of workflow systems, an update on the state of the art and the enrichment and rearrangement of parts of the taxonomy that is presented in the former in order to include new advances and features.

TAXONOMY OF DIFFERENT DISCOVERY MECHANISM CHARACTERISTICS

Service Discovery mechanisms can be categorized according to a vast number of characteristics. These features may include their functionality, offered features or implementation differentiations.

The major categories that have been identified are:

Mechanism Structure

This feature regards the design and implementation of the entire service discovery mechanism. This has an effect on the locality of the components as well as the protocols of communication.

The different SD mechanisms can be divided in two groups:

- *Adhoc SD:* This group comprises those mechanisms with the ability to look for services in ad-hoc networks with no fixed infrastructure. Such SD mechanisms do not usually have a need for a central repository but are limited to the concrete network they are located in and are not able to interact with nodes located in other networks. The most representative protocols of this type are: Service Location Protocol (SLP), Zeroconf (based on multicast DNS), UPnP, Jini and Bluetooth's SDP.
- *Wide Area SD or Infrastructure SD:* This group is used in infrastructure networks and involves a central repository where:
  - ◦ The descriptions of the available services are usually published by service providers, and
  - ◦ The service requestors perform their queries.

The scope for infrastructure SD mechanisms extends to more than one IP network comprising an administrative area network or a site. Implementations incorporate centralized solutions as well as distributed. Furthermore, with regard to the latter, further categorization may apply with regard to the specific nature of the implementation. Characteristic solutions include a hierarchical implementation or P2P implementations.

Information Retrieval

This feature regards the way the information is relayed to the SD mechanism. This can be either static, in the beginning of the advertisement, or it can be refreshed in a given interval. It can also incorporate interfaces and specifications for enabling support for mobile devices, like the SIP protocol, or based on specific events.

Knowledge Modelling

In order to represent knowledge with regard to the context of the registered services or resources in general, a number of ways exist in order to semantically represent this information. This may include semantic annotations and tagging for example through suitable keywords, or the simplest case, attributes in the form of key value pairs.

Another approach is to use structured semantics such as ontologies in order to store and correlate the information from the various sources. This helps in determining not only the important keywords but also hierarchically classify the numerous concepts that may be used to describe a service or resource. This also aids in avoiding different levels of semantic descriptions for the latter.

Knowledge Processing

Regardless of the way the semantic information is stored or represented, the processing of this information in order to perform matchmaking between requests and offers is of extreme importance. This matchmaking refers to the following cases

- Matching client requests to available services
- Matching service requests to available and suitable hardware resources
- Automated composition between different services in order to create adhoc applications with added value that meet the client's requirements in case a service is not found that satisfies the latter. This is mainly referred to as automated composition.

Specifically, this composition may be automated or user-aided, in the form of final approval of the composed workflow of services. Furthermore, the matchmaking may be based on partial or full success rates, use of techniques such as reasoning or based on the class hierarchy that is extracted from the ontology structures.

Specifications

A number of specifications and protocols exist for a variety of needs that arise in implementing an SD mechanism. The needs may vary from the form the registry is implemented, the way information is relayed in an ad hoc network (for the according cases), the way interfaces are going to be designed or the use of semantics in the mechanism.

(WSIL, 2007) is a specification (and XML schema) for aggregating pointers to service descriptions that already exist in repositories, in order not to duplicate them. These descriptions may be written in different formats. Furthermore, a set of rules for accessing this information is defined.

The basic technology standard for implementing service registries is based on the UDDI Specification (2004). The UDDI catalogue consists of three kinds of pages:

- Yellow pages that contain the taxonomy of services in order to locate them based on the category
- White pages that contain contact information and
- Green pages containing the technological information that describes the behaviors and support functions of a Web Service.

The Representational State Transfer protocol (Fielding, 2000) is based on a representation of entities and functionalities as resources. The management of these resources is based on specific standardized interfaces like the GET, PUT, POST and DELETE operations of HTTP. In contrast to the competitive SOAP protocol (http://www.

w3.org/TR/soap/), it does not allow users to specify their own interfaces in the style of inputs, outputs and operations. This leads to improved interoperability. An extensive description of the differences between SOAP and REST can be found in Zhao and Dossi (2009).

SIP is a protocol designed by the IETF (http://datatracker.ietf.org/wg/sip/charter/) for session control on IP-based networks. Although SIP is independent from session specific issues, it is commonly related with Voice over IP (VoIP) scenarios. A session in this context is understood as an exchange of data between associations of participants. This concept can be very useful for Internet applications that rely on a relationship between two or more participants, as it allows taking session handling logic out of specific application logic. SIP provides mechanisms to handle, i.e. create, modify and terminate, these sessions, independent of the type of session being handled. SIP was designed with modularity in mind.

(WS-DD, 2009) is an OASIS specification for allowing dynamic discovery of services by clients in ad-hoc or managed networks. The clients send a probe request while searching for a suitable service, which in turn replies to the sender. WS-DD supports also the use of a Discovery proxy for limiting multicast traffic in a managed network. Furthermore, a new service may send a notification to the same multicast group, to which the clients listen, in order to minimize the polling needs of the latter.

The Web Service Modeling Ontology (WSMO, 2005) is a conceptual framework and a formal language for describing the semantic aspects of Web Services, so that automated discovery and composition of Web Services can be achieved. Through its four elements, ontologies, WS descriptions, goals and mediators, the functional and behavioral aspects of a Web service, the user requirements and the automatic handling of interoperability issues may be addressed.

(WSDL, 2001) is "an XML format for describing network services as a set of endpoints operating on messages containing either document-oriented or procedure-oriented information. The operations and messages are described abstractly, and then bound to a concrete network protocol and message format to define an endpoint". It is the most adopted specification for expressing a service's functionality to the external world.

(SAWSDL, 2007) is the W3C recommendation of the Semantic Annotations for WSDL and XML Schema specification. Its main goal is not to define a language for semantically representing concepts but to propose mechanisms for connecting external semantic model concepts to internal WSDL or XML components.

Type of Advertised Information

With regard to the type of advertised information, various levels of detail can be followed. These may be complementary to one another. For example, the services or resources in general may advertise their state (available/unavailable) or status (current workload etc.). Furthermore, they may advertise non functional parameters (like QoS characteristics) that are supported by the specific service instance. This of course has an immediate correlation with the semantic representations that must be sufficiently rich in order to depict this. Finally, their functionality must be advertised, which mostly relates to their interfaces and their provided operations. Especially for services, this is mainly performed through the Web Services Description Language.

In the following figure (Figure 2), the taxonomy of Service Discovery in relation to the identified parameters and characteristics is portrayed.

STATE OF THE ART MECHANISMS: APPROACHES, IMPLEMENTATION AND COMPARISONS

In this section, an analysis of currently used Service Discovery mechanisms is given. This includes sample implementations from all of the above categories, however it must be stressed that due to the extension of the research topic in recent years, these solutions in many cases are limited to only parts of an SD functionality or characteristics as these were described above.. The latter are compared with regard to the aforementioned taxonomy, in order to extract their characteristics.

UDDI

As seen in Section 2, UDDI is a protocol for Service registries. Implementations based on UDDI have gained popularity during recent years. It is based on XML for message exchange but while it is widely adopted and implemented, it is extremely static. Services are registered initially but there is no dynamic monitoring of their state. If a registered service becomes unavailable then there is no notification to the user. Furthermore there is a major manual intervention, either for administrative purposes or for the user in order to make the required selection. The several UDDI processes and mechanisms cover solely operational aspects of the UDDI cloud, data management as well as replication aspects. They are designed and are suitable for dealing with explicitly published changes to the registry data. Such changes are typically performed by operators or publishers. While these processes can be regarded as an approach to automatically handle changes in the registry, they do not represent a solution for the problem of dynamic service invocation or fault tolerance.

Figure 2. Taxonomy of Service Discovery Features

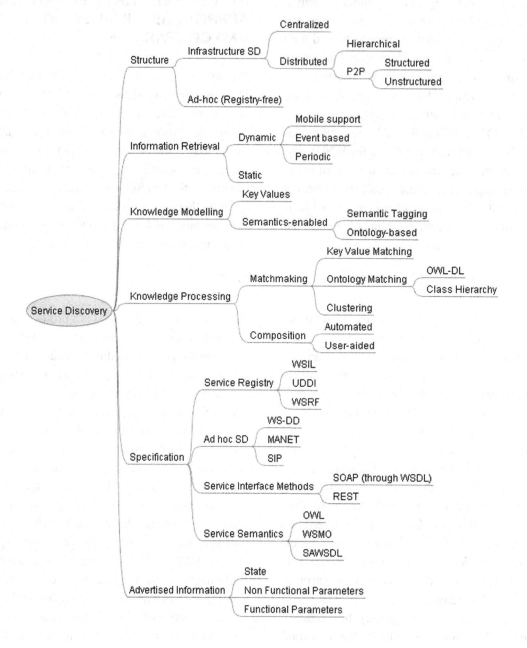

ebXML

Another approach to this kind of service is ebXML(http://www.ebxml.org). Its main goal is to make business processes easier and automated. It allows businesses to find another, define trading-partner agreements and exchange XML messages in support of business operations. Its messaging specification is based on SOAP with attachments, but does not use WSDL, a feature which can prove to be limiting. It is mainly focused for business exchange so its flexibility is also limited.

Sun Service Registry

As far as implementations are concerned, for UDDI there is a vast number of them but the one that prevails is the Sun Service Registry (2005), an open-source, Java based utility that implements UDDI and ebXML standards. It supports Web Service registry functions, organization, storage, control of any kind of service metadata or artefact, federated Web Service asset management across multiple repositories, core infrastructural support for service discovery, lifecycle management and SOA governance, security, APIs as well as database abstraction layer. It is tightly integrated into the Java Enterprise System but there is no report about monitoring capabilities or the support of a distributed architecture.

IBM WebSphere Registry

Another implementation is the IBM WebSphere Registry (http://www-01.ibm.com/software/integration/wsrr/). It is a proprietary solution that uses metadata repository for service interaction endpoint descriptions, supports both traditional Web Services (SOAP/HTTP) and SOA services (WSDL, XSD). It is more reliable than open-source packages and optimizes the use of services in SOA by exchanging rich service information with runtime monitoring tools and operational data stores. One question rises about the fact that it does not seem to manage service metadata across the whole SOA life cycle and of course the matter of cost and extensibility in comparison with open source solutions.

MDS

Another popular scheme is MDS, the Monitoring and Discovery Service of the Globus Toolkit 4 (http://www.globus.org/mds). This service also monitors the state of each resource and provides a multi-level hierarchy organization and multiple indexes. It also features WSRF implementation, VO (Virtual Organization- the dynamic concentration of resources for mutual use) support (good for collaborative applications), plug-in specialized functionality, common VO-level service functionality, monitoring and updating of the states of services and resources. Finally, WSRF implements large-scale, reliable distributed monitoring and systems. The main limiting feature of MDS is the query based information service for matchmaking between requests and resources. It is primarily focused on keyword matching

In order to deal with these inadequacies, various schemes have been proposed in order to combine the power of MDS with semantics. (RDF, 2004) is an XML specification/format for describing resources and their properties. Attributes of resources correspond to traditional attribute-value pairs but there are also properties that represent relationships between resources. In a way it is similar to object-oriented programming languages and their concepts and it is extensible. An extension of RDF is the Web Ontology Language (OWL). OWL uses the power of semantics in order to cope with the restrictions posed by keyword matching. A number of Web Services can be retrieved that may have similar functionality which is hidden when simply viewing their WSDL. With OWL, web services are modelled with ontologies and the semantic representation of concepts and their relations is exploited in order to achieve semantic matching. The basic languages to obtain semantic description from web services are DAML-S and OWL-S (2002). OWL can be added as another layer in existing implementations such as UDDI or MDS, allowing the creation of a hierarchy of concepts in manner that when a query is made the possible returned result is not necessarily syntactically the same with the requested but its relation with the wanted one is derived from the hierarchy. The relations between concepts are depicted in a knowledge tree.

gLite

A useful combination of MDS and semantics is the gLite system (Burke et al, 2007). It integrates MDS with the Relational Grid Monitoring Architecture (http://www.r-gma.org/) in an attempt to improve the query and matchmaking capabilities of the former. The GLUE information model (http://forge.gridforum.org/sf/projects/glue-wg), a standardized description of a Grid computing system to enable resources and services to be presented to users and external services in a uniform way, is used. RGMA supports relational database-like SQL queries and there are also a CLI, an API, and a Web browser interface available, so that users could publish their own data. The Producers (offered services or infrastructures) feed their information in this relational database, where Consumers (searching for services or infrastructures) subscribe to perform queries based on their constraints. Multiple rows with primary key and a timestamp for information freshness is used for the Producers, so that RGMA queries can be made concerning different time periods (latest, history, streaming results) according to the update requirements. Latest will give more accurate information but history means that there is a larger set of results. Servers collect data from both local clients (primary producers) and other servers (secondary producers).

GridBus

A very useful combination is the one in GridBus (Somasundaram et al., 2006) where MDS is used for the monitoring and management part and OWL is used for the registration and the matchmaking process. This system uses ontology templates, meaning domain specific ontologies that provide hierarchy of concepts along with properties to define their characteristics. Any resource can be modeled as an instance of a specific concept provided that the resource can be described using the properties defined in that concept. Upon resource registry, an instance of an appropriate resource concept in the ontology template is created. If an exact match is not found, then a higher level representation of what is requested by the user can be found. It is based on the knowledge tree and allows the avoidance of a total miss. Specifically, if the user provides a label that does not exist then instead of a failure the user inserts the level where the new label should be, in order to enrich the knowledge tree. A Protégé-OWL editor is used to create an extensible ontology template and Protégé-OWL libraries to dynamically create knowledge base of grid resources. An Algernon (http://algernon-j.sourceforge.net/doc/overview.html) query is used between users and OWL. Algernon is used in order to perform inference on data in knowledge bases and is compatible with the Protégé knowledge base.

S-MDS

In a similar architecture, the S-MDS implementation (http://wiki.dbgrid.org/index.php?smds) describes the resource properties (RP) using ontologies through a mapping procedure. Resource properties describe the resource/service state but they deal only with the document structures and not with its contained semantics/concept. This way querying problems appear. With S-MDS, through the mapping process these properties are transformed to ontologies and are stored and maintained in a WS or RDF repository so that it can be semantically queried. In the beginning there is a fully automatic correlation between RP and Domain Specific Ontologies (DSO), then a creation of a DSO instance based on values defined in the RP and afterwards an enrichment of the DSO by importing other ontologies (DSOE). Finally, a DSOE instance is created based on user inputs. SPARQL or RDF query language is used and a GUI is provided for easy SPARQL creation.

Decentralized Resource Discovery

Regarding other approaches, a decentralized Grid resource discovery system based on a spatial publish/subscribe index is presented in Ranjav et al.(2007). It utilizes a Distributed Hash Table (DHT) routing substrate for delegation of d-dimensional service messages. The Grid brokers create a Chord overlay, which collectively maintains the logical publish/subscribe index to facilitate a decentralized resource discovery process. *G*rid resource query rate directly affects the performance of the decentralized resource discovery system, and at higher rates the queries can experience considerable latencies. Furthermore, system size does not have a significant impact on the performance of the system, in particular the query latency. The basic dependency is the use of Chord and the main advantage the increased fault tolerance of this scheme. The same features exist in MDS and gLite, where also the refresh rate of information can be configured according to the administrator's needs and network performance. A P2P implementation of GT4 appears in Bharathi and Chervenak (2007).

NWS

A distributed system that monitors and predicts the performance of various resources of the Grid is the Network Weather Service (http://nws.cs.ucsb. edu/ewiki/). It has sensors that sample a number of parameters of the resources and then uses a range of algorithms and numerical models in order to predict the near-time performance of these resources. The best fitting algorithm is chosen for every resource according to the prediction success. This is a very attractive scheme that enables a very dynamic view of the network leading to a very high efficiency level. One question is about the speed of selection due to the fact that a number of algorithms has to be tested. Another point is the level of prediction success, especially in accordance with real-time attributes.

Collaborative Tagging

Fernandez et al (2008) present a method based on Collaborative Tagging for matchmaking services to requests. In SWS models, like OWL-S, DAML-S etc., the service provider has the responsibility to handle ontologies and semantic descriptions. However his/her approach may be different than the one the end user that is going to search for a service is following. In this paper, a combination of the ontologies in addition to free text tagging of services by end users is performed. Each service is semantically annotated by end users through tags. These tags constitute the tag-cloud of the service. Each tag has a different weight depending on whether it has been selected by many users. Different clouds exist for describing a service's input, output and operation. At the next level, a hierarchical dendrogram of tag descriptions is created based on clustering techniques that process the clouds from step 1. The basic advantage of this method with regard to semantic descriptions is the merge of two worlds, the service as this is described through its interfaces, and the user's notion regarding its context and usage in the real world.

EASY

EASY (Mohtar et al, 2008) is a framework that can be used on existing SD mechanisms in order to enrich the use of semantics for both functional and non functional (like QoS) characteristics. It is comprised of two main components. The EASY-L is a language for semantic service description that is extensible and contains required information for semantic service matching. EASY-M is a matchmaking mechanism for both functional and non functional parameters that enables both complete and partial matching. Furthermore, due to its rich descriptions, services can be matched with resources or other services. EASY is an add-on on existing SD mechanisms, however it must be deployed on every node participating to the discovery process. These mechanisms can be either centralized or distributed. If the request is not matched with the repository in the vicinity of the client, it is forwarded to other registries.

The major processing workload is during the service advertisement. Based on a DAG approach, the new service is entered on a existing ontology according to the semantics of its description. Thus the online matching is performed much faster. Furthermore, the partial matching of requests could potentially lead to the usage of this implementation for service composition also.

RESTful WSs

In (Zhao and Doshi, 2009), an approach using RESTful web services is presented. In this work, a formal description of the RESTful Web service composition problem is presented along with a formal model for classifying and describing RESTful WSs. The model is based on the description of RESTful WSs as ontology resources and "state transfer" of ontology resources. By using this formulation, a situation calculus based state transition system can be used for automating composition of services.

Publish/Subscribe Broker

In (Hu et al, 2008), an approach based on the publish/subscribe messaging paradigm is presented. In this case, a distributed system is used for the service composition part. This helps in scaling the performance of such a system, that in centralized service repositories is unfeasible. The authors exploit the fact that interaction relationships among the data senders and receivers in a pub/sub system is almost identical to the problems that are faced during service composition. Thus by modeling services using content-based pub/sub messages, existing work on matching of these messages is exploited. In the pub/sub case, each publisher produces data that are forwarded to a channel, to which subscribers have registered in order to

receive them. Constraints can be set as to what kind of information a subscriber may get. The use of semantically rich ways in order to express these constraints is not dealt with in this work, however this constraint matching is the basis of the composition functionality. A broker network is used, where service and request agents as well as brokers can join or leave at any time, thus resulting in a decentralized, highly dynamic infrastructure. The process search algorithm finds for a suitable DAG of services that meet the request made in the advertisement. Overall, it is a very promising approach. The semantic capabilities can be enhanced while the lack of any specification used for describing services may be a limiting factor.

Group-Based Service Discovey

Group-based Service Discovey (Chakraboty et al, 2006) is an SD mechanism based on the P2P paradigm. Its main goal is to exhibit a high rate of flexibility in order to include pervasive computing environments such as mobile agents in addition to standard distributed infrastructures. No central repository exists for the services or resources to register their existence but the approach is based on dynamic caching of advertisements. Due to the fact that syntactic matching is not efficient in pervasive autonomic environments due to heterogeneity of implementations and interfaces, the authors have used OWL. Through this implementation, semantic capabilities are exploited in order to describe capabilities of services and resources in this environment. The services are also classified into groups based on the class-subclass hierarchy of OWL. This group information is used in order to route the requests towards the most suitable available services. Due to this differentiation, this implementation is efficiently utilizing resources without the need for expensive, in terms of bandwidth and delay, solutions like broadcasting.

In general, the SD lies on three steps:

- Advertisement of services according to vicinity
- P2P dynamic caching of advertisements
- Forwarding of discovery requests based on the service group defined through the ontologies

More information regarding numerous P2P discovery systems in Grid computing can be found in Trunfio et al (2007).

FUSION

The FUSION Semantic Registry (Kourtesis et al, 2008) is built upon a UDDI registry, exploiting the fact that in the latter, references can be given towards the specification with which a description of the functional and non-functional characteristics of a service can be found (like in a WSDL document). In order to support however more fine-grained matchmaking between the requests and responses of the SD mechanism, the authors follow also SAWSDL semantically annotated descriptions of service interfaces in addition to OWL-DL for performing fine-grained matchmaking through DL reasoning.

Regarding the advertised information, FUSION supports both functional and non-functional properties (like QoS) and extensions can be performed in order to enrich the level of advertisements.

In terms of architecture, the FUSION Semantic Registry is independent from the UDDI server implementation and is external to the latter, with the main objective to increase the syntactic and matchmaking abilities. It exposes two interfaces for publication and discovery functions. Operations such as SAWSDL parsing, OWL ontology processing, and DL reasoning are performed internally.

Akogrimo Service Discovery (SIP and MDS)

The Session Initiation Protocol Service Discovery (SIP SD) is a mechanism implemented using the SIP technology (RFC 3261, IETF). This particular solution was developed within the frame of the Akogrimo IST project (http://www.mobilegrids.org/). This mechanism was developed to discover devices connected to the network, such as printers, webcams, proxies, time servers, etc. More information can be found regarding this implementation in Olmedo et al (2009). In general, the approach connects the Akogrimo EMS (Execution and Management System), a distributed system that utilizes the Globus MDS,, with a SIP enabled framework for discovery of mobile agents and resources. Due to the fact that the MDS has been thoroughly studied in the previous sections, and that SIP-enabled Discovery mechanisms, to the best of our knowledge, are very rare in the bibliography, the main focus of the analysis lies on the description of the SIP SD mechanism that follows.

The core of the SIP SD is based on two SIP extensions, namely "SIP – Specific Event Notification" (RFC 3265) and "SIP extension for Event State Publication" (RFC 3903). SIP (Specific Event Notification) creates a framework for communication of events between SIP nodes in an infrastructure. Event packages are used in order to define the events that can be communicated. The SIP extension for Event State Publication is used by a SIP node in order to forward the information to a corresponding agent This extension is used in the SIP SD mechanism to provide the agents with all the necessary data.

The SIP SD mechanism of the Akogrimo project provides some interesting characteristics:

- The ability to alert in case of service changes or subscription to services before they go online.

- Reduced network traffic, due to its compliance with the subscription- notification concept.
- A description language (XML) with more expressivity compared to common attribute-value pair approaches. This can be extended with enriched, semantic, XML based languages such as Ontologies.

Through these features, the mechanism enables higher levels of expressivity and functionality and enhances the classical SD concept with a more flexible and powerful implementation, that can also support mobile resources to be incorporated in the framework.

Publish/Subscribe Event-Based Mechanism

In Yan et al (2009), a resource discovery mechanism is presented that focuses mostly on the depiction of the state of the resources throughout time. The major contribution of this work lies on the fact that the status of the resources can be monitored in real time. Furthermore, the mechanism is event-based in order to notify the users, based on a publish/subscribe mechanism. The intermediate brokers deal with subscription for advertisements and routing of requests to the proper resources. The high level of dynamicity and scalability in this implementation are very attractive features. Four classes are implemented, regarding the level and flow of information, based on whether this information is static or dynamic. One disadvantage is the fact that the matchmaking is based on key value pairs, which has limited semantic capabilities. This solution is mostly aiming at resources and not services.

MUSIC

MUSIC (Rouvoy et al, 2009) is a component-based planning middleware and framework that has the goal of enabling discovery in ubiquitous environ-

ments. It is mostly focused on exchanging current services with replacement ones for self adaptation purposes, however the way this is performed can prove to be helpful for automated composition cases. It focuses also on QoS features. The application is modeled as a series of components with given functionalities. The latter can be dynamically configured with conforming component implementations. So the purpose of the framework is to search for alternative services that meet these requirements. Components (e.g. services) can be plugged in for replacing disappeared components with similar functionality. The planning capabilities of the platform are based on a meta-model. In this model, the composition is described as a set of Roles that are collaborating through Ports. The latter represent functionality that is provided or required from connected components. Properties are used to describe the association between QoS levels and the resource needs. Each port has a Type that represents its needs in terms of interfaces and protocol. So during an automated composition, the comparison of these can aid in determining whether the interconnection of two components is feasible. This feasibility involves also QoS features. This planning activity is key for selecting the fittest services that provide the end-to-end desirable output to the requester.

The MUSIC platform supports a number of SD protocols like SLP and UPnP. A service can register to these mechanisms and advertise its presence, along with a static description of its offered QoS, with regard to its non functional capabilities. For the dynamic QoS offered by the service, this is dependent on the node that hosts the former. So it is adapted later on, depending on the load. Discovery listeners may register to different MUSIC platforms in order to be aware of new services that register. It extends OSGI in order to be able to support distributed services and to be able to handle different communication and discovery protocols. The main disadvantage of this platform seems to be the fact that the services are bound to specific nodes of execution, a fact

Table 1. Implementations in relation to Service Discovery Taxonomy characteristics

Tool	Structure	Information Retrieval	Knowledge Modeling	Knowledge Processing	Automated Composition	Specification	Advertised Information
RESTful WSs (Zhao et al, 2009)	-	-	Ontologies	Situation Calculus	Yes	REST, OWL	Functional
EASY (Mokhtar et al, 2008)	Dependent on the underlying SD	Dynamic	Ontologies	Ontology matching (+partial+subsumption)	-	OWL	Functional and Non-Functional (QoS)
Pub/Sub Broker (Hu et al, 2008)	Distributed, Ad hoc	Dynamic	Key value pairs	Key value matching	Yes, DAG based	-	Functional
Akogrimo SIP SD (Olmedo et al,2009)	Distributed, Hierarchical	Dynamic, Mobile	Key value pairs	Key value matching	-	SOAP, WS-*, SIP	State, Non Functional
GSD (Chakraborty et al, 2006)	Distributed, P2P	Dynamic, Mobile	Ontologies	Ontology matching (+partial)	Yes	OWL	Functionality (in terms of OWL service group)
FUSION Semantic Registry (Kourtesis et al, 2008)	Centralized	Dynamic, service-driven	Ontologies, Semantic Annotations	OWL-DL	-	OWL, SAWS-DL, UDDI	Functional, Non Functional
Event-based (Yan et al, 2009)	Distributed	Dynamic, event-based	Key value pairs	Key value matching	-	Publish/Subscribe	State (or status) in real-time
MUSIC (Rouvoy et al, 2009	Distributed	Dynamic, event-based	Meta-model	Comparison of Meta-model characteristics	Yes, Meta-model based	OSGI, SLP, UPnP	Functional and Non-Functional (QoS)
GSO (Santos et al, 2009)	Centralized	-	Ontologies	Ontology matching (service-task-goal)	Yes, Goal oriented	OWL and WSMO (service descriptions in any language)	Functional and Non-Functional (QoS)

that is contrary to the modern Cloud Computing Stack, as this is described in the next Section. If this limitation is lifted then this solution is one of the most promising ones. Another hindering factor is the limited use of semantics. An addition of an ontology on top of the meta-model described earlier could help in the enhancement of this framework.

A thorough survey and classification especially for service composition frameworks can be found in (Ibrahim et al, 2009).

Goal-Based Service Ontology

Goal-based Service Ontology (Bonino da Silva Santos et al, 2009) is a framework that has the aim of assisting non-technology experts in service discovery and composition. It uses the concept of goal for representing abstract service requests. The approach is based on goal modeling and has as a prerequisite the need for shared domain specific ontologies between the involved parties. Through ontological representations, the tasks that are valid are correlated with the specific goals that domain users may have. Furthermore, the context-aware platform is based on the aforementioned semantic descriptions and uses contextual information from the user in order to select the appropriate tasks to aid in the fulfillment of the goal. The providers register their services and semantically annotate them by using the domain specific ontologies. The main focus is to link services with tasks and tasks with goals. Then, whenever a client inserts a new goal, the sequence of tasks and subtasks is defined through the semantic representations, allowing for the framework to deploy the necessary services.

Following, a comparative table (Table 1) of the most advanced solutions with relation to the aforementioned taxonomy features is presented.

What is shown from the above analysis is that there are numerous efforts, each with advantages and disadvantages. There is no clear solution that is fittest in comparison to all the others. Furthermore, there does not seem to be one solution that covers all aspects of the taxonomy. However, as it will be described in the following chapter, this may not be a limiting factor in the current computing environment.

Especially with regard to service composition, while considerable focus has been given on satisfying input and output criteria, the semantic functionality of services is not considered. Having the same I/O (or according descriptions) and protocol of communication, which are the basic criteria for composition approaches, may make two services compatible but it does not necessarily provide the functionality that is needed by the end user. For example, a service may have as input (and output) an image file, but the internal operations may be completely different (gray scale in one case or color enhancement in the other). So a gap that is worth pursuing is the ability to give services a functional semantic aspect regarding their internal operation on data.

FUTURE TRENDS AND REQUIREMENTS

In the future the most important feature will be the dynamic nature of networks and providers. Multiple Service or Infrastructure Providers will federate in order to achieve a better overall result and to increase their offered services with limiting cost by adding value from each contributor (The Future Of Cloud Computing, 2010). In order to manage such kinds of organizations the most necessary feature will be not just to discover resources but to also combine and monitor them and their availability. Furthermore, semantic matchmaking is another hot topic, due to the fact that an advanced solution in this field will allow the full automation of the selecting and negotiating procedure with minimal user intervention. Furthermore, the automatic comparison from multiple compatible sources will contribute to the discovery of more cost effective resources.

However, one issue that arises from the current business models, towards which modern Cloud solutions evolve, is the fact that with the creation of different roles for SaaS, PaaS and IaaS that are undertaken by separate entities, the flow of information from these layers to the Service Discovery mechanisms, typically residing in the PaaS layer, may be restricted. For example, an IaaS provider will certainly advertise information related to the supported types of infrastructures but will almost never do the same for information regarding the workload of these resources.

So, what is critical for an SD mechanism on the PaaS layer is to be able to express service and resource requirements in a semantically enriched way, including features such as functional and non-functional characteristics. In this level, three operations may be performed:

- Matchmaking of client requests to available services
- Composition of services, thus combining two or more services in an integrated

Figure 3. Cloud Computing Stack in relation to SD mechanisms

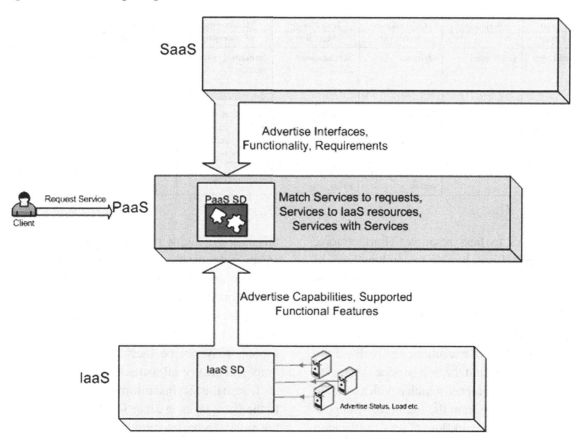

workflow level in case the first step is not successful

- Filtering of IaaS providers that can accommodate all or part of the workflow

With regard to the second point, this was not the case in the past. In most cases, the service provider was also the one that provided the infrastructures for execution. With the advent of Cloud computing however, additional matchmaking must be performed, between the offered SaaS and the final platform of execution.

In addition, regarding the last point, what is seen as the most recent trend in Cloud computing is the federation of different Cloud providers through a number of scenarios such as Cloud bursting or multi-cloud execution cases. Typical examples of this kind are the projects RESERVOIR

(http://www.reservoir-fp7.eu/) and OPTIMIS (http://www.optimis-project.eu/). The part that will be critical in such a distributed, multi-role environments, combining services from different providers with resources from potentially different providers, is the service composition and matchmaking part with semantic enhancements. This matchmaking may involve composing different services in order to add value and create more complicated and advanced combinations and matching these components to specific IaaS providers (from a functional point of view) that according to their advertisements are able to accommodate the former. The matchmaking capabilities are in general critical, as also identified in Carrascosa et al (2009).

So in the PaaS level that orchestrates this process, what is crucial is to be able to accom-

Table 2. Requirements for the SD mechanisms for each layer of the Cloud Computing Stack

Cloud Layer	Structure	Information Retrieval	Knowledge Modeling	Knowledge Processing	Automated Composition	Advertised Information
PaaS Layer	Distributed	Dynamic	Semantics-enabled	Semantic Match-making	Yes	Functional, Non Functional (with regard to service capabilities)
IaaS Layer External	Centralized	Dynamic	Semantics-enabled (Ontologies)	Needed in order to classify internal resources and advertise their type	No	Functional, Non Functional (with regard to service capabilities)
IaaS Layer Internal	Distributed	Extremely dynamic	Semantics-enabled	No	No	Non Functional and State

modate SaaS to IaaS resources. Furthermore, what is needed is to be able to combine SaaS in order to create new products, based on mash-ups of services. Another point of importance is that the semantic descriptions of the service must be able to address also functional requirements in terms of platform of execution. This will aid the PaaS provider to find the best service that meets the client's requirements, match it with a suitable hardware resource from the IaaS layer and possibly extend it to a workflow of services through automated composition. State information is not critical for this layer, due to the SaaS paradigm. Through this, the software services that are offered by the PaaS provider are deployed in the IaaS layer as many times as needed.

In the following figure (Figure 3), the various layers of the Cloud Computing Stack in relation to the different SD mechanisms are presented, with an analysis of their functionalities.

On the other hand, an SD mechanism that resides internally to the IaaS provider will be used in order to obtain information regarding the status of the resources. As seen in the previous paragraphs, the IaaS provider will almost never advertise, for competitive reasons, the workload or status of its resources. However, such an internal mechanism is critical in order to manage the infrastructure and proceed to intelligent and flexible decisions regarding allocation of tasks, for example with regard to scheduling decisions. For

this reason, a highly flexible and dynamic mechanism is required, that will be able to include information such as state and QoS characteristics. This information must be always up to date, with a very high refresh rate. Furthermore, a distributed mechanism is necessary because these resources may not be located in the same geographical area or infrastructure.

Due to the fact that information will be passed to the PaaS layer in order for the latter to select the most appropriate provider, what is also critical for an IaaS provider is to give this data with a semantically rich description. For this reason, an SD mechanism with specific semantic capabilities towards external PaaS providers is necessary. This will aid the PaaS provider to perform better matches with the according infrastructures.

So as a conclusion for the optimal selection of which SD mechanism to implement and which characteristics this must address, the answer is that this depends on the level of use of this component. In the following table (Table 2), a concentrated list of needed characteristics for each layer of the Cloud Computing Stack in relation to the taxonomy identified in Section 3 is presented. The SaaS layer is not considered in this approach due to the fact that in general software will be transformed in a service oriented implementation and be adapted to an existing platform. So the latter is the one that decides which information must be provided by the Application Developer in order for this adaptation to take place. For example, with what semantic representation this software service will be described in order to be included in the platform is a choice of the PaaS provider. Furthermore, automated composition is considered separately due to the fact that its importance is expected to be critical in the upcoming years.

Based on this analysis, there are solutions that can handle SD mechanisms, at least in the IaaS layer as seen from Table 1 of Section 3. What seems to be the most obvious gap in research up to date is the fact that service composition in many cases is user directed and actually semi-automatic. Furthermore, one issue that is critical for the future and is not addressed today is the need to merge ontologies from potentially different providers, either at the SaaS or PaaS layer. This merge should be performed automatically, however this ability does not exist in modern SD mechanisms.

CONCLUSION

This chapter has performed a taxonomy of the characteristics that a service/resource discovery mechanism may address. This includes a variety of features that can be a part of these mechanisms.

A number of indicative solutions that implement part of these features have been presented in detail and with regard to their position in the taxonomy.

The investigation of current Cloud-based business models (in the form of the Cloud Computing Stack) and their specific per layer requirements has also been performed, in an effort to identify what are the most attractive characteristics (and therefore appropriate mechanisms). Gaps have been identified with respect to these approaches and the current business models.

As a conclusion, in recent years a large number of efforts have been implemented in the Service Discovery and Information field. Solutions exist with various features, with regard to dynamicity, level of information stored, method of process-

ing, semantic annotation. Discovery mechanisms may be used for both hardware resources and software services, each one with a specific range of requirements for an efficient implementation.

There is no clear dominance of one solution over the others. Furthermore, the plug-in fashion of a number of these mechanisms is enabling their use with a number of different underlying technologies. Based on this and the analysis that has been made regarding each solution's characteristics and each layer's requirements, an actor may choose a suitable combination according to his/her needs and the level of complexity that is needed or wanted in each case. This selection may be further enhanced by what is foreseen to be the most critical characteristic for each provider, depending on the latter's nature and objectives.

REFERENCES

Bharathi, S., & Chervenak, A. (2007). Design of a scalable peer-to-peer Information System using the GT4 index service. In *Proceedings of the Seventh IEEE International Symposium on Cluster Computing and the Grid* (CCGrid'07).

Bonino da Silva Santos, L. O., Guizzardi, G., Silva Souza Guizzardi, R., Goncalves da Silva, E., Ferreira Pires, L., & van Sinderen, M. J. (2009). Gso: Designing a well-founded service ontology to support dynamic service discovery and composition. In *Proceedings of the 2nd International Workshop on Dynamic and Declarative Business Process* (DDBP 2009).

Burke, S., Campana, S., Delgado Peris, A., Donno, F., M´endez Lorenzo, P., Santinelli, R., & Sciab`a, A. (2007). *gLite-3-UserGuide, v.1.1.* CERN-LCG 2007.

Carrascosa, C., Giret, A., Julian, V., Rebollo, M., Argente, E., & Botti, V. (2009). Service oriented MAS: An open architecture. In *Proceedings of the AAMAS 09.*

Chakraborty, D., Joshi, A., Yesha, Y., & Finin, T. (2006). Toward distributed service discovery in pervasive computing environments. *IEEE Transactions on Mobile Computing, 5*(2), 97–112. doi:10.1109/TMC.2006.26

CORDIS. (2010). The future of cloud computing. *Expert Group Report.* Retrieved from http://cordis.europa.eu/fp7/ict/ssai/docs/cloud-report-final.pdf

DAML-S. (2002). *Describing Web services using DAML-S and WSDL.* Retrieved from http://www.daml.org/services/ daml-s/0.7/daml-s-wsdl.html

Fernandez, A., Hayes, C., Loutas, N., Peristeras, V., Polleres, A., & Tarabanis, K. (2008). Closing the service discovery gap by collaborative tagging and clustering techniques. In *Proceedings of ISCW 2008, Workshop on Service Discovery and Resource Retrieval in the Semantic Web.*

Fielding, R. T. (2000). *Architectural styles and the design of network-based software architecture.* PhD thesis, University of California, Irvine.

Handley, M., & Schulzrinne, H. (1999). *SIP: Session initiation protocol.* (RFC3261, IETF).

Hu, S., Muthusamy, V., Li, G., & Jacobsen, H.-A. (2008). Distributed automatic service composition in large-scale systems. In *Proceedings of DEBS, 2008,* 233–244. doi:10.1145/1385989.1386019

Ibrahim, N., & Le Mouël, F. (2009). A survey on service composition middleware in pervasive environments. *International Journal of Computer Science Issues, 1.*

Kourtesis, D., & Paraskakis, I. (2008). Combining SAWSDL, OWL-DL and UDDI for semantically enhanced Web service discovery. In *Proceedings of the 5th European Semantic Web Conference* (ESWC 2008) [Berlin/Heidelberg, Germany: Springer-Verlag.]. *Lecture Notes in Computer Science, 5021,* 614–628. doi:10.1007/978-3-540-68234-9_45

Mokhtar, S. B., Preuveneers, D., Georgantas, N., Issarny, V., & Berbers, Y. (2008). Easy: Efficient semantic service discovery in pervasive computing environments with QoS and context support. *Journal of Systems and Software, 81*(5).

Niemi, A. (2004). *Session initiation protocol (SIP) extension for event state publication. RFC 3903.* IETF.

Olmedo, V., Villagrá, V. A., Konstanteli, K., Burgosc, J. E., & Berrocal, J. (2009). Network mobility support for Web service-based grids through the session initiation protocol. *Future Generation Computer Systems, 25*(7). doi:10.1016/j.future.2008.11.007

OWL. (2009). *Ontology Web language version 2.* Retrieved from http://www.w3.org/TR/owl2-overview/

Ranjan, R., Chan, L., Harwood, A., Karunasekera, S., & Buyya, R. (2007). Decentralised resource discovery service for large scale federated Grids. In *Proceedings of the Third IEEE International Conference on e-Science and Grid Computing 2007* (pp. 379-387).

RDF. (2004). *RDF/XML syntax specification.* Retrieved from http://www.w3.org/TR/ REC-rdf-syntax

Roach, A. B. (2002). *Session initiation protocol (SIP) – Specific event notification. RFC 3265.* IETF.

Rouvoy, R., Barone, P., Ding, Y., Eliassen, F., Hallsteinsen, S., Lorenzo, J., et al. Scholz, U. (2009). MUSIC: Middleware support for self-adaptation in ubiquitous and service-oriented environments. In B. H. C. Cheng, et al. (Eds.), *Software engineering for self-adaptive systems. LNCS, vol. 5525.* Heidelberg, Germany: Springer.

SAWSDL. (2007). *Semantic annotations for WSDL.* Retrieved from http://www.w3.org/TR/sawsdl/

Somasundaram, T. S., Balachandar, R. A., Kandasamy, V., Buyya, R., Raman, R., Mohanram, R., & Varun, S. (2006). Semantic-based Grid resource discovery and its integration with the Grid service broker. In *Proceedings of the 14th International Conference on Advanced Computing and Communications* (ADCOM 2006) (pp. 84-89). Dec. 20-23. Piscataway, NJ: IEEE Press. ISBN: 1-4244-0715-X

Specification, U. D. D. I. (2004). Retrieved from http://www.uddi.org/pubs/ uddi_v3.htm

Sun Service Registry for SOA. (2005). Retrieved from http://xml.coverpages.org/ ni2005-06-15-a. html

Trunfio, P., Talia, D., Papadakis, H., Fragopoulou, P., Mordacchini, M., & Pennanen, M. (2007). Peer-to-Peer resource discovery in Grids: Models and systems. *Future Generation Computer Systems*, *23*(7), 864–878. doi:10.1016/j.future.2006.12.003

WS-Discovery Specification. (2009). Retrieved from http://docs.oasis-open.org/ ws-dd/dpws/1.1/ os/ wsdd-dpws-1.1-spec- os.html#wsdiscovery

WSDL. (2001). *Web service description language*. Retrieved from http://www.w3.org/TR/wsdl

WSIL specification. (2007). *Web services inspection language specification*. Retrieved from http://www.ibm.com/ developerworks/library/ specification/ws-wsilspec/

WSMO. (2005). *Web service modeling ontology*. Retrieved from http://www.w3.org/ Submission/ WSMO/

Yan, W., Hu, S., Muthusamy, V., Jacobsen, H.-A., & Zha, L. (2009). Efficient event-based resource discovery. In *Proceedings of the 2009 inaugural International Conference on Distributed Event-Based Systems*, Nashville, TN.

Yu, J., & Buyya, R. (2005). A taxonomy of scientific workflow systems for grid computing. *SIGMOD Record, 34*(3), 44-49. DOI= http://doi. acm.org/10.1145/ 1084805.1084814

Zhao, H., & Doshi, P. (2009). Toward automated restful Web service compositions. In *Proceedings of the 2009 IEEE International Conference on Web Services* (ICWS 2009), (pp. 189-196). IEEE Computer Society.

Chapter 6
Monitoring and Metering in the Cloud

Eduardo Oliveros
Telefónica Investigación y Desarrollo, Spain

Tommaso Cucinotta
Scuola Superiore Sant'Anna, Italy

Stephen C. Phillips
University of Southampton IT Innovation Centre, UK

Xiaoyu Yang
University of Southampton IT Innovation Centre, UK

Stuart Middleton
University of Southampton IT Innovation Centre, UK

Thomas Voith
Alcatel-Lucent, Germany

ABSTRACT

Monitoring and Metering are essential activities for Service Oriented Infrastructures (SOI) and Cloud services. The information collected through monitoring is necessary to ensure the correct execution of the applications in the Cloud and the monitoring of the SLA compliance.

This chapter will present the reasons and difficulties for monitoring and metering on Cloud infrastructures. The approaches for monitoring of the execution environment and the network on virtualised infrastructures will be described together with the existing monitoring tools present on different commercial and research platforms.

INTRODUCTION

Cloud Computing Overview

Cloud computing has become a new computing paradigm as it can offer dynamic IT infrastructure, configurable service and QoS guaranteed computing environment (Wang et al., 2008). Cloud computing can be illustrated from the following aspects:

SPI model – Cloud computing originates from the concept "Hardware as a Service" (HaaS), "Software as a Service" (SaaS). Cloud now advances from SaaS to "Platform as a Service" (PaaS) and "Infrastructure as a Service" (IaaS), known as SPI[1] model. In Cloud computing, customers can avoid capital expenditure on hardware and software by renting the usage from service provider

DOI: 10.4018/978-1-60960-827-9.ch006

of third party, rather than owning the physical infrastructure by themselves. The hardware and software are rendered to customers as IT services.

Scalability / elasticity – Klems and Gaw (in Geelan, 2008) claim that automatic scale of infrastructure for load balancing is a key element in Cloud computing. The delivered services can elastically / dynamically grow its capacity on an as-needed basis so that the Quality of Service (QoS) can be guaranteed: "on-demand services are all cloud computing based" (de Haaff, 2008).

"Pay-per-use" / "Pay-as-you-go" / "Utility computing" – There is also a vision that Cloud computing is more like a business revolution, rather than a technology evolution. Business model, or we call "pay-per-use", "pay-as-you-go", and "utility computing" is another feature of Cloud computing (Geelan, 2008; Watson, Lord, Gibson et al., 2008); Buyya, Yeo, Venugopal, 2009; McFedries, 2008). The usage of the resource will be metered and service customers will pay bill to service provider for the actual resource usage.

Data centre - Another view of Cloud presents the data centre as the basic unit of the Cloud infrastructure (Vaquero, Rodero-Merino, Caceres and Lindner, 2009). Data centre can offer huge amount of computing power and data storage. The capacity of the data centre can change dynamically when handling a task. According to Vaquero, Rodero-Merino, Caceres and Lindner (2009), this is associated with the concept "massive data scalability" proposed by Hand (2007).

Virtualisation - Cloud computing can also be regarded as a "virtualised hardware and software" (Sheynkman in Geelan, 2008). This perspective emphasizes the use of virtualisation technology in the Cloud computing. Virtualization technologies multiplex hardware and have made the flexible and scalable provision of resource as hardware and software on demand easier. Virtual machine techniques, such as VMware (http://www.vmware.com) and Xen (http://www.xen.org), offer virtualized IT-infrastructures on demand. Virtual network advances, such as Virtual Private Network

(VPN), support users with a customized network environment to access Cloud resources.

Why Does Cloud Need Metering and Monitoring

Monitoring tasks comprise a fundamental functionality in every distributed computing system. Every service should be monitored in order to check its performance and allow for corrective actions in case of failure. Monitoring data represents an operational snapshot of the system behaviour along the time axis. Such information is fundamental in determining the origin of the problems or for tuning different system components. For instance, fault detection and recovery mechanisms need a monitoring component to decide whether a particular subsystem or server should be restarted due to the information collected by the monitoring system (Litke et al., 2005).

Metering tasks are necessary for checking the disk space, network and memory usage from the machines of the platform. This information is vital to allocate services under conditions of optimum performance.

Metering and monitoring play an important role in Cloud computing, which can be attributed to the following reasons:

From Cloud computing SPI model perspective – Customer consumes services provided by a service provider and service provider outsources the service hosting to the dedicated infrastructure providers. Service Level Agreement (SLA) is usually employed to serve as a bilateral contract between two parties to specify the requirements, quality of service, responsibilities and obligations. SLA can contain a variety of service performance metrics with corresponding Service Level Objectives (SLO). Therefore we need to meter values of associated metrics defined in the SLA at the usage stage to monitor whether the specified service level objectives are achieved or not.

From Cloud computing "Pay-per-use" / "Pay-as-you-go" / "Utility computing" perspective–Cloud service provider delivers QoS-assured services and other commitments in exchange for financial commitments based on an agreed schedule of prices and payments. This requires the service / resource usage to be metered, based on which the bill can then be calculated.

From Cloud computing scalability / elasticity and data centre perspective – These two perspectives have a feature in common, that is, capacity on-demand or called on-demand resources provisioning. The service and resource usage need to be metered and monitored to support this dynamic scale feature on an as-needed basis. In the report "The Future of Cloud Computing" (Schubert, Jeffery, Neidecker-Lutz, et al., 2010) produced by the EC with the support of a group of external experts, it has been identified that Cloud computing is facing following challenges. From the technical aspects, the challenging issues are mainly related to: (i) scalability and elasticity, (ii) trust, security and privacy, (iii) handling data in Clouds is still complicated, especially large amount of data and heterogeneous data, and (iv) programming model are currently not aligned to highly scalable applications and thus cannot exploit the capabilities of Clouds. The Cloud scalability and elasticity issue which is directly related to monitoring and metering is listed at the top of the challenges that need to be addressed.

The Difficulties of Performing Monitoring and Metering in the Cloud

There are different ways of collecting monitoring data, for instance:

1. Obtain information from the Operating System or the Virtual Machine Unit (VMU) in relation to the CPU usage, the network interfaces and the storage connected to the machine.
2. Simple Network Management Protocol (SNMP) is used mostly on network system, and can be used to monitor the status of the

network and detect error events (SNMP traps enable an agent to notify the management station of significant events by way of an unsolicited SNMP message). Besides SNMP there are other protocols provided by network vendors to monitor and gather usage statistics, for instance NetFlow is a network protocol developed by Cisco Systems to run on Cisco IOS-enabled equipment for collecting IP traffic information.

3. Extract the information from the application log files, searching for specific patterns that provide information about interesting events in the application, for instance: error in the interaction with the client (this also could be related to denial of service (DoS) attacks) or number of client interactions performed.
4. Specific ad-hoc monitoring mechanism. Applications that do not provide standard mechanisms (like SNMP) to deliver monitoring data can implement a private API for monitoring. This mechanism could be a set of proprietary functions or more generically a SOAP interface with an XML specific message format.

The following steps are required for monitoring and link the raw monitoring data to the behaviour of the application (Heroix, 2006):

1. **Collect and correlate to reveal service performance**. One of the problems to perform correctly this correlation of information from the different sources is time synchronization. On a virtualized environment where the physical resources are shared by different applications and the infrastructure has the ability of reallocate the resources depending on the needs in each specific moment, one portion of a network or one server is not longer associated to a single service or application. The monitoring system will be unable to associate the corresponding data of the different systems to the applica-

tion unless a precise time synchronization mechanism is in place. Global Positioning System (GPS) (http://www.gps.gov) afford one way to achieve synchronization within several tens of μsec. Ordinary application of NTP (http://www.ntp.org/) may allow synchronization within several msec. The different granularities of those time synchronization mechanism determine the precision of the monitoring system at a whole (e.g. it is not possible to detect network delays of the order of milliseconds or less if the time difference of the clocks is also of this order).

2. **Interpret the business impact**. It is not trivial to deduce from the monitoring data collected from the different systems the performance of the application, and infer if the application is performing correctly. From one side, a complete outage in one segment of the network affecting some servers inside the application architecture could have no effect in the performance perceived by the user, for instance during low usage period where the rest of the service platform is able to provide the requested performance to the user. On the other side, a completely functional infrastructure could be insufficient to provide the QoS requested by the users. Accordingly, the monitoring system should gather information from the infrastructure and from the application components themselves to have a complete view of the execution and performance of the application.

3. **Resolve quickly; prevent when possible**. The ideal situation is the prevision of the user demand so that the provider can anticipate the requirements and adapt the application dynamically to support this demand. This is the promise of the cloud, the easy adaptation of the application to the changing environment that affects it. To support this, the application must be designed in advance to allow the dynamic deployment of application components, and the reconfiguration of the application to support these changes in the internal architecture of the application.

When an unexpected error occurs that affects the performance of the application, the cloud provider should provide the mechanism to detect those events and react to them to minimize as possible the negative effects on the clients. From an operational point of view the desired situation is when the monitoring application is able to suggest corrective actions to errors and events that can affect the application performance.

APPROACHES, IMPLEMENTATIONS AND COMPARISONS

There are several approaches in the design and development of monitoring and metering systems. This section presents briefly the techniques used to monitor the execution environment and the network on virtualised infrastructures. Finally, different monitoring tools of existing grid and cloud platforms are described, including commercial platforms like Amazon Web Services and Google App Engine; and monitoring systems used on open source and academic solutions like GRIA, Akogrimo, Edutain@Grid, Globus Toolkit and gLite.

Monitoring CPU Usage in Virtualized SOIs

Monitoring of actual resources usage in SOIs is of paramount importance due to the value that the corresponding information flow possesses in the overall resource allocation and management strategies. In fact, monitoring data may be used by resource providers for a variety of purposes, including:

- foreseeing the future loads for an optimum allocation of the available physical infrastructures;

- identifying possible bottlenecks within the infrastructure leading to either temporary or permanent performance degradations;
- fine-tuning their price lists and business model policies.

More specifically, monitoring data about the actual usage of *computing power* in a *distributed virtualized infrastructure* is particularly critical because not only the availability of CPU power is at the basis of providing compute-intensive services to the final users, but also for I/O intensive ones. In fact, retrieving selected portions/cuts of large amounts of data from remote disks and routing them to the final data consumers may require significant amounts of computing power for such tasks as:

- streaming the data on the network;
- selecting the requested data and/or aggregating or transforming it as requested (think of database applications);
- routing them among possibly virtualized gateway nodes.

Depending on the involved Operating Systems, the virtualization technologies in use, and specifically on the level of para-virtualization of the I/O and networking layers, the computing requirements due to a given data throughput may largely vary. Furthermore, when more VMUs run concurrently on the same physical node, a computing power shortage due for example to a CPU-intensive VMU may result in a degraded network throughput for another data-intensive VMU and vice-versa. Such situations need to be properly detected on-time and compensated (e.g., by live-migrating VMUs for load-balancing purposes), and monitoring plays a key role in this context.

However, monitoring of the CPU usage is not as easy as it is for other resources like network and memory, where objective metrics may be used for monitoring purposes, such as the number of transferred bytes. In fact, there are various factors that need to be properly considered in a monitoring process:

- the accuracy of the used sensors, in terms of time-precision by which they are capable of reporting CPU usage;
- the granularity at which the monitored data is collected, for example one may collect per-thread, per-process, per-VMU or per-node CPU usage data;
- CPU power-saving capability of the monitored physical nodes.

The accuracy of the monitoring data depends on the precision of the hypervisor and involved Operating Systems in accounting the processes load. In this section the focus is on the Linux Operating System and the kvm ("KVM, Kernel-based Virtualization Driver, Whitepaper", 2006) virtualization solution, both products are open source which allows a major customisation of the software. Using kvm, the Virtual Machine Units run as processes of the host Linux instance. Accuracy of monitoring of the CPU usage by individual VMUs depends on the accuracy of Linux in tracking the CPU usage of individual processes. Historically, the Linux kernel used to perform all of its time-related book-keeping activities, comprising measuring time and firing timers, at a precision depending on the frequency of the system tick, whose period is statically configured into the kernel to one of a few values between 1ms and 10ms. Even worse, the per-process monitoring data reported by the kernel used to be collected based on what observed at each system tick, independently of the actual CPU usage of a task between ticks, rather than on the actual time instants at which tasks where scheduled on the CPUs by the kernel. As a consequence, it was also possible for a properly designed unprivileged process in the system to consume nearly all of the available CPU power, still having the system report that the system was almost idle (Tsafrir, Etsion & Feitelson, 2007).

In order to mitigate such problems, it was once necessary to patch the kernel applying the well-known *high-resolution timers* patch, which introduced a much more fine-grained notion of time within the Operating System. Since the 2.6.16 version, Linux integrates (Corbet, 2006) such mechanism in the mainstream kernel, and in recent kernel versions the tasks accounting mechanism is done based on the actual CPU schedule. However, even though the kernel had high-resolution timers, it was not using them for accounting the CPU time consumed by processes. For this reason, in order to get a reliable CPU accounting information, it was usually necessary to introduce a custom mechanism flanking the scheduler. This was done, for example in the AQuoSA real-time scheduler for Linux (Palopoli, Cucinotta, Marzario & Lipari, 2009).

Also, another important issue to take into consideration is the possible CPU load due to system OS elements whose accounting is troublesome. One typical example is constituted by the CPU time consumed by *interrupt drivers*. These occur asynchronously with respect to the running processes and possible VMUs, and usually the OS accounts "randomly" the duration of the interrupt handlers onto the interrupted processes, what may produce additional undesired noise on the measured data. Such phenomenon may at least be controlled at a finer grain level by using the peempt-rt patchset (http://www.kernel.org/pub/linux/kernel/projects/rt)(Arthur, Emde & Mc Guire, 2007) by Ingo Molnar available on recent Linux kernel series. This introduces into the kernel, among others, an infrastructure for dealing with interrupt handlers into dedicated kernel threads. Basically, interrupt handling code formerly executing in interrupt context now is split into a demultiplexing logic which executes in response to the hardware interrupt, and the actual driver running into a kernel thread on its own and which is woken up by the interrupt driver. This allows not only for a finer

control on the way interrupt drivers are scheduled with respect to other activities in the system (Manica, Abeni & Palopoli, 2010), but also for a better monitoring of the elements that take up CPU power into a system.

Concerning the interfaces by which monitoring data is made available from the kernel to user-space processes, Linux offers various alternatives. First, it is possible to rely on POSIX (2004) compliant time measurement system calls, such as the clock_getcpuclockid(), clock_gettime() and pthread_getcpuclockid(). Using the special CLOCK_PROCESS_CPUTIME_ID and CLOCK_THREAD_CPUTIME_ID timers, it is possible to track the CPU power consumed by individual processes and threads, respectively. However, the implementation of such mechanisms in the Linux kernel is far from being stable, and the actual way it is done is still sensitive to the kernel version that is being used. The advantage of relying on standard system calls is of course portability of the software components across different Operating Systems.

On the other hand, custom extensions were proposed to get accurate CPU accounting information from the kernel. For example, in the AQuoSA real-time scheduler mentioned above (Palopoli, Cucinotta, Marzario & Lipari, 2009), a special API call was introduced for getting at once the overall CPU time consumed by the set of tasks attached to a real-time reservation.

Alternatively, on recent kernel versions, the Linux-specific cgroups (Menage, n.d.) virtual filesystem may be exploited for defining groups of processes in the system and attaching them a specific *controller*, which is capable of tracking the overall CPU consumption of all of the tasks in the group. This way it is possible to track the CPU consumption of an entire VMU (constituted by a set of threads composing a VMU process) or a group of VMUs. This method may be easily applied, for example, when using the IRMOS real-time scheduler (Checconi, Cucinotta, Faggioli & Lipari.2009) for achieving temporal isolation across multiple concurrently running VMUs (Cucinotta, Anastasi & Abeni. 2008), which already leverages the cgroups special filesystem for configuring real-time reservations and the tasks associated to them. In fact, when configuring (via the mount operation) the cgroups filesystem, it is possible to attach a CPU Accounting Controller to the same filesystem. This way, a special filesystem entry may be used in order to read the overall time spent by the tasks attached to the reservation in user-mode and kernel-mode. For example, this is extremely useful for the benchmarking (Boniface et al. 2010) phase while deploying real-time Virtual Machines (Cucinotta, Anastasi & Abeni. 2009) in the best possible (ideally optimum) way (Kostanteli et al. 2009; Cucinotta, Konstanteli & Varvarigou. 2009).

Power management usually done by modern CPUs by frequency switching and dynamic voltage scaling constitutes yet another source of uncertainty and unreliability, for a monitoring infrastructure. In fact, a host may figure out as being quite loaded simply because the power management system daemon is running the CPU at a reduced frequency. For example, the powernowd (http://www.deater.net/john/powernowd.html) daemon implements a simple utilization-control loop that aims to keep each CPU saturation level between the configurable thresholds, defaulting to 20% and 80%. If power management is active on a system, then CPU usage monitoring data needs to be accurately complemented by the data about the actual speed of the physical CPUs, in order to gather reliable and meaningful measurements. However, this may not be always done precisely, due to the fact that the monitoring infrastructure usually runs asynchronously with respect to the power management control logic. In such cases, reliable results may be obtained by implementing a custom power-management logic that is tightly integrated with the virtualized infrastructure management services. For example, this needs to be done anyway if one wants to provide real-time

guarantees and/or stable QoS levels to the hosted virtualized applications.

Finally, another possibility for taking into account frequency switching into monitoring data is to recur to cycle-counters as available on many CPUs, e.g., the RDTSC instruction on Intel 386 architectures. This way one would base the load information on the number of CPU cycles. However, while such data may easily be gathered for the entire system, differentiating the monitoring on a per-process basis may not be as easy.

Network Monitoring in the Cloud

Currently, in most cloud solutions the network is considered as granted and usually information about the network performance and its status inside the cloud infrastructure is not provided (Oberle et al., 2009). This is a major problem to support interactive real-time applications where the characteristics of the network are a key factor for maintaining the performance of the application.

In several IETF documents IP performance metrics have been specified (Paxson, Almes, Mahdavi & Mathis, 1998):

- The metrics must be concrete and well-defined.
- A methodology for a metric should have the property that it is repeatable, i.e. if the methodology is used multiple times under identical conditions, the same measurements should result in the same measurement results.
- The metrics must exhibit no bias for IP clouds implemented with identical technology.
- The metrics must exhibit well-understood and fair bias for IP clouds implemented with non-identical technology.
- The metrics must be useful to users and providers in understanding the performance they experience or provide.

For a given set of well-defined metrics, a number of distinct measurement methodologies may exist. Some examples are:

- **Direct** measurement of a performance metric using injected test traffic.

Example: measurement of the round-trip delay of an IP packet of a given size over a given route at a given time.

- **Projection** of a metric from lower-level measurements.

Example: given accurate measurements of propagation delay and bandwidth for each step along a path, projection of the complete delay for the path for an IP packet of a given size.

- **Estimation** of a constituent metric from a set of more aggregated measurements. Example: given accurate measurements of delay for a given one-hop path for IP packets of different sizes, estimation of propagation delay for the link of that one-hop path.
- **Estimation** of a given metric at one time from a set of related metrics at other times. Example: given an accurate measurement of flow capacity at a past time, together with a set of accurate delay measurements for that past time and the current time, and given a model of flow dynamics, estimate the flow capacity that would be observed at the current time.

When a quantity is quantitatively specified, we term the quantity a metric. Each metric will be defined in terms of standard units of measurement. The international metric system will be used (meters, seconds...). Appropriate related units based on thousands or thousandths of units are acceptable (e.g. km or ms, but not cm). The unit of information is the bit. When metric prefixes are used with bits or with combinations including bits, those prefixes will have their metric meaning (related to decimal 1000), and not the meaning conventional with computer storage (related to decimal 1024). When a time is given, it will be expressed in Universal Time Coordinated (UTC).

Metrics are specified but measurement methodologies are not formally standardized.

A methodology for a metric should have the property that it is repeatable: if the methodology is used multiple times under identical conditions, it should result in consistent measurements. In practice, as conditions usually change over time, it is enough to ask for "continuity", to describe a property of a given methodology: a methodology for a given metric exhibits continuity if, for small variations in conditions, it results in small variations in the resulting measurements.

Network measurement methods can broadly be classified into passive methods that rely on data collected at e.g. routers, and active methods based on observations of actively-injected probe packets. Network operators use active measurements because they are easy to conduct, have low overhead and, in contrast to passive data collection methods, measure exactly what normal data packets experience. One of the main disadvantages of active measurements is their limited accuracy due to the need to be non-intrusive, thus leaving the measured systems uninfluenced by the observation, fundamentally affecting accuracy (Machiraju, 2006).

Active techniques, in which traffic is injected into the network. The overall link can be characterized and they are not aware of application protocols. This is also known as intrusive measurements.

Passive techniques, in which existing traffic is recorded and analyzed. They may deal with connections (pair of IP addresses and ports) and they may distinguish between different protocol streams. This is also known as non-intrusive measurements.

For active monitoring, it is clear that as the number of resource pairs increases, the injected traffic incurs a significant disruption in the network, so usually such measurements are performed sequentially, measuring one or a few paths at a time. In contrast, a passive monitoring approach can provide an instant estimation across different paths, independently of their number.

It is recommended in a cloud to follow a strategy of doing passive monitoring rather than active monitoring. If active monitoring is unavoidable then it is preferred to do representative measurement (e.g. just one per network path) to be as minimal intrusive as possible.

Monitoring in Cloud Platforms

Amazon Web Services

One relevant area of monitoring is the so called 'Cloud' approaches for online access to virtualised and distributed resources and applications. Amazon's Web Service suite (http://aws.amazon.com/) is a good example. Amazon's Web Services include S3 for storage, EC2 for compute resource, SQS for queuing and SimpleDB for a database. Various vendors are adapting and porting their applications to run on the platform, including J2EE, Solaris and mySQL. Relevant to this section is the obvious need for consumers of 'cloud' services to monitor the performance and availability they are getting from the services, especially when using these services to deliver business critical applications.

Amazon CloudWatch (http://aws.amazon.com/cloudwatch/) is a web service that provides monitoring for AWS cloud resources, starting with Amazon EC2. It provides customers with visibility into resource utilization, operational performance, and overall demand patterns—including metrics such as CPU utilization, disk reads and writes, and network traffic. To use Amazon CloudWatch, clients simply have to select the Amazon EC2 instances they want to monitor;

Amazon CloudWatch will begin aggregating and storing monitoring data that can be accessed using the AWS Management Console, web service APIs or Command Line Tools.

Amazon CloudWatch provides two APIs: Query and SOAP API to collect programmatically monitoring information. The set of metrics that can be collected from the EC2 service are shown in Table 1 ("Amazon CloudWatch Development Guide", 2009).

These interfaces are now driving the emergence of specialised monitoring services, for example CloudStatus that provides online and live feeds on the status of Amazon's Web Services (http://www.cloudstatus.com) as well as longer term statistics on past performance (for example bandwidth for S3). CloudStatus is implemented using an open source monitoring and management infrastructure called Hyperic HQ (http://www.hyperic.com) which provides an extensible approach for application monitoring on SOIs.

Google App Engine Monitoring Tools

This section presents three monitoring tools available to monitor the activity of application running on Google App Engine (http://code.google.com/appengine/): Appstats library, application log files and the App Engine Scaffold plug-in system.

Appstats (Google, 2010) is a Python and Java library that is linked to the application to allow monitoring of the Remote Procedure Calls (RPC) of the application (van Rossum, 2010). This tool is included into the SDK provided by Google. Appstats integrates with the applicatoin using a servlet filter to record events, and provides a web-based administrative interface for browsing statistics.

The Appstats servlet filter adds itself to the remote procedure call framework that underlies the App Engine service APIs. It records statistics for all API calls made during the request handler, then stores the data in memcache ("Using Memcache", 2010). Appstats retains statistics for the most recent 1,000 requests (approximately). The

Table 1.

Metric	Description
CPUUtilization	The percentage of allocated EC2 compute units that are currently in use on the instance. This metric identifies the processing power required to run an application upon a selected instance. Units: *Percent*
NetworkIn	The number of bytes received on all network interfaces by the instance. This metric identifies the volume of incoming network traffic to an application on a single instance. Units: *Bytes*
NetworkOut	The number of bytes sent out on all network interfaces by the instance. This metric identifies the volume of outgoing network traffic to an application on a single instance. Units: *Bytes*
DiskWriteOps	Completed write operations to all hard disks available to the instance. This metric identifies the rate at which an application writes to a hard disk. This can be used to determine the speed in which an application saves data to a hard disk. Units: *Count*
DiskReadBytes	Bytes read from all disks available to the instance. This metric is used to determine the volume of the data the application reads from the hard disk of the instance. This can be used to determine the speed of the application for the customer. Units: *Bytes*
DiskReadOps	Completed read operations from all disks available to the instances. This metric identifies the rate at which an application reads a disk. This can be used to determine the speed in which an application reads data from a hard disk. Units: *Count*
DiskWriteBytes	Bytes written to all disks available to the instance. This metric is used to determine the volume of the data the application writes onto the hard disk of the instance. This can be used to determine the speed of the application for the customer. Units: *Bytes*

data includes summary records, about 200 bytes each, and detail records, which can be up to 100 KB each.

Besides this tool, App Engine also maintains a log of messages emitted by the application. App Engine records each request in the log. This log file can be browsed using the Admin Console. If a developer wants to perform more detailed analysis of the application's logs, he or she can download the log data to a file on their computer.

Finally, the App Engine Scaffold (http://support.hyperic.com/display/hypcomm/App+Engine+Plugin+Tutorial) is another tool that allows developers to monitor an application running on Google App Engine using Hyperic HQ. The scaffold is a set of files, a plugin descriptor, some Python scripts, and a shell script, that the developer can use as a starting point for building a special type HQ plugin that enables HQ com-

ponents to accept and manage metrics generated by an application running on App Engine

Together, Hyperic HQ and an HQ App Engine Plugin allow developers to:

- Chart and trend the application metrics over time, to answer questions like *"How many blog posts did I have in June?"*

- Execute and apply alerts to synthetic transactions. For instance, a developer can define an alert on the time it takes to create a new user, and be notified when the "create user" transaction takes longer than 2 seconds.

- Apply alerts to metrics, including those that indicate application usage. For instance, given a game application, it is possible to calculate a "games_played_today" metric, push it to HQ, and define an alert so that clients will be notified if the value is lower than a predefined threshold.

- Compare application metrics from different deployment environments. For instance, developers can compare how long it takes to run a particular transaction during development, QA, and production environments.

Akogrimo's Monitoring System

Akogrimo (http://www.akogrimo.org/) was an EU research project partially funded by the EC under the FP6-IST programme aiming at the definition and realization of a Mobile Grid Architecture ensuring the viability of this concept for the different stakeholders in the value chain by developing new business models for this commercial platform (Wesner, Järnert & Aránzazu).

Within the Akogrimo's framework an Execution Management System was developed on the basis of the OGSA and WSRF specifications. This system was therefore responsible for finding execution candidate locations, selecting the most suitable execution location, preparing, initiating and managing/monitoring the execution of services. In order to address these tasks and at the same time ensure continuous conformation to the terms of the SLA contract, EMS works closely together and involves numerous interactions with a Monitoring group of services.

The Akogrimo Monitoring group of services consists of the following three Grid services, developed on the GT4 platform:

- Metering service, which maintains runtime information on the performance parameters related to the business service execution, defined in the SLA. In particular, it measures low level performance parameters such as memory, CPU and disk usage. This low level information is communicated to the Monitoring service through a notification mechanism established between

the two services. The notification mechanism was developed on the basis of the WS-BaseNotification (Graham, Tibco & Murray, 2006), a specification that belongs to the WS-Notification family of specifications (OASIS Web Services Notification TC, 2006) that enables the use of the notification design pattern with Grid Services. In more detail, the Metering service has two main functionalities:

- To notify the Monitoring service about the changes in the following low level parameters related to the execution of a service:
  - CPU usage.
  - Memory usage.
  - Disk usage.
  - Wall clock time (time that elapsed while the business service was running).
- An aggregated version of the information that is calculated by the Metering service is communicated to the accounting $A4C^2$ system and used for accounting purposes at the end of the service execution.

- QoS Broker service, which is a bandwidth broker that can provide three bundles of network services, each one of them corresponding to a specific usage profile: audio, video or data. It handles QoS network requests, keeps records of information related to the client, such as network QoS levels the client is allowed to use according to the SLA contract and is also responsible for monitoring network parameters, such as network bandwidth throughout the execution of a service.

- Monitoring service, which is the link between the Metering group of services and the SLA Enforcement group of services. It receives notifications about the values of the QoS parameters related to the execution of the services from the Metering and

QoS Broker services and notifies the SLA Enforcement group of services. In more detail, the Monitoring component can be seen as a set of four components that provide the following functionalities:

- Remote control concerning enabling/ disabling of the monitoring process.
- Reception of low level parameters from the Akogrimo producer services (Metering service and QoS Broker service).
- Sending of QoS object to the SLA enforcement components.
- Storage of monitoring information about the different SLA/services being monitored.

More information on their functionality and their implementation can be found in (Litke et al., 2005, 2007; Inácio et al., 2005).

GRIA Monitoring System

GRIA (http://www.gria.org/) is a service-oriented infrastructure designed to support B2B collaborations through service provision across organisational boundaries in a secure, interoperable and flexible manner. GRIA uses Web Service protocols based on key interoperability specifications. GRIA is available free and open source (most of the software is LGPL).

The GRIA SLA Management Service was developed in the SIMDAT project (http://www.simdat.org/) to monitor and manage a wide range of services. The main objective of the SIMDAT project was to test and enhance grid technology for product development and production process design as well as to develop federated versions of problem-solving environments by leveraging enhanced Grid services.

The SLA Service in GRIA takes responsibility for pulling usage reports from managed services, evaluating the usage of the services against the SLAs in force and enacting the necessary management actions to maintain the service provider's commitments.

Each managed GRIA service is instrumented to place usage reports on a WS-BaseNotification (Graham, Tibco & Murray, 2006) pull-point which the SLA Service periodically polls. The usage reports are defined in terms of "metrics", loosely defined as "something measurable" such as the number of CPUs, amount of data or number of sessions. Each metric is represented by its own unique URI. These metrics are also used in to define the service's capacity, the quality of service offered in an SLA and the cost of usage.

The use of metrics is reported and recorded in terms of "instantaneous" and "cumulative" measurements. The cumulative usage is the numerical integration of the instantaneous measurements over time. For some metrics, data-transfer for example, the instantaneous measurement is best thought of as a rate (bytes per second) and the cumulative usage (the time integral, which in this case is the amount of data transferred) has no time dimension (bytes). For other metrics, such as CPU, the instantaneous measurement is just the quantity in use at the time (e.g. 3 CPUs) and it is the cumulative usage that has the time dimension, e.g. 180 CPU.seconds.

By using some basic assumptions, the SLA service can convert between the two. For instance, if the rate of data transfer is reported periodically then, with the assumption that the rate of a metric remains constant unless otherwise notified, the SLA service can compute the numerical time integral of this rate to give an approximation of the total data transfer (see Figure 1). Of course, there are easier ways to find the total data transferred, this example just demonstrates the concept of inferring one value of a metric from others.

Another example is CPU time. If a job runs on 1 CPU for 5 minutes then the SLA service will be notified that the instantaneous measurement of CPU usage went to 1 at the start and then to 0 five minutes later. The SLA service can infer that 300 seconds of CPU time have been used (1*5*60

Figure 1. The area under the curve can be approximated by sampling the rate (black dots) and performing numerical integration (the hatched area)

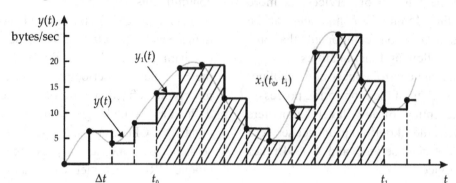

= 300 CPU seconds). Alternatively, if a service reported that it had used 120 units of a resource in a 1 minute period, the SLA service would infer that the average instantaneous measurement (rate of usage) had been 2 units/s.

All metrics have both instantaneous measurements and cumulative usage which may be recorded or inferred from each other. For some metrics one or other concept will not be useful, but the SLA manager has no idea of what it is counting, restricting or billing for in each metric, and so can cope with either type of measurement and can always infer the other from it.

A managed GRIA service can report usage of a metric in two main ways:

1. An instantaneous rate report: specifying the rate of usage of a metric at a particular instant in time. For instance, "the number of CPUs in use at 12:53 was 2.2".
2. A cumulative usage report: specifying the time-integral of a metric between two times. For instance, "the number of CPU seconds used between 10:20 and 10:30 was 1320".

For instance, the standard GRIA job service uses the following metrics:

• http://www.gria.org/sla/metric/activity/current-activities

This is set to one when a job is created and to zero when it is destroyed.

• http://www.gria.org/sla/metric/activity/job

This is set to one when a job is created and to zero when it is destroyed.

• http://www.gria.org/sla/metric/resource/cpu

As a job executes, the number of CPU.seconds used by the process as reported by the host operating system is repeatedly reported as cumulative reports.

The standard GRIA data service uses the following metrics:

• http://www.gria.org/sla/metric/activity/current-activities

This is set to one when a job is created and to zero when it is destroyed.

• http://www.gria.org/sla/metric/activity/data-stager

This is set to one when a data-stager is created and to zero when it is destroyed.

- http://www.gria.org/sla/metric/resource/disc

When data is stored in a data-stager, the disc space usage is recorded by setting this to the file size.

- http://www.gria.org/sla/metric/resource/data-transfer

When data is transferred to or from a data-stager, the transfer is recorded by setting the cumulative usage of this metric to the file size.

The information from these reports is stored in a database at the SLA Service and the individual data points or the inferred points in between can be queried. The data, along with the mathematical model encoded in the service, provide for flexible SLA terms. For instance:

- Constraining the total disc space permitted.
- Pricing disc space usage per GB/month (as Amazon S3).
- Pricing disc usage according to the maximum capacity (as many ISPs do).
- Constraining and pricing total data transfer.
- Monitoring (and potentially constraining) data transfer rate.
- Charging per job at a flat rate and/or according to the CPU time.
- Constraining the CPU time over a period.
- Constraining the maximum number of CPUs permitted at any one time.

All this is achieved without the SLA Service having any specific understanding of the metrics being monitored. When services are adapted to report usage to a GRIA SLA Service the developer chooses metrics appropriate to the service. Usage of these metrics is reported and the same variety of functionality is automatically available.

Cloud Metering and Monitoring in Edutain@Grid

Edutain@Grid (http://www.edutaingrid.eu/) is an EU-funded project which aimed to develop a scalable QoS-enabled business Grid environment for multi-user Real-time Online Interactive Applications (ROIA) (Fahringer, Anthes, Arragon, Lipaj et al., 2007). ROIAs (e.g. on-line games) are characterised by the high rate of interaction between users, requiring very fast updates of information being passed from one computer to another (Ploß, Glinka & Gorlatch, 2009). Large numbers of users may participate in a single session and are typically able to join or leave at any time. Thus an ROIA typically has an extremely dynamic distributed workload, making it difficult to host efficiently. In this project, a service-oriented infrastructure with elastic resource provisioning (both up and down) and enhanced security features was developed to support a business model where multiple independent infrastructure providers provide a level of QoS to ROIA service to customers.

The Edutain business model (Middleton, Surridge, Nasser & Yang. 2009) introduces a concept, namely the "Coordinator", which can be regarded as an organisation that plays the role of ROIA application service provider. However, the Coordinator itself may not have any physical infrastructure for running ROIA, instead it outsources the ROIA hosting services to one or more 'Hosters' (i.e. organisations that provide the infrastructure or platform for running ROIA applications). Each Hoster provides a collection of web services required for running the ROIA, QoS monitoring (QoS targets defined in a SLA) and invoicing facilities. The Coordinator has an account and a bipartite Service Level Agreement with each Hoster and the Hoster provides metered services to the Coordinator. When the hosting service finishes, the Hoster sends the bill to the Coordinator for the resource usage.

The combination of each autonomous Hoster and the Coordinator provides a scalable virtual environment for running the ROIA. The capacity of this virtual environment can dynamically grow or shrink through 'zone migration' and 'zone replication' across multiple Hosters during a live gaming session.

The GRIA middleware was employed in the implementation of the business layer of this system. The standard GRIA SLA Management Service adds together metric QoS measurements from across all activities.

In Edutain, six metrics to be monitored in the SLA were defined, namely,

- ServerTickDuration in milliseconds (a measure of server frame rate),
- AveragePacketLoss as a percentage,
- ServerThroughputIn in bytes per second,
- ServerThroughputOut in bytes per second,
- AveragePacketLatency in milliseconds, and
- ClientConnectionCount.

Associated pricing terms such as variable pricing and penalty costs were also defined for each metric. For some metrics such as ServerTickDuration, a penalty is incurred if its peak value exceeds the constraint defined in the SLA, whereas for other metrics such as ServerThroughputIn and ServerThroughputOut, a fee is calculated depending on the accumulated usage. Once an ROIA is in use, it is monitored and QoS measurement data of these metrics are reported back to the SLA service. The SLA service aggregates the data and generates the QoS measurement report on-demand to the Coordinator's SLA monitoring service. If the work load of a particular Edutain local session is predicted to exceed the threshold defined in SLA, Edutain 'zone migration' can be triggered either manually or automatically by to migrate the zone to an idle Edutain Hoster.

Globus Toolkit Monitoring

The Globus Toolkit (http://www.globus.org/toolkit/) is an open source middleware used for building Grid applications. The toolkit includes software services and libraries for resource monitoring, discovery, and management, security and file management in a Grid environment (Foster, Kesselman & Tuecke. 2001).

The Globus Toolkit provides a Monitoring and Discovery System (MDS) (http://www.globus.org/toolkit/mds/) which is the information services component and provides information about the available resources on the infrastructure and their status. MDS4 is a WSRF implementation of information services released with Globus Toolkit 4.0.

This version of MDS includes WSRF implementations of the Index Service, a Trigger Service, WebMDS (formerly known as the Web Service Data Browser) and the underlying framework, the Aggregator Framework.

The MDS is a suite of web services to monitor and discover resources and services. This system allows users to discover what resources are considered part of a *Virtual Organization (VO* and to monitor those resources. MDS services provide query and subscription interfaces to arbitrarily detailed resource data and a trigger interface that can be configured to take action when pre-configured trouble conditions are met. The services included in the WS MDS implementation (*MDS4*) acquire their information through an extensible interface which can be used to:

- query WSRF services for resource property information,
- execute a program to acquire data, or
- interface with third-party monitoring systems.

Different computing resources and services can advertise a large amount of data for many different use cases. MDS4 was specifically designed to address the needs of a Grid monitoring system – one that publishes data that is available to multiple people at multiple sites. As such, it is not an event handling system, like NetLogger, or a cluster monitor on its own, but can interface to more detailed monitoring systems and archives, and can publish summary data using standard interfaces.

MDS4 includes two WSRF-based services: an *Index Service* (The Globus Alliance, 2005c), which collects data from various sources and provides a query/subscription interface to that data, and a *Trigger Service* (The Globus Alliance, 2005a), which collects data from various sources and can be configured to take action based on that data. An *Archive Service*, which will provide access to historic data, is planned for a future release.

The *Index Service* is a registry similar to UDDI, but much more flexible. Indexes collect information and publish that information as *resource properties*. Clients use the standard WSRF resource property query and subscription/notification interfaces to retrieve information from an Index. Indexes can register to each other in a hierarchical fashion in order to aggregate data at several levels. Indexes are "self-cleaning"; each Index entry has a lifetime and will be removed from the Index if it is not refreshed before it expires.

The *Trigger Service* collects information and compares that data against a set of conditions defined in a configuration file. When a condition is met, or triggered, an action takes place, such as emailing a system administrator when the disk space on a server reaches a threshold.

In addition to the services described above, MDS4 includes several additional software components, including an *Aggregator Framework* (The Globus Alliance, 2005b), which provides a unified mechanism used by the Index and Trigger services to collect and aggregate data.

Currently, MDS4 includes the following sources of information:

- *Hawkeye Information Provider, and Ganglia Information Provider,* which in-

clude information about basic host data (name, ID), processor information, memory size, OS name and version, file system data, processor load data and other basic cluster data.

- *WS GRAM*: The job submission service component of GT4. This WSRF service publishes information about the local scheduler, including: queue information, number of CPUs available and free, job count information and some memory statistics.
- *Reliable File Transfer Service (RFT)*: The file transfer service component of GT4. This WSRF service publishes: status data of the server, transfer status for a file or set of files, number of active transfers and some status information about the resource running the service.
- And any other WSRF service that publishes resource properties.

Finally, MDS provides a web-based interface to WSRF resource property information called *WebMDS* that is available as a user-friendly front-end to the Index Service. WebMDS uses standard resource property requests to query resource property data and displays the results in various formats.

gLite-MON: gLite Monitoring System Collector Server

The gLite Monitoring System is based on R-GMA monitoring system collector server. R-GMA (Relational Grid Monotoring Architecture) (http://www.r-gma.org/) is an information system very similar to a standard relational database.

The R-GMA server is a Java servlet-based web application which provides a service for information, monitoring and logging in a distributed computing environment. R-GMA makes all the information appear like one large relational database that may be queried to find the information

Figure 2. Grid Monitoring Architecture (GMA) (http://www.r-gma.org)

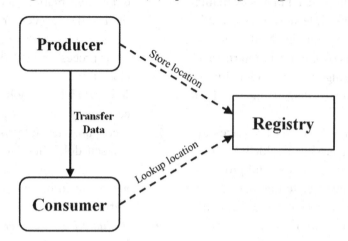

required. It consists of Producers which publish information into R-GMA, and Consumers which subscribe to the information.

In a distributed environment, such as a computing Grid, it is important to be able to find information on what resources are available. This may be information on what computers are available on various sites to run jobs, including their current load and what software they have available. Information may also be needed on mass data storage facilities, including the current status and maximum size and number of files that may be stored. It is also important to be able to monitor the progress of jobs, especially when the user will probably not know where the job is going to be executed when the job is submitted.

The Open Grid Forum (OGF) (http://www.ogf. org/) defined a basic architecture for monitoring within the Grid, called the 'Grid Monitoring Architecture' or 'GMA'. This architecture consists of three components: *Consumers, Producers* and a directory service (called *Registry*).

In the GMA Producers register themselves with the Registry and describe the type and structure of information they want to make available to the Grid. Consumers can query the Registry to find out what type of information is available and locate Producers that provide such information. Once this information is known the Consumer

can contact the Producer directly to obtain the relevant data. The Registry communication is shown by a dotted line and the main flow of data by a solid line. The GMA architecture was devised for monitoring but it also makes an excellent basis for combined information and monitoring system.

The *Relational Grid monitoring Architecture* (R-GMA) is an implementation of GMA, with two special properties:

- Anyone supplying or obtaining information from R-GMA does not need to know about the Registry, the Consumer and Producer handle the registry behind the scenes.
- The Information and monitoring system appears like one large relational database, and can be queried as such. Hence the 'R' GMA, a relational implementation of GMA.

Note that R-GMA provides a way of using the relational model in a Grid environment and that it is not a general distributed RDBMS. All the producers of information are quite independent. It is relational in the sense that Producers announce what they have to publish via an SQL CREATE TABLE statement and publish with an SQL IN-

SERT and that Consumers use an SQL SELECT to collect the information they need.

To interact with R-GMA APIs are available in various languages. Currently APIs are available in Java, C, C++, and Python.

A web browser is available, which allows users to browse the status of a Grid. And a command line tool is also available, which helps a user to understand and test out producers and consumers.

The R-GMA usage up to now has been as a Grid Information, Monitoring and Logging tool. When the user submits the job the Job Manager will need to find a suitable resource to run the job. The information System may be used to find the appropriate resource.

The user will also want to track progress of the job - R-GMA can be used to keep track of job progress. In this case the user submitting a job does not need to know about R-GMA, it is hidden from the user. Besides this, any system where a developer wishes to manage information in a distributed system can use R-GMA.

For a more detailed description of R-GMA see the R-GMA architecture (http://www.r-gma.org/arch-virtual.html).

CONCLUSION

There are currently a great number of tools for monitoring the diverse infrastructure resources and the status and performance of applications running on this infrastructure. This chapter has presented some tools that are particularly relevant for virtualized and distributed environments. The existing diversity on monitoring tools and the metrics used makes difficult the integration of monitoring systems as the infrastructure grows. To solve this problem the use of semantic tools could be a solution to allow a coherent data access providing a common understanding of the different metrics used by the different monitoring systems. It is therefore necessary to agree on a common and standardised ontology for monitoring

systems. In that sense, the IP traffic Measurement for Industrial Ontology Specification Group (ISG MOI) in ETSI is working in the specification of an ontology standard for IP traffic measurements. This work should be extended to cover the other parts of the infrastructure.

REFERENCES

Amazon (2009). *Amazon CloudWatch development guide* (API Version 2009-05-15). Retrieved June 25, 2010, from http://docs.amazonwebservices.com /AmazonCloudWatch/latest/ DeveloperGuide/index.html? arch-AmazonCloudWatch-metricscollected.html

Arthur, S., Emde, C., & McGuire, N. (2007). *Assessment of the real time preemption patches (RT-Preempt) and their impact on the general purpose performance of the system.* 9th Real-Time Linux Workshop, Linz, Austria.

Boniface, M., Nasser, B., Papay, J., Phillips, S. C., Servin, A., & Yang, X. …Kyriazis, D. (2010). Platform-as-a-service architecture for real-time quality of service management in clouds. *Proceedings of the Fifth International Conference on Internet and Web Applications and Services,* (pp. 155–160). Barcelona, Spain.

Buyya, R., Yeo, C. S., & Venugopal, S. (2009). Cloud computing and emerging IT platforms: Vision, hype, and reality for delivering computing as the 5th utility. *Future Generation Computer Systems, 25*(6), 599–616. doi:10.1016/j.future.2008.12.001

Checconi, F., Cucinotta, T., Faggioli, D., & Lipari, G. (2009). Hierarchical multiprocessor CPU reservations for the Linux kernel. In *Proceedings of the 5th International Workshop on Operating Systems Platforms for Embedded Real-Time Applications* (OSPERT 2009), Dublin, Ireland.

Corbet, J. (2006). *The high-resolution timer API.* Retrieved from http://lwn.net/Articles/167897

Cucinotta, T., Anastasi, G., & Abeni, L. (2008). Real-time virtual machines. In *Proceedings of the 29th Real-Time System Symposium* (RTSS 2008) -- Work in Progress Session, Barcelona.

Cucinotta, T., Anastasi, G., & Abeni, L. (2009). Respecting temporal constraints in virtualised services. In *Proceedings of the 2nd IEEE International Workshop on Real-Time Service-Oriented Architecture and Applications* (RTSOAA 2009), Seattle, Washington.

Cucinotta, T., Konstanteli, K., & Varvarigou, T. (2009). Advance reservations for distributed real-time workflows with probabilistic service guarantees. In *Proceedings of the IEEE International Conference on Service-Oriented Computing and Applications* (SOCA 2009).

de Haaff, B. (2008). Cloud computing – The jargon is back! *Computing Journal Electronic Magazine.* Retrieved from http://cloudcomputing.sys-con. com/ node/ 613070

Fahringer, T., Anthes, C., Arragon, A., Lipaj, A., Müller-Iden, J., Rawlings, C., & Prodan, R. (2007). The Edutain@Grid Project. In Veit, D. J., & Altmann, J. (Eds.), *GECON 2007. LNCS (Vol. 4685,* pp. 182–187). Heidelberg, Germany: Springer.

Foster, I., Kesselman, C., & Tuecke, S. (2001). The anatomy of the Grid: Enabling scalable virtual organizations. [from http://www.globus. org/alliance/publications/papers/anatomy.pdf]. *The International Journal of Supercomputer Applications, 15*(3), 200. Retrieved June 25, 2010. doi:10.1177/109434200101500302

Geelan, J. (2008). Twenty-one experts define cloud computing. Electronic magazine. Retrieved from http://cloudcomputing.sys-con.com /node/612375?page=0,1

Google. (2010). *Google app engine. Appstats for Java.* Retrieved June 25, 2010, from http://code. google.com/intl/es-ES /appengine/docs/java/ tools/appstats.html

Google. (2010). *Using Memcache.* Retrieved June 25, 2010, from http://code.google.com/intl/ en/ appengine/ docs/ python/ memcache/ using-memcache.html

Graham, S., Tibco, D., & Murray, B. (2006). *Web services base notification 1.3* (WS-BaseNotification). Retrieved June 25, 2010, from http://docs. oasis-open.org/wsn/ wsn-ws_base_notification-1.3-spec-os.pdf

Hand, E. (2007). Head in the Clouds. *Nature, 449,* 963. doi:10.1038/449963a

Heroix. (2006). *The best practices guide to developing and monitoring SLAs.* Whitepaper.

IEEE. (2008). *Standard for Information Technology – Portable operating system interface* (POSIX). Retrieved from http://www.opengroup. org/ onlinepubs/ 009695399

Inácio, N., et al. (2005). *D4.1.1. Mobile network architecture, design & implementation.* Retrieved June 25, 2010, from http://www.akogrimo.org/ download/ Deliverables / D4.1.1.pdf

ISG. (2010). *The measurement ontology for IP traffic ISG website.* Retrieved from http://portal. etsi.org/portal/ server.pt/ community/ MOI

Kernel. (2010*). CPU accounting controller.* Retrieved from http://www.kernel.org/doc/ Documentation/cgroups/ cpuacct.txt

Kostanteli, K., Kyriazis, D., Varvarigou, T., Cucinotta, T., & Anastasi, G. (2009). Real-time guarantees in flexible advance reservations. In *Proceedings of the 2nd IEEE International Workshop on Real-Time Service-Oriented Architecture and Applications* (RTSOAA 2009), Seattle, Washington.

KVM. (2006). *Kernel-based virtualization driver.* Whitepaper, Qumranet 2006. Retrieved from http://docs.huihoo.com/kvm /kvm-whitepaper.pdf

Litke, A., et al. (2005). *D4.3.1 -Architecture of the infrastructure services layer V1.* Akogrimo Consortium. Retrieved June 25, 2010, from http:// www.akogrimo.org/ modulese73d.pdf?name=Up Download&req=getit&lid=37

Litke, A., et al. (2007). *D4.3.4 -Consolidated report on the implementation of the infrastructure services layer version 1.0.* Akogrimo Consortium. Retrieved June 25, 2010, from http:// www.akogrimo.org/ modulesa3f9.pdf?name= UpDownload&req =getit&lid=121

Machiraju, S. (2006). *Theory and practice of non-intrusive active network measurements.* Doctoral Thesis. UMI Order Number: AAI3228413, University of California at Berkeley.

Manica, N., Abeni, L., & Palopoli, L. (2010). Reservation-based interrupt scheduling. *Proceedings of the 16th IEEE Real-Time and Embedded Technology and Applications Symposium* (RTAS 2010), April 2010, Stockholm, Sweden.

McFedries, P. (2008). The cloud is the computer. *IEEE Spectrum Online.* Retrieved from http:// www.spectrum.ieee.org/ aug08/6490

Menage, P. (n.d.). *CGROUPS, official Linux kernel documentation.* Retrieved from http://git.kernel. org/?p=linux/ kernel/git/torvalds /linux-2.6.git

Middleton, S. E., Surridge, M., Nasser, B. I., & Yang, X. (2009). *Bipartite electronic SLA as a business framework to support cross-organization load management of real-time online applications.* Real Time Online Interactive Applications on the Grid (ROIA 2009), Euro-Par 2009.

OASIS. (2010). *Web services notification (WSN) TC website.* Retrieved June 25, 2010, from http:// www.oasis-open.org/ committees/ tc_home. php?wg_abbrev=wsn

Oberle, K., Kessler, M., Stein, M., Voith, T., Lamp, D., & Berger, S. (2009). *Network virtualization: The missing piece.* 13th International Conference on Intelligence in Next Generation Networks, 2009. ICIN 2009, (pp. 1-6). Retrieved from http://irmosproject.eu/Files/ICIN2009_FinalVersion_Network Virtualization.pdf

Palopoli, L., Cucinotta, T., Marzario, L., & Lipari, G. (2009). AQuoSA - Adaptive quality of service architecture. *Software, Practice & Experience, 39*(1), 1–31. doi:10.1002/spe.883

Paxson, V., Almes, G., Mahdavi, J., & Mathis, M. (1998). *RFC2330 - Framework for IP performance metrics.*

Ploß, A., Glinka, F., & Gorlatch, S. (2009). *A case study on using RTF for developing multi-player online games. Euro-Par 2008 Workshops-Parallel Processing* (pp. 390–400). Springer.

Schubert, L., Jeffery, K., Neidecker-Lutz, B., et al. (2010). *The future of cloud computing-Opportunities for European cloud computing beyond 2010.* Retrieved June 25, 2010, from http://cordis.europa.eu/fp7/ict/ ssai/docs/cloud-report -final.pdf

The Globus Alliance. (2005). *GT 4.0 WS MDS trigger service.* Retrieved June 25, 2010, from http:// www.globus.org/toolkit /docs/4.0/info/trigger/

The Globus Alliance. (2005). *GT 4.0: Information services: Aggregator framework.* Retrieved June 25, 2010, from http://www.globus.org/ toolkit / docs/ 4.0/ info/ aggregator/

The Globus Alliance. (2005). *GT 4.0: Information Services: Index.* Retrieved June 25, 2010, from http://www.globus.org/ toolkit / docs/ 4.0/ info/ index /index.pdf

Tsafrir, D., Etsion, Y., & Feitelson, D. (2007). Secretly monopolizing the CPU without superuser privileges. In *Proceedings of the 16th USENIX Security Symposium,* (Boston, MA).

van Rossum, G. (2010). *Appstats - RPC instrumentation and optimizations for app engine*. Retrieved from http://code.google.com/intl /es-ES/events/ io/2010/ sessions/ appstatsrpc-appengine.html

Vaquero, L. M., Rodero-Merino, L., Caceres, J., & Lindner, M. (2009). A break in the clouds: Towards a cloud definition. *ACM SIGCOMM Computer Communication Review*, *39*(1), 50–55. doi:10.1145/1496091.1496100

Wang, L., et al. (2008). *Scientific cloud computing: Early definition and experience*. 10th IEEE International Conference on High Performance Computing and Communications, (pp. 825–830).

Watson, P., Lord, P., Gibson, F., et al. (2008). Cloud computing for e-science with CARMEN. *Proceedings of IBERGRID Conference*, (pp. 1-5). Porto, Portugal. May 12–14.

Wesner, S., Järnert, J. M., & Aránzazu, M. (n.d.). *Mobile collaborative business Grids – A short overview of the Akogrimo Project*. Retrieved June 25, 2010, from http://www.akogrimo.org/ download /White_Papers_and_Publications / Akogrimo_WhitePaper _Overview.pdf

ENDNOTES

[1]   SPI from SaaS, PaaS and IaaS
[2]   Authentication, Authorization, Accounting, Auditing and Charging

Chapter 7

Workflow Management Systems in Distributed Environments

Spyridon V. Gogouvitis
National Technical University of Athens,
Greece

Kleopatra G. Konstanteli
National Technical University of Athens,
Greece

Dimosthenis P. Kyriazis
National Technical University of Athens,
Greece

Gregory Katsaros
National Technical University of Athens,
Greece

Tommaso Cucinotta
Scuola Superiore Sant'Anna, Italy

Michael Boniface
University of Southampton IT Innovation
Centre, UK

ABSTRACT

With the advent of Service Oriented Architectures, more applications are built in a distributed manner based on loose coupled services. In this context, Workflow Management Systems play an important role as they are the means to both define the processes that realize the application goals as well as implement the orchestration of the different services. The purpose of the chapter is to give an overview of various solutions regarding workflow semantics and languages, as well as their enactment within the scope of distributed systems. To this end, major focus is given to solutions that are aimed at Grid environments. Scheduling algorithms and advance reservation techniques are also discussed as these are among the hottest research topics in Workflow Management Systems.

INTRODUCTION

The recent technological advances in the field of computing and networking have led to the rapid growth of the internet. People around the world started using it as a tool for not only information exchange, but also as a way to perform various tasks, from online shopping to working remotely. Enterprises were forced to keep up with the internet boom in order to increase profits both by cutting costs and fulfilling the drastically increasing demands of the customers. Organizational efficiency and responsiveness are critical factors in determining the profitability of an organization, especially in the today's global business environment, where resources and people tend to be geographically

DOI: 10.4018/978-1-60960-827-9.ch007

dispersed. The same can be said for the eScience community, where profit takes on a different form. For these reasons a process oriented view is used to formalize the business processes that take place within an organization, be it in the business or the science domain. A Business process is defined as (Coalition, Terminology, & Glossary, 1999) "a collection of activities that takes one or more kinds of input and creates an output that is of value to the customer". In essence a business process or workflow defines who needs to do what and in what order in order to achieve a specific goal. With the emergence of distributed environments such as grid and cloud infrastructures, which provide many benefits such as reliability, cost-effectiveness and scalability, workflow management systems have received great attention. Workflow management constitutes to the formalization of a business process and its automatic enactment. This provides many advantages since components that are responsible for executing a specific task can be autonomously developed without the need to incorporate any business logic within them. This task is left to the workflow management system. This also means that components can be reused in different workflows, while workflow can be easily changed in order to provide new functionalities. In this chapter we aim to define the core characteristics of workflow management systems and review some of the solutions proposed within the context of distributed environments.

BACKGROUND

The term 'workflow' is used with various meanings depending on the domain in which the term is used. The Workflow Management Coalition's definition is based on document oriented business processes: "*Workflow is the automation of a business process, in whole or part, during which documents, information or tasks are passed from one participant to another for action, according to a set of procedural rules*" (Coalition, et al., 1999).

In the Grid community, the term workflow is typically used in the context of electronic services that may, or may not, be distributed. For example "*Workflow is a pattern of business process interaction, not necessarily corresponding to a fixed set of business processes. All such interactions may be between services residing within a single data centre or across a range of different platforms and implementations anywhere*" (Treadwell, 2005).

In the eScience community, workflow is often used to refer to the use of workflow techniques to support the scientific process, i.e. for performing the activities that take place as part of scientific endeavour in a structured, repeatable and verifiable way. For example, in bioinformatics the scientific process can involve the use of 'in silico experiments', where local and remote resources to test a hypothesis, derive a summary or search for patterns (R. Stevens et al., 2003).

In the Business Process Management and Web Services domain, the term 'workflow' tends to mean programming and automation of processes that involve software exposed as services. This is applied in a variety of areas, e.g. enterprise application integration, supply chains, and business process automation.

WORKFLOW MANAGEMENT SYSTEMS

Overview

Traditionally, information systems have been implemented without the explicit consideration of a business process. Discreet components within a system need to be operated manually and their results propagated to the next component within the process chain. This has also led to the incorporation of process logic within application programs. While this solution can make a system work, it has many drawbacks. Management of the system becomes difficult and costly, as internal changes to any component may have an effect on others. It also lowers interoperability with other systems, thus hindering integration of new components or processes.

Service Oriented Architecture (SOA) (Erl, 2005) is an architectural style that emphasizes implementation of components as modular services that can be discovered and used by clients. Infrastructures based on the SOA paradigm are called Service Oriented Infrastructures (SOIs). Managing the application workflow operations within a SOI requires the orchestration of the distributed resources (Mayer et al., 2004). In that frame, workflow is an important factor for application composition promoting inter-organizational collaborations by integrating the teams involved in managing of different parts of a workflow. Besides, literature (Spooner, Cao, Jarvis, He, & Nudd, 2005) describes additional advantages of the workflow management such as the utilization of resources to increase throughput or reduce execution costs and the ability to build dynamic applications which orchestrate these resources. Workflow Management Systems enable the separation of the business process from the application program code. The process is defined in a workflow model both in task and structure level.

A Workflow Management System needs to support the full lifecycle of a workflow which can be divided into two main phases: *Modeling* of the workflow, where it is composed using some language and *enactment*, where the various tasks are executed according to the specification. There exists a multitude of languages for describing workflows, and a corresponding set of workflow engines to enact the defined processes. These range from the high level descriptions more geared toward the human understanding of processes, to the technically oriented approaches focused on the actual automation of the processes.

There are two types of workflow definitions, namely Abstract and Concrete (Deelman, Blythe, Gil, & Kesselman, 2004), (Deelman et al., 2004). In an abstract model, the tasks are described in an abstract form without referring to specific

resources for task execution since it provides the ability to the users to define workflows in a flexible way, isolating execution details. In the concrete model, the tasks of the workflow are bound to specific resources and therefore this model provides service semantic and execution information on how the workflow has been composed both for the service instances and for the overall composition (e.g. dataflow bindings, control flow structures). It has to be mentioned that the service instances do not necessarily correspond to resources since within a resource more than one service instances may be available and executable.

A Workflow Management System provides the ability to define, instantiate and enact an application workflow. A Workflow Model / Specification is used to define a workflow, both in task and structure level. An abstract workflow (or workflow template) defines the sets of services to be executed without explicitly mentioning the exact resources needed. In the usually workflow lifecycle, a mapping mechanism is needed which transforms the abstract workflow into an executable one (concrete workflow or workflow instance), that can be used by an enactment engine for the actual execution, as it contains specific resources to be used.

The main aim of a workflow 0management system is to execute a set of tasks according to a predefined order. Apart from this basic requirement there exists a set of requirements that needs to be fulfilled in order to make such a system viable.

Scalability. A WfMS needs to be able to handle multiple concurrent requests for workflow execution without impact on its performance.

Fault handling. Faults are bound to happen both on hardware as well as on software level. The WfMS must firstly be able to acknowledge these and also provide the capability to the application developer to define a set of corrective actions to be taken under certain circumstances.

Declaration of QoS requirements. There are numerous situations where an application user needs to be able to define QoS parameters either for the application workflow as a whole or parts thereof.

Workflow Monitoring. The WfMS must be able to monitor the execution of every running workflow and be able to present the current state to the user.

Security. While security tends to be neglected in such areas as scientific workflows, it is very vital when concerned with business workflows. A WfMS needs to provide the appropriate level of security for all involved parties, having a sound infrastructure for authentication, authorization and secure message exchange between services.

Legacy code support. While most WfMS are targeted towards the SOA paradigm it is also important to be able to execute tasks not developed in a service oriented function. This is feasible by creating service wrappers around legacy code and is important so as to allow for fast integration of legacy application into the SOA universe.

Workflow Semantics and Languages

The most widely used specifications for describing procedural workflows within businesses are XPDL (WfMC, 2005) and ebXML (OASIS, 2006), and the most widely used workflow specification with reference to service oriented architectures is WS-BPEL (OASIS, 2007). Besides the usual orchestration support, WS-BPEL provides mechanisms for specifying business roles and model actual behavior of participants in a business interaction. The W3C is currently working to provide a choreography framework described with WS-CDL (Kavantzas & others, 2005). The focus of BPEL and most business-oriented workflow languages is control flow.

However, extensive research on workflow control patterns has shown that all languages have limitations in terms of what can be easily expressed (Aalst, Hofstede, Kiepuszewski, & Barros, 2003). This insufficient expressivity and lack of rigorous semantics to allow automated checks on correctness and completeness mean that BPEL

and similar Web Service workflow standards have limitations when applied to a distributed environment. The work on workflow patterns led Van der Aalst (Van der Aalst) to provide an up-to-date and extensive comparison of workflow languages and implementations (open source and commercial). Van de Aalst has identified specific patterns grouped into control-flow, data, resource and exception handling.

However, it should be noted that workflow standards is a rapidly moving area and the evaluations by the workflow patterns group may, in some cases, lag behind the latest available specifications. For example, WS-BPEL 2.0 was released in summer 2007 and allows processes to be defined along with compensation and exception handlers. Support is already available in Open Source tools, such as the (ActiveBPEL).

Whilst the post-hoc evaluation of existing workflow languages against workflow patterns with well defined semantics allows useful comparison of standards or implementations, it does not address the problem of inherent lack of rigorous machine-interpretable semantics within each workflow language.

The semantic web service community, on the other hand, is producing rigorous models and logics for the semantic description of Web Services from the ground up. Several European projects inc. (SEKT), (DIP), (SUPER) and (ASG) are working together through the European Semantic Systems Initiative (ESSI) and have collaborated to develop the Web Service Modeling Ontology (WSMO) and Web Service Modeling Language (WSML), which has now been submitted for standardization through the W3C. Meanwhile work done by academia and industry through (SWSI) has resulted in the Semantic Web Service Framework (SWSF), which has both a language (SWSL), also submitted to the W3C for standardisation, and an ontology (SWSO) that include a process model. Indeed their complexity and lack of tool support is a barrier to take-up and is a factor that has to be considered when implementing a distributed environment.

At the other end of the spectrum, the practical application workflow technology, in research projects with applications in the engineering and scientific sectors have seen a proliferation of home-grown solutions. These applications are often data and computation intensive and often make use of grid infrastructure and grid workflow technologies. A typical example is the orchestration of compute resources to execute a large scale numerical simulation, e.g. for multi-scale modelling of biological systems (Lloyd et al., 2007). Some solutions are focused on providing support to scientific applications, e.g. Taverna (Oinn et al., 2006), Pegasus (Deelman, Blythe, Gil, Kesselman, et al., 2004) and Kepler (Bowers, Ludascher, Ngu, & Critchlow, 2006), while others are addressing more architectural issues like KWF-Grid (Neubauer, Hoheisel, & Geiler, 2006), Triana (Taylor, Shields, Wang, & Harrison, 2007) and Askalon (Fahringer et al., 2007), or the workflow components in Unicore (Sild, Maran, Romberg, Schuller, & Benfenati, 2005) and (Globus) The approach taken by these projects is often bespoke, including tailoring workflow solutions to specific domains e.g. processing of bioinformatics data, supporting specific requirements not addressed by existing standards e.g. service-to-service transfer of large datasets, or simply to use 'do it yourself' solutions because widely adopted workflow standards tend to lag behind the cutting edge functionality needed in these applications. For example, scientific processes in eScience can often involve user interaction with experiments during the data production, use and archiving lifecycle (Coles et al., 2006).

Whilst many of these projects have developed their own workflow languages and enactment engines rather than adopt existing standards, some have built upon existing formalisms and therefore provide good targets for extension or reuse. For example, Triana is based on Petri-Nets, Akogrimo uses BPEL and the semantic workflow language (OWL-WS) developed in NextGrid is an extension to OWL-S (Beco, Cantalupo, Giammarino, Matskanis, & Surridge, 2005). However, although some use of standards exists, the use of workflow in advanced Grid architectures, e.g. NextGrid and Akogrimo, has yet to see the emergence of a common approach. The consequent waste of effort in reinventing the wheel, the lack of interoperability, and the confusion in the community regarding the best way forward is a recognised problem (Beco, Cantalupo, & Terracina, 2006).

Workflow Scheduling

Workflow scheduling is considered to be a form of global task scheduling as it focuses on deciding where to execute a task and managing the execution of tasks that are inter-depended on shared resources. The resources may be heterogeneous both in terms of local configuration and as well as in terms of policies. The scheduling process should take into account users' QoS constraints in order to satisfy user requirements. Workflow scheduling taxonomy is divided into the following categories:

- *Scheduling architecture*: Workflow scheduling architectures can be divided into three major categories: centralized, hierarchical and decentralized. When a workflow enactment service has a centralized architecture, all scheduling decisions for all tasks in the workflow are taken by one central scheduler. Even though the resulted schedules might be efficient, there are concerns regarding scalability issues. In contrast to centralized scheduling, both hierarchical and decentralized scheduling shares the work among multiple schedulers. In comparison with centralized scheduling, hierarchical and decentralized schedulers are more scalable but this distributed pattern of work may lead to performance degradation for the overall workflow execution.

- *Decision making*: This is the task of mapping workflows onto resources and services. One option is that decision making can be focused on the information of a single task or of a section of the workflow, referred to as local decision making. Alternatively it can take into account information about the entire workflow, referred to as global decision.

- *Planning scheme*: This is the task of translating abstract workflows, i.e. a workflow described in an abstract manner without any reference to specific resources concrete workflows. Workflow planning schemes can be distinguished between static (where the dynamically changing state of the resources is not taken into account) and dynamic (where, in contrast to static, both dynamic and static information about resources is used to make scheduling decisions at run-time).

- *Scheduling strategy*: Workflow scheduling in a distributed system is an NP-complete problem (Fernandez-Baca, 1989). To this end, many heuristics have been developed for near-optimal solutions so as to match users' QoS constraints. Most of the current existing approaches are performance-driven, in the sense that they are focused on minimizing overall execution time. Unlike performance-driven scheduling strategies, market-driven schedulers take into consideration other parameters apart from performance, such as the cost. Trust-driven schedulers base their strategies on levels of trust that depend on security policy, accumulated reputation and attack history etc.

- *Performance estimation*: Performance estimation is one of the most critical tasks associated with workflow scheduling and workflow enactment engines in general. Workflow schedulers use performance estimation techniques to predict the performance of the tasks in a workflow applied on distributed heterogeneous resources, in order to decide on how and where the actual execution will take place. Performance estimation approaches include: simulation, analytical modeling, historical data, online learning, and hybrid.

Fault Tolerance

In a highly dynamic and heterogeneous SOI geographically and organizationally dispersed, heterogeneous resources are incorporated such as computing systems and software, storage systems, instruments, scientific equipment, specialized hardware, communication systems, data sources as well as human collaborators. In such a heterogeneous environment changes are numerous, highly variable and with unpredictable effects. These changes can lead to failure for various reasons: non-availability of required services or software components, overloaded resource conditions, memory shortage, and network fabric failures. For these reasons, workflow management in SOIs should be able to detect and manage failures in order to ensure reliable support of the execution environment.

Workflow failure handling techniques can be divided into two different levels: task-level and workflow-level (Soonwook & Kesselman, 2003). Whereas task-level techniques are concerned with masking the effects the service failures and their impact on the entire workflow, workflow-level techniques are focused on the manipulation of the workflow structure in order to deal with erroneous conditions.

Task-level techniques can be divided into the following categories:

- *Retry*: After failure, the same task is executed again on the same resource.
- *Alternate resource*: After failure, the same task is submitted and executed on a different resource.

- *Checkpoint/Restart*: After failure, task is moved to other resources and maintains its state, so that it can continue its execution from the point of failure.
- *Replication*: The task is executed simultaneously on different resources.

Workflow-level techniques include:

- *Alternate task*: After failure, another implementation of the same task is executed.
- *Redundancy*: Multiple alternative tasks are executed simultaneously on different resources.
- *User-defined exception handling*: Users are responsible for specifying corrective actions for a certain types of failure.
- *Rescue workflow*: This technique ignores failures and continues to execute the rest of the tasks in the workflow, if possible. Afterwards, information that includes statistics about the failures is generated for internal processing by the system and the client.

Advance Reservation

Lack of end-to-end QoS guarantees, especially when working with workflow service-oriented applications, is considered to be one of the most critical impediments to further penetration of SOIs into the industry world since it discourages both Service Providers (SPs) as well as potential clients from making more extended use of the facilities offered by a SOI. Advance reservation of resources is widely considered as a mechanism to address the aforementioned problem and offer to the users the specific QoS guarantees they want (Schwiegelshohn, Yahyapour, & Wieder, 2006). In essence, advance reservation allows the user to request resources from systems for a specific time interval, i.e. start time and end time, and obtain a sufficient number of resources during this time

interval to support the execution of the specific job for which the resources were reserved.

Deterministic Advance Reservation

Deterministic advance reservation consists of mathematical methods for reserving resources. It is based on deterministic algorithms for analyzing performance constraints by applying mathematical processes to the various layers and assumptions associated with each candidate node. In general this technique reduces the risk of missing deadlines and failures and increases the overall reliability of the system since they can be run on real-time environments efficiently. However, such methods do have limitations. Existing deterministic scheduling algorithms assume that the parameters for flexibility are static (Farooq, Majumdar, & Parsons, 2005) are mostly focused on minimizing the response time and do not promote resource sharing while in other cases all requests for execution that overlap with previous ones are rejected. Studies on the performance of these mechanisms (Netto, Bubendorfer, & Buyya, 2007) have demonstrated good results in terms of satisfying the given performance constraints. However, it is also shown that they lead in fragmentation of the resources and lower utilization.

Probabilistic Advance Reservation

The basic motivation behind probabilistic advance reservation is the fact that in many cases the input parameters and the run-time conditions are so many, that it is inefficient and sometimes even impossible to analytically examine the entire solution space. Probabilistic methods generally employ the principles behind decision theory and are influenced by prior probabilities that are derived from analytical methods coupled with benchmarking. These prior probabilities are used to determine the posterior probability of an advance reservation decision. These algorithms demonstrate better results in terms of resource utilization and lead to lower costs for the resources, but in general appear to be less reliable than deterministic methods in terms of the resulting performance granted to the running applications.

APPROACHES, IMPLEMENTATIONS AND COMPARISONS

A very interesting and well documented survey is found in (Yu & Buyya, 2005), indicating the characteristics of some of the major players in workflow management systems worldwide. One of the most interesting among them is GrADS (Berman et al., 2001). It is based on the Globus Toolkit, one of the most prevalent Grid middleware, and it aims specifically at applications with large computational and communication load. It supports a Directed Acyclic Graph (DAG) approach for workflows which means that dependencies between tasks are analyzed and their parallelization can be performed for enhanced scheduling purposes. It also supports QoS constraints through estimating the application execution time. This estimation is performed through analytical modelling and historical data. Furthermore it is based on a centralized architecture with both global and local decision making policies, a prediction based planning scheme and a task level rescheduling for fault tolerance purposes.

Another worth to mention implementation is that of Askalon project (Fahringer, et al., 2007), where attention is given to performance oriented applications and is based on the Globus Toolkit too. Performance estimation is also attempted within this project and a positive feature is the decentralized architecture but with a global decision making mechanism.

The GridBus Toolkit (Buyya & Venugopal, 2004) has been developed by the University of Melbourne and is based on market principles. It follows a hierarchical approach and allows the enactment of services that can be found through a grid registry. It supports the definition of QoS constraints, as the user is able to define total cost and task of overall workflow deadline, but not more complex conditions. Gridbus also offers monitoring of resources through the Gridscape plugin, but not for the status of a running workflow. As for fault tolerance the platform provides only the option for alternate resource.

Taverna (Oinn, et al., 2006) is the workflow management system of the myGrid (R. D. Stevens, Robinson, & Goble, 2003) project aimed to supporting data-intensive experiments in molecular biology. The system follows a centralized architecture which poses questions on the scalability of the system. Its scheduling strategy is performance-driven and not combined with estimation of performance. Taverna supports web services as well as programs coded as java classes, but does not provide any QoS guarantees. The system does provide monitoring of running workflows and a friendly environment for the users to manipulate them. As far as fault tolerance is concerned Taverna allows for the definition of either a retry operation or an alternate location of the same service.

In ICENI (S. McGough, Young, Afzal, Newhouse, & Darlington, 2004), another GT oriented implementation with a computationally intensive scope, the estimation is less efficient than the previous ones but it has a more market driven approach, with a global decision making policy, centralized architectural scheme and a varying scheduling strategy. In all of the above cases a very positive feature is that the workflow composition system can be extended by the user.

Pegasus (Deelman, Blythe, Gil, Kesselman, et al., 2004) is the workflow manager of GriPhyN (Deelman, Blythe, Gil, & Kesselman, 2004) and aims to map abstract workflows to grid resources. The abstract workflow is modeled as a Directed Acyclic Graph (DAG) containing logical files and application components and before being mapped to the actual resources an optimization step takes place. Pegasus is based on a centralized architecture and does not support QoS specifications or monitoring during the execution of a workflow. For fault tolerance Pegasus provides a remapping of an entire subworkflow to new resources.

UNICORE (Forum, 2003) is an approach which is becoming quite popular lately, mainly due to its extremely robust nature. It is mostly based on internal components rather than already circulating solutions for Grid integration and it comes with a number of disadvantages such as concrete workflow models. In a concrete model the user specifies which part of the workflow must be executed in a specific resource. This feature not only limits scheduling performance, as in the case when many users want to access a single resource while others are idle, but also is quite risky in dynamic environments where resources come and go unexpectedly. Nevertheless, one popular characteristic of UNICORE is that many of its mechanisms such as decision making, planning policy and strategy are designed in order to be extensible by the user. The workflow is modeled as a directed acyclic graph with temporal dependencies, even thought advanced flow control constructs, such as *if-then-else* and *repeat until* statements, are supported.

Karajan is part of the Java Commodity Grid (CoG) Kit (Laszewski, Hategan, & Kodeboyina, 2007) which aims to allow Grid users, Grid application developers, and Grid administrators to easily use, program, and administer grids from a high-level framework. The workflow engine, apart from the actual service enacted, interfaces with a visualization component, responsible for providing a representation of the workflow structure as well as monitoring of the execution and a checkpointing subsystem, which provides fault-tolerance to the system. The workflow can be defined in an XML format that provides primitives for generic sequential and parallel execution, sequential and parallel iterations, conditional execution and functional abstraction.

The Kepler workflow system (Ludascher et al., 2006) is an open source application that extends the work of the Ptolemy II (Eker et al., 2003) system to support scientific applications using a dataflow approach. It's main characteristic is that it is based on processing steps, called "actors", which have well defined input and output ports. Users are able to define workflows by selecting appropriate actors and connecting them within a visual user interface. A "director" component holds the overall execution and component interaction semantics of a workflow. The Kepler system provides a various fault-tolerant mechanisms, most important of which is the ability to define actors that are responsible for catching exceptions.

Relevant work in workflow management systems includes (Ming, Xian-He, & Yong, 2006). The authors of the specific paper investigate the effect of resource reservation on external applications as well as on local jobs, and introduce the design of efficient task scheduling algorithms considering the tolerance of local jobs to resource reservation. A new performance metric is proposed, the relative slowdown, to quantify the performance impact of resource reservation. The local job process is modeled with an M/G/1 queuing system and the effect of system parameters on relative slowdown is analyzed. They investigate both first-come-first-serve (FCFS) and round-robin (RR) queuing disciplines. Efficient algorithms are designed and implemented considering local jobs' tolerance to reservation. A user-level soft real-time CPU scheduler, DSRT, is updated to enable resource reservation in a general computing platform. They also define a new metric, the relative slowdown of local jobs on a resource for a given reservation which is the ratio of the average waiting time with reservation and the average waiting time without reservation. DSRT is the implementation of the CPU server of QualMan middleware. A major component of DSRT is the resource scheduler, named the dispatcher. A priority scheduling mechanism is applied to differentiate the processing of real-time (RT) processes and time-sharing (TS) processes. The dispatcher runs at the highest fixed-priority. The approach of the slowdown of running processes as a result of external tasks can be useful in studying the effects of new tasks assigned to resources in comparison with the time constraints.

Paper (Lilan, Tao, Zhanbei, & Minglun, 2004) presents the concept of Manufacturing Grid (MG) as the application of Grid technology. It follows the Open Grid Service Architecture (OGSA) as the system framework, and Globus Toolkit 3.0 (GT3) as the developing toolkit. A QoS-based Global Process Planning (GPP) and scheduling schema (Manufacturing Grid Resource Scheduling, MGRS) is presented and the corresponding module is implemented with the functions of GPP analyzing, resource discovery, AHP (Analytic Hierarchy Process)-based resource selection and fault-tolerant handling (re-scheduling). The goal of the schema is to be the supplement of the application Grid in manufacturing with better QoS performance, such as higher user satisfaction, product quality and service, as well as the lower failure rate, time-to-market, cost, etc. Its main features are:

- *GPP Analyzing*: Refers to analyzing the submitted task, and decomposing the complicated target task into a few serial or parallel simple, basic manufacturing subtasks, according to its QoS properties
- *Resource Selection*: Once the list of possible resources is known, MGRS will select a resource that is expected to meet the requirements mostly. In order to fulfil the restrictions, it has to gather dynamic information about resource accessibility, machining precision, machining capability, and resource status, etc
- *Fault-tolerant Handling*: This is also called re-scheduling. Manufacturing Grid is inherently a dynamic system where environmental conditions are subjected to unpredictable changes as: resource or network failures, system performance degradation, variations in the cost of resources, etc. Fault-tolerant handling is the efficient

way to guarantee that the submitted tasks are completed and that the user's requirements are met.

AHP is particularly useful for evaluating complex multi-attribute alternatives involving subjective criteria. The essential steps in the application of AHP are the following:

- Decomposing in a hierarchical manner, a general decision problem into sub-problems that can be easily comprehended and evaluated,
- Determining the priorities of the elements at each level of the decision hierarchy, and
- Synthesizing the priorities to determine the overall priorities of the decision alternatives.

The most limiting feature is the use of UDDI registry for resource discovery. As already mentioned previously, UDDI is generally static and lacks monitoring abilities. Moreover GT3 is considered obsolete, as the current working edition is version 4.

The workflow management service within the GRIDCC project (A. McGough et al., 2007) is tasked with optimizing the workflows and ensuring that they meet the pre-defined QoS requirements specified upon them. The project aims at utilizing instruments through Grid infrastructures, which means that there are serious real-time issues to be met. It also focuses on Web Services and SOA and implements a partner language to use with BPEL4WS. Instead of defining a new language for workflows with QoS requirements, or embedding QoS requirements within a language such as BPEL4WS, GRIDCC uses a standard BPEL4WS document along with a second document which points to elements within the BPEL4WS document and annotates this with QoS requirements. This allows to take advantage of standard BPEL4WS tooling for execution and manipulation as well as to provide QoS requirements. XPath notation to reference elements is used within the BPEL4WS document; therefore, this approach can be easily adapted to other (workflow) languages based on XML. The end-to-end workflow pipeline takes a user's design and implements it within the Grid, through reservation services and performance repository. Workflows are defined through a web based editor which allows the augmentation of QoS requirements by defining the user's expectations for the execution. The WfMS (Workflow Management Service) provides a mechanism for building QoS on top of an existing commodity, based on BPEL4WS engine, thus allowing the provision of a level of QoS through resource selection from a priori information together with the use of advanced reservation.

In the Phosphorus project (Deliverable D.5.2.), a number of scheduling algorithms are proposed in the context of fairness of resource assignment between users and their tasks. An interesting scheme is the fact that Phosphorus takes into consideration the time for completion and the deadline, in order to meet QoS requirements. Phosphorus also deals task workloads, which are either known or not known a priori, and advance reservation. The MetaScheduling Service (MSS) developed by the specific project can tackle complicated workflows allowing the end-user to execute the individual components of his application using the most appropriate resources available. MSS is able to orchestrate resources of different sites belonging to different administrative domains, while it is also responsible for the negotiation of agreements on resource usage with the individual local resource management systems. The main dependency of this implementation is the use of the UNICORE middleware.

In (Brandic, Benkner, Engelbrecht, & Schmidt, 2005) a QoS-aware Grid Workflow Language (QoWL), subset of Business Process Execution Language (BPEL) with QoS extensions and QoS-aware Grid Workflow Engine (QWE) is presented. Users may specify different QoS constraints addressing the overall workflow or individual workflow tasks. QWE comprises of a workflow planning component, which performs QoS negotiation and service selection, and a workflow execution component which executes the workflow by invoking the selected services. Based on the specified QoS constraints, the QWE negotiates with multiple candidate Grid services to select appropriate services which satisfy the specified QoS constraints. Performance prediction for QoS-aware VGE services is based on application-specific performance models which depend on metadata about the input data (e.g. matrix size) supplied by the client during QoS negotiation. VGE services rely on a generic QoS module which usually comprises of an application-specific performance model, a pricing model, a compute resource manager that supports advance reservation and a QoS manager. VGE relies on standard Web Services technologies such as WSDL, SOAP, WS-Security, Tomcat and Axis. VGE services enclose native HPC applications, usually parallel MPI (Message Passing Interface) (MPI) codes running on a cluster, and expose their functionality via a set of common operations for job execution, job monitoring, data staging and error recovery. One limiting factor is the dependency upon application nature.

Workflow has a major role in grid dynamics and is adopted as the core technology for applying grid dynamics in NextGRID. It provides the ability to compose and dynamically adapt grid services available in distributed systems and orchestrate their execution. The workflow components, the services and their environment compose an infrastructure that is described in NextGRID as the concept of Grid Virtual Infrastructure Model or Grid VIM. This infrastructure is designed to allow Grid applications and Grid business models and processes to be combined at run-time. The VIM is designed to provide a run-time adaptable infrastructure, in particular:

• Run-time bindings: workflows need not specify a binding of every task to a specific service, so that the bindings can be chosen at run-time.

- Selective enactment: a single service may provide multiple functions, and it must be possible to choose which is bound to an abstract task, supported by the service.
- Workflow substitution: some abstract tasks may be bound at run-time to more detailed workflows that can be inserted into the enactment at run-time. A common example is substitutions with template business operations such as account and billing workflows.
- Workflow prioritisation. Critical processes, which are either expensive in resources or define the result or the performance of the workflow, must have high priority in the evaluation order.

A key feature of the NextGrid approach is the abstraction of business processes in order for application developers to not have to encode business processes explicitly in their applications. This allows applications to remain functional even if a service provider wants to use a different business model or process (e.g. pay-as-you-go instead of subscription-based access to services). The result is NextGrid's workflow enactment model known as the Grid Virtual Infrastructure Model (Grid VIM) with a corresponding workflow enactment engine. This provides a way to dynamically assemble concrete application workflows using an abstract application workflow specification as a starting point, and introducing business processes at run-time as specified by the service providers and consumers involved in executing the application.

Advance Reservation Implementations

Askalon is a Grid development environment with main objective to simplify the development and optimization of Grid workflow applications. It conducts a performance estimation based both on historical data obtained from a training phase as well as analytical modeling. Furthermore, it uses a variety of predefined as well as user-defined QoS parameters for the discovery process. The approach presented in (Wieczorek, Siddiqui, Villazon, Prodan, & Fahringer, 2006) proposes an extension of Askalon's scheduling service to support advance reservation. The introduced approach performs resource mapping based on a fair-sharing principle that limits the number of resources offered to a single user at a time. Scheduling is based on a list-scheduling heuristic known as the Heterogeneous Earliest-Finish-Time (HEFT) (Topcuoglu, Hariri, & Min-You, 2002) algorithm which is proven to perform well with a low time complexity.

In contrast to most workflow enactment engines, ICENI (S. McGough, et al., 2004) is able to support advanced reservation in some cases. In particular, when it is determined that a resource will be required for a certain interval of time, a reservation is made through a WS-Agreement (*Grid Resource Allocation Agreement Protocol [December 2004]*) procedure. In order to determine the execution start time of each component in the workflow, a repository with historical information about their performance on different resources is used. This information is used during the reservation phase in order to get a prediction of the start time of each component in the workflow. If an agreement to reserve a resource is reached then the components to be deployed to that resource are placed into a queue until the resource reservation time is met. However, this work does not attempt to explore the entire problem space to find the optimal concrete workflow, as this is an NP-hard problem (McMahon & Florian, 1975). Instead, heuristics are used to approximate the optimal solution and a number of existing scheduling algorithms such as random and best-of-n-random have been made workflow aware so that they take the whole workflow into account when scheduling each component. Furthermore, the start time of the workflow executions is strictly defined and the system is responsible for starting the execution of the workflow during the interval of the reservation.

Relevant work includes (Claris, George, & Khaled, 2007) where the authors introduced an implementation of the best-fit scheduling algorithm with deadline constraints for minimizing resource fragmentation so as to employ advance reservation while maximizing utilization. The algorithm reuses concepts of computational geometry to deal effectively with resource fragmentation and deadline requirements, under a generic design that can be adopted to accommodate both network and computing resources. Specifically, it determines whether it is feasible to schedule the job so as to meet its deadline. If so, then it uses a set of criteria to select one of the (possibly multiple) servers who can handle this job, updates its schedule, and returns to the user a reference to this server. Otherwise, the job is dropped. However, the start time of the job is strictly defined and the client can run the job only once per reservation. Furthermore, the scheduling schema presented in this work focuses on trying to minimize the response time instead of maximizing utilization of the resource. Finally, the selection depends on the existence of idle periods between already reserved time periods on each server.

Similarly, the solution offered by the SSS algorithm (Farooq, et al., 2005)consists of periods of continuous utilization of the resource called blocks with idle periods separating the blocks. Scheduled-time of a certain task is the time at which it is scheduled to start its execution under the current schedule of the resource. Given the new request and the current resource schedule, the SSS algorithm accommodates the new request in the resource schedule if it is feasible to do so. The algorithm first identifies all those tasks in the resource schedule that can affect the feasibility of the new schedule with the new request and then tries to work out a feasible schedule for only that subset of tasks. Once this subset of tasks is known, an initial solution can be worked out for that subset and the new request, using any of the

well-known strategies such as the earliest-deadline first and the least-laxity-first. However, as in (Claris, et al., 2007) this work does not promote resource sharing and it also considers strict start times of execution.

Netto, Bubendorfer and Buyya in (Netto, et al., 2007) investigate the performance of scheduling with advance reservations. For this purpose they developed a QoS scheduler that uses SLAs to efficiently schedule advance reservations for computation services based on their flexibility. They also introduce the concept of adaptive time QoS parameters, in which the flexibility of these parameters is not static but adaptive according to the user needs and resource provider policies. However, as in (Claris, et al., 2007) and (Farooq, et al., 2005) the scheduling of a job consists on finding a free time-slot that meets the job requirements assuming that the start time of the job is known in advance. Thus, all incoming requests for advance reservation that overlap with any of the previously committed reservations are rejected.

Singh, Kesselman and Deelman in (Singh, Kesselman, & Deelman, 2006) propose a resource provisioning model that describes the resource availability in the form of slots with each slot representing the number of processors available for a certain timeframe at a certain cost. On this basis, they formulate a resource provisioning plan that reserves time slots on resources to optimize a parameterized metric, which combines the economic cost of the resource allocation and the expected application runtime. This resource provisioning planning is combined with two heuristic algorithms, the Min-Min and a genetic algorithm in conjunction with a list-scheduling algorithm. The solution is then tested against workflow-based applications. However, this work deals with optimization as seen from the user's perspective and ignores the utilization of the given resources, which is something that the resource owners are mostly interested in. In addition, this approach does not consider the deadlines that the tasks in the workflow may have.

Zhao and Sakellariou in (Zhao & Sakellariou, 2007) present an advance reservation model for DAG (Directed Acyclic Graph)-based workflows, taking into account the latest possible time that the execution of the whole workflow needs to be completed as specified by the user. Two different approaches are proposed in an attempt to make advance reservations for each task in the DAG by distributing the spare time among the tasks that comprise it. However, this work considers strict start times of execution for the DAGs and ignores resource sharing and maximum utilization.

CONCLUSION

With the advent of service oriented architectures (SOA), applications have started to move away from the monolithic approach towards a paradigm that emphasizes modular design. In such distributed systems workflows play an important role, as there needs to be a high-level component that can orchestrate the different services that make up an application. Most distributed WfMS today are targeted towards a Grid environment and thus have various advantages and disadvantages tied to the Grid ecosystem. In order for the WfMSs to move towards the Cloud paradigm new workflow approaches need to be used that allow dynamic workflow composition and evolution as well as dynamic service discovery and selection during workflow enactment, taking into consideration several QoS parameters. Moreover special attention needs to be paid to the scheduling capabilities a WfMS has to offer. To this end the use of advance reservation mechanisms needs to be researched further. The effectiveness of current advance reservation mechanisms is limited and in many cases not applicable to workflows, mainly due to concerns regarding the dynamic nature of the SOIs and the inability to adjust to the ever-changing resource availability and user demand without obvious consequences on the performance. Furthermore, most of the existing work on advance reservation assumes a precise start time when the workflow starts running, specified either by the user or the advance reservation system itself. Based on this start time, the start times of each task in the workflow are estimated using the end time of the preceding task. The existing studies on relaxed start time advance reservations, namely in cases where the start time of execution is not precise, either assume that the parameters for flexibility are static, or reallocate existing advance reservations at reservation time. At runtime, as the actual deadline approaches, the priority of the job with the flexible start time is increased to ensure that the execution completes prior to its deadline. To overcome these challenges, the mechanisms that perform the task of advance reservation in service-oriented environments should take into account future potential changes in the offered QoS level of a service and provide additional metrics and mechanisms for estimating the QoS level. In addition, such advance reservation mechanisms need to reflect more the real needs of the users by becoming more flexible and relieving the user of strict constrains, such as the start time of the execution and the number of allowed executions per reservation.

REFERENCES

Aalst, W. M. P. V. D., Hofstede, A. H. M. T., Kiepuszewski, B., & Barros, A. P. (2003). Workflow patterns. *Distributed and Parallel Databases, 14*(1), 5-51. doi: http://dx.doi.org/10.1023/A:1022883727209

ActiveBPEL. (2010). Retrieved from http://www.activevos.com/ community-open-source.php

ASG. (201). Retrieved from http://asg-platform.org/cgi-bin /twiki/view/Public

Beco, S., Cantalupo, B., Giammarino, L., Matskanis, N., & Surridge, M. (2005). *OWL-WS: A workflow ontology for dynamic Grid service composition* (pp. 148–155). IEEE Computer Society.

Beco, S., Cantalupo, B., & Terracina, A. (2006). *The role of workflow in next generation business oriented Grids: Two different approaches leading to a unified vision.* Paper presented at the Second IEEE International Conference on e-Science and Grid Computing (e-Science'06).

Berman, F., Chien, A., Cooper, K., Dongarra, J., Foster, I., Gannon, D., et al. (2001). The GrADS project: Software support for high-level Grid application development. *International Journal of High Performance Computer Applications, 15*(4), 327-344. doi: http://dx.doi.org/10.1177/109434200101500401

Bowers, S., Ludascher, B., Ngu, A. H. H., & Critchlow, T. (2006). *Enabling scientific workflow reuse through structured composition of dataflow and control-flow.* Paper presented at the 22nd International Conference on Data Engineering Workshops.

Brandic, I., Benkner, S., Engelbrecht, G., & Schmidt, R. (2005). *QoS support for time-critical Grid workflow applications.* Paper presented at the First International Conference on e-Science and Grid Computing.

Buyya, R., & Venugopal, S. (2004). *The Gridbus toolkit for service oriented grid and utility computing: An overview and status report.* Paper presented at the 1st IEEE International Workshop on Grid Economics and Business Models, 2004. GECON 2004.

Claris, C., George, N. R., & Khaled, H. (2007). *Efficient implementation of best-fit scheduling for advance reservations and QoS in Grid.* Paper presented at the 1st IEEE/IFIP Intl. Workshop on End-to-end Virtualization and Grid Management (EVGM).

Coles, S. J., Frey, J. G., Hursthouse, M. B., Light, M. E., Milsted, A. J., & Carr, L. A. (2006). An e-science environment for service crystallography - From submission to dissemination. *Journal of Chemical Information and Modeling, 46*(3), 1006–1016. doi:10.1021/ci050362w

Deelman, E., Blythe, J., Gil, Y., & Kesselman, C. (2004). *Workflow management in GriPhyN- Grid resource management: State of the art and future trends* (pp. 99–116). Kluwer Academic Publishers.

Deelman, E., Blythe, J., Gil, Y., Kesselman, C., Mehta, G., & Patil, S. (2004). Pegasus: Mapping scientific workflows onto the Grid. In Dikaiakos, M. D. (Ed.), *Grid computing* (*Vol. 3165*, pp. 131–140). Berlin / Heidelberg, Germany: Springer. doi:10.1007/978-3-540-28642-4_2

DIP. (2010). *QoS-aware resource scheduling DIP.* (Deliverable D.5.2., P. P). Retrieved from http://dip.semanticweb.org/

Eker, J., Janneck, J. W., Lee, E. A., Jie, L., Xiaojun, L., & Ludvig, J. (2003). Taming heterogeneity - The Ptolemy approach. *Proceedings of the IEEE, 91*(1), 127–144. doi:10.1109/JPROC.2002.805829

Erl, T. (2005). *Service-oriented architecture: Concepts, technology, and design.* Upper Saddle River, NJ: Prentice Hall.

ESSI. (2010). Retrieved from http://www.essi-cluster.org

Fahringer, T., Prodan, R., Duan, R., Hofer, J., Nadeem, F., & Nerieri, F. (2007). ASKALON: A development and Grid computing environment for scientific workflows. In Taylor, I. J., Deelman, E., Gannon, D. B., & Shields, M. (Eds.), *Workflows for e-science* (pp. 450–471). London, UK: Springer. doi:10.1007/978-1-84628-757-2_27

Farooq, U., Majumdar, S., & Parsons, E. W. (2005). *Efficiently scheduling advance reservations in Grids*. Ottawa, Canada: Dept. of Systems and Computer Engineering, Carleton University.

Fernandez-Baca, D. (1989). Allocating modules to processors in a distributed system. *IEEE Transactions in Software Engineering, 15*(11), 1427-1436. doi: http://dx.doi.org/10.1109/ 32.41334

Globus. (2010). *Globus Project*. Retrieved from http://www.globus.org

Kavantzas, N., et al. (2005). *Web services choreography description language*. W3C candidate recommendation: 9.

Laszewski, G., Hategan, M., & Kodeboyina, D. (2007). Java CoG kit workflow. In Taylor, I. J., Deelman, E., Gannon, D. B., & Shields, M. (Eds.), *Workflows for e-science* (pp. 340–356). London, UK: Springer. doi:10.1007/978-1-84628-757-2_21

Lilan, L., Tao, Y., Zhanbei, S., & Minglun, F. (2004). *A QoS-based global process planning and scheduling approach for manufacturing Grid*. Paper presented at the In Flexible Automation and Intelligent Manufacturing (FAIM 2004), Toronto, Canada.

Lloyd, S., Gavaghan, D., Simpson, A., Mascord, M., Seneurine, C., Williams, G., et al. (2007). Integrative biology - The challenges of developing a collaborative research environment for heart and cancer modelling. *Future Generations Computer Systems, 23*(3), 457-465. doi: http://dx.doi.org/10.1016/ j.future.2006.07.002

Ludascher, B., Altintas, I., Berkley, C., Higgins, D., Jaeger, E., Jones, M., et al. (2006). Scientific workflow management and the Kepler system: Research articles. *Concurrency and Computation: Practice and Experience, 18*(10), 1039-1065. doi: http://dx.doi.org/10.1002 /cpe.v18:10

Mayer, A., Mcgough, S., Furmento, N., Lee, W., Gulamali, M., Newhouse, S., et al. (2004). *Workflow expression: Comparison of spatial and temporal approaches*. Paper presented at the Workflow in Grid Systems Workshop, Berlin.

McGough, A., Akram, A., Guo, L., Krznaric, M., Dickens, L., Colling, D., et al. (2007). *GRIDCC: Real-time workflow system*. Paper presented at the 2nd Workshop on Workflows in support of large-scale science, Monterey, California, USA.

McGough, S., Young, L., Afzal, A., Newhouse, S., & Darlington, J. (2004, September). *Workflow enactment in ICENI*. Paper presented at the UK e-Science All Hands Meeting, Nottingham, UK.

McMahon, G., & Florian, M. (1975). On scheduling with ready times and due dates to minimize maximum lateness. *Operations Research, 23*(3), 475–482. doi:10.1287/opre.23.3.475

Ming, W., Xian-He, S., & Yong, C. (2006). *QoS oriented resource reservation in shared environments*. Paper presented at the Sixth IEEE International Symposium on Cluster Computing and the Grid, 2006. CCGRID 06.

MPI. (2010). Retrieved from http://www.mpi-forum.org/docs

Netto, M. A., Bubendorfer, K., & Buyya, R. (2007). *SLA-based advance reservations with flexible and adaptive time QoS parameters*. Paper presented at the 5th International Conference on Service-Oriented Computing, Vienna, Austria.

Neubauer, F., Hoheisel, A., & Geiler, J. (2006). Workflow-based Grid applications. *Future Generations Computer Systems, 22*(1-2), 6-15. doi: http://dx.doi.org/10.1016/ j.future.2005.08.002

OASIS. (2006). *OASIS standard v2.0.4- ebXML business process specification schema technical specification* v2.0.4.

OASIS. (2007). *Web services business process execution language*, version 2.0.

Oinn, T., Greenwood, M., Addis, M., Alpdemir, M. N., Ferris, J., Glover, K., et al. (2006). Taverna: Lessons in creating a workflow environment for the life sciences: Research articles. *Concurrency and Computing: Practice and Experience, 18*(10), 1067-1100. doi: http://dx.doi.org/10.1002/cpe. v18:10

Schwiegelshohn, U., Yahyapour, R., & Wieder, P. (2006). Resource management for future generation Grids. In Getov, V., Laforenza, D., & Reinefeld, A. (Eds.), *Future generation Grids* (pp. 99–112). Springer, US. doi:10.1007/978-0-387-29445-2_6

SEKT. (2010). Retrieved from http://www.sekt-project.com/

Sild, S., Maran, U., Romberg, M., Schuller, B., & Benfenati, E. (2005). OpenMolGRID: Using automated workflows in GRID computing environment. In Sloot, P. M. A., Hoekstra, A. G., Priol, T., Reinefeld, A., & Bubak, M. (Eds.), *Advances in Grid computing - EGC 2005* (*Vol. 3470*, pp. 464–473). Berlin/Heidelberg, Germany: Springer. doi:10.1007/11508380_48

Singh, G., Kesselman, C., & Deelman, E. (2006). *Application-level resource provisioning on the Grid.* Paper presented at the Second IEEE International Conference on e-Science and Grid Computing.

Soonwook, H., & Kesselman, C. (2003). Grid workflow: A flexible failure handling framework for the grid. *Proceedings of the 12th IEEE International Symposium on the High Performance Distributed Computing,* 2003.

Spooner, D. P., Cao, J., Jarvis, S. A., He, L., & Nudd, G. R. (2005). Performance-aware workflow management for Grid computing. *Comput. J., 48*(3), 347-357. doi: http://dx.doi.org/10.1093/comjnl/bxh090

Stevens, R., Glover, K., Greenhalgh, C., Jennings, C., Pearce, S., Li, P., et al. (2003). Performing in silico experiments on the Grid: A users perspective. *Proceedings of UK e-Science All Hands Meeting,* 2003.

Stevens, R. D., Robinson, A. J., & Goble, C. A. (2003). MyGrid: Personalized bioinformatics on the information Grid. *Bioinformatics (Oxford, England),* 19.

SUPER. (2010). Retrieved from http://www. ip-super.org/

SWSF. (2010). Retrieved from http://www.w3.org/ Submission /SWSF

SWSI. (2010). Retrieved from http://www.swsi.org

SWSL. (2010). Retrieved from http://www.w3.org/ Submission /SWSF-SWSL

SWSO. (2010). Retrieved from http://www.daml. org/services/ swsf/1.0/swso

Taylor, I., Shields, M., Wang, I., & Harrison, A. (2007). The Triana workflow environment: Architecture and applications. In Taylor, I. J., Deelman, E., Gannon, D. B., & Shields, M. (Eds.), *Workflows for e-science* (pp. 320–339). London, UK: Springer. doi:10.1007/978-1-84628-757-2_20

The Open Grid Forum. (2004). *Grid resource allocation agreement protocol.*

Topcuoglu, H., Hariri, S., & Min-You, W. (2002). Performance-effective and low-complexity task scheduling for heterogeneous computing. *IEEE Transactions on Parallel and Distributed Systems, 13*(3), 260–274. doi:10.1109/71.993206

Treadwell, J. (2005). *Open Grid services architecture glossary of terms.* (Global Grid Forum OGSA-WG. GFD-I, 044).

Unicore Forum. (2003). *Unicore plus final report: Uniform interface to computing resource.* Retrieved December, 2004, from http://www.unicore. eu/ documentation/files/ erwin-2003-UPF.pdf

Van der Aalst, W. (2010). *Workflow patterns*. Retrieved from http://www.workflowpatterns.com

WFMC. (1999). *Terminology and glossary- English*. (Document Number WFMC-TC-1011).

WFMC. (2005). *XML process definition language*. XPDL.

Wieczorek, M., Siddiqui, M., Villazon, A., Prodan, R., & Fahringer, T. (2006). *Applying advance reservation to increase predictability of workflow execution on the Grid*. Paper presented at the Second IEEE International Conference on e-Science and Grid Computing.

WSML. (2010). Retrieved from http://www.wsmo.org/wsml

WSMO. (2010). Retrieved from http://www.wsmo.org

Yu, J., & Buyya, R. (2005). A taxonomy of workflow management systems for Grid computing. *Journal of Grid Computing, 3*(3-4), 171–200. doi:10.1007/s10723-005-9010-8

Zhao, H., & Sakellariou, R. (2007). *Advance reservation policies for workflows*. Paper presented at the 12th International Conference on Job Scheduling Strategies for Parallel Processing, Saint-Malo, France.

Chapter 8
Service Level Agreements for Real-Time Service-Oriented Infrastructures

Roland Kübert
University of Stuttgart, Germany

Georgina Gallizo
University of Stuttgart, Germany

Theodoros Polychniatis
National Technical University of Athens, Greece

Theodora Varvarigou
National Technical University of Athens, Greece

Eduardo Oliveros
Telefónica Investigación y Desarollo, Spain

Stephen C. Phillips
University of Southampton IT Innovation Centre, UK

Karsten Oberle
Alcatel Lucent Bell Labs, Germany

ABSTRACT

Service Level Agreements (SLAs) are nowadays used as a cornerstone for building service-oriented architectures. SLAs have been closely investigated in the scope of distributed and Grid computing and are now gaining uptake in cloud computing as well. However, most solutions have been developed for specific purposes and are not applicable generally, even though the most approaches propose a general usability. Only rarely have SLAs been applied to real-time systems. The purpose of this chapter is to analyze different fields where SLAs are used, examine the proposed solutions, and investigate how these can be improved in order to better support the creation of real-time service-oriented architectures.

DOI: 10.4018/978-1-60960-827-9.ch008

Figure 1. OASIS SOA reference model for service description

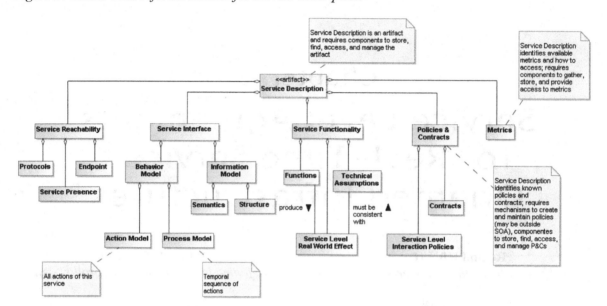

INTRODUCTION

In the context of service oriented architectures, a service is a mechanism to enable access to one or more capabilities, where the access is provided using a prescribed interface and is exercised consistent with constraints and policies as specified by the service description (OASIS).

An SLA is an agreement between the provider of the service and the consumer of the service that specifies the function performed by the service, the obligations on both the provider and consumer of the service, the agreed bounds of performance (Quality of Service, QoS) for the service, and how deviations are handled (exceptions and compensation). In this sense, an SLA is a contract between the participants in the service, which is typically the provider and the consumer of the service, but can also include mediators or other actors that are stakeholders in the service.

SLAs form part of wider frameworks used to describe, access, use and govern services (policies and contracts) for example as shown in Figure 1.

An SLA is made in some business context, which may include decisions made by each party

leading up to the agreement, the presence of an endorser for the agreement and simply some prior conditions that make the terms of the agreement acceptable to both sides. An SLA is typically established before deploying a service and covers the whole lifecycle including execution and monitoring through to decommissioning. However, it is also possible to form an SLA with an existing service, e.g. through a federation process orchestrated by an existing consumer that produces new interactions with other consumers. SLAs therefore have a huge influence on all aspects of the service, from as early as design time, to the infrastructure the service is deployed and executed on and the monitoring components that will be required for the provider to offer a service successfully in a cloud computing environment. While many aspects of context following the creation of an SLA can be shared or agreed (e.g. roots of trust, expected QoS, etc), some should not (e.g. no commercial service provider is likely to reveal their resource plan to a consumer).

On a more practical level, some examples of the use of SLAs in real systems are given. Within the academic Grid community SLAs, e.g.

as described in (Buyya, Abramson, & Venugopal, 2005),(Czajkowski, Foster, & Kesselman, 2005),(Yeo & Buyya, 2005), tend to focus on resources (e.g. computers, network bandwidth, storage devices) rather than services. This is appropriate for a community of experienced users running often experimental codes. However, in order to address the needs of business users (as opposed to technical users) the value of the service must be articulated at the appropriate business level rather than the resource level. The customer should not be concerned with the resources required to provide the service but just that the service exists and provides a clear business benefit. It is also important to consider SLA information when composing services to provide an integrated business solution. The NextGRID project (Snelling et al., 2008) proposes the use of bipartite (two-party) SLAs to describe both the functional and non-functional aspects of a service to allow consumers to make informed choices. NextGRID SLAs have a strong linkage to business impact for both the customer and provider so that the customer can assign and manage costs transparently within their business and the service provider can retain the flexibility in operations to strive to reduce the cost of delivery and ultimately the price paid by the customer (McKee, Taylor, Surridge, Lowe, & Ragusa, 2007). The notion of a well defined and bidirectional 'business level' SLA is an underlying concept in the NextGRID architecture for service oriented infrastructures, and the project takes the view that an SLA needs to be between two parties, modeling real business interactions. This is in contrast to the traditional Virtual Organization (VO) approach, where VO members contribute resources to a centrally managed "club" in order to get some benefit for themselves. NextGRID asserts that a future Grid is in many ways similar to the ways people and organizations interact in real business. Here the contract for service is based on setting expectations on both sides of the agreement (the customer and the provider) and the obligations on each side. The

use of bipartite business agreements encapsulated in SLAs provides a flexible foundation from which a wide range of value chains and business models can be constructed, which includes the traditional 'big VO' approach as well as conventional outsourcing and supply chain models.

Naturally, the three different concepts – resource-focused, service-focused and business-focused SLAs - shortly addressed above have different advantages and disadvantages. Resource-focused SLAs describe low-level, technical details and suitable for experienced users which have detailed knowledge about necessary technical requirements. Special code might be best executed on a special CPU architecture, a requirement that is not generally posed. Service-focused SLAs are situated on a higher layer and describe requirement on services themselves, disregarding low-level technical details. This seems to be a more generally viable approach, although it might not be able to cater to specific resource-level requirements. Business-focused SLAs are situated on an even higher layer, being more still more abstract than service-focused SLAs. The great advantage of this approach is that it can be modeled to comply with the "real world", for example with contractual law, and can model business relationships well. All three concepts have features that might be applicable in certain situations. In others, a mixture of these concepts might be needed.

This was a short overview of different concepts of SLAs as they are used in existing systems today. The following chapter provides a general overview of existing work on SLA's and how SLAs can be used to build service-oriented infrastructures today. Chapter 4 will give some outlook on future areas of work on SLA's especially in the context of usage for provisioning of interactive real-time services on service oriented infrastructures.

ANALYSIS OF EXISTING WORK ON SLAs

SLAs are a complex topic and have been used for various task, be they off-line or online. In order to perform a thorough analysis of the existing work that has been performed on SLAs and to structure the analysis, we identified the following topics:

- Languages and schemas
- SLA Negotiation
- Mapping of QoS parameters
- SLA management and enforcement

These four topics divide the complex field of SLAs into individual parts which we believe to capture all relevant topics. Languages and schemas are the foremost and most obvious topic as the question of "how does an SLA look like" is essential to its usage. Even though often mentioned and proposed in the same breath, SLA Negotiation is a complex field in itself and independent of individual languages and schemas, therefore we discuss negotiation approaches independently of schemas. From the general specification of SLAs follows the question of how to map parameters specified in an SLA to the infrastructure. Last but not least, After the establishment of an SLA, which is covered by the three points mentioned before, we have to investigate how SLAs can be managed and, of even more importance, how they can be enforced.

Languages and Schemas

Different proposals on how to specify SLAs electronically exist and have, mostly, different foci. This section analyzes various approaches on the specification of SLAs.

WS-Agreement

The Web Services Agreement Specification of the Open Grid Forum (OGF) describes a protocol for establishing an agreement on the usage of Services between the provider and the consumer of a service (known as initiator and responder, respectively). It defines a language and a protocol to represent the services of providers, create agreements based on offers and monitor agreement compliance during runtime. An agreement defines a dynamically established and dynamically managed relationship between two parties. The objective of such a relationship is the provision and delivery of a service by one of the parties. In the agreement each party agrees on the respective roles, rights and obligations. Thus in an agreement a provider offers a service according to conditions described within it, while a consumer enters into that agreement with the intention to obtain guarantees on the availability of one or more services offered by the provider. Agreements can also be negotiated by entities acting on behalf the provider and/or the consumer. The structure of a WS-Agreement consists of the following elements:

- **Context:** contains the participants and other information such as the termination time of the agreement.
- **Service Description:** contains domain-specific service descriptions and necessary information to interact with the service instance.
- **Guarantee Terms:** includes the condition collection under which a service will be executed, often referred to as Service Level Objectives (SLO).
- **Negotiability Constraints:** may describe rules for the negotiation phase

An agreement creation process usually consists of the following steps:

- The initiator retrieves a template from the responder, which advertises the types of offers the responder is willing to accept.
- The initiator then makes an offer, which is either accepted or rejected by the responder.

Furthermore, WS-Agreement Negotiation, which sits on top of WS-Agreement, describes the re/negotiation of agreements. The WS-Agreement Specification allows the usage of any domain specific or standard condition expression language to define SLOs. The specification of domain-specific term languages is explicitly left open (Akogrimo Deliverable D2.2.1, 2005; Jan Seidel, Oliver Wäldrich, Philipp Wieder, & Ramin Yahyapour and Wolfgang Ziegler; Web Service Agreement., 2004).

Web Service Level Agreement (WSLA)

WSLA is a framework developed by IBM for the specification and monitoring of Service Level Agreements (SLA) for Web Services (IBM Coorporation; IBM Corporation; Jan Seidel et al.). The framework is able to measure and monitor the QoS parameters of a Web Service and to report violations to the parties specified in the SLA. In a Web Service environment, services are usually subscribed dynamically and on demand. In this environment automatic SLA monitoring and enforcement helps to fulfill the requirements of both the service providers and the consumers. WSLA provides a formal language, based on XML Schema, to express SLAs and a runtime-architecture able to interpret this language. The runtime architecture comprises several SLA monitoring services, which may be outsourced to third parties (supporting parties) to ensure a maximum of objectivity. The WSLA language allows service customers and providers to define SLAs and their parameters and specify how they are measured. The WSLA monitoring services are automatically configured to enforce an SLA upon receipt. The SLA management life-cycle of WSLA consists of five distinct stages:

- *Negotiation/Establishment*: In this stage an agreement between the provider and the consumer of a service is arranged and signed. An SLA document is generated.

- *SLA Deployment*: The SLA document of the previous stage is validated and distributed to the involved components and parties.
- *Measurement and Reporting*: In this stage the SLA parameters are computed by retrieving resource metrics from the managed resources and the measured SLA parameters are compared against the guarantees defined in the SLA.
- *Corrective Management Actions*: If an SLO has been violated, corrective actions are carried out. These actions can be to open a trouble ticket or automatically communicate with the management system to solve potential performance problems. Before all actions regarding the managed system the Business Entity of the service provider is consulted to verify if the proposed actions are allowable.
- *SLA Termination*: The parties of an SLA can negotiate the termination the same way the establishment is done. Alternatively, an expiration date can be specified in the SLA.

SLAng (SLA Notification Generation)

SLAs capture the mutual responsibilities of the provider of a service and of its client with respect to non-functional properties. The SLAng language (Akogrimo Deliverable D2.2.1, 2005; Lamanna, Skene, J., Emmerich, & W., 2003) provides a format for the description of QoS properties, the means to capture these properties unambiguously for inclusion in SLAs and a language appropriate as input for automated reasoning systems or QoS-aware adaptive middleware.

SLAng introduces a reference model for inter-organisational service provision at storage, network, middleware, and application level for distributed component architecture. Figure 2 shows the depicted model.

This traditional layered architecture points out that service provisioning could occur at any

Figure 2. SLAng Service Provision Reference Model

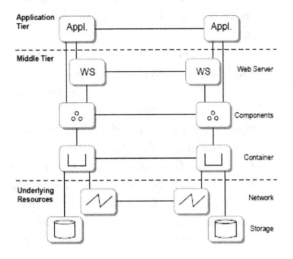

level of the architecture and different parties could provide or consume services. SLAng defines six different types of SLAs: three vertical and three horizontal. These types regulate the type of agreement occurring between the different types of parties of this architecture.

The vertical ones are:

- *Hosting*: between a service provider and a host.
- *Persistence*: between a host and a storage service provider.
- *Communication*: between a container and a network service provider.

The horizontal ones are:

- *Service*: between an Application or service and ASP.
- *Container*: between containers providers.
- *Networking*: between network providers.

This cross-layered architecture considers all the cases of interactions between the actors taking a share in an e-business model.

CGSL (Class of Grid Service Language)

CGSL (Yazhe Tang, Yubin Yang, Ming Zhao, Lei Yao, & Ya Li, 2007) is a language used to describe Class of Service (CoS). It has three main characteristics:

- It is XML-based.
- It is compatible with WSDL and is an augment of WSDL.
- It is optional for Grid services.

Service providers can decide whether there are QoS guarantees in their services. The main concepts of CGSL include: Class of Service (CoS), Constraint, Constraint Group (CG), CGSL Parameter and Management Information.

A CGSL file includes none or more CoSs. A CoS consists of at least one constraint, and it can have CGs and CoS management information (ServiceCoSObjective). A constraint is an expression of several CGSL parameters. Several constraints or CGs can make up a new CG, which will enhance the reusability of constraint. The ServiceCoSObjective and ServiceConstraintObjective (constraint management information) is included in the Management Information. The described functionality is illustrated in the figure that follows (Figure 3).

NextGRID SLA Primitives and SLA Schema

In NextGRID, bipartite SLAs support a set of federation primitives (e.g. encapsulation [Figure 4], sharing [Figure 6] and orchestration [Figure 5]) that can then be used to build more complex models, including VOs if necessary [Figure 7]. The key thing is to start with SLAs and a processes for dynamic composition (dynamic integration of application and business processes) to allow arbitrary business networks including VOs to be used as necessary rather than to prejudge the

Figure 3. Definition of CGSL

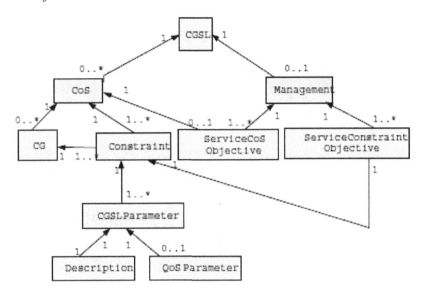

Figure 4. Resource Encapsulation Pattern (Hubert Herenger, Rene Heek, Roland Kuebert, & Mike Surridge, 2007)

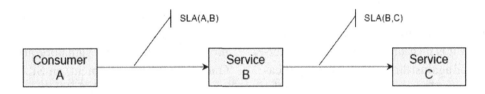

Figure 5. Resource Orchestration Pattern (Hubert Herenger et al., 2007)

Figure 6. Resource Sharing Pattern (Hubert Herenger et al., 2007)

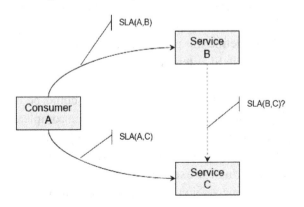
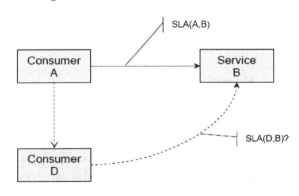

Figure 7. Use of federation primitives to build the Virtual Organisation (VO) model (Hubert Herenger et al., 2007)

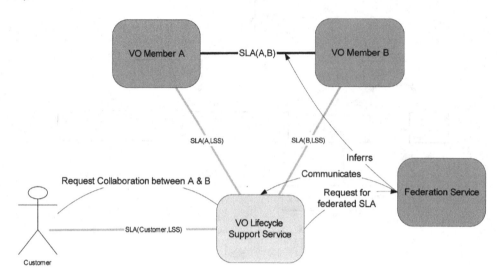

business model and impose a single approach from the outset.

The project has focused on SLA, and produced an XML schema for SLAs (Nextgrid).

NextGRID SLAs concentrate on the obligations on both sides of an agreement, and describes QoS and how it is measured. This has been internally validated against different partners' application experiments. The project has investigated the issues surrounding Grid business, and has taken a number of exemplar business models that illustrate important issues regarding the operation of a Grid for business, which have been analyzed using the questionnaire described above. The aim of this was to draw out the important points of the business models and test them for viability against the criteria laid out by the questionnaire.

SLA Negotiation Protocols

SLA Negotiation describes the different steps leading client and provider to agree an SLA. The process begins with the client specifying the desired performance conditions and it involves Service Discovery mechanisms and different matching policies as well as methods for selecting

and discarding the Service Provider (SP) offerings and re-negotiation. The key point is the existence of quotes, allowing all parties to negotiate by changing the offer provided by the other side. The client and provider have a common expression language through the use of templates, and the provider has the ultimate signature on the contract. Once there is an agreement, an SLA contract is established, containing information on the agreed QoS level and price.

In more detail, the SLA Negotiation is the process that allows a Client:

- to find a Service Provider able to provide the service with the required quality and acceptable price and
- to define the penalties in case of violation of the SLA terms.

The way the client selects an SP could be a simple process, with low flexibility, or a complex process involving internal business policies during the selection phase and re-negotiation methods (even during the execution of the service).

The next sections present different SLA messages and negotiation protocol specifications.

SNAP (Service Negotiation and Allocation Protocol)

SNAP (Akogrimo Deliverable D2.2.1, 2005; K. Czajkowski, I. Foster, C. Kesselman, V. Sander, & S. Tuecke, 2002) describes the requirements and procedures of a protocol for negotiating SLAs within Grid middleware. In particular it focuses on the multiphase nature of this negotiation process, initiated with service requests from the user and the discovery of appropriate providers, followed by negotiation and reservation, reaching up to configuration, monitoring, or re-negotiation. SNAP provides a model for the implementation of these steps.

SNAP addressed the fundamental problem of competing interests of service consumer and service provider within the service negotiation process. On one hand the service consumer is interested in a maximum level of understanding and insight. On the other hand the resource provider aims at retaining a maximum level of autonomy and control over the resources in his administrative domain. Even if the provider has not undisclosed all information about his resources, the user (or alternatively an automated system at Grid middleware, like a Grid broker service) has to be able to determine if a resource is appropriate for a given job and what performance and service characteristics can be anticipated. The most important disadvantage of SNAP is that it does not support renegotiation, and it is thus difficult to use this approach in fault tolerance situations.

WS-Agreement

The Web Services Agreement Specification (WS-Agreement), which has already been presented in the Languages and schemas section, also defines a simple protocol for establishing agreement between two parties, i.e. between a Service Provider and Consumer, as well as the process of obtaining agreement templates to facilitate discovery of compatible agreement parties (Global Grid Forum).

The goal of WS-Agreement is to standardize the terminology, concepts, overall agreement structure with types of agreement terms, agreement template with creation constraints and a set of port types and operations for creation, expiration and monitoring of agreements, including WSDL needed to express the message exchanges and resources needed to express the state.

In meeting these goals, the specification must address the following specific requirements:

- *Must allow the use of any service term:* It must be possible to create agreements for services defined by any domain specific service terms, such as job specification, data service specification, network topology specification and web service description language (WSDL). Service objective description will reference the elements defined in service description.

- *Must allow creation of agreements for existing and new services:* It must be possible to create agreements for predefined services and resources modelling service state. Additionally, service description can be passed as agreement terms for coordinated creation of agreements and new service specific resources.

- *Must allow the use of any condition specification language:* It must be possible to use any domain specific or other standard condition expression language in the definition of service level objectives and negotiability constraints.

- *Must enable symmetry of protocol:* A large number of scenarios are possible depending on whether a service provider or a consumer initiates the creation of an agreement, as well as on where the agreement state is maintained. The basic messages defined in this document can be applied for modelling various usage specific scenarios.

- *Must be "composable" with various negotiation models:* It must be compatible with different negotiation protocols.
- *Must be standalone:* simple agreement creation must be supported in the WS-Agreement specification, independent of any negotiation model.
- *Must allow independent use of different parts of the specification:* The specification of agreement structure can be used without any concern about whether or not this is created using message exchange defined via protocol or template as a starting point.

WSLA

The Web Service Level Agreement (WSLA)'s schema has been presented above; it mainly addresses service level management issues and challenges in a Web Services environment related to monitoring (IBM Coorporation). The project aims to address the following issues:

- Unambiguous and clear specification of SLAs (IBM Coorporation) that can be monitored by the service provider, customer or even by a third-party.
- Ease of SLAs creation via template-based authoring or possible automated negotiation, and an XML schema (IBM) to represent WSLAs, and
- A distributed monitoring framework that can be deployed in a single site or across multiple sites. It translates an SLA into configuration information for the individual service provider components and third party services to perform the measurement and supervision activities.

WSLAs are agreements between a service provider and a customer and as such they define the obligations of the parties involved. Primarily, it is the obligation of a service provider to perform a service according to agreed-upon guarantees for IT-level service parameters (such as availability, response time and throughput) for Web Services (IBM Coorporation).

An SLA also specifies the measures to be taken in case of deviation and failure of the provider to meet the asserted service guarantees. In that case, for example, a notification is sent to the customer. The assertions of the service provider are based on a detailed definition of service parameters including the algorithms–how basic metrics should be measured in systems and how they are aggregated into composite metrics and SLA parameters. In addition, a WSLA can express the operations of monitoring and managing the service. This may include third parties (such as Management Service Providers) that contribute to the measurement of metrics, supervision of guarantees or even the management of deviations of service guarantees. These multi-party constellations necessitate the definition of the interactions among the parties supervising the WSLA.

However, a WSLA only covers the agreed common view of a service between the parties involved. To actually participate in a WSLA, parties have various degrees of freedom to define an implementation policy for a service and its supervision. Typically, the obligations of a WSLA must be translated into system-level configuration information, which can be proprietary to each party involved.

Akogrimo

Akogrimo (Akogrimo Project) (Access to Knowledge through the Grid in a mobile World) is a European FP6 project that ended in September 2007. The aim of the project was to define a Grid architecture which would provide heterogeneity, privacy, security, mobility and QoS to the service providers and to the end users.

The SLA representation in Akogrimo is a mixture of the WS-Agreement and WSLA Specifications so as to take advantage of the two technologies and result in a flexible language that specifies metrics, penalties, SLA parameters and a way of measuring them. The *Negotiation* process follows the WS-Agreement specification and it can be summarised in the following steps(Akogrimo Deliverable D4.3.3, 2007):

- The negotiation service processes the low level parameters of the SLA and communicates with the discovery service.
- The discovery service queries the EMS index service (EMS-Execution Management System) finding order to find resources compliant with the client's requirements. A mobile registry is used instead of the index service in case of mobile devices.
- The negotiation service receives a list of candidate services
- The negotiation service checks the network availability of each service by contacting with the QoS Broker. The first service from the list that meets the network requirements is selected; otherwise the service is removed from the list.
- All the information related to the negotiation request and the discovered resources is stored to a Negotiation Resource (NR) and the EPR of this NR is returned to the EMS.

From the above it is evident that according to the WS-Agreement, the client either accepts or rejects the proposed SLA, without negotiating the SLA parameters. However the advantage of the above described process is that the network bandwidth is checked for every candidate service. The Negotiation Service is part of the EMS which is implemented with a leveraged version of Globus Toolkit-4 WS-GRAM and MDS4 using Java WS Core.

Quality of Service and SLAs

In order to provide an SLA offer to the client, the resources that will be used during the execution of the requested job need to be identified. This identification process is based on the estimation of the usage of resources and in principle consists of the following three steps:

- The first step is the estimation of the resources required by a job. The resources might comprise CPU cycles, available RAM, storage capacity and possibly licensing fees in the case of commercial applications. This is the basic step that needs to be accomplished for the next steps to follow.
- The second step is the investigation of the scheduling that should take place, as part of the selection process. During the negotiation of the SLA, there can be a number of offers from the SP side concerning the task completion time. These offers must be tested first against their realism to assure that they will not cause any SLA violations and the consequent penalties. This leads to an attempt to schedule all the pending tasks along with their time constraints and the estimated required.
- The final step is the pricing of the service according to the SP's business model, the required costs, the time constraints posed and the definition of the market policy that is going to be applied.

For the estimation of execution time, many methodologies have been proposed in bibliography. These methodologies focus mainly on the use of historical or empirical data from previous executions stored in databases. These data allow the deduction of conclusions about the statistical performance estimation, as long as there is a basic statistical correlation between the results. Analytical modeling is used in other cases that are based on "*a set of equations describing the performance of a computer system. In practical terms, it describes a collection of measured and calculated behaviors of different elements over a finite period of time within the computer system – workloads, hardware, software, and the CPU itself, and can even include the actions and behaviors of its users and support personnel*" (Zhengting He, Cheng Peng, & Aloysius Mok, 2006).

Other methodologies include source code examination to estimate the complexity of the service under investigation, while others incorporate data flow graph modeling for estimating the performance. Test executions can also be applied, especially in the case of parallel applications to estimate the effect that allocating multiple processors has on the execution of a parallel job. Estimation of WCET (Worst Case Execution Time) may be also applicable in cases of hard real-time constraints, with the disadvantage being the reduction of utilization due to the fact that the WCET occurs scarcely in reality and the resources are over-provisioned for the entire reserved period.

Approaches, Implementations and Comparisons

(Zhengting He et al., 2006) presents an approach to performance modeling of applications on digital signal processors (DSPs) by modeling an application through a conditional data-flow graph (CDFG) and the underlying hardware through a configurable hardware graph (HWG). The CDFG models tasks in the application and their dependencies and can be parametrized by the user in order to allow for more flexible performance estimation. A simulator takes CDFG and HWG as input parameters, maps the CDFG to the HWG and carries out a low-level simulation in order to determine estimate system performance and identify performance bottlenecks. The drawback of this approach is that the necessary modeling of application and hardware for elaborate systems beyond simple DSPs is very complex and, moreover, application-specific.

In (Siegfried Benkner & Gerhard Engelbrecht, 2006), a generic QoS infrastructure based with application-level support based on Web Services

is presented. QoS parameters can be arbitrary, but the approach is demonstrated by focusing on response time and pricing. If an application can support a client request for a specific QoS request is determined by a specific model – for example a performance model for response time and a pricing model for pricing. These models take as input request descriptors, which specify a clients requirements, and other models or information from the system-side, for example machine descriptors which describe the system hardware. The outputs are descriptors that describe which service level can be offered by the system. For applications where the provision of an analytical performance model is not feasible, a database is involved, relating typical problem parameters to resource needs in terms of main memory, disk space and execution time. This database is initially populated with data from representative test cases, and is able to expand dynamically to include historical data. Thus, although a mapping process is supported, it does not offer a generic solution and it does not scale well.

In (Yuan Chen, Subu Iyer, Xue Liu, Dejan Milojicic, & Akhil Sahai, 2007), a process for deriving low-level service level objectives (SLOs) from SLAs for multi-tier applications is described. This process is based on two steps, a performance profiling and a performance modeling step. During the performance modeling step, an application is run and benchmarked while certain factors, for example the CPU allocated to the application, are varied. With these measurements, functional mappings from system metrics to component performance metrics are derived using regression analysis. In a case study, the authors conclude that this is feasible because for all actions such as SQL transactions, web server requests etc. this is relatively static and repeating. But in the framework of generic applications there is no assurance that such a statistical/historical approach will have a satisfying accuracy. But even if this is the case, application profiling is a quite promising part of the final solution. The output of this stage is then used as input in the second step, which is the analytical performance model. This model aims at identifying the relationship between the overall application performance as a function of transaction workload, the application configuration, and the resource performance characteristics, by using queuing network models. This allows the estimation of how many resources must be allocated to each application in order to meet time constraints.

In (Jae W. Lee & Krste Asanovic, 2006) the authors use two modes of operation to provide QoS. In the first mode, called Enforcement, a QoS process cannot exceed its guaranteed resource share. This mode is used to execute the process with various resource reservation vectors in order to determine a minimal required resource reservation. In the second mode, called Deployment, the process is executed with at least the minimal resources allocated to it. Allocating surplus resources to the process can increase the safety margin for ensuring the required QoS. Since there is no generic model of a process' behavior, the main drawback is the necessity to test executions for every application instance. If more generic executions exist for each application then there is no guarantee that the estimation of these will be accurate for every instance executed in the grid.

In the EU funded project GEMSS (Siegfried Benkner, Gerhard Engelbrecht, Stuart E. Middleton, & Mike Surridge) a very interesting implementation is presented. The GEMSS service provider infrastructure employs a flexible QoS manager that can be configured by the service provider with an application specific performance model and a pricing model in order to determine the best possible QoS offered for a service request. In order to ensure the availability of appropriate computing resources for a service request, a backend scheduling system with support for advance reservation is utilized. The performance model receives as input a request descriptor with a set of request parameters representing application-specific input metadata supplied by the client during QoS negotiation. Then it generates a performance descriptor typically consisting of estimates for the required runtime, memory, and disk space. For example, in the case of an image reconstruction service, request parameters typically include image size and required accuracy. In the case of MPI applications, the performance model is usually parameterized by the number of processors. It may be executed repeatedly with a varying number of processors until the time constraints set by the client are met, or the range of feasible processors as specified in the machine descriptor is exceeded. The pricing model takes as input a resource descriptor and calculates the price for the required resources. Finally, a machine descriptor has to be specified containing details about the compute resources (e.g. maximum number of processors) that may be made available for an application service. GEMSS does not prescribe the actual nature of performance and pricing models; only an abstract interface is prescribed with XML-based input and output descriptors. Each descriptor comprises one or more parameters which have to be specified during service configuration using the deployment tool. The choice of model implementation is left to the service provider, with each model implemented as a Java library that can be plugged in and selected dynamically. For example, a performance model could be implemented based on an analytical model, or where this is not feasible, a neural network or a database could be used to map typical problem parameters to requirements in resources. GEMSS supports a flexible pricing policy that can be customized for each service offered by a SP. Two pricing models have been realized:

- A fixed price telephone pricing model where users are charged at a prearranged CPU hour rate and
- A dynamic pricing model where the CPU hour rate is dependent on the current load levels the service provider is experiencing.

Finally, the computational resource manager takes as input the performance descriptor generated by the performance model, and generates a resource descriptor containing details about temporarily reserved resources. The resource descriptor is then used as input to the pricing model to determine the price for a service request. The resource manager contacts the scheduler to check whether the required resources, as specified in the performance descriptor (number of processors for the estimated runtime) can be made available within the time frame (begin time, end time) specified in the client's QoS request. The result is that this approach offers a full scale implementation of the steps identified in the Overview Section especially as far as the framework services are concerned. It is also extensible in order to include new models. Its basic drawback is the fact that there is no tangible generic model for performance estimation but this has to be externally provided.

In (Peer Hasselmeyer, 2006) the authors present an architecture that addresses all the 3 steps identified in the beginning of this section. The proposed scheme consists of a Conversion Factory, a BLO (Business Level Objectives) Database, a Knowledge Database, a Complexity Database, and a Converter. The Converter is required for checking availability, configuring the system and monitoring the status. A Conversion Factory implements interfaces necessary to query the different databases in order to retrieve information about potential pre-calculated complexities or former business transactions. The Knowledge Databases stores information about system requirements for different complexities which have been obtained by running similar jobs in the past. The Complexity Database stores information about different complexity for previously run jobs. The BLO Database contains goals, which represent the service provider's policies. These can be used in order to favor or to disadvantage individual customers. All of the above modules take part in the final decision about the SLA terms to be proposed. It is an overall solution to the SLA

mapping process but its major disadvantage is the fact that it requires human intervention in cases when the complexity of the task is unknown. In that case an expert analyst has to decide what the order of the algorithm is.

In (Jarvis et al., 2006), an application performance prediction environment called PACE (Performance Analysis and Characterization Environment) is presented. PACE works by building models for applications and the underlying hardware, combining these resource to predict application execution. PACE takes non-linear effects into account when increasing resource allocation and allows accounts for mapping strategies (of processes to processors) and underlying computational algorithms. This approach is implemented both at intra-domain as well as inter-domain environments. The application tools provide a means of capturing the performance aspects of an application and its parallelization strategy in an application model. This is done by static source code analysis, which determines an application's control flow, frequency of operations and their communication structure. Although a large part of this process is automated, users can modify the performance scripts to account for data-dependent parameters and also utilize previously generated scripts stored in an object library. A similar process is followed for modeling hardware as well. Once the application and hardware models have been generated, they can be evaluated using the PACE Evaluation Engine. PACE allows:

- Evaluation of time predictions (for different systems, mapping strategies and algorithms);
- Investigation of the scalability of the application and the resources;
- Prediction of the utilization of the system resources (network usage, computation, idle time etc.), and
- Generation of predictive traces.

Overall it is a great approach but has the main drawback that application's source code must be available and that the main scope is about parallel applications.

SLA Management and Enforcement

The SLA Management covers different phases from the publication of services' descriptions and their capabilities, the negotiation and establishment of contractual bindings (the SLAs), the provisioning of the resources and supervision, monitoring, evaluation and enforcement of the SLA terms.

The management of an SLA is a complex task as the overall service quality depends on several aspects such as system behaviour, network reliability, external dependencies and even unexpected events. This makes the SLA Management and Enforcement a complex task that affects the way the internal resources are provisioned and managed. In case of service outage or failure that will cause an unavoidable SLA violation the service provider should take decisions based on its business relationships with clients, the current infrastructure status and incurred penalties, to try to minimize the global cost incurred by the SLA violation.

The monitoring of the own infrastructure and the capability to adapt the running processes and rescheduling of tasks is an essential capabilities of the Service Provider to perform SLA Enforcement.

The following sections describe different approaches taken by several projects in relation to SLA Management and Enforcement.

CQEF

CQEF (Yazhe Tang et al., 2007) is a QoS-enabled framework that offers quality assurance for Grid services. It brings CoS (Class of Service), which was initially used in WSOL (Web Service Offering Language) to express QoS levels a service provider can support, into grid environments. Briefly, CoS is

a simple way for users to express their demand for QoS in a lightweight SLA. While SLAs has been widely used in web service literature, sometimes CoS is more suitable for grid services. There are two reasons for this:

- In grid service environments, where transient services are met, the overhead to make SLAs between the transient service providers and users cannot be ignored
- Traditional grid services, such as services based on CPU power, may not need to distinguish among so many service levels (if each SLA is considered as a different service level). Instead, service providers only need to list a limited number of classes of services for users to pick up.

As CoS is the core point of the framework, CQEF covers different phases for CoS-based QoS management, such as:

- CoS definition and registration,
- CoS deployment,
- Service execution with CoS, and
- CoS monitoring.

CQEF has the following characteristics:

- A special Grid service description language (CGSL) is developed to describe the service level of grid service.
- It relies on CoS to offer QoS-aware service registration and discovery mechanism.
- A new grid resource management mechanism which is based on CoS is presented.
- It has a special monitoring mechanism to evaluate the compliance of CoS.

GRUBER/DI-GRUBER SLA Broker

GRUBER (C. Dumitrescu & I. Foster, 2005) is an architecture and toolkit for the SLA specification regarding resource utilisation and enforcement in grid environments. It allows the automatic selection of resources available within a VO, following restrictions and rules specified in the VO's policy (Matthias Hovestadt, 2006).

According to the GRUBER approach, a job is characterized by the properties of VO membership group (defining the execution context), including the required processor time and storage space. Thus the broker is seeking for an assignment that satisfies all policies and promotes maximum utilization in terms of provider, VO or other objectives.

The GRUBER system consists of five main components:

- The engine encompasses all algorithms necessary for determining optimized resource assignments.
- The site monitor is acting as data provider, publishing selective numbers about the local resource system to the Globus environment.
- The site selector is responsible for selecting a resource provider for execution of new tasks.
- The algorithms of this selection process are part of the engine, so that these two components are communicating.
- The queue manager is installed on submitting hosts, deciding which jobs can be executed at what time.

GRUBER has been implemented in Globus Toolkit versions 3 and 4, both for web-service and pre-web-service flavours. It is promoted as part of the official Globus Toolkit family, and therefore has significant impact in the Grid broker's domain. The DI-GRUBER (C. Dumitrescu, I. Raicu, & I. Foster, 2005) architecture is an enhancement of the GRUBER system, allowing it to work in a larger scale Grids. In contrast to GRUBER, DI-GRUBER has no single point within the system for taking scheduling decisions. Instead, schedulers are working independently, exchanging information only rarely and in a loosely coupled fashion.

Even if GRUBER is called to be an SLA broker service, the notion of an SLA differs significantly from the ideas of this work. Here, an SLA does not cover any service quality parameters, but only basic job profile information. This is due to the fact that GRUBER has been developed for the classic Globus environment, which is using queuing-based resource management systems only for realizing jobs. For GRUBER the specification of processor time and storage space is essential to find an optimal match to those systems.

GRUBER's main drawback is that instead of negotiating with these systems, it demands special services running on these machines that publish data, such as utilization, to the central GRUBER component. The latter takes the scheduling decision, without any interference from the local RMS. However, this approach does not take into consideration the fact that the majority of the commercial providers strive to obtain their local autonomy when providing their resources to Grid systems.

NextGRID

Within the NextGRID project a framework that concentrates on the set-up of SLAs was designed and implemented. It includes the discovery of service provider candidates that provide a certain service level as well as the negotiation with those candidates to reach an agreement (the SLA) at the service level requested and (ultimately) provided. It was implemented on Globus Toolkit 4, UNICORE, complied with the WS-Agreement whereas the template registry is set on an eXist XML database (Peer Hasselmeyer et al., 2007).

NextGRID platform aimed to address the following two issues:

- The customer should not deal with SLAs in form processed by the machines, but specify business objectives, requirements, and preferences in a preferably "natural" way. This implies that the user interface offers choices like e.g. "gold", "silver", or "bronze" service levels instead of presenting the SLA as an XML instance document to be edited within a text editor.

- The framework has to support the user in getting an agreed-upon SLA. The framework should therefore handle and automate all tasks surrounding the creation of an SLA, including:
  ◦ Discovery of service providers,
  ◦ Selection of providers that offer the required service,
  ◦ Retrieval of service offers (SLA templates),
  ◦ Visualization of SLA templates, and
  ◦ Establishment of an actual SLA.

The expected results are listed below:

- Fast and effective advertisement of services to the outside world,
- Fast and scalable search for matching service provider(s),
- Building on technologies which are accepted as (de-facto) standards,
- Adaptive to different negotiation protocols.

AssessGrid/OpenCCS

AssessGrid has been a European project that introduced risk management and assessment to Grid computing. Risk assessment helps providers to make decisions on suitable SLA offers by relating the risk of failure to penalty fees. Similarly, end-users get knowledge about the risk of an SLA violation by a resource provider that helps to take appropriate decisions regarding acceptable costs and penalty fees. A broker is the matchmaker between end-users and providers. The broker provides a time / cost / risk optimised assignment of SLA requests to SLA offers (AssessGrid Project; Jan Seidel et al.). AssessGrid used a distributed Resource Management System (RMS) called Computing Center Software (CCS or

openCCS). CCS provides interfaces to UNICORE and Globus Toolkit 4.

The WS-Agreement protocol has been implemented for openCCS. The major negotiable SLA parameters in openCCS are general parameters like number of nodes, amount of memory, job runtime, deadline for job completion, policies on security or migration, and fault tolerance requirements. The RMS is enhanced by risk assessment and risk management functionalities. A negotiator module is responsible for negotiating SLAs with external contractors using the WS-Agreement-Negotiation protocol. The negotiator defines the price, penalty and risk in the SLA according to policies. The risk is included in the SLA as an additional attribute. The Risk Assessor evaluates current monitoring information as well as aggregated statistical information to assess the risk for an SLA violation.

HPC4U/OpenCSS

HPC4U (HPC4U)(Highly Predictable Cluster for Internet-Grids) started working on an SLA-aware RMS, utilizing the mechanisms of process, storage, and network subsystems for realizing application-transparent fault tolerance. As central component of the HPC4U project the RMS OpenCCS has been selected, since its planning-based nature seemed to be well-suited for realizing SLA-awareness. Within the project all features required for SLA-awareness and SLA-compliance have been developed, namely an SLA-aware scheduler, mechanisms for transparent check-pointing of parallel applications, or the negotiation of new SLAs (Georg Birkenheuer, Matthias Hovestadt, Odej Kao, & Kerstin Voss; Hovestadt, 2005).

Planning is an alternative approach on system scheduling. In contrast to queuing that considers only currently free resources, planning takes into consideration resources are being used and assigns them to waiting jobs. Instead, planning-based systems also plan for the future, assigning a start time to all waiting requests. This way a schedule is generated, encompassing all jobs in the schedule. Having such a schedule available, the system scheduler is able to determine which jobs are scheduled to be executed at what time.

The process of SLA-negotiation differs significantly from the regular job submission interface of a resource management system. There, a user submits his job description, directly getting information about rejection or acceptance in return. In the latter case, the job has already entered the system schedule.

In the case of SLAs, a multi-phase negotiation is conducted before the job finally enters the system. The GRAAP working group of the Open Grid Forum (OGF) described such a negotiation process in the WS-Agreement Negotiation specification. Here the provider answers a job request with an SLA offer. The user has to commit to this offer before the SLA is actually enforced.

For the scheduling component of an RMS this negotiation process has significant implications: once the RMS has issued an SLA offer, it has to adhere to this offer until it has been committed or cancelled by the user. Timeout mechanisms ensure that SLA offers automatically expire after a given time period (e. g. some seconds). However, at least during this timeout period the system has to reserve system capacity for the job in negotiation.

For this purpose, a novel list is introduced into the system: the SLA-offer list (O-list). Jobs from this list are scheduled within the regular scheduling process in the following order: P-list before D-list before O-list before N-list. It is preferable to privilege jobs from D-list than O-list, since jobs in O-list are not yet affirmative, so that the system would not actually break an SLA-Contract but only an SLA-offer. Again, the general policy of handling failures is to not affect other jobs, rather than to keep the implication of a failure as local as possible.

Akogrimo (Access to Knowledge Through the Grid in a Mobile World)

Akogrimo (Akogrimo Project) developed one of the few approaches that include QoS enforcement in the SLA subsystem. The SLA Enforcement system is responsible for the appliance of the contract conditions (which are described in the SLA contract) of every running service. It can identify the violations of the contract that may occur and take the appropriate decisions to ensure the fulfillment of the contract. In Akogrimo two main services comprise the SLA Enforcement system:

- **The SLA-Controller:** This service detects deviations from the values defined in the client's SLA. It receives and processes all measurements related to the execution of a business service sent by the Monitoring service. It checks whether the measurements are within the thresholds defined in the SLA contract for QoS metrics. Whenever the execution of a business service does not satisfy these conditions, the SLA-Controller notifies (using a WS-Notification mechanism) the SLA-Decisor service, which is in charge of starting the appropriate recovery action.

- **The SLA-Decisor:** Receives and manages notifications from the SLA-Controller service. In turn, it contacts the Policy Manager Service in order to retrieve the most suitable affiliated policy, depending on the business execution context. This policy includes the actions that must be undertaken, such as showing informational messages, increasing priorities of processes, applying discounts, destroying the service, re-instantiating the service, etc. Depending on the seriousness of the violation, the context of the business service and the overall status of the system, this event can be solved at domain level or at VO level. In the first case, it may be only necessary to notify the EMS which will take corrective actions, whereas in the second case, it may be necessary to notify higher layers (e.g., workflow manager or other subsystem) to recover from the situation by taking global corrective actions.

In Akogrimo the enforcement process (Akogrimo Deliverable D4.3.3, 2007) during the execution is summarized through the following steps:

- The Metering service sends notification messages to Monitoring service.
- These notifications are being forwarded to the SLA-Decisor through the SLAController.
- When a violation is detected, the SLA-Decisor propagates the notification to the EMS along with the policy that should be applied.
- The EMS filters the message and propagates it the A4C system (Authentication, Authorization, Accounting, Auditing and Charging) and reallocates resources if needed.

The SLA Controller and Decisor were developed in Microsoft.NET platform and.NET Framework with WS Enhancements. The Controller makes use of WSRF.NET.

GRIA SLA Management

GRIA is a service-oriented infrastructure designed to support B2B collaborations through service provision across organizational boundaries ("Gria"). GRIA features an SLA Management Service in order to to meet the demands of distributed product development teams needing to share IT assets (Boniface, Phillips, & Surridge, 2006; EU IST SIMDAT Project). GRIA SLAs have some of the characteristics of NextGRID SLAs, for example, bi-partite agreements and high-level

business value exchange linked to low-level resourcing. It is important to note that the SLAs in SIMDAT and NextGRID projects attempt to present QoS issues on a higher abstraction level using business-specific terms rather than by using hardware level attributes such as CPU time, bandwidth and disk space.

The SLA management infrastructure developed in the GRIA project concentrates on issues on maximising resource utilisation whilst satisfying QoS commitments to existing customers. The GRIA project developed an advanced SLA Management Service that allows the service provider to offer SLAs described in terms of high-level metrics whilst incorporating strategies to manage SLA violations, mapping high-level SLA metrics to measured metrics and aggregation of QoS measurements across multiple customers. The main functions of the SLA Management Service are related to the process of agreeing, monitoring and enforcing an SLA between the customer and the service provider (Boniface, Phillips S., Sanchez-Macian Perez A., & Surridge):

- It provides controlled access to SLA "templates" that can be filled in and submitted by a potential consumer as service level "proposals".
- It decides, according to its capacity and the consumer's account status, whether to enter into a new SLA (with a given QoS) when proposed by a consumer, and responds accordingly.
- It decides whether a new requested "activity" at an application service is covered by the referenced SLA and accepts or denies the request accordingly.
- It detects when a consumer is exceeding the limits of an SLA, and initiates load reductions in the corresponding application service(s) to prevent this.
- It tracks the QoS actually delivered, and initiates charges when appropriate.

The GRIA SLA Management Service is designed to be very flexible and to support a wide range of application services. It retrieves usage information from application services (e.g. job and data services), records the usage and optionally constrains and/or bills for the usage. Different application services will want to report usage of different measurable quantities (metrics) which are identified by URIs. For example, a job service may report usage of CPU but a data service may report usage of disk space. The SLA Service does not understand the meaning of each metric, it records usage, aggregates the usage across the SLA and across the entire service and acts according to service provider policies when usage exceeds a constraint. This "lack of understanding", or rather "generalisation", is an advantage as it means that the SLA Service can be used to manage new, previously unimagined, services without alteration.

Constraints play a major role in GRIA's SLA definitions. An SLA can contain any number of constraints, each one defining a usage limit that defines the commitment made by the service provider which the consumer is not supposed to exceed. A constraint may act over the lifetime of the SLA or be repeating with a time period, such as a usage limit per month. Each constraint places a limit on a metric, for instance, at a low level:

- Amount of CPU time,
- Amount of disk space,
- Number of databases.

Or at a higher level:

- Number of simulation time steps,
- Size of mesh for CFD,
- Number of video frames rendered.

Each GRIA SLA template contains both public and private constraint terms. The public terms are presented to the consumer and the private ones are hidden. This provides a simple mechanism for translating from the high-level business terms re-

quired by the consumer and the low-level resource terms required to ensure that the service provider has sufficient capacity to service the SLAs. For instance, an SLA template may state (publicly) that the maximum number of video frames to be rendered each day is 1000 and state (privately) that the SLA requires up to 17 hours of CPU time per day. When such a template is proposed by the consumer, the SLA Service can compare the CPU time constraint against its configured CPU capacity to determine if the SLA can be serviced or not.

As well as constraining the usage of resources, an SLA can also (optionally) charge for resource usage. Metric-specific charges may be defined, either on the cumulative amount of a metric used in the period (e.g. a charge per CPU second) or on how many times a metric has been used (e.g. a charge per job executed). These metric-specific charges can also be augmented with usage pricing bands so that, for instance, the first slice of usage can be cheap, or included in the subscription, and additional usage can become increasingly more expensive. The billing period for each SLA can be defined and the SLA manager will place a single charge combining a subscription fee and a charge for the month's aggregated usage onto the users account at the end of each period.

RESERVOIR

RESERVOIR is a European Union FP7 funded project that aims to support the service-oriented computing paradim using virtualization technologies, transparently provisioned and managed on an on-demand basis at competitive costs with high quality of service.

One of the areas that the RESERVOIR project is investigating is the way RESERVOIR sites can provision their infrastructure and comply with SLAs under a dynamic request of resources from the clients (Martín et al., 2009).

For resource assignments RESERVOIR follows a schema called statistical multiplexing to satisfy the elastic needs of the demand. This concept comes from data networks where it is possible that the picks of requirements requested exceed the available capacity. It is based on the knowledge about the statistical distribution of the sources and technique improves the utilisation of the resources in comparison to other mutiplexing options.

The statistical adminision control mechanism (called Policy-Driven Probabilistic BSM-aligned Admission Control) is responsible for calculating the risk associated with not fulfiling an SLA and also estimates the impact this SLA violation has on the business goals of the site.

In RESERVOIR, each site has autonomy to manage its own business goals. But business goals are defined at such a high level of abstraction that there is a semantic gap between them and the ICT level management goals and policies. Bridging this gap is notoriously difficult. RESERVOIR aims at narrowing this gap and aligning between the high level business management goals and ICT- level management policies by introducing the notion of acceptable risk level (ARL) of capacity allocation congestion.

ARL can be defined as the probability of SLA violation of some services. The ARL is being controlled by the business policy of the site and its value is obtained by calculating the residual benefit resulting from specific SLA violations.

An SLA commitment for the new application service should be made if and only if the potential effect does not cause the residual benefit to fall below some predefined level, being controlled by the site's business policy. This decision process is referred to as BSM-aligned admission control.

Based on the elasticity rules of the service supplied in the manifest and on the historic resource allocation statistics, RESERVOIR's admission control algorithm calculates the equivalent capacity required to satisfy the resource demands of the service applications for the given ARL. The equivalent capacity is matched against the actual available capacity. If the equivalent capacity does not exceed the available physical capacity suitable

for placement of the application Virtual Execution Environments (VEE), the application passes admission control and is admitted to the site.

The equivalent capacity model was developed by Guerin et.al.(1991) for bandwidth dimensioning in data networks and RESERVOIR has extended this concept to VEE capacity allocation.

When a new service with unknown history arrives in the system, its mean capacity demand and standard deviation are conservatively estimated from the service elasticity rules and historic data known for other services.

Intuitively, RESERVOIR is interested in minimizing the costs of capacity over-provisioning while controlling the risk associated with capacity over-booking. From minimizing the cost of capacity over-provisioning, the project is interested in maximizing yield of the existing capacity. However, at some point, the conflicts (congestions) in capacity allocation may cause excessive SLA penalties that would off-set the advantages of yield maximization. Accounting for benefits from complying with SLAs and for costs of compliance and non-compliance due to congestions, residual benefit for the site can be computed. The target value of residual benefit can be controlled by a high-level business policy. To satisfy this business policy, an appropriate congestion probability needs to be calculated, ARL. ARL, in turn, would help to calculate equivalent capacity for the site to take an advantage of statistical multiplexing in a safe manner.

SLA@SOI

SLA@SOI aims at developing a comprehensive multi-layer SLA management framework for service-oriented software systems. It is targeted at providing these management capabilities to service providers, from business service providers all the way down to infrastructure service providers. Across all layers of an IT stack and across the various stakeholder perspectives the framework will support the provision of software systems or parts of them as services with a contractually fixed quality based on service-level agreements. Noteworthy, quality attributes span across multiple non-functional domains such as security, performance, availability, and reliability (Theilmann et al., 2009).

The following three key characteristics of this infrastructure shall support the dynamic provisioning of service as tradable goods:

- **Predictability and Dependability:** The quality characteristics of services can be predicted and enforced at run time.
- **Transparent SLA management:** SLAs defining the exact conditions under which services are provided/consumed can be transparently managed across the whole business and IT stack.
- **Automation:** The whole process of negotiating SLAs and provisioning, delivery and monitoring of services will be automated allowing for highly dynamic and scalable service consumption.

As already mentioned, the overall SLA management process may include different stakeholders, SLA@SOI has identified the following: Software Provider, Service Provider, Service Broker, Infrastructure Provider, Service Customer, and Service User.

SLAs will be associated with multiple elements of the stack at multiple layers and will be correlated with each other, e.g. SLAs for elements of the physical infrastructure, virtualized infrastructure, middleware, application level and process-level.

As today's business systems typically consist of complex layered systems, user-level SLAs cannot be directly mapped onto the physical infrastructure. Therefore, top-level SLAs do not allow service providers to either plan their IT landscapes according to possible, planned or agreed SLAs. Nor do they allow understanding why a certain SLA violation might have occurred. The reason for this is that SLA guarantee terms are typically not explicitly or directly related to actual performance metrics or configuration parameters.

The fundamental challenge for realizing this vision is how to properly correlate the different SLAs in such a scenario so that they form a well synchronized SLA hierarchy.

In SLA@SOI, the lifecycle considers six main phases. These are

- Design and Development
- Service Offering
- Service Negotiation
- Service Provisioning
- Service Operations
- Service Decommissioning

In SLA@SOI the area of design-time prediction deals with the gap between top-level SLAs and the multiple elements of the stack and the infrastructure. This area targets to

- Create a domain-specific metamodel that allows to model abstractions on the performance of a component- based system. This metamodel must include all information required for predicting the system's QoS.
- Provide a design-time prediction service supporting the prediction of a system's QoS properties without having to fully implement, deploy and execute the system.

The QoS metamodel consists of four parts corresponding to different roles involved in the service life-cycle: 1) service component model, 2) infrastructure model, 3) allocation model, and 4) usage model. Every role is responsible for providing its assigned model for QoS analysis. The required models can thereby be specified independently.

SLA@SOI provides a tool used during the automated SLA negotiation between customers and providers of a service: it allows service providers to calculate feasible QoS parameters they can offer. For this purpose, prediction has to be performed on the fly, as part of automatic negotiation between service customer and provider.

The prediction service (Momm et al., 2009) retrieves the different information and translates it into infrastructure models that can be processed by the simulation engine of the Palladio Component Model (PCM) (Becket et al., 2009).

The implementation of the framework is done in Java. For the purpose of prediction, the input model is automatically transformed into a Java code skeleton. The generated code is instrumented to collect performance and utilization data. Performance evaluation is done through simulation using the SSJ simulation engine.

When a SLA violation occurs in SLA@SOI, the adjustment module is the primary responsible of collecting all detected SLA violations or warnings and to trigger adjustment actions. It makes use of a set of adjustment patterns and a manageability model to achieve this.

The consequences of a SLA violation could be:

- Reporting the SLA violation which generally will conduct to penalties.
- Reprovision of the allocated infrastructure to overcome the violation (re-negotiation of the SLA)
- Reconfigures the running software stack to overcome a violation; note that this operation is highly application specific.

FUTURE RESEARCH DIRECTIONS

This chapter explains what future research can be done to improve the work presented in the previous chapters.

Languages and Schemas

Firstly, current languages and schemas miss the possibility to specify attributes of real-time applications and resources in a machine-readable way. Semantic enhancements could enable the

reasoning through software in order to facilitate automation. Secondly, there is a need to investigate how SLAs can better support complex value chains. In the NextGRID project, SLA federation through bipartite agreements was investigated, but this was only a simple scenario, less complex than the provisioning of real-time capabilities with the potential interaction of various providers, for example compute, network and storage. Additionally, the interaction of various providers along the value chain and intertwined SLAs between these providers, is not covered as of yet. This is detrimental as it is unlikely that a single provider can fulfill all of the specific requirements in a real-time infrastructure and, therefore, various providers will be part of a value chain. Thirdly, even though SLAs need a certain level of expressiveness, they should only capture what is strictly necessary in order not to be bloated and to maintain the privacy of both service provider and customer.

SLA Negotiation Protocols

Even though in general complex negotiation protocols exist, many SLA frameworks often propose only very simple protocols. Especially when complex parameters, like real-time and QoS constraints are encountered, there is the need for the development of a negotiation system with the following features:

- Simple and fast negotiation process.
- Lower level negotiation capabilities (it is necessary to negotiate the SLA parameters of an offered SLA/template, not just accept or reject it).
- Renegotiation of existing agreements.
- Partly automated negotiation system.
- Cooperating/Complying with WS-* specifications.

A very promising specification which is in its first draft version though, is the WS-Agreement-Negotiation (GGF GRAAP Working Group). The

Figure 8. WS-AgreementNegotiation Conceptual Layered Service Model (GGF GRAAP Working Group)

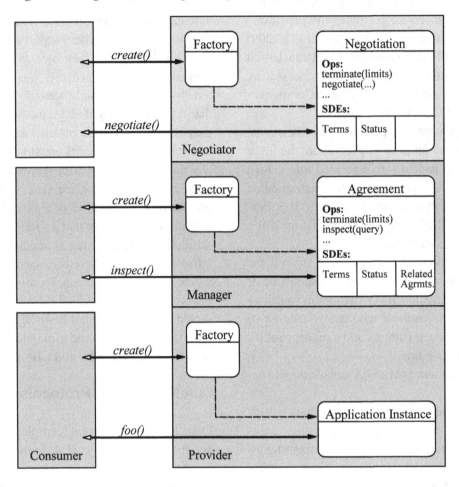

new specification introduces a new "negotiation" layer to the WS-Agreement conceptual model (see WS-Agreement Global Grid Forum). The new layer provides a Web service-based interface which:

- Allows the negotiation of an agreement to continue until it satisfies both parties. (This does not mean that there will be an agreement eventually, see next bullet).
- Can express negotiation offers with possible constraints that must be maintained in any counter offer.
- Allows the renegotiation of existing agreements.

- Allows the use of different negotiation protocols, other than WS-AgreementNegotiation, when appropriate.

The above are illustrated in Figure 8.

As the negotiator layer is simply an extension, sitting on top of the agreement layer, WS-Agreement Negotiation would solve the problem that a quote message is missing from the very simple negotiation proposed by WS-Agreement. Timeliness issues, which can easily occur in real-time systems, like requirements on the time allowed between response messages, is, unfortunately not foreseen in the protocol itself.

Quality of Service and SLAs

All methodologies regarding the assertion of QoS parameters presented up to this point have pros and cons. The fact is that neither of them has a generic approach, mainly due to the fact that the range of applications is very wide and with different features. Legal issues have also a specific impact. For example, estimation through code observation requires that the code is accessible by the estimator, which is not feasible for many proprietary applications. Furthermore, in many cases human intervention is necessary in order to cover some of the involved parameters. Additionally in the case of historical data, the estimation is rather easy but with no guarantees, since for a vast number of applications execution time varies greatly with time or varying input data and therefore historical data is of limited use.

Regarding the special case of real-time applications, there is no generally applicable solution. As real-time QoS requirements will be described on different layers, it is essential that a reliable and repeatable mapping can be performed.

In conclusion, the basic goal for this technological area is to fully support the automation of the mapping process and at the same time making it as generic as possible. This can be achieved using a combination of the practices described above. By combining the above methodologies each one's disadvantages can be compensated and most or all of the use cases can be covered.

SLA Management and Enforcement

One important aspect of SLA management that is not addressed adequately currently is the recognition that Service Providers in the real world will deliberately break SLAs and take the hit of any penalties that ensue if by doing so they better fulfill their business objectives, for example to maximize profit by giving priority service to preferred customers. This type of behavior can be seen in a range of industries, for example flights and hotels where resources are deliberately overbooked. The same is likely to happen in real-time SOI since there is a similar situation of resource reservation, multiple classes of customer, expensive resources and the need for providers to maximize the utilization. Therefore, approaches should target to supporting the management of a set of SLAs by a service provider according to policies that define when they are prepared to accept or break these SLAs.

CONCLUSION

This chapter has analysed the different facets regarding the usage of SLAs in real-time service-oriented infrastructures (SOIs) by analysing the aspects of languages & schemas, SLA negotiation, QoS & SLAs and SLA management and enforcement. For each of these areas we have presented and discussed implementations and realizations and have proposed missing pieces that are necessary to support for real-time applications.

None of the investigated solutions can in itself cover all requirements that a real-time enabled SOI demands from SLAs. Nonetheless there exist promising solutions in all areas and the selection and combination of various relevant developments can already provide good coverage. Further developments, however, are necessary to further the uptake of SLAs not only in the area of cloud computing but as well in the area of real-time. SLAs continue to be a promising technique for the provisioning of services with defined QoS.

REFERENCES

Akogrimo Deliverable D2. 2.1. (2005). *Report on state of the art,* vol. 2. Retrieved from http://www.akogrimo.org/ modules3653.pdf? name=UpDownload& req=getit& lid=16

Akogrimo Deliverable D4. 3.3. (2007). *Report on the implementation of the infrastructure services layer*. Akogrimo Project. Retrieved from http://www.akogrimo.org/ modules8128.pdf? name=UpDownload& req=getit& lid=116

Akogrimo Project. (2006). *Akogrimo: Access to knowledge through the Grid in a mobile world*. Retrieved from http://www.akogrimo.org

AssessGrid Project. (2009). *AssessGrid - Advanced risk assessment & management for trustable Grids*. Retrieved from http://www.assessgrid.eu

Benkner, S., & Engelbrecht, G. (2006). *A generic QoS infrastructure for Grid Web services*. AICT-ICIW.

Benkner, S., Engelbrecht, G., Middleton, S. E., & Surridge, M. (2007). *Supporting SLA negotiation for QoS-enabled simulation services in a medical Grid environment, Lecture Notes in Computer Science* (*Vol. 4699*). Berlin, Germany: Springer.

Birkenheuer, G., Hovestadt, M., Kao, O., & Voss, K. (2008). *Planning-based scheduling for SLA-Awareness and Grid integration*.

Boniface, M., Phillips, S., Sanchez-Macian Perez, A., & Surridge, M. (2007). *Non Functional Properties and Service Level Agreements in Service Oriented Computing Workshop, The 5th International Conference on Service Oriented Computing*. NFPSLA-SOC'07, September 17, 2007, Vienna, Austria.

Boniface, M., Phillips, S. C., & Surridge, M. (2006). *Grid-based business partnerships using service level agreements*.

Buyya, R., Abramson, D., & Venugopal, S. (2005). The Grid economy. *Proceedings of the IEEE, 93*, 698–714. doi:10.1109/JPROC.2004.842784

Chen, Y., Iyer, S., Liu, X., Milojicic, D., & Sahai, A. (2007). *SLA decomposition: Translating service level objectives to system level thresholds*. In Fourth International Conference on Autonomic Computing (ICAC'07).

Czajkowski, K., Foster, I., & Kesselman, C. (2005). *Proceedings of the IEEE, 93*(3), 631-643. ISSN: 0018-9219.

Czajkowski, K., Foster, I., Kesselman, C., Sander, V., & Tuecke, S. (2002). SNAP: A protocol for negotiating service level agreements and coordinating resource management in distributed systems. In *Proceedings of the 8th Workshop on Job Scheduling Strategies for Parallel Processing*.

Dumitrescu, C., & Foster, I. (2005). A Grid resource SLA-based broker. In *EuroPar*. Lisboa, Portugal: GRUBER.

Dumitrescu, C., Raicu, I., & Foster, I. (2005). A distributed approach in Grid resource brokering. In *Supercomputing*. Seattle, WA, USA: DI-GRUBER.

EU IST SIMDAT Project. (2010). *EU IST SIMDAT project*. Retrieved from http://www.simdat.org

GGF GRAAP Working Group. (2005). *Web services agreement negotiation specification*. Retrieved from http://forge.gridforum.org/ sf/ go/ doc15831

Global Grid Forum. (2010). *Web services agreement specification*.

Gria. (2010). Retrieved from http://www.gria.org

Hasselmeyer, P., Koller, B., Schubert, L., & Wieder, P. (2006). *Towards SLA-supported resource management*.

Hasselmeyer, P., Mersch, H., Koller, B., Quyen, H. N., Schubert, L., & Wieder, P. (2007). *Implementing an SLA negotiation framework*.

He, Z., Peng, C., & Mok, A. (2006). *A performance estimation tool for video applications*. RTAS.

Herenger, H., Heek, R., Kuebert, R., & Surridge, M. (2007). Operating virtual organizations using bipartite service level agreements. In D. Talia, R. Yahyapour, & W. Ziegler (Eds.), *Grid middleware and services: Challenges and solutions*. Retrieved from http://eprints.ecs.soton.ac.uk/ 15278/

Hovestadt, M. (2005). Fault tolerance mechanisms for SLA-aware resource management. *Parallel and Distributed Systems, 2*(2), 458–462.

Hovestadt, M. (2006). *Service level agreement aware resource management*. Paderborn.

HPC4U. (2010). *HPC4U*. Retrieved from http:// www.hpc4u.org

IBM. (1993). *Research WSLA*. Retrieved from http://www.research.ibm.com/ wsla/ WSLA093. xsd

IBM. (2003). *Web service level agreement (WSLA) language specification*. Retrieved from http:// www.research.ibm.com/ wsla/ WSLASpecV1-20030128.pdf

IBM. (2010). *Web service level agreements (WSLA) project*. Retrieved from http://www. research.ibm.com/ wsla/

Jarvis, S. A., Spooner, D. P., Keung, H. N., Cao, J., Saini, S., & Nudd, G. R. (2006). Performance prediction and its use in parallel and distributed computing systems. *Future Generations Computer Systems, 22*(7), 745-754. Retrieved from http:// dx.doi.org/10.1016/ j.future.2006.02.008

Lamanna, D. D., & Skene, J. Emmerich, & W. (2003). *SLAng: A language for defining service level agreements*. Distributed Computing Systems.

Lee, J. W., & Asanovic, K. (2006). *METERG: Measurement-based end-to-end performance estimation technique in QoS-capable multiprocessors*. RTAS.

McKee, P., Taylor, S., Surridge, M., Lowe, R., & Ragusa, C. (2007). *Strategies for the service marketplace*. GECON.

Nextgrid. (2010). *NextGRID SLA schema*. Retrieved from http://www.nextgrid.org/ GS/ management_systems/ SLA_management/ Next-GRID_SLA_schema.pdf

OASIS. (2010). *Service oriented architecture reference model*. Retrieved from http://www. oasis-open.org/ committees/ tc_home.php? wg_abbrev=soa-rm

Seidel, J., Wäldrich, O., Wieder, P., Yahyapour, R., & Ziegler, W. (2007). *Using SLA for resource management and scheduling - A survey*.

Snelling, D., Fisher, M., Basermann, A., Wray, F., Wieder, P., & Surridge, M. (2008). *NextGRID vision and architecture White Paper V5*. Retrieved from http://www.nextgrid.org/ download/ publications/ NextGRID_Architecture_White_Paper.pdf

Tang, Y., Yang, Y., Zhao, M., Yao, L., & Li, Y. (2007). *CoS-based QoS management framework for grid services*.

Web Service Agreement. (2004). *GFD: 107 proposed recommendation*.

Yeo, C. S., & Buyya, R. (2005). Service level agreement based allocation of cluster resources handling penalty to enhance utility. In *Proc. of the 7th IEEE International Conference on Cluster Computing Cluster*.

Chapter 9
Securing Real–Time Interactive Applications in Federated Clouds

Michael Boniface
University of Southampton IT Innovation Centre, UK

Bassem Nasser
University of Southampton IT Innovation Centre, UK

Mike Surridge
University of Southampton IT Innovation Centre, UK

Eduardo Oliveros
Telefónica Investigación y Desarollo, Spain

ABSTRACT

Enterprise adoption of cloud computing for real-time interactive applications processes is limited by their ability to meet inter-enterprise security requirements. Although some clouds' offerings comply with security standards, no solution today allows businesses to assess security compliance of applications at the business level and dynamically link to security countermeasures on-demand. In this chapter we examine cloud security, privacy, and trust issues from three levels: business, jurisdiction, and technical. Firstly, we look at the business level to identify issues arising from the motivations and concerns of business stakeholders. Secondly, we explore jurisdictional level to identify risks that arise from legislation, gaps in legislation, or conflicts between legislation in different jurisdictions related to a cloud deployment, given the concerns of stakeholders. Finally, we examine the technical level to identify issues that arise from technical causes such as ICT vulnerabilities, and/or require technical solutions, such as data confidentiality and integrity protection.

DOI: 10.4018/978-1-60960-827-9.ch009

INTRODUCTION

The cloud is such a general-purpose paradigm that it is impossible to consider 'the cloud' as a single set of business models with a single set of security, privacy and trust issues. To some extent, issues with cloud computing are necessarily related to the application purpose. However, using the cloud modalities (IaaS, PaaS and SaaS) it is possible to identify common stakeholders and concerns in each classification (Rimal, Choi, & Lumb, 2009).

Infrastructure as a service (IaaS): the provision of 'raw' machines (servers, storage and other devices) on which the service consumer installs their own software (usually as virtual machine images). The service is billed on a utility computing basis according to the amount of resources consumed. IaaS stakeholders include the IaaS hoster, provider and customer. The IaaS hoster must provide adequate resources in order to meet demands of its customers needs, together with appropriate availability contingencies. It will also need to avoid becoming liable for illegal uses of the software including licence violations. The IaaS provider must provide an interface in order for customers to configure and manage the resources they will use, to upload workloads and data. Utility billing or the resources used together with usage data must be provided. Today it is normal for the IaaS provider to also host the cloud resources, but in some research projects (Edutain@ Grid and RESERVOIR) multi-hosting models are being developed in which at least some hosters delegate the provision of customer-facing cloud management services to a separate entity (Ferris, Surridge & Glinka, 2009; Sotomayor, Montero, Llorente & Foster, 2009). The IaaS customer will be able to choose from a range of resources, services and SLAs that best meet their need. This may include tiered pricing for different kinds of configuration (performance, capacity), which may

be provisioned as shared or dedicated resources, or levels of security.

The PaaS stakeholders include the PaaS hoster, provider and user (developer). The PaaS hoster must provide adequate resources (typically via an IaaS model) in order to meet demands of its customers needs, together with appropriate availability contingencies. The PaaS provider provides an environment suitable for general developers to build web applications without deep domain expertise of back-end server and front-end client development or website administration. The PaaS user (developer) must have a browser-based development environment, the ability to deployment seamlessly to a hosted runtime environment, management and monitoring tools and pay as you go billing.

The SaaS stakeholders include hoster, provider, customer, consumers and application software vendors. The SaaS hoster needs to protect their infrastructure from misbehaving applications, and avoid becoming liable for illegal uses of the software including licence violations, etc. This stakeholder may be covered under IaaS, of course. The SaaS provider needs to restrict access to paying customers, and ensure the hoster provides the necessary performance and respects other consumer requirements such as confidentiality, personal data protection, etc. The SaaS customer needs to have adequate performance and pay only for what they used, protect sensitive application data (inputs, outputs and stored data) including protection of any personal data used, and may need the fact they used the service to be confidential. The SaaS consumers are people who use the service purchased by the SaaS customer – e.g. friends, colleagues or downstream customers – who may be owners or data subjects for some of the data being used in the service. The application software vendor needs to define and enforce a licensing model that compensates them for use of their application via SaaS, ensure effective user support, etc.

CHALLENGES FOR CLOUD SECURITY

Business Issues

The business issues associated with cloud security, privacy and trust must be analysed, in light of foreseeable technological capabilities. These include requirements for business responsibility, accountability and liability for cloud-based actions and processes, as well as business governance and regulatory compliance. Related to these we should add accreditation: providing a business-level assurance concerning technical capabilities and undertakings. The business benefits driving cloud adoption are being able to defer and avoid costs; fix the IT bottleneck; map supply and demand more effectively; and de-capitalize IT (Miller & Veiga, 2009). The perceived barriers are security; compliance issues (e.g. data location regulations) and application rewrites. The most important of these at this stage is security – indeed it is difficult to see any new trend or service take root in the IT realm without answering tough questions about security (Boniface, Surridge, Hall-May, Bertram, & Briscombe, 2010).

Unlike interoperability and portability efforts, which are both largely standards-process driven, excellent security does not require agreement between competing providers and vendors. In fact, customers of cloud software vendors and cloud providers will provide the impetus for a fully realized cloud security model as cloud request for proposals are constructed and refined. That being said, it will likely be several years before most cloud offers incorporate the level of security that is general considered 'enterprise grade' (Jensen, Schwenk, Gruschka, & Iacono, 2009). So far, cloud computing has been mostly concerned with running programs on remote computers. In future it will be processing workloads rich with data and other artefacts that will be the business of cloud computing. Accordingly, this is where business issues - responsibility, liability, accountability,

privacy, and data protection compliance – will need to be addressed. Cloud users will therefore need to devote significant time and resources to evaluating cloud providers in terms of their ability to support compliance requirements whether internal and/or regulatory in nature. For example, a consortium of industries, academia and governmental organizations has conducted a risks assessment on cloud computing business model and technologies providing practical recommendations (ENISA, 2009)

In the absence of other mechanisms SAS 70 Type II (NDB Accountants and Consultants, 2009) - the auditing standard used by US certified public accountants to evaluate the processing of transactions – and ISO 27001 (ISO, 2005) information security standards, are emerging as ways to evaluate cloud service provider security. However they remain very high level tools. Other standards such as PCI (Payment Card Industry) and Health Insurance Portability and Accountability Act (HIPAA) do not directly address requirements for cloud providers yet. Nevertheless some cloud providers (Amazon, RightScale) do now provide information on how to achieve HIPAA using their clouds (Amazon, 2009).

Vendor responses to the security question have seen the likes of Verizon (CaaS) and Unisys (Stealth) position new cloud offerings around their security credentials (PR Newswire, 2009; Unisys, 2010). Indeed most security and virtualization management vendors have strategies to support secure practices and/or products for the cloud, but these are only scratching the surface. Microsoft's Azure resides in an ISO27001k certified infrastructure (Microsoft, 2009). Meantime, industry-lead groups such as the Cloud Security Alliance and the Jericho Forum are focused on developing best practices and consensus (Cloud Security Alliance, 2009).

Cloud providers will of course want legal liabilities to remain with the customer and not be transferred to them. A fundamental aspect of the business issues associated with cloud security will be the availability of a contractual language that can adequately represent SLA requirements and liabilities on data security, regulatory needs and availability. The relationship expressed by cloud providers is mostly 'do it my way or take the highway'. This is especially evident in the Cloud Security Alliance's report 'Security Guidance for Critical Areas in Cloud Computing'. This provides a useful checklist of security and privacy concerns, but its guidelines also highlight the current immaturity of cloud offerings. These focus mainly on the need to analyse risks and exercise due diligence prior to negotiating cloud service level agreements. The value of clouds comes from the use of commodity components, and these include the terms and mechanisms of use. Detailed analysis and negotiation of security requirements and obligations is possible, but will drive up costs and erode the benefits clouds can offer. A simpler approach that can meet most security, trust and privacy requirements without protracted negotiation is clearly needed.

Jurisdictional and Legislative Issues

The jurisdictional and legislative issues associated with cloud security, privacy and trust must be analysed in light of current and future business issues and foreseeable technological capabilities. In some cases, the business requirements for cloud computing as identified above will need to be met by using regulatory rather than technical means.

Data protection: the lack of transparency associated with the cloud raises a significant issue when it comes to compliance with data protection and privacy requirements. Under European rules, a firm that processes personal data in the cloud cannot give up all control over the data processing (EC, 2005). Although most of the data processing is done by the firm, hosting, storage and back-up are likely to be performed by the service provider. In these cases the service provider will be considered as 'data processor' for data protection purposes. Three main issues need to be considered here:

- the features of the service must allow the firm to comply with data protection regulations
- the engagement of the cloud service provider must include terms that require appropriate (organizational and technical) measures to be taken against unauthorized and illegal processing of personal data, also applicable in case of loss or damage.
- the firm must know where the data is kept and processed in order to determine whether the rules on the adequacy of the data protection will apply, and how the firm can comply

Credit card numbers cannot be kept in the cloud as PCI mandates that we know where the numbers are kept. Rackspace (Rackspace, 2010) suggests users seeking PCI running its services use a PCI gateway (Rimal, Choi, & Lumb, 2009). But the bottom line is that owners of data have to take specific actions again to ensure that while engaged with a cloud provider's services that they do not lose their PCI compliance.

Due diligence and contractual protection: it is important to address, as starting point, what is, in legal terms, the agreement that encompasses the provision of cloud services. This depends on the applicable national legal framework but, in general it means to set up a service contract. The contractual freedom of the parties plays a fundamental role also regarding confidentiality obligations. This issue is particularly complex, but the relative clause should address at least the extension of the confidentiality obligations of the supplier and the client, duties of the parties and contractual and Court remedies, taking into account that the latter are heavily influenced by the applicable national legal framework. Exceptions to the rule, i.e. situations in which there are no confidentiality obligations.

More availability and better services are promised by the provider and are expected by the customer. This means that the Service Level

Agreements are expected to be more favourable to the customer. Various topics must be considered include the content of SLAs in cloud environments, e-negotiations from legal point of view, applicable law in international SLAs - B2C, B2B scenarios, and jurisdiction and SLAs in case of disputes. A set of principles designed to protect customers is being promoted--the so-called 'Cloud Computing Bill of Rights'. This document provides a checklist of protection with which to benchmark a supplier's offering and to ensure what is provided in the contract.

Jurisdiction: Most of the major cloud suppliers are US-based. What happens when European organizations use cloud services that are based outside of Europe? Europeans might not be in compliance with European data-protection law, as sensitive customer data could be inappropriately shared, or exposed through legal discovery. Cloud providers can try to address this issue by providing certification for datacenters to comply with regulatory rules, and offering services in the EU (e.g. Amazon provides datacenters in Ireland). Also, large organizations can encrypt data, or seek to address any problems contractually through agreed terms and conditions. In order to secure personal information in the cloud, regulators may have to answer questions such as which entities have jurisdiction over data as it flows across borders, and whether governments can access that information as it changes jurisdiction, and whether the risks of improper disclosure are accentuated by using (potentially multiple) datacenters in different jurisdictions.

Regulations and policies: Firms must assess the operational risk and compliance implications as they do with any other product or service. On the one hand, legislation such as the UK Data Protection Act (UK Parliament, 1998), and regulations such as PCI-DSS, need to be examined by companies considering cloud computing.

On the other hand, governments need to re-examine legislation in light of the new technologies and business scenarios they can support. The EU

is launching a broad consultation on whether it should consider revising the 1995 data protection directive. Technologies are not the same as they were in 1995, and cloud computing and new business models are really challenging current systems.

Cloud computing is accelerating in adoption, but the policy issues are a big impediment, and this is where governments have a role to play by addressing policy and regulation components including privacy assurances and access to data. With respect to privacy, Jim Dempsey from the Center of Democracy and Technology said that there's actually a loss of fourth amendment protection for US entities who are using cloud services. The reason behind this statement is that if there is a legal order, whether it be from a court or otherwise, but a legal order to provide data does not have to be served on the owner of the data. It can in fact be served on the cloud provider, and the owner of the data may not even know that the cloud provider was served with that legal order and has in fact turned over the customer's data to whatever government agency or court is requesting that data. Policies can make industry stronger, but at the same time, the wrong kind of policy-making can have huge impacts on technological dominance and on the unfolding of the cloud vision.

Technical Issues

The technical issues associated with cloud security, privacy and trust must be analysed in light of current and future business issues and regulatory environments. These include the technical requirements for implementing the consequences of trust decisions and trust relationships through a combination of management and security capabilities. That includes tight access controls, secure authentication, appropriate encryption of data, logging and playback, intrusion detection, anomaly detection, encrypted management mechanisms and more. Most current cloud offerings are all over the map on the security issue, from largely insecure for some commodity and private cloud offerings to about 50% of the way towards meeting this goal for the best enterprise public clouds. Certainly, as enterprises extend into the cloud they will be forced to examine how they use identity and ensure privacy and regulatory compliance. Business issues rather than strictly 'security' concerns will increasingly require attention.

Authentication: this is usually the starting point for technical security measures. Service hosters must know a user's identity and/or other attributes so they can determine whether their requested access to a service should be granted. Users need to know who is responsible for (and in control of) a service before sending information to it. The problems of authentication over the Internet are widely recognised: technical measures can be used based on digital signatures and X.509 or SAML authentication tokens attached to access requests and responses. However, the cost of establishing trust in these tokens can be high. In the cloud, the position is complicated by the fact that users and services will not have pre-established relationships with each other, and the organisation responsible for a service may not be the organisation who hosts it. Indeed, depending on what cloud facilities are used (IaaS, PaaS or SaaS) and whether the cloud is public or private, the party responsible for a service may actually be a cloud service consumer. This issue is not well addressed in current cloud offerings, where the consumer of cloud services is left to manage the issues at the application level. As a result, it is hard to ensure that all one's business and legal requirements are met – e.g. by ensuring that all the parties involved in providing a cloud service are bound to comply with EU privacy legislation. In future, it is likely that cross-hosting scenarios will be encountered for some (highly scalable) applications, at which point authentication models should allow one cloud hoster to identify potentially several parties associated with an access request from another cloud hoster.

Authorisation: this generic term describes the processes and decisions needed to determine whether access to a service (computing, data storage, etc) should be granted, and how the policies and user authentication tokens are managed and made consistent with each other. In the cloud, as in the Grid, the main challenge is to maintain an authorisation policy that meets the needs of the stakeholders of a service, and simultaneously to maintain consistency between this policy and the policies that regulate access to user identity/attribute authentication tokens. A key aspect is the ability to define which token sources are considered trustworthy, and attach these definitions to services (or data) wherever they may be. For example, the effect of (cloud-enabled) extended enterprise on identity and access management will mandate a need for federation. Securing data in motion and at rest across and between LANs, WANs and wireless will be a business issue for all stakeholders. Research from the Grid domain has shown that the most cost-effective approach is to use a dynamic policy model in which authorisation policies are provisioned along with other resources for individual services, and the policy incorporates rules for how it can be updated by users. This allows a 'self service' model for policy and trust management allowing trust decisions to be encoded directly by the various stakeholders. However, these mechanisms are not well addressed in current cloud offerings, and in future the management at scale of trust decisions (and their expression in policies) will remain a challenge even with such dynamic policy models.

Accountability: accountability is driven by the business issues of defining (through agreements) who is responsible for the consequences of actions implemented using cloud services, including payment of any fees or other costs associated with the action. At present, cloud operators typically assume no responsibility for anything, which implies that the consumer is responsible, but even this position is not explicitly defined. For example, AWS S3 services state that authorisation policies can be defined for stored data making it private to the service user, restricted to a list of users authenticated by AWS, made available to any user authenticated by AWS, or made available to anonymous users (Amazon, 2010). If data is accessed by anonymous users, the original S3 service user pays for any data transfer, but we are left to assume that authenticated users will pay if they access the data. In many cases this may not match the application users' business requirements.

Accountability is also a technical issue because it must be taken into account in the design of both authentication and authorisation measures, depending on the accountability rules agreed between the various parties. For example, technical solutions exist for non-repudiation based on storing information exchanged using authenticated protocols but the limits of authentication and accountability solutions means they are of limited use. Research in business Grids shows that accountability must be fine grained (related to individual data sets and computational processes), and possibly dynamic (so users can trade in data and other resources). This drives the need for fine-grained authorisation policy and trust management for large numbers of individual resources (see above). In future, software agents and physical devices will need to be incorporated into accountability models, and at this stage there are no good accountability models that address large numbers of non-human actors even within the research community.

Data confidentiality: normally a fundamental business pre-requisite, data confidentiality is usually achieved by controlling access to stored data (based on authentication and accountability), and using encryption to prevent eavesdropping. However, these techniques are not universally applied, and users are often left to configure them according to their needs. Not all users have the understanding or expertise to do this, and cloud providers may eventually have to take some responsibility for the consequences. For example, Google has been

asked by a group of leading security experts to enable HTTPS encryption by default on its most popular web apps, including Gmail and Google Docs, to avoid exposing users the risk of fraud from hackers when using an open or badly secured network, particularly public WiFi spots.

Confidentiality can also be compromised by flaws in self-service authorisation policy management systems, or in the technical measures used to enforce authorisation policies. For example, in Google Apps information or documents have been shared inappropriately with other customers, with at least one incident being caused by a flaw in the authorisation management system in Google Docs (Jensen, 2009). Other high-profile cases include inappropriate access to data from thousands of customers at VAServ, due to a flaw in the enforcement technology (in this case in the virtualisation software – see below). Some users may prefer to encrypt any data they store in the cloud, but this means they also have to provide keys to any processing they want to run on the data. Secure computing techniques to process data in encrypted form do exist, but the technology is still in its infancy, for a limited range of applications and typically with huge performance overheads.

Data integrity: just as important as confidentiality is the ability to ensure that user data stored or transferred in the cloud remains available and uncorrupted. Access control is a pre-requisite, as even if data is encrypted to prevent it being read, it can still be altered or deleted by a malicious user. For data being transferred across the network, it is impossible to prevent tampering in transit, so in practice the only defence is to check the data whenever it is transferred to or from a cloud service. Data integrity can be verified using the same techniques as authentication. For example, a digital signature can be created on the data plus other information such as the date, making it possible to verify that the data hasn't changed when retrieved at some later time. The biggest challenges arise when data has to be retained for many months or years, during which time:

- advances in computing power and digital cryptography may make it possible to break or fake an old digital signature; or
- the stored data may degrade through the accumulated effects of background radiation, physical deterioration of the media, or obsolescence of the technology needed to read it.

In long-term archives one has to actively preserve the data, by keeping redundant copies of the data, transferring it to new media as existing storage technology becomes outdated, and applying new integrity protection devices before existing protection becomes worthless. Note however that preservation is not without its costs (Addis, Wright & Miller, 2008), so it is important to manage the level of preservation used to balance costs against risks. Cloud service providers like Amazon currently do not provide any quantifiable integrity safeguards, but researchers are starting to analyse and formulate business models and QoS metrics for archival services in the cloud, making it feasible to offer high-integrity storage services in future (Addis, Lowe, Salvo, & Middleton, 2009).

Service availability: users need to feel confident that if they choose cloud resources to meet their needs, those resources will be available when they need them. Large numbers of virtualised resources can be packed into a small number of physical resources, but each virtual resource can then suffer from low performance. The problem therefore is not simply whether a resource can be contacted, but also whether it will perform adequately. At present, few cloud providers make any guarantees about this – they price services based on usage, leaving performance to vary depending on the prevailing load. One solution is to include performance QoS commitments in service level agreements. Experience from Grid and SOA research shows that such commitments will have to be bi-directional – if the provider guarantees performance then the consumer will have to make a commitment not to overload the

service. For example, the GRIA software (Boniface, Phillips, & Surridge, 2006) provides two options: the service provider can block access without penalty if a usage threshold is exceeded, or charge more for higher levels of usage so they do not lose out if an overload from one consumer leads to underperformance towards other consumers. Research in real-time QoS-management on virtualized infrastructures has shown that QoS guarantees can be provisioned and managed for VMUs deployed on the same physical resources, by exploiting isolation techniques at the CPU, network and storage scheduling levels (Boniface, Nasser, Papay, et al, 2010; Cucinotta, Anastasi, and Abeni, 2009). Commercial cloud providers also typically use price bands to discourage excessive usage (Amazon, 2010), but consumers can evade this by using multiple identities and spreading their usage between them. Providers can also reduce risks from customer contention for services by asking customers to commit to a usage level in advance. One option is to ask users to pay up front for a reservation, in exchange for a discount in the price per unit actually used (Amazon, 2010). This is less vulnerable to consumer evasion, but also less likely to discourage additional unexpected usage. IT Innovation conducted an in-depth study of the relationship between SLA terms and the management of availability/performance in the NextGRID project.

Even if users can trust cloud providers to allocate resources to meet their needs, any service that is accessed over a public network can also be rendered unavailable by a Denial of Service attack by a malicious third party wishing to harm the cloud provider or specific customers. There are two main forms of DoS attacks. In 'conventional' DoS, the attacker seeks to consume resources at the service making it unable to respond to legitimate request, as in the classic SYN flood attack that uses up available connections. These 'conventional' attacks can be mitigated using a range of technical measures including packet filtering firewalls (Patrikakis, Masikos, & Zouraraki, 2004). The other approach is to overload the network through which the target service is accessed, so it doesn't matter whether the service allocates resources to deal with malicious requests. Since cloud providers typically have very high capacity network connectivity, the only way to do this is through a distributed denial of service (DDoS) attack, using large numbers of compromised (zombie) machines on the Internet. DDoS is much harder to mitigate, as in most cases one has to locate the attacker and disrupt their communication with the zombie network, characterise the malicious traffic so it can be blocked through a coordinated effort by Internet backbone network operators, or find vulnerabilities in the zombie network through which they can be prevented from participating in the attack.

System integrity: the integrity of cloud systems is obviously essential if they are to fulfil users' expectations. There are two aspects to be considered:

- the integrity of cloud management infrastructure used to provision and monitor cloud resources for end users;
- the integrity of cloud resources once in service.

The integrity of cloud hardware must be considered – as hinted in the discussion of data integrity above. The evolution and take-up of multi-core technology is likely to have an impact on system integrity. At present, multi-core technology is widely used in data centres that host Grid/cloud services. However, the thrust of Grid/cloud management mechanisms is to use virtualisation to abstract away from the underlying architecture. However, as the number of cores per device grows, devices are more likely to experience failures affecting some cores, and are more likely to remain in service after a few of the cores have failed. This represents a new threat to cloud users: an increased likelihood that the hardware executing their applications may have undetected faults.

The integrity of cloud management infrastructure is also a cloud-specific security challenge, for which responsibility lies with the service provider. In IaaS, protecting the management interfaces is a key concern, and for Public Clouds these interfaces have to be open to any potential customer. Security is typically handled via simple authentication against a previously registered username-password. PaaS and SaaS typically use a similar approach but with a more complex authorisation model restricting each user to services they have paid for. European research projects such as NextGRID and SIMDAT have gone well beyond these simple approaches, using dynamic federated security models supported by X509, SAML and Web Service Security specifications, as implemented in GRIA (Ahsant et al, 2006) These provide much greater sophistication but are not supported by any commercial provider.

The integrity of monitoring and accounting systems is also essential for service providers especially where they are used to generate billing information – if the billing system is compromised, some users may get services for free, and others may refuse to pay bills if they believe they may not be trustworthy. The integrity of virtualisation systems is critical to ensure segregation between users sharing the same set of physical resources. Finally, once a cloud resource has been provisioned, its integrity must also be protected. This is really no different from any other system, except that cloud resources cannot be protected by disconnecting them (logically or physically) from the Internet. The usual measures therefore need to be applied: the amount of software installed should be minimised to avoid unnecessary vulnerabilities, intrusion detection systems and anti-virus software should be used, and security updates should be applied promptly. Firewalls may also be used to block unnecessary traffic. With PaaS and SaaS services, the service provider will normally be responsible for these measures, and while they are unlikely to accept liability for any breaches, they may agree to use independently accredited security procedures. With IaaS the consumer is responsible for the integrity of installed software and must implement their own procedures. Some IaaS providers provide some support for self-service security configuration – e.g. Amazon's management Web Service interface allows users to configure firewall settings for provisioned virtual hosts. However, few non-corporate users have the expertise to use this facility (which is based on IP Tables configuration). It remains to be seen whether clouds become an attractive target for malicious compromise. In theory cloud resources should be better protected than home computer systems, but without more user-friendly self-service security configurations this may not be the case, and compromised cloud resources may be a more profitable target for criminals if they have corporate co-tenants, for example. Multitenancy, the reason virtualisation is so attractive to cloud service hosters is that it allows them to share a device between multiple users. Most users do not need dedicated use of even a single device, so by sharing a device it is possible to serve more users with the same physical resources. However, when users share resources (even if only the networking resources), it is important that one user cannot access information and other assets belonging to another. The integrity of virtualisation technology (see above) is critical to enforce the necessary segregation between co-tenants of the same cloud infrastructure. Breaches have occurred – the disclosure (and loss) of data belonging to many thousands of customers at cloud provider VAServ (Register, 2009) was caused by a flaw in the underlying HyperVM virtualisation technology from LXLabs.

FUTURE RESEARCH DIRECTIONS

The current state of the art in commercial cloud service provision is currently behind the state of the art in European FP6 and FP7 research projects. For example, commercial Cloud operators are not using fine-grained dynamic federated security models, or privacy enhancing technologies (Meissner & Schallaböck, 2009) that would enable them to better address European concerns over privacy, accountability, etc. A significant emphasis will therefore be to highlight where research results can be used in conjunction with more familiar technology, some of which may need to be adapted to mitigate business risks that are currently not well addressed by cloud operators:

Compliance: Compliance and security are intersecting but non-identical issues. A computer system may be secure but not compliant, or compliant but not secure. Nevertheless, in regulated industries such as finance, healthcare and the public sector, cloud tools for enforcing compliance with the relevant regulatory regimes are a non-negotiable checklist item. The industry may even see the evolution of specialized clouds guaranteeing compliance with, for example, the Health Information Portability and Accountability Act or the Payment Card Industry Data Security Standard. So glad would enterprises be to outsource the burden of compliance that this could become a driver for cloud adoption.

Firewalls: While firewalls would seem an excellent candidate for inclusion in the 'common ground' section, due to their largely commoditized status, not just any firewall can be used in a cloud environment. It's exactly the opposite – a very specific set of features is necessary to ensure safe and economical cloud deployment and operation. Cloud firewalls must operate with a large number of simultaneous, virtual and parallel rule sets, and be configurable via a rich API to allow integration into cloud management structures and a rapid provisioning of new virtual networks.

Log management: Log management is a common function in today's IT security architecture, but the ability to manage and integrate the logs of numerous virtual machines, keeping each set of VM logs separate and discrete, yet providing correlation within each set, is somewhat complex. It is vital that this capability be supported in order for a log management element to be included in cloud architectures. Sophisticated API access, to allow log information to be communicated with management front ends, is also necessary.

Identity management: Identity solutions for cloud architectures face many of the same issues as those for log management, including the need to support discrete sets of virtual machines or storage volumes without providing any visibility into assets that do not belong to a particular user. Identity solutions must also allow federated identity between in-house IT (or private clouds) and public clouds through standards-based protocols. Neither is well supported by existing cloud offerings, but could be achieved by adopting results from recent EU research in Grids and SOA, and where appropriate (e.g. in public commodity clouds for individual citizens) privacy enhancing technology.

Intrusion detection: Similar to issues surrounding firewalls, intrusion detection and prevention systems (IDPS) must be capable of supporting numerous virtual and discrete networks, must be rapidly provisionable and must support integration via management APIs. While some cloud architectures skirt issues of IDPS being able to handle discrete internal networks by placing IDPS far outside of the cloud infrastructure entirely, that will not protect one user's virtual cloud infrastructure from another's, which necessitates IDPS between users, as well as at the network boundary.

CONCLUSION

In this chapter we have presented the current and future challenges for securing real-time interaction applications in federated cloud environments. We expect the evolution of clouds to be largely driven by the convergence of networks, services, content and things that is leading to the Future Internet as envisioned in Europe. This will raise additional issues:

- service users may be continuously connected and never actually 'log on' to use a service – raising new challenges for authentication by service vendors or hosters;
- service users may be autonomous devices – raising new challenges for accountability for the consequences of using a service;
- composition of different services by consumers will become easier – increasing the need for interoperable 'inter-hoster' and 'inter-cloud' security and trust models;
- cloud intermediaries may emerge, e.g. coordinators of multi-hoster clouds, or brokers selling to consumers using wholesale hosting markets, leading to increasingly complex trust networks between cloud service providers and consumers;
- composition of services with content (including sensor data and media content) will also lead to more complex trust networks of cloud providers and content stakeholders (data subjects, intellectual property owners, sensor operators, etc).

Moreover, as the take-up of cloud computing increases, the cloud will increasingly become a critical infrastructure in its own right, so it is necessary to consider vulnerabilities and interdependency issues on a 'global' scale. For example, society may become more vulnerable to DDoS if more business and government ICT is cloud based, and compromised clouds may make it easier for malicious agents to perpetrate attacks on other clouds. The success of the Conficker worm in maintaining communication with its criminal controllers despite efforts to prevent this means at least one large-scale compromised cloud (with largely unsuspecting hosters) already exists. Interdependency issues may mean that efforts to manage clouds (both malicious and legitimate) may have indirect and unforeseen consequences – e.g. a 'trust crunch' may drastically reduce the availability of computing capacity in the same way the credit crunch reduced access to liquid funds.

Some of these issues go beyond the scope of the proposed study, but we will seek to identify areas where further work (possibly including RTD in the Framework programme) is likely to be needed.

We believe that by combining technical mitigation strategies with robust business models and agreements in the context of the European regulatory framework, cloud stakeholders can address many of the security, trust and privacy issues that are not well handled by existing cloud offerings. This will involve going beyond current operational practices, including those advocated in the Cloud Security Alliance guidelines, and adopting results of ongoing research, combined with policy initiatives from governments to encourage safer and more trustworthy clouds. This vision will incorporate and be supported by state of the art security technologies including results from past and present EC RTD projects, and also foreseeable or desirable extensions beyond the current state of the art in the next 5-10 years. However, we expect that some gaps will remain that cannot be filled without further research and/or updates to the legal and regulatory framework in which clouds operate.

REFERENCES

Addis, M., Lowe, R., Salvo, N., & Middleton, L. (2009, September). *Reliable audiovisual archiving using unreliable storage technology and services.* Conference of the International Broadcasting Convention, Amsterdam, Netherlands.

Addis, M., Wright, R., & Miller, A. (2008, September). The significance of storage in the cost of risk of digital preservation. In *Proceedings of the Fifth International Conference on Preservation of Digital Objects* (iPRES 2008), British Library, London, UK.

Ahsant, M., Surridge, M., Leonard, T. A., Krishna, A., & Mulmo, O. (2006). *Dynamic trust federation in Grids.* The 4th International Conference on Trust Management, 16 - 19 May 2006, Pisa, Tuscany, Italy. ISBN 978-3-540-34295-3

Amazon. (2009). *Creating HIPAA-compliant medical data applications with AWS.* Retrieved on June 30, 2009, from http://aws.amazon.com/about-aws/whats-new/2009/04/06/whitepaper-hipaa/

Amazon. (2010). *Amazon EC2 banded pricing.* Retrieved July 5, 2010 from http://aws.amazon.com/ec2/#pricing

Amazon. (2010). *Amazon EC2's reserved instances model.* Retrieved July 5, 2010 from http://aws.amazon.com/ec2/#pricing

Amazon. (2010). *What is AWS?* Retrieved July 5, 2010 from http://aws.amazon.com/what-is-aws/

Boniface, M., Nasser, B., Papay, J., Phillips, S., Servin, A., Zlatev, Z., et al. Kyriazis, D. (2010) *Platform-as-a-service architecture for real-time quality of service management in clouds.* Internet and Web Applications and Services, ICIW 2010 Fifth International Conference, May 2010, Barcelona.

Boniface, M., Surridge, M., Hall-May, M., Bertram, S., & Briscombe, N. (2010). *On-demand dynamic security for risk-based secure collaboration in clouds.* IEEE International Conference on Cloud Computing 2010, July 2010, Miami, USA.

Boniface, M. J., Phillips, S. C., & Surridge, M. (2006, October). *Grid-based business partnerships using service level agreements.* Cracow Grid Workshop, Cracow, Poland.

Cloud Security Alliance. (2009). *Security guidance for critical areas of focus in cloud computing.* Retrieved June 30, 2010 from http://www.cloudsecurityalliance.org/guidance/csaguide.pdf

Cucinotta, T., Anastasi, G., & Abeni, L. (2009, July). Respecting temporal constraints in virtualised services. *Proceedings of the 2nd IEEE International Workshop on Real-Time Service-Oriented Architecture and Applications* (RTSOAA 2009), Seattle, Washington.

EC. (2005, November). Principles relating to data quality. *Official Journal of the European Communties, 281*(40).

European Network and Information Security Agency (ENISA). (2009). *Cloud computing: Benefits, risks and recommendations for information security.* Retrieved June 10, 2010, from http:// www.enisa.europa.eu/ act/ rm/ files/ deliverables/ cloud-computing-risk-assessment

Ferris, J., Surridge, M., & Glinka, F. (2009). *Securing real-time online interactive applications in edutain@grid.* Workshop on Real-Time Online Interactive Applications on the Grid, Las Palmas de Gran Canaria, Spain, Lecture Notes in Computer Science.

Gilbert Miller, H., & Veiga, J. (2009). Cloud computing: Will commodity services benefit users long term? *IT Professional, 11*(6), 57–59. doi:10.1109/MITP.2009.117

ISO. (2005 October). *ISO 20001 Information security management systems — Requirements.* Retrieved from http://www.27000.org/ iso-27001. htm

Jensen, M., Schwenk, J., Gruschka, N., & Lo Iacono, L. (2009). *On technical security issues in cloud computing.* IEEE International Conference on Cloud Computing, (pp. 109-116).

Meissner, S., & Schallaböck, J. (2009). *Requirements for privacy enhancing service oriented infrastructures.* EC IST Primelife Project. Retrieved on June 30, 2009 from http://www.primelife.eu/ images/ stories/ deliverables/ h6.3.1-requirements_for_ privacy_enhancing_ soas-public.pdf

Microsoft. (2009). *Securing Microsoft's cloud infrastructure.* Retrieved June 30, 2009, from http://www.globalfoundationservices.com/ security/ documents/ SecuringtheMSCloud May09.pdf

NDB Accountants and Consultants. (2009). *Statement on auditing standards.* No. 70 (SAS Primer) Retrieved on Dec. 09 from http://www. sas70.us.com/

Newswire, P. R. (2009). *Verizon business offers tips on how enterprises can secure the cloud.* Retrieved on June 30, 2009, from http://www.prnewswire. com/ news-releases/ verizon-business-offers-tips -on-how-enterprises -can-secure-the-cloud -96784414.html

UK Parliament. (1998). *Data protection act 1998.*

Patrikakis, C., Masikos, M., & Zouraraki, O. (2004). Distributed denial of service attacks. *The Journal of Internet Protocol, 7*(4), 13–35.

Rackspace. (2010). *The PCI toolbox.* Retrieved July 5, 2010, from http://www.rackspace.com/ managed_hosting/ services/ security/ pci.php

Register. (2009). *Webhost attack.* Retrieved June 30, 2009 from http://www.theregister.co.uk/ 2009/ 06/ 08/ webhost_attack/

Rimal, B. P., Choi, E., & Lumb, I. (2009). A Taxonomy and survey of cloud computing systems. In R. Dienstbier (Ed.), *Fifth International Joint Conference on Networked Computing and Advanced Information Management,* (pp. 44-51).

Sotomayor, B., Montero, R. S., Llorente, I. M., & Foster, I. (2009). *Virtual infrastructure management in private and hybrid clouds.* IEEE Internet Computing. ISSN: 1089-7801

Unisys. (2010). *Secure cloud solution service brief.* Retrieved on July 5, 2010, from http://www. unisys.com/ unisys/ ri/ pub/ bl/ detail.jsp?id= 10020100026

KEY TERMS AND DEFINITIONS

Federation: Processes and mechanisms where 2 or more administration domains can reach agreement for the exchange of information and services, and how the exchange is governed.

Inter-Enterprise: The exchange of information and services between enterprises using the Internet.

Privacy: Processes and mechanisms by which personally identifiable information is protected from unintended use.

Regulation: Legal restrictions placed by governments on a market.

Risk: The combination of the probability of an event and its consequences, positive and negative.

Security: Processes and mechanisms by which information, services and other property are protected from theft, corruption and failure.

Trust: The belief that an entity is capable of acting reliably, dependably, and securely for a specific interaction.

Chapter 10
Web Service Specifications Relevant for Service Oriented Infrastructures

Eduardo Oliveros
Telefónica Investigación y Desarrollo, Spain

Jesús Movilla
Telefónica Investigación y Desarrollo, Spain

Andreas Menychtas
National Technical University of Athens, Greece

Roland Kuebert
University of Stuttgart, Germany

Michael Braitmaier
University of Stuttgart, Germany

Stuart Middleton
University of Southampton, UK

Stephen C. Phillips
University of Southampton, UK

Michael Boniface
University of Southampton, UK

Bassem Nasser
University of Southampton, UK

ABSTRACT

Service Oriented Infrastructures (SOIs) have recently seen increased use, mainly thanks to technologies for data centre virtualization and the emergence and increasing commercial offering of Cloud solutions. Web Services have been seen as a tool to implement SOI solutions thanks to their versatility and interoperability, but at the same time, Web Services have been considered not suitable for providing interactive real-time solutions. In this chapter the state of the art of the Web service technology will be analysed, and their different communication mechanisms and the existing implementations will be compared. Firstly, the different standardisation bodies working on Web service specifications relevant to SOI will be introduced. The various approaches to implement Web services will be described followed by the Web service specifications and the middleware that make use of those specifications, including the description of the commercial interfaces and development tools to create services for the cloud. In the last part of the chapter, the interoperability problems present on the different frameworks and the existing solutions to minimize those interoperability problems will be explained.

DOI: 10.4018/978-1-60960-827-9.ch010

INTRODUCTION

The most well known and widely used connection technology for building SOIs are web services. A web service is a software system designed to support interoperable machine-to-machine interaction over a network. There are currently two types of web services: the SOAP web services and the RESTful web services.

In the SOAP web services the interface is described in a machine-processable format, Web Service Description Language (WSDL), which provides a model and an XML format for describing web services. WSDL enables one to separate the description of the abstract functionality offered by a service from concrete details of a service description such as "how" and "where" that functionality is offered (Chinnici et al. 2003). WSDL describes a web service in two fundamental levels: the *abstract level* and the *concrete level*. Within each of these two levels, the description uses a number of constructs to promote reusability of the description and separate independent design concerns.

At the *abstract level*, WSDL describes a web service in terms of the messages it sends and receives; messages are described independent of a specific wire format using a type system, typically XML Schema. An operation associates a message exchange pattern with one or more messages. A message exchange pattern identifies the sequence and cardinality of messages sent and/or received as well as to whom they are logically sent to and/or received from. An interface groups together operations without any commitment to transport or wire format.

At the *concrete level*, a binding specifies transport and wire format details for one or more interfaces. An endpoint associates a network address with a binding. And finally, a service groups together endpoints that implement a common interface (Chinnici et al., 2003).

Other systems interact with a web service in a manner prescribed by its description using SOAP messages, typically conveyed using HTTP with an XML serialization in conjunction with other web-related standards (Booth et al., 2004).

Web services provide a standard means of interoperating between different software applications, running on a variety of platforms and/or frameworks. Their complexity and orientation to large software vendors rather than open source software are often regarded as the major drawbacks of web services. Other criticism on web services is their performance, due to the fact of using XML as a message format and SOAP for the envelop.

The following list outlines the steps involved in a web service invocation using the SOAP approach:

1. The client application uses a client stub, which offers remote operations as seemingly local method calls, to turn its request into a proper SOAP request. This is often called the *marshalling* or *serializing* process.

2. The SOAP request is sent over a network using the HTTP protocol. The server receives the SOAP requests and passes it to a server stub. The server stub *unmarshals/deserializes* the SOAP request.

3. The server stub invokes the service implementation of the requested operation, which carries out the work.

4. The result of the requested operation is handed to the server stub and converted into a SOAP response message.

5. The SOAP response is sent over a network using the HTTP protocol. The client stub receives the SOAP response and *unmarshals/deserializes* it.

6. Finally the client receives the result of the web service operation.

The Representational State Transfer (REST) is another style of creating web service that has emerged as an alternative to SOAP implementation for web services. RESTful web services are implemented using HTTP and focused on interactions with stateful resources rather than messages and operations. The resources are identified and accessed using directory structure-like URIs (e.g. http://www.example.com/myservice/users/123) and the service actions for create, read, update, and delete (CRUD) are performed with the standard HTTP methods GET, POST, PUT and DELETE. The web service architectures that are based on REST can either use WSDL to describe SOAP messaging over HTTP or can be created without using SOAP at all. REST being an architectural approach, and not a protocol, is not following any "official" standards; nevertheless there are several REST implementations for all programming languages.

This chapter will present the existing web service specifications that are relevant to SOIs and the standardisation bodies working on those specifications. The existing research and commercial development frameworks that make use of those specifications are also described at the end of the chapter.

STANDARDISATION ORGANISATIONS OF WEB SERVICE SPECIFICATIONS

The World Wide Web Consortium (W3C)

The World Wide Web Consortium (W3C) is an international community that works to develop web standards (http://www.w3.org/standards). W3C's mission is to lead the Web to its full potential.

Probably the most important Web standards are provided by the W3C, like HTTP (with IETF), HTML and CSS. But most specifically in relation to web services Standards, the W3C is responsible for the specification (among others) of SOAP, WSDL, WS-Addressing, WS-Policy, XML Schema and has published some working drafts for the WS-Transfer, web services Resource Transfer (WS-RT) (Reistad et al., 2006), WS-

Enumeration (Davis et al., 2009), WS-Metadata Exchange (Davis et al., 2009b) and WS-Eventing (Davis et al., 2009c) specifications.

A complete list of standards is available in (http://www.w3.org/TR/Overview) and specifically regarding web services specifications in (http://www.w3.org/2002/ws/).

Organization for the Advancement of Structured Information Standards (OASIS)

OASIS (Organization for the Advancement of Structured Information Standards) (http://www.oasis-open.org) is a global consortium that drives the development, convergence and adoption of open standards for the global information society. The consortium produces more Web services standards than any other organization along with standards for security, e-business, and standardization efforts in the public sector and for application-specific markets. Founded in 1993, OASIS has more than 5,000 participants representing over 600 organizations and individual members in 100 countries.

OASIS is distinguished by its transparent governance and operating procedures. Members themselves set the OASIS technical agenda, using a lightweight process specifically designed to promote industry consensus and unite disparate efforts. Completed work is ratified by open ballot. Governance is accountable and unrestricted. Officers of both the OASIS Board of Directors and Technical Advisory Board are chosen by democratic election to serve two-year terms. Consortium leadership is based on individual merit and is not tied to financial contribution, corporate standing, or special appointment.

The Consortium hosts two of the most widely respected information portals on XML and Web services standards, Cover Pages (http://xml.coverpages.org/) and XML.org (http://www.xml.org/).

OASIS is responsible for the Web Services Resource Framework (WSRF), BPEL, ebXML and the WS-DD set of specifications, just to name a few. A complete list of the OASIS Committees working on web services is available in (http://www.oasis-open.org/committees/tc_cat. php?cat=ws).

The Open Grid Forum (OGF)

The Open Grid Forum (OGF) (http://www.ogf. org/) is a community of users, developers, and vendors leading the global standardization effort for grid computing. The OGF community consists of thousands of individuals in industry and research, representing over 400 organizations in more than 50 countries. OGF works to accelerate adoption of grid computing worldwide because they believe grids will lead to new discoveries, new opportunities, and better business practices.

The work of OGF is carried out through community-initiated working groups, which develop standards and specifications in cooperation with other leading standards organizations, software vendors, and users. OGF is funded through its Organizational Members, including technology companies, academic and government research institutions. OGF hosts several events each year to further develop grid-related specifications and use cases and to share best practices.

The OGF community reflects the near universal interest in and applicability of distributed systems, and includes leaders and practitioners drawn from academia, enterprises, vendors and government organizations. OGF is open to everyone who is willing to participate.

Applied distributed computing environments include everything from distributed high performance computing resources (traditional 'Grids') to horizontally scaled transactional systems supporting Service Oriented Architectures to Clouds, across all scales and for all application domains.

Applied distributed computing environments take advantage of many technologies, e.g. virtualization, multi-Core, web services, SOA, etc.

Some of the specifications provided by OGF are: JSDL, WS-Agreement, WS Data Access and Integration (WS-DAI).

Distributed Management Task Force, Inc. (DMTF)

DMTF (http://www.dmtf.org) enables more effective management of millions of IT systems worldwide by bringing the IT industry together to collaborate on the development, validation and promotion of systems management standards. The group spans the industry with 160 member companies and organizations, and more than 4,000 active participants crossing 43 countries. The DMTF board of directors is led by 16 innovative, industry-leading technology companies. They include Advanced Micro Devices (AMD); Broadcom Corporation; CA, Inc.; Citrix Systems, Inc.; Dell; EMC; Fujitsu; HP; Hitachi, Ltd.; IBM; Intel Corporation; Microsoft Corporation; Novell; Oracle; Sun Microsystems, Inc. and VMware, Inc. With this deep and broad reach, DMTF creates standards that enable interoperable IT management. DMTF management standards are critical to enabling management interoperability among multi-vendor systems, tools and solutions within the enterprise. Information about DMTF technologies and activities can be found at (http://www.dmtf.org).

For more in-depth information about DMTF's standards, visit the standards (http://www.dmtf. org/standards/) page, where WS-Management is one of the specifications defined by DMTF.

DIFFERENT APPROACHES AND IMPLEMENTATION OPTIONS

Web Services

The World Wide Web Consortium's (W3C) web service definition (Booth et al., 2004) specifies clients and servers that communicate with each other using XML messages that follow the SOAP standard (http://www.w3.org/TR/soap/). In this context, WSDL (Christensen et al., 2001), although not a requirement of a SOAP endpoint, is a prerequisite for automated client-side code generation in many Java and .NET SOAP frameworks such as Spring (http://www.springsource.org/), Apache Axis2 (http://ws.apache.org/axis2/) and Apache CX (http://cxf.apache.org/).

Mostly object-oriented programming languages are used to develop web services. This section provides a brief background on the most widely-known and commonly used object-oriented programming languages for the development of web services. The main object programming languages are listed below:

- *Java* (http://www.java.com) is an object-oriented, platform-independent, multi-threaded, programming environment. Software written in the Java programming language is compiled to byte code. The Java virtual machine interprets that byte code to any platform on which the Java virtual machine is installed. Web services are developed using Java Technology APIs and tools provided by an integrated web services Stack. This stack consisting of Java API for XML Web Services (JAX-WS) (https://jax-ws.dev.java.net/), Java Architecture for XML Binding (JAXB) (https://jaxb.dev.java.net/), and Web Services Interoperability Technologies (WSIT) (https://wsit.dev.java.net/), enables developers to create and deploy secure, reliable, transactional, interoperable web services and clients.
- *C#* is an object-oriented programming language that enables programmers to build solutions for the Microsoft .NET development environment. The framework allows C# components to become XML web services that are available across the Internet, from any application running on any platform.
- *C++* is an object-oriented programming language with a bias towards systems programming that also supports the development of web services through gSOAP (http://gsoap2.sourceforge.net/), which is an open source set of web service-enabling tools for C and C++ applications.
- *PHP* is a scripting language widely used for web development, mobile applications such as SMS center or desktop widgets. PHP has a number of extensions that provide support for Web Services (including SOAP messages, XML-RPC or OAuth).

The basic two applications servers that provide middleware services for security and state maintenance, along with data access and persistence are Java applications servers based on J2EE or subsequent specifications or Microsoft's .NET.

From Web Services to Grid Services

Although not stated explicitly in their definition, simple web services are considered to be unable to maintain state, i.e. web service have no memory of the interactions that take place and therefore cannot maintain the state between invocations. However, Grid applications often imply the need for stateful interactions and do generally require some form of persistency between invocations where one invocation should influence the execution of the succeeding ones. So, the challenge was to enable web services to maintain information about state while still keeping them stateless. This was achieved by splitting the web service from the state and keeping them completely separate. In more detail, state is stored inside a separate entity that is called a resource that has a unique key we can use to interact with it.

More formally, a WS-Resource (Graham et al.,2006) is the composition of a resource and a web service through which the resource can be accessed. The aforementioned objects are illustrated in the following figure.

A WS-Resource is further defined as follows:

- A reference to a WS-Resource is represented by an endpoint reference (EPR), or more precisely an XML element type which is, or is derived from (by extension), the complexType named EndpointReferenceType defined by the WS-Addressing specification. Such EPRs must reference exactly one WS-Resource.
- The set of properties of the resource must be expressed using an XML Infoset (Booth & Haas, 2004) described by XML schema. The WS-Resource must support accessing resource properties through message exchanges defined by the WS-ResourceProperties specification (Graham &Treadwell, 2006).
- A WS-Resource may support the message exchanges defined by the WS-ResourceLifetime specification (Srinivasan & Banks, 2006).

For a given WS-Resource there may be many references. The way two references are compared for equality is implementation-specific and not defined by this specification (Graham et al.,2006).

Restful Web Services

In recent years, RESTful web services (Fielding, 2000) are becoming popular again. REST is an architectural style that can be used to design web services. Although it meets the W3C definition, REST does not require XML messages or WSDL service-API definitions and while REST is not a standard itself, it makes use of other well-established standards such as HTTP, URL, XML and HTML among others.

The basic concept behind REST is the existence of sources of specific information, called resources, each of which can be referred to using a URI. The management of these resources is controlled by components that communicate via a standardized interface (e.g. HTTP) and exchange representations of these resources.

It should be noted that web services, either written in C#/C++ and running on .NET platforms or written in Java and running on Java EE platforms,

Figure 1. Stateful WS-Resources

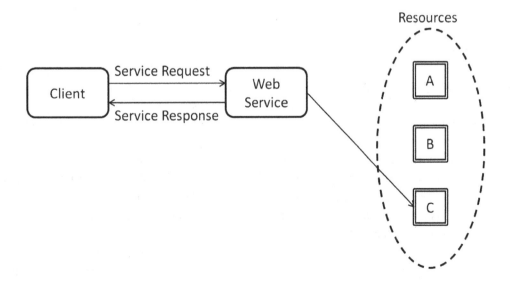

can be consumed by another service or client running on other platform. There are implementations of web services in other languages/platforms too, but in a much smaller scale.

The REST interface uses the standard HTTP requests, as defined in RFC 2616 (Fielding et al., 1999), to communicate with the service. You can see Amazon Simple Storage Service Developer Guide for a reference about how the request to Simple Storage Service provided by Amazon is built.

In Amazon 85% of the API usage is of REST interfaces (O'Reilly, 2003). It is clear that the complexity of using the SOAP alternative makes companies (especially SMEs) to prefer the simple approach of the SOAP interface that can be implemented easily. Google and PayPal have traditionally provided its services using SOAP, but recently Google has published a new service: "Google Storage for Developers" that only has a REST interface. There is a clear trend in the market to provide REST style of interfaces over SOAP alternatives.

The advantages of REST are (Singh and Singh, 2009):

- Lightweight, less bandwidth
- Caching
- Use of standard technologies (HTTP, URI, etc).
- Simpler, no development tool
- Easy to test

The advantages of SOAP are:

- Type checking
- Management of large amounts of data.
- Server-side complexity. To expose a method using SOAP is supported by most of the programming languages and development tools, and it is more challenging to create the same interface with a REST approach.

WEB SERVICES SPECIFICATIONS

There are a number of web service specifications that are relevant to Service Oriented Infrastructure. In this section the different specifications will be presented together with their scope and functionality provided.

Web Services Resource Framework

The purpose of the Web Services Resource Framework (WSRF) is to define a generic framework for modelling and accessing WS-Resources using web services so that the definition and implementation of a service and the integration and management of multiple services is made easier (Graham et al., 2006). WSRF is frequently described as the convergence of Grid technologies and web services technologies, where WSRF is seen as the means to incorporate state in the resource following a web service compliant way. WSRF replaces Open Grid Services Infrastructure (OGSI) (Tuecke et al., 2003) as the initial attempt to extend web services to support stateful resources.

The central component of WSRF is the WS-Resource which contains a set of properties that encapsulate "the state" required by Grid applications and that can be accessed following the WS-ResourceProperties specification. WSRF is based on the following collection of specifications:

WS-ResourceProperties: The relationship between web services and stateful resources is defined in WS-Resource in terms of a WS-Resource which represents the composition of a stateful resource and a web service as a WS-Resource. One characteristic of a WS-Resource is the set of properties associated with the resource. The WS-ResourceProperties specification (Graham & Treadwell, 2006) standardizes the means by which the definition of the properties of a WS-Resource may be declared as part of the web service interface. The declaration of the WS-Resource's properties represents a projection of or a *view* on the resource's state. The projection is defined in terms of a resource properties document. This resource properties document serves to define a basis for access to the resource properties through the web service interface. This specification also defines a standard set of message exchanges that allow a client to query or update the resource property values. The set of properties defined in the resource properties document, and associated with the service interface, defines the constraints on the valid contents of these message exchanges.

WS-ResourceLifetime: The lifetime of a WS-Resource is defined as the period between its instantiation and its destruction. The WS-ResourceLifetime specification (Srinivasan & Banks, 2006) standardizes the means by which a WS-Resource can be destroyed. The specification also defines the means by which the lifetime of a WS-Resource can be monitored. However, this specification does not prescribe the means by which a WS-Resource is created. Normally, a service requestor's interest in a WS-Resource is for some period of time - rarely is it indefinite. In many scenarios, it is appropriate for clients of a WS-Resource to cause its immediate destruction. The immediate destruction of a WS-Resource may be accomplished using the message exchanges defined in this specification. In addition, this specification defines the means by which a resource may be destroyed after a period of time. In a distributed computing environment, a client may become disconnected from the service provider's endpoint and therefore may be unable to, or unwilling to, cause the immediate destruction of the WS-Resource. This specification defines the means by which any client of a WS-Resource may establish and extend the scheduled termination time of a WS-Resource. If that time expires, the WS-Resource may self-destruct without the need for an explicit destroy request message from a client. Periodically extending the termination time of a WS-Resource can serve to extend its lifetime. WS-ResourceLifetime defines a standard message exchange by which a service requestor can establish and renew a scheduled termination

time for the WS-Resource, and defines the circumstances under which a service requestor can determine that this termination time has elapsed.

WS-ServiceGroup: The WS-ServiceGroup specification, inspired by a portion of the Global Grid Forum's "Open Grid Services Infrastructure (OGSI) Version 1.0" specification (Maguire, Snelling & Banks, 2006), defines a means by which web services and WS-Resources can be aggregated or grouped together for a domain specific purpose. In order for requestors to form meaningful queries against the contents of the ServiceGroup, membership in the group must be constrained in some fashion. The constraints for membership are expressed by intension using a classification mechanism. Further, the members of each intension must share a common set of information over which queries can be expressed. In this specification, the ServiceGroup membership rules, membership constraints and classifications are expressed using the resource property model WS-ResourceProperties. Groups are defined as a collection of members that meet the constraints of the group. The ServiceGroupRegistration interface extends the basic ServiceGroup capabilities with message exchanges for managing the membership of a ServiceGroup. The ServiceGroup and ServiceGroupRegistration interfaces are commonly expected to be composed with other application domain specific interfaces, which define more specialized interaction with the service group and/or with the services that are members of the service group. For example, specialized interfaces may offer means of querying the contents of the ServiceGroup, and for performing collective operations across members of the ServiceGroup.

WS-BaseFaults: Finally, the WS-BaseFaults specification (Liu & Meder, 2006) provides a standard way of representing faults in case of failures when interacting with a WS-Resource. A designer of a web services application often uses interfaces defined by others. Managing faults in such an application is more difficult when each interface uses a different convention for representing common information in fault messages. Support for problem determination and fault management can be enhanced by specifying web services fault messages in a common way. When the information available in faults from various interfaces is consistent, it is easier for requestors to understand faults. It is also more likely that common tooling can be created to assist in the handling of faults.

WS-Notification and WS-Addressing

Apart from the WSRF family of specifications, WS-Notification (Graham, Hull & Murray, 2006) and WS-Addressing (Box, 2004) are two other collections of specifications that are closely related to it, although not a part of WSRF. WS-Notification allows notification consumers to subscribe to a web service that acts as a notification producer, in order to receive asynchronous notifications about well-defined topics of interest. This means that if a change occurs in the state of a WS-Resource, this change will be notified to all the clients that have previously subscribed to receive notifications about this event.

WS-Addressing provides transport-neutral and generic mechanisms to address web services. XML elements are used to define the endpoint to a web service and to secure end-to-end identification in messages. One of the biggest benefits of this specification is that it enables the transmission of messages through firewalls and gateways in a transport-neutral manner.

Web Services Distributed Management

The Web Services Distributed Management (WSDM) standard (Bullard, Murray & Wilson, 2006) specifies how the manageability of a resource is made available to manageability consumers via web services. The focus of the WSDM architecture is the manageable resource which must be represented as a web service. In other words, management information regarding the resource must be accessible through a web service endpoint. To provide access to a resource, this endpoint must be able to be referenced by an endpoint reference, or EPR, as defined in the WS-Addressing standard. Endpoints that support access to manageable resources are called manageability endpoints. The implementation behind those endpoints must be capable of retrieving and manipulating the information related to a manageable resource.

The EPR provides the target location to which a manageability consumer directs messages. The manageable resource may also direct notifications of significant events to a manageability consumer, provided the consumer has subscribed to receive notifications. Thus, WSDM covers three modes of interaction between a manageable resource and a manageability consumer. These modes of interaction are as follows:

- A manageability consumer can retrieve management information about the manageable resource. For example, the consumer can retrieve the current operating status of the manageable resource or the current state of the process running on the manageable resource.
- A manageability consumer may affect the state of some manageable resource by changing its management information.
- A manageable resource may inform, or notify, a manageability consumer of a significant event. This mode of interaction requires the manageability consumer to subscribe to receive events on a desired topic.

Web Services Distributed Management (WSDM 1.0) is an approved OASIS standard (2006), built upon non-approved OASIS specifications including WSRF and WSN. WSDM management functionality comes in three parts:

- **WSDM-MUWS Part 1:** covers basic resource manageability functionality.
- **WSDM-MUWS Part 2:** defines specific message formats for specific situations to support interoperability between implementations of WSDM-MUWS.
- **WSDM-MOWS:** covers manageability of Web Services using WSDM.

MUWS Part 1 describes a basic notification event schema, and three "manageability capabilities" for identity, creatable properties (properties that should be identical between any two web services that provide access to the same resource), and manageability characteristics (a capability for publishing other management capabilities).

MUWS Part 2 builds upon this, describing a more detailed notification schema covering "situations", which include the situation time/category, optional priority, severity and success status elements, the last of which is used to report situations that resulted from management commands. MUWS Part 2 also defines manageability capabilities for:

- **OperationalStatus:** a simple descriptive property describing whether a resource is partially or fully available, plus an associated notification topic and metadata.
- **State:** describes resource states, transitions, current state and last transition, plus an associated notification topic and metadata.
- **Configuration:** describes resource properties linked to configuration parameters that can be used to change the operational behaviour of a resource, plus an associated notification topic and metadata.
- **Metrics:** describes resource properties linked to measurable characteristics of the managed resource, plus an associated notification topic and metadata.

The last of these includes a schema for associated attributes describing the temporal nature of the underlying measurements (e.g. measurements over an time interval, at a single instant, since the last reset, etc), how the result can change (e.g. counters versus gauges, etc), when they are updated (regular or irregular intervals, on demand, etc), and provides a way to associate metrics with metric groups.

The MUWS Part 2 metrics are quite generic, and at first glance appear useful for describing QoS in a very general way. However, it turns out that they describe only instantaneous values, even those that are collected over an interval. The "interval" is defined as an xsd:duration type, which is an amount of time (e.g. 1 hour) not an absolute interval (e.g. between 1605 and 1705 UTC on Tuesday 28 Feb 2006). The time-scope properties of a MUWS Part 2 metric describe how a value is measured (e.g. a time average) and not its temporal relationship to other measurements or events.

The MOWS specification describes how MUWS can be applied to the management of web services via a MUWS-type management web service. The following specific metrics are defined by MOWS:

- **NumberOfRequests:** the number of requests received.
- **NumberOfFailedRequests:** the number of requests for which the service response was a SOAP fault.
- **NumberOfSuccessfulRequests:** the number of requests for which any other response was made.
- **ServiceTime:** a duration describing the total time spent processing requests, whether successful or not.
- **MaxResponseTime:** a duration describing the maximum time spent processing any requests.
- **LastResponseTime:** the amount of time spent processing the last request.

These properties may be useful for some purposes, but they don't cover resource usage or limits, and they provide only a crude description of consumer-centric QoS.

WSDM uses Web services as a platform to provide essential distributed computing functionality, interoperability, loose coupling, and implementation independence. Therefore, the WSDM specifications depend on the WS-I Basic Profile (BP) plus other Web services foundation specifications being standardized in OASIS:

- WS-Resource Framework (WS-RF) Resource Properties (WSRP) for properties
- WS-Notification (WSN) Base Notifications (WSBN) for management event transport
- WS-Addressing (WSA) for service references

WSDM also utilizes WS-RF Service Groups (WSSG) and WS-Notification. WS-Topics (WST) in optional function.

WS-Management

The *web services for Management (WS-Management) Specification* describes a Web services protocol based on SOAP for use in management-specific domains. These domains include the management of entities such as PCs, servers, devices, Web services and other applications, and other manageable entities. Services can expose only a WS-Management interface or compose the WS-Management service interface with some of the many other Web service specifications. A crucial application for these services is in the area of systems management. To promote interoperability between management applications and managed resources, this specification identifies a core set of Web service specifications and usage requirements that expose a common set of operations central to all systems management. This includes the ability to do the following:

- Get, put (update), create, and delete individual resource instances, such as settings and dynamic values
- Enumerate the contents of containers and collections, such as large tables and logs
- Subscribe to events emitted by managed resources
- Execute specific management methods with strongly typed input and output parameters

In each of these areas of scope, this specification defines minimal implementation requirements for conformant Web service implementations. An implementation is free to extend beyond this set of operations, and to choose not to support one or more of the preceding areas of functionality if that functionality is not appropriate to the target device or system. This specification intends to meet the following requirements:

- Constrain Web services protocols and formats so that Web services can be implemented with a small footprint in both hardware and software management services.
- Define minimum requirements for compliance without constraining richer implementations.
- Ensure backward compatibility and interoperability with WS-Management version 1.0.
- Ensure compatibility with other Web services specifications.

These are some systems that provide a WS-Management interface:

- Windows Vista and Windows Server 2008 provide remote management through WS-Management.
- SUSE Linux Enterprise Server 11 supports WS-Management.

- WS-Management (named WinRM by Microsoft) is also available for Windows XP and Windows Server 20031.

WS-Management uses WS-Eventing, WS-Enumeration, WS-Transfer and SOAP 1.2 via HTTP.

WS-Security

WS-Security (Web Services Security, short WSS) specification (OASIS Web Services Security (WSS) TC, 2004, http://www.oasis-open.org/committees/wss/) describes enhancements to SOAP messaging to provide message integrity and confidentiality. The specified mechanisms can be used to accommodate a wide variety of security models and encryption technologies.

This specification also provides a general-purpose mechanism for associating security tokens with message content. No specific type of security token is required, the specification is designed to be extensible (i.e.. support multiple security token formats). For example, a client might provide one format for proof of identity and provide another format for proof that they have a particular business certification. Additionally, this specification describes how to encode binary security tokens, a framework for XML-based tokens, and how to include opaque encrypted keys. It also includes extensibility mechanisms that can be used to further describe the characteristics of the tokens that are included with a message.

WS-Security describes three main mechanisms:

- How to sign SOAP messages to assure integrity. Signed messages provide also non-repudiation.
- How to encrypt SOAP messages to assure confidentiality.
- How to attach security tokens.

WS-Security allows the communication of various security token formats, such as SAML, Kerberos, X.509 and UserID/Password credentials. Its main focus is the use of XML Signature and XML Encryption to provide end-to-end security.

The specification is meant to provide extensible framework and flexible syntax, with which one could implement various security mechanisms. This framework and syntax by itself does not provide any guarantee of security. When implementing and using this framework and syntax, one must make every effort to ensure that the result is not vulnerable to any one of a wide range of attacks. This specification intentionally does not describe explicit fixed security protocols.

Therefore, key management, trust bootstrapping, federation and agreement on the technical details (ciphers, formats, algorithms) is outside the scope of WS-Security.

WS-Security adds significant overhead to SOAP-processing due to the increased size of the message on the wire, XML and cryptographic processing, requiring faster CPUs and more memory and bandwidth.

WS-Transfer

The WS-Transfer specification (Alexander et al., 2006) defines a mechanism for acquiring XML-based representations of entities using the Web service infrastructure. It defines two types of entities:

- Resources, which are entities addressable by an endpoint reference that provide an XML representation
- Resource factories, which are Web services that can create a new resource from an XML representation

Specifically, it defines two operations for sending and receiving the representation of a given resource and two operations for creating and deleting a resource and its corresponding representation.

It should be noted that the state maintenance of a resource is at most subject to the "best efforts" of the hosting server. When a client receives the server's acceptance of a request to create or update a resource, it can reasonably expect that the resource now exists at the confirmed location and with the confirmed representation, but this is not a guarantee, even in the absence of any third parties. The server may change the representation of a resource, may remove a resource entirely, or may bring back a resource that was deleted.

For instance, the server may store resource state information on a disk drive. If that drive crashes and the server recovers state information from a backup tape, changes that occurred after the backup was made will be lost.

A server may have other operational processes that change resource state information. A server may run a background process that examines resources for objectionable content and deletes any such resources it finds. A server may purge resources that have not been accessed for some period of time. A server may apply storage quotas that cause it to occasionally purge resources.

In essence, the confirmation by a service of having processed a request to create, modify, or delete a resource implies a commitment only at the instant that the confirmation was generated. While the usual case should be that resources are long-lived and stable, there are no guarantees, and clients should code defensively.

There is no requirement for uniformity in resource representations between the messages defined in this specification. For example, the representations required by Create or Put may differ from the representation returned by Get, depending on the semantic requirements of the service. Additionally, there is no requirement that the resource content is fixed for any given endpoint reference. The resource content may vary based on environmental factors, such as the

security context, time of day, configuration, or the dynamic state of the service.

As per the SOAP processing model, other specifications may define SOAP headers which may be optionally added to request messages to require the transfer of subsets or the application of transformations of the resource associated with the endpoint reference. When the Action URIs defined by this specification are used, such extension specifications must also allow the basic processing models defined herein.

This specification intends to meet the following requirements:

- Provide a SOAP-based protocol for managing resources and their representations.
- Minimize additional mechanism beyond the current web services architecture.

Web Services Resource Transfer

This specification (Davis, Malhotra, Warr and Chou, 2009) defines extensions to WS-Transfer (Alexander et al., 2006). While its initial design focuses on management resource access its use is not necessarily limited to those situations.

This specification is intended to form an essential core component of a unified resource access protocol for the Web services space.

The operations described in this specification constitute an extension to the WS-Transfer specification, which defines standard messages for controlling resources using the familiar paradigms of "get", "put", "create", and "delete". The extensions deal primarily with fragment-based access to resources to satisfy the common requirements of WS-ResourceFramework and WS-Management.

This specification intends to meet the following requirements:

- Define a standardized technique for accessing resources using semantics familiar to those in the system management domain: get, put, create and delete.

- Define WSDL 1.1 portTypes, for the Web service methods described in this specification, compliant with WS-I Basic Profile 1.1 (Ballinger, 2006).
- Define minimum requirements for compliance without constraining richer implementations.
- Compose with other Web service specifications for secure, reliable, transacted message delivery.
- Provide extensibility for more sophisticated and/or currently unanticipated scenarios.
- Support a variety of encoding formats including (but not limited to) both SOAP 1.1 (Box et al., 2000) and SOAP 1.2 (Gudgin et al., 2007) Envelopes.

The Web Services Resource Transfer (WS-RT) specification was developed jointly by IBM, Hewlett-Packard, Intel, and Microsoft to provide a unified resource access protocol for web services.

In many scenarios, vendors and customers building solutions using Web services could find that the existing specifications support their scenarios. Vendors and customers may use the new specifications and functions when needing the common capabilities. The common functionality this specification covers includes (Cline et al., 2006):

- **Resources:** The ability to create, read, update and delete information using Web services.
- **Events:** The ability to connect Web services together using an event driven architecture based on publish and subscribe.
- **Management:** Provide a Web service model for building system and application management solutions, focusing on resource management.

Moreover the common interoperable collection of specifications is designed such that organizations can easily extend the specifications to cover additional advanced scenarios. Today there are many specifications that provide Web service capabilities for resources, events, and management. Some examples are:

- WS-Transfer
- WS-Enumeration
- WS-Eventing
- WS-MetadataExchange
- WS-ResourceFramework
  - WS-Resource
  - WS-ResourceProperties
  - WS-ResourceLifetime
  - WS-ServiceGroup
  - WS-BaseFaults
- WS-Notification
  - WS-BaseNotification
  - WS-BrokeredNotification
  - WS-Topics
- WS-Management
- Web Services Distributed Management
  - Management Using Web Services (Part 1)
  - Management Using Web Services (Part 2)
  - Management of Web Services

WS-RT aims to provide a convergent view of these specifications, to simplify interoperability, solution development, and the process of standardizing a new common set of specifications.

Usage Record

The OGF Usage Record (UR) Working Group has defined a usage accounting record schema (Mach, R. et al., 2005) that allow Grid sites to exchange usage data in a mutually understood format. The base properties of a usage record are defined to include:

- a global usage record identifier.
- global and local job identifiers, and local process id (PID).
- the global (e.g. DN) and local user name.
- the total charge in the local system's accounting units.
- the job status (aborted, completed, failed, held, queued, started, suspended, etc).
- the start and end time of the job, and the wall-clock and CPU-time duration of the job.
- the descriptive name and hostname of the machine that ran the job, and the hostname of the machine from which the job was submitted.
- the queue to which the job was submitted.
- the network and disk resource (scratch, temp), and the memory and swap space used.
- the number of nodes and CPU used.
- the service level (an optional string).

The specification allows other properties to be defined as extensions by individual sites or groups of sites. Finally, it allows usage records to be aggregated to provide summary information over multiple jobs, in which case the job-specific identifiers and PID are not used.

Job Submission Description Language

The OGF Job Submission Description Language (JSDL) Working Group has published a specification (Anjomshoaa et al, 2005) for describing the requirements of computational jobs for submission to resources, including but not limited to Grid environments. Where UR focuses on records of job resource usage during and primarily after execution, JSDL focuses on specifying resource requirements (i.e. upper limits) at submission time. The main components of JSDL job description are:

- **Job identification:** the job name (a string) and description plus any annotations and projects.
- **Application:** the application name (a string), version and description.
- **Resources:** the resource requirements for the job, which may include
  ○ a set of named hosts on which the job may execute.
  ○ file systems needed (mount point, type, disk space, etc).
  ○ whether the job needs exclusive access to the specified resources.
  ○ the operating system type and version.
  ○ the CPU architecture (e.g. Sparc, Intel, etc).
  ○ upper and lower bounds for the CPU speed (in Hz), CPU time (in seconds), CPU count, network bandwidth (bits/second), physical and virtual memory (bytes) and disk space (bytes) per resource used.
  ○ upper and lower bounds on the total CPU time, CPU count, physical and virtual memory and disk space, and number of resources across all resources used.
- **DataStaging:** describes file transfer actions between remote source or destination URI and local filenames on file systems specified for the job, including overwrite/append and post-execution deletion flags.

JSDL allows for extensions by attribute or element, and specifies a set of extensions for POSIX-style application description.

In addition to JSDL and UR, there are two other OGF working groups that address relevant topics:

- The OGSA Resource Usage Service Working Group (https://forge.gridforum.org/projects/rus-wg) aims to define a usage service for tracking resource usage (in the Unix accounting sense), working with the

OGF Usage Record working group and the OGF Grid Economic Services Architecture working group.

- The OGF Distributed Resource Management Application API (DRMAA) Working Group has published an API specification (Rajic, 2004). This is primarily designed to allow programmers to submit and interact with jobs executed on the Grid, but it does include interfaces to query and specify resource usage and usage limits.

DEVELOPMENT FRAMEWORKS

In this section we are going to review some of the different commercial and open source options to create applications on Service Oriented Infrastructures, which are the interfaces provided by those solutions and a brief description of the available features.

Amazon Web Services

Amazon provides commercial cloud services under the name of Amazon Web Services (AWS) (http://aws.amazon.com/). They have a portfolio of solutions from the execution environment (Elastic Cloud 2) to the storage (S3) and other solutions like simple database (SimpleDB), payments services (FPS) and a simple queue service (SQS) to deliver short messages between computers.

The services in Amazon are provided by 3 APIs: two REST-based APIs (REST and Query) and the traditional web service SOAP interface. All services have a WS SOAP interface and also a combination of the REST-based interfaces (Murty 2008).

Amazon's Elastic Compute Cloud (EC2) provides an environment for running virtual servers on demand. The client can manage each virtual server like a physical machine, installing the software needed and configure it to work as required, or the client can use pre-prepared servers created by third parties. The service allows the creation of resizable pool of servers for handling computing tasks. The client can start as many virtual servers as necessary to perform a task, increase or decrease the number of servers as demand rises and falls, and stop them all when the task is finished. The client only pays for the computing resources use. In addition to scaling out by increasing the number of servers that will work on a task, the computing power can be scaled up or down by using more or less powerful virtual server types.

The EC2 service provides an API interface to launch and manage servers and to create customized servers.

The service's API can also be used to start, stop, configure, and monitor EC2 server instances, and manage the Amazon Machine Images (AMIs) that will store the customized servers.

A client can create his or her own customized servers and store them permanently as AMIs that can be executed later on by the client.

The Amazon Machine Images (AMI) is a virtual machine image that can be created from scratch or the client can use one of the pre-configured images provided by Amazon.

The set of actions that can be performed in Amazon EC2 include:

- Managing AMIs (registering, deregistering), Listing available AMIs, modifying image attributes
- Starting instance
- Stopping running instance
- Listing running instances

A client can configure different security mechanisms: The firewall doesn't allow the access to any instance except if it is explicitly allowed. This firewall is controlled by IP rules and group rules. With IP rules the user can specify the kind of traffic that has access to the machine inside a specified subnet. The group rules control the access from other instance inside EC2. This mechanism allows an easy way to communicate instances inside the EC2 network (without using IPs).

Google App Engine

Google App Engine (GAE) follows a PaaS solution, this means that developers don't have to interact with the platform directly, but create their services in the form of a Servlet (for instance) and the platform provides the automatic scalability of the application.

Google App Engine provides SDKs for Java and Python (http://code.google.com/intl/en/appengine/downloads.html). Those SDKs contains the classes to use the internal services of the platform (like the datastore), the application for Google App Engine are web applications that use the standard Python or Java technologies (like Servlets or JSP).

Google Storage for Developers

Google Storage for Developers (http://code.google.com/intl/en/apis/storage/) is a new service for developers to store and access data in Google's cloud. It offers developers direct access to Google's scalable storage and networking infrastructure as well as powerful authentication and data sharing mechanisms.

Google Storage for Developers is a RESTful service for storing and accessing application's data on Google's infrastructure. In addition, Google Storage for Developers offers a web-based interface for managing the storage and GSUtil (http://code.google.com/apis/storage/docs/gsutil.html), an open source command line tool and library. The service is also compatible with many existing cloud storage tools and libraries. This service follows a pay-per-use pricing model.

The Google Storage API is a RESTful interface that lets clients programmatically manage data on Google Storage. As a RESTful API, the Google Storage API relies on method information and scoping information to define the different operations. The developer can specify the method information with standard HTTP methods, such as DELETE, GET, HEAD, and PUT. And he or she can specify the scoping information with a publicly-accessible endpoint (URI) and various scoping parameters. In this case, the primary scoping parameter is a path to a resource, which consists of an object name (file name) and bucket name (container name). Used together, the object name, bucket name, and public URI create a unique URL to a given resource—a resource on which users can perform operations with HTTP methods. Developers can further scope their operations by using HTTP headers and query string parameters.

Microsoft Azure

The Microsoft Azure platform (http://www.microsoft.com/windowsazure) is a PaaS solution, this means that users are limited to a set of programming languages and tools supported by the platform to develop solutions. The two main products provided by Microsoft Azure are:

- **Windows Azure**: operating system as an online service. Developers can create web applications with the tools provided by Microsoft, like Visual Studio 2010 (or 2008) and certain tools that extend the functionalities to support the deployment in Windows Azure. The development environment is basically the same used by the developers to create web applications for the Internet Information Services (IIS), with additional tools to upload the application to the Windows Azure Cloud and execute the application in that environment. The SDK allows developers to test the application locally before uploading to the Cloud.
- **Microsoft SQL Azure**: Microsoft SQL Azure Database is a cloud-based relational database platform built on SQL Server technologies. By using SQL Azure, devel-

opers can easily provision and deploy relational database solutions to the cloud, and take advantage of a distributed data centre that provides enterprise-class availability, scalability, and security with the benefits of built-in data protection and self-healing.

SQL Azure will seem very familiar to developers and administrators because data is stored in SQL Azure just like it is stored in SQL Server, by using Transact-SQL. Conceptually similar to an on-premise instance of SQL Server, a SQL Azure server is logical group of databases that acts as an authorization boundary.

Within each SQL Azure server, developers can create multiple databases that have tables, views, stored procedures, indices, and other familiar database objects. This data model are compatible with existing relational database design and make use of Transact-SQL, simplifying the process of migrating existing on-premise database applications to SQL Azure. Furthermore, SQL Azure servers and databases are virtual objects that do not correspond to physical servers and databases.

Microsoft provides SOAP and REST interfaces to the SQL Data Service. The operations that can be performed using those interfaces are: Creating an authority, creating and deleting a container, creating, retrieving, updating, querying and deleting entities.

GRIA

GRIA is a Service Oriented Architecture (SOA) middleware designed to meet the needs of industry. GRIA was initially developed within the EC ICT GRIA project (http://www.gria.org/), which ended in 2004. GRIA continues to be enhanced to meet the needs of industry through developments in many projects including EC NextGRID, EC SIMDAT, EC BRIDGE, EC edutain@grid, EC BEinGRID, EC ArguGRID, EC GridEcon, EC BREIN, ECIRMOS (http://www.irmosproject.

eu/), UK TSB projects Avatar-M, UK TSB MUPPITS, EC SERSCIS and EC PRESTOPRIME.

The latest version of GRIA, version 5.3.1 (Dec 2008), is a modular service-oriented architecture, based on use of key Web Service interoperability standards including an industrial WSRF profile using the WS-I doc/literal profile, and updated security features based on WS-Trust/WS-Federation token-based security patterns. It contains four principle components:

- **Service provider infrastructure:** services to provision and control both server side data storage and server side application execution.
- **Client framework:** API for easy client-side application development, GUI for interacting with server side job, data and management services.
- **Service provider management:** services to track invoicing for provisioning of server-side resources, negotiate bi-partite service level agreements (SLA's) and metrics to measure quality of service delivered.
- **Client management:** services to issue security tokens, discover services / resources and provide policy-driven federation with service providers.

The GRIA middleware addresses barriers to adoption such as integration with enterprise identity systems (MS ActiveDirectory / LDAP), policy-driven service and resource selection and improved interoperability with .NET through the Windows Communication Foundation (WCF) Client API.

Latest initiatives for the GRIA 6 research and development include integration of media delivery and preservation, dynamic resource management and governance application areas.

In the area of cloud computing experiments are being conducted by the GRIA team to take proven GRIA service oriented architecture management capabilities and use them to manage the business relationships associated with specific cloud resource deployments. This approach has already been successfully piloted in the edutain@ grid project (http://www.edutaingrid.eu/), which applied GRIA to dynamically control provision of massively multiplayer online (MMO) gaming servers in an elastic way across multiple organizations; such state of the art deployments are helping to shape this technology as it transfers from classic service oriented architecture to cloud provisioning environments.

Globus Toolkit Version 4

Globus Toolkit version 4 (GT4) (http://www.globus.org) is an open source Grid middleware that provides the necessary functionality required to build and deploy fully operational Grid Services. It includes software for security, information infrastructure, resource management, data management, communication, fault detection, and portability. It supports the core specifications that define the web services architecture. It also supports and implements the WS-Security (Lawrence, 2004) and other specifications relating to security, as well as the WSRF, WS-Addressing and WS-Notification specifications used to define, name, and interact with stateful resources.

The GT4 includes many high-level services, developed to take advantage of the potentials that the toolkit offers to the fullest. The Globus Toolkit provides a suite of web services, collectively termed "WS-GRAM", with which clients can interact to submit, monitor, and cancel jobs on local or remote computing resources within a GT4 based Grid. MDS4 ("GT 4.0 Component Fact Sheet") is a WSRF implementation of information services released with GT4. MDS4 builds on query, subscription, and notification protocols and interfaces defined by the WSRF and WS-Notification families of specifications and implemented by the GT4 Web Services Core.

UNICORE

UNICORE (Uniform Interface to Computing Resources) (Erwin et al., 2003) is a Grid middleware which includes client and server software (command line based and graphical). It is a platform-independent system which runs on Linux, Mac or Windows. A high level overview of the UNICORE architecture is depicted in Figure 2.

UNICORE is an open source project written in Java that supports the latest version of WSRF 1.2.

The current release, UNICORE 6, was released a short time ago and provides many advantages over previous versions, including better performance, better scalability, support for current versions of specifications and an easily extensible core.

UNICORE uses state of the art web service tools and provides a small and powerful web service stack based on XFire, XmlBeans and Jetty; web service development is simple and straightforward. The final WSRF Specification v1.2 is supported, as is WS-ServiceGroup, WS-BaseNotifications and "plain" WS-I web services. UNICORE 6 has a built-in support for security, file transfer, monitoring, etc. and features a very easy installation procedure.

A great advantage of UNICORE versus, for example, the Globus Toolkit, is that the project seems very active and is releasing updates and new versions regularly and seems to a have a solid developer base. Unfortunately, documentation coverage is not very good, but at least introductory lessons and manuals exist.

gLite

The gLite (http://glite.web.cern.ch/glite/) distribution is an integrated set of components designed to enable resource sharing. In other words, this is middleware for building a grid.

The gLite middleware is produced by the EGEE (http://www.eu-egee.org/) project. In addition to

Figure 2. The UNICORE Architecture (http://www.unicore.eu)

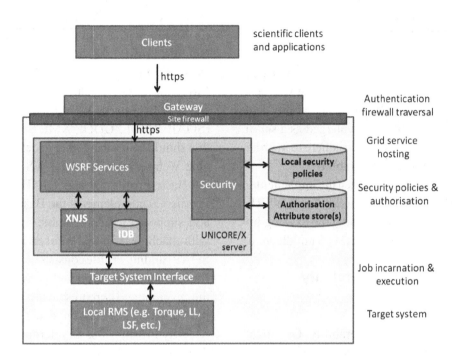

code developed within the project, the gLite distribution pulls together contributions from many other projects. The distribution model is to construct different services ('node-types') from these components and then ensure easy installation and configuration on the chosen platforms (currently Scientific Linux (https://www.scientificlinux.org/) versions 4 and 5, and also Debian 4 (http://www.debian.org/) for worker nodes).

gLite middleware is currently deployed on hundreds of sites as part of the EGEE project and enables global science in a number of disciplines. The EGEE project has a main goal of providing researchers with access to a geographically distributed computing Grid infrastructure, available 24 hours a day. It focuses on maintaining and developing the gLite middleware and on operating a large computing infrastructure for the benefit of a vast and diverse research community.

WSRF.NET

WSRF.NET (Humphrey & Wasson, 2005) is another popular middleware used to develop Grid Services. WSRF.NET is developed by the Grid Computing Group of the University of Virginia.

Like GT4, WSRF.NET fully implements the WSRF and WSN families of specifications. It also provides a set of software libraries, tools and applications on top of .NET that can be used to easily create Grid Services and clients. WSRF.NET allows service authors to easily build WSRF-compliant web services by adding meta-data to their ASP.NET web service logic.

WSRF.NET builds heavily on many Microsoft Technologies, such as WSE, ADO.NET and IIS.

WEB SERVICES INTEROPERABILITY: PROBLEMS AND SOLUTIONS

The section presents the existing solutions to solve interoperability problems among web service implementations. WS-Interoperability and the WS-I Basic Profile have emerged as a set of guidelines web services should adhere to in order to achieve optimum interoperability.

The interoperability between the implementations of WSRF by Globus Toolkit 4 and WSRF. NET is also analysed, describing the existing interoperability problems of these two middleware.

Web Services Interoperability Organization

The Web Services Interoperability Organization (WS-I) (http://www.ws-i.org) is an open industry organization chartered to establish Best Practices for Web services interoperability, for selected groups of Web services standards, across platforms, operating systems and programming languages.

WS-I comprises a diverse community of Web services leaders from a wide range of companies and standards development organizations (SDOs). WS-I committees and working groups create Profiles and supporting Testing Tools based on Best Practices for selected sets of Web service standards. The Profiles and Testing Tools are available for use by the web service community to aid in developing and deploying interoperable web services. Companies interested in helping to establish Best Practices for web services are encouraged to join WS-I.

Profiles are guidelines based on Best Practices for the selected groups of Web services standards to assist the Web services community in developing and deploying interoperable Web services. They are available to the public for download at no charge from (http://www.ws-i.org/deliverables/Default.aspx).

The key Profiles are the Basic Profile1.1 (Ballinger, 2006), Attachments Profile1.0 (Ferris, Karmarkar & Kevin, 2006), Simple SOAP Binding Profile1.0 (Nottingham, 2004) and the Basic Security Profile1.0 (McIntosh, Gudgin, Morrison & Barbir, 2007). The WS-I Basic Profile establishes core Web services specifications (SOAP, WSDL, UDDI, XML Schema, HTTPS) that should be used together to develop interoperable Web services. To date, WS-I has produced the Basic Profile 1.0 and 1.1. The Attachments Profile 1.0 complements the Basic Profile 1.1 to add support for interoperable SOAP Messages with attachments-based Web services. The Simple SOAP Binding Profile consists of those Basic Profile 1.0 requirements related to the serialization of the envelope and its representation in the message, incorporating any errata to date. The WS-I Basic Security Profile 1.0 is an interoperability Profile that addresses transport security, SOAP message security and other security considerations, and composes with other WS-I Profiles. It references existing specifications and standards, including the OASIS Web Services Security 1.0 and SOAP Message Security 1.0 specifications, and provides clarification and guidance designed to promote interoperability of Web services created according to those specifications.

The goal of web services is to enable communication between different software and hardware systems. These systems typically differ in both their hardware and software configurations. These differences have been overcome through the definition of standard protocols, such as those employed in building web services. Occasionally, incompatibility issues arise even when using these standard protocols, which can lead to interoperability problems. For addressing these interoperability problems, the WS-Interoperability specifications and the WS-I Basic Profile have emerged as a set of guidelines web services should adhere to in order to achieve optimum interoperability. In this way, developers can expose their own services in an environment and use policies that define how these web services are allowed to interact with other clients and services (Mandal and Silberman, 2007).

WSRF GT4 vs. WSRF.net

The Akogrimo architecture specifies many interactions between services that were built on GT4 and WSRF.NET. For this reason, these interactions were not only challenging in terms of design and efficiency but in terms of interoperability as well, since it allowed for checking whether these two popular Grid development tools implement the WSRF and WS-related specifications in a transparent and interoperable way.

During the establishment of communication between them, a number of inconsistencies were detected and were handled in different ways and at different levels with some of them even requiring changing the form of the SOAP messages. All the problems found can be categorized as follows:

- Incorrect implementation of specifications.
- Web services tool bugs.
- Incorrect application of WS-I recommendations.

These interoperability problems (along with their solutions-if found) have been gathered in a report that was presented in the OGF meeting (ETSI GRID TC) in Manchester, May 2007.

GRIA Interoperability with other SOA Platform Technologies

The GRIA middleware comes with a java API for clients and a set of Apache Tomcat services with python wrappers for server side application installations. There have been a number of projects that have used GRIA services and/or clients to interoperate with different middleware technologies.

GRIA and .NET

The CRISP project (http://crisp-project.org/) looked at using GRIA with .NET web services implementing the WS security stack. A .NET client was created for GRIA services by linking with the GRIA client java libraries; this interoperated well using the WS security stack. Security tokens (X.509 certificates etc) are well standardized now and interoperate well in both systems. In the BREIN project (http://www.eu-brein.com/) a portal was created to allow GRIA clients to communicate with .NET services using the WS security stack.

GRIA and Globus

The NextGRID project (http://www.nextgrid. org/) developed Globus Toolkit (http://www.globus.org/toolkit/) client code to interoperate with GRIA services and vice versa. This was achieved but there were practical difficulties with library management since GRIA and Globus use different versions of the same AXIS libraries (Globus AXIS 1.2, GRIA AXIS 1.4).

GRIA and Apache CXF

The BEinGRID project demonstrated interoperability between GRIA services and Apache AXIS CXF services. Here GRIA SLA services were integrated directly into an Apache CXF governance service deployment.

GRIA and g-Eclipse

The g-Eclipse project (http://www.geclipse.eu/) created a number of Eclipse clients allowing interoperability with a variety of Eclipse supported GRID infrastructures. These included Amazon EC2, Amazon S3, gLite EGEE and GRIA.

GRIA and CNGrid GOS

The CN GRID GOS project (http://www.cngrid. org) validated the use of GRIA with the Chinese GRID middleware GOS. The underlying use of WS security by GOS made this relatively simple.

CONCLUSION

This chapter has presented the different standardisation bodies and the specifications relevant to Service Oriented Infrastructures. The existing development frameworks that make use of those specifications have been described together with the commercial interfaces currently in the market to develop distributed system on the cloud.

It is noticed that there is a clear trend on the consumers of the cloud services in using RESTful interfaces, instead of the more complex SOAP interfaces. And companies that traditionally have provided only SOAP interfaces (like Google) are now moving to offer REST type of interfaces, this is an important trend because this is what the market and particularly SMEs are demanding.

In the last part of the chapter the interoperability problems that affect the different development frameworks has been presented, those interoperability problems are mainly caused by the use of different specification versions in the implementation of the solutions. These problems are what the WS-I organisation is trying to solve with the production of guidelines with the aim of minimising the interoperability issues that could appear among different vendors' platforms.

We are now at the beginning of a new era of cloud services, where infrastructure resources are managed and used in a much more dynamic way, and where new services are emerging around this new SOI, which provide solutions to the main concerns companies have in relation to security, performance and monitoring, among others. The challenge for the future is to solve the great interoperability problems that exist between the emerging cloud platforms: how to manage and migrate applications among cloud infrastructures and how to connect services or application components deployed on different clouds.

REFERENCES

Alexander, J., et al. (2006). *Web services transfer* (WS-Transfer). Retrieved June 25, 2010, from http://www.w3.org/ Submission/ WS-Transfer/

Amazon. (2006). *Simple storage service developer guide* (API Version 2006-03-01). Retrieved June 25, 2010, from http://docs.amazonwebservices. com/ AmazonS3/ 2006-03-01/ index.html? RESTAPI.html

Anjomshoaa, A., et al. (2005). *Job submission description language (JSDL) specification*, version 1.0. Retrieved from http://www.gridforum. org/ documents/ GFD.56.pdf

Ballinger, K., et al. (2006). *Basic profile*, version 1.1. Retrieved June 25, 2010, from http://www. ws-i.org/ Profiles/ BasicProfile-1.1.html

Banks, T. (2006). *Web services resource framework (WSRF) – Primer*, v1.2. Retrieved June 25, 2010, from http://docs.oasis-open.org/ wsrf/ wsrf-primer-1.2- primer-cd-02.pdf

Booth, D., Haas, H., McCabe, F., Newcomer, E., Michael, I., Ferris, C., & Orchard, D. (2004). Web services architecture. Retrieved June 25, 2010, from http://www.w3.org/ TR/ ws-arch/

Box, D., et al. (2000). *Simple object access protocol* (SOAP) 1.1. Retrieved June 25, 2010, from http://www.w3.org/ TR/ 2000/ NOTE-SOAP-20000508/

Box, D., et al. (2004). *Web services addressing* (WS-Addressing). Retrieved June 25, 2010, from http://www.w3.org/ Submission/ ws-addressing/

Bullard, V., Murray, B., & Wilson, K. (2006). *An introduction to WSDM*. Retrieved June 25, 2010, from http://www.oasis-open.org/ committees/ download.php/ 16998/ wsdm-1.0-intro-primer -cd-01.doc

Chinnici, R., Gudgin, M., Moreau, J., Schlimmer, J., & Weerawarana, S. (2003). *Web services description language (WSDL) version 2.0 part 1: Core language*. Retrieved June 25, 2010, from http://www.w3.org/ TR/ 2003/ WD-wsdl20-20031110/

Christensen, E., Curbera, F., Meredith, G., & Weerawarana, S. (2001). *Web services description language* (WSDL) 1.1. Retrieved June 25, 2010, from http://www.w3.org/ TR/wsdl

Cline, K., et al. (2006). *Toward converging Web service standards for resources, events, and management*. Retrieved June 25, 2010, from http:// download.boulder.ibm.com/ ibmdl/ pub/ software/ dw/ webservices/ Harmonization_Roadmap.pdf

Cowan, J., & Tobin, R. (2004). *XML information set*, 2nd ed. Retrieved June 25, 2010, from http:// www.w3.org/ TR/ xml-infoset/

Davis, D., Malhotra, A., Warr, K., & Chou, W. (2009). *Web services resource transfer* (WS-RT). Retrieved June 25, 2010, from http://www.w3.org/ TR/ 2009/ WD-ws-resource- transfer-20090317/

Davis, D., Malhotra, A., Warr, K., & Chou, W. (2009). *Web services enumeration* (WS-Enumeration). Retrieved June 25, 2010, from http://www.w3.org/ TR/ 2009/ WD-ws- enumeration-20090924/

Davis, D., Malhotra, A., Warr, K., & Chou, W. (2009). *Web services metadata exchange* (WS-MetadataExchange) Retrieved June 25, 2010, from http://www.w3.org/ TR/ 2009/ WD-ws-metadata-exchange-20090924/

Davis, D., Malhotra, A., Warr, K., & Chou, W. (2009). *Web services eventing* (WS-Eventing). Retrieved June 25, 2010, from http://www.w3.org/ TR/ 2009/ WD-ws- eventing-20090924/

Erwin, D., et al. (2003). *UNICORE plus final report - Uniform interface to computing resources*. Retrieved June 25, 2010, from http://www.unicore. eu/ documentation/ files/ erwin-2003-UPF.pdf

Ferris, C., Karmarkar, A., & Kevin, C. (2006). *Attachments profile*, version 1.0. Retrieved June 25, 2010, from http://www.ws-i.org/ profiles/ attachmentsprofile-1.0.html

Fielding, R., et al. (1999). *Hypertext transfer protocol -- HTTP/1.1*. Retrieved June 25, 2010, from http://tools.ietf.org/ html/rfc2616

Fielding, R. T. (2000). *Architectural styles and the design of network-based software architectures*. PhD Dissertation. Dept. of Information and Computer Science, University of California, Irvine. Retrieved June 25, 2010, from http://www. ics.uci.edu/ ~fielding/ pubs/ dissertation/ top.htm

Globus. (2010). *GT 4.0 component fact sheet: WS MDS WebMDS*. Retrieved June 25, 2010, from http://www.globus.org/ toolkit/ docs/ 4.0/ info/ webmds/ WSMDSWeb MDSFacts.html

Graham, S., Hull, D., & Murray, B. (2006). *Web services base notification 1.3* (WS-Base Notification). Retrieved June 25, 2010, from http://docs. oasis-open.org/ wsn/ wsn-ws_base_notification -1.3-spec-os.pdf

Graham, S., Karmarkar, A., Mischkinsky, J., Robinson, I., & Sedukhin, I. (2006). *Web services resource 1.2* (WS-Resource). Retrieved June 25, 2010, from http://docs.oasis-open.org/ wsrf/ wsrf-ws_resource- 1.2-spec-os.pdf

Graham, S., & Treadwell, J. (2006). *Web services resource properties 1.2* (WS-ResourceProperties). Retrieved June 25, 2010, from http://docs.oasis-open.org/ wsrf/ wsrf-ws_resource_properties-1.2-spec-os.pdf

Gudgin, M., et al. (2007). *SOAP version 1.2 part 1: Messaging framework* (2nd ed). Retrieved June 25, 2010, from http://www.w3.org/ TR/ soap12-part1/

Humphrey, M., & Wasson, G. (2005). Architectural foundations of WSRF.NET. *International Journal of Web Services Research, 2*(2), 83-97. Retrieved June 25, 2010, from http://www. cs.virginia.edu/ ~gsw2c/ wsrf.net.html

Lawrence, K., et al. (2004). *Web services security: SOAP message security 1.1* (WS-Security 2004). Retrieved June 25, 2010, from http://www.oasis-open.org/ committees/ download.php/ 16790/ wss-v1.1-spec-os- SOAPMessage Security.pdf

Liu, L., & Meder, S. (2006). *Web services base faults 1.2* (WS-BaseFaults). Retrieved June 25, 2010, from http://docs.oasis-open.org/ wsrf/ wsrf-ws_base_faults- 1.2-spec-os.pdf

Mach, R., et al. (2005). *Usage record format recommendation.* GGF draft recommendation. Retrieved June 25, 2010, from http://www. psc.edu/ ~lfm/ PSC/ Grid/ UR-WG/ UR-WG-Spec-20050925 -tracked.pdf

Maguire, T., Snelling, D., & Banks, T. (2006). *Web services service group 1.2* (WS-ServiceGroup). Retrieved June 25, 2010, from http://docs.oasis-open.org/ wsrf/ wsrf-ws_service_group- 1.2-spec-os.pdf

Mandal, M., & Silberman, H. (2007). *Understanding Web services specifications, part 6: WS-interoperability.* Retrieved June 25, 2010, from http://www.ibm.com/ developerworks/ edu/ ws-dw-ws-understand- web-services6.html

McIntosh, M., Gudgin, M., Morrison, K. S., & Barbir, A. (2007). *Basic security profile*, version 1.0. Retrieved June 25, 2010, from http://www. ws-i.org/ profiles/ basicsecurityprofile-1.0.html

Murty, J. (2008). *Programming Amazon Web services*. O'Reilly Press.

Nottingham, M. (2004). *Simple SOAP binding profile*, version 1.0. Retrieved June 25, 2010, from http://www.ws-i.org/ Profiles/ SimpleSoapBinding Profile-1.0.html

O'Reilly, T. (2003). *REST vs. SOAP at Amazon.* Retrieved from http://www.oreillynet.com/ pub/ wlg/ 3005

OASIS. (n.d.). *Web services distributed management (WSDM) TC.* Retrieved June 25, 2010, from http://www.oasis-open.org/ committees/ tc_home. php ?wg_abbrev =wsdm

Rajic, H., et al. (2004). *Distributed resource management application API,* specification 1.0. Retrieved from https://forge.gridforum.org/ projects/ drmaa-wg

Reistad, B., et al. (2006). *Web services resource transfer* (WS-RT). Retrieved June 25, 2010, from http://www.ibm.com/ developerworks/ library/ specification/ ws-wsrt/ ?S_TACT=105AGX04 &S_CMP=LP

Singh, T., & Singh, K. (2009). *REST vs. SOAP – The right Web service.* Retrieved from http:// www.taranfx.com

Srinivasan, L., & Banks, T. (2006). *Web services resource lifetime 1.2* (WS-ResourceLifetime). Retrieved June 25, 2010, from http://docs.oasis-open.org/ wsrf/ wsrf-ws_resource _lifetime-1.2-spec -os.pdf

Tuecke, S., et al. (2003). *Open Grid services infrastructure* (OGSI), version 1.0, Retrieved June 25, 2010, from http://www.ggf.org/ documents/ GFD.15.pdf

ENDNOTE

[1] http://www.microsoft.com/ downloads/ details.aspx? displaylang=en& FamilyID=845289ca -16cc-4c73- 8934-dd46b5ed1d33

Section 3
Infrastructure as a Service

Chapter 11
Execution and Resource Management in QoS–Aware Virtualized Infrastructures

Dominik Lamp
University of Stuttgart, Germany

Sören Berger
University of Stuttgart, Germany

Manuel Stein
Alcatel-Lucent Bell Labs, Germany

Thomas Voith
Alcatel-Lucent Bell Labs, Germany

Tommaso Cucinotta
Scuola Superiore Sant'Anna, Italy

Marko Bertogna
Scuola Superiore Sant'Anna, Italy

ABSTRACT

Both real-time systems and virtualization have been important research topics for quite some time now. Having competing goals, research on the correlation of these topics has started only recently. This chapter overviews recent results in the research literature on virtualized large-scale systems and soft real-time systems. These concepts constitute the fundamental background over which the execution environment of any large-scale service-oriented real-time architecture for highly interactive, distributed, and virtualized applications will be built in the future. While many aspects covered in this chapter have already been adopted in commercial products, others are still under intensive investigation in research labs all over the world.

INTRODUCTION

Traditional real-time methodologies focus on hard real-time safety-critical systems, where applications have associated a set of temporal constraints (e.g., deadlines) which must never be violated, as otherwise the system as a whole will fail – with potentially fatal consequences such as loss of human lives. However, a class of soft real-time applications exists, for example in the multimedia domain, in which an approach to meet the desired timing constraints under all circumstances is neither needed nor practical. In fact, for those applications, violations of the temporal constraints lead to degrations in Quality of Service (QoS), rather than an entire system failure. Thus, they are

DOI: 10.4018/978-1-60960-827-9.ch011

usually tolerated as long as their frequency and severity remains within sensible limits.

Different service-oriented architecture (SOA) and cloud management approaches exist that possess specific features to provide increased service reliability, scalability, host virtualization, application failure detection, global resource management, and optimized server utilization. However, in case of deployment of real-time interactive distributed applications, such features need to be complemented by taking the timing constraints that are in place for the applications into proper consideration during the various decision processes and run-time mechanisms. The challenge that has to be addressed is that the goals of virtualization and real-time-compliance are competing: Virtualization is used to exploit multiplex gains by sharing physical resources among multiple tasks so that *statistically* the resource usage is maximized. On the other hand, real-time systems are designed to guarantee response times even for the worst case scenario, resulting in resource underutilization in the average case.

The remainder of this chapter is structured as follows. First, an overview of real-time scheduling is given. Section two discusses how virtualization mechanisms improve resiliency and utilization optimization. The third part of the chapter covers host virtualization mechanisms. The chapter concludes with an overview of mechanisms to give real-time guarantees in virtualized environments.

REAL-TIME SCHEDULING

Real-time theory and methodologies are gaining applicability in the field of soft real-time systems. In this domain, applications possess precise timing and performance requirements, but occasional failures in meeting them may be easily tolerated by the system, causing a graceful degradation in the quality of the provided service.

The real-time literature on soft real-time technologies for General purpose operating systems

(GPOSes) is growing, and the major research branches are those in relation to: multiprocessor scheduling, soft real-time scheduling, QoS control in distributed real-time applications and adaptive QoS control, as detailed below.

Scheduling Real-Time Task Sets on Multiprocessor Platforms

Even if the concept of multiprocessing has always been present in the real-time community, only recently it is receiving a significant attention, thanks to the increasing industrial interest on such platforms, and their consequent increasing availability. While the scheduling problem for uniprocessor systems has been widely investigated for decades, producing a considerable variety of publications and applications, there are still many open problems regarding the schedulability analysis of multiprocessor systems. As pointed out by Liu in his seminal paper (C. L. Liu, 1969): *"few of the results obtained for a single processor generalize directly to the multiple processor case: bringing in additional processors adds a new dimension to the scheduling problem"*.

Unfortunately, predicting the behaviour of a multiprocessor system requires in many cases a considerable computing effort. To simplify the analysis, it is often necessary to introduce pessimistic assumptions. This is particularly needed when modelling globally scheduled multiprocessor systems, in which the cost of migrating a task from one processor to another can significantly vary over time. The presence of caches and the frequency of memory accesses have a significant influence on the worst-case timely parameters that characterize the system. To bind the variability of these parameters, often real-time literature focuses on platforms with multiple processors but with no caches, or whose cache miss delays are known. Also, the cost of pre-emption and migration on multi-processor systems is a very important issue that still needs to be properly considered in real-time methodologies. Some research in the domain of hardware architectures moves towards partially mitigating such issues. Recently, a few architectures have been proposed that limit penalties associated to migration and cache misses, for example the ARM's MPCore. Some researchers have recently proposed (Audsley & Bletsas, 2004; Furunäs, 2000; Kuacharoen, Shalan & Vincent J. Mooney III, 2003; Lindh, Stärner & Furunäs, 1995; Ward & Audsley, 2002) hardware implementations of some parts of the operating system, allowing one to reduce the scheduling penalties of multiprocessor platforms.

Approaches, Implementations and Comparisons

Scheduling on Multiprocessors

When deciding which kind of scheduler to adopt in a multiple processor system, there are two main options: *partitioned* scheduling and *global* scheduling:

Partitioned Scheduling

In a partitioned scheduler, there are multiple ready queues, one for each processor in the system, and it is possible to leave a processor in idle state even when there are ready tasks needing to execute. Each queue is managed according to (well-known) uni-processor scheduling algorithms, and task migration is not allowed. The placement of tasks among the available processors is a critical step. The problem of optimally dividing the workload among the various queues, so that the computing resources are well utilized, is analogous to the bin-packing problem, which is known to be NP-hard in the strong sense (Garey & Johnson, 1979; Leung & Whitehead, 1982). This complexity is typically avoided using sub-optimal solutions provided by polynomial and pseudo-polynomial time heuristics. Examples of policies used for this purpose are First Fit, Best Fit, Next Fit, and First Fit with decreasing utilizations (Burchard, Liebeherr, Oh & Son, 1995; Lauzac, Melhem &

Mossé, 2003; López, Díaz & García, 2004; López & García, 2003).

Global Scheduling

For task sets with highly varying computational requirements, instead of wasting computational power by repeatedly invoking complex load-balancing algorithms, it is better to use a global scheduler (Andersson & Jonsson, 2000). This way, tasks are extracted from a single system-wide queue and scheduled onto the available processors. The load is thus intrinsically balanced, since no processor is idled as long as there is a ready task in the global queue.

A class of algorithms, called Pfair schedulers (Sanjoy Baruah, Neil Cohen, Greg Plaxton & Donald Varvel, 1996), is able to ensure that the full processing capacity can be used, but unfortunately at the cost of a potentially large run-time overhead. Migrative and non-migrative algorithms have been proposed (Anand Srinivasan & Sanjoy Baruah, 2002; Andersson & Eduardo Tovar, 2006; Baker, Cirinei & Bertogna, 2008; Bertogna, Michele Cirinei & Giuseppe Lipari, 2005) modifying well-known solutions adopted for the single processor case and extending them to deal with the various anomalies (Dhall & C. L. Liu, 1978) that arise on a parallel computing platform.

Complications in using a global scheduler mainly relate to the cost of inter-processor migration, and to the kernel overhead due to the necessary synchronization among the processors for the purpose of enforcing a global scheduling strategy. Even if there are mechanisms that can reduce the migration cost, such kind of schedulers could nevertheless cause a significant schedulability loss (i.e., the guaranteed bandwidth that is wasted due to pre-emption and migration overhead) when tasks have a large context associated. Therefore, the effectiveness of a global scheduler is rather conditioned by the application characteristics and by the architecture in use.

Hybrid Schedulers

In addition to the above classes, there are also intermediate solutions, like hybrid- and restricted-migration schedulers. A hybrid-migration scheduler (John M. Calandrino, James H. Anderson & Dan P. Baumberger, 2007) limits the number of processors among which a task can migrate in order to limit the number of caches in which the task image is present. In this way, a fewer amount of cache misses is expected, and the cost of migration and context changes is smaller. This method is more flexible than a rigid partitioning algorithm without migration, and it is particularly indicated for systems with a high number of processors (with tens of CPUs), where it would be very difficult and time-consuming to move a task image from a computing unit to a distant one.

A restricted-migration scheduler is instead a scheduler that allows task migration, but only at job boundaries, i.e., before a job starts executing or at the end of its execution. In this way, the amount of information that must be transferred while migrating a task from a processor to another is likely to be less than in the full migration case (Baruah & Carpenter, 2003). A similar method consists in using a global scheduler without pre-emption: in this way, once a job starts executing on a CPU, it is not possible to interrupt it until the end of execution, so that migration can never take place (Baruah, 2006). However, non-pre-emptive systems can have significant schedulability overhead, due to potential delays caused by long chunks of code that can execute without being interrupted.

Scheduling and Exclusive Access to Shared Resources

There are well-known efficient protocols to arbitrate the exclusive access to shared resources for real-time task sets scheduled on a single processor platform: Priority Inheritance (PI), Priority Ceiling Protocol (PCP), Dynamic Priority Ceiling Protocol (DPCP), and Stack resource Policy (SRP). Each one of these protocols allows solving the "priority-inversion" problem that takes place when a task is blocked by a lower priority one at the beginning of a critical section accessing a shared resource. The SRP ensures that a task can never be blocked once it started executing. This minimizes the number of context switches, allows all tasks to be executed on a single stack, and prevents deadlocks.

Soft Real-Time Scheduling

Different scheduling algorithms have been proposed to support the specific needs of soft real-time applications. A first important class approximates the Generalized Processor Sharing concept of a *fluid flow* allocation, in which each application using the resource marks a progress proportional to its weight. Among the algorithms of this class, we can cite Proportional Share (Ian Stoica et al., 1996) and Pfair (Sanjoy Baruah, Neil Cohen, Greg Plaxton & Donald Varvel, 1996). The underlying principles of a family of algorithms known as Resource Reservation schedulers (Luca Abeni & Giorgio Buttazzo; Raj Rajkumar, Kanaka Juvva, Anastasio Molano & Shuichi Oikawa, 1998) are similar. In the Resource Kernels project (Raj Rajkumar et al., 1998), the resource reservation approach has been successfully applied to different types of resources (including disk and network). Also, it is noteworthy to mention that the current scheduler in the main-stream Linux kernel, known as Completely Fair Scheduler (CFS), is basically a variation of the Proportional-Share idea. The Resource Reservation framework has been adapted to partitioned multiprocessor systems in (Sanjoy Baruah & Giuseppe Lipari, 2004) and (S. Baruah & G. Lipari, 2004) for respectively, the CBS and TBS servers.

Design of Distributed Real-Time Applications

The problem of designing scheduling parameters for distributed real-time applications has received a constant attention in the past few years. In (Neil C., 1995), the authors introduce a notion of transaction for real-time databases characterized by periodicity and end-to-end constraints and propose a methodology to identify periods and deadlines of intermediate tasks. A similar approach is taken in (Gerber, R., Seongsoo Hong & Saksena, M, 1995), in which activation periods of the intermediate tasks that comply with end-to-end real-time requirements are synthesized by an optimization problem. In (Dong-In Kang, Richard Gerber & Manas Saksena, 2000), the same idea is applied to soft real-time applications. In this case, the authors use performance analysis techniques to decide the bandwidth allocated to each task that attain a maximum latency and a minimum average throughput for the chain of computation.

Concerning the modelling of timing requirements of real-time applications, usually models similar to synchronous dataflow networks (Walid A. Najjar & Edward A., 1999) are used. As shown in (Shuvra S. Battacharyya & Edward A., 1996), synchronous data flow networks lend themselves to an effective code generation process, in which an offline schedule is synthesized that minimizes the code length and the buffer size. The models used in (L. Palopoli & T. Cucinotta, 2007) and (Steve Goddard & Kevin Jeffay, 2001) are also a special case of synchronous dataflow, but, due to the inherently distributed and dynamic nature of the considered applications, the aim is not an optimized offline scheduling of activities, but an efficient on-line scheduling mechanism.

Future Trends and Current Research Directions

Basically, scheduling solutions based on a partitioned scheduling approach seem the most promising, but traditional approaches like Fixed Priority or Earliest Deadline First exhibit usually a high number of pre-emptions per task, or an unacceptably short duration of the time-slice dedicated to each task execution in the schedule. This may be dramatically negative for the performance if the activity that is scheduled is a virtual machine that may experience further context changes on its own. Appropriate solutions in this field are probably based on an appropriate control of pre-emptability by the scheduler, so to achieve appropriate trade-offs between the overall performance (computational throughput) of the hosted activities and their responsiveness/latency when considered individually.

Resiliency, Recovery, and Utilization Optimization

Both resiliency and recovery target at achieving high availability rates. In Information and Communication Technology, availability is a metric for the probability of a system failure and is calculated from parameters like the (statistical) age-related failure rate of HW components for a system of given architecture (reliability structure) and the predicted time required to put a failed system back into operational mode. Therefore, the calculation uses stochastic methods for determining the overall probability of a given architecture of age-related failure rate of components. Mean Time Between Failures (MTBF) is the average time between failure of hardware components and is estimated by the respective manufacturer. The time it takes to repair or replace a defective component is called Mean Time To Repair (MTTR).

If MTBF and MTTR are known, the availability of a system can be estimated as

$$Availability = \frac{MTBF}{MTBF + MTTR}$$

As a consequence, the availability depends on how fast a failing component can be replaced or repaired. A typical value for a carrier-grade system is 99.999%, often also referred to as "five nines availability".

When assessing the quality of an availability estimation, it is essential to also consider the time frame for which a certain maximum outage is guaranteed: Within a one year period, five nines would allow a maximum outage of about 5 minutes. That means that the prepared component (standby component) must be in operational mode within 5 minutes for a maximum of 1 failure per year. When five nines are required and the respective timeframe is a month, then the recovery time must be less than 30 seconds.

Both the desired service quality and fines for the case that the negotiated service quality is not achieved are usually specified in a Service Level Agreement (SLA). On the technical level, Quality of Service (QoS) mechanisms are implemented to ensure that the SLA is kept. Two important techniques to ensure QoS, namely redundancy and migration, are described in the following sections.

Approaches, Implementations and Comparisons

Redundancy

Redundant systems are built in a way that the failure of one or more components does not affect the overall system. This is done by replicating the system's critical components. The way that components are replicated and hold available can differ significantly. However, the key concepts are cold standby and hot standby.

Cold standby means that the prepared components are available, but are kept separate from the "live" infrastructure. Usually, cold standby components have to be manually integrated into the system in the event of failure.

As they are not actively participating in service delivery during normal operation, the failure of a cold standby component does not affect the over-all service availability provided that the primary components are in service.

Hot standby on the other hand means that the standby component is an active part of the infrastructure of the system and that it is kept up and running, being able to step in at any time.

A hot standby system can be passive, which means that the backup components are not adding to the system's performance. As long as the active component is not failing, the standby component does not execute any designated task. However, the backup component might perform the same operations as the primary unit in order to be able to immediately take over at any point.

In active hot standby environments, all components are actually carrying out tasks. By using load balancing mechanism, the load is distributed among multiple components. In the case of failure, the tasks of the failed component are redistributed among the remaining components. If the system shall be able to run without degradation in such a scenario, then the system needs to be overprovisioned in the non-failure scenario.

A variation of hot standby is used in critical systems: Here, multiple active systems perform the same task in parallel. The result of those systems is compared and considered valid only if the majority of systems provide the same result.

Depending on the required resiliency level, redundancy can be achieved in different ways. For critical components that are crucial for the overall availability, protection by dedicated standby components (1+1, 1:1 redundancy) is common. For less critical components, N active components of the system can be protected by a single standby component (N+1, N:1 redundancy).

In both cases, after recovery from the failure the original component might take over processing again (1:1/N:1) or might become a standby component (1+1/N+1).

The advantage of 1+1/N+1 redundancy is that only one disruption occurs. In 1:1/N:1 configurations, two disruptions take place; one when the fault occurs and a second after recovery when a fall forward to the original system occurs. If the original system suffers from an intermittent failure, fall back and fall forward also occur intermittently, thus potentially disrupting the service multiple times.

Frequently, the term 1+1 is also used to refer to an active/active setup, since in most cases these two cases go hand in hand.

Basically, the same also applies to N:M and N+M, respectively. Here, N active components/ links are protected by M redundant components/ links. The difference is that in the "N+M" case, any system can replace any other. After repair of the failed one, there is no need to return back. The repaired system will become standby for all the active ones. In the "N:M" case, any system can replace any of the components, but only once. After repair of the failing system, a reversion is needed to get back to the original redundancy level.

In addition to the different means to provide additional resources to provide the desired QoS even in the case of failure, it also needs to be discussed how the take over process is prepared. This preparation process is heavily application-dependant, but three main concepts exist:

- *Stateless replacement.* The replacing system does not care about any states of the failing system. It is just brought in operation mode. This is normally the fastest way to come back to active operation mode. Existing sessions might be lost and need to be re-established. Thus, stateless replacement is best suited for stateless processes and short-running processes that can be easily re-run. The MTTR phase ends when the standby system has become active. Examples include web-servers serving static information.
- *Stable state protection.* During normal operation mode of active system, the stable states are synchronized to a standby system or to an external database. When the failover occurs to standby, the standby

system will become active immediately, initialized with the stable state information or, after the states are recovered from this external database. The unstable states are lost. As an example for communication protocol stacks in telecom environment, this is known as stable call preservation. It is e.g. required that after a switchover 90% of the calls are preserved and just 10% of the transient calls are lost. The replacement scenario phase ends when standby system is able to run with the 90% of stable calls and accepting new calls.
- *Seamless protection.* normally goes hand in hand with an active/active operational mode, but it covers a different scope. The protected system is continuously exchanging the state changes to the standby system, so that, in case of a failing, the standby can immediately overtake the task from the failing one without losing any states. If there is any outage time during switchover, the replacement scenario phase ends when the standby is operational for the transferred tasks.

Migration

Migration is the relocation of running computational processes from one resource to another. This migration can be motivated by environmental changes that make it beneficial (cheaper, improve overall performance, etc.) to reallocate a certain process or bundle of processes. Migration however will impose an overhead either in time, resources utilization or costs that needs to be taken into account.

There are two different types of migration, *Single Process Migration* and *Virtual Machine Migration*.

Single Process Migration means that a single process is moved across different nodes. In order to migrate at process level, a system is needed that is able to reallocate processes among machines in a transparent way. One of the first examples is the Sprite implementation (Douglis & Ousterhout, 1991) for SPARCstation 1 workstations. The proposed mechanism is used to offload computationally expensive tasks to idle workstations within the same domain. This is done by spawning processes on remote workstations and by migrating them to idle machines as soon as the local user requires the machine's resources.

Virtual Machine Migration: The use of virtualization enables the migration of processes by replicating the whole environment, including the operating system, they run in. Although certain computing overhead is inherent to this approach, a lot more flexibility is achieved, as no specific requirements are imposed to the running code or to the host environment (except for the support of virtualization). While this approach has gained quite some popularity with the open source Xen hypervisor (Ian Pratt, 2003), *live migration* is nowadays available in most modern virtualization solutions for x86 platforms. Current implementations do not support migration beyond the borders of the ISO/OSI Layer 2 Network the virtual machine is connected to.

Migration is also a suitable technology to avoid some outage scenarios. As an application running in an environment that allows migration is not bonded to a dedicated physical host, it can be moved to another location when an outage of the hardware is imminent. Thus, a physical host can be freed of all tasks before it is taken down for maintenance or before a critical condition (e.g., a faulty fan or a hard drive showing recoverable errors) becomes terminal. On a large scale, migration technology can even be used to evacuate complete data centres either to save energy by concentrating computational power in one location and shut down completely other locations or in the case of predicted disasters that might affect a whole area.

To support migration of processes or operating system instances, it is common to utilize virtualization technology as introduced in the upcoming section.

Virtualization

Virtualization is a key building block of modern IT infrastructures as it increases system resiliency, eases error and disaster recovery, and is a key pillar of modern systems to optimize system utilization. It is used to hide actual physical resources and to provide logical resources instead. This enables the use of one single physical resource to be rendered as several of them (1:n), the use of several physical resources to be rendered as a single logical resource (n:1) or the use of several physical resources to render several logical resources (n:n). Decoupling the fixed physical resources from the resources that are used in first instance enables great flexibility in the dimensioning of the resources needed. Resources can be created on demand tailored for a specific use.

A key aspect of virtualization is that the kind of resources is not changed, i.e., the virtual resources are equivalent to the underlying physical resources. If resources which differ from the available physical resources are required, a different technology called *emulation* is used. An emulator fully resembles a resource. Common examples are the emulation of cellular handsets on a desktop PC, the emulation of end-of-life hardware, or of hardware like graphics cards or network adapters for which operating systems provide driver support out of the box.

Approaches, Implementations and Comparisons

Platform virtualization enables the virtualization of a whole Operating System environment. In this case, one can distinguish the Host OS on top of which the virtualized Guest OSs run. Regarding virtualization for software resources, the following distinctions can be made:

- *Application virtualization*: Virtualizes resources for certain applications, with a virtualization layer between the OS and the application.

- *OS-level virtualization:* All resources are virtualized at the OS level, i.e., the OS running on the physical hardware "duplicates" itself and provides multiple instances of itself. *OS-level virtualization* can be restricted to the OS kernel or also include system libraries and tools.
- *Software-based virtualization:* The operating system is run under the control of a virtualization program. While operations that cannot affect other processes are executed 1:1 on the underlying hardware, operations that could have side effects are intercepted and transformed into a safe command sequence.
- *Hardware-assisted virtualization:* Similar to the *Native Virtualization* scenario, the *Hardware* layer provides special support to for virtualization through a concrete set of instructions, e.g. Intel VT-d, AMD IOMMU. Usually, some hardware like network cards is emulated or paravirtualized.
- *Paravirtualization:* Does not fully simulate the hardware but an API is provided to the guest OS to access the physical resources. To this end, the guest system needs to be modified.

Often multiple of the above mechanisms are combined: While the core components of a system (like CPU and memory) are virtualized, other components like network adapters might be emulated or paravirtualized. It is common to restrict paravirtualization to I/O-intensive resources as paravirtualization provides the highest performance gain for these devices.

Some examples are:

- *Java* (Gosling & McGilton, 1996) is a programming language developed at Sun Microsystems. It fundamental difference from programming popular at the time

of its creation is the fact that its compiler does not produce binaries native to a certain processor, but so-called byte-code that is interpreted by the Java Virtual Machine at runtime. As a result, Java programs are platform independent and can be run on any host platform that provides the appropriate runtime environment.

- *.NET* is a framework developed by Microsoft (Microsoft Corporation). It is very similar to Java in that source code is compiled to an intermediate form, the common language runtime, that is executed by a runtime environment independent of the underlying system. Programs for .NET can be written in a number of languages such as C#, C++, or Visual Basic.
- *Solaris Zones* are an integral concept of the Solaris operating system. Zones basically are execution environments within a single instance of Solaris OS (Menno Lageman, 2005). While Zones share the same (running) Kernel, they are isolated against each other.
- *FreeBSD Jails* have been introduced in (Kamp & Robert N. M. Watson, 2000). The jail(2) system call of the FreeBSD kernel can be used to jail processes into separate environments. It limits access to a certain area of the file system as well as to other resources such as IP addresses.
- *Virtuozzo* (Parallels Holdings Ltd.) is a product that separates an operating system into several logical containers. It is thus similar to the Zones and Jails concepts described above. Virtuozzo is available for Linux and Windows. Parts of the Linux implementation are also available as open source under the name *OpenVZ*.
- *VMWare,* a software family developed by VMWare, Inc. The company's first product, VMWare Workstation, was released in 1999 and actually the first solution to bring virtualization to the x86 platform. Over

time, the product range has extended to hypervisor-based products for server virtualization (VMWare Inc.). Current releases support live migration of virtual machines as well as fault tolerance through replicated, parallel execution of virtual machines on multiple physical hosts (VMware, 2009).

- *VirtualBox* is a cross-platform virtualization software that runs on top of Windows, Linux, Mac OS, and OpenSolaris operating systems. It is distributed as both Open Source under the GPL and with an extended feature set under a proprietary license (Oracle Corporation).

- *Kernel-based Virtual Machine (KVM),* which is another full virtualization solution for Linux on x86 hardware containing virtualization extensions (Intel VT or AMD-V). It consists of a loadable kernel module, which provides the core virtualization infrastructure, and a processor specific module. KVM also requires a modified QEMU although work is underway to get the required changes upstream. Using KVM, one can run multiple virtual machines running unmodified Linux or Windows images. Each virtual machine has private virtualized hardware: a network card, disk, graphics adapter, etc. KVM is a free open-source software (Qumranet).

- *Xen,* which is an x86 virtual machine monitor which allows multiple commodity operating systems to share conventional hardware in a safe and resource managed fashion but without sacrificing either performance or functionality. Although XenSource Inc. sells enterprise versions of the software, the company also support open source project. The research originated at the University of Cambridge led by Ian Pratt (Ian Pratt, 2003).

Virtualized Real-Time Service-Oriented Infrastructures

When Service-Oriented Infrastructures are built using virtualized environments, the temporal interferences among multiple virtual machines concurrently running on the same physical node may completely disrupt the quality of service of the hosted applications. Therefore, appropriate node-level mechanisms are needed in order to guarantee correct scheduling of concurrent virtualized real-time services within the same node. The need for real-time support within SOAs is witnessed by the RTSOA paradigm (Cucinotta, Anastasi & Abeni, 2008; McGregor & Eklund, 2008), and by the increasing need for real-time support within the Grid community (Cuzzocrea, 2008). Unfortunately, most of the works in these directions do not consider time-shared or virtualised nodes. For example, (P.A. Dinda et al., 2008) proposed the use of time-shared systems, but their work did not address the issues concerned with low-level real-time scheduling algorithms. Steps in this direction have been moved by (L. Almeida et al., 2008), who applied real-time scheduling theory to the problem of guaranteeing temporal guarantees to distributed applications built as a network of composeable services, focusing on the distribution aspects. Also, (Cucinotta et al., 2009) recently proposed a real-time service-oriented architecture for distributed real-time applications in the industrial automation context.

The problem of QoS provisioning to virtualized applications has been addressed in some previous work, but the level of determinism needed to run real-time applications inside a virtual machine has not been reached yet.

For example, Xen (Ian Pratt, 2003) uses an EDF-based reservation mechanism (called S-EDF) to enforce temporal isolation between the different VMUs. However, the S-EDF scheduler lacks a solid theoretical foundation, and is not guaranteed to work correctly in presence of dynamic activations and deactivations. As a result, it seems to have problems in controlling the amount of CPU allocated to the various domains. In fact, in (Freeman, Foster I. T. et al., 2006), it is shown that the Xen scheduler is not able to properly control CPU allocations for I/O intensive operations.

If virtual machines are scheduled using proper real-time algorithms, the entire ensemble constituted by the host and the guests Operating Systems can be modelled as a hierarchy of schedulers. Therefore, its real-time performance can be evaluated by using hierarchical scheduling analysis techniques, such as the one proposed by Saewong and Rajkumar who extended resource reservations to support hierarchical reservations (Saewong, Rajkumar, Lehoczky, Klein & M. H., 2002). Shin and Lee proposed a different approach based on a compositional real-time scheduling framework (Shin & Lee, 2004), where the timing requirements of complex real-time components are analysed in isolation and subsumed into an abstract specification called interface, then combined to check schedulability of the overall system. A multiprocessor extension of this model has been presented in (Bini, Bertogna & Baruah, 2009; Bini, Buttazo & Bertogna, 2009).

Mok and others (Feng & Mok, 2002; Mok & Feng, 2001) presented a general methodology for hierarchical partitioning of a computational resource, where schedulers may be composed at arbitrary nesting levels. Specifically, they associate to each resource partition a characteristic function that identifies, for each time window of a given duration, the minimum time that the processor is allocated to the partition. On the other hand, (Lipari & Bini, 2004) addressed the problem of how to optimally tune the scheduling parameters for a partition, in order to fulfil the demand of contained real-time task sets. The latter technique has been applied by (Cucinotta et al., 2008) to analyse the schedulability of real-time tasks running in a virtualized Operating System, and to compute suitable scheduling parameters at the root scheduling level, complementing experimental results which showed how virtualized services may actually

be run with predictable QoS levels on Linux by using a soft resource-reservation scheduler built inside the kernel. The more complex problem of considering applications that may share global resources has been considered by (Bertogna, Fisher & Baruah, 2009).

Future Trends in QoS-Compliant Virtualization

There is a lot of effort in the direction of allowing more and more different environments to be able to virtualize a greater number of virtualized guests with maximum performance. Another trend is the development of means to enable the hot-dynamic adjustments of virtualized resources at run time.

The virtualization trend opens a new bunch of possibilities in the field of customer-tailored services tied to an on-the-fly purpose specific SLA, specially the real-time component comes on stage. To this end necessary mechanisms need to be created to allow the use of resources with real-time constrains, independently of whether these resources are network resources or software.

Resource Optimization

In traditional real-time literature, the criticality of tasks and the consequent hard nature of their deadlines leave the problem of resource usage or optimization only as a secondary concern. However, when focusing on soft real-time systems, the research efforts shift completely on the problem of finding appropriate trade-offs between an efficient/optimum resource usage and the guarantees provided to the real-time activities. In this context, QoS optimization and adaptive QoS control for soft real-time tasks are particularly relevant research areas, as detailed below.

Approaches, Implementations and Comparisons

Global QoS Control

Concerning the choice of optimum scheduling parameters for maximizing the QoS of a distributed system where multiple applications may share different resources, (Ragunathan Rajkumar, Chen Lee, John P. Lehoczky & Daniel P. Siewiorek) proposed Q-RAM, a very general model that allows each task to be associated with a custom utility function which relates the resource consumption to the QoS experienced by the application. An optimization algorithm is then run to decide a recommended vector of resource allocations that optimizes the overall utility function of the system. In the original paper this is a static allocation scheme, for it is very computationally demanding (the optimization problem is NP-Hard). In (Sourav Ghosh, Jeffery Hansen, Ragunathan Rajkumar & John Lehoczky), the authors adapt the Q-RAM approach to a radar system. Another interesting work is described in (Fumiko Harada, Toshimitsu Ushio & Yukikazu Nakamoto, 2007), where an on-line adaptation algorithm based on a discrete integral controller, executed at periodic sampling instants, decides the resource allocation based on the knowledge of upper and lower bounds to the utility function. The approach in (L. Palopoli & T. Cucinotta, 2007) considers instead a more specific class of applications, for which the QoS is tightly related to the latencies and to the delays (thus no utility function is needed), trading generality for accuracy in QoS control, and it uses very efficient control algorithms that need to be activated potentially for each job of the application.

Adaptive QoS Control

The motivation for research on feedback-based scheduling is that a static design can be highly inefficient when applications exhibit high time-varying workloads. For example, for multimedia applications, the extensive use of compression technologies leads to a high variability in the computational as well as network/disk workloads, despite the typical periodic nature of the application.

In order to keep under control the evolution of application QoS parameters, it is possible to use two main approaches: application-level and resource-level adaptation. In the first case (Hideyuki Tokuda & Takuro Kitayama, 1993; Scott Brandt & Gary Nutt, 2002; Tatsuo Nakajima, 1998; Wust, Steffens, Bril & Verhaegh, 2004), in response to time-varying application requirements and availability of shared resources, a software infrastructure (typically a middleware) influences run-time parameters of the applications to make their requirements fit in the instantaneous resource availability.

Many papers in the past few years propose to govern the resource allocation based on a constant monitoring of the QoS experienced by the application. The application, in principle, can run almost unaware of the underlying ongoing adaptation. In (Anton Cervin, Johan Eker, Bo Bernhardsson & Karl-Erik, 2002) the authors propose to adjust the scheduling priorities to maximize the performance of a set of feedback controllers. Recently, in (Fumiko Harada et al., 2007; Sourav Ghosh et al.) a work inspired to the Q-RAM framework has been done. The idea is to associate each task with a custom utility function relating the resource consumption to the QoS. An on-line optimization problem is then solved to compute the optimal assignment of resources.

Focusing on soft real-time applications, in (Lu, Stankovic, Tao & Son, 2002) the authors use an EDF scheduling algorithm trying to dynamically adapt the deadline miss ratio. A research line based on a well-founded dynamical model of the system, from a QoS evolution perspective, was first introduced in (Luca Abeni, Luigi Palopoli, Giuseppe Lipari & Jonathan Walpole, 2002) for a single resource. The model introduces a QoS metric based on measurements of the finishing time of the jobs, and relies on an underlying resource-reservation scheduling policy. The authors propose to split the controller into a prediction component and a feedback correction action, while the work is extended to a stochastic characterization of applications in (Cucinotta T., Palopoli L. & Marzario L., 2004), and to distributed applications in (L. Palopoli & T. Cucinotta, 2007).

A similar approach was the one proposed in (Ashvin Goel, Jonathan Walpole & Molly Shor), where a controller is used to regulate the progress rate of each task (real-rate scheduling), defined as the difference between a time-stamp associated to a computation and the actual time this computation is performed at. The approach is generalized to pipelines of tasks in (Steere, Shor, Goel & Walpole, 2000).

Finally, many papers have considered the problem of QoS adaptation from a software architecture point of view. For instance, the use of adaptation techniques inside general-purpose Operating Systems is discussed in (John Regehr & John A. Stankovic). In other papers, some authors propose to perform resource adaptation in a middleware layer (Eric Eide, Tim Stack, John Regehr & Jay Lepreau, 2004; Gill et al., 2005; Shankaran, Koutsoukos, Schmidt, Xue & Lu, 2006a). The latter work revolves around the QuO (Krishnamurthy et al., 2001) middleware framework, which is particularly noteworthy for it utilizes the capabilities of CORBA to reduce the impact of QoS management on the application code. A CORBA-oriented approach may also be found in (Shankaran, Koutsoukos, Schmidt, Xue & Lu, 2006b), where traditional control theory based on linearization, proportional control and linear systems stability is applied to the context of controlling resources allocation for a real-time object tracking system.

Future Trends

A good design for a soft real-time system is based on appropriate trade-offs between interactivity and responsiveness of individual applications or software components, and global utilization of the available resources. Basically, this leads to an overbooking of resources, usually based on statistical analysis of the application behaviour. However, whenever SLA agreements come in the loop, it may happen that a deadline miss, or the impossibility to sustain a certain throughput due to temporary or persistent overload conditions, even if not fatal for the system, may involve monetary consequences due to the presence of SLA agreements between service providers and end users.

The possibility not only to dynamically fine-tune the resources allocation for a given activity on a given host, but also to dynamically migrate activities on more powerful hosts opens up a new way of adapting resource availability to application requirements, based on the optimization of cost functions that may mix-in technical ingredients (expected capability for applications to meet their timing constraints) as well as business related ones (cost of occupying extra-resources out of the original plan, expected losses due to deadline misses).

CONCLUSION

Both Real-Time systems and virtualized infrastructures are already fairly well understood by themselves. The combination of these two paradigms, however, still poses quite some challenges. As most services do not require hard Real-Time constraints but have "only" soft Real-Time constraints, Real-Time aware service-oriented infrastructures that provide services on top of virtualized infrastructure are likely to become widely available in the not too distant future. This will enable also smaller companies to satisfy peak loads by exploiting the cost-effectiveness of using cloud resources while still being in control of the customer experience.

REFERENCES

Abeni, L., & Buttazzo, G. (1998). Integrating multimedia applications in hard real-time systems. *Proceedings of the IEEE Real-Time Systems Symposium,* December 1998, Madrid.

Abeni, L., Palopoli, L., Lipari, G., & Walpole, J. (2002). Analysis of a reservation-based feedback scheduler. *Proc. of the Real-Time Systems Symposium.*

Almeida, L., et al. (2008). Solutions for supporting composition of service-based RT applications. In *Proceedings of the 11th IEEE Symposium on Object Oriented Real-Time Distributed Computing* (pp. 42–49).

Andersson, B., & Jonsson, J. (2000). *Fixed-priority preemptive multiprocessor scheduling: To partition or not to partition* (pp. 337–346). Cheju Island, South Korea: RTCSA.

Andersson, B., & Tovar, E. (2006). Multiprocessor scheduling with few preemptions. In *Proceedings of the International Conference on Real-Time Computing Systems and Applications (RTCSA).*

Audsley, N., & Bletsas, K. (2004). Fixed priority timing analysis of real-time systems with limited parallelism. In *Proceedings of the Euromicro Conference on Real Time Systems.* Catania, Italy.

Audsley, N. C., Burns, A., Richardson, M. F., & Wellings, A. J. (1995). Data consistency in hard real-time systems. *Informatica, 19*(2).

Baker, T. P., Cirinei, M., & Bertogna, M. (2008). EDZL scheduling analysis. *Real-Time Systems: The International Journal of Time-Critical Computing, 40*(3), 264–289.

Baruah, S. (2006). The non-pre-emptive scheduling of periodic tasks upon multiprocessors. *Real-Time Systems: The International Journal of Time-Critical Computing, 32*(1-2), 9–20.

Baruah, S., & Carpenter, J. (2003). Multiprocessor fixed-priority scheduling with restricted interprocessor migrations. In *Proceedings of the EuroMicro Conference on Real-time Systems.* Porto, Portugal: IEEE Computer Society Press.

Baruah, S., Cohen, N., Plaxton, G., & Varvel, D. (1996). Proportionate *progress: A notion of fairness in resource allocation.*

Baruah, S., & Lipari, G. (2004). *A multiprocessor implementation of the total bandwidth server.* International Parallel and Distributed Processing Symposium (IPPDS 04), Santa Fe.

Baruah, S., & Lipari, G. (2004). *Executing aperiodic jobs in a multiprocessor constant-bandwidth server implementation.* Euromicro Conference on Real-Time Systems (ECRTS 04), Catania (Italy).

Battacharyya, S. S., Lee, E. A., & Murthy, P. K. (1996). *Software synthesis from dataflow graphs.* Kluwer Academic Publishers.

Bertogna, M., Cirinei, M., & Lipari, G. (2005). New schedulability tests for real-time tasks sets scheduled by deadline monotonic on multiprocessors. In *Proceedings of the 9th International Conference on Principles of Distributed Systems.* Pisa, Italy: IEEE Computer Society Press.

Bertogna, M., Fisher, N., & Baruah, S. (2009). Resource-sharing servers for open environments. *IEEE Transactions on Industrial Informatics, 5*(3), 202–220. doi:10.1109/TII.2009.2026051

Bini, E., Bertogna, M., & Baruah, S. (2009). Virtual multiprocessor platforms: Specification and use. In *Proceedings of 30th IEEE Real-Time Systems Symposium.*

Bini, E., Buttazo, G., & Bertogna, M. (2009). The multi supply function resource abstraction for multiprocessors: The global EDF case. In *Proceedings of the 15th IEEE International Conference on Embedded and Real-Time Computing Systems and Applications.*

Brandt, S., & Nutt, G. (2002). *Flexible soft real-time processing in middleware*. Real-Time Systems Journal, Special Issue on Flexible Scheduling in Real-Time Systems.

Burchard, A., Liebeherr, J., Oh, Y., & Son, S. H. (1995). New strategies for assigning real-time tasks to multiprocessor systems. *IEEE Transactions on Computers, 44*(12), 1429–1442. doi:10.1109/12.477248

Calandrino, J. M., Anderson, J. H., & Baumberger, D. P. (2007). A hybrid real-time scheduling approach for large-scale multicore platforms. In *Proceedings of the Euromicro Conference on Real-Time Systems.* Pisa.

Cervin, A., Eker, J., Bernhardsson, B., & Arzen, K.-E. (2002). Feedback-feedforward scheduling of control tasks. *Real-Time Systems, 23*(1/2). doi:10.1023/A:1015394302429

Cucinotta, T., Anastasi, G., & Abeni, L. (December 2008). Real-time virtual machines. In *Proceedings of the 29th Real-Time System Symposium (RTSS2008).*

Cucinotta, T., Mancina, A., Anastasi, G., Lipari, G., Mangeruca, L., Checcozzo, R., & Rusinà, F. (2009). A real-time service-oriented architecture for industrial automation. *IEEE Transactions on Industrial Informatics, 5*(3).

Cucinotta, T., Palopoli, L., & Marzario, L. (2004). Stochastic feedback-based control of QoS in soft real-time systems. In *Proceedings of the 43rd IEEE Conference on Decision and Control.*

Cuzzocrea, A. (2008). Towards RT data transformation services over grids. In *Proceedings of the 32nd Annual IEEE International Computer Software and Applications Conference* (pp. 1143–1149).

Dhall, S. K., & Liu, C. L. (1978). On a real-time scheduling problem. *Operations Research, 26,* 127–140. doi:10.1287/opre.26.1.127

Dinda, P. A. (2008). Resource virtualization renaissance. *Computer, 38*(5), 28–31.

Douglis, F., & Ousterhout, J. (1991). Transparent process, igration: Design alternatives and the Sprite implementation. *Software, Practice & Experience, 21*(8), 757–785. doi:10.1002/spe.4380210802

Eide, E., Stack, T., Regehr, J., & Lepreau, J. (2004). Dynamic CPU management for real-time middleware-based systems. *Proceedings of 10th IEEE Real-Time and Embedded Technology and Applications Symposium.*

Feng, X., & Mok, A. K. (2002). A model of hierarchical real-time virtual resources. In *Proceedings of the 23rd IEEE Real-Time Systems Symposium.*

Freeman, T., & Foster, I. T. (2006). *Division of labor: Tools for growing and scaling grids* (pp. 40–51). ICSOC.

Furunäs, J. (2000). Benchmarking of a real-time system that utilises a booster. In *Proceedings of the International Conference on Parallel and Distributed Processing Techniques and Applications, PDPTA2000.*

Garey, M. R., & Johnson, D. S. (1979). *Computers and intractability: A guide to the theory of NP-completeness.* New York, NY: W. H. Freeman and Company.

Gerber, R., Hong, S., & Saksena, M. (1995). Guaranteeing real-time requirements with resource-based calibration of periodic processes. *IEEE Transactions on Software Engineering, 21*(7). doi:10.1109/32.392979

Ghosh, S., Hansen, J., Rajkumar, R., & Lehoczky, J. (2008). Integrated resource management and scheduling with multi-resource constraints. *Proceedings of the 25th IEEE International Real-Time Systems Symposium (RTSS04).*

Gill, C. D., Gossett, J. M., Corman, D., Loyall, J. P., Schantz, R. E., Atighetchi, M., & Schmidt, D. C. (2005). *Integrated adaptive (QoS) management in middleware: A case study, real-time systems.*

Goddard, S., & Jeffay, K. (2001). Managing latency and buffer requirements in processing graph chains. *The Computer Journal, 44*(6). doi:10.1093/comjnl/44.6.486

Goel, A., Walpole, J., & Shor, M. (2004). Real-rate scheduling. *Proceedings of Real-time and Embedded Technology and Applications Symposium.*

Gosling, J., & McGilton, H. (1996). *The Java™ language environment: A White Paper.* Mountain View.

Harada, F., Ushio, T., & Nakamoto, Y. (2007). Adaptive resource allocation control for fair QoS management. *IEEE Transactions on Computers, 56*(3). doi:10.1109/TC.2007.39

Kamp, P.-H., & Watson, R. N. M. (2000). Jails: Confining the omnipotent root. In *Proc. 2nd Intl. SANE Conference.*

Kang, D.-I., Gerber, R., & Saksena, M. (2000). Parametric design synthesis of distributed embedded systems. *IEEE Transactions on Computers, 49*(11).

Krishnamurthy, Y., Kachroo, V., Karr, D. A., Rodrigues, C., Loyall, J. P., Schantz, R. E., & Schmidt, D. C. (2001). *Integration of QoS-enabled distributed object computing middleware for developing next-generation distributed application.* LCTES/OM.

Kuacharoen, P., Shalan, M. A., & Mooney, V. J., III. (2003). A configurable hardware scheduler for real-time systems. In *Proceedings of the International Conference on Engineering of Reconfigurable Systems and Algorithms.*

Lageman, M. (2005). *Solaris containers: What they are and how to use them* (Sun blueprints online). Retrieved from http://www.sun.com/blueprints

Lauzac, S., Melhem, R., & Mossé, D. (2003). An improved rate-Monotonic admission control and its application. *IEEE Transactions on Computers, 58*(3).

Leung, J. Y. T., & Whitehead, J. (1982). On the complexity of fixed-priority scheduling of periodic, real-time tasks. *Performance Evaluation, 2*, 237–250. doi:10.1016/0166-5316(82)90024-4

Lindh, L., Stärner, J., & Furunäs, J. (1995). From single to multiprocessor real-time kernels in hardware. In *Proceedings of the IEEE Real Time Technology and Applications Symposium.* Chicago.

Lipari, G., & Bini, E. (2004). A methodology for designing hierarchical scheduling systems. *Journal of Embedded Computing, 1*(2).

Liu, C. L. (1969). Scheduling algorithms for multiprocessors in a hard real-time environment. *JPL Space Programs Summary, 37*(60), 28–31.

López, J. M., Díaz, J. L., & García, D. F. (2004). Utilization bounds for EDF scheduling on real-time multiprocessor systems. *Real-Time Systems: The International Journal of Time-Critical Computing, 28*(1), 39–68.

López, J. M., & Garcia, M. (2003). Utilization bounds for multiprocessor rate-Monotonic scheduling. *Real-Time Systems: The International Journal of Time-Critical Computing, 24*(1), 5–28.

Lu, C., Stankovic, J., Tao, G., & Son, S. (2002). Feedback control real-time scheduling: Framework, modeling and algorithms. *Journal on Control-Theoretic Approaches to Real-Time Computing, 9.*

McGregor, C., & Eklund, J. M. (2008). RT SOAs to support remote critical care: Trends and challenges. In *COMPSAC '08: Proceedings of the 2008 32nd Annual IEEE International Computer Software and Applications Conference* (pp. 1199–1204).

Microsoft Corporation. (2010). *NET framework conceptual overview. NET framework 4*. Retrieved from http://msdn.microsoft.com/ library/zw4w595w.aspx

Mok, A. K., & Feng, X. A. (2001). Towards compositionality in real-time resource partitioning based on regularity bounds. In *Proceedings of the 22nd IEEE Real-Time Systems Symposium*.

Najjar, W. A., Lee, E. A., & Gao, G. R. (1999). Advances in the dataflow computational model. *Parallel Computing, 25*, 13–14. doi:10.1016/S0167-8191(99)00070-8

Nakajima, T. (1998). *Resource reservation for adaptive QoS mapping in real-time mach*.

Oracle Corporation. (n.d.). *VirtualBox website*. Retrieved from http://www.virtualbox.org/

Palopoli, L., & Cucinotta, T. (2007). Feedback scheduling for pipelines of tasks. In *Proceedings of the 10th Conference on Hybrid Systems Computation and Control*.

Parallels Holdings Ltd. (n.d.). *Parallels virtuozzo containers*. Retrieved from http://www.parallels.com/ products/ virtuozzo/ lib/ download/ wp/

Pratt, I. (2003). Xen and the art of virtualization. In *Proceedings of the Nineteenth ACM Symposium on Operating Systems Principles*.

Qumranet. (2010). *KVM - Kernal-based virtualization machine - White paper*.

Rajkumar, R., Juvva, K., Molano, A., & Oikawa, S. (1998). Resource kernels: A resource-centric approach to real-time and multimedia systems. *Proceedings of the SPIE/ACM Conference on Multimedia Computing and Networking*.

Rajkumar, R., Lee, C., Lehoczky, J. P., & Siewiorek, D. P. (1998). *Practical solutions for QoS-based resource allocation*.

Regehr, J., & Stankovic, J. A. (2001). Augmented CPU reservations: Towards predictable execution on general-purpose operating systems. In *Proceedings of the IEEE Real-Time Technology and Applications Symposium* (RTAS 2001), May 2001, Taipei.

Saewong, S., Rajkumar, R., & Lehoczky, J. P. Klein & M. H. (2002). Analysis of hierarchical fixed-priority scheduling. In *Proceedings of the IEEE Euromicro Conference on Real-Time Systems*.

Shankaran, N., Koutsoukos, X. D., Schmidt, D. C., Xue, Y., & Lu, C. (2006). Hierarchical control of multiple resources in distributed real-time and embedded systems. In *Proceedings of the 18th Euromicro Conference on Real-Time Systems*.

Shin, I., & Lee, I. (2004). Compositional real-time scheduling framework. In *Proceedings of the 25th IEEE International Real-Time Systems Symposium* (pp. 57–67).

Srinivasan, A., & Baruah, S. (2002). Deadline-based scheduling of periodic task systems on multi-processors. *Information Processing Letters, 84*(2), 93–98. doi:10.1016/S0020-0190(02)00231-4

Steere, D., Shor, M. H., Goel, A., & Walpole, J. (2000). Control and modeling issues in computer operating systems: Resource management for real-rate computer applications. In *Proceedings of 39th IEEE Conference on Decision and Control*.

Stoica, I., Abdel-Wahab, H., Jeffay, K., Sanjoy, K., Baruah, J. E., Gehrke, C., & Plaxton, G. (1996). A proportional share resource allocation algorithm for real-time, time-shared systems. *Proceedings of the IEEE Real-Time Systems Symposium.*

Tokuda, H., & Kitayama, T. (1993). Dynamic QoS control based on real-time threads. *NOSSDAV '93: Proceedings of the 4th International Workshop on Network and Operating System Support for Digital Audio and Video.*

VMware Inc. (2009). *Protecting mission-critical workloads with VMware fault tolerance.* Retrieved from http://www.vmware.com/ resources/ techresources/ 1094

VMWare Inc. (2010). *VMWare media resource center - Company milestones.* Retrieved from http://www.vmware.com/ company/ mediaresource/ milestones.html

Ward, M., & Audsley, N. (2002). Hardware implementation of programming languages for real-time. *Proceedings of the 8th IEEE Real-Time and Embedded Technology and Applications Symposium.*

Wust, C. C., Steffens, L., Bril, R. J., & Verhaegh, W. F. J. (2004). QoS control strategies for high-quality video processing. In *Proceedings of the 16th Euromicro Conference on Real-Time Systems.*

KEY TERMS AND DEFINITIONS

Quality of Service (QoS): Summary of mechanisms used to deliver an agreed service level.

Real-Time: Real-Time systems guarantee a maximum response time. Responses become worthless after the set deadline.

Scheduling: Determining when, i.e., the time interval, and where, i.e. on which processor, a job is executed.

Service Level Agreement (SLA): Contract defining the level at which a service is to be provided. It defines parameter s such as maximum delay and jitter, guaranteed bandwidth, and service availability.

Temporal Interference: Influence the execution of a virtual machine has on the timing of execution of another virtual machine on the same host.

Virtualization: Decoupling physical from logical entities. Multiple physical entities may be aggregated to form a single logical entity or a single physical entity may provide multiple logical entities.

Chapter 12
Network Management in Virtualized Infrastructures

Manuel Stein
Alcatel-Lucent Bell Labs, Germany

Karsten Oberle
Alcatel-Lucent Bell Labs, Germany

Thomas Voith
Alcatel-Lucent Bell Labs, Germany

Dominik Lamp
University of Stuttgart, Germany

Sören Berger
University of Stuttgart, Germany

ABSTRACT

Service Oriented Infrastructures (SOI) build upon previous advancements in Distributed Systems, Grid Computing, Cloud Computing, Virtualization, SOA, and technologies alike. Capabilities merged under the banner of SOI offer a solution that serves long-standing business needs, but also meets increasing demand for infrastructures, enabling the fast and flexible deployment of new services.

However, typical current SOI realizations, e.g., Grid or Cloud solutions, do not take the network infrastructure, necessary for flawless service interaction, sufficiently into consideration. In most cases, those frameworks focus on providing huge and extremely divisible applications with hardware resources possibly distributed over several provider domains. They manage just computing related resources like CPU and RAM or Storage (e.g. Amazon Web Services), but network connectivity is typically taken for granted while network Quality of Service (QoS) aspects (e.g., jitter, delay) of the data exchange is usually not considered. Consequently, the data exchange between changeably deployed components cannot be comprehensively treated.

DOI: 10.4018/978-1-60960-827-9.ch012

This chapter provides an overview on related state of the art technologies regarding topics such as QoS provisioning, virtualization, and network resource management. This background is enriched with latest research results on future trends and advances in state of the art in network management.

INTRODUCTION

Host virtualization has changed the landscape of hosting services over the past years from traditional server hosting towards rentable virtual machines. Under the concept of Cloud Computing, those virtual machines can be also be rented on-demand under a negotiated service level agreement (SLA), which makes Clouds coveted for outsourcing of application delivery networks from in-house data centers to a serviced infrastructure. At the same time, network virtualization could likewise facilitate on-demand provisioning of network services under negotiated SLAs. Yet, network management in virtualized infrastructures is challenged by current and emerging virtualization solutions to cope with differing parameter sets for virtual machine endpoints, networking QoS level agreements and multiple tenancies.

Cloud providers operate on geo-distributed data centers for reliability and redundancy, but argue that it is necessary to expand from large-scale computational silos towards a higher network distribution in order to improve efficiency both in operational cost and networking (Church, Greenberg, Hamilton, 2008). The operational expenses of a data center can be reduced if commodities (e.g. facilities, energy and networking) were used to build smaller and highly distributed data centers. In a more detailed reflection on video service provisioning (Norton, 2008), the author reports that strongly increasing traffic demands exhaust Internet exchange capacities, which, after a foretold period of higher transit pricing might leave transit wholesale with a traffic profile pricing scheme similar to the telephone system, making it worthwhile to consider construction of smaller data centers at the last mile. In such a distributed data center scenario, network management design

has to consider higher propagation delays and capacity bottlenecks to remote data center locations in order to maintain its responsiveness. Techniques developed in the fields of distributed systems and agent communications are required to account for the stability of Network Management.

Future Internet research has adopted the trend of multi-homed service providers to develop the concept of a virtual service provider, whose infrastructure can span across multiple ISPs using network virtualization. Approaches exist to provide a multitude of virtual networks on the global infrastructure that would provision point-to-point and point-to-multipoint links or other topologies of virtual links under a negotiated SLA with assured QoS for mission-critical application delivery across existing carrier networks. This concept of network virtualization closes the market gap between investment in a costly, dedicated network infrastructure and rental of an over-provisioned IP transit that is subject to varying cross traffic conditions when interconnecting remote data center locations. In the pursuit for cost savings, the data center operator is unlikely to rely on a single option among these but rather employs several types of transport services in order to map cloud traffic onto individual transport resources, i.e. depending on the negotiated QoS terms of virtual machine communication. Hence, Network Management in Virtualized Infrastructures is facing an increased complexity to map virtual machine traffic onto resources, since it has to manage multiple transitions among data centers as opposed to the simple transit model that is unfit to provide network QoS among data center locations.

In the following, we have a closer look at network virtualization techniques developed in the context of Future Internet research and the Cloud business. We further look at network QoS provisioning, i.e. network metrics that are likely to describe the negotiable SLA between a cloud provider and its customers as well as possible architectures that can account for negotiated network QoS. Eventually, we look at current works on network resource management technologies and approaches that can be applied in the distributed data center model and finally, we sketch possible future research directions for Cloud management to support network QoS provisioning in distributed infrastructures.

ANALYSIS OF PAST WORKS ON NETWORK VIRTUALIZATION

The term network virtualization is divergently attributed in literature. Although network technologies using the attribute "virtual" have already some history (e.g. VC, VLAN, VPN), the concept of network virtualization is yet vaguely settled in research, leaving it to create both hype and confusion in the market.

ISPs and carriers alike have developed services to diversify infrastructure offers. The Internet itself started as an overlay to the circuit-switched telephony network. Its success has lead to a steady replacement of dial-up access infrastructures by TDM switching systems (SDH, frame-relay, ATM) and subsequently a purely packet-switched access infrastructure (Carrier-/Metro-Ethernet). In ATM networks, the term "Virtual Circuit" was introduced to describe a connection-oriented transport service that, despite being realized over cell-oriented ATM, behaves as a bidirectional communication channel, i.e. virtualization has freed the circuit from its original implication that it requires its own physical channel. The virtual LAN technology provides the coexistence of multiple LANs on a single Ethernet infrastructure. The original conception of a closed, physical switching environment has been breached to segment the address space into self-contained Ethernet stratums on a shared infrastructure. The approach

is designed to reduce the extent of flooding, allows individual aging and filtering per VLAN, theoretically frees the LAN concept from the uniqueness of MAC addresses (VLAN switches forward packets based on both VLAN identifier and MAC destination) and repels the uniqueness of MAC routing tables in a switch. Virtual Private Networks as compared to their non-virtual counterparts can span across public infrastructures by applying mechanisms that preserve privacy across third-party networks. Virtualization of private networks breaks the implication that privacy can only be supported in an owned infrastructure, i.e. the unique correlation of the private network and a self-contained infrastructure can be dropped.

In 2003, Joseph D. Touch et al. conceived the generic idea of a Virtual Internet Architecture (Touch, Wang, Eggert, Finn, 2003), i.e. the decoupling the Internet's unique existence upon various link layer bindings in order to allow for the creation of a "virtual" Internet of hosts, routers and links, supporting multi-hop paths, unique endpoint addresses, address resolution, etc. The term "virtual" was leaned from virtual memory in such that the virtualization technology provides *isolation*-based address protection and *abstraction* of the underlying complexity. In the Virtual Internet Architecture, an IP layer is used on top of the Internet IP endpoints to model a reconfigurable link-layer substrate that serves as a virtual topology to an additional Virtual Internet IP layer. Interestingly here is the use of IP-in-IP encapsulation giving birth to the attribute of *recursion*, i.e. a virtual network could subsequently serve as a substrate for additional virtual network architectures. The explicit modeling of a link-layer between the Internet IP layer and the Virtual Internet layer also allows for *concurrence* and *revisitation*, i.e. an Internet host can be a member of concurrent Virtual Internets and a Virtual Internet can have multiple of its virtual endpoints on the same Internet host respectively, allowing revisitation of the very same Internet host for either of the virtual link-layer endpoints.

Lastly, the attribute *inheritance* is used to state that the Virtual Internet is ultimately bound to the characteristics of the underlying Internet.

Future Internet research targets to overcome the impasse of Internet evolution that is stuck with hierarchical address space separation and simple point-to-point routing while being challenged by impeding address space exhaustion and increasing demand for smaller Autonomous Systems. In this context, network virtualization was first perceived as a way to experiment with new architectures (Anderson, Peterson, Shenker, Turner, 2005) in order to develop technologies for the next generation Internet, also known as the purist approach, whereas Nick Feamster et al. (Feamster, Gao, Rexford, 2007) argue that virtualization itself should be a crucial feature of the Future Internet architecture and propose to split the traditional ISP role into an infrastructure provider role and a service provider role, a.k.a. the pluralist approach - as in the plurality of serviced virtual networks running on a shared infrastructure. As a result, N.M. Mosharaf Kabir Chowdhury et al have derived a definition of network virtualization (Chowdhury, Boutaba, 2009) as the decoupling of the infrastructure provider role from the service provider role, i.e. breaking up the unite role of traditional ISPs. Clearly, the interpretation from a business viewpoint conceals the technological characterization of the term network virtualization, but fulfills its purpose with regards to Future Internet incentives.

Victor Moreno describes the term "Network Virtualization" in his eponymous book (Moreno, Reddy, 2006) figuratively as an architectural approach to providing separate logical networking environments created over a single shared network infrastructure that provide each the network services of a traditional non-virtualized network, hence perceived by the user as dedicated networks with dedicated resources (cmp. Moreno, Reddy, 2006 chapter 1, §2). Further, in the context of Cloud research, Marcus Kessler et al have derived 4 characteristics of network virtualization (Oberle, Kessler, Stein, Voith, Lamp, Berger 2009), i.e. *isolation* of virtual networks from the infrastructure and each other, *segmentation* of the infrastructure resources to employ subsets and partial resources [cmp. concurrence], *aggregation* to let virtual networks span across infrastructure domains and *encapsulation* that hides the underlying complexity (cmp. abstraction) and preserves recursion of an approach, sometimes titled "clean" virtualization.

Despite the diverging perception of the term "network virtualization", we can summarize that it can be rather used as a paradigm to decouple a network's singularities from its original architecture in order to provide plurality over the uniqueness in the nature of its non-virtualized counterpart. The decomposition of settled singularities explains the hype and expectations around virtualization, because getting rid of yet undiscovered constraints is considered disruptive to the linear evolution of computer networking and can cause impact proportional to the extent of its use.

Network Virtualization Layer

In contrast to few, settled virtualized technologies (virtual memory, virtual machine, virtual LAN, etc.), the term network virtualization, general in its wording, collectively applies to a large set of computer network virtualization technologies. Chowdhury and Boutaba (Chowdhury, Boutaba, 2010) attempt to classify solutions by 4 attributes, i.e. the networking layer that is being virtualized (e.g. IP/ATM), the layer that is used to create a virtual network substrate (physical layer, link layer, network layer, application layer), the functional scope of virtualization (called the architectural domain, e.g. network management, resource management) and the infrastructure extent of virtualization (called granularity, e.g. nodes, links, routers, etc.). In the following, we will revisit these attributes in contemplation on an approach for distributed SOIs.

The protocol layer that is suitable to interconnect dynamically deployed service components on a SOI varies depending on the technological viewpoint. From a host virtualization perspective, Ethernet data link layer virtualization seems appropriate since virtual machines are typically provisioned with one or more emulated Ethernet interface cards that exchange Ethernet frames. In fact, numerous approaches share this layer of virtualization. In 2003, Xuxian Jiang and Dongyan Xu proposed an application-level substrate of UDP connections as isolated virtual link topology upon which a virtual Ethernet can be provisioned that consists of virtual hosts and virtual switches (Jiang, Xu, 2003). The advantage of an application-layer overlay is its wide applicability on existing infrastructures. Unlike lower layer substrates, application transport layer connections provide variable payloads to encounter the mismatch between virtual Ethernet MTU sizes and available substrate payload sizes, notably at additional connection setup and IP fragmentation cost. As a result of research conducted in the Virtual Network Infrastructure project (VINI), Bhatia et al have employed Ethernet over GRE tunneling (Bhatia, Motiwala, Mühlbauer, Mundada, Valancius, Bavier, Feamster, Peterson, Rexford, 2008) that reduces superfluous application transport protocol overhead (checksum, 4-tupel connection identification, user-level socket implementation) to a better performing link virtualization with a small, fixed encapsulation overhead (4-byte key, OS kernel implementation). While the above-mentioned transport layer encapsulation is resilient to network address translation, a direct encapsulation of Ethernet frames over the Internet IP address space would be thinkable, but a simple IP-pair identification of a virtual link identification does not suffice the propounded virtualization requirements for concurrence and isolation at the same time, i.e. either the virtual Ethernet address space is shared and requires unique, managed MAC addresses as in the IP link layer substrate of the Virtual Internet Architecture or, otherwise, a virtual link identified by an IP-pair could not be reused among virtual Ethernet networks. This restriction

derives from the lack of a virtual network identifier in the IP substrate. Any layer below IP could not be driven as an overlay across the existing Internet IP infrastructure to encapsulate Ethernet. However, a cloud operator can rely on L2VPN network services from ISPs to interconnect data center locations that allow the continuation of a substrate for link layer virtualization across the WAN infrastructure, such as Ethernet-over-MPLS paths or Ethernet-over-SDH leased lines. An encapsulation of Ethernet-in-Ethernet could employ VLAN identifier (12bit) as a link layer substrate to distinguish virtual networks but is limited to a comparatively small number (4096) of virtual Ethernet networks. Workarounds exist that propose either VLAN translations among data center locations or VLAN stacking (IEEE Standard 802.1ad Provider Bridges, 2006).

In addition to the above-mentioned choices for link layer virtualization, recent Cloud approaches to overcome the scalability caveats of WAN Ethernet use a hybrid virtualization approach where the necessity for recursion is dropped, i.e. the virtual MAC endpoint addresses are not encapsulated but chosen by network management as a unique address in the SOI. The hybrid approach has risen from the evolution of data centers to support multiple virtual machines on a single host – yet without consideration to provide a customer with a dedicated virtual network. Network interface controller virtualization, either through multithreaded networking cards (SUN™ Neptune, 2007) or memory virtualization for directed I/O (Abramson, Jackson, Muthrasanallur, Neiger, Regnier, Sankaran, Schoinas, Uhlig, Vembu, Wiegert, 2009), allows for the dynamic spawning of multiple MAC endpoints on a shared interface card, so that each virtual machine can directly leverage the physical network infrastructure without the requirement for software-emulated network controllers. Here, virtual networks can be either distinguished by a unique MAC address' affinity to a virtual network and/or by using VLAN identifiers to explicitly identify the virtual network.

Constructing the virtual network from unique MAC addresses alone implies that a switching element in the network domain maintains the virtual network affinity, i.e. a large table of endpoints to enforce isolation among the virtual networks. Proposals exist to solve the switching complexity in such an architecture by introducing best practices, e.g. by hierarchical MAC address space organization (Scott, Crowcroft, 2008) with the downside of choosing in appropriate mask lengths or by applying DHT-based forwarding (Kim, Caesar, Rexford, 2008) with a fixed 2-hop delivery and the downside that the network paths vary by the chosen MAC address. Constructing virtual networks by VLAN identifiers faces the same scalability problems as the use of VLAN identifiers with Ethernet-in-Ethernet encapsulation, yet with the additional constraints of having the endpoint addresses chosen uniquely by the data center network management.

The problem of Ethernet scalability lies in the maintenance of its bridging topology and link states, a combination of learning by flooding and auto-aging of information. Though the Spanning Tree Protocol, its optimized derivate Rapid-STP and the VLAN-enabling derivate Multiple-STP can provide a loop-free routing topology for each VLAN stratum, STP does not fit to a distributed mesh of virtual machines. The time for the tree topology to converge makes it difficult to provide seamless live migration of virtual machines within the infrastructure. With the current introduction of virtual switches at each virtualization host to bridge virtual machine traffic, the complexity of the bridge topology increases. Further, if geographical distribution of the virtual mesh is targeted, e.g. to meet application delivery latency requirements, STP's inherent reduction of a virtual mesh to a tree topology, spanning across the WAN to several remote locations, is not appreciable. The latter has been addressed by TRILL (Touch & Perlman, 2009) Transparent Interconnection of lots of links), that introduces routing bridges to terminate site-local STP and realize pair-wise

forwarding among data center locations. Yet, flooding and aging mechanisms are required in the link layer stratum, even in the virtualized MSTP/VLAN-RBridges environment. By introducing pair-wise routing to the data link layer among RBridges, the switching complexity increases. As of the interconnection of sites with IP commodity access (e.g. Cisco Overlay Transport Virtualization), Ethernet-in-IP encapsulation across the WAN remains and imposes a high protocol overhead. It is questionable whether a virtualization of the Ethernet protocol layer is amiable. It allows customers to interconnect virtual machines with a wider range of protocols, such as HyperSCSI and multimedia Ethernet protocols, but appears over-engineered for Internet application delivery (i.e. TCP+UDP/IP).

From an Internet application viewpoint, the IP layer virtualization seems to be appropriate to interconnect virtual machine meshes. In host virtualization, there is yet no equivalent to the Ethernet interface card virtualization, i.e. no device driver exist that would offload address resolution and Ethernet framing to the virtualization host, so instead, the link layer control within the virtual machine has to be tricked into local communication with the virtualization host by preempting address resolution and routing IP packets among virtualization hosts. Nortel's IP VPN-Lite architecture is an IP-in-IP VPN solution that uses MP-BGP-like extensions to control the VPN architecture, similar to the RFC4364 BGP/MPLS IP VPNs architecture, yet without MPLS. However, the approach is as promising, since IP routing apparently provides advantages in the virtual topology creation over Ethernet level virtualization since route metrics can be used to balance traffic across the infrastructure and multiple data center interconnections can be leveraged for individual communication flows among virtual machines. The network management's notion of IP endpoints within the virtual topology allows for additional IP flow classification, flow policing, shaping and filtering. Traffic classification and diversified routing of IP flows among two virtual machines is crucial to consider QoS aspects (e.g. jitter, delay) of the data exchange and is required to comprehensively treat virtual machine communications. The IRMOS project Path Manager Architecture (Stein, Oberle, Voith, Kübert, Gallizo, Berger, Lamp, Fürst, Neple, 2009) describes an approach to network management that evaluates a virtual machine mesh's IP flows to find an optimal mapping onto the distributed data center infrastructure, taking the existence of multiple, available transit connections into account that interconnect data center locations.

Further up the protocol stack, an Internet application could largely profit from virtualization of protocols that use application-specific addressing (e.g. URLs). Note, that the application transport layer (e.g. UDP and TCP) does not contain endpoint addressing but relies on IP virtualization instead. Application protocols using URLs for addressing (e.g. HTTP, SIP), a.k.a. Internet overlays, could be provided by the virtualization host towards the virtual machine by introducing new kinds of virtual devices. A kernel-based approach (Völker, Martin, El Khayat, Werle, Zitterbart, 2009) promotes the flexible composition of protocol stacks to serve user-level applications, similar to the above mentioned introduction of application protocol device emulation for virtual machines. Web application servers offer a similar level of communication services to application modules, though applications are not isolated at the machine level but by providing sandboxed execution spaces at the process level (cmp. Java™ Virtual Machines). Application protocol virtualization would allow for offloading of several computational tasks such as DNS lookup, SSL encryption, packetization, application load balancing, TCP multiplexing, etc. into the virtualization platform. Currently, those communication interfaces are implemented as user-level libraries and have no standardized API equivalent in the device driver domain, so their introduction would not only require modifications at the OS level, but change the way how user-level applications interface with the OS. An approach to virtualize application protocols allows for a wide range of diversification. The notion of application protocol's traffic behavior through a virtual device offers a great opportunity in respect to resource mapping, flow control and computation offload but tends to be solution-specific regarding the ongoing evolution of application overlay protocols.

Our brief review across the protocol layers has shown a strong development at the Ethernet layer virtualization with the benefits of a generic connectivity but a significant protocol overhead if encapsulated across the WAN, a lack of routing metrics and a lack of flow classification to enforce QoS. We see that IP virtualization has yet to be adopted in machine virtualization but seems a promising solution to comprehensively treat application flows in a virtual machine mesh. Lastly, application overlay virtualization would require application adaptation but offers efficiency benefits and a wide area of market diversification. We conclude that it is unlikely to state that one network virtualization fits all purposes. Instead, network management in distributed SOIs should be able to select virtualized network resources according to the application's requirements. A detailed notion of the application flow composition can be leveraged by the SOI network management for resource matching, topology mapping and optimization of the resource allocation. In turn, the migration of application delivery networks onto SOIs can benefit from a better predictable performance, topology diversity, auto-scaling and timely responsiveness of mission-critical components.

Performance Guarantees in Virtualized Networks

Having reviewed past works on network virtualization, we now take a closer look at IP flow performance metrics. Web application delivery networks (search engines, web market places, social networking platforms, logistic information support systems etc.), Software-as-a-Service offers (customer relationship management, sales force automation, web-based office applications, e-Learning platforms, etc.), real-time interactive multimedia services (web conferencing, virtual and augmented reality, video-on-demand, gaming-on-demand, etc.) altogether require the timely delivery of a service to ensure customer quality of experience. An essential task of advanced network management systems in distributed SOIs is the automated QoS provisioning for multi-component services across different locations under consideration of soft end-to-end service guarantees. One of the key components required to fulfill this ambitious task is to have strict Quality of Service guarantees provided in the transport network below the virtualization layer where required - due to the inheritance of network characteristics. QoS demands can only be answered with over-provisioning of bandwidth which is not sufficient especially for real-time services. Network virtualization concepts subdivide the physical router nodes and the connected links in an infrastructure provider's transport network into virtualized ones. A service provider can "own" such virtualized nodes and links from which it builds up its dedicated QoS-enabled and fully controlled "virtual" network infrastructure. In the following we give an overview on QoS management schemes which are likely available from a transport operator's network infrastructure. There are two core approaches for providing QoS in IP transport networks, namely integrated services and differentiated services.

Integrated Services Approach

First there is the "Integrated Services" (IntServ) approach which performs QoS management on a per micro flow granularity to support real-time services (Clark, Shenker, & Zhang, 1992), (Braden, Clark, & Shenker, 1994). The "Resource Reservation Protocol" (RSVP) is used to manage resources across such an IntServ network. Each router along the negotiated path reserves the required networking resources, which are needed to guarantee the pre-negotiated QoS. In principle this approach can provide hard QoS guarantees in IP based transport networks. But one must keep in mind that this approach performs resource reservation on a micro flow level. Hence there are severe issues with regards to scalability, as routers within such a network have to maintain per flow session information. Even more each router independently needs to perform traffic classification to identify which packet belongs to which micro-flow to ensure pre-negotiated packet forwarding behavior for each QoS negotiated session.

Differentiated Services Approach

Second there is the "Differentiated Services" (DiffServ) approach, defining an architecture that offers scalable service differentiation on IP packet level (Blake, Blake, Carlson, Davies, Wang, Weiss, 1998). This scheme gives precedence to certain types of traffic in the transport network. Aggregated traffic flows, combining micro flows with similar service characteristics are passed with similar forwarding behavior across a DiffServ enabled network.

Traffic classification mechanisms, which are performed at the edge of a DiffServ enabled network, map IP packets onto a limited set of traffic classes. Each of these traffic classes represents the aggregated traffic of one service class in the network. In the inner part of the network, no micro flow specific knowledge needs to be maintained. Instead all packets are forwarded based on their classification being applied at the edge of the network. Routers in the inner part of the network only perform a limited number of forwarding schemes optimized to fulfill the service requirements of the traffic classes they are assigned to. In contrast to the IntServ approach this scheme does not imply a scalability issue, as in the inner part of the network, no flow-specific packet process-

Figure 1. Taxonomy of applications

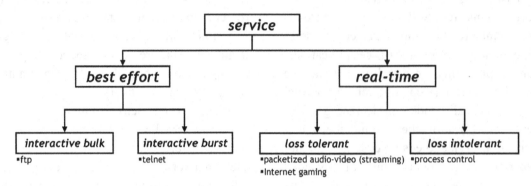

ing is necessary and only a limited number of per hop forwarding behaviors need to be performed by the routers, preserving the stateless hop-per-hop IP forwarding paradigm. The drawback of this approach is that due to the coarse-granular mapping of micro flows onto a limited number of traffic classes no hard QoS guarantees can be easily achieved.

QoS Characteristics

Notably, delay and jitter are associated with the term QoS guarantees for network traffic coming from the so called loss tolerating real-time applications. But also ensured bandwidth and minimizing of loss rate needs to be taken into account for getting a satisfying user experience in respect to QoS.

The authors of (Peterson, Davie, 1996) introduce taxonomy of network applications, as shown in Figure 1. The main characterization distinguishes between real-time and elastic application. Elastic applications have no time constraints in respect to the delivery of data. They are usually not loss-tolerant: i.e., they require reliable data transfer. For this class of applications, it is sufficient to provide best-effort data transport. For dedicated cases, e.g., signaling traffic, one distinguishes between best-effort traffic guaranteeing a minimal bandwidth and best-effort without any guarantees. Real-time applications

require the delivery of data within a specified time frame. The real-time class is sub-classified into loss-tolerant and loss-intolerant applications. The differentiation criteria at the base of Figure 1 (e.g., non-adaptive or rate-adaptive) are relevant for end points only.

Certain QoS guarantees of the transport network would improve user experience.

Especially best-effort application mainly benefits from ensured bandwidth. The throughput for an application decreases in a manner as the delay increases. Loss-tolerant real-time applications, especially audio and video, benefit from certain delays and jitter guarantees. The strongest applications are the loss-intolerant real-time applications, which require zero packet loss. Loss-intolerant real-time applications can just be realized with a reasonable expense in closed well known local network premises.

It is a big challenge to define a service model, which meets the requirements of a wide range of applications and even allows for future applications. Due to the bad experience with IntServ scalability a DiffServ like approach classifying the network traffic is a preferred solution for larger approaches with the necessity to scale.

Ensuring Bandwidth

The objective of ensuring bandwidth for applications is impacted by packet loss, since it impacts the throughput for elastic applications and the user quality experience of real-time loss-tolerant systems. Real-time loss-tolerant applications like audio and video transmissions are very sensitive in respect to packet loss rate.

Packet loss may occur due to corrupted packets caused on the transport medium, due to defect HW in network elements or due to faulty SW dealing with network packets. An operator has to supervise the network elements and have to take steps against faulty network elements or degrading transport mediums.

Other causes for packet loss are overloaded network elements. Allowing as many packets as possible into a network causes full buffer queues at each routing network element with the risk of loosing packets due to limited buffer sizes (overload). Longer queues cause also longer delay in the network. For providing QoS to applications the network traffic needs to be controlled and therefore managed for minimizing loss and delay by avoiding overload of network elements. This could be done by explicit reservation on each network element on the network path of each flow (intserv) or by just prioritizing the traffic by classifying it (diffserv) in conjunction with a managed limitation of the network traffic at the network's edge avoiding the overload of network elements within the network.

Delay and Jitter

Real-time traffic (e.g. video) is characterized mainly by stronger requirements in respect to delay and jitter. Delay is determined mainly by the propagation delay i.e. the amount of time it takes for the network packet to send over a medium like copper wires or optical fiber. In a virtualized infrastructure, queuing and transmission delays in the hidden underlying physical infrastructure account for the overall delay experienced on a flow between two virtual machines. Notably, the locality of an application impacts the propagation delay and needs to be considered for component

placing. Research conducted by Asgari et al (Asgari, Trimintzios, Irons, Pavlou, Egan, & Van Den Berghe, 2002) shows that propagation delay can be regarded purely additive across network segments.

Jitter is influenced by cross-traffic, for which a real-time traffic is confronted on the way through a network. Without knowing the amount of expected cross-traffic of same or higher priority, a prediction of jitter in a specified range is not feasible. Classifying the traffic of an application can be used for using different transport network paths. For example for real-time traffic with very strong delay and jitter requirements leased lines over SDH can be used. Managing the amount of traffic and the possibility of using different transport network paths depending on classified network traffic allows the prediction of jitter in a specified range. The receiving endpoint of an isochronous real-time stream removes the jitter impact by using a jitter buffer. A jitter buffer is a buffer with queued packets, which are picked out with a certain delay. This can be also done inside a network known as traffic shaper, but it has to be done per flow, which is a memory-expensive operation and does therefore not scale. In addition, buffering influences the overall end-to-end delay.

Why Managed Network is Mandatory for Getting QoS?

Concluding the QoS issues as discussed we can say:

- Managing of network traffic would ensure that the multiplex stages always get a controlled load of traffic *avoiding packet loss* due to congested buffer queues.
- The managing of location of application and the selection of network paths would make it possible for calculating *the delay* mainly affected by the propagation delay.
- The managing of the amount of traffic of same or higher priority level or selection

of network path avoiding additional jitter allows the prediction of the *maximum jitter* caused by well-known concurrent traffic, if any.

CURRENT WORK AND FUTURE TRENDS OF NETWORK MANAGEMENT IN VIRTUALIZED INFRASTRUCTURES

Regarding the traditional ITU-T basic objectives and general requirements of a Telecommunications management network (ITU-T Recommendation M.3010, 2000) based on the Open Systems Interconnection model (ISO/IEC 7498-1, 1996), the network management has to account for fault-, configuration-, accounting-, performance- and security-management (FCAPS) of network services. As of the TMN functional architecture targeted to perform these tasks, a logical layering is recommended. The lowest layer consists of the network elements, each exposing functionality to the next layer. Individual elements are then grouped by similar functionality to bundle their functions through an *element management layer* towards the overall *network management layer* that maps requested edge-to-edge service functionalities onto the managed network domain. This functional OSS architecture would be topped by a *service management layer* for service order handling, including interfacing with the customer, information collection, deployment coordination and interaction with federated service providers. Within each provider domain, service managers underlie the control and goal-setting influence of a *business management layer* that is kept proprietary to the network operator. The service management layer mediates between internal business goals (usually high-utilization) and customer requirements, i.e. the SLA. The OSI TMN logical layered architecture can be found in differing forms of Grid management and Cloud data center management architectures proposed in current research.

To clarify the use of the terms Grid, Clouds and SOIs in the comparison of architectures, the separation of Buyya et al. (Buyya, Yeo, Venugopal, Broberg and Brandic, 2009) serves to distinguish Grids and Clouds. Accordingly, Clouds are the evolution of data centers with host virtualization, on-demand provisioning, SLA negotiation and late provider binding through Web Service interfacing. Instead, Grids strongly underline the autonomy of resource sites, did originate from scientific computing without on-demand contracting and billing and historically do not employ host virtualization. Neither category considers ISP services, i.e. carrier network services for on-demand site/application interconnection – the core driver of Future Internet network virtualization. In the extended Cloud services model (Infrastructure-/Platform-/Software-as-a-Service), the term Intelligent Service-Oriented Network Infrastructure (ISONI) coined by Kessler et al. (Kessler, Reifert, Lamp & Voith, 2008) considers the creation of an IaaS provider from both computational host virtualization, data storage and network virtualization services. As a result of the infrastructure evolution, the exposure of virtual infrastructure elements as on-demand services imposes more frequent service request handling by the network management architecture and introduces shorter lifecycles which would not return profitable if it wasn't for intelligent infrastructure management automation that can autonomously find and execute deployment decisions. At the same time, network management is seeing a tighter integration with host and storage resource management. A compound virtual infrastructure service carried out by a joint *service management layer* requires the alignment of the competing service *business layer* goals for utilization of resource kinds (e.g. link stress vs. node stress, cmp Zhu & Ammar, 2006) and the information collection and correlation of networking, processing and storing functions to carry out the virtual infrastructure service request. Eventually, the multitude of evolving Infrastructure-as-a-Service provider domains drives the ideal of a virtual resource trade market where customers can compose virtual infrastructures by picking from multiple SOI offers. Therefore, the customer interfacing of the *service management layer* is required to expose resource offerings in electronic advertisement form and interoperability negotiation to settle interworking of virtual resources also across sites and across provider domains.

The RESERVOIR Model and Architecture for Open Federated Cloud Computing (Rochwerger, Breitgand, Levy, Galis, Nagin, Llorente, Montero, Wolfsthal, Elmroth, Caceres, Ben-Yehuda, Emmerich, Galán, 2009) considers host virtualization and the provisioning of so called Virtual Execution Environments (VEE) as the crucial functionality and hence groups VEE Hosts of different Hypervisor technologies under a VEE Manager (VEEM), which contains both *element management layer* functions, such as the deployment, configuration and migration of VEEs among hosts at a RESERVOIR site (data center), but also contains *service management layer* functions such as the coordination of the overall VEE Group (VM Cloud). The research contribution is a federative concept where a primary VEEM employs one or more remote VEEMs analogous to TMN interworking at *service management layer* where each site-local VEEM keeps control over resource selection and yet utilization of the site resources. However, after resource allocation, the primary VEEM gains control over the employed VEEs analogous to TMN *element management layer* functionality which arises from the melting of both element configuration and coordination functions within the primary VEEM function. Further, the primary VEEM is chosen per provided service (VEE Group) and chosen in advance to virtual infrastructure provisioning. The imminent lack of a dedicated *element management layer* derives from the fact that focus has been laid on host virtualization (VEE service) and no differentiation of functionalities (e.g. network virtualization) has been considered to be provided under collaborating

element managers. Eventually, every RESERVOIR site provides a so called Service Manager that is reduced to customer interfacing, accounting and billing while the other *service management layer* functionality for information collection, deployment coordination and interaction with federated reservoir sites remain with the primary VEEM. In comparison with the TMN architecture model, the RESERVOIR architecture subsumes *element-*, *network-* and *service-management layer* functionality within the VEEM and extracts the *service management layer* functionality for customer interaction, accounting and billing to the Service Manager that is site-local. Lastly, a TMN *business management layer* equivalent or interface to define and enforce business goals is not contained in the RESERVOIR site management architecture. As of resource selection and VM placement decision support in RESERVOIR, VEE constraints (memory, CPU, bandwidth, disk size, range of instances) are considered by the VEEM to locate VMs. These customer-provided VEE manifests are intended to allow the platform a higher degree of autonomy in defragmenting and utilizing computational infrastructure than a customer-driven selection and employment lifecycle could achieve. However, being derived from traditional SOIs, the manifest is not intended to describe VEE Group internetworking constraints, Internet locality or component affinity and due to a lack of TMN network management layer, the architecture leaves no place for a function to evaluate a compound trade-off among competing constraints of different functionalities (e.g. virtual machine placement versus data locality versus bandwidth requirements). Rather, the RESERVOIR architecture follows the idea of deployments that resize at a primary starting site and utilize federation neighbors when required similar to Zhu & Ammar's approach called assignment without reconfiguration that favors the least utilized spot in the resource pool to evolve the virtual infrastructure deployment around it – an approach which has been found efficient for mapping virtual networks alone as carried out by Lu & Turner (Lu & Turner, 2006). But the customer's primary site selection in the RESERVOIR infrastructure could hinder to meet constraints not yet covered by the VEE manifest, such as the site's available bandwidth to accommodate the full VEE Group mesh, an enforced geographical distribution of redundant VMs for availability or statutory regulations on data and processing co-location for security.

The IRMOS project's IaaS architecture called Intelligent Service-Oriented Network Infrastructure (Kessler, Reifert, Lamp & Voith, 2008) preserves autonomy of different data center sites (called ISONI Nodes) over the resources and technologies similarly to RESERVOIR. However, each ISONI Node contains *element managers* of diverse functionality, namely Execution (host virtualization), Networking (IP-over-GRE encapsulation) and Storage (object-based NAS) services. Further, each site contains a site-local *network management* function that combines these multiple element services to realize the local sub-graphs of the virtual infrastructure deployments. On top of all the sites, an ISONI domain-level serves as service management layer that collects abstracted resource availability information from the sites' offered functionality to assist in selection of sites for a virtual service network deployment.

The domain-level's service deployment coordination (resource selection and control) is incorporated in the Deployment Manager while customer interfacing (SLA negotiation, invoice handling, contract supervision) is separately performed by the SLA Manager. At negotiation, the Deployment Manager queries the domain-level informational support functions for a site-mapping first, chooses a compound trade-off and then contacts sites for deployment reservation and orchestration of sub-parts of the virtual application delivery network. At the sites, the *element manager* for virtualization hosts – called Resource Manager Node - also takes the role of a promoted site-local *network management* entity to coordinate site-local virtualization service provisioning (VMs,

virtual links and storage objects) with the other site-local *element managers,* i.e. Path Manager Node and Storage Manager Node.

As of resource selection and placement, IRMOS foresees to let the IaaS customer deliver a descriptive document to the infrastructure provider that contains the model and service level objectives of the complete virtual infrastructure deployment, called Virtual Service Network (VSN). The IRMOS ISONI uses a modeled RDF graph description of the virtual service network with all constraints interlinked under an extensible ontology (Web Ontology Language), i.e. QoS requirements, virtual machines, interlinking, resource class affinity, etc. By employing Semantic Web technologies and adopting their Open World assumption, the model framework remains extensible to additional virtual resource types (e.g. relational databases, firewalling) and applicable to inference of complex coherences in the overall model. Yet, the adoption of Semantic Web technologies to empower autonomous self-reconfiguration of the IaaS alone introduces a large knowledge complexity to the network management system. A unified ontology of Cloud computing (Youseff, Butrico & Da Silva 2008), including Platform- and Software-as-a-Service layers, has been proposed for various reasons, e.g. a better understanding, teaching, application development, etc. to facilitate the adoption of Cloud computing. Oberle et al (Oberle, Stein, Voith, Gallizo & Kuebert, 2010) formalize a unified ontology with Semantic Web technologies to describe abstract virtual infrastructure requests that serve as deployment SLA and that allow the virtual elements to be described in form of requirements, so that each can subsequently be mapped regardless of the [virtualization] technology available at the provider site. The ontology is envisioned a standard to equip Cloud service management with knowledge in form of an extensible meta-data model and with rule-based support functions to drive the multi-constraint resource discovery, mapping, advance reservation and configuration of virtual infrastructure deployments. The resource allocation process in IRMOS, as opposed to RESERVOIR, takes the notion of graph splitting to divide the virtual infrastructure request into subparts deployed site-locally. The approach dominates the 2-level hierarchy in the ISONI architecture. However, this approach to an autonomous, decision-making *service management layer* requires efficient, reliable rule sets that infer sustainable decisions from the deployment context, i.e. from service level objectives expressed by the customer, business goals set by the infrastructure operator and run-time infrastructure reports.

Regarding RESERVOIR and IRMOS architectures with respect to the TMN model, we can find two very different approaches to carry out virtual infrastructure services. RESERVOIR combines the TMN element management, network management and partly service management in the single, site-local VEEM function and applies a so-called federation principle among VEEMs while customer interaction is separated into a site-local Service Manager entity. In IRMOS, a site implements element management and network management while service management remains a domain-wide layer. However, both architectures decouple customer interaction from deployment configuration, i.e. the decoupling of SLA Manager and Deployment Manager as well as the decoupling of Service Manager and the primary VEEM. IRMOS proposes a more fine-grained component architecture while the VEEM incorporates both resource and deployment management in a single entity. The virtual resource elements in RESERVOIR are limited to separate VEEs and VEE Groups, i.e. virtual machines of different configuration extent that share default interconnection. IRMOS on the other hand tries to incorporate storage, network and computing resources in its common 2-layer hierarchical management architecture.

With regard to shorter lifecycles and increased request complexity, RESERVOIR has successfully condensed computing management into (mostly) flat federation architecture where groups of virtual machines grow locally from the primary site while IRMOS splits the infrastructure request at domain-level to have the virtual infrastructure deployment carried out in parallel and jointly by the selected sites.

The integration of computing, networking and storing services into a combined management architecture has been tackled by IRMOS. The architecture accounts for the different resource kinds and promotes site-local management and a global directory function for each to drive the site selection and deployment process. In RESERVOIR, the interworking among virtual machines, storage spaces and connectivity is not explicitly managed, i.e. either networking and storing services external to the VEE Group would be employed in separate contractual agreements or proprietary services within a RESERVOIR federation would be employed by configuration of the VEE. The resulting

Yet, neither of the architectures reflects the explicit role of a business management functionality that would formulate business goals towards the service management. IRMOS preserves the consideration of competing business goals for different resource kinds, i.e. the computing, network and storing site-mapping functionality may implement business strategies in the selection of sites as well as in the site-local selection and configuration of resources. These decisions have to be found against the requested virtual infrastructure SLA, i.e. the customer's service level objectives. RESERVOIR names Business Service Management as related work and does not specify further the objectives but argues that in carrying out the customer's SLA, basic business targets should be followed.

Finally, regarding the ideal of a virtual resource trading market, RESERVOIR proposes independent RESERVOIR sites that employ each other as required. Note, that each relationship between the primary site and a secondary site requires the negotiation of an SLA for the resource employment. IRMOS describes several levels of federation at its hierarchical architecture, i.e. in order to let an IRMOS deployment span multiple providers, an agreement among operators is required to register sites with each other's domain levels - similar to the federation agreement required for the interworking of RESERVOIR sites. Conclusively, both projects argue, that the interrelations within a virtual infrastructure (ordered start-up and configuration for RESERVOIR or the compound virtual resource topology in IRMOS) does not allow for a distribution of the deployment control, i.e. RESERVOIR VEE Groups and IRMOS VSN, hence both projects propose resource federation rather than federation in carrying out the virtual infrastructure deployment. However, the ontological approach to standardize interrelations among virtual resource components and their configuration in a single service request appears promising to have an IaaS customer's virtual infrastructure realized from multiple SOI offerings.

CONCLUSION AND FUTURE RESEARCH DIRECTIONS

For efficient network management in a globally virtualized federated infrastructure, Cloud service providers would benefit from control over the transport networks which connect the different locations their services are executed at. Unfortunately in today's networks this requires intense coordination with the transport provider(s) from which the service provider leases the required transport resources, if possible at all. As in Future Internet propositions, efforts focus on a network architecture of two "actors", which are infrastructure providers (own and manage the physical network infrastructure) and service providers (offer end-to-end service, run network protocols) under the slogan "Concurrent Architectures are Better than One" (Feamster, Gao, Rexford, 2007). For Cloud service model (IaaS), such an environment

for network virtualization can be seen as one key component, which could allow IaaService providers to simultaneously provision multiple QoS enabled end-to-end services over equipment owned by (different) infrastructure providers. While currently, simple Internet transit leaves Cloud providers with single choice of encapsulating traffic of a group of virtual machines over IP (Cisco Overlay Transport Virtualization), clearly the CABO approach would change that network infrastructure provisioning would be reduced to dedicated network resource offerings whereas IaaS offers on top (CABO service provider) themselves have full control over the network allowing them to provision their own virtual internetworking to Cloud virtual application delivery networks with dedicated and optimized QoS management schemes and protocols. As of the plain infrastructure offerings, in the past few years in the context of Network Resource Management Multiprotocol Label Switching (MPLS) has been getting a lot of attention. This attention is mainly caused by the sophisticated MPLS traffic engineering concepts which merges the best of connection oriented traffic engineering concepts (like the Permanent Virtual Connection establishment mechanisms in Asynchronous Transfer Mode (ATM)) with the IP routing paradigms. It avoids a lot of the drawbacks of IP over ATM but preserves IP's flexibility and preserves the concept of class of service differentiation. In that sense MPLS combines the beneficial mechanisms of the IntServ and DiffServ approach allowing traffic aggregation into traffic classes for which dedicated transport resources can be reserved via a MPLS extended RSVP-Traffic Engineering management protocol in a scalable manner. Even more MPLS also easily allows the setup of virtual private network services what makes it especially attractive to network providers, as VPN is a service they can sell to their customers. MPLS also provides means for efficient protection and restoration in the network. In case of link or node failures MPLS provides mechanisms which allow a fast reroute around affected links or nodes. Consequently MPLS is widely deployed and used by network operators to make QoS-aware offerings with their networks and offer high quality site interconnection services to data center operators.

In a federation of network and data center operators, virtual network services and cloud computing services can be combined to allow network computing where placement, geographical extent, capacity planning, migration/growth/consolidation can holistically consider intelligent end-to-end provisioning.

REFERENCES

Abramson, D., Jackson, J., Muthrasanallur, S., Neiger, G., Regnier, G., Sankaran, R., et al. Wiegert, J. (August 2006). Intel® virtualization technology for directed I/O. *Intel Technology Journal, 10*(3). Retrieved from http://www.intel.com/ technology/ itj/ 2006/ v10i3/

Anderson, T., Peterson, L., Shenker, S., & Turner, J. (2005). Overcoming the Internet impasse through virtualization. [Los Alamitos, CA: IEEE Computer Society Press.]. *IEEE Journal Computer, 38*(4), 34–41.

Asgari, A., Trimintzios, P., Irons, M., Pavlou, G., Egan, R., & Van Den Berghe, S. (2002, December). A scalable real-time monitoring system for supporting traffic engineering. In *Proceedings of the IEEE Workshop on IP Operations and Management* (pp. 202-207).

Bhatia, S., Motiwala, M., Mühlbauer, W., Mundada, Y., Valancius, V., Bavier, A., et al. Rexford, J. (2008). Trellis: A platform for building flexible, fast virtual networks on commodity hardware. In *CoNEXT '08: Proceedings of the 2008 ACM CoNEXT Conference* (pp. 1-6). New York, NY: ACM.

Blake, S., Blake, D., Carlson, M., Davies, E., Wang, Z., & Weiss, W. (1998, December). *An architecture for differentiated services.* (Internet Engineering Task Force, RFC 2475). Retrieved May 21, 2008, from http://tools.ietf.org/ html/ rfc2475

Braden, R., Clark, D., & Shenker, S. (1994, June). *Integrated services in the internet architecture: An overview.* (Internet Engineering Task Force, RFC 1633). Retrieved May 15, 2008, from http:// tools.ietf.org/ html/ rfc1633

Buyya, R., Yeo, C. S., Venugopal, S., Broberg, J., & Brandic, I. (2009, June). Cloud computing and emerging IT platforms: Vision, hype, and reality for delivering computing as the 5th utility. *Future Generation Computer Systems, 25*(6), 599–616. doi:10.1016/j.future.2008.12.001

Chowdhury, N. M. M. K., & Boutaba, R. (2009, July). Network virtualization: State of the art and research challenges. *IEEE Communications Magazine, 47*(7), 20–26. doi:10.1109/ MCOM.2009.5183468

Chowdhury, N. M. M. K., & Boutaba, R. (2010, April). A survey of network virtualization. [Elsevier.]. *Computer Networks, 54*(5), 862–876. doi:10.1016/j.comnet.2009.10.017

Church, K., Greenberg, A., & Hamilton, J. (2008). *On delivering embarrassingly distributed cloud services.* Seventh ACM Workshop on Hot Topics in Networks (HotNets-VII).

Clark, D., Shenker, S., & Zhang, L. (1992). Supporting real-time applications in an integrated services packet network: Architecture and mechanism. [ACM.]. *ACM SIGCOMM Computer Communication Review, 22*(4), 14–26. doi:10.1145/144191.144199

Feamster, N., Gao, L., & Rexford, J. (2007, January). How to lease the Internet in your spare time. [ACM.]. *ACM SIGCOMM Computer Communications Review, 37*(1), 61–64. doi:10.1145/1198255.1198265

ISO/IEC JTC 1. (1996, June). *ISO/IEC 7498-1 open systems interconnection model.*

ITU-T Study Group 4. (2000, February). *ITU-T recommendation M.3010 rev. 200002.* Approved under the WTSC Resolution No. 1 procedure on 4 February 2000.

Jeffree, T. (Ed.). (2006). *Provider bridges.* (ANSI/ IEEE Standard 802.1ad). New York, NY: IEEE. Retrieved from http://www.oracle.com/ us/ products/ servers-storage/ networking/ 049259.pdf

Jiang, X., & Xu, D. (2004). VIOLIN: Virtual internetworking on overlay infrastructure. *Lecture Notes in Computer Science, 3358,* 937–946. doi:10.1007/978-3-540-30566-8_107

Kessler, M., Reifert, A., Lamp, D., & Voith, T. (2008). A service-oriented infrastructure for providing virtualized networks. *Bell Labs Technical Journal, 13*(3), 111-128. Wiley Periodicals, Inc. DOI: 10.1002/bltj.20328

Kim, C., Caesar, M., & Rexford, J. (2008). Floodless in SEATTLE: A scalable Ethernet architecture for large enterprises. In *SIGCOMM '08: Proceedings of the ACM SIGCOMM 2008 Conference on Data Communication* (pp. 3-14). New York, NY: ACM.

Lu, J., & Turner, J. (2006, June). *Efficient mapping of virtual networks onto a shared substrate.* (Technical Report WUCSE-2006—35). Department of Computer Science and Engineering - Washington University in St. Louis, MO.

Moreno, V., & Reddy, K. (2006). *Network virtualization.* Cisco Press.

Norton, W. B. (2008). *Video Internet: The next wave of massive disruption to the U.S. peering ecosystem* (v1.6). Retrieved December 17, 2009, from http://www.drpeering.net/ a/ Internet_Peering_White_ Papers_files/ Video Internet 1.6.pdf

Oberle, K. Stein., M., Voith, T., Gallizo, G., & Kuebert, R. (2010, October). The network aspect of infrastructure as a service. In *Proceedings of 14th International Conference on Intelligence in Next Generation Networks,* 2010.

Oberle, K., Kessler, M., Stein, M., Voith, T., Lamp, D., & Berger, S. (2009). Network virtualization: The missing piece. *Bell Labs Technical Journal, 13*(3), 111–128.

Peterson, L. L., & Davie, B. S. (1996). *Computer networks: A systems approach.* San Francisco, CA: Morgan Kaufmann.

Rochwerger, B., Breitgand, D., Levy, E., Galis, A., Nagin, K., Llorente, I., … Galán, F. (2009). The RESERVOIR model and architecture for open federated cloud computing. *IBM Journal of Research & Development, 53*(4), Paper 4.

Scott, M., & Crowcroft, J. (2008, April). *MOOSE: Addressing the scalability of Ethernet.* Poster session presented at EuroSys 2008, Glasgow, Scotland.

Stein, M., Oberle, K., Voith, T., Kübert, R., Gallizo, G., Berger, S., ... Neple, T. (2009, May). *Initial version of path manager architecture. Interactive real-time multimedia applications on service oriented infrastructures.* (ICT FP7-214777).

Touch, J., & Perlman, R. (2009, May). *Transparent interconnection of lots of links (TRILL): Problem and applicability statement.* (Internet Engineering Task Force, RFC 5556). Retrieved February 20, 2010, from http://tools.ietf.org/ html/ rfc5556

Touch, J., Wang, Y.-S., Eggert, L., & Finn, G. (2003, March). *A virtual Internet architecture.* Future Developments of Network Architectures (FDNA) at ACM Sigcomm, August 2003. (ISI Technical Report ISI-TR-570, March 2003).

Völker, L., Martin, D., El Khayat, I., Werle, C., & Zitterbart, M. (2009). A node architecture for 1000 future networks. In *Proceedings of IEEE International Conference on Communications Workshops, 2009*, 1–5. doi:10.1109/ICCW.2009.5207996

Youseff, L., Butrico, M., & Da Silva, D. (2008, November). *Toward a unified ontology of cloud computing.* In Grid Computing Environments Workshop, 2008. GCE '08, (pp. 1-10).

Zhu, Y., & Ammar, M. (2006, April). Algorithms for assigning substrate network resources to virtual network components. In *Proceedings of the IEEE International Conference on Computer Communications.* DOI: 10.1109/INFOCOM.2006.322

Chapter 13
Data Storage in Cloud Based Real–Time Environments

Sai Narasimhamurthy
Xyratex, UK

Fabio Checconi
Scuola Superiore Sant'Anna, Italy

Malcolm Muggeridge
Xyratex, UK

Tommaso Cucinotta
Scuola Superiore Sant'Anna, Italy

Stefan Waldschmidt
Digital Film Technology, Germany

ABSTRACT

The service oriented infrastructures for real-time applications ("real-time clouds[1]") pose certain unique challenges for the data storage subsystem, which indeed is the "last mile" for all data accesses. Data storage subsystems typically used in regular enterprise environments have many limitations which impedes direct applicability for such clouds, particularly in their ability to provide Quality of Service (QoS) for applications. Provision of QoS within storage is possible through a deeper understanding of the behaviour of the storage system under a variety of conditions dictated by the application and the network infrastructure. We intend to arrive at a QoS mechanism for data storage keeping in view the important parameters that come into play for the storage subsystem in a soft real-time cloud environment.

INTRODUCTION

The cloud environment mandates multiple "tiers" of functionality before the applications eventually get access to storage. These tiers bring about a disconnect between application requirements and storage functionality. The problems of providing a predictable and reliable storage subsystem is

further exacerbated when real-time applications need to be serviced by the cloud.

The storage subsystem for distributed real-time applications within clouds requires the following storage optimization characteristics:

a. Capability of dealing with rapidly fluctuating demand from hundreds of applications accessing storage
b. Ability to leverage commodity storage subsystems to increase the Return on Investment

DOI: 10.4018/978-1-60960-827-9.ch013

and reduce costs for storage service providers within the cloud

c. Scalability to accommodate an ever increasing number of applications

d. Use of readily available, mostly open source software components to implement storage

e. End user performance that does not get affected with constant increases in storage capacity as noted in (c)

f. More flexibility of provisioning and managing storage than currently available in standard enterprise storage implementations

Storage QoS which is fundamentally absent in enterprise storage gains significance in real-time application based clouds. QoS defined at various tiers of real-time clouds percolates to storage specific Service Level Agreements (SLAs), which needs to be reliably adhered to.

This chaper is organised through the following sections:

- **Storage Optimization:** This section discusses current day storage subsystems optimized for soft real-time environments through an understanding disk drive technologies, Storage virtualization technologies and file system technologies. The chapter also discusses the state of the art on research in Storage QoS. The arguments lead in to the use of Lustre™[2] based storage solution with the QoS innovations we provide.

- **Storage Platform Processing:** This section discusses a Lustre file system based storage platform and how it fits in to the overall soft real-time cloud environment framework.

- **Providing QoS:** This section discusses our Storage QoS model implemented for our storage platform.

- **Conclusions and future work:** Concludes the chapter highlighting next steps.

STORAGE OPTIMIZATION

Storage Characteristics

The primary QoS parameters for storage are storage capacity, storage bandwidth and storage latency. Storage capacity denotes the total storage that is available for use by applications (in units of MegaBytes, Gigabytes, TeraBytes, Petabytes etc). Storage bandwidth denotes the throughput with which this data can be accessed by applications (in units of MegaBytes/s, Gigabytes/s etc). Storage latency denotes the delay incurred by requests accessing storage (in units of time).

These parameters should be defined in SLAs which address fine-grained infrastructure requirements for a cloud-based platform environment. Such an approach has been followed successfully, in the IRMOS project (Gallizo et al., 2008). These parameters have presented different challenges. Capacity is the simplest to guarantee. Capacity is in abundance on the storage network as disk drives are available with very high capacities (which at this time stand at 1TB). There are well known technologies based on the concepts of Storage Area Networking (Preston, 2002) and Network Attached Storage (Preston, 2002) providing large aggregates of these disk drives providing extremely high capacities to applications.

Guaranteeing of bandwidth is more difficult to realise. Bandwidth incorporates the ability of the drives in the storage subsystem as well as the storage subsystem as a whole. Latency is a function of bandwidth. Latency for individual storage requests amounts to a net bandwidth for applications over a large period of time.

In the following sections, we study these parameters and then provide a deeper understanding of the disk drive components affecting these parameters.

Understanding Bandwidth

The bandwidth per disk is quite low compared to the capacity of disks, which can be readily observed by attempting to write or read a whole TB drive. This disk bandwidth is not in abundance, it is regularly the bottleneck to applications. It must be shared out and guaranteed.

Storage bandwidth is a function of:

1. User access patterns (Sequentiality), transfer sizes, access profiles (or read/write mix) and the number of competing clients.
2. The storage system software architecture, caching mechanisms and other storage related hardware elements.

"Access pattern" implies the chance of the application's IO requests causing the disks in the storage system to "seek" for the required data. Seeking is inefficient as it is time where no data transfer is being performed from the disks. Transfer size is the size of each individual IO operation. This could be small (1KB) for some applications, or very large (8MB) for others. "Access profiles" denotes the percentage of read and write requests as issued by the application. The number of competing client connection implies the number of applications, or, Application Service Components (ASCs) within different virtual machines (and possibly in different client machines) accessing the same storage system.

Randomness of IO requests have a large effect on the bandwidth that can be provided by drives. Drives do not have a single absolute bandwidth number that can be measured and then divided linearly amongst concurrent access streams. The measure of disk bandwidth depends heavily on the way the data is accessed by the ASC. The more the disk has to seek to collect the data requested, the less data is delivered per time interval and hence lower the bandwidth. Therefore to know how much data can be delivered off a disk, either:

1. The access pattern and transfer size of the user(s) must be pre-determined, or,
2. A guarantee must be made assuming a random access pattern (as random access involves a high proportion of seek time).

Traditional hard real-time approach typically assumes the second case. Choosing this case means that the guarantee will only be a small proportion of the possible best case maximum bandwidth. Here, this possible best case maximum bandwidth is the number most often quoted by vendors. It is single stream sequential access, with sufficiently large block sizes.

There are two types of storage bandwidth guarantee scenario:

1. An application requires less bandwidth than can be provided by a single disk or RAID array of disks acting as a Logical Unit:

   That application can then share a disk with other application(s) if their combined access pattern, I/O size and the disk seek and caching is within the capabilities of the disk. In this case it is then necessary to use a scheduling mechanism to ensure that each application gets its required access to the disk resources.

2. An application requires greater bandwidth than can be provided by a single disk or RAID array of disks acting as a Logical Unit:

   That application is given multiple disks that are virtualised together as a single disk that can provide the performance it requires.

Many applications require low bandwidth random access so the first approach can be used to share disk bandwidth to these applications. For these applications, the access to the disk may be throttled when one application competes with another affecting performance. Thus a mechanism to QoS guarantees is required.

Real-time applications can be envisioned in the near future, where a large number of users interface over a network through a virtual environment and there is a need for synchronisation in user experiences. Such applications can be very successfully used for distance learning("eLearning") and education. These type of applications need storage for databases (to store the eLearning content) with very low bandwidth requirement. Multiple instances of such eLearning scenarios could be serviced from the same storage, each requiring guaranteed bandwidth for users.

Some very bandwidth intensive applications which are I/O bound use custom-built or dedicated storage set ups which are tuned to give best performance for access patterns matching their applications. These applications push the limits of what is physically possible from a storage system. To support the needs of these applications, the second approach would be used to collect together enough "commodity/low cost" disk drives on commodity hardware platforms to provide the required bandwidth Such applications can be envisioned for digital film post production for the upcoming digital movie industry. In that, streaming of very large video files is needed from the storage subsystem and there would be very intense bandwidth requirements ensuing from that.

Once SLAs are granted for a particular access profile from an application in a real-time environment, a policing and reporting policy needs to be in place to detect a violation of the access pattern. If the application requested "sequential" bandwidth and then used random access and thus did not receive the performance it had intended, this should be detected and reported. Thus any claim from the application that their SLA was not met can be addressed on the grounds that the access profile was incorrect at the time of decreased performance.

Broadly, the process of delivering storage QoS should be as follows:

1. Receive information about the application:
   a. Requested bandwidth.
   b. Transfer size.
   c. Access pattern.
   d. Access profile
2. Work out whether this can be shared on one disk, or requires combining multiple disks.
3. Allocate the storage pool and assign the connection.
4. For shared disk access have a mechanism in place to allocate application bandwidth and storage system resources based on SLAs.

Delivering (4) is the complex task that is accompalished by our storage QoS modelling.

Understanding Disk Drives

Primary Components

Disk drives are non-volatile storage devices (they can retain stored information even when not powered) that store digitally encoded data on rotating platters with a magnetic coating. Primary components of a disk drive are a mechanism and a controller (Ruemmler and Wilkes, 1994):

- **Mechanism:** The mechanism of a disk drive is a number of rotating platters with a magnetic surface upon which binary data is stored. These platters are spun at high speed (7200rpm or 15000rpm are typical). The data on these surfaces are arranged into concentric circles called tracks and platters are stacked on top of each other into a spindle. A set of tracks at the same radius on each platter in a spindle is called a cylinder.

  Read/write heads are used to change the magnetization of the material (and thus the value of the binary data). There is one head for each platter. Additionally, an actuator arm is used to simultaneously move a head for positioning and following tracks. The arms are attached to the same pivot so all heads move simultaneously.

- **Controller:** The disk controller is the component which allows the CPU to communicate with the hard disk. Similarly, a Host Bus Adaptor is the device responsible for connecting the CPU to a storage infrastructure (such as Infiniband switches, Serial Attach Scsi). The controller contains a buffer cache and a processor.

Working Characteristics

- **Seeking:** This is the speed of head movement across the disk. A seek is composed of a speed up where the arm is accelerated, a coast at maximum velocity, a slowdown where the arm is decelerated to rest on the track and a settle where the controller adjusts the head to access the data.

  Very short seeks are described as those that are dominated by settling time, while short seeks are those that spend most of their time in the acceleration phase (their time is proportional to the square root of the seek distance(Ruemmler et al., 1994)). Long seeks spend most of their time at constant speed (so their time is proportional to distance). In general, short seeks are most common but their frequency is a function of the access pattern to the disk.

- **Data layout:** Each track on a disk is divided into sectors. The number of sectors per track varies depending on the location of the track on the disk (i.e. outer tracks have more sectors). Sectors, along with heads and cylinders, are the fundamental units of data access on a disk drive. However, Logical Block Addressing is used to simplify access to disks. This is to allow devices drives and operating systems to communicate with the disk without having to understand the internal geometry of each manufacturer's hard disk drives. LBA 0 is cylinder 0, sector 0, head 0 and increase in number along each sector of a track, then each track in a cylinder, then along each cylinder from outer to inner. As the angular velocity is constant, tracks on the outside (lower LBA) have higher linear velocity and thus higher maximum sustained data rate (as a rule of thumb, at the middle of the range of LBAs around 10-15% of performance is lost).

- **I/O Latency:** We can view I/O latency as the total amount of time it takes to complete a single I/O operation. As an example, a user may interact with an ASC using a human interface device (i.e. keyboard) that tells the operating system of a virtual machine to access a file. This request is mapped through to the clients on a Physical Host (PH) which then transmits this as requests to the relevant storage servers (or Object Storage Servers [OSS], for Lustre, as discussed later) across an infiniband storage network. The OSS then maps this request to a OSS specific file system call which interacts with the RAID subsystem and finally the disks themselves to read or write the data. The payload then returns along the same path back to the ASC. The time this entire process takes can be regarded as application I/O latency.

Taking into account all of this, there are many sources of latency:

- **Operating system latency:** Once the user request is made, the OS can choose to adjust the scheduling of a program in an ASC, the execution of an IO request can then be postponed if other processes are also executing.

- **Infrastructure latency:** The round trip delay, or light travel time through the physical cabling and switches in the system.

- **Device latency:** Such as processing time in the host bus adaptor or within the disk controller.
- **Protocol latency:** The delays associated with the additional data (headers, CRC etc.) that must be sent with the IO payload.
- **Protocol translation latency:** SAS disk interfaces needing to be converted to SATA commands etc.
- **Disk access latency:** This is the mechanical latency of accessing the disks, including seek time, data transfer rate and rotational latency. This is the largest source of latency.
- **Caching latency:** Delays caused by reading ahead extra data and from write back caching to protect data integrity.
- **RAID latency:** Delay caused by calculating parity data, and delays associated with the performance penalty of partial stripe writes.

Some of these delays only minimally impact performance, others are addressed within their own mechanisms by the use of caching or are minimal, constant and can be easily measured. However, mechanical latency and the effect of caching (not just the latency but also the performance increase from successful cache hits for sequential reads) can give vast performance differences based on how the data is accessed.

Caching

- **Command Queuing:** Command queuing allows the disks, server or RAID to service commands in parallel rather than waiting for each request to complete before starting the next one. This can provide an improved overall latency at the cost of possibly increased latency for particular requests. In general, the greatest performance from a storage system is achieved when commands can be queued on the disk drives.

- **Read Ahead:** Disk drives have a cache on the controller which can be used for caching reads and writes. File systems (such as Lustre) use a cache for read ahead as do RAID controllers. The basic idea of a read ahead cache is as follows: An algorithm is in place that detects whether the recent disk accesses are "sequential" (or perhaps step in predictable and small increments), the algorithm then determines that the disk should continue reading beyond the last request and place this data in cache. When the next sequential request comes, the data is already in cache and results in a potentially large performance increase. This is termed a "Cache Hit". The disadvantage is when the read ahead algorithm is incorrect in its prediction; in that, the data has been read from the disk unnecessarily, the cost of transferring the unnecessary data is still incurred and performance is actually decreased. A further disadvantage is that typically read ahead algorithms for components like disk drives and RAID controllers are not disclosed by manufacturers. This however is not the case with mechanisms in Linux or the Lustre file system which are open source components.
- **Write caching:** Write caching is the process of delaying writes to the disk with the hope that multiple writes can be combined and serviced together. This gives particular benefit in RAID configurations using parity data as the performance overhead of recalculating parity data can be quite high and hence caching writes until a full stripe can be written gives a performance boost. Typically write caching is disabled on the disks in a RAID array to ensure that data integrity is maintained (for example, in a power failure situation). In this case, the RAID system will perform the write cache functionality and provide a mechanism to protect this cache. As write and reads re-

quests to a single drive are not interleaved, in a RAID configuration, write performance suffers when multiple write commands are issued as the RAID array can only have one write stripe sequence active at a time.

- **Throughput:** Disk throughput is measured in both I/O operations completed per second (IOPs) and "bandwidth" which is number of MB/s. The maximum performance of a storage system is limited by the storage interface for low latency non-TCP/IP interconnects. If the storage device had an Infiniband interface that can deliver a maximum of 4Gb/s there is no way of delivering more from the back end storage server. While this provides a limit on the total data rate, typically, however, it is the disk drives themselves which are the bottleneck for the individual users of a system. Their access pattern to the disks, and the seeking that it causes determines the performance.

- **IOPs:** One measure of performance is IOPs. This is used for applications that require a large number of operations to be executed as quickly as possible. Applications like this include transactional databases that typically access their data randomly using small transfer sizes (e.g. less than 32kB). High IOs can also be required in an environment with many users attempting to access the same storage resource.

To provide a high IOPs the storage should perform efficient command queuing to allow the device to receive commands simultaneously rather than waiting on the completion of each command in turn and the number of spindles (disk drives) should be increased to provide a higher availability to service the I/O commands.

- **Random vs. sequential access:** Sequential access provides better performance than random access. Sequential access demonstrates the maximum performance of the system. This is because of reduced disk seeks and read ahead caching schemes as discussed previously.

- **Transfer size:** Along with randomness vs. sequentiality of the access profile to the data, transfer size is the most important factor in performance. However, the transfer size seen at the disks may not be what started out at the ASC as the request gets translated from the virtual machines, through the file system software layers, through RAID controllers and finally to the disks themselves. Firstly, an application that indicates 8MB files at a time will not necessarily result in 8MB transfers on the disks. For example, the operating system splits requests into smaller chunks and sends them as sequential requests, while the RAID mechanism will access data based on its chunk and stripe size. When determining the access pattern of the application, it is therefore necessary to understand the intermediate layers in the I/O chain.

- **Access patterns:** Taking the information described above, the access pattern of an application consists of the transfer size, the randomness (as defined by the chance that a seek will occur) and the proportion of requests that are reads as opposed to writes. Together these factors define the performance an application can receive from a disk or storage system. Some example access patterns are given in Table 1 based on a study by Enterprise Strategy Group (ESG Labs, 2010).

- **RAID:** RAID combines two or more physical hard disks into a single logical unit. This can either be accomplished by a dedicated RAID controller or by using software (for example Linux software RAID). There are two primary reasons for combining disks into a RAID configuration; to increase data reliability (through redundan-

Table 1. ESG Lab Industry Application Workloads

Application	Measurement point	Transfer Size (kB)	% of total workload	Reads (%)	Randomness (%)
4k OLTP	Application	4	100	67	100
8k OLTP	Application	8	100	67	100
File Server	Application	0.5	10	80	100
		1	5	80	100
		2	5	80	100
		4	60	80	100
		8	2	80	100
		16	4	80	100
		32	4	80	100
		64	10	80	100
Web Server	Application	0.5	22	100	100
		1	15	100	100
		2	8	100	100
		4	23	100	100
		8	15	100	100
		16	2	100	100
		32	6	100	100
		64	7	100	100
		128	1	100	100
		512	1	100	100
Exchange Data	Disk	4	90	73	100
		4	7	100	0
		4	3	0	0
Exchange Logs	Disk	64	100	0	0
Windows Media Player	Application	32	100	100	0
Exchange Streaming Media Database	Disk	128	67	100	0
		128	33	0	0

cy) or to increase data throughput (via increased number of spindles). The fundamental unit of data in a RAID array is a chunk, with a typical chunk size being 64KB. Data is stored in chunks across all the disks in an array, this is called a stripe.

- **Non-parity RAID:** To increase reliability, two disks can be combined together into a redundant pair (called mirroring or RAID 1). In this configuration, each write request is mirrored to the other disk. Read performance can be increased (almost doubled) as the two disks can be read from simultaneously.

To increase performance to sequential applications, disks can be combined together into a stripe or RAID 0, where the logical block addresses are split now across not only the sectors, heads and cylinders of a disk, but also the disks (spindles) in a stripe. This can increase performance and capacity.

Striping and mirroring can be combined together to create large redundant arrays (RAID 10).

- **Parity RAID:** Parity RAID (RAID 5 and 6) combine the concept of striping together disks while also providing a level of redundancy. In RAID 5, one chunk per stripe is reserved for parity data which can be used to reconstruct data in event of an error; RAID 6 uses two chunks for parity data. Parity RAID allows multiple concurrent access but has a higher overhead for writes due to the calculation of parity data per stripe. Because of this, write caching is often used to defer writing until a full stripe can be written to mitigate some of the cost of parity calculation.

Storage Virtualization

Storage Virtualization is a process of separating logical storage as seen by applications and physical storage where data actually resides. The logical storage pools together physical data blocks that could be located either anywhere on the same device, or elsewhere on a storage network with possibly multivendor storage devices. Storage Virtualization brings about the same benefits inherent in Server Virtualization, which is, cost savings and easy manageability by better consolidation of existing physical resources.

Storage Virtualization software is typically used here, which maintains a mapping of contiguous logical blocks, and physical blocks. Storage devices from multiple vendors could be part of the physical storage system. Logical storage is created from "storage pools" of aggregated physical storage.

Storage Virtualization leads to better storage subsystem disk utilization, easy scale out of storage as required by real-time cloud applications and non-disruptive migration of physical data without affecting unpredictable access patterns inherent in these type of applications. Storage virtualization thus prevents "storage sprawl", or, too many underutilized storage resources for a cloud service provider. Further, the ability to incrementally add storage, helps in the realization of Thin Provisioning, or the "capacity on the go" feature.

Existing Approaches

The commericial providers of Storage Virtualization either offer a software solution, or a Storage Virtualization enabling appliance. The software vendors include Falconstor (Falconstor, 2010) and DataCore software (Data Core Software, 2010). Many of the enterprise storage appliance vendors are now beginning to offer an appliance solution (IBM, Hitachi, etc). These solutions suffer from high costs and lack of scalability needed for real-time cloud applications.

Some academic research work has been carried out on the topic in recent years. We briefly mention two of them here.

The *"Stonehenge"* project by Huang et al. (2004) described a multi-dimensional storage virtualization system which virtualizes a cluster-based physical storage system along multiple dimensions, including bandwidth, capacity, and latency.

The *V: Drive* (Brinkmann et al., 2004) approach virtualizes storage and creates storage pools based on various factors such as age of data and speed of the disks. Volumes that are accessible by the clients are created on top of these pools.

Specialised File Systems

A filesystem is a methodology used in end systems to gain access to files and directories in a storage device. We now look into the type of file system that would best fit our class of applications within a cloud architechture.

1. The real-time cloud architechture consists of many tiers with components on multiple clients executed on several different hosts that would need to read and write data simultaneously to support corresponding application requests, which should be supported by the file system.
2. The file system has to take into account "moving" components distributed over a network without perceived application degradation.
3. The components need data storage that scales, which the file system must support.
4. There should be a methodology in place within the file system to parallelize reads and writes so as to not affect application performance. Further, the file system should be able to support very high speed interconnects to accommodate massive amounts data traffic to/from storage from the components.

Existing Approaches

Disk based File Systems such as ext3 (Bovet and Cesati, 2006) acts upon requests for read and write blocks to/from a single storage device, or a single set of storage devices within a host.

Distributed File Systems such as NFS accomodates reads and writes to/from multiple hosts (and hence components), but are restricted by the processing power of a single appliance which acts upon these Read/Write requests from the components. An NFS based solution hence cannot scale with an increasing number of requesting components.

Shared data access is not possible in a Storage Area Network (SAN), where each client needs a dedicated storage unit or a "Logical Unit Number" assigned to it. *Shared Disk File Systems* such as MelioFS (Melio File System, 2010) enables block based shared data access in SANs. These file systems have severe limitations in terms of scalability and performance.

Parallel Distributed File Systems cater to storage requests from multiple clients, and have the ability to parallelize reads and writes from clients to bring forth increasing performance that scales with storage capacity. Parallel Distributed file systems support the characteristics as needed by our applications.

Lustre

Lustre is a Parallel Distributed file system that can be implemented on commodity hardware, and comes with an Open Source Licence (GNU GPL). Lustre aims at providing simultaneous read and write access to tens of thousands of clients, with potentially enormous amounts of storage access (in the range of Petabytes). We therefore consider Lustre as a viable option for real-time cloud based environments.

STORAGE QUALITY OF SERVICE APPROACHES

Providing reliable Quality of Service (QoS) for applications is a unique requirement for real-time clouds as discussed earlier. Considering the importance, we next discuss at some length, some background work done in the area of providing QoS in storage subsystems.

Storage QoS has been explored to some depth in the research literature. However, there is no consolidated approach for providing this. There are a variety of techniques that can be used to deliver guarantees on storage performance which range across the elements of the entire storage system; from the application level, the file system, the network connection, block device I/O and the disks themselves. Typically, the solutions proposed are focused on one of these areas and seek to solve a particular aspect of the larger challenge of storage QoS.

We next look into the various methodologies that exist to provide Storage QoS.

Disk Modeling/Simulation

One approach to providing QoS is to create a detailed model of the disk drive to provide accurate timing data to each disk request. The idea here is to understand the various overheads involved in seeking and caching the data to provide accurate timings for the block I/O layer. This information could be used to model QoS.

Thorncock et al. (1997) used trace data to construct simulation models for disk drives and thus constructed statistical models to understand Disk Drive behaviour, which can be further modelled to provide QoS.

Ruemmler and Wilkes of HP Labs gave an overview of disk drive modeling in (Ruemmler et al., 1994) and a detailed account of the mechanical operations involved in a disk drive's operation. Simulators such as DiskSim (Disk Simulation Environment, 2010) developed at the University of Michigan and Carnegie Mellon University claims more accuracy than that provided by the model in (Ruemmler et al., 1994). Using such a direct model, it is possible to achieve very high accuracy provided that the model contains enough of the features of a real disk.

We question the applicability of these models as storage capacity in our environment scales rapidly and hence rule these out.

Networked I/O Throttling

One approach to providing QoS to multiple I/O streams is to use a form of I/O throttling, either at the network level, or at an application or block device level. Either way, these methods follow an approach to QoS that is used in networking which is to use a *token bucket* or other scheduling method to ensure that some amount of throughput is "fairly" dealt out to each access stream

Façade by Lumb et al. (2003) of HP labs propose the use of a controller to throttle requests between the client and the host on the storage network.

Argon (Wachs et al., 2007) from Carnegie-Mellon University is a storage server designed to "insulate" storage access streams from one another to guarantee a certain fraction of total performance to each stream. The system aims to control disk head interference and cache interference. It does this by controlling disk utilization for each stream and by using a partitioned cache. It is implemented at the application level rather than disk level.

Throttling techniques from the realm of networking require care if they are to be applied to storage. As an example, dropping SCSI commands to relieve congestion is not an option. We hence rule out these methodologies.

Disk Scheduling

Another approach is to manage the QoS at the disk I/O scheduler in the operating system. We first explain these different methodologies here under the context of different processes in an operating system competing for a single storage device.

When a component of the OS wishes to read or write data from a disk, it creates a request to do so (block devices generally hold pending requests in a *request queue*). This request is not satisfied by the kernel as soon as it is created but instead it is *scheduled* to occur at some later point. By delaying individual requests and waiting to potentially combine them together with newer requests (and optionally reorder them) means that when the disk is finally accessed it can be done more sequentially. At a basic level, the idea is to reduce seeks and thus increase performance (Bovet et al., 2006). This was the primary purpose of an earlier generation of disk schedulers namely, SSTF (Shortest Seek Time First), versions of SCAN (Reddy et at., 1993) and the two versions of LOOK (Reddy et at., 1993).

Provision of QoS through disk scheduling entails a focus on two primary parameters.

1. Throughput to the individual requesting entities (or processes)
2. Fairness with regards to latency and bandwidth allocation.

We present here some of most recent disk schedulers implemented in current day end systems and worked on by the storage research community, bringing into perspective the above issues.

The Anticipatory scheduler (Iyer and Druschel, 2001) was the default disk scheduler implemented in the 2.6 Linux kernel until 2.6.18. The anticipatory scheduler focuses on providing higher throughput to the individual requesting entities by "anticipating" requests ahead of time and thus has a mechanism for dealing with the Deceptive Idleness problem (Iyer et al., 2001), which affected an earlier generation of disk schedulers. In that, the scheduler would switch to servicing a different process as soon as work was completed for a current process, with no time lag. Hence there was no account for the time a process would take to complete the service before issuing the next request, with a possible sequential access pattern for disk blocks. This incurred unnecessary seek times when the process got back the time slice for getting its requests serviced. The anticipatory scheduler introduced a delay after completing a request on behalf of a process with "anticipation" that the process might issue another sequential request for disk blocks. The anticipatory scheduler greatly improves throughput for a process because of "forcing" sequential access. However, fairness to individual processes with regards to latency and bandwidth allocation has been an issue (Valente and Checconi, 2010).

The CFQ, or Completely Fair Queuing (Axboe, 2010) divides the process requests into different priority queues, with each process given a time slice. The processes within a priority queue follow a round robin policy. CFQ further introduces the elements of request "anticipation" by waiting for a small period of time before switching out a process request queue. CFQ is the default disk scheduler in most linux distributions with kernels after 2.6.18.

One of the main issues with CFQ is that processes with the same time slice would get different throughputs as a function of the position of the head on the disk. This comes in the way of fairness in bandwidth distribution. The worst case delay and jitter follows O(N) with N being the number of requesting processes.

YFQ (Yet another Fair Queuing) (Bruno et al, 1999) is a scheduling algorithm designed with the intent of providing bandwidth sharing on disks for multiple requests. YFQ is claimed to provide fairness and low delay, and hence provides certain QoS guarantees. YFQ splits incoming requests into resource reservation queues and then dispatches requests to the disk in "batches" from these queues.

The accuracy of throughput distribution within YFQ depends on the accuracy with which the request service times of the disk can be predicted, which is very difficult to do. (Valente et al., 2010) shows better fairness characteristics for BFQ (discussed later) as compared to YFQ.

SCAN EDF (Reddy et al., 1993) is a combination of the SCAN, which is an earlier seek optimization algorithm and EDF, or the Earliest Deadline First which brings in the element of deadlines or completion of requests within a given period of time. This is in line with the requirements of real-time applications. SCAN EDF however requires an accurate knowledge of some of the disk physical parameters, just like YFQ. Further, though SCAN EDF addresses fairness, BFQ (Valente et al., 2010) discussed next is shown to have better fairness characteristics among competing requests.

BFQ (Budget fair queuing) provides strong throughput guarantees, throughput distribution as well as good approximations on upper bounds for latency for each individual requesting applications. Budget fair queuing schedules processes based on the number of sectors they need to transfer (called the "budget"), and the budget is varied based on the nature of the application to ensure good throughput distribution and fairness. BFQ focuses on applications that submit synchronous requests (where each request is submitted only after the completion of a subsequent request), and tackles the deceptive idleness problem, that affects a vast majority of previous schedulers. BFQ works through splitting incoming requests into various queues based on the budgets they have requested, and schedules queues according to a weighted fair queuing algorithm, WF2Q+ (Bennet and Zhang, 1997). Within each queue a simple version of LOOK is used to schedule requests.

Valente et al. (2010) has shown that BFQ has better fairness and throughput distribution characteristics as compared to the previously discussed schedulers. BFQ also does not need accurate knowledge of disk parameters. BFQ is shown to have excellent fairness characteristics for media applications.

Fahrrad real-time scheduler by Povzner et al. (2008) of IBM Research takes the approach of providing QoS in the form of disk utilization time (as opposed to throughput) for multiple streams. This approach is based around the claim that utilization based control makes more efficient use of the disk resource than basing the QoS on throughput.

Cello by Shenoy et al. (1997) is an example of a disk scheduler that uses the concept of QoS classes. It manages QoS from the point of view of both throughput and disk utilization. They conclude that disk utilization management is more suitable for admission control algorithmic approach to storage QoS while throughput management is more suitable for environments where different files have different record sizes.

Bruno et al. (1999) of Bell Labs as part of the Eclipse operating system implement their real-time disk scheduling by intercepting read and write system calls. The calls are placed in queues which manage requests to ensure that different streams receive fair access based on disk utilization time. Their approach is to allocate disk access time to each stream so that the majority of time is spent on disk access and minimal time is spent on seeking.

An approach similar to these disk scheduling mechanisms can be used in a Parallel Distributed file system framework of Lustre to provide QoS, as described in the next few sections.

Object Based Storage QoS

Object based storage has been promoted in the literature as being suitable for inclusion of QoS mechanisms (Wu and Brandt, 2007). "Object" storage is a concept, not necessarily tied to one implementation or standard. The basic premise is that data is organised in logically connected objects (for example, as whole files) on the storage device. The IO commands that are sent to retrieve this data are constructed in terms of these objects rather than lower-level block IO entities such as blocks, sectors, cylinders etc. The Luster methodology which we use inherently adopts the Object based storage concept.

We next look into the Lustre based storage processing platform that could be used for real-time clouds.

STORAGE PROCESSING PLATFORM

Overview

The Lustre based Storage Processing platform for real-time clouds is as depicted in Figure 1.

Real-time applications executing across clouds are divided into multiple Service Components. These Service Components are physically executed in virtual machines as depicted in Figure 1. These virtual machines are contained in physical hosts that contain the Lustre client module. These Lustre client modules communicate over a high speed/low latency networking interface with Object based Storage Targets (OSTs) and issue

Figure 1. Lustre based Storage Processing Platform

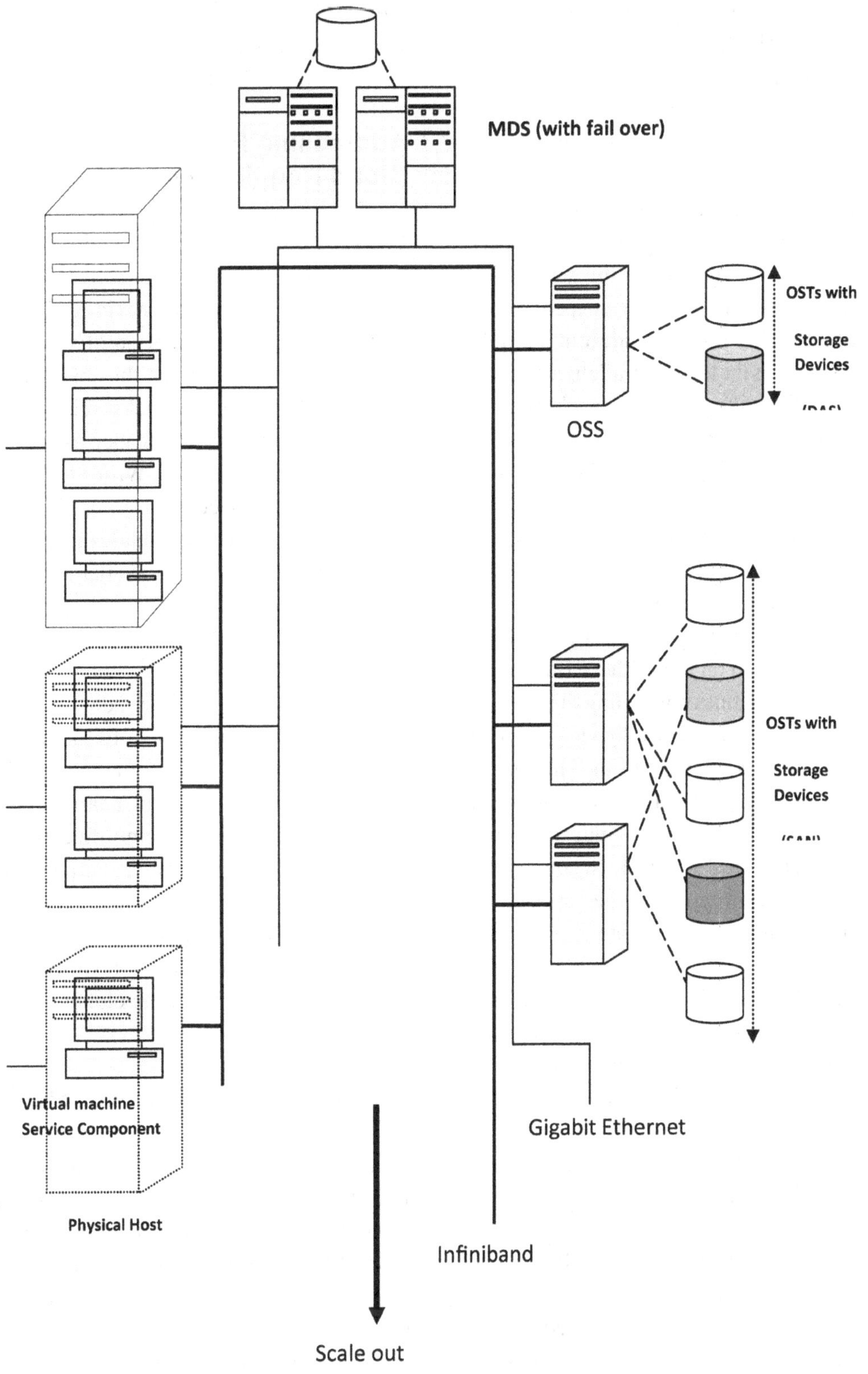

MDS (with fail over)

OSTs with Storage Devices (DAS)

OSS

OSTs with Storage Devices (SAN)

Virtual machine Service Component

Physical Host

Gigabit Ethernet

Infiniband

Scale out

read/write requests on files, which the OSTs contain. The OSTs are managed by Object Storage Servers (OSSs), The Metadata servers (MDSs) contain the "file header data" which provides the information regarding the location of file data to the Lustre clients before they issue read/write requests.

A key premise of Lustre is that file granularity is in terms of variable sized objects as previously discussed. These objects contain the actual disk blocks. The file data is typically striped across muliptle objects that could reside on multiple OSTs. This feature is the key to parallelizing reads/writes accross to multiple OSTs, and hence the key to scalability of storage.

The Physical Hosts which contain the Lustre clients can typically scale to tens of thousands to accommodate an increasing number of Service Components across the cloud. The Lustre clients are typically linux machines with the Lustre client modules installed. The server virtualization hypervisor is installed on top of these Lustre clients. The virtual machines containing the Service Components are on top of the hypervisor. The luster client modules connect to the infiniband networking subsystem through the associated driver subsystem. Figure 2 contains a simple depiction of the physical hosts which contain the Lustre clients. The virtual machines are shown with Service Components executing on behalf of the cloud application.

The Metadata Server (MDS), which is arranged with failover modules, contains "inodes" for files that are stored on OSTs. These inodes contain information about the location of the objects for a given file and other important access parameters. The MDS is used for file lookups by the Lustre clients before they start the actual Reads/Writes on the files.

The OSSs intercept Read/Write calls for objects from the infiniband network and convert them to simple Reads/Writes as defined by the local filesystem (such as ext3) on the OSS's. The OSTs can be connected as Direct Attached

Storage (DAS), or could be connected through the SAN to the OSS's. The OST's may consist of very disperate storage devices, and could already be subjected to RAID.

Addressing Real-Time Cloud Requirements

The Lustre physical hosts could scale to tens of thousands of nodes, and the corresponding OSTs can scale to thousands, providing PetaBytes of storage. A rapid proliferation of service components across the cloud can thus be easily accommodated. Adding additional service components does not affect the performance as seen by these components as the Reads/Writes to OSTs are effectively parallelized.

The Lustre software modules are open sourced under GNU GPL and are available for free. The OSTs are typically commodity storage hardware. This leads to very low costs of adoption for the service provider.

The OSTs can be easily added/removed in a way that is non destructive to the applications. There is failover build into the OSSs/OSTs. Lustre systems are capable of adapting to rapidly fluctualting demand as exemplified by large scale implementations (Lustre was implemented in 7 out of the top 10 supercomputers in the world at the end of 2008 as indicated by Sun Microsystems Press Release, 2008). These flexibility characteristics are ideal for real-time clouds.

PROVIDING QUALITY OF SERVICE

One of the features that is currently lacking in the Lustre architechture is QoS capabilities and the management features as specifically needed by real-time applications. A framework through which the Lustre based architechture provides QoS is provided next.

The essence of the proposed framework for the provision of Quality of Service (QoS) is:

Figure 2. Physical Hosts with Lustre Client

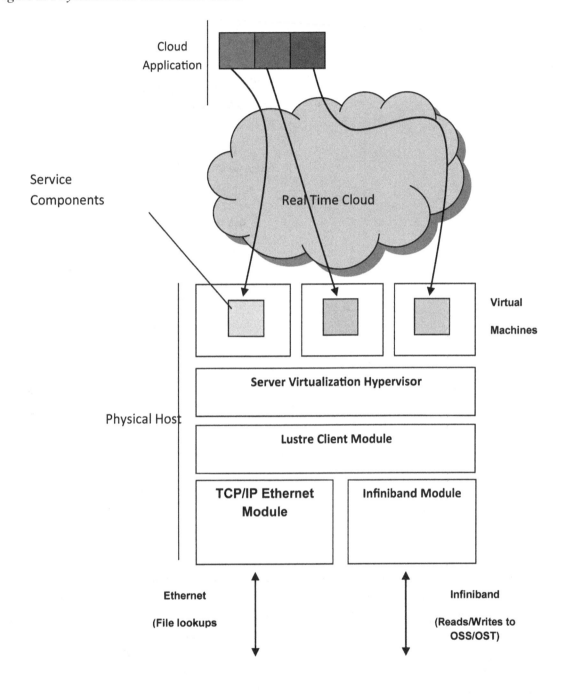

1. A throttling mechanism in place within the Lustre OSS to throttle client bandwidth (and hence introduce latencies) to applications based on the respective strengths of their Service Level Agreement (SLA) requests.

2. Ability of the system to accept and reject these SLA requests based on the "net" capability of the Lustre storage subsystem.

Figure 3. Quality of Service Framework for Storage

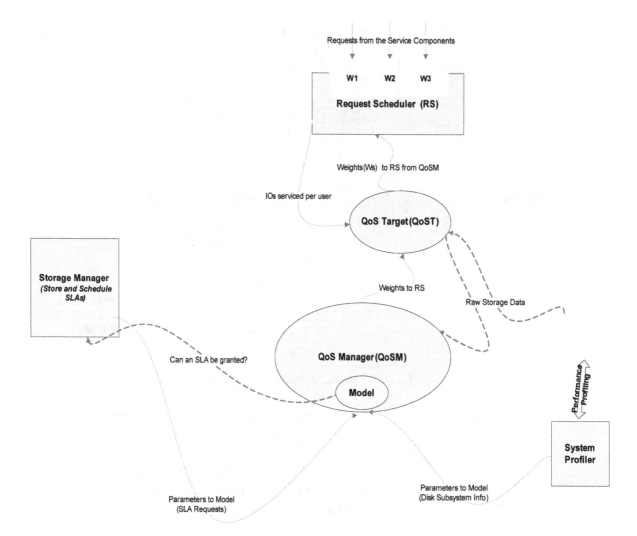

There are several modules that can be envisioned for implementation, that could work together to realize the QoS for data storage

- Storage Manager
- QoS Manager
- System Profiler
- QoS Target
- Storage Network Request Scheduler

We briefly describe the following below using Figure 3.

Storage Manager

This module forms the interface to the rest of the cloud based real-time environment. The Storage manager stores and schedules SLAs for storage requests accumulated from applications.

QoS Manager

This is the module that determines whether an SLA can be granted by the storage system. It communicates with the Storage Manager. It takes as input the data from the System Profiler (below) and the SLA request parameter (bandwidth or latency) from the Storage Manager. It passes these to the model to determine the cost in terms of storage system resources and whether an SLA can be granted by the Storage Manager.

As a further output of the model, the QoS Manager also calculates the weights for a request scheduler. These are passed to the QoS Target to input into the storage request scheduler to throttle access to the storage system for different users based on their SLA.

The QoS Manager is also responsible for the Reporting and Monitoring functionality. Information for these reports is created from raw storage performance data collected from each QoS Target. This data has to be translated by the QoS Manager into a format suitable for the rest of the cloud environment.

System Profiler

This module benchmarks the storage system to provide the parameters for the model that is used by the QoS Manager.

The profiler runs a one time benchmark against the storage system for various block sizes, sequentialities, access profiles and number of client connections. The data set is used to generate an analytical model for QoS by the QoS Manager. The analytical model determines whether an SLA can be granted.

QoS Target

This is the interface between the QoS manager and the storage request scheduler.

The QoS target inserts weights into the scheduler given to it by the QoS Manager to throttle and manage the bandwidth to each user.

The QoS target also collects raw storage performance data from log files on the OSS whose information is passed back to the QoS manager to be used in the Monitoring and Reporting functionality.

Storage Request Scheduler

The request scheduler is written as a module in Lustre that ensures that the correct proportion of each application's IO requests is serviced. This essentially implements the Bandwidth throttling mechanism.

Each user is assigned his own queue for his IO requests. This queue is assigned a weight from the QoS target. The requests in the queues are serviced in proportion to the weights they are assigned. The weights are simple numerical equivalents of the requested SLAs.

Quality of Service Model

The Lustre based storage server subsystem consists of many components with a variety of capabilities. A small subset of these are identified below:

- The disks interactions (as discussed in the previous section)
- The disk caches
- RAID subsystem (discussed later)
- Back end File system architecture on the OSS
- OSS Storage server operating system memory subsystem
- Networking stack for the OSS
- Hardware capabilities such as Bus bandwidths, and processor speeds
- Interaction of processor cores
- Infiniband driver subsystem

Providing Quality of Service (QoS) capabilities for such a system entails the ability to make predictions and precise decisions regarding the capability of the system to accept storage requests. Further the interactions of the above components are not driven by simple mathematical relations of the individual component capabilities. This makes the storage subsystem very chaotic which makes the problem of building a predictive model very complex. There is hence very little or no

Figure 4. System Capability Parameters

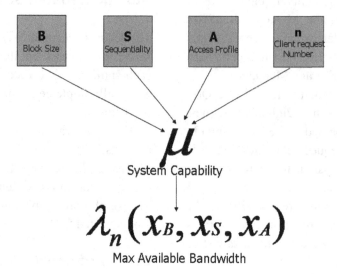

work done in the area of storage QoS modelling especially for high scalable, multi-tenent cloud based environments.

The following are the objectives of an analytical QoS Model for a Storage subsystem:

1. Whether a request for an SLA, that is, the *request for a given bandwidth* access to the storage subsystem can be granted.
2. *Prediction of estimated delay* for client requests which have been granted.
3. Characterization of the system in terms of a *new parameter termed System Capability*, which denotes the ability of the system to process requests.

The model also helps us to clearly visualize the changes in the "net system capability" available to process new requests in a very dynamic environment where clients' connections enter and leave the system. The storage system is highly parallel and distributed, and the clients are able to generate a potentially very large quantity of asynchronous and outstanding IO requests and as such, a model which accommodates both the time taken for the storage sytem to service the individual requests and the effect of queueing of these requests is required.

There is a need to accurately characterize the system in terms of changing performances with changes in block size, sequentiailty of reading/ writing from the storage system and access profiles. Changes along each of the dimensions has the effect of changing the maximum bandwidth that can be allocated to the storage system.

"System Capability" (μ) is a single parameter that takes in block size, sequentiality, access profile and the number of the clients as inputs and gives a numerical measure that characterizes the capability that is available to soft real-time applications. The System Capability has the same units as throughput and denotes the maximum theoretical throughput that can be accommodated by a storage system. We study probability distributions of latencies and apply ideas from queuing models for the final characterization of System Capability.

The practical maximum throughput, t$\lambda_n(x_B, x_S, x_A)$ hat is available to the system for block size(B), sequentiality(S), access profile(A) and the nth client connections can be derived from μ. Figure 4 pictorially depicts the input parameters for μ and its relation to $\lambda_n(x_B, x_S, x_A)$. On the storage OSS side, request for any throttled bandwidth

Figure 5. Reducing System Capability with new clients

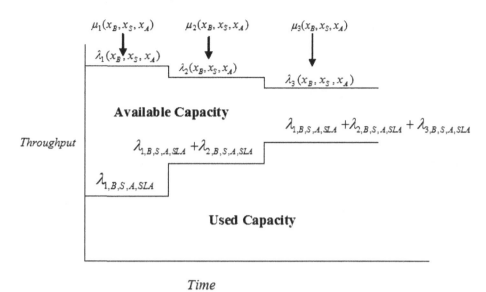

($\lambda_{n,B,S,A,SLA}$) from a client can be accepted/rejected after comparing with the maximum practical throughput. Once a given throttled bandwidth is accepted, the expected value of delay introduced by the storage system for the client I/Os can also be derived from the model. Figure 5 is a pictorial depiction of how the System Capabilities vary with added number of clients.

Figure 6 shows an example of System Capability measured in our Lustre storage system setup measured along two dimensions, block size and sequentiality, so that it can be visualised in 3D space.

The System capability is a truly holistic approach to determine the ability of the storage system to accept and reject connections based on SLAs.

FUTURE RESEARCH DIRECTIONS

Cloud computing environments require very highly scalable and user shareable infrastructures which should be capable of supporting a wide variety of applications. The issues of real-time applications working seamlessly in clouds has started getting focus from the research community and the industry only recently. Our proposed QoS approaches for storage to tackle those issues are currently being adopted for the IRMOS project. The IRMOS project entails the provision of Quality of Service to real-time applications in a cloud computing environment addressing all the "tiers", namely the application interfaces to cloud platform, the cloud computing platform itself and the infrastructure elements within the cloud, namely, networking, computing and data storage. The vision of seamlessly working real-time applications over a cloud are being investigated and prototyped by IRMOS for various application scenarious such as eLearning, Digital Film Postproduction and Virtual Reality, with users being spread across the cloud infrastructure. The first use cases of the proposed real-time Quality of Service for storage over clouds would hence be realised in IRMOS.

Figure 6. System capability along two dimensions (Block Size and Sequentiailty), visualised in 3D space

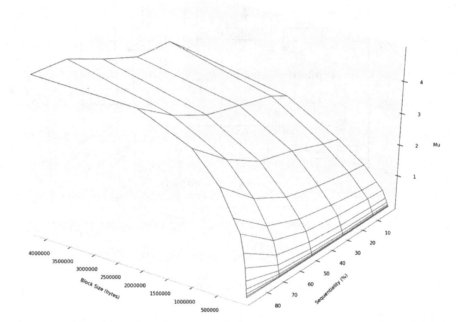

CONCLUSION

In this chapter we have discussed some of the storage specific rquirements for real-time applications for cloud architechtures. We discussed some of the associated background work and then discussed a storage platform processing architechture to address the issues along with a QoS model.

Current ongoing work is focussed on the tighter integration of the model into the IRMOS cloud based environment. There is also work ongoing to develop graphical user interfaces that accurately and simplistically describe the concept and helps a non-technical end user understand the behaviour of the Lustre based storage subsystem. The System Capability model can be extended to other types of storage subsystems utilizing a variety of file system technologies. Further, we have used bandwidth as the main parameter to describe System Capability. It is possible to have an inverse System Capability model based on latencies, which is relatively simple given simple mathematical relations between bandwidth and latency.

Folowing are some of the technical areas being investigated:

1. The current QoS model focuses on a single or a few OSSs. Scalability and interaction implications of having 100s of OSSs needs to be carefully studied.

2. Detailed mathematical characterization of our "credit" based Throttling mechanism needs to be done.

3. Understandng the statistics of Jitter (which is the Variance in Latency) and incorporation into the Model.

4. The Lustre system as a Parallel Distributed file system has some inherent limitations in scalability beyond tens of PetaBytes primarily because of metadata server limitations. These limitations have to be carefully studied.

5. Incorporation of content awareness into storage especially for multimedia cloud based environments has interesting implications in terms of performance, cost and reduction of raw storage requirements. This might be the next big step in developing a more intelligent storage solution.

REFERENCES

Axboe, J. (2010). *CFQ IO scheduler*. Retrieved on March 4, 2010, from http://mirror.linux.org.au/pub/linux.conf.au/2007/video/talks/123.pdf

Bennet, J. C. R., & Zhang, H. (1997). Hierarchical packet fair queuing algorithms. *IEEE Transactions on Networking, 5*(5).

Bovet, D. P., & Cesati, M. (2006). *Understanding the Linux kernel*. O'Reilly.

Brinkmann, A., Heidebuer, M., Meyer, F., Heide, A., Rückert, U., Salzwedel, K., & Vodisek, M. (2004). V: Drive - Costs and benefits of an out-of-band storage virtualization system. *Proceedings of the 21st IEEE Conference on Mass Storage Systems and Technologies.*

Bruno, J., Brustoloni, J., Gabber, E., Ozden, B., & Silberschatz, A. (1999). Disk scheduling with quality of service guarantees. *Proceedings of the IEEE International Conference on Multimedia Computing and Systems.*

Data Core. (2010). *Software*. Retrieved June 2010 from http://www.datacore.com/

DiskSim. (2010). *Simulation environment*. Retrieved on June 3, 2010, from http://www.pdl.cmu.edu/DiskSim/

Falconstor. (2010). Retreived June 2010 from http://www.falconstor.com/

Gallizo, G., Kuebert, R., Oberle, K., Menychtas, A., & Konstanteli, K. (2008). Service level agreements in virtualised service platforms. *Proceedings of the eChallenges 2009 Conference* eChallenges 2009, Istanbul, Turkey, October 2008.

Huang, L., Peng, G., & Chiueh, T. (2004). Multidimensional storage virtualization. *Proceedings of the 2004 ACM SIGMETRICS Conference on Measurement and Modeling of Computer Systems.*

Iyer, S., & Druschel, P. (2001). Anticipatory scheduling: A disk scheduling framework to overcome deceptive idleness in synchronous IO. *Proceedings of the 18th ACM Symposium on Operating Systems Principles.*

Labs, E. S. G. (2010). *Website*. Retrieved March 2010 from http://www.enterprisestrategygroup.com/

Lumb, C. R., Merchant, A., & Alvarez, G. A. (2003). Façade: Virtual storage devices with performance guarantees. *Proceedings of the 2003 USENIX Conference on File and Storage Technologies.*

Povzner, A., Brandt, A., Golding, R., Wong, T., & Maltzahn, C. (2008). *Virtualizing disk performance with Fahrrad*. USENIX Conference on File and Storage Technologies.

Preston, W. C. (2002). *Using SANs and NAS*. O Reilly.

Reddy, A. L. N., Wyllie, J., & Wijayaratne, K. B. R. (1993). Disk scheduling in a multimedia I/O system. *Proceedings of the first International Conference on Multimedia.*

Ruemmler, C., & Wilkes, J. (1994). An introduction to disk drive modeling. *IEEE Computer, 27*(3).

Sanbolic. (2010). *Melio file system*. Retrieved March 2010 from http://www.sanbolic.com/melioFS.htm

Shenoy, P., & Vin, H. M. (1997). *Cello: A disk scheduling framework for next generation operating systems*. ACM Sigmetrics Conference.

Sun Microsystems. (2008). *Press release*. Retrieved November 2008 from http://www. hpcwire.com/ specialfeatures/ sc08/ offthewire/ Suns_Lustre_ File_System _Powers_Top _Supercomputers.html

Thorncock, N. C., Tu, X., & Flanagan, J. K. (1997). A stochastic disk I/O simulation technique. *Proceedings of the 1997 Winter Simulation Conference.*

Valente, P., & Checconi, F. (2010). High throughput disk scheduling with deterministic guarantees on bandwidth distribution. *IEEE Transactions on Computers*, *59*(9). doi:10.1109/TC.2010.105

Wachs, M., Abd-El-Malek, M., Thereska, E., & Ganger, G. R. (2007). Argon: Performance insulation for shared storage servers. *Proceedings of the 2007 USENIX Conference on File and Storage Technologies.*

Wu, J., & Brandt, S. A. (2007). Providing quality of service support in object-based file system. *Proceedings of the 24th IEEE Conference on Mass Storage Systems and Technologies.*

ENDNOTES

[1] Real-time is used to imply "Soft Real-time", which is our main focus

[2] Lustre is an open source project, original trademark being owned by Cluster File Systems, Inc, which was eventually acquired by Sun Microsystems and then Oracle.

Chapter 14
Fault Detection and Recovery Mechanisms and Techniques for Service Oriented Infrastructures

Andreas Menychtas
National Technical University of Athens, Greece

Kleopatra G. Konstanteli
National Technical University of Athens, Greece

ABSTRACT

The need for guaranteed QoS and efficient management in Service Oriented Infrastructures is an essential requirement for the deployment, execution, and management of modern business applications. In that frame, the capabilities for fault detection and recovery in all layers of a Service Oriented Infrastructure are essential for the smooth operation of the business applications and the wide adoption of these solutions in the global market. In this chapter, we present the concepts of fault detection and recovery, including terminology, classification of faults, and analysis of the key processes taking place in a system in order to diagnose and recover from failures. The state of the art mechanisms and techniques for fault detection and recovery are also analyzed, while recommendations for applying them in Service Oriented Infrastructure are presented.

INTRODUCTION

Service Oriented Infrastructures, and generally the Distributed Systems, are increasingly considered to be ideal candidates for implementing platforms capable to support business applications. This is tightly coupled with the need for high quality of service (QoS) provisioning for the applications not only to guarantee their smooth operation

and management but also to support the primary capabilities of such systems for scalability, service orchestration, autonomous management and abstraction of the systems' complexity. In this frame, fault tolerance functionality is necessary to achieve high QoS provisioning for both the system and the applications. The advantage of Service Oriented Infrastructures from the fault tolerance perspective is significant. These systems can be easily made redundant, which is the corner-stone for all fault tolerance techniques. Unfortunately,

DOI: 10.4018/978-1-60960-827-9.ch014

distribution also means that the imperfect and fault prone physical world cannot be ignored, so that as much as they help in supporting fault tolerance, distributed systems may also be the source of many failures.

On the other hand, the building blocks and components of the SOIs are independent of each other and therefore are independent points of failure. Even though this may be an advantage for the end users, it is also a complex problem for the developers and administrators in terms of synchronization and management. In fault tolerant distributed systems, a component failure means that the other components and services have to detect and handle that failure to keep the system running and maintain the QoS level for the applications and end users to an acceptable level. This involves redistributing the functionality from the failed component to other, or it may mean switching to some king of emergency mode for the operation of the systems and the execution of the application.

Providing fault tolerant design for every component is normally not an option. In such cases the following criteria may be used to determine which components should be fault tolerant:

- How critical is the component? In a car, the radio is not critical, so this component has less need for fault tolerance.
- How likely is the component to fail? Some components, like the drive shaft in a car, are not likely to fail, so no fault tolerance is needed.
- How expensive is it to make the component fault tolerant? Requiring a redundant car engine, for example, would likely be too expensive both economically and in terms of weight and space, to be considered.

In the next sections of introduction we present the terminology related with fault detection and fault tolerance systems since many of these terms are confused. In addition we have catego-

rized the faults that may occur in SOIs based on their duration, cause and effect and we analyze their most important drawbacks. In section two, the key processes that take place in such systems to provide the fault tolerance functionality are described. Section three presents the state of the art mechanisms and techniques for the fault tolerance while section four concludes our work and highlights the future trends.

Terminology

Nowadays mechanisms and techniques that maintain the desired QoS levels and smooth operation of systems, services and applications are widely adopted and used, while in terms of implementation and design, they span in various different domains following different approaches. Often the terms related with the technologies for fault tolerance, detection and recovery are confused and hard to distinguish, for instance the terms "failure" and "error" or the techniques of "redundancy" and "replication". In this section we introduce the key terms for the fault tolerant systems based on Randell, B., Lee, P., and Treleaven, P. C., (1978), Selic B., (2004), IFIP 10.4 Working Group on Dependable Computing and Fault Tolerance, (2010) and Ding, S.X., (2008).

- **Fault Tolerance:** Fault tolerance is the ability of a system to perform its function correctly even in the presence of internal faults. The purpose of fault tolerance is to increase the dependability of a system.
- **Fault Prevention:** Fault Prevention refers to techniques, such as inspection, whose intent is to eliminate the circumstances by which faults arise.
- **Fault Detection:** is the detection of occurrence of faults in functional units of the process, which lead to undesired or intolerable behavior of the whole system.
- **Fault Isolation:** describes the process of localization (classification) of different faults.

- **Fault Analysis or identification:** is the determination of the type, magnitude and cause of a fault.
- **Failure:** A failure occurs when an actual running system deviates from this specified behaviour. The cause of a failure is called an error.
- **Error:** An error represents an invalid system state, one that is not allowed by the system behaviour specification. The error itself is the result of a defect in the system or fault. It should be noted that an error is the symptom of a fault meaning that a fault may result to one or multiple errors. Similarly, a single error may lead to multiple failures.
- **Reliability:** Reliability characterizes the ability of a system to perform its service correctly. Reliability is defined as the probability that a system will perform correctly up to a given point in time.
- **Availability:** Availability means that the system is available to perform the service when it is asked to do so. Availability is defined as the probability that a system is operational at a given point in time. A typical availability metric is the time required to restore the system to service once a failure occurs.
- **Dependability:** describes the trustworthiness of a computing system which allows reliance to be justifiably placed on the service it delivers.
- **Redundancy:** Providing multiple identical instances of the same system and switching to one of the remaining instances in case of a failure (failover).
- **Replication:** Providing multiple identical instances of the same system or subsystem, directing tasks or requests to all of them in parallel, and choosing the correct result.

Faults Classification

The question is what type of faults we should expect in a modern computing infrastructure. From the duration perspective there two types faults, the permanent and the transient. A system under permanent fault can recover only with the support of an external system, while the transient faults are only temporary. Even though the permanent faults are considered of higher importance since they are more likely to cause complete failures to the system, in the transient ones is more difficult to identify the cause and proceed afterwards to corrective actions.

Based on the cause of the fault, the faults can be categorized in design faults and operational faults. The design faults appear when a system is not carefully designed, like coding bugs. The operational faults occur during the lifetime of the system due to external or physical causes, such as disk or network failures.

Finally, we can classify the faults based on the effect that the fault has on the system. From this perspective, there are four categories of faults, crash faults, where the system either completely stops operating or never returns to an acceptable operational state, omission faults, where the system is operational but fails to deliver the requested services, timing faults, where the system cannot complete the requested service on time and finally byzantine faults (Castro, M. and Liskov, B., 2002), where the system is processing requests incorrectly, corrupting their local state, and/or producing incorrect or inconsistent outputs.

Fault Tolerant Systems Drawbacks

While the fault tolerant design advantages are obvious, many of the disadvantages are not. In next paragraphs we summarize the most important drawbacks for systems implementing fault tolerant solutions.

- **Interference with fault detection in another component.** Another variation of this problem is when fault tolerance in one component prevents fault detection in a different component. For example, if component B performs some operation based on the output from component A, then fault tolerance in B can hide a problem with A. If component B is later changed (to a less fault tolerant design) the system may fail suddenly, making it appear that the new component B is the problem. Only after the system has been carefully scrutinized will it become clear that the root problem is actually with component A.
- **Reduction of priority of fault correction.** Even if the operator is aware of the fault, having a fault tolerant system is likely to reduce the importance of repairing the fault. If the faults are not corrected, this will eventually lead to system failure, when the fault tolerant component fails completely or when all redundant components have also failed.
- **Test difficulty.** For certain critical fault tolerant systems, such as a nuclear reactor, there is no easy way to verify that the back-up components are functional. The most infamous example of this is Chernobyl, where operators tested the emergency backup cooling by disabling primary and secondary cooling. The backup failed, resulting in a core meltdown and massive release of radiation.
- **Cost.** Both fault tolerant components and redundant components tend to increase cost. This can be a purely economic cost or can include other measures, such as weight. Manned spaceships, for example, have so many redundant and fault tolerant components that their weight is increased dramatically over unmanned systems, which don't require the same level of safety.

- **Inferior components.** A fault tolerant design may allow for the use of inferior components, which would have otherwise made the system inoperable. While this practice has the potential to mitigate the cost increase, the use of multiple inferior components may lower the reliability of the system to a level equal to, or even worse than, a comparable non-fault tolerant system.

FAULT RECOVERY PROCESSES

According to IBM (Selic B., 2004) the generic fault tolerance procedures can be grouped in the following four phases:

- **Error Detection**, identification that the system is in an invalid state;
- **Damage Confinement**, limitation and isolation of the error effecting particular system components;
- **Error Recovery**, recovery from the error and system restoration to a valid state;
- **Fault Treatment**, isolation of the fault and system repair.

Error Detection

The error detection process can be performed with the following techniques:

- **Replication checks**. The replication checks in a system are achieved through multiple replicas of a component working simultaneously and any discrepancy of the outputs is an indication of an error. In hardware level a typical approach of this is the triple-modular redundancy (TMR), in which the output of three independent components is compared, and the output of the majority of the components is considered as the correct one. In software level, replication checks are realized with multiple independently developed instances of the same component, known as N-version programming (Knight, J.C. & Leveson, N.G., 1986).

- **Diagnostic checks**. The diagnostic checks determine whether a component is functioning correctly applying known input for which the correct output is also known.
- **Run-time constraints checking**. In the run-time constraints checking, the error detection mechanisms check if the values of system variables are within an acceptable operational range. Checksums for data structures is an example of this technique.
- **Timing checks**. The timing checks approach is used to detect timing errors. For each operation of the component, a timer is used to detect if the time to compete an operation exceeds the expected time. The problem with timers is in cases where there is variation in the execution of a function where it is dangerous to set the timer too tightly or too loosely that would either indicate false errors or delayed detection of errors respectively.

Damage Confinement

The damage confinement procedure is used to determine and isolate the parts of the systems and the particular component(s) where the error occurred.

Error Recovery

In the error recovery phase the system is restored to a valid state. There are two general approaches to achieving this, the backward error recovery and the forward error recovery. In the backward error recovery, checkpointing techniques are used and the system is restored to a previous known valid state. In the forward error recovery the system is moved to a new valid state following a precise

detection and isolation of the fault that caused the error.

Fault Treatment

This is the phase where the system is repaired and the actions that are required depend on the type of the fault. More particularly, the fault is isolated to the particular problematic system components which are thereafter replaced by non-failing ones. To maintain a high QoS provisioning lever for the system, standby components are required. However, the integration of the standby components into the system is a difficult process in which the state of the standby components should be synchronized with the rest of the system.

There are three general types of standby schemes:

- **Cold standby**: In the cold standby approach the standby component is not operational, and a synchronization of it state is necessary during its initialization, a process that requires additional time for the complete system recovery with the tradeoff of not introducing overhead during the normal operation of the system.
- **Warm standby**: In warm standby, the standby components keep the last valid state of the operational component (checkpoints) and when the principal component fails, the standby components are integrated in the system with the last checkpoint state.
- **Hot standby**: The hot standby practice requires the standby component to be fully active, duplicating the function of the primary component. Therefore, in the case that an error occurs, recovery can be practically instantaneous but the overhead that is introduced is much higher than in the previous schemes and standby requires continuous communications between the primary and the standby. The main dif-

ference with the warm standby is that the synchronization is performed on a constant basis and not only during checkpoints.

STATE OF THE ART MECHANISMS AND TECHNIQUES

In this section we describe the state of the art mechanisms and approaches for fault tolerance and detection in Service Oriented Infrastructures.

Workflows

In a highly dynamic and heterogeneous SOI, geographically and organizationally dispersed, heterogeneous resources are incorporated such as computing systems, software, storage systems, instruments, scientific equipment, specialized hardware, communication systems, data sources as well as human collaborators. In such a heterogeneous environment changes are numerous, highly variable and with unpredictable effects. These changes can lead to failure for various reasons: non-availability of required services or software components, overloaded resource conditions, memory shortage, and network fabric failures. For these reasons, workflow management in SOIs, in general, and especially those supporting workflows execution with real-time applications, should be able to detect and manage failures in order to ensure reliable support of the execution environment.

Workflow failure handling techniques can be divided into two different levels: task-level and workflow-level (Hwang S. and Kesselman C., 2003). Whereas task-level techniques are concerned with masking the effects the failures of the services impose on the entire workflow, workflow-level techniques are focused on the manipulation of the workflow structure in order to deal with erroneous conditions.

Task-level techniques can be divided into the following categories:

- *Retry*: After failure, the same task is executed again on the same resource.
- *Alternate resource*: After failure, the same task is submitted and executed on a different resource.
- *Checkpoint/Restart*: After failure, task is moved to other resources and maintains its state, so that it can continue its execution from the point of failure.
- *Replication*: The task is executed simultaneously on different resources.

Workflow-level techniques include:

- *Alternate task*: After failure, another implementation of the same task is executed.
- *Redundancy*: Multiple alternative tasks are executed simultaneously on different resources.
- *User-defined exception handling*: Users are responsible for specifying corrective actions for a certain types of failure.
- *Rescue workflow*: This technique ignores failures and continues to execute the rest of the tasks in the workflow, if possible. Afterwards, information that includes statistics about the failures is generated for internal processing by the system and the client.

It is evident that SOIs need to support fault tolerance in order to be economically viable. This can be seen by the fact that most grid frameworks already provide some of the techniques mentioned in the overview and plan to implement more. On the task level, the technique of *Retry* can be implemented, as this is the easiest and most straightforward method. It should be noted here that it will be investigated whether this is superseded by the Migration technique, as the IaaS provide redundancy and thus the Alternate Resource method can be implemented. Therefore, it is possible that after failure, the same task will be submitted and executed on another resource that is already reserved by IaaS and not executed again on the same machine that failed, thus saving time and keeping the workflow within its constraints. The Check-pointing method will be seriously considered as it can save a serious amount of time, especially for services that last for long. The overhead that this imposes is relatively small when this method is used on task level (light-weight check-pointing) and can therefore be used to keep a workflow within its timing constraints after a failure.

In addition on the workflow level, Exception Handling is another option. By Exception Handling it is meant that certain corrective actions will be taken when specific failures occur. This is done by the platform and not propagated to the user, as this will most certainly break any timing guarantees. In addition, Rescue workflow is considered as a failure of a service may not have detrimental effects on the whole workflow. It is also possible that heavy-weight check-pointing can be implemented.

There are several approaches in the design and development of systems that aim to handle failures in the context of workflow enactment. In the sequel, the most relevant ones are presented.

ASKALON

The goal of ASKALON (Thomas Fahringer, et. al., 2005) is to simplify the development and optimization of Grid workflow applications. The Enactment Service is the central service of the ASKALON middleware responsible for executing a workflow application. The Enactment Service provides fault tolerance for the middleware. It does so in three different levels:

- *Activity level*: For the activity level, retry and replication methods are used.
- *Control flow level*: For control flow level, light-weight checkpointing and migration are used. With this method, the workflow state and URL references to intermediate data are saved and can be recovered in case of a failure. This is very fast, but poses the disadvantage that the intermediate data are stored on possibly unsecured file systems.
- *Workflow Level*: For the workflow-level fault tolerance the methods of alternative task, redundancy and checkpointing are used. The last differs from light-weight checkpointing in that it stores backup copies of intermediate data into a database and execution can be restored and resumed at any time from any Grid location. This method posses the disadvantage of increased overhead.

Akogrimo

In Akogrimo Project (http://www.akogrimo.org) once the execution of a business service has started, it is managed and monitored in order to achieve continuous conformance to the contractual terms of SLAs. In case of execution failure or failure to meet the SLA criteria and depending on the explicit type of failure, Execution Management System - EMS is able to reallocate the execution. In order to detect possible failures and maintain the state of the execution between possible reallocations, a fault detection in conjunction with a recovery scheme is being used. The EMS establishes a WS-Notification mechanism with the business services in order to receive notification messages every time a property of the business resource changes its value. Resource properties provide to the EMS a view on the current state of the resource. Every time the EMS receives a notification message it stores the new value of the resource property. If a failure occurs during the execution of the business service and the creation of new business resource is needed (either on the same or different location), the EMS will set the resource properties to the last known ones before the failure occurs. This approach makes use of the WS-Resource specification in order to maintain the state of the business resources.

ProActive

ProActive (Baude F., et. al., 2005) is a middle-ware for parallel, distributed and multi-threaded computing. ProActive provides fault tolerance capabilities through two different protocols:

- *Communication-Induced Checkpointing protocol* (CIC) and
- *Pessimistic Message Logging protocol* (PML)

The fault tolerant applications following CIC protocol implement checkpointing mechanisms for their components. Each component has to checkpoint at least every Time-To-Checkpoint (TTC) seconds and at the time all components have completed the process, a global state is formed from which the application restores its status in case of a failure. The efficiency of this approach depends on the frequency of failures and the value of the TTC parameter. Small TTC values require frequent global state creation introducing overhead to the system but the advantage of this is small rollbacks in the application execution when many failures occur and vice versa.

For components of the applications using the PML protocol checkpointing should take place every TTC seconds but in contrast with CIC all the messages delivered to a component are stored to a common location. In that way each checkpoint is independent and global synchronization is not required. In this approach, the various application processes and their checkpoints are independent and in case of a failure, only a specific process has to restore its state. In comparison with the CIP approach the recovery time is lower if the failures involve only parts of the application or independent processes but has more overhead when the application operates smoothly.

Process Migration

Migration is the practice of relocating running computational processes from one resource to another. This migration can be triggered by environmental changes and conditions that make it beneficial (cheaper, improved overall performance, etc) to reallocate a certain process or bundle of processes. Migration however imposes an overhead either in time and resources utilization or in costs that needs to be taken into account.

Process migration is the act of transferring a process between two machines (Dejan S. et. al., 2000). Among others it enables fault resilience which is very important for distributed systems and supercomputers. Migration improves the fault resilience of a system on abnormal and unstable situations e.g. a partially failed node, or in the case of long-running applications when failures of different kinds (network, devices) are probable. Fault resilience is frequently mentioned as a benefit of process migration. So far the major contribution of process migration for fault resilience is through combination with checkpointing mechanisms, such as in Condor (Litzkow, M. and Solomon, M., 1992).

Failures play an important role in the implementation of process migration as they can happen on a source or target machine or even on the communication medium. It should be noted the various migration schemes are more or less sensitive to each type of failure. Migration can be considered as a trade-off between efficiency and reliability, since overusing migration solutions may have a negative impact on fault resilience and of course on the total system efficiency. Fault resilience can be improved in several ways e.g. by maintaining process state on both the source and destination sites until the destination site instance is successfully promoted to a regular process. We present below the fault tolerance related characteristics for the most important systems that implement process migration base on the survey conducted by Dejan S. Milojicic et al., (2000).

An initial process migration approach was implemented in MOSIX systems (Barak, A., Guday, S., and Wheeler, R. G., 1993) where nodes can dynamically join and leave a MOSIX cluster at will. A unique feature of MOSIX is that it operates on the process-level, in contrast with the other approaches that operate on the job-level. Following a process-level approach the system adapts and redistributes during runtime the workload to the computational nodes when the number of processes of a job and/or their demands changes. The advantage of MOSIX based solutions if for parallel jobs. In addition, the resent versions of MOSIX enabled Linux Kernels allow applications to start initially on workstation or a cluster and then run in remote nodes on other clusters, e.g. on Clouds, without pre-copying files to these remote nodes, providing among other, fault resilience capabilities.

Sprite process migration (Douglas, F., 1987) was rather intolerant of fault since there are cases during migration that a failure could result in the termination of the migrating process. En example for this is when open files have to be moved to the target machine. In addition after migration, the failure of either the home machine or the process's current host could result in the termination of the process. Also there was no facility to migrate away from a home machine that was about to be shut down, since there would always be some residual dependencies on that machine.

The fault tolerance capabilities of Mach task migration (Milojicic, D. et. al., 1993) were limited by the default transfer strategy, but even more by the implemented Distributed Inter-Process Communication - DIPC and Distributed Memory Management - DMM modules. Both modules heavily employ the lazy evaluation principle, leaving residual dependencies throughout the nodes of a distributed system. For example, in the case of DIPC, proxies of the receive capabilities remain on the source node after receive capability is migrated to a remote node while in the case of DMM, the established paging paths remain bound

to the source node even after performing copying of pages to the destination node.

Redundancy

Redundancy is a technique used to increase the reliability of a system by replicating components so that for the system to fail completely, all replicated components need to fail at the same time. Depending on the nature of the component to be made fail-safe, there are different approaches to achieve redundancy.

Redundancy types can be categorized as follows:

- *Stand-by*
  - *Cold:* In Stand-by redundancy concepts, one component has one or more identical replicated components. When a malfunction is detected, operation is transferred to the Stand-by component. In cold stand-by, the second component is off or not synchronized with the first one, which might have an impact on resilience depending on the application, due to the large downtime.
  - *Hot:* The second component performs the same tasks in parallel so that the downtime is minimized when a failure is detected.
- *Modular:* Several systems work in parallel and the output is chosen by voting. More than three replicas are needed for this approach.
- *M:N redundant*: It is modular system with N replicas backed-up by M stand-by replicas.

Fault Tolerant Servers

In the era of SOIs and cloud computing the demand of server systems to be *up and running* all the time is even higher, something that is translated in technical level to increased demand of high availability servers. The high availability systems cost in the past millions of dollars and the target organizations for such investments were mainly the telecom and financial industries. The recent years, the market conditions have changed and the fault tolerant server systems are getting affordable for customers with usual internet applications such as retail transactions.

Fault tolerant server systems include redundant components that run the same set of operations in parallel, at the same time, so that if one component fails, the other picks up and the system keeps running. High-end systems such as NonStop servers from HP (HP, 2010) are massively parallel systems that run two copies of every job running on the server. In this approach, the system can have better protection against software faults but at a lower cost than traditional fault tolerant boxes.

HP NonStop technology provides 24/7 application availability out of the box and allow the most critical and complex processes to run continuously in a straightforward manner. To this direction enterprise businesses are able to boost the performance and efficiency of their data centers while are significantly lowering their cost per transaction. The Integrity NonStop BladeSystem doubles the performance of previous high-end NonStop systems in half the footprint while providing the same trusted 24/7 NonStop availability, scalability, and data integrity.

One of the first companies that produced such lower-priced systems was Stratus Technologies with the ftServer Systems (http://www.stratus.com). Stratus servers deliver five nines (99.999%) availability. The Stratus approach to availability is automatic and transparent for the users since every aspect of a Stratus system is designed and implements to provide high availability levels.

Another company with fault tolerant server solutions is NEC. NEC Fault Tolerant (FT) servers, (2010) provide an innovative solution to address planned and unplanned downtime for the most important applications. NEC server systems are able to deliver continuous uptime through fully redundant and modular hardware and provide high availability through hardware redundancy in all components: CPU, memory, motherboards, I/O, hard disk drives, and cooling fans.

According to NEC: *"IT industry trends indicate that virtual machine densities per server are increasing as more applications and users are consolidated onto virtualized servers"* as it will be presented in next section. However, many IT organizations are concerned that if the host server fails there is a risk of losing all virtual machines. Modern FT servers are able to overcome these concerns providing high and scalable CPU performance for each virtual machine and continuous operation-without data loss and high performance for applications even in the cases of the worst failure scenarios.

Virtualization

Platform virtualization is performed on a given hardware platform by host software (a control program), which creates a simulated computer environment, a virtual machine, for its guest software. The guest software is not limited to user applications and many hosts allow the execution of complete operating systems. In virtualization environments, the guest software executes as if it were running directly on the physical hardware accessing the physical system resources (such as the network access, display, keyboard, and disk storage) in a transparent way. However guest software and operating systems are often restricted from accessing specific peripheral devices, or may be limited to a subset of the device's native capabilities, depending on the hardware access policy implemented by the virtualization host.

VMware

According to VMware (http://www.vmware.com), a key player in virtualization area, *"as server virtualization becomes commonplace in the enterprise, IT organizations are growing increasingly reliant on the associated virtualization benefits: higher server consolidation ratios, better resource utilization, lower power consumption, greater workload mobility via technologies such as VMotion, and the general ease of system management"*

However, these benefits also introduce new availability requirements to virtualized environments. As more business-critical workloads are deployed in virtual machines, a catastrophic failure of a single physical server might lead to an interruption of a large number of services.

The advancements of VMware Fault Tolerance (FT), (2010) are based on the idea of building high availability directly into the ESX hypervisor and in that way they provide hardware style fault tolerance to virtual machines eliminating the need of custom hardware or software modifications in operating system or application level. VMware fault tolerance solution is based on the VMware vLockstep technology. The various virtual machines are continuously synchronized during runtime with secondary ones using the vLockstep technology. As explained by VMware, the secondary virtual machine resides on a different host, executes exactly the same sequence of virtual (guest) instructions as the primary virtual machine and is ready to take over at any time without any data loss or interruption of service should the primary fail. Even though that the virtual machines are managed as a single unit, they are hosted on different physical machines with the possibility of more distributed approaches in physical and geographical level such as different buildings. The advantage of this solution is that system administrators can easily implement fault tolerance with just a few clicks minimizing deployment, configuration, licensing, and operating costs without touching the guest operating systems and applications.

VMware fault tolerance solution is able to increase the total system availability and recover from failures and any abnormal operation. The basic requirement for successful migration of virtual machines is the correct synchronization of their states. The vLockstep technology guarantees that the states of the primary and secondary virtual machines are identical at any point by having the primary and the secondary execute identical sequences of x86 instructions. In order to detect any hardware failures of the physical machine running (either the primary or the secondary virtual machine) and trigger the necessary migration actions, the hypervisors on the physical machines establish a system of heartbeat signals and mutual monitoring during the vLockstep process. In that way any failure of either physical machine is noticed by the other in a timely fashion and it is able to take over and continue running the protected virtual machine seamlessly via transparent failover.

XEN

Another approach that provides fault detection and tolerance is available for the XEN hypervisor (http://www.xen.org) named Kemari project (http://www.osrg.net/kemari). Kemari aims to keep virtual machines transparently running in times of hardware failures and to achieve this objective a synchronization mechanism is proposed. There are two main approaches proposed in Kemari to synchronizing the state of virtual machines across physical machines. The first approach is lock-stepping, in which external events are logged on the primary virtual machine and replayed on the secondary virtual machine. Although this approach enables efficient synchronization, it requires complicated implementation to handle differences between processor families. The second approach is continuous checkpointing, in which the state of the primary virtual machine is frequently transferred to the secondary virtual machine. However, outputs to devices are delayed for a specific period of time because they are buffered to keep the state of the virtual machines and the attached devices consistent.

Kemari was designed to take advantage of both approaches. It transfers the state of the primary virtual machine to the secondary virtual machine when an event occurs. In that way, it enables the primary virtual machine and the secondary virtual machine to be kept in sync with less complexity compared to lock-stepping. Furthermore, Kemari does not require external buffering mechanisms that impose output latencies, which is necessary in continuous checkpointing and synchronizes the virtual machines when the primary virtual machine is about to send an event to some device.

At the point a primary virtual machine tries send en event to a device such as to read or write to the storage, it outputs an event to the storage. As explained before, given that this event will change the state of the storage device, the system will pause the primary virtual machine, and update the secondary one to the current state of the primary virtual machine. After the synchronization, the primary virtual machine continues is operation and therefore the secondary virtual machine can continue transparently when the primary virtual machine fails. In case of a hardware failure, the system switches to the secondary virtual machine, which will start running from the latest state for which the secondary virtual machine and the virtual disk are consistent.

REMUS

Remus (Brendan Cully et. al.,2008) is a software system that provides OS and application agnostic high availability on commodity hardware. One of the advantages of Remus is the fault tolerance capabilities with stateful system migration and small downtime. Remus includes mechanisms that synchronize continuously the states of the primary and backup virtual machines providing high availability for mid and low-end systems.

The Remus systems implement active-passive configuration for paired servers based on three pillars:

- Replication using virtualization solutions,
- Speculative execution decoupling the external output from the synchronization points and
- Asynchronous synchronization.

Remus team exploits virtualization to run pairs of servers, synchronized using the lock-step technique enhanced with additional functionality to ensure that the primary and secondary virtual machines are at the same state. The problems of this approach is that on one hand this solution is highly architecture-specific in order to interpret the external events and on the other it introduces severe overhead for multi-processor systems that require shared memory communication between the processors. In addition, given that it is likely the state of a machine is different if the machine is rolled back and executes the operations for the same input, the state the virtual machines should be synchronized once the output of the primary becomes externally visible. To this direction, Remus system, buffers the output performing computation speculatively ahead of synchronization points, allowing the system administrators to decide between output latency and runtime overhead. Implementing buffering for the output, replication can take place asynchronously with overlapped execution between the primary and backup virtual machines allowing efficient overall operation and high performance.

Amazon Web Services

The Amazon Web Services cloud infrastructure also offer fault tolerance capabilities (AWS, 2010). The application developers can build fault tolerant applications by placing the Amazon EC2 instances in multiple Availability Zones. Availability Zones are distinct locations that are engineered to be insulated from failures in other zones and provide inexpensive, low latency network connectivity between them and in that way by launching instances in separate Availability Zones, the applications can be protected from failure of a single location.

Another solution to achieve even more fault tolerance with less manual intervention is the Elastic Load Balancing functionality that can be implemented. Elastic Load balance can provide improved fault tolerance by managing the various computing instances and automatically balance traffic across multiple instances and multiple Availability Zones in order to ensure that only healthy Amazon EC2 instances receive traffic. An Elastic Load Balancer can be setup to load balance incoming application traffic across instances in a single Availability Zone or multiple Availability Zones and then the Elastic Load Balancing can detect which ones have a healthy status and which not. When it detects unhealthy instances, it no longer routes traffic to those unhealthy ones and distributes the load across the remaining healthy Amazon EC2 instances. The developer has the option to set up instances in various Availability zones and in the extreme case that all Amazon EC2 instances of the application in a particular Availability Zone are unhealthy, Elastic Load Balancing forwards the traffic to the healthy Amazon EC2 instances in those other zones. As soon as the original Amazon EC2 instances are restored to a healthy state, load balancing will redistribute the load and forward the traffic back to them.

Network Fault Tolerance

The network fault tolerance aspects of Service Oriented Infrastructures are critical for the smooth operation and high availability of applications and services. A wide variety of approaches–detailed in Medhi (1999)–can be implemented for detection and recovery of network failures. The objective of the fault tolerance methods in networks is to initially identify if something is wrong in the communication medium between the sender and the receiver and in sequel recover from this situation. There are several fault tolerance solutions, path-based, link-based, hybrid and solution in higher levels of network stack. For example backbone networks implement both path and link based solutions exploiting the advantages of both. In most cases, the network protocols already include redundancy techniques for the data transmission.

The failure detection methods implemented in backbone networks are related with the overall strategy for restoring circuits in cases of failures in links and networking components. The path-based solutions do not provide information for failure localization and careful investigation is required to detect the exact location and nature of the fault. In addition, with this solution the failure information should be transmitted to both endpoints of the path to achieve fault detection which introduces further delay. The link-based solutions provide rapid response to failures with the failure information to be available to both endpoints of a link, which can be also exploited for dynamic routing and reconstruction of the future paths.

The aforementioned strategies are also implemented for the network fault tolerance functionality of SOIs since in these infrastructures a high number of failures come from the communication medium. The communication problems can vary from permanent failures to QoS degradation such as increased delay and jitter. An approach to overcome permanent failures is to partition the system in independent parts to easily isolate faults and avoid conflicts and interference of faults in many parts of the system. The cases of intermittent failures, where messages travelling through a communication medium are lost, reordered, or duplicated which are not always due to hardware failures, are also important for SOIs stability according to Selic B., (2004). For instance, a message may be lost because the system may have temporarily run out of memory for buffering it and message reordering may occur due to successive messages taking different paths through the communication medium. Also duplication can occur in a number of ways such as retransmission due the assumption that the original message was lost. Regarding unreliable communication problems and in order to confirm that a message that was sent by a source component has been received the destination component, a common technique is the positive acknowledgement protocol, where the receiver notifies the sender when it receives a message. However, this approach does not address completely the problem since there is the possibility that the acknowledgement message is lost.

In cases of lost messages, the most common technique for fault detection is by using time-outs for the transmitted messages. If a component does not get a positive acknowledgement within a predefined time interval, it is concluded that the message was lost somewhere between the source and destination. This approach has also drawbacks. There cases where is difficult to distinguish whether a message (or its acknowledgement) is delayed or really lost. Therefore, when the time-out interval is too short, the risk of duplicating messages and reordering is high while if the interval too long, then the system becomes unresponsive.

Even though transmission delays cannot be considered always as failures, there is always a possibility to lead to failures. The message delays can be classified in variable delays (jitter) and in constant delays. In SOIs with increased jitter for communication between the various components, the time it takes for a message to reach its destination may vary significantly affection the smooth operation of applications with high QoS requirements for network. In cases where the transmission delay is constant, the process to fault detection process (to identify if a message has been lost) is easier and based on that fact there are many communication networks designed as synchronous networks. In that way the delay values are fixed and known in advance. However, even in this case if the delays experienced are greater than the time required to change from one state to the next, such as during a migration process,

the information in these messages will be out of date leading to unstable systems.

Therefore the network fault tolerance solutions in Service Oriented Infrastructures have to be tightly coupled with global fault tolerant strategy of the system. Network failures that are not corrected in a reasonable time frame may affect the stability of the platform and to total system failure. In addition, because of the fact that the components of the distributed platforms require continuous communication and synchronization to achieve efficient overall management and operation, the network management should be considered as inextricable part of the system management process. To this direction, the network failures can be reported to higher system management layers that have a complete knowledge of the system status. These failures can be treated in indirect methods triggering corrective actions in other subsystems. For instance, a domain network failure, permanent or transient, which is reported to platform management, may trigger redeployment of the application components and migration of the services to new domain as described before regarding Amazon Web Services. Furthermore, in order to overcome networking failures, distributed management approaches can be applied. These approaches include independent management domains, in which the components in the domain can maintain their stability and upkeep the QoS for applications and services even if the cross or intra-domain networking links in other domains are failing.

CONCLUSION

In this chapter we presented the state of the art mechanisms and techniques for providing fault detection and recovery functionality in Service Oriented Infrastructures. Furthermore we clarified the terminology around the fault detection and recovery concept as well as the main processes taking place to accomplish this objective. In order to achieve the key requirements in Services Oriented Infrastructures for guaranteed QoS and efficient management of applications and resources, fault detection and recovery approaches have to be implemented in such systems and in that frame we examined the available solutions from various perspectives, from the workflows in application layer to the hardware solutions for fault tolerant servers and networking. The analysis of these solutions concluded that the various fault detection and recovery mechanisms of each layer need to be carefully designed and synchronized with each other considering them as fractions of the overall fault detection and recovery strategy of the system. The efficiency of each approach could be significantly enhanced following similar methodologies in the other system layers and orchestrating a comprehensive solution.

REFERENCES

Amazon Web Services. (2010). *Elastic load balancing*. Retrieved from http://aws.amazon.com/ elasticloadbalancing

Barak, A., Guday, S., & Wheeler, R. G. (1993). *The MOSIX distributed operating system: Load balancing for UNIX*. New York, NY: Springer-Verlag, Inc.

Baude, F., Caromel, D., Delbe, C., & Henrio, L. (2005). A hybrid message logging-CIC protocol for constrained checkpointability. *Proceedings of EuroPar* 2005, Lisbon, Portugal.

Castro, M., & Liskov, B. (2002). Practical Byzantine fault tolerance and proactive recovery. *ACM Transactions on Computer Systems*, *20*(4), 398–461. doi:10.1145/571637.571640

Cully, B., Lefebvre, G., Meyer, D., Feeley, M., Hutchinson, N., & Warfield, A. (2008). Remus: High availability via asynchronous virtual machine replication. *Proceedings of the 5th USENIX Symposium on Networked Systems Design and Implementation*, (pp. 161-174). April 16-18, 2008, San Francisco, California.

Ding, S. X. (2008). *Model-based Fault Diagnosis Techniques: Design Schemes, Algorithms, and Tools*. Berlin: Springer.

Douglis, F. (1987). *Process migration in the Sprite operating system. (Technical Report, UMI Order Number: CSD-87-343)*. University of California at Berkeley.

Fahringer, T., Prodan, R., Duan, R., Nerieri, F., Podlipnig, S., Qin, J., et al. Wieczorek, M. (2005). *ASKALON: A Grid application development and computing environment*. The 6th IEEE/ACM International Workshop on Grid Computing.

HP. (2010). *HP integrity nonstop server evolution*. Retrieved from http://www.hp.com/ products1/ evolution/ nonstop

Hwang, S., & Kesselman, C. (2003). *Grid workflow: A flexible failure handling framework for the Grid*. In 12th IEEE International Symposium on High Performance Distributed Computing (HPDC'03), Los Alamitos, CA: IEEE CS Press. Seattle, Washington, USA, USA, June 22 - 24, 2003.

IFIP. (2010). *10.4 working group on dependable computing and fault tolerance*. Retrieved from http://www.dependability.org/ wg10.4

Knight, J. C., & Leveson, N. G. (1986). An experimental evaluation of independence in multi-version programming. *Transactions on Software Engineering*, *12*, 96–109.

Litzkow, M., & Solomon, M. (1992). Supporting checkpointing and process migration outside the UNIX kernel. *Proceedings of the USENIX Winter Conference*, (pp. 283–290).

Medhi, D. (1999). Network reliability and fault tolerance. In *Wiley encyclopedia of electrical and electronics engineering*. New York, NY: John Wiley. doi:10.1002/047134608X.W5322

Milojicic, D. S., Douglas, F., Paindaveine, Y., Wheeler, R., & Zhou, S. (2000). Process migration. *ACM Computing Surveys*, *32*(3). doi:10.1145/367701.367728

Milojicic, D. S., Giese, P., & Zint, W. (1993). *Experiences with load distribution on top of the mach microkernel*. In USENIX Systems on USENIX Experiences with Distributed and Multiprocessor Systems - Volume 4 (San Diego, California, September 22 - 23, 1993). USENIX Association, Berkeley, CA, 2-2.

NEC. (2010). *Fault tolerant (FT) servers*. Retrieved from http://www.necam.com/Servers/FT

Randell, B., Lee, P., & Treleaven, P. C. (1978). Reliability issues in computing system design. *ACM Computing Surveys*, *10*(2), 123–165. doi:10.1145/356725.356729

Selic, B. (2004). *Fault tolerance techniques for distributed systems*. IBM Technical Library.

VMware. (2010). *Fault tolerance* (FT). Retrieved from http://www.vmware.com/resources/techresources/1094

Chapter 15
Real–Time Attributes in Operating Systems

Tommaso Cucinotta
Scuola Superiore Sant'Anna, Italy

Spyridon V. Gogouvitis
National Technical University of Athens, Greece

ABSTRACT

General-Purpose Operating Systems (GPOSes) are being used more and more extensively to support interactive, real-time, and distributed applications, as found in the multimedia domain. In fact, the wide availability of supported multimedia devices and protocols, together with the wide availability of libraries and tools for handling multimedia contents, make them an almost ideal platform for the development of this kind of complex applications. However, contrarily to Real-Time Operating Systems, General-Purpose ones used to lack some important functionality needed for providing proper scheduling guarantees to application processes. Recently, the increasing use of GPOSes for multimedia applications is gradually pushing OS developers towards enriching the kernel of a GPOS so as to provide more and more real-time functionality, thus enhancing the performance and responsiveness of hosted time-sensitive applications. In this chapter, an overview is performed over the efforts done in the direction of enriching GPOSes with real-time capabilities, with a particular focus on the Linux OS. Due to its open-source nature and wide diffusion and availability, Linux is one of the most widely used OSes for such experimentations.

INTRODUCTION

New generation interactive distributed applications have significant demands on processing, storage and networking capabilities, as well as stringent timing requirements, such as various multimedia, virtual collaboration and e-learning applications. These are, among others, types of applications that have been undergoing in the last few years a very steep demand on the side of end-to-end interactivity level, response time, and throughput. This is also due to the growing availability of affordable broadband Internet connections. This allowed people to realize that most of the activities they used to carry on through offline workflows (especially when relatively high

DOI: 10.4018/978-1-60960-827-9.ch015

data volumes were involved) now could be done within on-line collaborative systems, in a much more interactive way.

For a long time, these applications have been made available to end-users in the form of costly professional solutions running on dedicated hardware. BHowever, the growth in computation capabilities of computing systems has led to a growing interest in providing such applications in the form of applications that may be run on General-Purpose Operating Systems (GPOSes). This allows for sharing a set of physical resources among different applications or application instances, thus scaling down the costs needed to deploy and run them.

Unfortunately, GPOSes are not designed to provide the run-time support that is necessary for meeting timing requirements of individual applications. In fact, in the traditional hard real-time domain, a Real-Time Operating System (RTOS) is used for such purpose. A RTOS usually provides those features that allow for a well-known, predictable and analysable timing behaviour of hosted applications: all kernel segments are characterized through well-known worst-case durations, scheduling latencies and interrupt latencies which may be controlled through the appropriate tuning of the interrupt and process schedulers. A set of real-time scheduling policies is available for the system designer and programmers. Time may be measured (and timers may fire) with a high precision (typically sub-millisecond) while there are tools available for Worst-Case Execution Time (WCET) estimation and (off-line) analysis, as well as for schedulability analysis. Unfortunately, such OSes are designed for embedded control applications, thus they imply serious constraints on the supported hardware and available high-level software infrastructures.

Therefore, in recent years, various efforts have been done towards the integration of real-time technologies within GPOSes, particularly within Linux, for the availability of its kernel as open-source and its worldwide diffusion.

Various drawbacks make the Linux kernel, as well as most of the GPOSes, particularly unsuitable for running real-time applications: the monolithic structure of the kernel and the wide variety of drivers that may be loaded within; the impossibility to keep under control all the non-preemptable sections possibly added by such drivers; the general structure of the interrupt management core framework that privileges portability with respect to latencies; and others.

As a result, the latency experienced by time-sensitive activities can be as large as tens or hundreds of milliseconds. This makes GPOSes non-suitable for hard real-time applications with tight timing constraints. Though, soft real-time applications may run quite well within such an environment, especially when the original kernel is modified so as to integrate the necessary real-time capabilities.

Objective of this chapter is to provide an overview of the approaches appeared in the research literature aiming to integrate real-time capabilities within General-Purpose Operating Systems, with a particular focus on Linux.

BACKGROUND

Although not being a real-time system, the 2.6 Linux kernel includes a set of features making it particularly suitable for soft real-time applications. First, it is a fully preemptable kernel, like most of the existing real-time operating systems, and a lot of effort has been spent on reducing the length of non-preemptable sections (the major source of kernel latencies). It is noteworthy that the 2.6 kernel series introduced a new scheduler with a bounded execution time, resulting in a highly decreased scheduling latency. Also, in the latest kernel series, a modular framework has been introduced that allows for an easier integration of other scheduling policies. Second, although being a general-purpose time-sharing kernel, it includes such real-time extensions to the POSIX standard (POSIX 2004) as: the SCHED_FIFO and SCHED_RR process scheduling policies, the priority inheritance protocol for avoiding the well-known priority inversion problem, the real-time POSIX extensions related to signals and timers. Also, there seems to be a growing interest in implementing the SCHED_SPORADIC real-time scheduling class as well. These features may result useful for developing real-time systems. Third, the recently introduced support in the kernel mainstream of the support for high-resolution timers is of paramount importance for the realization of high-precision customized scheduling mechanisms, and for the general performance of soft real-time applications.

Furthermore, recent patches proposed by the group of Ingo Molnar to the interrupt-management core framework, aimed at encapsulating device drivers within kernel threads, are particularly relevant as such approaches would highly increase predictability of the kernel behaviour.

Concerning the process scheduler, recently it has undergone two major changes: from the 2.4 series to the 2.6 series, the scheduler was reengineered so as to cut its computational complexity, from linear in the number of tasks to the so advertised O(1) scheduler. From the 2.6.23, a new modular framework has been introduced by Ingo Molnar, along with a complete rewrite of the default scheduling policy (the SCHED_OTHER POSIX class), now called Completely Fair Scheduler (CFS). It basically aims to exhibit fairness properties among running processes, resembling a Generalized Proportional Fair (GPF) system (in its use of a timestamping mechanism), but unfortunately it does not correspond to any algorithm with well-known properties in scheduling literature. Tasks are characterized by a configurable weight, and a run-time quantity called vruntime. Each time a task is executed for a time t, its vruntime value is incremented by t*task_weight/total_weight, where total_weight is the total weight of the currently running tasks. When a task is reactivated, it is assigned a vruntime that varies according to

the configuration of the system and to various heuristics, which tend to give a small vruntime to interactive processes.. Finally, tasks are scheduled in increasing vruntime order. As of now, no formal guarantees have been derived for the service provided to individual tasks scheduled using CFS.

Also, the current Linux kernel has a partial support for hierarchical scheduling, a feature typical of real-time OSes. Both real-time and SCHED_OTHER tasks can be organized in groups and for each group it is possible to limit the CPU time consumed by its real-time tasks, as well as configure the CPU share used by its SCHED_OTHER tasks.

Due to the internal architecture of the scheduler (that is not fully hierarchical in a traditional sense) a combination of the two effects cannot be obtained. In other words, it is not possible to limit the CPU time of a whole group (real-time + SCHED_OTHER tasks) and it is not possible to limit the CPU share assigned to a whole group. The intention of enhancing the real-time limiting (throttling) mechanism has been expressed on public discussions, but no code has been written in that direction, as of now.

Concluding, the mainline Linux kernel (a.k.a., Vanilla), despite recent improvements in the scope of real-time support, currently lacks a CPU scheduler able to fulfil the timing requirements of increasingly needed distributed real-time applications.

In what follows, related work in the area of real-time support for GPOSes is presented. Various modifications of GPOSes have appeared in the literature for supporting real-time scheduling policies at the kernel-level, for various types of resources. First, related work in the area of real-time scheduling for the CPU is surveyed. Then, approaches in which scheduling of multiple heterogeneous, possibly distributed, resources is integrated into a common framework, are described. Then, the most relevant and recent approaches, among the identified ones, are described in somewhat more detail, for the sake of completeness.

APPROACHES, IMPLEMENTATIONS AND COMPARISONS

Real-Time CPU Scheduling in GPOSes

Various GPOS kernels exist that are compliant with the POSIX real-time extensions (POSIX 2004). However, the main drawback of such extensions is that there are various optional parts, and most of the implementations limit themselves to Fixed-Priority scheduling, sometimes with the addition of high-resolution timers and the Priority Inheritance protocol for avoiding Priority Inversion (Sha 1990). Also, one key feature which is usually not implemented is the temporal isolation property (Buttazzo 2005), such as provided by the Sporadic Server (POSIX 2004) scheduling policy. Without such a mechanism, a higher priority task runs undisturbed until it blocks, independently of the computation time that may have been considered at system analysis/design time. This results in the potential disruption of the guarantees offered to lower priority tasks. Therefore, such approaches are suitable for the traditional hard real-time settings where everything running into the system has been thoroughly checked, if not formally proved.

For real-time scheduling of the CPU, hard real-time modifications to the Linux kernel have been proposed, like RT-Linux (http://www.rtlinuxfree.com), proposed by Yodaiken et al. (Yodaiken 1997) and RTAI (http://www.rtai.org), proposed by Dozio et al. (2003). In these approaches, a real-time micro-kernel layer is added between the real hardware and the Linux OS, which runs as the background/idle activity whenever there are no hard real-time tasks active in the system. This allows for respecting the very tight timing constraints (microsecond-level) typical of industrial automation and robotic applications. Main drawbacks of such approaches are due to the limitations that (hard) real-time applications exploiting real-time scheduling are subject to,

i.e., they are typically required to be written as kernel modules. Therefore, these hardly constitute solutions suitable for the large class of multimedia and interactive applications, which would greatly benefit from real-time scheduling policies. However, a detailed description of these approaches follows below, due to their historical importance.

In order to overcome these limitations, other approaches targeted explicitly soft real-time applications, by adding a real-time scheduling policy as an extension to a GPOS kernel itself, typically comprising a temporal isolation mechanism. Such an approach, which is also exploited by the work in this paper, allows for the coexistence of soft real-time and best-effort applications, all within a GPOS kernel with potentially long non-preemptive sections, what leads to the impossibility to provide hard real-time guarantees. However, for soft real-time applications like multimedia ones, that approaches allowed for great enhancements achieved on the side of the predictability in the temporal behaviour exhibited by applications, which resulted in significant improvements in the QoS experienced by users. An overview of these approaches has been carried out by Gopalan (2001). Just to mention a few, remarkable works are the ones for adding resource reservations (Mercer 1993) to Microsoft Windows NT by Jones (1999) (Rialto/NT), and the ones by Rajkumar et al. in the Linux/RK project (Rajkumar 1998). The latter constitutes a modification to the Linux kernel, largely inspired by prior work of the same authors on RT-Mach. Such code has also been designed so as to be portable across multiple GPOS kernels (Oikawa 1999), but it has been implemented on Linux only, to the best of authors' knowledge. An effort on portability of a real-time scheduler across various Operating Systems (from Microsoft, UNIX and Linux families), is constituted by the DSRT scheduler (http://cairo.cs.uiuc.edu/software/DSRT-2/dsrt-2.html) by Yuan et al. (Yuan 2003). However, similarly to the GRACE (Vardhan 2005) series of architectures, the focus seems to be limited exclusively on CPU scheduling.

Also, soft real-time schedulers for Linux have been investigated and implemented in the context of various European Projects like the CBS implementation on Linux developed during the OCERA Project, and its subsequent evolution, the AQuoSA (Palopoli 2009) scheduler for Linux, developed by Tommaso Cucinotta during the FRESCOR Project. More details about OCERA, FRESCOR and AQuoSA follow below dedicated sections.

More recently, the IRMOS Project (Interactive Real-Time Multimedia Applications on Service-Oriented Infrastructures, European Project n. FP7-214777, http://www.irmosproject.eu), is also investigating on the use of real-time scheduling on high-performance Linux machines, with a strong focus on virtualized distributed real-time applications. In the context of IRMOS, the most recent real-time extensions to the Linux scheduler have been proposed: Faggioli et al. proposed a POSIX compliant implementation (Faggioli 2008) of the FP-based Sporadic Server algorithm (and variations) for enhancing the current primitive throttling mechanism of the Linux kernel with improved possibility of predictability, temporal isolation and analysability; Checconi et al. designed a novel hierarchical hybrid scheduling framework (Checconi 2009), based on a combination of partitioned EDF and global FP, designed so as to fit as much as possible (and impact as less as possible) in the current real-time scheduling class code base. A similar work is being done in the context of the ACTORS Project (Adaptivity and Control of Resources in Embedded Systems, European Project n.216586, http://www.actors-project.eu), but with a focus on single-node embedded multi-core systems, without any distributed features. Here, both partitioned EDF (Faggioli 2009) and Global EDF (Lelli 2010) are being investigated.

Integrated Scheduling of Multiple Resources

Prior works exist that integrate real-time scheduling of heterogeneous resources and an architecture for their management for real-time applications, like the one by Stankovic et al. (Zhang 2002), or Hola QoS by Valls et al. (2002). The latter is an architecture specifically tied to the needs of consumer electronics embedded multimedia systems, providing flexible resource management and adaptivity. The Eclipse/BSD (Blanquer 1999) Project integrates real-time scheduling of CPU, network and disk access, and exposes to applications a file-system based user-space interface. However, the project does not deal with distributed real-time applications. More recently, Gopalan et al. (2007) proposed MURALS, a distributed real-time architecture built upon TimeSys Linux (http://www.timesys.com), supporting real-time applications with end-to-end constraints making use of distributed heterogeneous resources, such as disks, CPUs and network links. The architecture embeds a global admission control scheme that takes into account the entire dependency graph of the application.

The above mentioned Nahrstedt research group also worked on QualMan (Nahrstedt 1998), a distributed real-time resource allocation architecture supporting also network, disk and memory allocation, with prototype implementation on the Solaris OS. However, the same authors highlight that the modularity degree of their architecture is somewhat limited and that it would benefit from a CORBA-oriented design.

In fact, the CORBA specification has been extended to address reusability in the CORBA Component Model (CCM), which also considers QoS aspects. For example, this has been implemented in the Component-Integrated ACE ORB (Schmidt 2003). TAO (Schmidt 1997) constitutes a C++ implementation of the Real-Time CORBA specification (Wolfe 1997), which exposes fundamental functionality of distributed real-time applications via the CORBA paradigm.

Also, TAO has been integrated with QuO (Krishnamurty 2001), a framework that exploits the capabilities of CORBA to reduce the impact of QoS management on the application code.

The result (Schantz 2003) is a middleware for adaptive QoS control using real-time scheduling facilities at the computation and network levels. Recently, such an architecture has been used by Shankaran et al. within their HiDRA (Shankaran 2006) architecture for hierarchical management of multiple resources in distributed real-time systems. However, these works are focused on issues related to the monitoring of the run-time application behaviour, and the dynamic adaptation of resource allocations and/or application behaviour to their continuously changing needs, so they consider only marginally issues strictly related to the low-level mechanisms needed for guaranteeing the respect of timing constraints needed by real-time applications. Eide et al. (Eide 2004) also presented a CORBA-based middle-ware for the management of the CPU in distributed systems, however they didn't consider other resources.

Furthermore, it is worth to mention the architecture (Cucinotta 2009) developed in the context of the RI-MACS project for distributed real-time applications in the factory automation domain. The architecture relies on the capabilities of service-oriented infrastructures for providing discovery of resources and their real-time capabilities, self-configuration, fault-tolerance and scheduling parameters negotiation. The RI-MACS architecture also exploits AQuoSA (Palopoli 2009) as the low-level CPU scheduler (as this work does), but it lacks both the support for so many multiple heterogeneous resources as the present paper has (cable and wireless network, CPU, disk), and the well-defined unified API enabling applications to exploit such real-time capabilities.

In 2002, Ravindran introduced a conceptual framework (Ravindran 2008) encompassing the elements necessary in a middleware for distributed real-time applications: a system description language comprising real-time and QoS requirements specification, and run-time components for management of resources, fault detection and recovery, and detection of violations of real-time constraints and recovery actions (i.e., dynamic changes in the resources allocation). However, the work is quite abstract, and even if it refers to a prototype implementation in C on the Solaris OS, it does not address some essential details like the type of scheduling that is used at the resources level, or whether or not the implementation is anyway portable. Furthermore, the Ravindran framework highlights the need for the capability of migrating applications across nodes for tolerating hardware failure at the host level, or for enhancing the performance of applications whose workload requirements is deviating from the one predicted at deployment time, but it does not give any detail on how such a mechanism could be implemented and supported by the middleware (i.e., there is no discussion about the possible use of virtualization technologies or check-pointing). Also, the framework uses TCP/IP primitives for communications at the middleware level. Ttherefore, it has to re-implement such features as service registration and discovery, which are standard in a modern distributed middleware like CORBA.

More recently, Rajkumar et al. (Lakshmanan 2008) proposed Distributed Resource Kernels, an extension of Linux/RK adding support for distributed real-time applications. Linux/RK is geared towards a model of non-modifications to applications, because real-time support for legacy applications is one of its crucial features. So, applications are not necessarily aware that they are receiving service-guarantees by the OS, but rather the system is administered and configured in such a way that real-time scheduling services, for the various resources, is automatically activated each time a given application is launched in the system. Major drawbacks of Linux/RK are that, for improved efficiency, the kernel includes functionality for the distributed management and allocation of resources, by means of dedicated kernel threads which exchange messages over UDP in order to communicate to each other. Therefore, the kernel includes various components that are traditionally present at a higher level, in user-space, in other OSes, like an HTTP server, a DNS-like

Figure 1. The RT-Linux Architecture

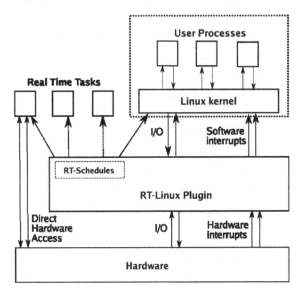

server, and an NTP-like server. Implementation of such services in user-space, instead, is highly beneficial and recommended for security and robustness purposes.

RTLinuxFree and RTAI

RTLinuxFree is the evolution of RT-Linux (see Figure 1), a modification (patch) to the Linux kernel aimed to support hard real-time applications, initially developed by Victor Yodaiken at University of New Mexico, then carried on by FSMLabs, which was acquired by WindRiver in 2007. It works as a small executive with a hard real-time scheduler that, in addition to the hard real-time tasks, executes the entire Linux OS (both the kernel and the user-space applications) as one of its low priority tasks (Setz 2007).

RTLinuxFree adds a hard real-time executive between the hardware and the Linux kernel, which takes direct control of the interrupts of the hardware, passing them to the Linux OS only when they are not relevant for the hard real-time tasks. This way, hard real-time tasks run undisturbed and without interferences from the entire Linux OS.

Real Time Application Interface (RTAI) is a modification of the Linux kernel made by Prof. Paolo Mantegazza from Dipartimento di Ingegneria Aerospaziale at Politecnico di Milano (DI-APM). RTAI is an open-source project that builds on the original idea of RT-Linux, but has been considerably enhanced. RTAI allows to uniformly mix hard and soft real-time by symmetrically integrating the scheduling of RTAI proper kernel tasks, Linux kernel threads and user space tasks. However, similarly to RT-Linux, in RTAI Linux tasks run in the background with respect to the hard real-time kernel. Linux only executes when there are no real-time tasks to run, and the real-time kernel is inactive. Furthermore, the Linux OS can never block interrupts or prevent itself from being preempted by the real-time kernel (Ripoll 2002).

Both approaches aim to integrate hard real-time tasks and standard Linux tasks within the same system. This allows, for example, running a set of real-time tasks that control an industrial plant together with the high-level software infrastructure and applications that allow monitoring of the plant from remote or from complex GUI-oriented interfaces. The main drawback of these approaches is that the real-time tasks cannot really exploit the full power of the hosting GPOS, and can only access a very limited set of peripherals (e.g. serial ports). A complex multimedia streaming application, that needs at least TCP/IP networking, heavy use of the disk and access to audio and video adapters would not be suitable to run on such a system.

OCERA and FRESCOR

A different approach has been undertaken in the open-source Linux/OCERA variant, developed as a result of the OCERA (Open Components for Embedded Real-time Applications, European Project n. IST2001-35102, http://www.ocera.org) European project, that embeds within the Linux OS itself a reservation-based scheduling policy (Mercer 1993) typical of real-time systems. This way, standard Linux applications, making use of the full set of resources available through OS services and libraries, may at the same time exploit the benefits of predictable timing behavior and temporal isolation for those threads that are most computation intensive. Actually, OCERA provided a customized distribution of the Linux kernel suitable for both hard and soft real-time activities, that integrates: RT-Linux, a set of drivers useful in the context of industrial control (i.e., for the CAN Bus), Linux with soft real-time extensions at the scheduler level enriched with a feedback-based QoS controller useful for continuous adaptation of the scheduling parameters to the actual task requirements. A unified kernel configuration interface allows one to decide what components to compile in the OCERA kernel.

An approach similar to OCERA has also been adopted by Linux/RT, a commercial variant of Linux supported by TimeSys Inc. and based upon the original Linux Resource Kernel (Linux/RK) from Carnegie Mellon University (Rajkumar 1998). In Linux/RT the kernel has been directly modified so to provide CPU, network and disk reservations directly to user processes. This allows the provision of timing guarantees to legacy Linux applications in a transparent way. Moreover, it is possible to access a specific API to take advantage of the reservations and of quality of service management facilities.

The OCERA soft real-time scheduler inside the Linux kernel has been almost rewritten within the on-going FRESCOR (Framework for Real-Time Embedded Systems based on Contracts, European Project n. FP6/2005/IST/5-034026, http://www.frescor.org) European project, also due to the main changes undergone by the kernel from the 2.4 to the 2.6 series, resulting in the AQuoSA framework, described below. Furthermore, the FRESCOR project focused on development of components for supporting distributed and multi-resource applications, and realizing more complex QoS control strategies that also account for power-scaling issues typical of embedded applications, and that are also suitable for dis-

tributed embedded applications. In fact, as of now, in FRESCOR there are kernel components for providing resource reservation capabilities at the CPU, disk and networking level, that may be accessed through a uniform API designed around the POSIX well-known real-time extensions API. Also, hard real-time components are being developed for hard real-time OSes, in the project.

Generally, the main objective of the FRESCOR project is to develop the enabling technology and infrastructure required to effectively use the most advanced techniques developed for real-time applications with flexible scheduling requirements, in embedded systems design methodologies and tools, providing the necessary elements to target reconfigurable processing modules and reconfigurable distributed architectures.

The approach integrates advanced flexible scheduling techniques directly into an embedded systems design methodology, covering all the levels involved in the implementation, from the OS primitives, through the middleware, up to the application level. This is achieved through a contract model that specifies which are the application requirements with respect to the flexible use of the processing resources in the system, and also what are the resources that must be guaranteed if the component is to be installed into the system, and how the system can distribute any spare capacity that it has, to achieve the highest usage of the available resources.

The main disadvantage of FRESCOR is its focus on embedded systems, so, for example, multiprocessor capabilities of the platform are only marginally addressed, and the Linux components developed at the scheduler level do not support it. Instead, in the context of the IRMOS European Project, a real-time scheduler for Linux has been developed (Checconi 2009) with full support for multi-processor and multi-core platforms.

Figure 2. The AQuoSA architecture

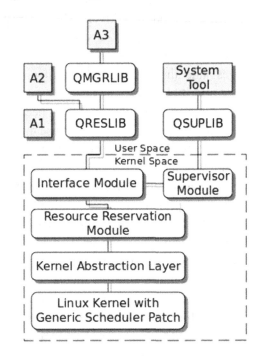

Adaptive Quality of Service Architecture (AQuoSA)

The AQuoSA framework (http://aquosa.source-forge.net) enhances a standard GNU/Linux system with scheduling strategies based on the Resource Reservation techniques. AQuoSA has a layered architecture as depicted in Figure 2.

At the lowest level, there is a small patch (Generic Scheduler Patch, GSP) to the Linux kernel that allows dynamically loaded modules to customize the CPU scheduler behaviour, by intercepting and reacting to scheduling-related events such as: creation and destruction of tasks, blocking and unblocking of tasks on synchronization primitives, receive by tasks of the special SIGSTOP and SIGCONT signals. A Kernel Abstraction Layer (KAL) aims at abstracting the higher layers from the very low-level details of the Linux kernel (which may change from version to version of the kernel), by providing a set of C functions and macros that abstract the needed

kernel functionalities. The Resource Reservation Module implements a variant of the CBS scheduling policy on top of an internal EDF scheduler. The Interface Module allows user-space applications to request reservations of the CPU, letting all of the posted requests go through the Supervisor Module. The latter implements an appropriately designed access control model (Cucinotta 2008), by means of which AQuoSA is available to non-privileged users under a security policy that may be configured by the system administrator. Most of other real-time extensions to Linux, instead, allow only privileged users to take advantage of the available real-time functionality.

A well designed user-space library allows user-space applications to take advantage of the AQuoSA functionality. In addition to the resource reservation library (QRESLIB), used by unprivileged applications to reserve the CPU, a supervisor library (QSUPLIB) is used by a system tool in order to provide to the kernel the access-control policy configured by the system administrator. Finally, a QoS Management Library (QMGRLIB) is available implementing adaptive reservations, and providing various bandwidth controllers potentially of general interest for developers, especially in the case of periodic applications.

An interesting feature of the AQuoSA architecture is that it does not replace the default Linux scheduler, but coexists with it, giving to soft real-time tasks a higher priority than any non-real-time Linux task. Furthermore, the AQuoSA architecture follows a non-intrusive approach by keeping at the bare minimum (the GSP patch) the modifications needed to the Linux kernel. Unfortunately, in the current version, AQuoSA only supports single-processor systems.

The IRMOS Real-Time Scheduler

Here we recall the basic characteristics of the real-time scheduler developed in the context of the IRMOS project (http://www.irmosproject.

eu) reminding to (Checconi 2009) for a more complete description.

The IRMOS real-time scheduler allows to reserve a „slice" of the processing capability of a system to a group of threads and/or processes (shortly, tasks). This is done by specifying two scheduling parameters for each group: a budget Q and a period P, with the meaning that the tasks in the group are entitled to run on each of the CPUs (processor, or cores when present) available to the OS, for Q time units every period of P time units. This constitutes a scheduling guarantee and a limitation at the same time. This is achieved by a hard-reservation variant of the EDF-based Constant Bandwidth Server (CBS) scheduler (Abeni 1998), implemented as a partitioned scheduling strategy, where each CPU has its own private task queue, and it is scheduled independently. However, when a group is entitled to run on each CPU, the IRMOS scheduler employs a POSIX priority-based real-time scheduling strategy (POSIX 2004) among its tasks, in such a way that, if there are m CPUs, (at most) the m tasks with the highest priority are the ones which actually run. The system performs admission control over admitted reserved groups, so that the overall system capacity may be properly partitioned among concurrently running activities in the system, without overloading it.

Also, the scheduler has a hierarchical configuration capability, by which it is possible to define groups and nested subgroups of real-time tasks with given scheduling parameters.

Solaris 10

Solaris 10 provides real-time capabilities (Litchfield, 2007). Its main characteristics include:

- Fully preemptible kernel: If a RT process becomes runnable, it will immediately be placed on a CPU if its priority is higher than the thread running on that CPU.
- Interrupts as threads: Interrupts are converted into threads with their own data structures. Interrupts can block on kernel synchronization primitives. This enables the ability to protect data structures in the Solaris kernel with synchronization primitives rather than raising and lowering interrupt priority levels.
- Real-time scheduling: Entities needing real-time response latencies can use the real-time scheduling class which offers two options: round-robin or FIFO scheduling.
- Priority inheriting synchronization primitives: The primary synchronization primitive in the Solaris kernel is the mutex. They are adaptive in that if the entity owning the mutex is not currently running then the entity attempting to gain the mutex is put to sleep as there is no chance of gaining the mutex while the current owner is sleeping. Mutexes (and other primitives) offer the possibility of "priority inversion." Solaris mutexes implement the basic priority inheritance protocol. When the high level entity blocks, all of the entities blocking it are given the high level entity's priority. When they cease to block the thread, their priorities revert to their previous level.
- POSIX Compliance: Solaris 10 has almost full support for POSIX 1003.1b and full support for POSIX 1003.1c.

Others

There is also a number of commercially available OSes that are real-time capable, comprising Linux-based ones such as SUSE Linux Enterprise Real Time 10 and Red Hat Enterprise MRG 1.0. The discussion of the features of these other OSes is outside the scope of this document.

CONCLUSION

In this chapter, an overview was done about the real-time support in GPOSes with a particular focus on Linux. As evident from the discussion, there is a growing interest in integrating real-time support at the kernel level, even in General-Purpose Operating Systems, like Linux, other UNIX-es as Solaris, or Microsoft OSes. In fact, these constitute excellent development platforms for a wide variety of soft real-time applications, such as interactive and multimedia applications, thanks to the wide availability of multimedia and compression libraries, and the support for widespread multimedia devices and supports.

Looking at the development trend within the Linux kernel, it is evident how in the last few years, despite the growing computational capabilities of the hardware on which the kernel runs, such issues as interrupt and scheduling latencies, preemptability, timer precision and scheduling policies are gaining more and more importance in the community of users and developers. The current Linux scheduler for non-real-time processes already embeds concepts borrowed from the world of real-time scheduling, even if not in a completely effective way for the purpose of real-time applications.

It is expected that, in the next years, each GPOS will integrate more real-time mechanisms than nowadays, in order to better meet the growing requirements of time sensitive applications.

REFERENCES

Blanquer, J., Bruno, J., Gabber, E., Mcshea, M., Ozden, B., Silberschatz, A., & Singh, A. (1999). Resource management for QoS in Eclipse/BSD. In *Proceedings of the FreeBSD'99 Conference*. Berkeley, CA.

Buttazzo, G., Lipari, G., Abeni, L., & Caccamo, M. (2005). *Soft real-time systems predictability vs. efficiency. (Springer Series in Computer Science no. 10.1007/0-387-28147-9-3)*. Springer.

Checconi, F., Cucinotta, T., Faggioli, T., & Lipari, G. (2009). Hierarchical multiprocessor CPU reservations for the Linux kernel. In *Proceedings of the 5th International Workshop on Operating Systems Platforms for Embedded Real-Time Applications* (OSPERT 2009). Dublin, Ireland.

Cucinotta, T. (2008). *Access control for adaptive reservations on multi-user systems*. 14th IEEE Real-Time and Embedded Technology and Applications Symposium. St. Louis, MO, United States.

Cucinotta, T., Mancina, A., Anastasi, G. F., Lipari, G., Mangeruca, L., Checcozzo, R., & Rusinà, F. (2009). A real-time service-oriented architecture for industrial automation. *IEEE Transactions on Industrial Informatics, 5*(3).

Dozio, L., & Mantegazza, P. (2003). Real time distributed control systems using RTAI. In *Proceedings of the 6th IEEE International Symposium on Object-Oriented Real-Time Distributed Computing* (ISORC 2003), (pp. 11–18). Washington DC, USA.

Eide, E., Stack, T., Regehr, J., & Lepreau, J. (2004). Dynamic CPU management for real-time, middleware-based systems. In *Proceedings of 10th IEEE Real-Time and Embedded Technology and Applications Symposium*. Toronto, Canada.

Faggioli, D., Checconi, F., Trimarchi, M., & Scordino, C. (2009). *An EDF scheduling class for the Linux kernel*. 11th Real-Time Linux Workshop. Dresden, Germany.

Faggioli, D., Mancina, A., Checconi, F., & Lipari, G. (2008). Design and implementation of a POSIX compliant sporadic server. In *Proceedings of the 10th Real-Time Linux Workshop* (RTLW). Mexico.

Garcìa-Valls, M., Alonso, A., Ruiz, J., & Groba, A. M. (2002). An architecture of a quality of service resource manager middleware for flexible embedded multimedia systems. [Springer.]. *Lecture Notes in Computer Science, 2596*, 36–55. doi:10.1007/3-540-38093-0_3

Gopalan, K. (2001). *Real-time support in general purpose operating systems*. Research Proficiency Exam Report. Dept. of Computer Science. State University of New York at Stony Brook.

Gopalan, K., & Kang, K.-D. (2007). Coordinated allocation and scheduling of multiple resources in real-time operating systems. In *Proceedings of Workshop on Operating Systems Platforms for Embedded Real-Time Applications* (OSPERT). Pisa, Italy.

Jones, M. B. (1999). CPU reservations and time constraints: Implementation experience on Windows NT. In *Proceedings of the 3rd USENIX Windows NT Symposium*, (pp. 93–102). Seattle, Washington.

Krishnamurthy, Y., Kachroo, V., Karr, D. A., Rodrigues, C., Loyall, J. P., Schantz, R. E., & Schmidt, D. C. (2001). *Integration of QoS-enabled distributed object computing middleware for developing next-generation distributed application* (pp. 230–237).

Lakshmanan, K., & Rajkumar, R. (2008). Distributed resource kernels: OS support for end-to-end resource isolation. In *Proceedings of the 2008 IEEE Real-Time and Embedded Technology and Applications Symposium* (RTAS 2008), (pp. 195–204). Washington, DC: IEEE Computer Society.

Lelli, J. (2010). *Design and development of deadline based scheduling mechanisms for multiprocessor systems*. Thesis presented for the partial fulfilment of the Master Degree in Computer Engineering at the University of Pisa.

Litchfield, J. (2007). *The foundations of Solaris real-time*. Retrieved from http://blogs.sun.com/thejel/ entry/ the_foundations_of_ solaris_real-time

Mercer, C. W., Savage, S., & Tokuda, H. (1993). *Processor capacity reserves for multimedia operating systems*. (Technical Report CMU-CS-93-157). Pittsburgh, PA: Carnegie Mellon University.

Nahrstedt, K., Chu, H.-H., & Narayan, S. (1998). QoS-aware resource management for distributed multimedia applications. *Journal of High Speed Networks, 7*(3-4), 229–257.

Oikawa, S., & Rajkumar, R. (1999). Portable RK: A portable resource kernel for guaranteed and enforced timing behavior. In *Proceedings of the 5th IEEE Real-Time Technology and Applications Symposium* (RTAS'99), (p. 111). Washington, DC: IEEE Computer Society.

Palopoli, L., Cucinotta, T., Marzario, L., & Lipari, G. (2009). A QuoSA—Adaptive quality of service architecture. *Software, Practice & Experience, 39*(1), 1–31. doi:10.1002/spe.883

POSIX. (2004). *IEEE standard for Information Technology – Portable operating system interface (POSIX) – System interfaces*. (IEEE Std. 1003.1).

Rajkumar, R., Juvva, K., Molano, A., & Oikawa, S. (1998). Resource kernels: A resource-centric approach to real-time and multimedia systems. In *Proceedings of the SPIE/ACM Conference on Multimedia Computing and Networking* (MMCN 2008), (pp. 150–164). San Jose, California.

Ravindran, B. (2008). Engineering dynamic real-time distributed systems: Architecture, system description language, and middleware. *IEEE Transactions on Software Engineering, 28*(1), 30–57. doi:10.1109/32.979988

Ripoll, I., Pisa, P., Abeni, L., Gai, P., Lanusse, A., Saez, S., & Privat B. (2002). *OCERA project deliverable D1.1 – RTOS state of the art analysis*.

Schantz, R. E., Loyall, J. P., Rodrigues, C., Schmidt, D. C., Krishnamurthy, Y., & Pyarali, I. (2003). Flexible and adaptive QoS control for distributed real-time and embedded middleware. In *Proceedings of the ACM/IFIP/USENIX 2003 International Conference on Middleware* (pp. 374–393). New York, NY: Springer-Verlag New York, Inc.

Schmidt, C., Levine, D. L., & Mungee, S. (1997). The design of the TAO real-time object request broker. *Computer Communications, 21*, 294–324. doi:10.1016/S0140-3664(97)00165-5

Setz, J. (June 2007). *Inter-process communication in RTAI and RTLinux*. Saarland University Seminar Report.

Sha, L., Rajkumar, R., & Lehoczky, J. P. (1990). Priority inheritance protocols: An approach to real-time synchronization. [IEEE Computer Society.]. *IEEE Transactions on Computers, 39*(9), 1175–1185. doi:10.1109/12.57058

Shankaran, N., Koutsoukos, X. D., Schmidt, D. C., Xue, Y., & Lu, C. (2006). Hierarchical control of multiple resources in distributed real-time and embedded systems. In *ECRTS'06: Proceedings of the 18th Euromicro Conference on Real-Time Systems*, (pp. 151–160). Washington, DC: IEEE Computer Society.

Vardhan, V., Sachs, D. G., Yuan, W., Harris, A. F., Adve, S. V., Jones, D. L., et al. Nahrstedt, K. (2005). Integrating finegrain application adaptation with global adaptation for saving energy. In *Proceedings of the 2nd International Workshop on Power-Aware Real-Time Computing* (PARC). Jersey City, New Jersey, USA.

Wolfe, V. F., DiPippo, L. C., Ginis, R., Squadrito, M., Wohlever, S., Zykh, I., & Johnston, R. (1997). *Real-time CORBA*. In IEEE Real Time Technology and Applications Symposium (RTAS 1997), (p. 148). Montreal, Canada: IEEE Computer Society.

Yodaiken, V., & Barabanov, M. (1997). Introducing real-time Linux. *Linux Journal, 5.*

Yuan, W., & Nahrstedt, K. (2003). Energy-efficient soft real-time CPU scheduling for mobile multimedia systems. In *Proceedings of the 19th ACM symposium on Operating systems principles* (SOSP'03), (pp. 149–163). New York, NY: ACM.

Zhang, R., Lu, C., Abdelzaher, T. F., & Stankovic, J. A. (2002). ControlWare: A middleware architecture for feedback control of software performance. In *Proceedings of the International Conference on Distributed Computing Systems*. Vienna, Austria.

Compilation of References

Aalst, W. M. P. V. D., Hofstede, A. H. M. T., Kiepusze-wski, B., & Barros, A. P. (2003). Workflow patterns. *Distributed and Parallel Databases, 14*(1), 5-51. doi: http://dx.doi.org/10.1023/ A:1022883727209

Abeni, L., & Buttazzo, G. (1998). Integrating multimedia applications in hard real-time systems. *Proceedings of the IEEE Real-Time Systems Symposium,* December 1998, Madrid.

Abeni, L., Palopoli, L., Lipari, G., & Walpole, J. (2002). Analysis of a reservation-based feedback scheduler. *Proc. of the Real-Time Systems Symposium.*

Abramson, D., Jackson, J., Muthrasanallur, S., Neiger, G., Regnier, G., Sankaran, R., et al. Wiegert, J. (August 2006). Intel® virtualization technology for directed I/O. *Intel Technology Journal, 10*(3). Retrieved from http:// www.intel.com/ technology/ itj/ 2006/ v10i3/

Abstratt Technologies. (2010). *TextUML toolkit.* Retrieved from http://abstratt.com/

ActiveBPEL. (2010). Retrieved from http://www.active-vos.com/ community-open-source.php

Addis, M., Zlatev, Z., Mitchell, W., & Boniface, M. (2009). *Modelling interactive real-time applications on service oriented infrastructures. 2009 NEM Summit – Towards Future Media Internet.* St Malo.

Addis, M., Lowe, R., Salvo, N., & Middleton, L. (2009, September). *Reliable audiovisual archiving using unreliable storage technology and services.* Conference of the International Broadcasting Convention, Amsterdam, Netherlands.

Addis, M., Wright, R., & Miller, A. (2008, September). The significance of storage in the cost of risk of digital preservation. In *Proceedings of the Fifth International Conference on Preservation of Digital Objects* (iPRES 2008), British Library, London, UK.

Ahsant, M., Surridge, M., Leonard, T. A., Krishna, A., & Mulmo, O. (2006). *Dynamic trust federation in Grids.* The 4th International Conference on Trust Management, 16 - 19 May 2006, Pisa, Tuscany, Italy. ISBN 978-3-540-34295-3

Aisopos, F., Tserpes, K., Kardara, M., Panousopoulos, G., Phillips, S., & Salamouras, S. (2010). Information exchange in business collaboration using Grid technologies. *Identity in the Information Society, 2,* 189–204. doi:10.1007/s12394-009-0028-0

Akogrimo Deliverable D2. 2.1. (2005). *Report on state of the art,* vol. 2. Retrieved from http://www.akogrimo. org/ modules3653.pdf? name=UpDownload& req=getit& lid=16

Akogrimo Deliverable D4. 3.3. (2007). *Report on the implementation of the infrastructure services layer.* Akogrimo Project. Retrieved from http://www.akogrimo. org/modules8128.pdf? name=UpDownload& req=getit& lid=116

Akogrimo Project. (2006). *Akogrimo: Access to knowledge through the Grid in a mobile world.* Retrieved from http:// www.akogrimo.org

Alexander, J., et al. (2006). *Web services transfer* (WS-Transfer). Retrieved June 25, 2010, from http://www. w3.org/ Submission/ WS-Transfer/

Almeida, L., et al. (2008). Solutions for supporting composition of service-based RT applications. In *Proceedings of the 11th IEEE Symposium on Object Oriented Real-Time Distributed Computing* (pp. 42–49).

Alrifai, M., & Risse, T. (2010). Efficient QoS-aware service composition. In Alrifai, M., Risse, T., Calisti, M., Walliser, M., Brantschen, S., & Herbstritt, M. a. (Eds.), *Emerging Web services technology* (*Vol. III*, pp. 75–87). Whitestein Series in Software Agent Technologies and Autonomic Computing, Birkhäuser Basel. doi:10.1007/978-3-0346-0104-7_5

Alur, R., & Yannakakis, M. (1999). Model checking of message sequence charts. In *Proceedings of the Tenth International Conference on Concurrency Theory, LNCS 1661*, (pp 114–129). Springer.

Amazon (2009). *Amazon CloudWatch development guide* (API Version 2009-05-15). Retrieved June 25, 2010, from http://docs.amazonwebservices.com /Amazon-CloudWatch/latest/ DeveloperGuide/index.html? arch-AmazonCloudWatch- metricscollected.html

Amazon EC2 API. (n.d.). Retrieved from http://docs.amazonwebservices.com /AWSEC2/2009-11-30/ APIReference/

Amazon EC2. (n.d.). Retrieved from http://aws.amazon.com/ec2/

Amazon Web Services. (2010). *Elastic load balancing*. Retrieved from http://aws.amazon.com/ elasticloadbalancing

Amazon. (2006). *Simple storage service developer guide* (API Version 2006-03-01). Retrieved June 25, 2010, from http://docs.amazonwebservices.com/ AmazonS3/ 2006-03-01/ index.html? RESTAPI.html

Amazon. (2008). *Service level agreement for ec2*. Retrieved from http://aws.amazon.com/ ec2-sla

Amazon. (2009). *Creating HIPAA-compliant medical data applications with AWS*. Retrieved on June 30, 2009, from http://aws.amazon.com/ about-aws/ whats-new/ 2009/ 04/ 06/ whitepaper-hipaa/

Amazon. (2010). *Amazon EC2's reserved instances model*. Retrieved July 5, 2010 from http://aws.amazon.com/ ec2/ #pricing

Amazon. (2010). *What is AWS?* Retrieved July 5, 2010 from http://aws.amazon.com/ what-is-aws/

Anderson, T., Peterson, L., Shenker, S., & Turner, J. (2005). Overcoming the Internet impasse through virtualization. [Los Alamitos, CA: IEEE Computer Society Press.]. *IEEE Journal Computer*, *38*(4), 34–41.

Andersson, B., & Jonsson, J. (2000). *Fixed-priority preemptive multiprocessor scheduling: To partition or not to partition* (pp. 337–346). Cheju Island, South Korea: RTCSA.

Andersson, B., & Tovar, E. (2006). Multiprocessor scheduling with few preemptions. In *Proceedings of the International Conference on Real-Time Computing Systems and Applications (RTCSA)*.

Anjomshoaa, A., et al. (2005). *Job submission description language (JSDL) specification*, version 1.0. Retrieved from http://www.gridforum.org/ documents/ GFD.56.pdf

Apache. (2010). Apache ServiceMix. Retrieved from http://servicemix.apache.org /home.html

Arthur, S., Emde, C., & McGuire, N. (2007). *Assessment of the real time preemption patches (RT-Preempt) and their impact on the general purpose performance of the system*. 9th Real-Time Linux Workshop, Linz, Austria.

ASG. (201). Retrieved from http://asg-platform.org/cgi-bin /twiki/view/Public

Asgari, A., Trimintzios, P., Irons, M., Pavlou, G., Egan, R., & Van Den Berghe, S. (2002, December). A scalable real-time monitoring system for supporting traffic engineering. In *Proceedings of the IEEE Workshop on IP Operations and Management* (pp. 202-207).

AssessGrid Project. (2009). *AssessGrid - Advanced risk assessment & management for trustable Grids*. Retrieved from http://www.assessgrid.eu

Audsley, N. C., Burns, A., Richardson, M. F., & Wellings, A. J. (1995). Data consistency in hard real-time systems. *Informatica*, *19*(2).

Audsley, N., & Bletsas, K. (2004). Fixed priority timing analysis of real-time systems with limited parallelism. In *Proceedings of the Euromicro Conference on Real Time Systems*. Catania, Italy.

Axboe, J. (2010). *CFQ IO scheduler*. Retrieved on March 4, 2010, from http://mirror.linux.org.au/ pub/ linux.conf.au/ 2007/ video/ talks/ 123.pdf

Bajaj, S., Box, D., & Chappell, D. (2006). *Web services policy framework* (WS-Policy). Retrieved from http://www-128.ibm.com/ developerworks/library/ specification/wspolfram/

Baker, T. P., Cirinei, M., & Bertogna, M. (2008). EDZL scheduling analysis. *Real-Time Systems: The International Journal of Time-Critical Computing, 40*(3), 264–289.

Balasubramanian, K., Balasubramanian, J., Parsons, J., Gokhale, A., & Schmidt, D. C. (2007). A platform-independent component modeling language for distributed real-time and embedded systems. *Journal of Computer and System Sciences, 73*(2), 171–185. doi:10.1016/j.jcss.2006.04.008

Ballinger, K., et al. (2006). *Basic profile*, version 1.1. Retrieved June 25, 2010, from http://www.ws-i.org/ Profiles/ BasicProfile-1.1.html

Banks, T. (2006). *Web services resource framework (WSRF) – Primer*, v1.2. Retrieved June 25, 2010, from http://docs.oasis-open.org/ wsrf/ wsrf-primer-1.2-primer-cd-02.pdf

Barak, A., Guday, S., & Wheeler, R. G. (1993). *The MOSIX distributed operating system: Load balancing for UNIX*. New York, NY: Springer-Verlag, Inc.

Baruah, S. (2006). The non-pre-emptive scheduling of periodic tasks upon multiprocessors. *Real-Time Systems: The International Journal of Time-Critical Computing, 32*(1-2), 9–20.

Baruah, S., & Carpenter, J. (2003). Multiprocessor fixed-priority scheduling with restricted interprocessor migrations. In *Proceedings of the EuroMicro Conference on Real-time Systems*. Porto, Portugal: IEEE Computer Society Press.

Baruah, S., & Lipari, G. (2004). *A multiprocessor implementation of the total bandwidth server*. International Parallel and Distributed Processing Symposium (IPPDS 04), Santa Fe.

Baruah, S., & Lipari, G. (2004). *Executing aperiodic jobs in a multiprocessor constant-bandwidth server implementation*. Euromicro Conference on Real-Time Systems (ECRTS 04), Catania (Italy).

Baruah, S., Cohen, N., Plaxton, G., & Varvel, D. (1996). Proportionate *progress: A notion of fairness in resource allocation*.

Bastida, L., Berre, A. J., Elvesæter, B., Hahn, C., Johnsen, S. G., Kämper, S.,... Stollberg, M. (2009). *Model-driven methodology and architecture specification*. (SHAPE project deliverable D2.1).

Battacharyya, S. S., Lee, E. A., & Murthy, P. K. (1996). *Software synthesis from dataflow graphs*. Kluwer Academic Publishers.

Baude, F., Caromel, D., Delbe, C., & Henrio, L. (2005). A hybrid message logging-CIC protocol for constrained checkpointability. *Proceedings of EuroPar 2005*, Lisbon, Portugal.

Beco, S., Cantalupo, B., Giammarino, L., Matskanis, N., & Surridge, M. (2005). *OWL-WS: A workflow ontology for dynamic Grid service composition* (pp. 148–155). IEEE Computer Society.

Beco, S., Cantalupo, B., & Terracina, A. (2006). *The role of workflow in next generation business oriented Grids: Two different approaches leading to a unified vision*. Paper presented at the Second IEEE International Conference on e-Science and Grid Computing (e-Science'06).

Benkner, S., & Engelbrecht, G. (2006). *A generic QoS infrastructure for Grid Web services*. AICT-ICIW.

Benkner, S., Engelbrecht, G., Middleton, S. E., & Surridge, M. (2007). *Supporting SLA negotiation for QoS-enabled simulation services in a medical Grid environment, Lecture Notes in Computer Science* (Vol. 4699). Berlin, Germany: Springer.

Bennet, J. C. R., & Zhang, H. (1997). Hierarchical packet fair queuing algorithms. *IEEE Transactions on Networking, 5*(5).

Berman, F., Chien, A., Cooper, K., Dongarra, J., Foster, I., Gannon, D., et al. (2001). The GrADS project: Software support for high-level Grid application development. *International Journal of High Performance Computer Applications, 15*(4), 327-344. doi: http://dx.doi.org/10.1177/109434200101500401

Bertogna, M., Fisher, N., & Baruah, S. (2009). Resource-sharing servers for open environments. *IEEE Transactions on Industrial Informatics, 5*(3), 202–220. doi:10.1109/TII.2009.2026051

Bertogna, M., Cirinei, M., & Lipari, G. (2005). New schedulability tests for real-time tasks sets scheduled by deadline monotonic on multiprocessors. In *Proceedings of the 9th International Conference on Principles of Distributed Systems.* Pisa, Italy: IEEE Computer Society Press.

Bharathi, S., & Chervenak, A. (2007). Design of a scalable peer-to-peer Information System using the GT4 index service. In *Proceedings of the Seventh IEEE International Symposium on Cluster Computing and the Grid* (CCGrid'07).

Bhatia, S., Motiwala, M., Mühlbauer, W., Mundada, Y., Valancius, V., Bavier, A., et al. Rexford, J. (2008). Trellis: A platform for building flexible, fast virtual networks on commodity hardware. In *CoNEXT '08: Proceedings of the 2008 ACM CoNEXT Conference* (pp. 1-6). New York, NY: ACM.

Bini, E., Bertogna, M., & Baruah, S. (2009). Virtual multiprocessor platforms: Specification and use. In *Proceedings of 30th IEEE Real-Time Systems Symposium.*

Bini, E., Buttazo, G., & Bertogna, M. (2009). The multi supply function resource abstraction for multiprocessors: The global EDF case. In *Proceedings of the 15th IEEE International Conference on Embedded and Real-Time Computing Systems and Applications.*

Birkenheuer, G., Hovestadt, M., Kao, O., & Voss, K. (2008). *Planning-based scheduling for SLA- Awareness and Grid integration.*

Blake, S., Blake, D., Carlson, M., Davies, E., Wang, Z., & Weiss, W. (1998, December). *An architecture for differentiated services.* (Internet Engineering Task Force, RFC 2475). Retrieved May 21, 2008, from http://tools.ietf.org/ html/ rfc2475

Blanquer, J., Bruno, J., Gabber, E., Mcshea, M., Ozden, B., Silberschatz, A., & Singh, A. (1999). Resource management for QoS in Eclipse/BSD. In *Proceedings of the FreeBSD '99 Conference.* Berkeley, CA.

Blum, A. (2004, June 4). *UDDI as an extended Web services registry: Versioning, quality of service, and more.* SOA & WOA: Article.

Bocchi, L., Laneve, C., & Zavattaro, G. (2003). A calculus for long-running transactions. In *Proceeding Conference on Formal Methods Open Object-based Distributed Systems* (FMOOD), *LNCS 2884,* (pp. 124–138).

Boniface, M. J., Phillips, S., Sanchez-Macian Perez, A., & Surridge, M. (2007). *Dynamic service provisioning using GRIA SLAs.* NFPSLA-SOC'07. Vienna.

Boniface, M. J., Phillips, S. C., & Surridge, M. (2006, October). *Grid-based business partnerships using service level agreements.* Cracow Grid Workshop, Cracow, Poland.

Boniface, M., Nasser, B., Papay, J., Phillips, S. C., Servin, A., & Yang, X. …Kyriazis, D. (2010). Platform-as-a-service architecture for real-time quality of service management in clouds. *Proceedings of the Fifth International Conference on Internet and Web Applications and Services,* (pp. 155–160). Barcelona, Spain.

Boniface, M., Phillips, S., Sanchez-Macian Perez, A., & Surridge, M. (2007). *Non Functional Properties and Service Level Agreements in Service Oriented Computing Workshop, The 5th International Conference on Service Oriented Computing.* NFPSLA-SOC'07, September 17, 2007, Vienna, Austria.

Boniface, M., Phillips, S. C., & Surridge, M. (2006). *Grid-based business partnerships using service level agreements.*

Boniface, M., Surridge, M., Hall-May, M., Bertram, S., & Briscombe, N. (2010). *On-demand dynamic security for risk-based secure collaboration in clouds.* IEEE International Conference on Cloud Computing 2010, July 2010, Miami, USA.

Bonino da Silva Santos, L. O., Guizzardi, G., Silva Souza Guizzardi, R., Goncalves da Silva, E., Ferreira Pires, L., & van Sinderen, M. J. (2009). Gso: Designing a well-founded service ontology to support dynamic service discovery and composition. In *Proceedings of the 2nd International Workshop on Dynamic and Declarative Business Process* (DDBP 2009).

Booth, D., Haas, H., McCabe, F., Newcomer, E., Michael, I., Ferris, C., & Orchard, D. (2004). Web services architecture. Retrieved June 25, 2010, from http://www.w3.org/ TR/ ws-arch/

Bovet, D. P., & Cesati, M. (2006). *Understanding the Linux kernel.* O'Reilly.

Bowers, S., Ludascher, B., Ngu, A. H. H., & Critchlow, T. (2006). *Enabling scientific workflow reuse through structured composition of dataflow and control-flow.* Paper presented at the 22nd International Conference on Data Engineering Workshops.

Box, D., et al. (2000). *Simple object access protocol* (SOAP) 1.1. Retrieved June 25, 2010, from http://www.w3.org/ TR/ 2000/ NOTE-SOAP- 20000508/

Box, D., et al. (2004). *Web services addressing* (WS-Addressing). Retrieved June 25, 2010, from http://www.w3.org/ Submission/ ws-addressing/

Braden, R., Clark, D., & Shenker, S. (1994, June). *Integrated services in the internet architecture: An overview.* (Internet Engineering Task Force, RFC 1633). Retrieved May 15, 2008, from http://tools.ietf.org/ html/ rfc1633

Brandic, I., Benkner, S., Engelbrecht, G., & Schmidt, R. (2005). *QoS support for time-critical Grid workflow applications.* Paper presented at the First International Conference on e-Science and Grid Computing.

Brandt, S., & Nutt, G. (2002). *Flexible soft real-time processing in middleware.* Real-Time Systems Journal, Special Issue on Flexible Scheduling in Real-Time Systems.

Brinkmann, A., Heidebuer, M., Meyer, F., Heide, A., Rückert, U., Salzwedel, K., & Vodisek, M. (2004). V: Drive - Costs and benefits of an out-of-band storage virtualization system. *Proceedings of the 21st IEEE Conference on Mass Storage Systems and Technologies.*

Broy, M., Krugger, I., & Meisinger, M. (2007). A formal model of services. *ACM Transactions on Software Engineering and Methodology*, *16*(1). doi:10.1145/1189748.1189753

Bruni, R., Melgratti, H. C., & Montanari, U. (2005). *Theoretical foundations for compensations in flow composition languages.* In Symposium on Principles of Programming Languages (PoPL), (pp. 209–220).

Bruno, J., Brustoloni, J., Gabber, E., Ozden, B., & Silberschatz, A. (1999). Disk scheduling with quality of service guarantees. *Proceedings of the IEEE International Conference on Multimedia Computing and Systems.*

Buco, M. J., Chang, R. N., Luan, L. Z., Ward, C., Wolf, J. L., & Yu, P. S. (2004). *Utility computing SLA management based upon business objectives.*

Bullard, V., Murray, B., & Wilson, K. (2006). *An introduction to WSDM.* Retrieved June 25, 2010, from http://www.oasis-open.org/ committees/ download.php/ 16998/ wsdm-1.0-intro-primer -cd-01.doc

Burchard, A., Liebeherr, J., Oh, Y., & Son, S. H. (1995). New strategies for assigning real-time tasks to multiprocessor systems. *IEEE Transactions on Computers*, *44*(12), 1429–1442. doi:10.1109/12.477248

Burke, S., Campana, S., Delgado Peris, A., Donno, F., M´endez Lorenzo, P., Santinelli, R., & Sciab`a, A. (2007). *gLite-3-UserGuide, v.1.1.* CERN-LCG 2007.

Buttazzo, G., Lipari, G., Abeni, L., & Caccamo, M. (2005). *Soft real-time systems predictability vs. efficiency. (Springer Series in Computer Science no. 10.1007/0-387-28147-9-3).* Springer.

Buyya, R., Abramson, D., & Venugopal, S. (2005). The Grid economy. *Proceedings of the IEEE*, *93*, 698–714. doi:10.1109/JPROC.2004.842784

Buyya, R., Yeo, C. S., Venugopal, S., Broberg, J., & Brandic, I. (2009, June). Cloud computing and emerging IT platforms: Vision, hype, and reality for delivering computing as the 5th utility. *Future Generation Computer Systems*, *25*(6), 599–616. doi:10.1016/j.future.2008.12.001

Buyya, R., & Venugopal, S. (2004). *The Gridbus toolkit for service oriented grid and utility computing: An overview and status report.* Paper presented at the 1st IEEE International Workshop on Grid Economics and Business Models, 2004. GECON 2004.

Calandrino, J. M., Anderson, J. H., & Baumberger, D. P. (2007). A hybrid real-time scheduling approach for large-scale multicore platforms. In *Proceedings of the Euromicro Conference on Real-Time Systems.* Pisa.

Cao, J., Huang, J., Wang, G., & Gu, J. (2009). *QoS and preference based Web service evaluation approach.* Eighth International Conference on Grid and Cooperative Computing, (pp. 420-426).

Carrascosa, C., Giret, A., Julian, V., Rebollo, M., Argente, E., & Botti, V. (2009). Service oriented MAS: An open architecture. In *Proceedings of the AAMAS 09.*

Castro, M., & Liskov, B. (2002). Practical Byzantine fault tolerance and proactive recovery. *ACM Transactions on Computer Systems, 20*(4), 398–461. doi:10.1145/571637.571640

Cervin, A., Eker, J., Bernhardsson, B., & Arzen, K.-E. (2002). Feedback-feedforward scheduling of control tasks. *Real-Time Systems, 23*(1/2). doi:10.1023/A:1015394302429

Chaari, S., Badr, Y., & Biennier, F. (2008). *Enhancing Web service selection by QoS-based ontology and WS-policy.* ACM Symposium on Applied Computing, SAC '08 (pp. 2426-2431). Fortaleza, Ceara, Brazil: ACM.

Chakraborty, D., Joshi, A., Yesha, Y., & Finin, T. (2006). Toward distributed service discovery in pervasive computing environments. *IEEE Transactions on Mobile Computing, 5*(2), 97–112. doi:10.1109/TMC.2006.26

Checconi, F., Cucinotta, T., Faggioli, T., & Lipari, G. (2009). Hierarchical multiprocessor CPU reservations for the Linux kernel. In *Proceedings of the 5th International Workshop on Operating Systems Platforms for Embedded Real-Time Applications* (OSPERT 2009). Dublin, Ireland.

Chen, Y., Iyer, S., Liu, X., Milojicic, D., & Sahai, A. (2007). *SLA decomposition: Translating service level objectives to system level thresholds.* In Fourth International Conference on Autonomic Computing (ICAC'07).

Chinnici, R., Gudgin, M., Moreau, J., Schlimmer, J., & Weerawarana, S. (2003). *Web services description language (WSDL) version 2.0 part 1: Core language.* Retrieved June 25, 2010, from http://www.w3.org/ TR/ 2003/ WD-wsdl20- 20031110/

Chowdhury, N. M. M. K., & Boutaba, R. (2009, July). Network virtualization: State of the art and research challenges. *IEEE Communications Magazine, 47*(7), 20–26. doi:10.1109/MCOM.2009.5183468

Chowdhury, N. M. M. K., & Boutaba, R. (2010, April). A survey of network virtualization. [Elsevier.]. *Computer Networks, 54*(5), 862–876. doi:10.1016/j.comnet.2009.10.017

Christensen, E., Curbera, F., Meredith, G., & Weerawarana, S. (2001). *Web services description language (WSDL) 1.1.* Retrieved June 25, 2010, from http://www.w3.org/ TR/wsdl

Church, K., Greenberg, A., & Hamilton, J. (2008). *On delivering embarrassingly distributed cloud services.* Seventh ACM Workshop on Hot Topics in Networks (HotNets-VII).

Claris, C., George, N. R., & Khaled, H. (2007). *Efficient implementation of best-fit scheduling for advance reservations and QoS in Grid.* Paper presented at the 1st IEEE/IFIP Intl. Workshop on End-to-end Virtualization and Grid Management (EVGM).

Clark, D., Shenker, S., & Zhang, L. (1992). Supporting real-time applications in an integrated services packet network: Architecture and mechanism. [ACM.]. *ACM SIGCOMM Computer Communication Review, 22*(4), 14–26. doi:10.1145/144191.144199

Clark, A., & Gilmore, S. (2006). Evaluating quality of service for service level agreements. In L. Brim & M. Leucker (Eds.), *Proceedings of the 11th International Workshop on Formal Methods for Industrial Critical Systems, LNCS vol. 4346* (pp. 181—194). Springer-Verlag.

Cline, K., et al. (2006). *Toward converging Web service standards for resources, events, and management.* Retrieved June 25, 2010, from http://download.boulder.ibm.com/ ibmdl/ pub/ software/ dw/ webservices/ Harmonization_Roadmap.pdf

Cloud Security Alliance. (2009). *Security guidance for critical areas of focus in cloud computing.* Retrieved June 30, 2010 from http://www.cloudsecurityalliance.org/ guidance/ csaguide.pdf

Coles, S. J., Frey, J. G., Hursthouse, M. B., Light, M. E., Milsted, A. J., & Carr, L. A. (2006). An e-science environment for service crystallography - From submission to dissemination. *Journal of Chemical Information and Modeling, 46*(3), 1006–1016. doi:10.1021/ci050362w

Compare, E. M. F. (2010). *EMF Compare.* Retrieved from http://wiki.eclipse.org/index.php /EMF_Compare

Cook, N., Shrivastava, S., & Wheater, S. (2003, November). Middleware support for non-repudiable transactional information sharing between enterprises. In *Proceedings of 4th IFIP International Conf. on Distributed Applications and Interoperable Systems.*

COPE. (2010). *COPE – Coupled evolution of metamodels and models.* Retrieved from http://cope.in.tum.de/ pmwiki.php

Corbet, J. (2006). *The high-resolution timer API.* Retrieved from http://lwn.net/Articles/167897

CORDIS. (2010). The future of cloud computing. *Expert Group Report.* Retrieved from http://cordis.europa.eu/ fp7/ict/ ssai/docs/cloud-report-final.pdf

Cowan, J., & Tobin, R. (2004). *XML information set,* 2nd ed. Retrieved June 25, 2010, from http://www.w3.org/ TR/ xml-infoset/

Cucinotta, T. (2008). *Access control for adaptive reservations on multi-user systems.* 14th IEEE Real-Time and Embedded Technology and Applications Symposium. St. Louis, MO, United States.

Cucinotta, T., Anastasi, G., & Abeni, L. (2008). Real-time virtual machines. In *Proceedings of the 29th Real-Time System Symposium* (RTSS 2008) -- Work in Progress Session, Barcelona.

Cucinotta, T., Anastasi, G., & Abeni, L. (2009). Respecting temporal constraints in virtualised services. In *Proceedings of the 2nd IEEE International Workshop on Real-Time Service-Oriented Architecture and Applications* (RTSOAA 2009), Seattle, Washington.

Cucinotta, T., Anastasi, G., & Abeni, L. (December 2008). Real-time virtual machines. In *Proceedings of the 29th Real-Time System Symposium (RTSS2008).*

Cucinotta, T., Checconi, F., Abeni, L., & Palopoli, L. (2010). *Self-tuning schedulers for legacy real-time applications.* EuroSys '10, 5th European Conference on Computer Systems (pp. 55-68). Paris, France: ACM.

Cucinotta, T., Konstanteli, K., & Varvarigou, T. (2009). Advance reservations for distributed real-time workflows with probabilistic service guarantees. In *Proceedings of the IEEE International Conference on Service-Oriented Computing and Applications* (SOCA 2009).

Cucinotta, T., Mancina, A., Anastasi, G. F., Lipari, G., Mangeruca, L., Checcozzo, R., & Rusinà, F. (2009). A real-time service-oriented architecture for industrial automation. *IEEE Transactions on Industrial Informatics, 5*(3).

Cucinotta, T., Palopoli, L., & Marzario, L. (2004). Stochastic feedback-based control of QoS in soft real-time systems. In *Proceedings of the 43rd IEEE Conference on Decision and Control.*

Cully, B., Lefebvre, G., Meyer, D., Feeley, M., Hutchinson, N., & Warfield, A. (2008). Remus: High availability via asynchronous virtual machine replication. *Proceedings of the 5th USENIX Symposium on Networked Systems Design and Implementation,* (pp. 161-174). April 16-18, 2008, San Francisco, California.

Cuzzocrea, A. (2008). Towards RT data transformation services over grids. In *Proceedings of the 32nd Annual IEEE International Computer Software and Applications Conference* (pp. 1143–1149).

CXF. (2010). *Apache CXF: An open source service framework.* Retrieved from http://cxf.apache.org/

Czajkowski, K., Foster, I., & Kesselman, C. (2005). *Proceedings of the IEEE, 93*(3), 631-643. ISSN: 0018-9219.

Czajkowski, K., Foster, I., Kesselman, C., Sander, V., & Tuecke, S. (2002). SNAP: A protocol for negotiating service level agreements and coordinating resource management in distributed systems. In *Proceedings of the 8th Workshop on Job Scheduling Strategies for Parallel Processing.*

DAML-S. (2002). *Describing Web services using DAML-S and WSDL*. Retrieved from http://www.daml.org/services/daml-s/0.7/daml-s-wsdl.html

Data Core. (2010). *Software*. Retrieved June 2010 from http://www.datacore.com/

Davis, D., Malhotra, A., Warr, K., & Chou, W. (2009). *Web services resource transfer* (WS-RT). Retrieved June 25, 2010, from http://www.w3.org/ TR/ 2009/ WD-ws-resource- transfer-20090317/

Davis, D., Malhotra, A., Warr, K., & Chou, W. (2009). *Web services enumeration* (WS-Enumeration). Retrieved June 25, 2010, from http://www.w3.org/ TR/ 2009/ WD-ws- enumeration-20090924/

Davis, D., Malhotra, A., Warr, K., & Chou, W. (2009). *Web services metadata exchange* (WS-MetadataExchange) Retrieved June 25, 2010, from http://www.w3.org/ TR/ 2009/ WD-ws-metadata- exchange-20090924/

Davis, D., Malhotra, A., Warr, K., & Chou, W. (2009). *Web services eventing* (WS-Eventing). Retrieved June 25, 2010, from http://www.w3.org/ TR/ 2009/ WD-ws-eventing-20090924/

de Haaff, B. (2008). Cloud computing – The jargon is back! *Computing Journal Electronic Magazine*. Retrieved from http://cloudcomputing.sys-con.com/node/613070

Debusmann, M., & Keller, A. (2003). *SLA-driven management of distributed systems using the common information model*. IFIP/IEEE International Symposium on Integrated Management. Kluwer Academic Publishers.

Deelman, E., Blythe, J., Gil, Y., & Kesselman, C. (2004). *Workflow management in GriPhyN- Grid resource management: State of the art and future trends* (pp. 99–116). Kluwer Academic Publishers.

Deelman, E., Blythe, J., Gil, Y., Kesselman, C., Mehta, G., & Patil, S. (2004). Pegasus: Mapping scientific workflows onto the Grid. In Dikaiakos, M. D. (Ed.), *Grid computing* (*Vol. 3165*, pp. 131–140). Berlin / Heidelberg, Germany: Springer. doi:10.1007/978-3-540-28642-4_2

Deltacloud. (n.d.). Retrieved from http://www.deltacloud.org/

Denaro, G., Polini, A., & Emmerich, W. (2004, January). Early performance testing of distributed software applications. In *Proceedings of the 4th Int. Workshop on Software and Performance*, San Francisco, ACM Press.

Dhall, S. K., & Liu, C. L. (1978). On a real-time scheduling problem. *Operations Research, 26,* 127–140. doi:10.1287/opre.26.1.127

Dinda, P. A. (2008). Resource virtualization renaissance. *Computer, 38*(5), 28–31.

Ding, S. X. (2008). *Model-based Fault Diagnosis Techniques: Design Schemes, Algorithms, and Tools*. Berlin: Springer.

Ding, Q., Li, X., & Zhou, X. H. (2008). *Reputation based service selection in Grid environment*. International Conference on Computer Science and Software Engineering, 3, (pp. 58-61).

DIP. (2010). *QoS-aware resource scheduling DIP*. (Deliverable D.5.2., P. P). Retrieved from http://dip.semanticweb.org/

DiskSim. (2010). *Simulation environment*. Retrieved on June 3, 2010, from http://www.pdl.cmu.edu/ DiskSim/

DMTF. (n.d.). *DSP0243 open virtualization format specification 1.1.0*.

Douglis, F., & Ousterhout, J. (1991). Transparent process, igration: Design alternatives and the Sprite implementation. *Software, Practice & Experience, 21*(8), 757–785. doi:10.1002/spe.4380210802

Douglis, F. (1987). *Process migration in the Sprite operating system. (Technical Report, UMI Order Number: CSD-87-343)*. University of California at Berkeley.

Dozio, L., & Mantegazza, P. (2003). Real time distributed control systems using RTAI. In *Proceedings of the 6th IEEE International Symposium on Object-Oriented Real-Time Distributed Computing* (ISORC 2003), (pp. 11–18). Washington DC, USA.

Dumitrescu, C., & Foster, I. (2005). A Grid resource SLA-based broker. In *EuroPar*. Lisboa, Portugal: GRUBER.

Dumitrescu, C., Raicu, I., & Foster, I. (2005). A distributed approach in Grid resource brokering. In *Supercomputing*. Seattle, WA, USA: DI-GRUBER.

EC. (2005, November). Principles relating to data quality. *Official Journal of the European Communties, 281*(40).

Eclipse. (2010a). *Eclipse modeling framework* (EMF). Retrieved from http://www.eclipse.org/ modeling/emf/

Eclipse. (2010b). *Graphical modeling project* (GMP). Retrieved from http://www.eclipse.org/ modeling/gmp/

Eclipse. (2010c). *Java emitter templates* (JET) Retrieved from http://www.eclipse.org/ modeling/m2t/?project=jet

Edapt. (2010). *Edapt - Framework for Ecore model adaptation and instance migration.* Retrieved from http://www.eclipse.org /proposals/edapt/

Eide, E., Stack, T., Regehr, J., & Lepreau, J. (2004). Dynamic CPU management for real-time middleware-based systems. *Proceedings of 10th IEEE Real-Time and Embedded Technology and Applications Symposium.*

Eide, E., Stack, T., Regehr, J., & Lepreau, J. (2004). Dynamic CPU management for real-time, middleware-based systems. In *Proceedings of 10th IEEE Real-Time and Embedded Technology and Applications Symposium.* Toronto, Canada.

Eker, J., Janneck, J. W., Lee, E. A., Jie, L., Xiaojun, L., & Ludvig, J. (2003). Taming heterogeneity - The Ptolemy approach. *Proceedings of the IEEE, 91*(1), 127–144. doi:10.1109/JPROC.2002.805829

Emeakaroha, C. V., Brandic, I., Maurer, M., & Dustdar, S. (2010). *Low level metrics to high level SLAs - LoM2HiS framework: Bridging the gap between monitored metrics and SLA parameters in cloud environments.* IEEE 3rd International Conference on Cloud Computing.

Enea, O. S. E. O. S. (n.d.). Retrieved from http://www.enea.com/Templates/ Product____27035.aspx

Epsilon. (2010). *Epsilon.* Retrieved from http://www.eclipse.org/ gmt/epsilon/

Equinox. (2010). *Equinox.* Retrieved from http://www.eclipse.org/ equinox/

Erl, T. (2005). *Service-oriented architecture: Concepts, technology, and design.* Upper Saddle River, NJ: Prentice Hall.

Erwin, D., et al. (2003). *UNICORE plus final report - Uniform interface to computing resources.* Retrieved June 25, 2010, from http://www.unicore.eu/ documentation/ files/ erwin-2003-UPF.pdf

ESSI. (2010). Retrieved from http://www.essi-cluster.org

ETSI. (2001). *Methodological approach to the use of object-orientation in the standards making process. ETSI EG, 201,* 872.

EU IST SIMDAT Project. (2010). *EU IST SIMDAT project.* Retrieved from http://www.simdat.org

EuGENia. (2010). *EuGENia.* Retrieved from http://www.eclipse.org/gmt/ epsilon/doc/eugenia/

European Network and Information Security Agency (ENISA). (2009). *Cloud computing: Benefits, risks and recommendations for information security.* Retrieved June 10, 2010, from http://www.enisa.europa.eu/ act/ rm/ files/ deliverables/ cloud-computing-risk-assessment

Evidence. (2010). *ERIKA Enterprise and RT-Druid website.* Retrieved from http://www.evidence.eu.com / content/view/28/51/

Faggioli, D. (n.d.). *POSIX SCHED_SPORADIC implementation for tasks and groups.* Retrieved from http://lwn.net/Articles/293547/

Faggioli, D., Checconi, F., Trimarchi, M., & Scordino, C. (2009). *An EDF scheduling class for the Linux kernel.* 11th Real-Time Linux Workshop. Dresden, Germany.

Faggioli, D., et al. (2010). Sporadic server revisited. *Proceedings of 25th ACM Symposium On Applied Computing.* Sierre, Switzerland.

Faggioli, D., Mancina, A., Checconi, F., & Lipari, G. (2008). Design and implementation of a POSIX compliant sporadic server. In *Proceedings of the 10th Real-Time Linux Workshop* (RTLW). Mexico.

Fahringer, T., Prodan, R., Duan, R., Hofer, J., Nadeem, F., & Nerieri, F. (2007). ASKALON: A development and Grid computing environment for scientific workflows. In Taylor, I. J., Deelman, E., Gannon, D. B., & Shields, M. (Eds.), *Workflows for e-science* (pp. 450–471). London, UK: Springer. doi:10.1007/978-1-84628-757-2_27

Fahringer, T., Anthes, C., Arragon, A., Lipaj, A., Müller-Iden, J., Rawlings, C., & Prodan, R. (2007). The Edutain@ Grid Project. In Veit, D. J., & Altmann, J. (Eds.), *GECON 2007. LNCS* (*Vol. 4685*, pp. 182–187). Heidelberg, Germany: Springer.

Fahringer, T., Prodan, R., Duan, R., Nerieri, F., Podlipnig, S., Qin, J., et al. Wieczorek, M. (2005). *ASKALON: A Grid application development and computing environment.* The 6th IEEE/ACM International Workshop on Grid Computing.

Falconstor. (2010). Retreived June 2010 from http://www.falconstor.com/

Farooq, U., Majumdar, S., & Parsons, E. W. (2005). *Efficiently scheduling advance reservations in Grids.* Ottawa, Canada: Dept. of Systems and Computer Engineering, Carleton University.

Feamster, N., Gao, L., & Rexford, J. (2007, January). How to lease the Internet in your spare time. [ACM.]. *ACM SIGCOMM Computer Communications Review, 37*(1), 61–64. doi:10.1145/1198255.1198265

Feng, X., & Mok, A. K. (2002). A model of hierarchical real-time virtual resources. In *Proceedings of the 23rd IEEE Real-Time Systems Symposium.*

Fernandez, A., Hayes, C., Loutas, N., Peristeras, V., Polleres, A., & Tarabanis, K. (2008). Closing the service discovery gap by collaborative tagging and clustering techniques. In *Proceedings of ISCW 2008, Workshop on Service Discovery and Resource Retrieval in the Semantic Web.*

Fernandez-Baca, D. (1989). Allocating modules to processors in a distributed system. *IEEE Transactions in Software Engineering, 15*(11), 1427-1436. doi: http://dx.doi.org/10.1109/ 32.41334

Ferretti, S., Ghini, V., Panzieri, F., Pellegrini, M., & Turrini, E. (2010). QoS–aware clouds. IEEE 3rd International Conference on Cloud Computing.

Ferris, C., Karmarkar, A., & Kevin, C. (2006). *Attachments profile*, version 1.0. Retrieved June 25, 2010, from http://www.ws-i.org/ profiles/ attachmentsprofile-1.0.html

Ferris, J., Surridge, M., & Glinka, F. (2009). *Securing real-time online interactive applications in edutain@grid.* Workshop on Real-Time Online Interactive Applications on the Grid, Las Palmas de Gran Canaria, Spain, Lecture Notes in Computer Science.

Fielding, R. T. (2000). *Architectural styles and the design of network-based software architecture.* PhD thesis, University of California, Irvine.

Fielding, R. T. (2000). *Architectural styles and the design of network-based software architectures.* PhD Dissertation. Dept. of Information and Computer Science, University of California, Irvine. Retrieved June 25, 2010, from http://www.ics.uci.edu/ ~fielding/ pubs/ dissertation/ top.htm

Fielding, R., et al. (1999). *Hypertext transfer protocol -- HTTP/1.1.* Retrieved June 25, 2010, from http://tools.ietf.org/ html/rfc2616

Filman, R., Elrad, T., Clarke, S., & Aksit, M. (2004). *Aspect-oriented software development.* Addison Wesley.

Floros, N., Meacham, K., Papay, J., & Surridge, M. (1999). Predictive resource management for unitary meta-applications. *Future Generation Computer Systems, 15*, 723–734. doi:10.1016/S0167-739X(99)00022-9

Force, D. M. (1999, June). *Common information model (CIM) version 2.2.* Specification.

Foster, I., Kesselman, C., & Tuecke, S. (2001). The anatomy of the Grid: Enabling scalable virtual organizations. [from http://www.globus.org/alliance/publications/papers/anatomy.pdf]. *The International Journal of Supercomputer Applications, 15*(3), 200. Retrieved June 25, 2010. doi:10.1177/109434200101500302

Foster, I., Kesselman, C., Nick, J., & Tuecke, S. (2002, July). Retrieved from Globus Project.

Foster, I., Yong Zhao Raicu, I., & Lu, S. (2008). *Cloud computing and Grid computing 360-degree compared.* Grid Computing Environments Workshop, GCE.

Fowler, M., & Pearson, R. (2010). *Domain specific languages.* Addison Wesley.

Freeman, T., & Foster, I. T. (2006). *Division of labor: Tools for growing and scaling grids* (pp. 40–51). ICSOC.

FRESCOR – Framework for Real-time Embedded Systems. (n.d.). *European project no. FP6/2005/IST/5-034026.* Retrieved from http://www.frescor.org

Furunäs, J. (2000). Benchmarking of a real-time system that utilises a booster. In *Proceedings of the International Conference on Parallel and Distributed Processing Techniques and Applications,* PDPTA2000.

Gallizo, G., Kuebert, R., Oberle, K., Menychtas, A., & Konstanteli, K. (2008). Service level agreements in virtualised service platforms. *Proceedings of the eChallenges 2009 Conference* eChallenges 2009, Istanbul, Turkey, October 2008.

García, J. M., Ruiz, D., Ruiz-Cortés, A., Martín-Díaz, O., & Resinas, M. (2007). *An hybrid, QoS-aware discovery of Semantic Web services using constraint programming.* 5th International Conference on Service-Oriented Computing, (pp. 69-80). Vienna.

Garcìa-Valls, M., Alonso, A., Ruiz, J., & Groba, A. M. (2002). An architecture of a quality of service resource manager middleware for flexible embedded multimedia systems. [Springer.]. *Lecture Notes in Computer Science, 2596,* 36–55. doi:10.1007/3-540-38093-0_3

Garey, M. R., & Johnson, D. S. (1979). *Computers and intractability: A guide to the theory of NP-completeness.* New York, NY: W. H. Freeman and Company.

Geelan, J. (2008). Twenty-one experts define cloud computing. Electronic magazine. Retrieved from http://cloudcomputing.sys-con.com /node/612375?page=0,1

Gerber, R., Hong, S., & Saksena, M. (1995). Guaranteeing real-time requirements with resource-based calibration of periodic processes. *IEEE Transactions on Software Engineering, 21*(7). doi:10.1109/32.392979

GGF GRAAP Working Group. (2005). *Web services agreement negotiation specification.* Retrieved from http://forge.gridforum.org/ sf/ go/ doc15831

Ghosh, S., Hansen, J., Rajkumar, R., & Lehoczky, J. (2008). Integrated resource management and scheduling with multi-resource constraints. *Proceedings of the 25th IEEE International Real-Time Systems Symposium (RTSS04).*

Gilbert Miller, H., & Veiga, J. (2009). Cloud computing: Will commodity services benefit users long term? *IT Professional, 11*(6), 57–59. doi:10.1109/MITP.2009.117

Gill, C. D., Gossett, J. M., Corman, D., Loyall, J. P., Schantz, R. E., Atighetchi, M., & Schmidt, D. C. (2005). *Integrated adaptive (QoS) management in middleware: A case study, real-time systems.*

Global Grid Forum. (2010). *Web services agreement specification.*

Globus. (2010). *Globus Project.* Retrieved from http://www.globus.org

Globus. (2010). *GT 4.0 component fact sheet: WS MDS WebMDS.* Retrieved June 25, 2010, from http://www.globus.org/toolkit/docs/4.0/info/webmds/WSMDSWebMDSFacts.html

Goddard, S., & Jeffay, K. (2001). Managing latency and buffer requirements in processing graph chains. *The Computer Journal, 44*(6). doi:10.1093/comjnl/44.6.486

Goel, A., Walpole, J., & Shor, M. (2004). Real-rate scheduling. *Proceedings of Real-time and Embedded Technology and Applications Symposium.*

Goiri, Í., Julià, F., Fitó, J. O., Macías, M., & Guitart, J. (2010). Resource-level QoS metric for CPU-based guarantees in cloud providers. In *Economics of Grids, clouds, systems, and services, LNCS 6296* (pp. 34-47).

González Harbour, M., et al. (2008). *FRESCOR deliverable D-AC2v2 – Architecture and contract model for integrated resources II.*

Google App Engine. (n.d.). Retrieved from http://code.google.com/appengine/

Google. (2010). *Google app engine. Appstats for Java.* Retrieved June 25, 2010, from http://code.google.com/intl/es-ES /appengine/docs/java/ tools/appstats.html

Google. (2010). *Using Memcache.* Retrieved June 25, 2010, from http://code.google.com/intl/en/ appengine/docs/python/memcache/ usingmemcache.html

Gopalan, K. (2001). *Real-time support in general purpose operating systems.* Research Proficiency Exam Report. Dept. of Computer Science. State University of New York at Stony Brook.

Gopalan, K., & Kang, K.-D. (2007). Coordinated allocation and scheduling of multiple resources in real-time operating systems. In *Proceedings of Workshop on Operating Systems Platforms for Embedded Real-Time Applications* (OSPERT). Pisa, Italy.

Gosling, J., & McGilton, H. (1996). *The Java™ language environment: A White Paper*. Mountain View.

Graham, S., Hull, D., & Murray, B. (2006). *Web services base notification 1.3* (WS-Base Notification). Retrieved June 25, 2010, from http://docs.oasis-open.org/ wsn/ wsn-ws_base_notification -1.3-spec-os.pdf

Graham, S., Karmarkar, A., Mischkinsky, J., Robinson, I., & Sedukhin, I. (2006). *Web services resource 1.2* (WS-Resource). Retrieved June 25, 2010, from http://docs. oasis-open.org/ wsrf/ wsrf-ws_resource- 1.2-spec-os.pdf

Gria. (2010). Retrieved from http://www.gria.org

Gu, X., Nahrstedt, K., Yuan, W., Wichadakul, D., & Xu, D. (2002). An XML-based quality of service enabling language for the Web. *Journal of Visual Languages and Computing, 13*(1), 61–95. doi:10.1006/jvlc.2001.0227

Gudgin, M., et al. (2007). *SOAP version 1.2 part 1: Messaging framework* (2nd ed). Retrieved June 25, 2010, from http://www.w3.org/ TR/ soap12-part1/

Guidi, C. (2007, March). *Formalizing languages for service oriented computing*. (Technical Report, UBLCS-2007-07), Department of Computer Science, University of Bologna.

Guidi, C., Lucchi, R., Gorrieri, R., Busi, N., & Zavattaro, G. (2006). SOCK: A calculus for service oriented computing. In *International Conference on Service Oriented Computing (ICSOC), LNCS 4294*, (pp. 327–338).

Hahn C., Cerri, D., Panfilenko, D., Benguria, G., & Sadovyhk, A. (2009). *Model transformations and deployment – From UPMSHA to WSA, agents, P2P, grid and SWS platforms*. (SHAPE project deliverable D5.3).

Hand, E. (2007). Head in the Clouds. *Nature, 449*, 963. doi:10.1038/449963a

Handley, M., & Schulzrinne, H. (1999). *SIP: Session initiation protocol*. (RFC3261, IETF).

Harada, F., Ushio, T., & Nakamoto, Y. (2007). Adaptive resource allocation control for fair QoS management. *IEEE Transactions on Computers, 56*(3). doi:10.1109/ TC.2007.39

Hasselmeyer, P., Koller, B., Schubert, L., & Wieder, P. (2006). *Towards SLA-supported resource management*.

Hasselmeyer, P., Mersch, H., Koller, B., Quyen, H. N., Schubert, L., & Wieder, P. (2007). *Implementing an SLA negotiation framework*.

He, Z., Peng, C., & Mok, A. (2006). *A performance estimation tool for video applications*. RTAS.

Herenger, H., Heek, R., Kuebert, R., & Surridge, M. (2007). Operating virtual organizations using bipartite service level agreements. In D. Talia, R. Yahyapour, & W. Ziegler (Eds.), *Grid middleware and services: Challenges and solutions*. Retrieved from http://eprints.ecs. soton.ac.uk/ 15278/

Heroix. (2006). *The best practices guide to developing and monitoring SLAs*. Whitepaper.

Hey, T., Papay, J., & Surridge, M. (2005). The role of performance engineering techniques in the context of the Grid. *Concurrency and Computation: Practice and Experience, 17*(2-4), 297-316. ISSN 1532-0626

Hiles, A. N. (1994). Service level agreements: Panacea or pain? *The TQM Magazine, 6*(2), 14–16. doi:10.1108/09544789410053966

Hovestadt, M. (2005). Fault tolerance mechanisms for SLA-aware resource management. *Parallel and Distributed Systems, 2*(2), 458–462.

Hovestadt, M. (2006). *Service level agreement aware resource management*. Paderborn.

HP. (2010). *HP integrity nonstop server evolution*. Retrieved from http://www.hp.com/ products1/ evolution/ nonstop

HPC4U. (2010). *HPC4U*. Retrieved from http://www. hpc4u.org

Hu, S., Muthusamy, V., Li, G., & Jacobsen, H.-A. (2008). Distributed automatic service composition in large-scale systems. In *Proceedings of DEBS, 2008*, 233–244. doi:10.1145/1385989.1386019

Huang, L., Peng, G., & Chiueh, T. (2004). Multi-dimensional storage virtualization. *Proceedings of the 2004 ACM SIGMETRICS Conference on Measurement and Modeling of Computer Systems.*

Humphrey, M., & Wasson, G. (2005). Architectural foundations of WSRF.NET. *International Journal of Web Services Research, 2*(2), 83-97. Retrieved June 25, 2010, from http://www.cs.virginia.edu/ ~gsw2c/ wsrf.net.html

Hwang, S., & Kesselman, C. (2003). *Grid workflow: A flexible failure handling framework for the Grid.* In 12th IEEE International Symposium on High Performance Distributed Computing (HPDC'03), Los Alamitos, CA: IEEE CS Press. Seattle, Washington, USA, USA, June 22 - 24, 2003.

IBM jrtj. (n.d.). Retrieved from http://www.ibm.com/ developerworks/java/library/ j-rtj1/index.html?S_ TACT=105AGX02& S_CMP=EDU

IBM. (1993). *Research WSLA.* Retrieved from http://www.research.ibm.com/ wsla/ WSLA093.xsd

IBM. (2003). *Web service level agreement (WSLA) language specification.* Retrieved from http://www.research.ibm.com/ wsla/ WSLASpecV1- 20030128.pdf

IBM. (2010). *Web service level agreements (WSLA) project.* Retrieved from http://www.research.ibm.com/ wsla/

Ibrahim, N., & Le Mouël, F. (2009). A survey on service composition middleware in pervasive environments. *International Journal of Computer Science Issues, 1.*

IEEE. (2008). *Standard for Information Technology – Portable operating system interface* (POSIX). Retrieved from http://www.opengroup.org/ onlinepubs/009695399

IFIP. (2010). *10.4 working group on dependable computing and fault tolerance.* Retrieved from http://www.dependability.org/ wg10.4

Inácio, N., et al. (2005). *D4.1.1. Mobile network architecture, design & implementation.* Retrieved June 25, 2010, from http://www.akogrimo.org/ download/Deliverables /D4.1.1.pdf

ISG. (2010). *The measurement ontology for IP traffic ISG website.* Retrieved from http://portal.etsi.org/portal/ server.pt/community/MOI

ISO. (2005 October). *ISO 20001 Information security management systems — Requirements.* Retrieved from http://www.27000.org/ iso-27001.htm

ISO/IEC JTC 1. (1996, June). *ISO/IEC 7498-1 open systems interconnection model.*

ITU-T Study Group 4. (2000, February). *ITU-T recommendation M.3010 rev. 200002.* Approved under the WTSC Resolution No. 1 procedure on 4 February 2000.

Iyer, S., & Druschel, P. (2001). Anticipatory scheduling: A disk scheduling framework to overcome deceptive idleness in synchronous IO. *Proceedings of the 18th ACM Symposium on Operating Systems Principles.*

Jarvis, S. A., Spooner, D. P., Keung, H. N., Cao, J., Saini, S., & Nudd, G. R. (2006). Performance prediction and its use in parallel and distributed computing systems. *Future Generations Computer Systems, 22*(7), 745-754. Retrieved from http://dx.doi.org/10.1016/ j.future.2006.02.008

Java, A. P. I. (n.d.). Retrieved from http://code.google.com/ appengine/docs/java/ overview.html

Javolution. (n.d.). Retrieved from http://javolution.org

jClouds. (n.d.). Retrieved from http://code.google.com/p/ jclouds/

Jeffree, T. (Ed.). (2006). *Provider bridges.* (ANSI/IEEE Standard 802.1ad). New York, NY: IEEE. Retrieved from http://www.oracle.com/ us/ products/ servers-storage/ networking/ 049259.pdf

Jensen, M., Schwenk, J., Gruschka, N., & Lo Iacono, L. (2009). *On technical security issues in cloud computing.* IEEE International Conference on Cloud Computing, (pp. 109-116).

Jiang, X., & Xu, D. (2004). VIOLIN: Virtual internetworking on overlay infrastructure. *Lecture Notes in Computer Science, 3358,* 937–946. doi:10.1007/978-3-540-30566-8_107

Jones, M. B. (1999). CPU reservations and time constraints: Implementation experience on Windows NT. In *Proceedings of the 3rd USENIX Windows NT Symposium,* (pp. 93–102). Seattle, Washington.

Jouault, F., & Kurtev, I. (2006). *Transforming models with ATL*. In Satellite Events at the MoDELS 2005 Conference, Revised Selected Papers, volume 3844 of Lecture Notes in Computer Science. Springer. Kent, S. (2002). Model driven engineering. *Proceedings of IFM2002, LNCS 2335* (pp. 286-298). Springer.

Kamp, P.-H., & Watson, R. N. M. (2000). Jails: Confining the omnipotent root. In *Proc. 2nd Intl. SANE Conference*.

Kang, D.-I., Gerber, R., & Saksena, M. (2000). Parametric design synthesis of distributed embedded systems. *IEEE Transactions on Computers, 49*(11).

Kang, H., Yang, X., & Yuan, S. (2007, September). Modeling and verification of Web services composition based on CPN. In *Proceedings of IFIP international Conference on Network and Parallel Computing Workshops*, (pp. 613-617). NPC. Washington, DC: IEEE Computer Society.

Kavantzas, N., et al. (2005). *Web services choreography description language*. W3C candidate recommendation: 9.

Kaveh, N., & Emmerich, W. (2003). Validating distributed object and component designs in formal methods for software architecture. [Springer Verlag.]. *Lecture Notes in Computer Science, 2804*, 63–91. doi:10.1007/978-3-540-39800-4_5

Keller, A., & Ludwig, H. (2002). *The WSLA framework: Specifying and monitoring of service level agreements for Web services. Research report.* IBM.

KENAI Project. (n.d.). Retrieved from http://kenai.com

Kernel. (2010*). CPU accounting controller.* Retrieved from http://www.kernel.org/doc/ Documentation/cgroups/cpuacct.txt

Kessler, M., Reifert, A., Lamp, D., & Voith, T. (2008). A service-oriented infrastructure for providing virtualized networks. *Bell Labs Technical Journal, 13*(3), 111-128. Wiley Periodicals, Inc. DOI: 10.1002/bltj.20328

Kim, C., Caesar, M., & Rexford, J. (2008). Floodless in SEATTLE: A scalable Ethernet architecture for large enterprises. In *SIGCOMM '08: Proceedings of the ACM SIGCOMM 2008 Conference on Data Communication* (pp. 3-14). New York, NY: ACM.

Kim, H. J., Lee, D. H., Lee, J. M., Lee, K. H., Lyu, W., & Choi, S. G. (2008). *The QoE evaluation method through the QoS-QoE correlation model.* Fourth International Conference on Networked Computing and Advanced Information Management, NCM '08, (pp. 719-725).

Knight, J. C., & Leveson, N. G. (1986). An experimental evaluation of independence in multiversion programming. *Transactions on Software Engineering, 12*, 96–109.

Koch, N., Mayer, P., Heckel, R., Gönczy, L., & Montangero, C. (2007). *D1.4a: UML for service-oriented systems, Sensoria software engineering for service-oriented overlay computers.* Retrieved from http://www.pst.ifi.lmu.de/ projekte/Sensoria/ del_24/D1.4.a.pdf

Kostanteli, K., Kyriazis, D., Varvarigou, T., Cucinotta, T., & Anastasi, G. (2009). Real-time guarantees in flexible advance reservations. In *Proceedings of the 2nd IEEE International Workshop on Real-Time Service-Oriented Architecture and Applications* (RTSOAA 2009), Seattle, Washington.

Kourtesis, D., & Paraskakis, I. (2008). Combining SAWSDL, OWL-DL and UDDI for semantically enhanced Web service discovery. In *Proceedings of the 5th European Semantic Web Conference* (ESWC 2008) [Berlin/Heidelberg, Germany: Springer-Verlag.]. *Lecture Notes in Computer Science, 5021*, 614–628. doi:10.1007/978-3-540-68234-9_45

Kraiss, A., Schoen, F., Weikum, G., & Deppisch, U. (2001). Towards response time guarantees for e-service middleware. *A Quarterly Bulletin of the Computer Society of the IEEE Technical Committee on Data Engineering, 24*(1), 58–63.

Krishnamurthy, Y., Kachroo, V., Karr, D. A., Rodrigues, C., Loyall, J. P., Schantz, R. E., & Schmidt, D. C. (2001). *Integration of QoS-enabled distributed object computing middleware for developing next-generation distributed application.* LCTES/OM.

Krishnamurthy, Y., Kachroo, V., Karr, D. A., Rodrigues, C., Loyall, J. P., Schantz, R. E., & Schmidt, D. C. (2001). *Integration of QoS-enabled distributed object computing middleware for developing next-generation distributed application* (pp. 230–237).

Krugger, I., & Matthew, R. (2004). Systematic development and exploration of service-oriented software architectures. In *Proceedings of the 4th Working IEEE/IFIP Conference on Software Architecture* (WICSA) (Oslo), (pp. 177–187).

Kuacharoen, P., Shalan, M. A., & Mooney, V. J., III. (2003). A configurable hardware scheduler for real-time systems. In *Proceedings of the International Conference on Engineering of Reconfigurable Systems and Algorithms*.

KVM. (2006). *Kernel-based virtualization driver.* Whitepaper, Qumranet 2006. Retrieved from http://docs.huihoo.com/kvm /kvm-whitepaper.pdf

KVM. (n.d.). Retrieved from http://www.linux-kvm.org

Kyriazis, D., Tserpes, K., Menychtas, A., Sarantidis, I., & Varvarigou, T. (2009, April). Service selection and workflow mapping for Grids: An approach exploiting quality-of-service information. *Concurrency and Computation, 21*(6), 739–766. doi:10.1002/cpe.1343

Labs, E. S. G. (2010). *Website.* Retrieved March 2010 from http://www.enterprisestrategygroup.com/

Lageman, M. (2005). *Solaris containers: What they are and how to use them* (Sun blueprints online). Retrieved from http://www.sun.com/ blueprints

Lakshmanan, K., & Rajkumar, R. (2008). Distributed resource kernels: OS support for end-to-end resource isolation. In *Proceedings of the 2008 IEEE Real-Time and Embedded Technology and Applications Symposium* (RTAS 2008), (pp. 195–204). Washington, DC: IEEE Computer Society.

Lamanna, D., Skene, J., & Emmerich, W. (2003). *SLAng: A language for defining service level agreements.* The Ninth IEEE Workshop on Future Trends of Distributed Computing Systems (FTDCS'03), (pp. 100- 106).

Lapadula, A., Pugliese, R., & Tiezzi, F. (2007). *Calculus for orchestration of Web services.* In *Proc. European Symposium on Programming* (ESOP). *LNCS, vol. 4421,* (pp. 33–47). Heidelberg, Germany: Springer. Retrieved from http://rap.dsi.unifi.it/cows

Lassila, O., & Swick, R. R. (n.d.). *Resource description framework (RDF) model and syntax.* Retrieved from http://citeseerx.ist.psu.edu/ viewdoc/download?doi=10.1.1.44.6030&rep=rep1&type=pdf

Laszewski, G., Hategan, M., & Kodeboyina, D. (2007). Java CoG kit workflow. In Taylor, I. J., Deelman, E., Gannon, D. B., & Shields, M. (Eds.), *Workflows for e-science* (pp. 340–356). London, UK: Springer. doi:10.1007/978-1-84628-757-2_21

Lauzac, S., Melhem, R., & Mossé, D. (2003). An improved rate-Monotonic admission control and its application. *IEEE Transactions on Computers, 58*(3).

Lawrence, K., et al. (2004). *Web services security: SOAP message security 1.1* (WS-Security 2004). Retrieved June 25, 2010, from http://www.oasis-open.org/ committees/download.php/ 16790/wss-v1.1-spec-os- SOAPMessage Security.pdf

Lee, J. W., & Asanovic, K. (2006). *METERG: Measurement-based end-to-end performance estimation technique in QoS-capable multiprocessors.* RTAS.

Lelli, J. (2010). *Design and development of deadline based scheduling mechanisms for multiprocessor systems.* Thesis presented for the partial fulfilment of the Master Degree in Computer Engineering at the University of Pisa.

Leung, J. Y. T., & Whitehead, J. (1982). On the complexity of fixed-priority scheduling of periodic, real-time tasks. *Performance Evaluation, 2,* 237–250. doi:10.1016/0166-5316(82)90024-4

Li, J., He, J., Zhu, H., & Pu, G. (2007). Modeling and verifying Web services choreography using process algebra. In *Proceedings of the 31st IEEE Software Engineering Workshop,* (pp. 256-268). Washington, DC: IEEE Computer Society. (March 06-08, 2007).

Li, W., Liang, X., Song, H., & Zhou, X. (2007, June). QoS-driven service composition modeling with extended hierarchical CPN. In *Proceedings of the First Joint IEEE/IFIP Symposium on Theoretical Aspects of Software Engineering,* (pp. 483-492). Washington, DC: IEEE Computer Society. Retrieved from http://dx.doi.org/10.1109 /TASE.2007.39

libCloud. (n.d.). Retrieved from http://ci.apache.org/projects/libcloud

Lilan, L., Tao, Y., Zhanbei, S., & Minglun, F. (2004). *A QoS-based global process planning and scheduling approach for manufacturing Grid*. Paper presented at the In Flexible Automation and Intelligent Manufacturing (FAIM 2004), Toronto, Canada.

Lindh, L., Stärner, J., & Furunäs, J. (1995). From single to multiprocessor real-time kernels in hardware. In *Proceedings of the IEEE Real Time Technology and Applications Symposium.* Chicago.

Lipari, G., & Bini, E. (2004). A methodology for designing hierarchical scheduling systems. *Journal of Embedded Computing, 1*(2).

Litchfield, J. (2007). *The foundations of Solaris real-time.* Retrieved from http://blogs.sun.com/ thejel/ entry/ the_foundations_of_ solaris_realtime

Litke, A., et al. (2005). *D4.3.1 -Architecture of the infrastructure services layer V1.* Akogrimo Consortium. Retrieved June 25, 2010, from http:// www.akogrimo.org/ modulese73d.pdf?name=Up Download&req=getit&lid=37

Litke, A., et al. (2007). *D4.3.4 -Consolidated report on the implementation of the infrastructure services layer version 1.0.* Akogrimo Consortium. Retrieved June 25, 2010, from http://www.akogrimo.org/ modulesa3f9. pdf?name= UpDownload&req =getit&lid=121

Litzkow, M., & Solomon, M. (1992). Supporting checkpointing and process migration outside the UNIX kernel. *Proceedings of the USENIX Winter Conference,* (pp. 283–290).

Liu, C. L. (1969). Scheduling algorithms for multiprocessors in a hard real-time environment. *JPL Space Programs Summary, 37*(60), 28–31.

Liu, L., & Meder, S. (2006). *Web services base faults 1.2* (WS-BaseFaults). Retrieved June 25, 2010, from http://docs.oasis-open.org/ wsrf/ wsrf-ws_base_faults-1.2-spec-os.pdf

Li-Yuan, L., Wen-An, Z., & Jun-De, S. (2006). *The research of quality of experience evaluation method in pervasive computing environment.* 1st International Symposium on Pervasive Computing and Applications, (pp. 178-182).

Lloyd, S., Gavaghan, D., Simpson, A., Mascord, M., Seneurine, C., Williams, G., et al. (2007). Integrative biology - The challenges of developing a collaborative research environment for heart and cancer modelling. *Future Generations Computer Systems, 23*(3), 457-465. doi: http://dx.doi.org/10.1016/ j.future.2006.07.002

Lo, N., & Wang, C.-H. (2007). *Web services QoS evaluation and service selection framework - A proxy-oriented approach.* IEEE Region 10 Conference TENCON 2007, (pp. 1-5).

Lodi, G., Panzieri, F., Ross, D., & Turrini, E. (2007, March). SLA-driven clustering of QoS-aware application servers. *IEEE Transactions on Software Engineering, 33*(3). doi:10.1109/TSE.2007.28

López, J. M., Díaz, J. L., & García, D. F. (2004). Utilization bounds for EDF scheduling on real-time multiprocessor systems. *Real-Time Systems: The International Journal of Time-Critical Computing, 28*(1), 39–68.

López, J. M., & Garcia, M. (2003). Utilization bounds for multiprocessor rate-Monotonic scheduling. *Real-Time Systems: The International Journal of Time-Critical Computing, 24*(1), 5–28.

Lu, C., Stankovic, J., Tao, G., & Son, S. (2002). Feedback control real-time scheduling: Framework, modeling and algorithms. *Journal on Control-Theoretic Approaches to Real-Time Computing, 9.*

Lu, J., & Turner, J. (2006, June). *Efficient mapping of virtual networks onto a shared substrate.* (Technical Report WUCSE-2006—35). Department of Computer Science and Engineering - Washington University in St. Louis, MO.

Ludascher, B., Altintas, I., Berkley, C., Higgins, D., Jaeger, E., Jones, M., et al. (2006). Scientific workflow management and the Kepler system: Research articles. *Concurrency and Computation: Practice and Experience, 18*(10), 1039-1065. doi: http://dx.doi.org/10.1002 /cpe.v18:10

Lumb, C. R., Merchant, A., & Alvarez, G. A. (2003). Façade: Virtual storage devices with performance guarantees. *Proceedings of the 2003 USENIX Conference on File and Storage Technologies.*

Ma, Q., Wang, H., Li, Y., Xie, G., & Liu, F. (2008). *A semantic QoS-aware discovery framework for Web services*. IEEE International Conference on Web Service, ICWS '08, (pp. 129-136).

Mach, R., et al. (2005). *Usage record format recommendation*. GGF draft recommendation. Retrieved June 25, 2010, from http://www.psc.edu/ ~lfm/ PSC/ Grid/ UR-WG/ UR-WG-Spec-20050925 -tracked.pdf

Machiraju, S. (2006). *Theory and practice of non-intrusive active network measurements*. Doctoral Thesis. UMI Order Number: AAI3228413, University of California at Berkeley.

Maguire, T., Snelling, D., & Banks, T. (2006). *Web services service group 1.2* (WS-ServiceGroup). Retrieved June 25, 2010, from http://docs.oasis-open.org/ wsrf/ wsrf-ws_service_group- 1.2-spec-os.pdf

Mandal, M., & Silberman, H. (2007). *Understanding Web services specifications, part 6: WS-interoperability*. Retrieved June 25, 2010, from http://www.ibm.com/ developerworks/ edu/ ws-dw-ws-understand- web-services6.html

Manica, N., Abeni, L., & Palopoli, L. (2010). Reservation-based interrupt scheduling. *Proceedings of the 16th IEEE Real-Time and Embedded Technology and Applications Symposium* (RTAS 2010), April 2010, Stockholm, Sweden.

Marte, O. S. (n.d.). Retrieved from http://marte.unican.es

Mathworks. (2010). *MATLAB - The language of technical computing*. Retrieved from http://www.mathworks.com/ products/matlab/

Maximilien, E. M., & Singh, M. P. (2002). Conceptual model of web service reputation. *SIGMOD Record, 31*(4), 36–41. doi:10.1145/637411.637417

Maximilien, E. M., & Singh, M. P. (2004). *Toward autonomic Web services trust and selection*. 2nd International Conference on Service Oriented Computing, ICSOC '04 (pp. 212-221). New York, NY: ACM.

Mayer, A., Mcgough, S., Furmento, N., Lee, W., Gulamali, M., Newhouse, S., et al. (2004). *Workflow expression: Comparison of spatial and temporal approaches*. Paper presented at the Workflow in Grid Systems Workshop, Berlin.

McFedries, P. (2008). The cloud is the computer. *IEEE Spectrum Online*. Retrieved from http://www.spectrum. ieee.org/ aug08/6490

McGough, A., Akram, A., Guo, L., Krznaric, M., Dickens, L., Colling, D., et al. (2007). *GRIDCC: Real-time workflow system*. Paper presented at the 2nd Workshop on Workflows in support of large-scale science, Monterey, California, USA.

McGough, S., Young, L., Afzal, A., Newhouse, S., & Darlington, J. (2004, September). *Workflow enactment in ICENI*. Paper presented at the UK e-Science All Hands Meeting, Nottingham, UK.

McGregor, C., & Eklund, J. M. (2008). RT SOAs to support remote critical care: Trends and challenges. In *COMPSAC '08: Proceedings of the 2008 32nd Annual IEEE International Computer Software and Applications Conference* (pp. 1199–1204).

McIntosh, M., Gudgin, M., Morrison, K. S., & Barbir, A. (2007). *Basic security profile*, version 1.0. Retrieved June 25, 2010, from http://www.ws-i.org/ profiles/ basicsecurityprofile-1.0.html

McKee, P., Taylor, S., Surridge, M., Lowe, R., & Ragusa, C. (2007). *Strategies for the service marketplace*. GECON.

McMahon, G., & Florian, M. (1975). On scheduling with ready times and due dates to minimize maximum lateness. *Operations Research, 23*(3), 475–482. doi:10.1287/ opre.23.3.475

Meacham, K. E., Floros, N., & Surridge, M. (1998). *Industrial stochastic simulations on a European meta-computer*. Euro-Par'98 Parallel Processing, Springer. *Lecture Notes in Computer Science, 1470*, 1131–1139. doi:10.1007/BFb0057975

Medhi, D. (1999). Network reliability and fault tolerance. In *Wiley encyclopedia of electrical and electronics engineering*. New York, NY: John Wiley. doi:10.1002/047134608X.W5322

Meissner, S., & Schallaböck, J. (2009). *Requirements for privacy enhancing service oriented infrastructures*. EC IST Primelife Project. Retrieved on June 30, 2009 from http://www.primelife.eu/ images/ stories/ deliverables/ h6.3.1-requirements_for_ privacy_enhancing_ soas-public.pdf

Menage, P. (n.d.). *CGROUPS.* Retrieved from http://www.mjmwired.net/ kernel/Documentation/ cgroups.txt

Menage, P. (n.d.). *CGROUPS, official Linux kernel documentation.* Retrieved from http://git.kernel.org/?p=linux/kernel/git/torvalds /linux-2.6.git

Mercer, C. W., Savage, S., & Tokuda, H. (1993). *Processor capacity reserves for multimedia operating systems.* (Technical Report CMU-CS-93-157). Pittsburgh, PA: Carnegie Mellon University.

MetaCase. (2010). *Domain-specific modeling with MetaEdit+.* Retrieved from http://www.metacase.com/

Microsoft Corporation. (2010). *NET framework conceptual overview. NET framework 4.* Retrieved from http://msdn.microsoft.com/ library/ zw4w595w.aspx

Microsoft. (2009). *Securing Microsoft's cloud infrastructure.* Retrieved June 30, 2009, from http://www.globalfoundationservices.com/ security/ documents/ SecuringtheMSCloud May09.pdf

Microsoft. (2010a). *C# programming guide on generics.* Retrieved from http://msdn.microsoft.com/ en-us/library/ ms379564(VS.80).aspx

Microsoft. (2010b). *C# programming guide on partial classes.* Retrieved from http://msdn.microsoft.com/en-us/library/ wa80x488(VS.80).aspx

Middleton, S. E., Surridge, M., Nasser, B. I., & Yang, X. (2009). *Bipartite electronic SLA as a business framework to support cross-organization load management of real-time online applications.* Real Time Online Interactive Applications on the Grid (ROIA 2009), Euro-Par 2009.

Milojicic, D. S., Douglas, F., Paindaveine, Y., Wheeler, R., & Zhou, S. (2000). Process migration. *ACM Computing Surveys, 32*(3). doi:10.1145/367701.367728

Milojicic, D. S., Giese, P., & Zint, W. (1993). *Experiences with load distribution on top of the mach microkernel.* In USENIX Systems on USENIX Experiences with Distributed and Multiprocessor Systems - Volume 4 (San Diego, California, September 22 - 23, 1993). USENIX Association, Berkeley, CA, 2-2.

Ming, W., Xian-He, S., & Yong, C. (2006). *QoS oriented resource reservation in shared environments.* Paper presented at the Sixth IEEE International Symposium on Cluster Computing and the Grid, 2006. CCGRID 06.

Mitchell, B. (2005). Resolving race conditions in asynchronous partial order scenarios. *IEEE Transactions on Software Engineering, 31*(9), 767–784. doi:10.1109/TSE.2005.104

Mitchell, B. (2008). Characterising communication channel deadlocks in sequence diagrams. *IEEE Transactions on Software Engineering, 34*(3), 305–320. doi:10.1109/TSE.2008.28

Mok, A. K., & Feng, X. A. (2001). Towards compositionality in real-time resource partitioning based on regularity bounds. In *Proceedings of the 22nd IEEE Real-Time Systems Symposium.*

Mokhtar, S. B., Preuveneers, D., Georgantas, N., Issarny, V., & Berbers, Y. (2008). Easy: Efficient semantic service discovery in pervasive computing environments with QoS and context support. *Journal of Systems and Software, 81*(5).

MOLA. (2010). *MOLA - Model transformation language.* Retrieved from http://mola.mii.lu.lv/

Molina-Jimenez, C., Shrivastava, S., Crowcroft, J., & Gevros, P. (2004). *On the monitoring of contractual service level agreements.* First IEEE International Workshop on Electronic Contracting, (pp. 1- 8).

Moorsel, A. V. (2001). *Metrics for the Internet age: Quality of experience and quality of business.* 5th Performability Workshop.

Moreno, V., & Reddy, K. (2006). *Network virtualization.* Cisco Press.

MPI. (2010). Retrieved from http://www.mpi-forum.org/docs

Muller, P. A., Fleurey, F., & Jézéquel, J.-M. (2005). Weaving executability into object-oriented meta-languages. In *Model Driven Engineering Languages and Systems, 8th International Conference, MoDELS, volume 3713 of Lecture Notes in Computer Science,* (pp. 264–278). Springer.

Muñoz Frutos, H., Kotsiopoulos, I., Vaquero Gonzalez, L. M., & Rodero Merino, L. (2009). *Enhancing service selection by semantic QoS.* 6th European Semantic Web Conference on the Semantic Web: Research and Applications (pp. 565 - 577). Heraklion: LNCS.

Murty, J. (2008). *Programming Amazon Web services.* O'Reilly Press.

Nahrstedt, K., Chu, H.-H., & Narayan, S. (1998). QoS-aware resource management for distributed multimedia applications. *Journal of High Speed Networks, 7*(3-4), 229–257.

Najjar, W. A., Lee, E. A., & Gao, G. R. (1999). Advances in the dataflow computational model. *Parallel Computing, 25*, 13–14. doi:10.1016/S0167-8191(99)00070-8

Nakajima, T. (1998). *Resource reservation for adaptive QoS mapping in real-time mach.*

NDB Accountants and Consultants. (2009). *Statement on auditing standards.* No. 70 (SAS Primer) Retrieved on Dec. 09 from http://www.sas70.us.com/

NEC. (2010). *Fault tolerant (FT) servers.* Retrieved from http://www.necam.com/ Servers/ FT

Netto, M. A., Bubendorfer, K., & Buyya, R. (2007). *SLA-based advance reservations with flexible and adaptive time QoS parameters.* Paper presented at the 5th International Conference on Service-Oriented Computing, Vienna, Austria.

Neubauer, F., Hoheisel, A., & Geiler, J. (2006). Workflow-based Grid applications. *Future Generations Computer Systems, 22*(1-2), 6-15. doi: http://dx.doi.org/10.1016/j.future.2005.08.002

Newswire, P. R. (2009). *Verizon business offers tips on how enterprises can secure the cloud.* Retrieved on June 30, 2009, from http://www.prnewswire.com/ news-releases/ verizon-business-offers-tips -on-how-enterprises -can-secure-the-cloud -96784414.html

Nextgrid. (2010). *NextGRID SLA schema.* Retrieved from http://www.nextgrid.org/ GS/ management_systems/ SLA_management/ NextGRID_SLA_schema.pdf

Niemi, A. (2004). *Session initiation protocol (SIP) extension for event state publication. RFC 3903.* IETF.

Norton, W. B. (2008). *Video Internet: The next wave of massive disruption to the U.S. peering ecosystem* (v1.6). Retrieved December 17, 2009, from http://www.drpeering.net/ a/ Internet_Peering _White_ Papers_files/ Video Internet 1.6.pdf

Nottingham, M. (2004). *Simple SOAP binding profile,* version 1.0. Retrieved June 25, 2010, from http://www.ws-i.org/ Profiles/ SimpleSoapBinding Profile-1.0.html

OASIS. (2006). *OASIS standard v2.0.4- ebXML business process specification schema technical specification* v2.0.4.

OASIS. (2007). *Web services business process execution language,* version 2.0.

OASIS. (2010). *Service oriented architecture reference model.* Retrieved from http://www.oasis-open.org/ committees/ tc_home.php? wg_abbrev=soa-rm

OASIS. (2010). *Web services notification (WSN) TC website.* Retrieved June 25, 2010, from http://www.oasis-open.org/ committees/tc_home. php?wg_abbrev=wsn

OASIS. (n.d.). *Web services distributed management (WSDM) TC.* Retrieved June 25, 2010, from http://www.oasis-open.org/ committees/ tc_home.php ?wg_abbrev =wsdm

Obeo. (2010). *Acceleo: MDA generator.* Retrieved from http://www.acceleo.org /pages/home/en

Oberle, K., Kessler, M., Stein, M., Voith, T., Lamp, D., & Berger, S. (2009). Network virtualization: The missing piece. *Bell Labs Technical Journal, 13*(3), 111–128.

Oberle, K. Stein., M., Voith, T., Gallizo, G., & Kuebert, R. (2010, October). The network aspect of infrastructure as a service. In *Proceedings of 14th International Conference on Intelligence in Next Generation Networks,* 2010.

Oberle, K., Kessler, M., Stein, M., Voith, T., Lamp, D., & Berger, S. (2009). *Network virtualization: The missing piece.* 13th International Conference on Intelligence in Next Generation Networks, 2009. ICIN 2009, (pp. 1-6). Retrieved from http://irmosproject.eu/Files/ ICIN2009_ FinalVersion_Network Virtualization.pdf

OCCI specification. (n.d.). Retrieved from http://forge.ogf.org/sf/docman /do/listDocuments/projects.occiwg / docman.root.drafts. occi_specification

OCCI. (n.d.). Retrieved from http://www.occi-wg.org

OCERA – Open Components for Embedded Real-time Applications. (2001). (European Project No. IST-2001-35102). Retrieved from http://www.ocera.org

OCERA Project deliverable D1.1 - RTOS. (n.d.). Retrieved from http://www.ocera.org/download /documents/ documentation/wp1.html

OGF. (n.d.). *Cloud storage for cloud computing.* Retrieved from http://ogf.org/Resources/ documents/CloudStorageForCloudComputing.pdf

Oikawa, S., & Rajkumar, R. (1999). Portable RK: A portable resource kernel for guaranteed and enforced timing behavior. In *Proceedings of the 5ᵗʰ IEEE Real-Time Technology and Applications Symposium* (RTAS'99), (p. 111). Washington, DC: IEEE Computer Society.

Oikawa, S., et al. (1999). *Portable RK: A portable resource kernel for guaranteed and enforced timing behavior.* Fifth IEEE Real-Time Technology and Applications Symposium. Vancouver.

Oinn, T., Greenwood, M., Addis, M., Alpdemir, M. N., Ferris, J., Glover, K., et al. (2006). Taverna: Lessons in creating a workflow environment for the life sciences: Research articles. *Concurrency and Computing: Practice and Experience, 18*(10), 1067-1100. doi: http://dx.doi.org/10.1002/cpe.v18:10

Oldevik, J., Neple, T., Grønmo, R., Aagedal, J. Ø., & Berre, A.-J. (2005). Toward standardised model to text transformations. In Hartman, A., & Kreische, D. (Eds.), *ECMDAFA 2005. LNCS* (*Vol. 3748*, pp. 239–253). Heidelberg, Germany: Springer.

Olmedo, V., Villagrá, V. A., Konstanteli, K., Burgosc, J. E., & Berrocal, J. (2009). Network mobility support for Web service-based grids through the session initiation protocol. *Future Generation Computer Systems, 25*(7). doi:10.1016/ j.future.2008.11.007

OMG. (2002). UMLTM profile for modeling quality of service and fault tolerance characteristics and mechanisms, *2002.*

OMG. (2008). *A UML profile for MARTE: Modeling and analysis of real-time embedded systems*, 2008.

OMG. (2008a). *UML profile for modeling quality of service and fault tolerance characteristics and mechanisms*, v1.1. Retrieved May 31, 2010, from http://www.omg.org /spec/QFTP/

OMG. (2008b). *OMG systems modeling language* (OMG SysML) version 1.1. Retrieved June 7, 2010, from http://www.omg.org/ spec/SysML/

OMG. (2009a). *Business process model and notation* (BPMN) *FTF beta 1 for version 2.0.* OMG. Retrieved June 12, 2010, from http://www.bpmn.org/

OMG. (2009b). *UML profile for MARTE: Modeling and analysis of real-time embedded systems*, version 1.0. Retrieved June 3, 2010, from http://www.omg.org /spec/MARTE/

OMG. (2009c). *Service oriented architecture modeling kanguage (SoaML) - Specification for the UML profile and metamodel for services* (UPMS). Retrieved June 12, 2010, from http://www.omg.org/ spec/SoaML/

OMG. (2010a). *Object management group.* Retrieved from http://www.omg.org

OMG. (2010b). *OMG's meta-object facility.* Retrieved from http://www.omg.org/mof/

OMG. (2010c). *Unified modeling language, infrastructure version 2.3.* Retrieved June 3, 2010, from http://www.omg.org/ spec/UML/

OMG. (2010d). *MOF support for semantic structures RFP.* (Document ad/06-06-08). Retrieved from http://www.omg.org/ cgi-bin/doc?ad/2006-6-8

OpenArchitectureWare. (2010a). *OpenArchitectureWare.* Retrieved from http://www.openarchitectureware.org/

OpenArchitectureWare. (2010b). *Xpand language.* Retrieved from http://wiki.eclipse.org/ Xpand

Opennebula. (n.d.). Retrieved from http://www.opennebula.org/

Oracle Corporation. (n.d.). *VirtualBox website.* Retrieved from http://www.virtualbox.org/

O'Reilly, T. (2003). *REST vs. SOAP at Amazon.* Retrieved from http://www.oreillynet.com/ pub/ wlg/ 3005

Overton, C. (2002). On the theory and practice of Internet SLAs. *Journal of Computer Resource Measurement, 32*–45.

OWL. (2009). *Ontology Web language version 2*. Retrieved from http://www.w3.org/TR/owl2-overview/

Palopoli, L. (2008). A QuoSA - Adaptive quality of service architecture. *Software, Practice & Experience, 39*(1).

Palopoli, L., Cucinotta, T., Marzario, L., & Lipari, G. (2009). AQuoSA — Adaptive quality of service architecture. *Software, Practice & Experience, 39*(1), 1–31. doi:10.1002/spe.883

Palopoli, L., & Cucinotta, T. (2007). Feedback scheduling for pipelines of tasks. In *Proceedings of the 10th Conference on Hybrid Systems Computation and Control*.

Papyrus. (2010). *Papyrus*. Retrieved from http://www.papyrusuml.org

Parallels Holdings Ltd. (n.d.). *Parallels virtuozzo containers*. Retrieved from http://www.parallels.com/ products/ virtuozzo/ lib/ download/ wp/

Parasuraman, A., Zeithaml, V. A., & Leonard, L. (1985). A conceptual model of service quality and its implications for future research. *Journal of Marketing, 49*(4), 41–50. doi:10.2307/1251430

Partikle. (n.d.). Retrieved from http://www.e-rtl.org/ partikle

Patel, P., Ranabahu, A., & Sheth, A. (2009). *Service level agreement in cloud computing. OOPSLA 2009, 24th ACM SIGPLAN*. ACM.

Patrikakis, C., Masikos, M., & Zouraraki, O. (2004). Distributed denial of service attacks. *The Journal of Internet Protocol, 7*(4), 13–35.

Paxson, V., Almes, G., Mahdavi, J., & Mathis, M. (1998). *RFC2330 - Framework for IP performance metrics*.

Peterson, L. L., & Davie, B. S. (1996). *Computer networks: A systems approach*. San Francisco, CA: Morgan Kaufmann.

Petri, C. A. (1962). *Kommunikation mit Automaten*. Schriften des Rheinisch- 6 Westfälischen Institutes für Instrumentelle Mathematik an der Universität Bonn Nr. 2, 1962.

Ploß, A., Glinka, F., & Gorlatch, S. (2009). *A case study on using RTF for developing multi-player online games. Euro-Par 2008 Workshops-Parallel Processing* (pp. 390–400). Springer.

POSIX. (2004). *IEEE standard for Information Technology – Portable operating system interface (POSIX) – System interfaces*. (IEEE Std. 1003.1).

Povzner, A., Brandt, A., Golding, R., Wong, T., & Maltzahn, C. (2008). *Virtualizing disk performance with Fahrrad*. USENIX Conference on File and Storage Technologies.

Prandi, D., & Quaglia, P. (2007). Stochastic COWS. In *Proc. 5th International Conference on Service Oriented Computing, ICSOC~'07. LNCS vol. 4749*.

Pratt, I. (2003). Xen and the art of virtualization. In *Proceedings of the Nineteenth ACM Symposium on Operating Systems Principles*.

Preston, W. C. (2002). *Using SANs and NAS*. O Reilly.

Python, A. P. I. (n.d.). Retrieved from http://code.google.com/ appengine/docs/python/ overview.html

Qumranet. (2010). *KVM - Kernal-based virtualization machine - White paper*.

Rackspace. (2010). *The PCI toolbox*. Retrieved July 5, 2010, from http://www.rackspace.com/ managed_hosting/ services/ security/ pci.php

Raimondi, F., Skene, J., & Emmerich, W. (2008). *Efficient online monitoring of Web-service SLAs*. 16th ACM SIGSOFT International Symposium on Foundations of Software Engineering. Atlanta, GA: ACM.

Rajic, H., et al. (2004). *Distributed resource management application API*, specification 1.0. Retrieved from https:// forge.gridforum.org/ projects/ drmaa-wg

Rajkumar, R., Juvva, K., Molano, A., & Oikawa, S. (1998). Resource kernels: A resource-centric approach to real-time and multimedia systems. In *Proceedings of the SPIE/ACM Conference on Multimedia Computing and Networking* (MMCN 2008), (pp. 150–164). San Jose, California.

Rajkumar, R., Lee, C., Lehoczky, J. P., & Siewiorek, D. P. (1998). *Practical solutions for QoS-based resource allocation.*

Ran, S. (2003). *A model for Web services discovery with QoS. SIGecom Exch* (pp. 1–10). ACM.

Randell, B., Lee, P., & Treleaven, P. C. (1978). Reliability issues in computing system design. *ACM Computing Surveys, 10*(2), 123–165. doi:10.1145/356725.356729

Ranjan, R., Chan, L., Harwood, A., Karunasekera, S., & Buyya, R. (2007). Decentralised resource discovery service for large scale federated Grids. In *Proceedings of the Third IEEE International Conference on e-Science and Grid Computing* 2007 (pp. 379-387).

Ravindran, B. (2008). Engineering dynamic real-time distributed systems: Architecture, system description language, and middleware. *IEEE Transactions on Software Engineering, 28*(1), 30–57. doi:10.1109/32.979988

RDF. (2004). *RDF/XML syntax specification.* Retrieved from http://www.w3.org/TR/ REC-rdf-syntax

Reddy, A. L. N., Wyllie, J., & Wijayaratne, K. B. R. (1993). Disk scheduling in a multimedia I/O system. *Proceedings of the first International Conference on Multimedia.*

Regehr, J., & Stankovic, J. A. (2001). Augmented CPU reservations: Towards predictable execution on general-purpose operating systems. In *Proceedings of the IEEE Real-Time Technology and Applications Symposium* (RTAS 2001), May 2001, Taipei.

Register. (2009). *Webhost attack.* Retrieved June 30, 2009 from http://www.theregister.co.uk/ 2009/ 06/ 08/ webhost_attack/

Reistad, B., et al. (2006). *Web services resource transfer* (WS-RT). Retrieved June 25, 2010, from http://www.ibm.com/ developerworks/ library/ specification/ ws-wsrt/ ?S_TACT=105AGX04 &S_CMP=LP

Reservoir Project. (n.d.). Retrieved from http://www.reservoir-fp7.eu

Rimal, B. P., Choi, E., & Lumb, I. (2009). A Taxonomy and survey of cloud computing systems. In R. Dienstbier (Ed.), *Fifth International Joint Conference on Networked Computing and Advanced Information Management,* (pp. 44-51).

Ripoll, I., Pisa, P., Abeni, L., Gai, P., Lanusse, A., Saez, S., & Privat B. (2002). *OCERA project deliverable D1.1 – RTOS state of the art analysis.*

Risse, T., Wombacher, A., Surridge, M., Taylor, S., & Aberer, K. (2001, August). Online scheduling in distributed message converter systems. *Proceedings of 13th Parallel and Distributed Computing and Systems* (PDCS 2001), Anaheim, CA.

Roach, A. B. (2002). *Session initiation protocol (SIP) – Specific event notification. RFC 3265.* IETF.

Rochwerger, B., Breitgand, D., Levy, E., Galis, A., Nagin, K., Llorente, I., … Galán, F. (2009). The RESERVOIR model and architecture for open federated cloud computing. *IBM Journal of Research & Development, 53*(4), Paper 4.

Rosenberg, F., Platzer, C., & Dustdar, S. (2006). *Bootstrapping performance and dependability attributes of Web service.* ICWS.

Rouvoy, R., Barone, P., Ding, Y., Eliassen, F., Hallsteinsen, S., Lorenzo, J., et al. Scholz, U. (2009). MUSIC: Middleware support for self-adaptation in ubiquitous and service-oriented environments. In B. H. C. Cheng, et al. (Eds.), *Software engineering for self-adaptive systems. LNCS, vol. 5525.* Heidelberg, Germany: Springer.

RT-Druid. (2004). *RT-Druid: A tool for architecture level design of embedded systems.* White paper, Evidence S.r.l. 2004.

RTSC. (2010). *Real-time software components.* Retrieved from http://www.eclipse.org/ proposals/rtsc

Rtsj. (n.d.). Retrieved from http://www.rtsj.org/specjavadoc /book_index.html

Ruemmler, C., & Wilkes, J. (1994). An introduction to disk drive modeling. *IEEE Computer, 27*(3).

Saewong, S., Rajkumar, R., & Lehoczky, J. P. Klein & M. H. (2002). Analysis of hierarchical fixed-priority scheduling. In *Proceedings of the IEEE Euromicro Conference on Real-Time Systems.*

Sahai, A., Machiraju, V., Sayal, M., Jin, L. J., & Casati, F. (2002). *Automated SLA monitoring for Web services.* HP.

Sanbolic. (2010). *Melio file system.* Retrieved March 2010 from http://www.sanbolic.com/ melioFS.htm

SAWSDL. (2007). *Semantic annotations for WSDL.* Retrieved from http://www.w3.org/TR/sawsdl/

SCA. (2010). *STP service component architecture project.* Retrieved from http://www.eclipse.org/ stp/sca/

Schantz, R. E., Loyall, J. P., Rodrigues, C., Schmidt, D. C., Krishnamurthy, Y., & Pyarali, I. (2003). Flexible and adaptive QoS control for distributed real-time and embedded middleware. In *Proceedings of the ACM/IFIP/ USENIX 2003 International Conference on Middleware* (pp. 374–393). New York, NY: Springer-Verlag New York, Inc.

Schlosser, M., Sintek, M., Decker, S., & Nejdl, W. (2002). *A scalable and ontology-based P2P infrastructure for Semantic Web services.* Second International Conference on Peer-to-Peer Computing (P2P'02), (p. 104).

Schmidt, C., Levine, D. L., & Mungee, S. (1997). The design of the TAO real-time object request broker. *Computer Communications, 21,* 294–324. doi:10.1016/ S0140-3664(97)00165-5

Schmidt, K., & Stahl, C. (2004). A Petri net semantic for BPEL4WS validation and application. In *Proceedings of the 11th Workshop on Algorithms and Tools for Petri Nets,* (pp. 1-6).

Schruben, L. (2000). *Mathematical programming models of discrete event system dynamics.* In: Winter Simulation Conference 2000, (pp. 381-385). Retrieved from http:// ieeexplore.ieee.org/ iel5/7220/19454/00899742.pdf

Schubert, L., Jeffery, K., Neidecker-Lutz, B., et al. (2010). *The future of cloud computing-Opportunities for European cloud computing beyond 2010.* Retrieved June 25, 2010, from http://cordis.europa.eu/fp7/ict/ ssai/docs/ cloud-report -final.pdf

Schwiegelshohn, U., Yahyapour, R., & Wieder, P. (2006). Resource management for future generation Grids. In Getov, V., Laforenza, D., & Reinefeld, A. (Eds.), *Future generation Grids* (pp. 99–112). Springer, US. doi:10.1007/978-0-387-29445-2_6

Scilab. (2010). *The free platform for numerical computation.* Retrieved from http://www.scilab.org/

Scott, M., & Crowcroft, J. (2008, April). *MOOSE: Addressing the scalability of Ethernet.* Poster session presented at EuroSys 2008, Glasgow, Scotland.

Seidel, J., Wäldrich, O., Wieder, P., Yahyapour, R., & Ziegler, W. (2007). *Using SLA for resource management and scheduling - A survey.*

SEKT. (2010). Retrieved from http://www.sekt-project. com/

Selic, B. (2004). *Fault tolerance techniques for distributed systems.* IBM Technical Library.

Serhani, M., Dssouli, R., Hafid, A., & Sahraoui, H. (2005). *A QoS broker based architecture for efficient Web services selection.* IEEE International Conference on Web Services, ICWS 2005, (pp. 113- 120).

Setz, J. (2007). *Inter-process communication in RTAI and RTLinux.* Saarland University.

Sha, L., Rajkumar, R., & Lehoczky, J. P. (1990). Priority inheritance protocols: An approach to real-time synchronization. [IEEE Computer Society.]. *IEEE Transactions on Computers, 39*(9), 1175–1185. doi:10.1109/12.57058

Shankaran, N., Koutsoukos, X. D., Schmidt, D. C., Xue, Y., & Lu, C. (2006). Hierarchical control of multiple resources in distributed real-time and embedded systems. In *ECRTS'06: Proceedings of the 18th Euromicro Conference on Real-Time Systems,* (pp. 151–160). Washington, DC: IEEE Computer Society.

SHAPE. (2010). *SHAPE project.* (EU STREP – fp7 ICT-2007-216408). Retrieved from http://www.shape-project.eu

Shenoy, P., & Vin, H. M. (1997). *Cello: A disk scheduling framework for next generation operating systems.* ACM Sigmetrics Conference.

Shin, I., & Lee, I. (2004). Compositional real-time scheduling framework. In *Proceedings of the 25th IEEE International Real-Time Systems Symposium* (pp. 57–67).

Sild, S., Maran, U., Romberg, M., Schuller, B., & Benfenati, E. (2005). OpenMolGRID: Using automated workflows in GRID computing environment. In Sloot, P. M. A., Hoekstra, A. G., Priol, T., Reinefeld, A., & Bubak, M. (Eds.), *Advances in Grid computing - EGC 2005* (*Vol. 3470*, pp. 464–473). Berlin/Heidelberg, Germany: Springer. doi:10.1007/11508380_48

Singh, G., Kesselman, C., & Deelman, E. (2006). *Application-level resource provisioning on the Grid*. Paper presented at the Second IEEE International Conference on e-Science and Grid Computing.

Singh, T., & Singh, K. (2009). *REST vs. SOAP – The right Web service*. Retrieved from http://www.taranfx.com

Skene, J., Raimondi, F., & Emmerich, W. (2009). Service-level agreements for electronic services. *IEEE Transactions on Software Engineering*, *99*, 288–304.

Sloane, E. (2007, April). A hybrid approach to modeling SAO systems of systems using CPN and MESA/EXTEND. In *Proceedings of 1st IEEE Systems Conference Waikiki Beach*, Honolulu, Hawaii, USA. Retrieved from http://ieeexplore.ieee.org/ iel5/4258845/4258846/ 04258897.pdf

Snelling, D., Fisher, M., Basermann, A., Wray, F., Wieder, P., & Surridge, M. (2008). *NextGRID vision and architecture White Paper V5*. Retrieved from http://www.nextgrid. org/ download/ publications/ NextGRID_Architecture _White_Paper.pdf

Somasundaram, T. S., Balachandar, R. A., Kandasamy, V., Buyya, R., Raman, R., Mohanram, R., & Varun, S. (2006). Semantic-based Grid resource discovery and its integration with the Grid service broker. In *Proceedings of the 14th International Conference on Advanced Computing and Communications* (ADCOM 2006) (pp. 84-89). Dec. 20-23. Piscataway, NJ: IEEE Press. ISBN: 1-4244-0715-X

Soonwook, H., & Kesselman, C. (2003). Grid workflow: A flexible failure handling framework for the grid. *Proceedings of the 12th IEEE International Symposium on the High Performance Distributed Computing*, 2003.

Sotomayor, B., Montero, R. S., Llorente, I. M., & Foster, I. (2009). *Virtual infrastructure management in private and hybrid clouds*. IEEE Internet Computing. ISSN: 1089-7801

Specification, U. D. D. I. (2004). Retrieved from http://www.uddi.org/pubs/ uddi_v3.htm

Spillner, J., & Schill, A. (2009). *Dynamic SLA template adjustments based on service property monitoring*. IEEE Conference on Cloud Computing.

Spooner, D. P., Cao, J., Jarvis, S. A., He, L., & Nudd, G. R. (2005). Performance-aware workflow management for Grid computing. *Comput. J.*, *48*(3), 347-357. doi: http://dx.doi.org/10.1093/ comjnl/bxh090

Srinivasan, A., & Baruah, S. (2002). Deadline-based scheduling of periodic task systems on multiprocessors. *Information Processing Letters*, *84*(2), 93–98. doi:10.1016/S0020-0190(02)00231-4

Srinivasan, L., & Banks, T. (2006). *Web services resource lifetime 1.2* (WS-ResourceLifetime). Retrieved June 25, 2010, from http://docs.oasis-open.org/ wsrf/ wsrf-ws_resource _lifetime-1.2-spec -os.pdf

Stanovich, M., et al. (2009). *Defects of the POSIX sporadic server and how to correct them*.

Steere, D., Shor, M. H., Goel, A., & Walpole, J. (2000). Control and modeling issues in computer operating systems: Resource management for real-rate computer applications. In *Proceedings of 39th IEEE Conference on Decision and Control*.

Stein, M., Oberle, K., Voith, T., Kübert, R., Gallizo, G., Berger, S.,... Neple, T. (2009, May). *Initial version of path manager architecture. Interactive real-time multimedia applications on service oriented infrastructures*. (ICT FP7-214777).

Stevens, R. D., Robinson, A. J., & Goble, C. A. (2003). MyGrid: Personalized bioinformatics on the information Grid. *Bioinformatics (Oxford, England)*, 19.

Stevens, R., Glover, K., Greenhalgh, C., Jennings, C., Pearce, S., Li, P., et al. (2003). Performing in silico experiments on the Grid: A users perspective. *Proceedings of UK e-Science All Hands Meeting*, 2003.

Stoica, I., Abdel-Wahab, H., Jeffay, K., Sanjoy, K., Baruah, J. E., Gehrke, C., & Plaxton, G. (1996). A proportional share resource allocation algorithm for real-time, time-shared systems. *Proceedings of the IEEE Real-Time Systems Symposium*.

Sturm, R., Morris, W., & Jander, M. (2000). *Foundations of service level management*. SAMS Publishing.

Sun Microsystems. (2008). *Press release*. Retrieved November 2008 from http://www.hpcwire.com/ special-features/ sc08/ offthewire/ Suns_Lustre_ File_System _Powers_Top _Supercomputers.html

Sun Microsystems. (n.d.). *SUN Cloud*. Retrieved from http://developers.sun.com/cloud/

Sun Service Registry for SOA. (2005). Retrieved from http://xml.coverpages.org/ ni2005-06-15-a.html

SUPER. (2010). Retrieved from http://www.ip-super.org/

Swordfish. (2010). *Swordfish SOA runtime framework project*. Retrieved from http://www.eclipse.org/ swordfish/

SWSF. (2010). Retrieved from http://www.w3.org/Submission /SWSF

SWSI. (2010). Retrieved from http://www.swsi.org

SWSL. (2010). Retrieved from http://www.w3.org/Submission /SWSF-SWSL

SWSO. (2010). Retrieved from http://www.daml.org/ services/ swsf/1.0/swso

Takeuchi, H., & Quelch, J. (1983). Quality is more than making a good product. *Harvard Business Review*.

Tang, Y., Yang, Y., Zhao, M., Yao, L., & Li, Y. (2007). *CoS-based QoS management framework for grid services*.

Taylor, I., Shields, M., Wang, I., & Harrison, A. (2007). The Triana workflow environment: Architecture and applications. In Taylor, I. J., Deelman, E., Gannon, D. B., & Shields, M. (Eds.), *Workflows for e-science* (pp. 320–339). London, UK: Springer. doi:10.1007/978-1-84628-757-2_20

The Globus Alliance. (2005). *GT 4.0 WS MDS trigger service*. Retrieved June 25, 2010, from http://www.globus.org/toolkit /docs/4.0/info/trigger/

The Globus Alliance. (2005). *GT 4.0: Information services: Aggregator framework*. Retrieved June 25, 2010, from http://www.globus.org/toolkit /docs/4.0/info/aggregator/

The Globus Alliance. (2005). *GT 4.0: Information Services: Index*. Retrieved June 25, 2010, from http://www.globus.org/toolkit /docs/4.0/info/index /index.pdf

The Open Grid Forum. (2004). *Grid resource allocation agreement protocol*.

Thorncock, N. C., Tu, X., & Flanagan, J. K. (1997). A stochastic disk I/O simulation technique. *Proceedings of the 1997 Winter Simulation Conference*.

Tian, M., Gramm, A., Naumowicz, T., Ritter, H., & Schiller, J. (2003). *A concept for QoS integration in Web service*. Fourth International Conference on Web Information Systems Engineering Workshops (WISEW'03), (pp. 149-155). Rome.

Timesys. (n.d.). Retrieved from http://www.timesys.com/java

Tokuda, H., & Kitayama, T. (1993). Dynamic QoS control based on real-time threads. *NOSSDAV '93: Proceedings of the 4th International Workshop on Network and Operating System Support for Digital Audio and Video*.

Tong, H., & Zhang, S. (2006). *A fuzzy multi-attribute decision making algorithm for Web services selection based on QoS*. IEEE Asia-Pacific Conference on Services Computing, APSCC '06., (pp. 51-57).

Topcuoglu, H., Hariri, S., & Min-You, W. (2002). Performance-effective and low-complexity task scheduling for heterogeneous computing. *IEEE Transactions on Parallel and Distributed Systems, 13*(3), 260–274. doi:10.1109/71.993206

Touch, J., & Perlman, R. (2009, May). *Transparent interconnection of lots of links (TRILL): Problem and applicability statement*. (Internet Engineering Task Force, RFC 5556). Retrieved February 20, 2010, from http://tools.ietf.org/ html/ rfc5556

Touch, J., Wang, Y.-S., Eggert, L., & Finn, G. (2003, March). *A virtual Internet architecture*. Future Developments of Network Architectures (FDNA) at ACM Sigcomm, August 2003. (ISI Technical Report ISI-TR-570, March 2003).

Treadwell, J. (2005). *Open Grid services architecture glossary of terms*. (Global Grid Forum OGSA-WG. GFD-I, 044).

Trunfio, P., Talia, D., Papadakis, H., Fragopoulou, P., Mordacchini, M., & Pennanen, M. (2007). Peer-to-Peer resource discovery in Grids: Models and systems. *Future Generation Computer Systems*, *23*(7), 864–878. doi:10.1016/j.future.2006.12.003

Tsafrir, D., Etsion, Y., & Feitelson, D. (2007). Secretly monopolizing the CPU without superuser privileges. In *Proceedings of the 16th USENIX Security Symposium*, (Boston, MA).

Tserpes, K., Kyriazis, D., Menychtas, A., & Varvarigou, T. (2008). A novel mechanism for provisioning of high-level quality of service information in Grid environments. *European Journal of Operational Research*, *191*(3), 1113–1131. doi:10.1016/j.ejor.2007.07.012

Tserpes, K., Aisopos, F., Kyriazis, D., & Varvarigou, T. (2010). Service selection decision support in the Internet of services. In J. Altmann, & O. Rana (Ed.), *GECON 2010. LNCS 6296*, (pp. 16-33). Springer.

Tserpes, K., Kyriazis, D., Menychtas, A., Litke, A., Christogiannis, C., & Varvarigou, T. (2008). *Evaluating quality provisioning levels in service oriented business environments*. 12th International IEEE Enterprise Distributed Object Computing Conference, (pp. 309-315).

Tuecke, S., et al. (2003). *Open Grid services infrastructure* (OGSI), version 1.0, Retrieved June 25, 2010, from http://www.ggf.org/ documents/ GFD.15.pdf

UK Parliament. (1998). *Data protection act 1998*.

Unicore Forum. (2003). *Unicore plus final report: Uniform interface to computing resource*. Retrieved December, 2004, from http://www.unicore.eu/ documentation/files/ erwin-2003-UPF.pdf

Unisys. (2010). *Secure cloud solution service brief*. Retrieved on July 5, 2010, from http://www.unisys.com/ unisys/ ri/ pub/ bl/ detail.jsp?id= 10020100026

Valente, P., & Checconi, F. (2010). High throughput disk scheduling with deterministic guarantees on bandwidth distribution. *IEEE Transactions on Computers*, *59*(9). doi:10.1109/TC.2010.105

van der Aalst, W. M. P., ter Hofstede, A. H. M., Kiepuszewski, B., & Barros, A. P. (2003). Workflow patterns. *Distributed and Parallel Databases*, *14*(1), 5–51. doi:10.1023/A:1022883727209

Van der Aalst, W. (2010). *Workflow patterns*. Retrieved from http://www.workflowpatterns.com

van Rossum, G. (2010). *Appstats - RPC instrumentation and optimizations for app engine*. Retrieved from http:// code.google.com/intl /es-ES/events/io/2010/ sessions/ appstatsrpc-appengine.html

Vaquero, L. M., Rodero-Merino, L., Caceres, J., & Lindner, M. (2009). A break in the clouds: Towards a cloud definition. *ACM SIGCOMM Computer Communication Review*, *39*(1), 50–55. doi:10.1145/1496091.1496100

Vardhan, V., Sachs, D. G., Yuan, W., Harris, A. F., Adve, S. V., Jones, D. L., et al. Nahrstedt, K. (2005). Integrating finegrain application adaptation with global adaptation for saving energy. In *Proceedings of the 2nd International Workshop on Power-Aware Real-Time Computing* (PARC). Jersey City, New Jersey, USA.

Varvarigou, T., Tserpes, K., Kyriazis, D., Silvestri, F., & Psimogiannos, N. (2010). A study on the effect of application and resource characteristics on the QoS in service provisioning environments. *International Journal of Distributed Systems and Technologies*, *1*(1), 55–75. doi:10.4018/jdst.2010090804

vCloud API Programming Guide. (n.d.). Retrieved from http://communities.vmware.com /servlet/JiveServlet/previewBody/ 12463-102-1-13007/ vCloud_API_Guide.pdf

VMware Inc. (2009). *Protecting mission-critical workloads with VMware fault tolerance*. Retrieved from http:// www.vmware.com/ resources/ techresources/ 1094

VMWare Inc. (2010). *VMWare media resource center - Company milestones*. Retrieved from http://www.vmware.com/ company/ mediaresource/ milestones.html

VMware vCloud. (n.d.). Retrieved from http://www.vmware.com/ products/vcloud/

VMware. (2010). *Fault tolerance* (FT). Retrieved from http://www.vmware.com /resources/ techresources/ 1094

Völker, L., Martin, D., El Khayat, I., Werle, C., & Zitterbart, M. (2009). A node architecture for 1000 future networks. In *Proceedings of IEEE International Conference on Communications Workshops, 2009*, 1–5. doi:10.1109/ ICCW.2009.5207996

Vu, L.-H., Hauswirth, M., & Aberer, K. (2005). *QoS-based service selection and ranking with trust and reputation management. CoopIS; DOA; ODBASE. On the move to meaningful Internet systems.* Springer.

Vu, L. H., Hauswirth, M., & Aberer, K. (2005). *Towards P2P-based Semantic Web service discovery with QoS support.* Workshop on Business Processes and Services (BPS). Nancy.

Wachs, M., Abd-El-Malek, M., Thereska, E., & Ganger, G. R. (2007). Argon: Performance insulation for shared storage servers. *Proceedings of the 2007 USENIX Conference on File and Storage Technologies.*

Waheed Iqbal, M. D. (2009). *SLA-driven adaptive resource management for Web applications on a heterogeneous compute cloud. Lecture Notes in Computer Science.* LNCS.

Wang, H.-C., Lee, C.-S., & Ho, T.-H. (2007). Combining subjective and objective QoS factors for personalized Web service selection. *Expert Systems with Applications, 32*(2), 571–584. doi:10.1016/j.eswa.2006.01.034

Wang, C. H., & Wang, F. J. (2007). An object-oriented modular Petri nets for modeling service oriented applications. In *Proceedings of the 31st Annual international Computer Software and Applications Conference* (pp. 479-486). COMPSAC. Washington, DC: IEEE Computer Society. Retrieved from http://dx.doi.org/10.1109/COMPSAC.2007.68

Wang, L., et al. (2008). *Scientific cloud computing: Early definition and experience.* 10th IEEE International Conference on High Performance Computing and Communications, (pp. 825–830).

Wang, X., Vitvar, T., Kerrigan, M., & Toma, I. (2006). A QoS-aware selection model for semantic Web Services. In A. Dan, & W. Lamersdorf (Ed.), *ICSOC 2006. LNCS 4294,* (pp. 390–401). Springer.

Wang, Y., & Vassileva, J. (2007). *A review on trust and reputation for Web service selection.* 27th International Conference on Distributed Computing Systems Workshops, ICDCSW '07, (p. 25).

Ward, M., & Audsley, N. (2002). Hardware implementation of programming languages for real-time. *Proceedings of the 8th IEEE Real-Time and Embedded Technology and Applications Symposium.*

Watson, P., Lord, P., Gibson, F., et al. (2008). Cloud computing for e-science with CARMEN. *Proceedings of IBERGRID Conference,* (pp. 1-5). Porto, Portugal. May 12–14.

Web Service Agreement. (2004). *GFD: 107 proposed recommendation.*

Wesner, S., Järnert, J. M., & Aránzazu, M. (n.d.). *Mobile collaborative business Grids – A short overview of the Akogrimo Project.* Retrieved June 25, 2010, from http://www.akogrimo.org/download/White_Papers_and_Publications/Akogrimo_WhitePaper_Overview.pdf

WFMC. (2005). *XML process definition language.* XPDL.

WFMC. (1999). *Terminology and glossary- English.* (Document Number WFMC-TC-1011).

Wieczorek, M., Siddiqui, M., Villazon, A., Prodan, R., & Fahringer, T. (2006). *Applying advance reservation to increase predictability of workflow execution on the Grid.* Paper presented at the Second IEEE International Conference on e-Science and Grid Computing.

Wikipedia. (2010). *Unified modeling language.* Retrieved from http://en.wikipedia.org/wiki/Unified_Modeling_Language

Windows Azure. (n.d.). Retrieved from http://www.microsoft.com/windowsazure/windowsazure/

Wolfe, V. F., DiPippo, L. C., Ginis, R., Squadrito, M., Wohlever, S., Zykh, I., & Johnston, R. (1997). *Real-time CORBA.* In IEEE Real Time Technology and Applications Symposium (RTAS 1997), (p. 148). Montreal, Canada: IEEE Computer Society.

WS-Discovery Specification. (2009). Retrieved from http://docs.oasis-open.org/ws-dd/dpws/1.1/os/wsdd-dpws-1.1-spec-os.html#wsdiscovery

WSDL. (2001). *Web service description language.* Retrieved from http://www.w3.org/TR/wsdl

WSIL specification. (2007). *Web services inspection language specification.* Retrieved from http://www.ibm.com/developerworks/library/specification/ws-wsilspec/

WSML. (2010). Retrieved from http://www.wsmo.org/wsml

WSMO. (2005). *Web service modeling ontology.* Retrieved from http://www.w3.org/ Submission/WSMO/

WSMO. (2010). Retrieved from http://www.wsmo.org

Wu, C., Chang, E., & Thomson, P. (2005). A decision support system for QoS-enabled distributed Web services architecture. In H. Hess, L. Franquelo, A. Malinowski, & M. Chow (Ed.), *Industrial Electronics Society Conference*, IECON 2005.

Wu, J., & Brandt, S. A. (2007). Providing quality of service support in object-based file system. *Proceedings of the 24th IEEE Conference on Mass Storage Systems and Technologies.*

Wust, C. C., Steffens, L., Bril, R. J., & Verhaegh, W. F. J. (2004). QoS control strategies for high-quality video processing. In *Proceedings of the 16th Euromicro Conference on Real-Time Systems.*

Xu, Z., Martin, P., Powley, W., & Zulkernine, F. (2007). *Reputation-enhanced QoS-based Web services discovery.* IEEE International Conference on Web Services, ICWS 2007, (pp. 249-256).

Yan, W., Hu, S., Muthusamy, V., Jacobsen, H.-A., & Zha, L. (2009). Efficient event-based resource discovery. In *Proceedings of the 2009 inaugural International Conference on Distributed Event-Based Systems*, Nashville, TN.

Yeo, C. S., & Buyya, R. (2005). Service level agreement based allocation of cluster resources handling penalty to enhance utility. In *Proc. of the 7th IEEE International Conference on Cluster Computing Cluster.*

Yodaiken, V., & Barabanov, M. (1997). Introducing real-time Linux. *Linux Journal, 5.*

Youseff, L., Butrico, M., & Da Silva, D. (2008, November). *Toward a unified ontology of cloud computing.* In Grid Computing Environments Workshop, 2008. GCE '08, (pp. 1-10).

Yu, J., & Buyya, R. (2005). A taxonomy of workflow management systems for Grid computing. *Journal of Grid Computing, 3*(3-4), 171–200. doi:10.1007/s10723-005-9010-8

Yu, J., & Buyya, R. (2005). A taxonomy of scientific workflow systems for grid computing. *SIGMOD Record, 34*(3), 44-49. DOI= http://doi.acm.org/10.1145/1084805.1084814

Yuan, W., & Nahrstedt, K. (2003). Energy-efficient soft real-time CPU scheduling for mobile multimedia systems. In *Proceedings of the 19th ACM symposium on Operating systems principles* (SOSP '03), (pp. 149–163). New York, NY: ACM.

Zhang, R., Lu, C., Abdelzaher, T. F., & Stankovic, J. A. (2002). ControlWare: A middleware architecture for feedback control of software performance. In *Proceedings of the International Conference on Distributed Computing Systems.* Vienna, Austria.

Zhang, Y., Zheng, Z., & Lyu, M. R. (2010). *WSExpress: A QoS-aware search engine for Web services.* IEEE International Conference on Web Services, ICWS 2010, (pp. 91-98).

Zhao, H., & Doshi, P. (2009). Toward automated restful Web service compositions. In *Proceedings of the 2009 IEEE International Conference on Web Services* (ICWS 2009), (pp. 189-196). IEEE Computer Society.

Zhao, H., & Sakellariou, R. (2007). *Advance reservation policies for workflows.* Paper presented at the 12th International Conference on Job Scheduling Strategies for Parallel Processing, Saint-Malo, France.

Zhu, Y., & Ammar, M. (2006, April). Algorithms for assigning substrate network resources to virtual network components. In *Proceedings of the IEEE International Conference on Computer Communications.* DOI: 10.1109/INFOCOM.2006.322

About the Contributors

Dimosthenis P. Kyriazis received the diploma from the Dept. of Electrical and Computer Engineering of the National Technical University of Athens, Athens, Greece in 2001, the MS degree in Techno-Economic Systems (MBA) co-organized by the Electrical and Computer Engineering Dept - NTUA, Economic Sciences Dept - National Kapodistrian University of Athens, Industrial Management Dept - University of Piraeus and his Ph.D. from the Electrical and Computer Engineering Department of the National Technical University of Athens in 2007. He is currently a Research Engineer in the Telecommunication Laboratory of the Institute of Communication and Computer Systems (ICCS). Before joining the ICCS he worked in the private sector as Telecom Software Engineer. He has participated in numerous EU / National funded projects (such as IRMOS, NextGRID, Akogrimo, BEinGRID, HPC-Europa, GRIA, Memphis, CHALLENGERS, HellasGRID, etc) and currently serves as the Technical Coordinator of the IRMOS EU project. His research interests include Grid computing, scheduling, Quality of Service provision, and workflow management in heterogeneous systems and service oriented architectures.

Theodora A. Varvarigou received her B. Tech degree from the National Technical University of Athens, Athens, Greece in 1988, MS degrees in Electrical Engineering (1989) and in Computer Science (1991) from Stanford University, Stanford, California in 1989, and her Ph.D. from Stanford University in 1991. She worked at AT&T Bell Labs, Holmdel, New Jersey between 1991 and 1995. Between 1995 and 1997 she worked as an Assistant Professor at the Technical University of Crete, Chania, Greece. Since 1997, she was elected as an Assistant Professor, and since 2007, she is a Professor at the National Technical University of Athens, and Director of the Postgraduate Course "Engineering Economics Systems." Prof. Varvarigou has great experience in the area of semantic Web technologies, scheduling over distributed platforms, embedded systems, and grid computing. In this area, she has published more than 170 papers in leading journals and conferences. She has participated and coordinated several EU funded projects such as IRMOS, SCOVIS, POLYMNIA, Akogrimo, NextGRID, BEinGRID, Memphis, MKBEEM, MARIDES, CHALLENGERS, FIDIS, and others.

Kleopatra G. Konstanteli was born in Athens, Greece in 1981. She received her diploma in Electrical and Computer Engineering in 2004 from the National Technical University of Athens (NTUA). In 2007 she received a Master in Techno-economical Systems by the NTUA in cooperation with University of Athens and University of Piraeus. She is currently pursuing her doctoral-level research in computer science while at the same working as a research associate in the Telecommunications Laboratory of Electrical and Computer Engineering of NTUA and participating in EU funded projects. Her research interests are mainly focused in the field of distributed service-oriented computing.

* * *

Matthew Addis is a project manager at IT Innovation (12 years). Current responsibilities include WP leader in the EC FP7 PrestoPrime Integrated Project where he leads the work on automated data management. Matthew led the information security risk analysis and stochastic process modelling work in IRMOS. Matthew has been involved in a wide range of data analysis and multimedia processing projects over the past 10 years that range from data mining techniques of retail and finance databases, content-based analysis of fine art images, military network intrusion detection, and high throughput processing of video for broadcast archives. Matthew co-authored a report on data mining and data fusion commissioned by the Office of Science and Innovation as part of the UK Government's Foresight project, informing policy at a national level. Matthew has a PhD in physics.

Fotis Aisopos received his diploma from the Dept. of Electrical and Computer Engineering of the National Technical University of Athens (NTUA), Greece in 2007. He is currently pursuing his PhD in Grid Computing at the Telecommunications Laboratory of the Dept. of Electrical and Computer Engineering of the National Technical University of Athens and is a researcher for the Institute of Communication and Computer Systems (ICCS), where he has participates in the EU funded projects BEinGRID, +Spaces, and SocIoS. His research interests include information engineering, distributed systems and architectures, Web services, Web portals, and Grid computing.

Sören Berger reached his Dipl.-Inf. degree at the University of Stuttgart in 2008 where he was working on open source VoIP campus solutions and robustness and reliability in future IT infrastructures and distributed systems. Now he works at the Rechenzentrum Universität Stuttgart (RUS) at the University of Stuttgart and carries out research on resource management in distributed systems and visualization of network and computing resources in cloud infrastructures.

Marko Bertogna is an Assistant Professor at the Scuola Superiore Sant'Anna, Pisa, Italy. He graduated (summa cum laude) in telecommunications engineering from the University of Bologna, Italy, in 2002. He received the Ph.D. degree in computer science from Scuola Superiore Sant'Anna, in 2008. His research interests include scheduling and schedulability analysis of real-time multiprocessor systems, protocols for the exclusive access to shared resources, hierarchical systems, and reconfigurable devices. He is author of more than 30 papers in international journals and peer-reviewed conferences. He received the 2009 Best Paper for the IEEE Transactions on Industrial Informatics, the 2005 Best Paper Award at the IEEE/Euromicro Conference on Real-Time Systems (ECRTS'05), the 2009 and 2010 Best Paper Awards at the IEEE International Conference on Embedded and Real-Time Computing Systems and Applications (RTCSA'09 and RTCSA'10).

Michael Boniface is Technical Director of the IT Innovation Centre. He joined IT Innovation in 2000 after several years at Nortel Networks developing infrastructure to support telecommunications interoperability. His roles at IT Innovation include technical strategy of RTD across IT Innovation's project portfolio, technical leadership, and business development. He has over 10 years experience of RTD into innovative distributed systems for science and industry using technologies such as Semantic Web, Grid, and service-oriented architectures. He leads IT Innovation's contribution to the Future Internet initiative through Expert Groups including leadership of the FIA socio-economic working group. Michael provides architecture and business modelling direction in RTD projects including scientific leadership of ICT

SIMDAT, leadership of sustainability activities in IST BonFIRE and FIRESTATION, socio-economic impact assessment of Future Internet technologies in SESERV, and he provides overall technical co-ordination for the open source software, GRIA. Michael has a BEng in multimedia communications.

Michael Braitmaier has worked at HLRS on Virtual and Augmented Reality (VR/AR) collaboration environments in general and collaborative visualization environments specifically since 2004. He actively participated in the development and adaptation of a collaborative visualisation environment on the basis of software COVISE to the IRMOS framework and in this context presented approaches improving the user experience of VR and AR users by the means of guaranteed Quality of Service on the IRMOS framework. With his application-oriented knowledge, he contributed to the conception and development of service engineering tool to support application developers to easily adapt to service-oriented infrastructures and their frameworks.

Fabio Checconi is a postdoc in the Multicore Computing group at IBM Research. He received his PhD in Computer Engineering from the Real-Time Systems Laboratory, Scuola Superiore S. Anna in 2010. His research is focused on real-time operating systems and parallel programming.

Luis Costa is a researcher in the Cooperative and Trusted Systems department at SINTEF, currently working in the FP7 projects IRMOS and ENVISION. He has worked on the FP6 project SWING that focused on the interoperability of Semantic Web services for geospatial decision making. He has also been the project leader of the distributed resource center for Portuguese Linguateca from 2007 to 2009. The mission of this center is to raise the quality of Portuguese language processing, through the removal of difficulties for the researchers and developers involved. He has worked previously in the industry as a software engineer. Luis holds a computer science degree from Universidade Tιcnica de Lisboa.

Tommaso Cucinotta graduated in Computer Engineering at the University of Pisa in 2000, and received the PhD degree from Scuola Superiore Sant'Anna in 2004. He is Assistant Professor at the real time systems laboratory of Scuola Superiore Sant'Anna in Pisa. His main research activities are in the areas of real-time and embedded systems, with a particular focus on real-time support for general purpose operating systems and virtualised real-time applications.

Georgina M. Gallizo Rueda is a senior researcher with a broad experience in European research projects in the fields of Grid and cloud computing. She holds a MSc in Electrical and Computer Engineering from Universidad Politécnica de Madrid. She joined HLRS (High Performance Computing Center Stuttgart) in 2008, where she is currently the HLRS team leader for the EU research projects IRMOS and OPTIMIS, on cloud computing. She worked in Telefónica I+D since 1999, where she was initially involved in different projects for the Telefónica Group and, since 2003, actively participated in research projects related to multimedia communications over broadband networks and next generation networks (IST FP6 MUSE and MediaNet). Afterwards, she was involved in the coordination of the AKOGRIMO IST FP6 project on Grid technologies and mobility. Furthermore, she has been deeply involved in the preparation of new European project proposals (Eureka, IST FP6 and ICT FP7).

Spyridon V. Gogouvitis was born in Athens, Greece in 1982. He received the Dipl. -Ing. from the School of Electrical and Computer Engineering of the National Technical University of Athens (NTUA) in 2006. He is currently pursuing his PhD while working as a Researcher in the Telecommunication Laboratory of the Institute of Communication and Computer Systems (ICCS). In the past he has worked as a developer for the Hellenic Army Information Systems Support Centre and as a consultant for the General Secretariat for Information Systems of the Hellenic Ministry of Economy and Finance. He has also been involved in various European projects. His research interests include Grid and cloud computing, Web services and service oriented architectures, and mobile and ubiquitous computing.

Roy Grønmo has been working as a research scientist at SINTEF since 1998. He holds a doctor degree in Computer science at the University of Oslo. He has numerous publications since 1999 in international conferences and journals. At the IFIP International Conference on Distributed Applications and Interoperable Systems in 2005, he received a "best paper award." In 2010, he held the keynote speech at the International Workshop on Models and Model-driven Methods for Service Engineering. He has been a member of several programme committees of international conferences and workshops, and he has been a reviewer for a few journals. The main research topics are model-driven development, model and graph transformation, service-oriented modeling, and aspect-oriented modeling. During his time at SINTEF, he has been involved in European and Norwegian research and industrial projects.

Magdalini Kardara has obtained a Diploma in Electrical and Computer Engineering in 2004 from the National Technical University of Athens and an MSc in Advanced Computing from Imperial College London in 2006. She is a PhD candidate in the department of Electrical and Computer Engineering of NTUA and is currently working as Research Associate and Software engineer in the Telecommunications Laboratory. She has a significant expertise on Web services and Grid technologies through participation in related EU and national projects, like BEinGRID and GRIA.

Gregory Katsaros received the diploma from the Dept. of Electrical and Computer Engineering of the National Technical University of Athens, Athens, Greece in 2006 and the MS degree in Techno-Economic Systems (MBA) co-organized by the NTUA, National Kapodistrian University of Athens, University of Piraeus, in 2008. Currently, he is a PhD candidate under the supervision of Prof. Theodora Varvarigou while he is also working as an Associate Researcher in the Telecommunications Laboratory of the Institute of Communications and Computer Systems (ICCS) of NTUA. He has been involved in several European funded research projects such as NextGRID, BEinGRID, EchoGRID, and the last two years, he is working on the IRMOS FP7 project. His responsibilities within the IRMOS project are the design and implementation of the IRMOS portal and monitoring mechanism of IRMOS framework as well as contributing to publications and deliverables. His research interests include Grid computing, software engineering, license management, and Cloud computing.

George Kousiouris received his diploma in Electrical and Computer Engineering from the University of Patras, Greece in 2005. He is currently pursuing his PhD in Grid Computing at the Telecommunications Laboratory of the Dept. of Electrical and Computer Engineering of the National Technical University of Athens and is a researcher for the Institute of Communications and Computer Systems (ICCS), where he has participated in the EU funded projects BEinGRID, IRMOS, Challengers, and the National project GRID-APP. In the past he has worked for private telecommunications companies (OTE March 2005-October 2005) and the Hellenic Air Force (March 2006-March 2007). His interests are mainly computational intelligence, optimization, computer networks, and Web services discovery.

Roland Kübert received his diploma degree in Computer Science from the University of Würzburg in 2006. Since then he is employed as a research assistant at the High Performance Computing Center in Stuttgart where he is doing his PhD. He has been involved in several German-funded research projects like FinGRID and SLA4D-Grid as well as in European-funded research projects such as NextGRID and BEinGRID. He has been participating in the IRMOS project from the beginning and is responsible for the design and implementation of SLA negotiation protocols and components. His areas of interest are software engineering, Web services, service level agreements, and programming languages.

Dominik Lamp studied computer science at the Technische Universität Kaiserslautern and received his Dipl.-Inf. degree in 2006. In parallel to his studies, he worked as software developer for 1&1 Internet AG, Montabaur before joining the Rechenzentrum Universität Stuttgart (RUS) as scientific staff member in 2006. There, he is involved in multiple national and international research projects such as MAMS and IRMOS as well as in setting up the university's voice-over-ip (VoIP) laboratory.

Neil Loughran is a Research Scientist in the Cooperative and Trusted Systems group at SINTEF in Oslo, Norway. He holds a PhD from Lancaster University in the UK and has worked on several EU projects (e.g. CESAR, SESAR, IRMOS, AMPLE, AOSD-Europe) over the past six years covering language modelling, requirements modelling, service composition, variability management, product-line engineering, and aspect-oriented software development. Recently, he has served on the program committees for SC2009, FOSD2010, ACOM2010, and NESEA2010.

Patrick Mandic holds a MSc. Degree from the University of Stuttgart in Information Technology and studied telecommunication engineering at the Universitat Politecnica de Catalunya (UPC). He was co-founder of the barcelonawireless.net project (2001). His main research interests are oriented towards security, mobility, and service discovery in Next Generation Networks (NGN). Patrick Mandic is currently employed in the Communication Systems department at the Rechenzentrum Universitat Stuttgart (Center of Information Technologies Stuttgart). He has worked in several ICT European Projects (FP6 and FP7) in the area of telecommunications and Internet technologies such Daidalos, Akogrimo, and IRMOS. He was work package leader in the IRMOS project.

Andreas Menychtas graduated from the School of Electrical and Computer Engineering, National Technical University of Athens (NTUA) in 2004. In 2009, he received his Ph.D. in area of Distributed Computing from the School of Electrical and Computer Engineering of the National Technical University of Athens. He worked in the private sector as computer and network engineer and has been involved in several EU and National funded projects such as GRIA, NextGRID, EGEE, IRMOS, HellasGRID, and GRID-APP. His research interests include distributed systems, Web Services, object oriented programming, service oriented architectures, security and information engineering. Currently, he works as research engineer in the Institute of Communication and Computer Systems (ICCS) of National Technical University of Athens.

Stuart Middleton has 17 years experience with research interests in the areas of recommender systems, machine learning, ontologies, and media/sensor systems. Stuart has over 23 publications, is on several programme committees, and is an active member of the Open Geospatial Consortium. Stuart has managed six framework ICT programme projects including POLYMNIA, covering the digital content chain, and SANY, covering in situ sensor networks and the semantic integration of fusion processing services working with ad-hoc and mobile sensors. Prior to joining the University of Southampton, Stuart worked commercially for 7 years for Lloyd's of London, Racal, and then DERA.

Vrettos Moulos was born in Athens, Greece in 1983. He has obtained a Diploma in Information & Communication Systems Engineering from the Aegean University, an MSc in Advanced Computing from Imperial College of London in 2007, and another MSc in Computing IT Law & Management from King's College of London in 2008. He is a PhD candidate in the department of Electrical and Computer Engineering of NTUA and is currently working as Research Associate and Software engineer in the Telecommunications Laboratory. His research interests are mainly focused on the field of social network anti data mining and privacy.

Jesús M. Movilla is a doctor in Optical Physics in the Universidad Computense of Madrid. The topic of his dissertation was the characterisation of non-uniformly polarised laser beams. However, during the last 7 years, he changed his research interests and moved to the Information Technologies/ Systems and concentrated in the area of Grid technology and Cloud. He has been involved in several European funded projects in the area of Grid and Cloud, and currently, he is working on the IRMOS project in the framework services layer.

Malcolm Muggeridge is VP of Emerging Technologies in the Network Storage Solutions Business at Xyratex, the world's largest supplier of data storage equipment to other equipment manufacturers (OEM) such as Network Appliance, IBM and Dell. He has been with the company through its creation as a management buyout from IBM in 1994 growing the Storage Systems business from concept in 1997 to a projected 1.2B$ in 2010. Malcolm has a background through his prior period with IBM in the technology, manufacturing, quality, and reliability of disk drives and networked data storage systems, architecting and managing designs and new technologies across many products. More recently he has been focused on strategic innovation and business development, research, technology, and company innovation culture. Malcolm has a B.Eng degree in Electronics from Liverpool University.

Sai Narasimhamurthy is Lead Research Engineer for Xyratex Emerging Technologies working on Research and Development for next generation storage systems. Previously (2005 - 2009), Sai was CTO and Co-founder at 4Blox, inc, a venture capital backed storage infrastructure software company based in San Jose, CA focused on addressing performance issues in Internet Protocol(IP) based Storage Area Networks(SANs). Sai received both his Master's (2003) and PhD (2005) in the field of Storage Networking from Arizona State University and a Bachelor's degree in Electronics and Communication Engineering from Bangalore University (1999), India. Sai also worked with Intel Research and Development in the early stages of the RDMA Consortium (formed by IBM, Cisco, and Intel) in 2002, with focus on the upcoming 10Gigabit Ethernet based storage technologies. Earlier in his career, he worked with the verification and regression team for Nortel's SONET products (OC-12, OC-48, OC-192) through Wipro, India.

Bassem Nasser has a Ph.D. in networks and telecommunication from the University of Paul Sabatier, Toulouse, France. His research activities at UPS focused on designing inter-domain security architectures for collaborative workspaces in the European CASH, IMAGE, and VIVACE projects. He then moved to the University of Kent, contributing to the DyCom and VPMan projects, enhancing and integrating the PERMIS authorisation system with Grid infrastructures. His main research interests include risk management, identity management, trust, security models, and security policy specification. Currently, Bassem is working at IT Innovation on IRMOS and Edutain projects focusing on security architectures for interactive, real-time, online multimedia and e-learning applications. Bassem has published over conference and journal articles.

Karsten Oberle received the Dipl.-Ing. (FH) degree in communications engineering from the University of Applied Sciences "Fachochschule für Technik" Mannheim, Germany, in 1998. In the same year, he joined the Alcatel Research Center in Stuttgart. Currently, he is Project Manager in the Bell Labs Service Infrastructure research department of Alcatel-Lucent Germany. The service infrastructure research domain invents, analyzes, and builds disruptive technologies – related to distributed communications and computing infrastructures – that provide a superior foundation for Alcatel-Lucent's application enablement strategy. In 2008 he was awarded for his technical excellence inside Alcatel-Lucent by becoming a member of the Alcatel-Lucent Technical Academy. He has participated in numerous national and European projects. Accompanying he is active in standardization at ETSI since 2006; since June 2008 he holds the position of the Vice-Chairman of ETSI CLOUD. Since 2007, he has authored and co-authored more than 20 papers for conferences and journals. Furthermore he has filed more than 20 patents.

Eduardo Oliveros Dvaz holds a Telecommunication Engineer Degree from Universidad Politιcnica de Madrid (1997). He worked for Future Space(1998) where he participated in the project Infomail (Multimedia Messaging Server) of Telefonica R&D. He joined Telefσnica R&D in 2000, in the "Messaging Services" division, participating in the development of different e-mail systems, directory, and voice portals solutions for Spain and South America. Following he joined the "Real-time communications services" division (2005) where he was involved in several Telefσnica Corporation innovation projects concerning directory and unified messaging systems. He has participated in the European project Akogrimo (IST FP6) involved in exploitation activities and in the Administrative Coordination in the European project BREIN (IST FP6). Currently, he is working in the IRMOS project (IST FP7).

Athanasios Papaoikonomou received his diploma in Electrical and Computer Engineering from the National Technical University of Athens, in 2008. He completed his thesis titled "Verification of interoperability issues in a Grid environment and establishment of secure communication between Globus toolkit 4 and WSRF .NET" to the sector of telecommunication, electronics, and computer systems of NTUA. He is a PhD candidate in the department of Electrical and Computer Engineering of NTUA. He has participated in the EU funded project IRMOS. His research interests include SOA and social computing.

Juri Papay is a senior research engineer at the IT Innovation Centre in Southampton. He has a PhD in Computer Science from the University of Warwick (UK) and an engineering degree from the Electrotechnical Institute (LETI) of St-Petersburg. Juri has over twenty years of experience in research and development. He worked on numerous EC and UK funded projects involving engineering simulations, performance prediction of parallel computers, distributed infrastructure development, bioinformatics, and modelling of real time systems and multimedia applications. Juri has published over twenty research papers in journals and conference proceedings.

Stephen C Phillips joined IT Innovation nearly six years ago after gaining degrees in mathematics and chemistry, a chemistry PhD, and three years experience as a post-doctoral researcher at the University of Southampton. Since joining IT Innovation, Stephen has worked on many collaborative R&D projects, notably helping design and integrate a distributed workflow system in the SIMDAT project using tools from Inforsense, ModelCenter, and Matlab. Recently, Stephen has led IT Innovation's work in BEinGRID, linking financial institutions through secure and managed information exchange. Currently, Stephen is working on two EU funded projects: IRMOS, looking at application resource modelling, and PrestoPRIME where he leads a large work-package looking at topics including business process modelling for data-centric workflows and digital preservation, including long-term data retention.

Theodoros Polychniatis was born in Athens, Greece in 1981. He received the diploma from the Dept. of Electrical and Computer Engineering of the National Technical University of Athens (NTUA) in 2005. He received the MS degree in Techno-Economic Systems (MBA) co-organized by the Electrical and Computer Engineering Dept - NTUA, Economic Sciences Dept - National Kapodistrian Univ. of Athens, Industrial Management Dept – Univ. of Piraeus in 2007. He is currently working as a Researcher in the Telecommunication Laboratory of the Institute of Communication and Computer Systems (ICCS). Before joining the ICCS he has worked in the private sector as Software Developer. His research interests are focused on Grid Computing and Service Oriented Architectures.

Arturo Servin has a PhD in Artificial Intelligence from University of York following his Master's in Telecommunications Management. Arturo's research interests include network modelling, machining learning, and autonomous agents. Arturo worked on the IRMOS project focusing on how to optimize resourcing solutions for real-time applications deployed on the cloud. Arturo's work integrated SLA negotiation with application system models to deliver predictions of reliability for key performance indicators relevant to applications. Arturo has since left IT Innovation and is now working as CTO at Latin American and Caribbean Internet Addresses Registry (LACNIC).

Manuel Stein was born in Hadamar, Germany, in 1983. He received the Dipl.-Inf. (BA) degree in Information Technology from the University of Cooperative Education in Stuttgart in 2005. He is currently a researcher at the Bell Labs Service Infrastructure research department of Alcatel-Lucent Germany. After completing his studies, he conducted research on distributed service delivery platforms for IP Multimedia Subsystem (3GPP IMS) evolution. His current research activity focuses on network virtualization and application of Semantic Web technologies for network resource management in distributed cloud infrastructures. His main fields of interest include Future Internet design and autonomous network management.

Mike Surridge has a PhD in Theoretical Physics, and over 20 years experience in Information Technology research. Since the mid-1990s, he has focused on Grid and service oriented architectures, especially dynamic security and adaptation. He coordinated the FP5 GRIA project, was Principal Investigator of the UK Semantic Firewall project, and led the Grid Dynamics workpackage in the IST NextGrid project on workflow and dynamic security. He provides advice on Grid and Web service architecture, business models, and security to several commercial and research projects including the FP6 Edutain@Grid and BREIN projects, and is coordinator of the SERSCIS project on dynamic SOA for critical infrastructure protection. He was a co-founder of the UK e-Science Security Task Force, and is currently chair of the EC ICT Software and Service Working Group on Trust and Security (see http://www.eu-ecss.eu/contents/private-area/trust-security/trust-and-security/).

Konstantinos Tserpes is a senior researcher in the Telecommunication Laboratory of the ICCS, Athens, Greece. He graduated from the Computer Engineering and Informatics department, University of Patras, Greece. In 2006, he received his Master's degree in Information Systems Management from NTUA. In 2008, he acquired his Ph.D. in the area of Service Oriented Architectures from the school of Electrical and Computer Engineers of NTUA. He has been involved in several EU and National funded (e.g. NextGRID, HPC-Europa, BEinGRID, AkoGRIMO, EchoGRID, CHALLENGERS, HellasGRID, USNES) projects and his research interests include service oriented computing and its application and business extensions.

Thomas Voith is a senior scientist in Bell Labs Services Infrastructure Domain in Stuttgart, Germany. He received his Dipl.-Ing. Degree in electrical engineering from the University Stuttgart, Germany. Currently he is working on disruptive technologies – related to infrastructure as a service – that provide a superior foundation for Alcatel-Lucent's application enablement strategy. Mr. Voith worked on innovative architecture designs for next generation infrastructure in conjunction with European and national German research programs. He was an active member and editor of International Telecommunication Union, Telecommunication Standardization Sector Study Group 11 (ITU-T SG11) for several years. He joined the European Telecommunications Standards Institute (ETSI) – Telecommunication and Internet converged Services and Protocols for Advanced Networks (TISPAN) during preparation of TISPAN's Next-Generation Network (NGN) Release 1.

Stefan Waldschmidt is a professional software developer in the broadcast and multimedia industry since 1995. His main areas of work include real-time applications, control of external devices, data transmission, and image processing, with the focus on high performance and high quality, defining and applying mature development processes. Stefan received his Dipl.-Informatiker (Computer Science) from Darmstadt University of Technology where he also had the position of a scientific assistant for 3 years in the area of massive parallel systems.

Xiaoyu Yang has a PhD in Systems Engineering from De Montford University with a thesis titled "Methodology and Tools for Realising Product Service Systems for Consumer Products." Xiaoyu has a broad knowledge of distributed systems and a keen interest in the changing landscape of the Grid, Cloud, virtualization, and SOA. On the Edutain project, he researched and developed a business level monitoring infrastructure for real-time quality of service management on multi-hosted clouds. On the IRMOS project, his research focused on how to combine actual QoS data with predictive models for increased accuracy of resourcing predictions.

Zlatko Zlatev is a research engineer at the University of Southampton IT Innovation Centre, where he is involved in a number of collaborative R&D projects. Zlatko's current work is in the areas of data fusion, statistical learning, and systems performance modelling and estimation. His previous experience is in business analysis and design and implementation of enterprise Information Systems in the industry. He holds an MSc Degree in Machine Learning & Data Mining from the University of Bristol in the UK and also an MSc Degree in Computing Machines & Technologies from the Technical University of Varna, Bulgaria.

Index

A

activity diagrams 5-6, 18-19, 21
ad-hoc networks 77
Amazon.com 43, 49-50, 53, 55-57, 61, 69, 97, 102, 107, 111, 162, 164, 166-167, 169, 171, 180, 189, 195-196, 198, 218, 270-273
Amazon Machine Images (AMI) 49-50, 189
Amazon Web Services (AWS) 49-50, 53, 57, 69, 102, 165-166, 171, 189, 270, 273
analytical modeling 120, 126, 143
analytic hierarchy process (AHP) 124
application requirements 28, 211-212, 236, 282
application service components (ASC) 238, 240, 242

B

biological systems 119
business level objectives (BLO) 146
Byzantine faults 261, 273

C

class diagrams 5-6, 18-19, 21
class of services (CoS) 138, 147
cloud computing 1-2, 5-6, 11-12, 41-44, 46, 49-50, 52-58, 60, 66, 68-72, 75, 79, 87-92, 94-97, 100, 102, 107, 111-114, 116, 128, 133-134, 157, 160-172, 174, 189-192, 196, 201, 212, 218-222, 228-230, 232-237, 244-245, 250, 252-257, 259, 267, 270
cloud computing environments 134, 255
cloud computing stack 75, 87, 89-91
cloud infrastructures 43, 69, 94-95, 100, 116, 169-170, 172, 196, 255, 270
cloud modalities 161
cloud security 160, 162-164, 171
cloud software vendors 162
cloud solutions 43, 49, 56, 88, 100, 172, 174, 218

command queuing 241-242
commodity grids (CoG) 123, 130
communications as a service (CaaS) 162
completely fair scheduler (CFS) 203, 277
complete meta object facilities (CMOF) 17
complexity databases 146
composit structure diagrams 18-19
computational silos 219
computing power 95, 98, 167, 189
conditional data-flow graphs (CDFG) 144
constraint groups (CG) 47-48, 138
continuous time Markov chains (CTMC) 8, 10
control flow structures 117
C++ programming language 16, 33, 35, 50, 55, 111, 178-179, 208, 279
create, read, update, and delete (CRUD) 54, 176
CRISP project 195

D

data centres 95-96, 116, 168, 174, 191, 207
dataflow bindings 117
denial of service (DoS) attacks 96, 167
description logic (DL) 64, 85
digital signal processors (DSP) 57, 144
directed acyclic graphs (DAG) 84, 122, 128
discrete event simulations (DES) 11, 39
distributed hash tables (DHT) 83
Distributed Management Task Force, Inc. (DMTF) 57, 177
distributed systems 4-5, 8, 13, 70, 72, 83-85, 111, 115, 120, 125, 128, 130-131, 158-159, 177, 196, 211, 213, 218-219, 259-260, 266-267, 274, 280, 286-329
distributed virtualized infrastructures 98
domain specific languages (DSL) 37
domain specific ontologies (DSO) 82
dynamic compositions 138
dynamic pricing models 145